Social Research Methods

Second Canadian Edition

Social Research Methods

Alan Bryman   James J. Teevan   Edward Bell

OXFORD
UNIVERSITY PRESS

OXFORD
UNIVERSITY PRESS

70 Wynford Drive, Don Mills, Ontario M3C 1J9
www.oupcanada.com

Oxford University Press is a department of the University of Oxford.
It furthers the University's objective of excellence in research, scholarship,
and education by publishing worldwide in

Oxford   New York

Auckland   Cape Town   Dar es Salaam   Hong Kong   Karachi
Kuala Lumpur   Madrid   Melbourne   Mexico City   Nairobi
New Delhi   Shanghai   Taipei   Toronto

With offices in

Argentina   Austria   Brazil   Chile   Czech Republic   France   Greece
Guatemala   Hungary   Italy   Japan   Poland   Portugal   Singapore
South Korea   Switzerland   Thailand   Turkey   Ukraine   Vietnam

Oxford is a trade mark of Oxford University Press
in the UK and in certain other countries

Published in Canada
by Oxford University Press

Library and Archives Canada Cataloguing in Publication Data

Bryman, Alan
Social research methods / Alan Bryman, James J. Teevan, Edward Bell. —
2nd Canadian ed.

Includes bibliographical references and index.
ISBN 978-0-19-542986-2

1. Social sciences—Research—Textbooks.
2. Social sciences—Methodology—Textbooks.
I. Bell, Edward A. (Edward Allan), 1955–   II. Teevan, James J., 1942–
III. Title.

H62.B78 2009   300'.72   C2009-901085-2

Cover image: Image Source Photography/Veer

This book is printed on permanent acid-free paper ∞.

Printed and bound in Canada.

1 2 3 4—12 11 10 09

Contents

Guide to the Book   *xvi*
Acknowledgements   *xxii*

Part I   1

1   General Research Orientations   2

Chapter overview   2
Introduction   2
Theory and research   3
   Degree of abstraction   3
   Deductive and inductive approaches   5
Epistemological considerations   7
   Positivism   7
   Interpretivism   7
Ontological considerations   9
   Relationship to social research   11
General orientations: quantitative and qualitative research   11
Influences on the conduct of social research   13
   Values   13
   Politics in social research   15
   Practical considerations   17
Key points   19
Questions for review   19

2   Research Designs   21

Chapter overview   21
Introduction   21
Criteria for evaluating social research   22
   Reliability   22
   Replicability   22
   Validity   22
   Relationship with the general research orientation   23

Research designs   24
    Experimental design   24
    Cross-sectional design   33
    Longitudinal design(s)   36
    Case study design   38
Bringing research orientation and design together   40
Key Points   42
Questions for review   42

Part II   45

3   The Nature of Quantitative Research   46

Chapter overview   46
Introduction   46
The main steps in quantitative research   46
Concepts and their measurement   48
    What is a concept?   48
    Why measure?   48
    Indicators   49
    Using multiple-item measures in survey research   49
    Dimensions of concepts   51
Reliability and measurement validity   52
    Reliability   52
    Measurement validity   53
Reflections on reliability and validity   55
The main goals of quantitative researchers   55
    Measurement   55
    Establishing causality   55
    Generalization of findings to those not studied   57
    Replication   57
Critiques of quantitative research   58
    Criticisms of quantitative research   58
Is it always like this? Reality and practice   60
Key points   60
Questions for review   61

4   Survey Research: Structured Interviewing and Questionnaires   62

Chapter overview   62
Introduction   62
The structured interview   62
    Reducing error due to interviewer variability   63
    Accuracy and ease of data processing   63
    Dealing with interviewer effects   64
Interview contexts   64
    More than one interviewer or interviewee   64

In person or by telephone?   65
Computer-assisted interviewing   66
Using online personal interviews   66
Conducting interviews   67
Know the interview schedule   67
Introducing the research   67
Rapport   68
Topics and issues to include in an introductory statement   68
Asking questions   69
Recording answers   69
Question order   69
Probing   69
Prompting   70
Leaving the interview   70
Training and supervision   70
Questionnaires   71
Advantages of the questionnaire over the structured interview   71
Disadvantages of questionnaires versus structured interviews   71
Online social surveys   72
Researcher-driven diaries as a form of questionnaire   74
Respondent problems   76
Response sets   76
The issue of meaning   77
The feminist critique   77
Key points   78
Questions for review   78

5   Asking Questions   80

Chapter overview   80
Introduction   80
Open or closed questions?   80
Open questions   80
Closed questions   82
Types of questions   84
Rules for designing questions   85
General rules of thumb   85
Specific rules when designing questions   85
Designing the questionnaire   91
Clear presentation   91
Vertical or horizontal closed answers?   91
Identifying response sets in a Likert scale   92
Clear instructions about how to respond   92
Keep question and answers together   94
Vignette questions   94
Pilot studies and pre-testing questions   95
Using existing questions   96
Key points   98
Questions for review   98

6   Structured Observation   99

Chapter overview   99
Introduction   99
Problems with survey research   99
So why not just observe behaviour directly?   99
The observation schedule   101
Strategies for observing behaviour   102
Issues of reliability and validity   102
    Reliability   102
    Validity   104
Field experiments as a form of structured observation   104
Criticisms of structured observation   106
    On the other hand . . .   107
Key points   107
Questions for review   107

7   Other Sources of Data   109

Chapter overview   109
Introduction   109
Personal documents   110
    Diaries, letters, and autobiographies   110
    Visual objects   111
Government documents   113
Official documents from private sources   114
Mass media outputs   115
Virtual outputs and the Internet as objects of analysis   115
Introduction to secondary analysis   117
    Advantages of secondary analysis   117
    Limitations of secondary analysis   120
Official statistics   121
    Reliability and validity   123
    Condemning and resurrecting official statistics   124
Official statistics as an unobtrusive measure   124
Key points   125
Questions for review   125

Part III   127

8   The Nature of Qualitative Research   128

Chapter overview   128
Introduction   128
The main steps in qualitative research   129
Theory and concepts in qualitative research   130

Reliability and validity in qualitative research   131
    Adapting reliability and validity for qualitative research   131
    Alternative criteria for evaluating qualitative research   132
    Overview of the issue of criteria   134
The main goals of qualitative researchers   134
    Seeing through the eyes of the people being studied   134
    Description and the emphasis on context   135
    Emphasis on process   136
    Flexibility and limited structure   136
Critiques of qualitative research   137
    Qualitative research is too subjective   137
    Difficult to replicate   137
    Problems of generalization   138
    Lack of transparency   139
Is it always like this?   139
Some contrasts between quantitative and qualitative research   139
Key points   140
Questions for review   141

9   Ethnography and Participant Observation   142

Chapter overview   142
Introduction   142
Access   143
    Overt versus covert ethnography   143
    Access to closed settings   145
    Access to open settings   146
    Ongoing access   147
    Key informants   148
Roles for ethnographers   148
    Active or passive?   150
Field notes   151
    Types of field notes   152
The rise of visual ethnography   152
The end   154
Can there be a feminist ethnography?   155
Key points   156
Questions for review   157

10   Interviewing in Qualitative Research   158

Chapter overview   158
Introduction   158
Differences between structured and qualitative research interviews   158
Unstructured and semi-structured interviewing   159
    Preparing an interview guide   160

Kinds of questions   163
Recording and transcription   166
Focus groups: an introduction   168
Conducting focus groups   168
How many groups?   168
Size of groups and selecting participants   169
Asking questions and level of moderator involvement   171
Recording and transcription   171
Group interaction in focus group sessions   172
Limitations of focus groups   173
Online interviews and focus groups   174
Online qualitative interviews   174
Online focus groups   174
Feminism and interviewing in qualitative research   175
The focus group as a feminist method   178
Qualitative interviewing (without immersion in a social setting) versus ethnography   179
Advantages of ethnography compared to qualitative interviewing   179
Advantages of qualitative interviewing in comparison to ethnography   180
Overview   182
Key points   183
Questions for review   183

Part IV   185

11   Sampling   186

Chapter overview   186
Introduction   186
Sampling error   189
Types of probability sample   189
Simple random sample   189
Systematic sample   191
Stratified random sampling   191
Multi-stage cluster sampling   192
The qualities of a probability sample   193
Sample size   193
Absolute and relative sample size   193
Non-response   196
Heterogeneity of the population   197
Kind of analysis   197
Types of non-probability sampling   197
Convenience sampling   197
Snowball sampling   198
Quota sampling   199
Structured observation and sampling   200
Limits to generalization   201
Sampling problems   201

Qualitative sampling   202
    Theoretical sampling   202
    Not just people   203
Content analysis sampling   203
    Sampling media   203
    Sampling dates   204
Reducing non-response   205
    Improving response rates to mailed questionnaires   205
    Virtual sampling issues   206
    Overview   207
One last point   207
Key points   208
Questions for review   208

12   Quantitative Data Analysis   210

Chapter overview   210
Introduction   210
A small research project   210
    Missing data   212
Getting started in SPSS   215
    Introduction   215
    Entering data in the Data View   216
    Defining variables: variable names, missing values, variable labels, and value labels   217
    Saving the data   219
    Retrieving data   219
Types of variables   219
Univariate analysis   222
    Frequency tables   222
    Diagrams   225
Data analysis with SPSS   226
    Generating a frequency table   226
    Generating a bar chart   226
    Generating a pie chart   226
    Generating a histogram   228
    Printing output   228
More univariate analysis and SPSS   230
    Measures of central tendency   230
    Measures of dispersion   230
    Generating the arithmetic mean, median, standard deviation, and range   231
Bivariate analysis   232
    Contingency tables   232
    Generating a contingency table   233
    Pearson's r   234
    Generating scatter diagrams   234
    Generating Pearson's r   237
    Generating Kendall's tau-b   238

Generating Cramér's V   238
Comparing means and eta   239
Amount of explained variance   239
Statistical significance and inferential statistics   240
Correlation and statistical significance   241
The chi-square test   242
Comparing means and statistical significance   243
Multivariate analysis   243
Is the relationship spurious?   243
Is there an intervening variable?   243
Is there an interaction?   244
Generating a contingency table with three variables   244
Other uses for multivariate analysis   244
Key points   248
Questions for review   248

13   Qualitative Data Analysis   251

Chapter overview   251
Introduction   251
General strategies of qualitative data analysis   252
Analytic induction   252
Grounded theory   252
Basic operations in qualitative data analysis   257
Steps and considerations in coding   257
Turning data into fragments   258
Learning NVivo   259
Coding   261
Searching text   263
Memos   268
Saving and retrieving an NVivo project   269
Opening an existing NVivo project   269
General thoughts on using NVivo   269
Problems with coding   269
Narrative analysis   271
Key points   273
Questions for review   273

Part V   275

14   Breaking Down the Quantitative/Qualitative Divide   276

Chapter overview   276
Introduction   276
The natural science model and qualitative research   277
Quantitative research and interpretivism   278
Quantitative research and constructionism   278

Research methods and epistemological and ontological considerations   279
Problems with the quantitative/qualitative contrast   279
    Behaviour versus meaning   279
    Theory and concepts tested in research versus those emerging from the data   280
    Numbers versus words   280
    Artificial versus natural   280
The mutual analysis of quantitative and qualitative research   281
    A qualitative research approach to quantitative research   281
    A quantitative research approach to qualitative research   282
Quantification in qualitative research   282
    Thematic analysis   282
    Quasi-quantification in qualitative research   282
    Combating anecdotalism through limited quantification   283
Key points   283
Questions for review   283

15   Combining Quantitative and Qualitative Research   285

Chapter overview   285
Introduction   285
The argument against multi-strategy research   285
    The embedded methods argument   286
    The paradigm argument   286
Two positions in the debate about quantitative and qualitative research   286
Approaches to multi-strategy research   287
    The logic of triangulation   287
    Qualitative research facilitates quantitative research   288
    Quantitative research facilitates qualitative research   289
    Filling in the gaps   289
    Static and process features   289
    Researcher and participant perspectives   289
    The problem of generality   290
    Qualitative research may help to interpret the relationship between variables   290
    Studying different aspects of a phenomenon   290
    Solving a puzzle   292
Reflections on multi-strategy research   292
Key points   293
Questions for review   294

16   Content Analysis   295

Chapter overview   295
Introduction   295
What things are to be counted?   296
    Words   296
    Subjects and themes   297
    Value positions   297

Coding   297
   Coding schedule   298
   Coding manual   298
   Potential pitfalls in devising coding schemes   299
Qualitative content analysis   300
   Semiotics   300
   Hermeneutics   301
Readers and audiences—active or passive?   302
Two approaches to the study of language   302
Conversation analysis   302
   Assumptions of conversation analysis   303
   Transcription and attention to detail   303
   Some basic tools of conversation analysis   304
   A final note on conversation analysis   305
Discourse analysis   305
   Producing facts   307
   Overview   309
Advantages of content analysis   310
Disadvantages of content analysis   310
Key points   311
Questions for review   312

17   Writing Up Social Research   313

Chapter overview   313
Introduction   313
Writing up quantitative research: an example   313
   Introduction   314
   Theory   315
   Data   315
   Measurement   315
   Methods and models   315
   Results   315
   Conclusions   315
   Lessons   316
Writing up qualitative research: an example   316
   Introduction   317
   The analysis of the social dimensions of food and eating   317
   Studies of vegetarianism   317
   The design of the study   317
   The findings of the study   318
   Explaining contemporary vegetarianism   318
   Conclusions   318
   Lessons   318
Postmodernism and its implications for writing   319
Writing up ethnography   320
   Experiential authority   321
   Typical forms   321

The natives' points of view   322
Interpretative omnipotence   322
Bibliography   322
Key points   323
Questions for review   323

18   Conducting a Research Project   325

Chapter overview   325
Introduction   325
Know what is expected by your institution   325
Identifying research questions   325
Using a supervisor   326
Managing time and resources: start thinking early about the research area   327
Searching the existing literature   329
Preparing for research   330
Doing research and analyzing results   330
Writing up research   331
Start early   331
Be persuasive   331
Get feedback   332
Avoid sexist, racist, and other prejudicial language   332
Structure your writing   333
Finally   337

Appendix   338
Glossary   342
References   349
Index   362

An invitation to students

Why are you here?

That's a good question to ask oneself when starting something new.

So why are you here? Why are you reading this book? If you're like most students, you're here because you have to be. The methodology course you are taking is a required course, and to do well on the exams and assignments you have to read this book.

If you are here out of necessity, that's all right. But what if there were more to it than that? What if this book actually explored topics that were meaningful and useful to you? I'll be making the case here that with a little effort you can experience intellectual stimulation and growth, and get some valuable practical applications to go along with that, by reading this book.

What might the intellectual payoff be to learning about social research methods? In most courses in the social sciences, students spend their time absorbing, and sometimes challenging, claims made about the social world. For example, you may learn that men are more likely to commit violent crimes than women. You may come to understand what it feels like to be homeless. Or perhaps you'll encounter a theory of why some countries are rich and powerful while others are not. That sort of activity—learning of and reflecting on claims to knowledge—is a worthwhile endeavour, but it will not be what concerns us here. Instead we will focus on how those types of claims are *generated* and how they come to be accepted, by some at least, as knowledge. In other words, rather than exploring the body of facts, concepts, theories, and interpretations that social scientists use to make sense of the world, we'll look at how all of that comes about.

One of the most profound questions that can be asked of someone making a claim to knowledge is, 'How do you *know* that?' That simple question is at the heart of what this book is about. And like so many simple questions, it has no simple answer. In fact, since ancient times, philosophers, scientists, and others have been grappling with the issue of what knowledge is and how it is to be acquired. One branch of philosophy, *epistemology*, deals with matters of that sort, such as the nature of truth, what sorts of things can be known, what should be accepted as knowledge, and how knowledge is to be sought.

It may come as a surprise to you, but those kinds of epistemological debates are still alive and well and can be found in the social sciences. In fact, they rage on even among researchers in the same discipline, such as sociology. The epistemological issues we will examine in this book involve different and sometimes conflicting positions on what procedures should be used to know things about society. For example, should the methods used in the natural sciences (such as physics, chemistry, and biology) be used to study people and the social order? If not, what are the alternatives? To what extent should values affect the research process? Do human beings have free will to some extent? If so, does that make it impossible to predict their behaviour? These and many other issues impinge on social research in a variety of ways and will be confronted at different stages of the book. While knowing how to do research—how to design a questionnaire, how to observe, how to analyze the mass media, and so on—is crucial to an education in research methods, so too is an appreciation of those sorts of wider issues.

A related division of philosophy, *ontology*, is concerned with the nature of reality and existence, what 'reality' means, and what should be considered as real. Here again, age-old controversies have carried over into modern times. There is no shortage of broadly different assertions and positions taken in the social sciences, especially within sociological circles, regarding what is real. We will explore some of the more salient disagreements on that topic and see how they are reflected in social research and the claims to knowledge made by social scientists.

Learning about various approaches to social knowledge and how such knowledge may be generated can be of immense benefit to you as a social thinker. Just like learning how clothes are made can help you to tell the difference between a good pair of jeans and a shoddy pair, understanding where social knowledge comes from will help you to distinguish between sound ideas and fatuous ones.

The practical implications of improving your critical thinking skills in this way are many. First of all, having a solid background in social research methods will help you to make sense of the material you will be expected to understand in your social science courses. Secondly, at various points in your university career you will probably be called upon to do some small research projects. The knowledge you will gain here can put you at an advantage with that sort of undertaking, and it could even be a starting point for more sophisticated research if you decide to go on to graduate school or to become a professional social scientist.

Finally, in everyday life you will be inundated with claims about people, society, and the world at large—how men and women are different (or the same), why divorce occurs, how children should be educated, how the country should be governed, and so on. The knowledge and skills you can acquire through learning about various social research methods will be of use to you when you have to evaluate those types of claims in order to make decisions in your life. And you may not be the only beneficiary of what you will learn. The people who are affected by your decisions could benefit as well, and if you decide to become active in your community or in some larger social grouping, the ripple effects may be large indeed.

Who would benefit from reading this book?

This book was written for undergraduate students taking a research methods course, most often in sociology departments but also in other social science disciplines, such as social work and education. It

covers a wide range of methods, approaches to research, and ways of carrying out data analysis.

Research methods are not tied to a particular nation. The principles underlying them transcend national boundaries and the genesis of this book gives it a wide-ranging and international flavour. The original text by Alan Bryman was written with the needs of UK post-secondary students in mind but was widely adopted in Europe and Canada as well. Feedback from adopters and reviewers suggested the book could be made even more useful for Canadian instructors and students through the addition of Canadian and, more broadly, North American examples, sources, and research studies. James Teevan's and Edward Bell's adaptations of the book have preserved the qualities that contributed to its initial success—its clarity, comprehensiveness, and presentation of social research methods in an international context—and have expanded on those strengths by incorporating elements that are integral to North American and especially Canadian courses in the discipline.

Structure of the book

One of the most fundamental distinctions in social research occurs between its quantitative and qualitative varieties. This distinction lies behind the structure of the book and the way in which issues and methods are approached. It is divided into five parts.

Part One comprises two scene-setting chapters. It deals with basic ideas about the nature of social research.

- Chapter 1 examines such issues as the nature of the relationship between theory and research and the degree to which a natural science approach is an appropriate framework for the study of society. It is here that the distinction between quantitative and qualitative research is first encountered— they are presented as different *research orientations* with different ways of conceptualizing how people and society should be studied. This chapter also includes a discussion of *research questions*—what they are, their importance, and how they come to be formulated.
- In Chapter 2, the idea of a *research design* is introduced. It provides an introduction to the basic frameworks within which social research is

carried out, such as social survey research, case study research, and experimental research. These two chapters provide the basic building blocks for the rest of the book.

Part Two contains five chapters concerned with quantitative research.

- Chapter 3 explores the nature of quantitative research and provides a context for the later chapters. The next two chapters are largely concerned with aspects of social survey research.
- Chapter 4 is concerned with the kind of interviewing that takes place in survey research, that is, structured interviewing, and with the design of questionnaires. This involves a discussion of how to devise self-completion questionnaires.
- Chapter 5 examines the issue of how to ask questions for questionnaires and structured interviews.
- Chapter 6 covers structured observation, a method developed for the systematic observation of behaviour.
- Chapter 7 looks at the analysis of data collected by other researchers or by official bodies.

Part Three contains three chapters on aspects of qualitative research.

- Chapter 8 plays the same role in relation to Part Three as Chapter 3 plays in relation to Part Two. It provides an overview of the nature of qualitative research and as such provides the context for the other chapters in this part.
- Chapter 9 is concerned with ethnography and participant observation. The two terms are often used interchangeably and refer to the immersion of the researcher in a social setting, the source of some of the best-known studies in social research.
- Chapter 10 deals with the kinds of interviewing that qualitative researchers conduct—typically semi-structured interviewing or unstructured interviewing—and with focus groups in which groups of individuals are interviewed on a specific topic.

Part Four looks at sampling in both quantitative and qualitative research and then at data analysis, including computer aids.

- Chapter 11 deals with sampling—how to select a sample and the considerations involved in assessing what can be inferred from different kinds of samples. Most texts place sampling near their discussion of survey research. The placement here reflects how sampling is also crucial in qualitative research.
- Chapter 12 presents a range of basic non-technical tools for quantitative analysis. The emphasis is on how to choose a method of analysis and how to interpret findings. No formulae are presented. Instead SPSS, the most widely used social science computer software for analyzing quantitative data, is explained; mastering it means the computer performs the actual calculations.
- Chapter 13 explores some approaches to the analysis of qualitative data and also includes an introduction to using computer software in qualitative research analysis.

Part Five contains chapters that go beyond the quantitative/qualitative research contrast.

- Chapter 14 deals with some of the ways in which the distinction between quantitative and qualitative research is less fixed than sometimes supposed.
- Chapter 15 presents some ways in which they can be combined to produce what is referred to as multi-strategy research.
- Chapter 16 then applies these principles to content analysis, a method that provides a framework for the analysis of things like letters, documents, newspapers, movies, chat lines, books, radio and television, etc. and usually seen as the domain of quantitative research. It also examines two ways to analyze language: conversation analysis and discourse analysis.
- Chapter 17 provides guidance on writing up research, an often-neglected area in the teaching of the research process.
- Chapter 18 offers advice on conducting a research project, taking readers through the main steps involved.

Special features of the book

Several special features make the text more helpful:

- *Examples.* Students can learn by reading how others have carried out research and what lessons they seem to have learned. In view of this, most major points include an example or two, usually from published research. Students generally do not have the resources to conduct a similar level of research. In these instances the most that can be asked of them is an awareness of how their early efforts are governed by the principle of looking for what is satisfactory, rather than what is optimal, and the implications of doing so.

- *Boxes.* The text is full of them. Boxes do a variety of things—besides creating a break in the text, making it less imposing and more readable. Sometimes boxes provide examples; sometimes they define key terms ('What is . . .?'); sometimes they list a series of important points. They also provide a focus for definitions and key examples.

- *Ethical Issues boxes.* Several chapters contain a special type of box that considers how ethical issues impinge on researchers and the kinds of principles involved.

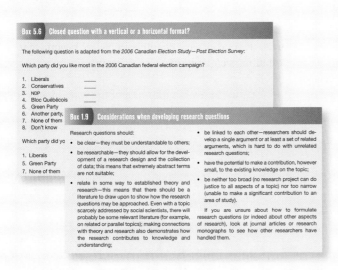

Box 1.1 Grand theory and social research

Giddens' (1984) structuration theory attempts to bridge the gulf between notions of structure and agency in social life. This theoretical issue is explored in empirical research by Dinovitzer et al. (2003) on the educational attainment of immigrant youth. The specific focus [is] suburban Toronto immigra[nts] to 1995. The data were q[uestioned] through structured intervie[ws] researchers was to tease ou[t] of structural variables (such [as] the youths' family backgrou[nd] ables more under their con[trol] and cutting classes) on achie[vement]

The authors found that bo[th] (gender and father's occupa[tion] factor (intellectual investme[nt] cation, and that bilingual E[SL] than those immigrants for w[hom] language. They are not brig[hter] harder, but they have greate[r] and, perhaps partly as a res[ult]

Box 1.2 The need for theory

Teevan and Dryburgh (2000) collected data from 57 male adolescents concerning their participation in various deviant activities, such as truancy, theft, vandalism, and fighting, and asked them why they acted the way they did. Then the boys were read specially adapted sociological explanations of such behaviour. The goal was to let them be sociologists and evaluate the theories. The idea was tied to giving marginalized groups a voice and to seeing the issue in question from the point of view of those studied, two things that are commonly done in qualitative research. The idea was great, some journal reviewers said, but the relevance of the findings for sociological theory needed to be explored. Eventually the authors dug up and fashioned the minimal amount of theory required to have the article published.

Box 5.6 Closed question with a vertical or a horizontal format?

The following question is adapted from the *2006 Canadian Election Study—Post Election Survey*:

Which party did you like most in the 2006 Canadian federal election campaign?

1. Liberals ____
2. Conservatives ____
3. NDP ____
4. Bloc Québécois ____
5. Green Party
6. Another party, ____
7. None of them
8. Don't know

Which party did yo[u]

1. Liberals
5. Green Party
7. None of them

Box 1.9 Considerations when developing research questions

Research questions should:

- be clear—they must be understandable to others;
- be researchable—they should allow for the development of a research design and the collection of data; this means that extremely abstract terms are not suitable;
- relate in some way to established theory and research—this means that there should be a literature to draw upon to show how the research questions may be approached. Even with a topic scarcely addressed by social scientists, there will probably be some relevant literature (for example, on related or parallel topics); making connections with theory and research also demonstrates how the research contributes to knowledge and understanding;

- be linked to each other—researchers should develop a single argument or at least a set of related arguments, which is hard to do with unrelated research questions;
- have the potential to make a contribution, however small, to the existing knowledge on the topic;
- be neither too broad (no research project can do justice to all aspects of a topic) nor too narrow (unable to make a significant contribution to an area of study).

If you are unsure about how to formulate research questions (or indeed about other aspects of research), look at journal articles or research monographs to see how other researchers have handled them.

Ethical issue 4.1

Mentioning sponsorship

At one Ontario university, ethical rules prohibit including the name of the sponsor of the research in the cover letter. The rule is based on the consideration that people may feel pressured or coerced by reading, for example, that the research is sponsored by the Canadian Cancer Society. At another university, it is unethical *not* to supply that information as it is thought to be part of informed consent. For example, some people may not want the government to know anything about them, so if the federal Ministry of Fisheries is funding the study, they would want to be informed so they can choose not to participate. But listing the sponsor does not guarantee informed consent, because a sponsoring body (even a highly controversial one) may be virtually unknown to the general public. Ethical issues are never simple!

- *Practical tips.* Most chapters have at least one box of practical tips—special points to think about or to watch out for—on certain recurring but easily avoidable mistakes that students make.

Practical Tip

Referring to websites

There is a growing practice in academic work that when referring to websites, the date they were consulted should be included. This convention is very much associated with the fact that websites often disappear and frequently change, so that if subsequent researchers want to follow up any findings, or even to check on them, they may find that they are no longer there or that they have changed. Citing the date(s) the site was visited may help to relieve any anxieties about such problems.

- *Checklists.* Most chapters include checklists of issues that should be borne in mind when engaging in certain activities, such as doing a literature review, devising a structured interview schedule, or conducting a focus group. Checklists are meant to highlight key points encountered in the text and to remind students what to look out for or consider when doing their own research.

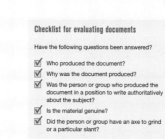

Checklist for evaluating documents

Have the following questions been answered?

- ☑ Who produced the document?
- ☑ Why was the document produced?
- ☑ Was the person or group who produced the document in a position to write authoritatively about the subject?
- ☑ Is the material genuine?
- ☑ Did the person or group have an axe to grind or a particular slant?

- ☑ Is the document typical of its kind, and if not, is it possible to establish how atypical it is and in what ways?
- ☑ Is the meaning of the document clear?
- ☑ Can the events or accounts presented in the document be corroborated?
- ☑ Are there different interpretations of the document from the one you offer, and if so what are they? Have you discounted them? If so, why?

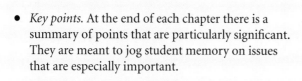

- *Chapter overviews.* Each chapter begins with a chapter overview that alerts readers to what they can expect to learn by the end of each chapter—a route map of what is to follow.

- *Key points.* At the end of each chapter there is a summary of points that are particularly significant. They are meant to jog student memory on issues that are especially important.

- *Questions for review.* At the end of each chapter there is also a series of questions to help test understanding of key concepts and ideas.

- *Glossary.* At the end of the book there is a glossary of definitions of central terms. Many repeat definitions in the 'What is . . .?' boxes, and they also provide a convenient way of recalling the meaning of key terms.

Companion website

Social Research Methods is accompanied by an inter-active website (**www.oupcanada.com/SRM**). The website provides additional teaching and learning material, including:

- instructor's guide;
- PowerPoint slides;
- examples drawn from real research of the main methods outlined in the book;
- links to social research websites; and
- summaries of key debates and controversies in social research.

The website also contains a **Methods and Skills Toolkit** designed to help guide students through the research process. This resource provides a guide to the practicalities and problems that students face when asked to do a research project. The toolkit covers a range of issues, from dealing with a super-visor to ways of organizing and writing a paper or thesis for maximum effect. The toolkit also shows students how the larger research issues and contro-versies dealt with in *Social Research Methods* may have an impact on their own experiences of con-ducting a research project.

How to use the book

The book can be used in many ways. Some instruc-tors, for reasons of time or preference, may not want to include all chapters or all sections of a specific chapter.

- *Wider philosophical and methodological issues.* If a full appreciation of the wider philosophical context of inquiry in social research is not needed, Chapter 1 can largely be ignored, except for the part on formu-lating a research question. If an emphasis on such issues *is* of interest, Chapter 1, along with Chapter 14, should be a particular focus of attention.

- *Practical issues concerned with doing quantitative research.* This is the province of the whole of Part Two. Chapter 2 is a good introduction because it maps out the main research designs, such as experimental and cross-sectional, used by quan-titative researchers.

- *Practical issues concerned with doing qualitative research.* This is the province of the whole of Part Three. Again, Chapter 2 maps out the research designs frequently employed, such as the case study, in qualitative research.

- *Analyzing data.* Chapters 12 and 13 explore the analysis of quantitative and qualitative research data respectively, including an introduction to the use of computer software for this analysis. Even if the module is taught without actual computer applications, exposure to them is useful for later work and for reinforcing the textual material.

- *The quantitative/qualitative research contrast.* The distinction between quantitative and qualitative research is used in two ways: to organize the dis-cussion of current research methods and methods of analysis and to introduce some wider philo-sophical issues about social research. Chapter 1 outlines the chief areas of difference between quantitative and qualitative research. Some of the limitations of adhering to an excessively strict demarcation between the two research strategies are presented in Chapter 14, while Chapter 15 explores ways of integrating them. If time is an issue these chapters can be skimmed.

- *Writing.* Writing up research is as much a part of the research process as is data collection. Chapter 17 discusses a variety of issues to do with writing up research and should be read.

- *Doing a research project.* As already mentioned in this guide, the whole book is relevant to student research projects or mini-projects, but Chapter 18 is where specific advice relating to this issue is located along with a discussion of writing a thesis or similar product.

Acknowledgements

Many people have helped me with this book, many of them unwittingly. Generations of research methods students at the University of Western Ontario have tested its contents. I wish to thank several people at or connected with OUP: David Stover, who had to persevere to initiate the project, Phyllis Wilson, who guided its early phases and never complained of my missing deadlines, and to a dedicated copy editor, Pamela Erlichman, for her suggestions. I am grateful to Sarah Pink for her permission to use an image from her research on women and bullfighting.

Two people deserve the greatest appreciation: Alan Bryman and my wife, Bonnie. He wrote the British text on which this book is based. He put into clear prose the many things I tried to impart to my students in lectures, from philosophy of science issues to showing the common aspects of qualitative and quantitative methods, making my adaptation so much easier. My wife put up yet again with the late nights and daily tensions that a book like this entails. Thank you both.

James J. Teevan

Many thanks must go to Alan Bryman, who wrote the original version of this book, and to James J. Teevan, who produced the First Canadian Edition. Their diligent work made this Second Canadian Edition possible. Both men were also very helpful in providing information and answering my queries as I prepared this version of the book.

Jacqueline Mason and Dina Theleritis of Oxford University Press did a fine job of marshalling this project from its initial stages to its completion.

Pamela Erlichman once again proved that she is a first-rate copy editor and writer. Thanks to all of you for what you have done.

My family—Jennifer Wakefield and Ted and Angelica Bell—had to endure a number of sacrifices as I worked on this book, but were unfailingly supportive of me nonetheless. Thank you for your kindness.

Edward Bell

Part I

Part I of this book is concerned with two ideas that recur again and again throughout the text—the notion of general research orientations and the idea of research designs. In Chapter 1, two general orientations are identified—the quantitative and qualitative approaches—along with a variety of considerations that affect the practice of social research. Chapter 2 presents different kinds of research design and identifies the criteria used to evaluate social research. Together these chapters provide the basic conceptual building blocks that are returned to later in the book. Some of the issues may seem remote from actual research practices, but they are in fact crucial for understanding them.

1

General Research Orientations

Chapter overview

The aim of this chapter is to examine the fundamental assumptions upon which social research is based. An important distinction commonly drawn among practitioners of social research—between the *quantitative* and *qualitative* approaches—is explored in relation to those considerations. We will consider:

- the relationship between theory and research—in particular, whether theories and the hypotheses derived from them are tested by gathering data (a *deductive* approach) or whether data gathering is used as a means to create theory (an *inductive* approach);
- *epistemological* issues, such as whether a natural science model like the one used in chemistry

or biology is suitable for the study of the social world;

- *ontological* issues, such as whether the social world should be regarded as a reality external to individuals over which they have little or no control or as something that social actors may fashion into their personal realities;
- the ways *values* and *practical issues* impinge on the research process; and
- how these issues relate to both quantitative and qualitative research; a preliminary discussion, followed up in Chapters 14 and 15, suggests that while the quantitative and qualitative orientations may be different, they can complement each other.

Introduction

This book is about social research. It would be easy to 'cut to the chase' by explaining how to choose among the various research procedures and describing how to implement them. But the practice of social research does not exist in a vacuum, sealed off from philosophical debates and contested assumptions. Several questions may arise, for example: Are people passive reactors to the social world or active creators of social reality? Can the methods of the natural sciences be applied to the social world or does social science need unique methods to deal with its subject matter? Must past research be the source for current research? The explanations scholars provide for social phenomena and their choice of research methods often depend on how they answer those sorts of questions.

Social research can arise from a variety of motives. Quite often, the goal is to assess the adequacy of a particular social theory, such as a theory of prejudice or crime. In other cases the aim is to gather information to create theories; for example, a sociologist may pose as a street person to find out how the homeless are treated by the public. Sometimes simple 'fact-finding' or exploratory work is carried out. For instance, Milgram's (1963) famous study of obedience was done partly to see how far subjects would go in obeying an authority figure's commands, and the results were astounding—many people appeared to be willing to inflict pain on innocent others. Similarly, Bell's (2007) study of the western-Canadian separatist movement was motivated in part by a desire to know how much public support the movement had, and it produced evidence that the movement was more popular than previously thought.

In other instances, research is driven by what is seen as a pressing social problem. In fact the discipline of sociology came into being in the eighteenth and nineteenth centuries partly as a way of understanding the social crises associated with modern life, and that tradition continues to this day. Hier (2002), for example, investigated raves when they became an area of official concern following the 1999 ecstacy-related deaths of three young adults in Toronto. Yet another stimulus for research is personal experiences (Lofland and Lofland 1995). Sugiman (2004), who is a 'sansei' or third-generation Japanese, investigated Japanese-Canadian women's experiences of internment during the Second World War after hearing about the personal histories of her family and friends.

Regardless of the motivation for doing research, the data gathered are usually viewed in relation to theories. That's because theories are an attempt to 'make sense of it all,' to find order and meaning in a seemingly infinite mass of information. How is that done?

Theory and research

The connection between theory and research is not straightforward. There are several issues at stake here, but two stand out: first, the form of the theory; and second, the relationship between data and theory.

Degree of abstraction

The term 'theory' is used in a variety of ways, but its most common meaning is *an explanation of observed regularities or patterns*, such as the finding that schizophrenia is more common in the working class than in the middle class, or that more men than women are alcoholics. Theories are composed of interrelated and usually verifiable statements or propositions. The statements and propositions come in varying forms and different types that may be combined in the same theory. Here are some of the common components of a theory:

1. *definitions*, which specify what the key terms in the theory mean; for example, 'Crime is any

violation of the *Canadian Criminal Code* and includes arson, embezzling, etc.';
2. *descriptions of the phenomena of interest*; for example, 'Arson involves the illegal setting of fires and is often done at night, either to abandoned buildings or houses when no one is home. There were 438 cases of arson last year, with estimated damage over $2 billion.';
3. *relational statements*, which connect two or more variables; knowing the value of one variable conveys information about the other; for example, 'As the economy experiences a downturn, the arson rate increases.' Relational statements can be:

   a. *deterministic*, which means the two variables go together all of the time; for example, 'as the economy shrinks by 1 per cent, the arson rate increases by 5 per cent.' If research uncovers an instance in which the variables are not related in this way, the relational statement must be modified.
   b. *probabilistic*, which means the two variables go together with some degree of regularity, but the relationship is not one of inevitability; for example, 'regions of the country with growing economies are more likely to experience a decrease in the arson rate than regions in which the economy is shrinking.' Here, finding a case that does not fit the pattern does not lead to a rejection of the theory—it could be one of the times they are not related in that way.

There are different types of theories. One distinction that is sometimes made is between *theories of the middle range* (Merton 1967) and *grand theories*. The former are more limited in scope, and can be tested directly by gathering empirical evidence. For instance, Durkheim's (1952 [1897]) theory of suicide, which maintains that suicide is a function of the level of social integration, is a theory of the middle range. One way to test it would be to compare suicide rates for married people with those for single, divorced, or widowed individuals. Grand theories, on the other hand, are more general and abstract. They include theories such as structural-functionalism, symbolic interactionism, critical theory, post-structuralism, and so on. Grand theories generally offer few direct indications of how to collect evidence to test them.

So, if someone were to try to test one, the level of abstraction would make it difficult to link the theory as a whole with the real world. For that reason, Merton argued that grand theories are of limited use for research purposes. However, as the example in Box 1.1 suggests, with some ingenuity an abstract theory like Giddens' structuration theory (1984) can be applied to a specific situation and yield some important insights.

Usually, then, it is not grand theory that directly guides social research—middle range theories are much more likely to be the focus of empirical inquiry. Merton's (1938) anomie theory, which suggests that crime is more common when a society instils a desire for wealth in everyone but provides insufficient means for all to achieve it, is another example of a theory of the middle range. Such theories fall somewhere between grand theories and particularistic explanations. They represent attempts to understand and explain a limited aspect of social life.

Although theory plays a crucial role in the social sciences, there may be no allusions to theories in some studies. For example, some qualitative writers strive to provide a rich description of the experiences of a group of people without trying to come up with a comprehensive theory that would explain those experiences. Nonetheless, as Box 1.2 shows, social scientists are often under pressure from their peers to relate their work to theories of some kind.

As Box 1.2 indicates, some social scientists are prone to reject research that has no direct connection to theory in either the grand or middle range sense of the term. However, as suggested earlier in this chapter, some non-theoretical work may provide qualitative insights that are useful or revealing in their own right. McKeganey and Barnard's (1996) research on British prostitutes and their clients is a case in point. The authors related their research findings to investigations of prostitutes in a number of other countries, and what they describe offers good illustrations of ideas that form an important part of the sociologist's conceptual toolkit. Although it is not possible to tell whether the authors had the concept in mind when they collected their data, their work offers real-life examples of Goffman's (1963) notion of 'stigma' and the way in which stigmatized individuals, here prostitutes and clients, manage a spoiled identity. Their work also illuminates Hochschild's (1983) concept of 'emotional labour', a term she coined to denote how flight attendants feign friendliness when dealing with difficult passengers. Similarly, it would be unwarranted to ignore the numerous studies that are directed towards providing data that could eventually be used to evaluate or devise a theory.

Box 1.1   Grand theory and social research

Giddens' (1984) structuration theory attempts to bridge the gulf between notions of structure and agency in social life. This theoretical issue is explored in empirical research by Dinovitzer et al. (2003) on the educational attainment of immigrant youth. The specific focus of their research was suburban Toronto immigrants in the years 1976 to 1995. The data were quantitative, generated through structured interviews. The goal of the researchers was to tease out the relative influence of structural variables (such as class, gender, and the youths' family background) and individual variables more under their control (such as studying and cutting classes) on achieving higher education.

The authors found that both structural variables (gender and father's occupation) and an individual factor (intellectual investment) affect higher education, and that bilingual ESL students do better than those immigrants for whom English is a first language. They are not brighter, nor do they work harder, but they have greater parental supervision and, perhaps partly as a result, plan better.

Box 1.2   The need for theory

Teevan and Dryburgh (2000) collected data from 57 male adolescents concerning their participation in various deviant activities, such as truancy, theft, vandalism, and fighting, and asked them why they acted the way they did. Then the boys were read specially adapted sociological explanations of such behaviour. The goal was to let them be sociologists and evaluate the theories. The idea was tied to giving marginalized groups a voice and to seeing the issue in question from the point of view of those studied, two things that are commonly done in qualitative research. The idea was great, some journal reviewers said, but the relevance of the findings for sociological theory needed to be explored. Eventually the authors dug up and fashioned the minimal amount of theory required to have the article published.

Our discussion of what theory is and what its importance is invites consideration of another question: What is the relationship between theory and research? Up to this point we have focused primarily on how theory can guide research, in particular on how the collection and analysis of data can be used to test theories. But this notion of research as essentially 'theory testing' does not provide a complete picture of what social scientists do. Theory may also *follow upon* or *arise from* the collection and analysis of data. One begins to see here two different ways to go about acquiring knowledge—the *deductive* and *inductive* approaches.

Deductive and inductive approaches

The deductive method represents the most common approach to social research. The sequence of steps taken in deductive research is depicted in Figure 1.1. Note that the researcher starts by coming up with a theory that seeks to explain a particular phenomenon, and then deduces specific hypotheses from it that are tested with empirical data (see Box 1.3 for a concrete example). The hypotheses are either confirmed or rejected. In Kelley and De Graaf's research described in Box 1.3, their hypotheses were supported. If, however, the data gathered do not support the researchers' hypotheses, the theory has to be revised or rejected.

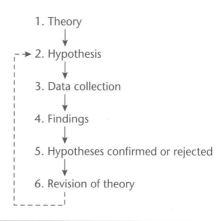

Figure 1.1 The process of deduction

It is also important to bear in mind that when this deductive approach is put into operation, there are many instances in which a researcher does not follow the exact linear sequence shown in Figure 1.1. For example, a new hypothesis may come to mind during the data-gathering stage; or the relevance of the data for a *second* theory may become apparent *after* the data have been collected. In fact, although the process of deduction outlined in Figure 1.1 often occurs, it is best considered as a general process that is not strictly followed in all cases.

In some research *no* attempt is made to follow the sequence outlined in Figure 1.1. Some investigators

Box 1.3   A deductive study

Based on their readings of previous studies of what affects religious beliefs—things like parents, schools, and friends—Kelley and De Graaf (1997) argued that there are good grounds to think that the nation into which one is born is also an important factor. These reflections constitute what they referred to as the 'theory' that guided their research and from which the following hypothesis was derived: 'People born into religious nations will, in proportion to the orthodoxy of their fellow-citizens, acquire more orthodox beliefs than otherwise similar people born into secular nations' (1997: 641). The authors hypothesized further that the religious orientation of the individual's family (whether devout or secular) would affect the nature of the relationship between national religiosity and religious orthodoxy.

To test the hypotheses, Kelley and De Graaf examined large-sample survey research from 15 nations. Religious orthodoxy was measured by four survey questions about religious belief: (1) whether the person believed in God; (2) past beliefs about God; (3) how close the individual felt to God; and (4) whether they had a belief that God cares about everyone. To measure national religiosity, the 15 nations were classified into one of five categories, from secular to religious. The classification was derived by averaging parental religious attendance measured on a scale of five levels and religious belief in the nation as a whole (1997: 647). The hypotheses were broadly confirmed and the authors concluded that the 'religious environment of a nation has a major impact on the beliefs of its citizens' (1997: 654).

Note how this study demonstrates the process whereby hypotheses are deduced from existing theory and then guide the process of data collection so that the theory can be tested.

Deductive approach

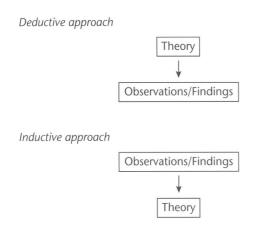

Inductive approach

Figure 1.2 Deductive and inductive approaches to the relationship between theory and research

prefer an *inductive* approach in which theory is the *outcome* of research. In inductive social science, the researcher begins not by coming up with a theory to be tested, but by *gathering or examining data* relevant to the phenomenon being investigated—see Figure 1.2, which illustrates the difference between induction and deduction. Box 1.4 provides an example: Wilson (2002) offered theories to explain raves only *after* he had gathered qualitative information on the topic. When the inductive method is used, data are gathered not to test a theory, but to come up with the information needed to *construct* a theory. That's why with induction data gathering comes

first, and the effort to create concepts and theories out of it comes later. After some theoretical reflection has occurred, a researcher may want to collect more data to establish the conditions in which the newly emerged theory does or does not hold. Such a general strategy is often called *iterative*: it involves a weaving back and forth between data and theory. The practice of deriving theories from qualitative data is sometimes referred to as *grounded* theory.

In actual research situations it is impossible to conduct a study that is *purely deductive* or *purely inductive*. Just as deduction entails an element of induction (theories do not emerge from a pristine state of mind lacking all awareness of data and observations), the inductive process is likely to entail a modicum of deduction (observation is usually made with at least some awareness of applicable theories). Often some combination of both can be found in the same research.

While some researchers using induction undoubtedly try to develop theories, sometimes the result of inductive research is little more than empirical generalizations, however useful they may be. An example is the recent Statistics Canada finding that from 1997 to 2007, salaries stagnated for blue-collar employees in manufacturing and for clerical employees and retail salespeople, yet the earnings of private-sector managers grew by 20 per cent in that period (see www.statcan.ca/Daily).

The next section examines some epistemological issues that impinge on the conduct of social research.

Box 1.4   An inductive study

Wilson (2002) examined the experiences of young adults who attend raves and in one phase of his research conducted semi-structured interviews with 10 females and 27 males. He also looked at underground magazines, flyers advertising raves, and recordings of raves. He found that the reasons for going to raves varied from something as simple as escape, to intentional rejection of the traditionally gendered and racially segregated bar scene, to a shallow resistance to conventional status hierarchies. Concerning the use of the drug ecstacy, one male university student asked: 'Do you really need social barriers, do we really need the defenses that we have

and would life be better off if we didn't have some of [them]?' (Wilson 2002: 396). But Wilson found that some ravers, in their disdain of the rave spinoffs and rave clubs, try to maintain an elite status.

In this inductive study, Wilson's explanations came after, rather than before, the data were gathered and examined. This was his expressed preference when he sought 'the meanings that youth give to their activities' (2002: 399). He tried to understand raves from the participants' points of view, an issue on which the existing literature was inconsistent. The qualitative data then led him to offer his explanations of their behaviour.

Epistemological considerations

Those who do social research base their work on a number of epistemological assumptions—notions of what can be known and how knowledge can be acquired. One important epistemological issue in the social sciences concerns the question of what should be regarded as acceptable knowledge. A fundamental controversy in this context is whether the social world should be studied according to the same principles and procedures as those used in the natural sciences.

Positivism

One epistemological position that affirms the importance of following the natural sciences is *positivism*. Although definitions of the term vary, positivism is generally taken to entail the following:

1. Only phenomena and regularities confirmed by the senses (such as sight and hearing) can be accepted as knowledge—the principle of *empiricism*. In other words, ideas must be subjected to the rigours of empirical testing before they can be considered knowledge.
2. A key purpose of theory is to generate hypotheses that can be tested and thereby allow explanations of observed laws and principles to be assessed (*deduction*).
3. Knowledge can also be arrived at through the gathering of facts that provide the basis for generalizations or laws (*induction*).
4. Science must (and presumably can) be conducted in a way that is value-free. Researchers used to call this *objectivity*; today they are more likely to call it *intersubjectivity*, meaning that different researchers, even those with different values, would reach the same conclusions given the same data.
5. There is a clear distinction between scientific statements, which describe how and why social phenomena operate the way they do, and normative statements, that outline whether certain acts or social conditions are morally acceptable. The former are held to be the true domain of science; the latter are seen as belonging in the realms of philosophy or religion, but not science. This idea is implied by point 1 above,

because the truth of moral claims cannot be confirmed by the senses.

It is possible to see in these five points a link with some of the issues already raised about the relationship between theory and research. Positivism assumes a fairly sharp distinction between theory and research and includes elements of both deduction and induction. One role of research is to test theories and to provide information for the development of laws, somewhat similar to the laws of science like Boyle's law. There is also an implication that it is possible to collect observations in a manner not influenced by pre-existing theories, and to derive theories from those observations. Finally, theories and propositions not directly testable through empirical observation are often not considered to be genuinely scientific.

A common mistake is to treat positivism as synonymous with science and the scientific. In fact, philosophers of science and social science differ quite sharply over how best to characterize scientific practice, and since the early 1960s positivism has acquired some negative connotations. It began to be viewed with dissatisfaction partly because some researchers in the positivist tradition ignored some fundamental differences between human beings and the often inanimate or not fully conscious entities studied by natural scientists. Unlike subatomic particles or plants, for example, we humans have thoughts, feelings, and values, and according to some at least, we have some capacity for volition. Those aspects of human behaviour were often not addressed in the leading positivistic theories of the day. Also, dissatisfaction developed concerning the positivist idea that science can or should be value-free. Critics pointed out that 'neutral' social scientists often took at least implicit moral positions on social issues—for example, theories that imply that social equilibrium or harmony are normal seemed to be saying that social change is not needed or desirable. Some critics went further and claimed that it is the duty of the social scientist to help bring about social change in order to create a better world.

Interpretivism

Interpretivism to some extent grew out of the epistemological critique of positivism, and provides an alternative to the sort of social science typically done by positivists. Interpretive researchers maintain that it is the role of social scientists to grasp the subjective *meanings* of people's actions. They make the point that people act on the basis of the meanings that they attribute to their acts and to the acts of others. Using their own common-sense constructs, individuals interpret the reality of their daily lives and it is these thoughts that motivate their behaviour.

Interpretivists claim that it is the job of the social scientist to gain access to the 'common-sense thinking' of the people they study and hence to interpret people's actions and their social world *from the point of view of the actors*. Thus any thoughts constructed by the social scientist to grasp this social reality must be founded upon the common-sense interpretations of those they study: people living their daily lives within their own social world (Schutz 1962: 59). Many interpretive social scientists argue that the subject matter of the social sciences—people, groups, and institutions—is fundamentally different from that of the natural sciences. For them it follows that the study of the social world requires a different logic and research procedure, one that reflects what they see as the distinctiveness of humans as against other living things or inanimate objects. This clash reflects a division between an emphasis on the *explanation* of human behaviour that is the chief ingredient of the positivist approach to the social sciences, and the preference for an *empathetic understanding*

and *interpretation* of human behaviour. This contrast reflects long-standing debates that preceded the emergence of modern social science, but find their expression in Max Weber's (1864–1920) notion of *Verstehen* (which means 'empathetic understanding'). Weber described sociology as a 'science which attempts the interpretive understanding of social action in order to arrive at a causal explanation of its course and effects' (1947: 88). Weber's definition seems to embrace both explanation *and* understanding here, but the crucial point is that the task of 'causal explanation' is undertaken with reference to the 'interpretive understanding of social action.' This is a different emphasis from a more Durkheimian view in which the external forces that affect behaviour may not be perceived by those involved, or at least may have no meaning for them. For a Marxist view, see Box 1.5.

Symbolic interactionism is an example of a sociological perspective that falls under the heading of interpretivism. The ideas of the founders of symbolic interactionism, in particular those of George Herbert Mead (1863–1931) who maintains that one's *self-concept* emerges through an appreciation of the perceptions of others, have been hotly debated. Symbolic interactionists argue that interaction takes place in such a way that individuals are continually interpreting the symbolic meaning of their environment (including the actions of others) and acting on the basis of that imputed meaning (cf. Collins

Box 1.5   Research methods used by Marxists

Almost all who adopt a Marxist approach are critical of the positivist notion that social researchers should take a value-neutral stance regarding their subject matter. But they are also critical of narrowly interpretive perspectives on social life, arguing that social research has to go beyond acquiring knowledge of how people in society interpret their world. Marxists argue that those who own the means of production deceive, constrain, and exploit the weak. The masses could be free if social scientists, by asking embarrassing questions and making pointed arguments, would uncover exploitation, expose hypocrisy, and reveal to the general populace the nature and extent of their oppression. This would transform the masses from what Marx called a *class an sich* (a class in itself, an objective reality) into a *class für*

sich (a class for itself, one with an awareness of its exploitation).

Marxists reject the idea that it is the role of the scientist to be detached. Instead, they see the role of social scientist as one of unmasking the unjust conditions in the world, thus allowing the downtrodden to see the sources of their ills. They maintain that research should be action-oriented, that it should involve *praxis*: putting one's theoretical and academic positions into practice. The idea of praxis is contained in Marx's famous dictum that 'philosophers have only *interpreted* the world in various ways; the point, however, is to change it' (Marx 1998 [1845]: 574). Smashing myths and uncovering contradictions are just the first part of that process (cf. Neuman 2003).

1994). In research terms, according to Blumer (1962: 188), 'the position of symbolic interaction requires the student to catch the process of interpretation through which [actors] construct their actions.'

Taking an interpretative stance can result in surprising findings, or at least findings that appear surprising if a position from outside the particular social context being studied is adopted. Box 1.6 provides an interesting example of that possibility.

Of course, as the example in Box 1.6 suggests, when social scientists adopt an interpretive stance, they are not simply laying bare how members of a social group interpret the world around them. The social scientist almost certainly aims to place those interpretations into a social scientific framework. Thus there is a double interpretation going on: the researcher is providing an interpretation of others' interpretations. Indeed, there is a third level of interpretation going on, because the researcher's interpretations have to be further interpreted in terms of the concepts, theories, and literature of a discipline. Thus, taking the suggestion from Box 1.6 that Riverside is not perceived as a high-crime area by residents is Foster's interpretation of her subjects' interpretations. She then had the additional job of placing her findings into a social scientific framework, which she accomplished by relating them to existing concepts and discussions in criminology, things like informal social control, neighbourhood watch schemes, and the role of housing style as a possible cause of criminal activity.

The aim of this section has been to outline how epistemological considerations—especially those relating to the question of whether a natural science or a positivist approach can supply legitimate knowledge of the social world—are related to research practice. Among the key points mentioned is the idea that the deductive approach is often taken by positivists, although they do concede that it is possible to generate theories using induction. By contrast, we've seen that interpretive researchers typically adopt an inductive strategy. However, while such interconnections between epistemological issues and research practice exist, it is important not to overstate them, since they represent tendencies rather than a rigid adherence to a particular way of doing research. Thus, particular epistemological principles and research practices do not necessarily go hand in hand in a neat, unambiguous manner. Often hybrid approaches are taken, which combine different positions and approaches. This point will be made again on several occasions.

Ontological considerations

There are two ontological debates that are of particular interest to social scientists. The first is concerned with the following questions: Do social phenomena have an objective reality, one that is independent of our perceptions? Or is what passes for reality merely a set of mental constructions? If you answer 'yes' to

---

Box 1.6   Interpretivism in practice

Foster (1995) conducted ethnographic research using participant observation and semi-structured interviews in a housing estate in East London referred to as Riverside, a residential complex experiencing a high level of crime according to official statistics. However, she found that residents did not perceive the estate to be a high-crime area, nor were they overly anxious about becoming victims of crime. These perceptions can be attributed to a number of factors, but a particularly important influence is the existence of 'informal social control,' which was used in conjunction with more formal methods such as policing. People expect a certain level of crime, but feel fairly secure because informal social control allows the level of crime to be contained.

Informal social control has a number of different aspects. One is that neighbours often look out for each other. In the words of one of Foster's interviewees: 'If I hear a bang or shouting I go out. If there's aggravation I come in and ring the police. I don't stand for it.' Another aspect of informal social control is that people often feel secure because they know each other. A second respondent said: 'I don't feel nervous . . . because people do generally know each other. We keep an eye on each other's properties.... I feel quite safe because you know your neighbours and you know they're there . . . they look out for you' (Foster 1995: 575).

the first question, that puts you in the objectivist camp. People on this side of the debate maintain that there is such a thing as social reality, and that it is the job of social scientists to discover what that reality is. An affirmative answer to the second question means that you agree with the *constructionist* position. People holding this view are in sympathy with Nietzsche's (1910: 12) famous aphorism that there are no facts, only interpretations. Such people maintain that there is no objective social reality against which our conceptions and views of the world may be tested. (The discussion of postmodernism in Chapter 17 further examines this viewpoint.) However, a middle ground or 'soft constructionist' position is possible and is held by many. It maintains that there may be an objective social reality, but many of our ideas do not reflect that reality at all, but instead are constructed to justify or rationalize various forms of domination. Box 1.7 provides two illustrations of the less stringent form of constructionism.

A second debate revolves around these questions: Is social reality akin to how most people view the physical world—largely fixed and 'out there,' something that individuals and groups have to confront but over which they have little or no control, like a snowstorm? Or is social reality not necessarily pre-existing and fixed, but is instead created through our actions? A 'yes' to the first question indicates support for a variant of objectivism, and agreement with the second affirms a kind of constructionism. In this chapter we'll focus mainly on that second debate—whether social reality can be created.

Some social scientists suggest that social phenomena confront individuals as external facts beyond their reach or influence. For example, an organization has rules and regulations and adopts standardized procedures for getting things done. A division of labour assigns people to different jobs. There is a hierarchy of authority, a mission statement, and so on. Objectivists see any organization as possessing a reality external to any of the specific individuals who inhabit it; they may leave but it will stay. Moreover, the organization represents a social order in that it exerts pressure on individuals to conform to organizational requirements. People learn and apply the rules and regulations and follow the standardized procedures. They do the jobs to which they are appointed. If they do not do these things, they may be reprimanded or even fired. The organization is therefore a constraining force that acts on and inhibits its members. To a large extent, this is the 'classic' way of conceptualizing an organization.

Box 1.7   Constructionism in action

Lantz and Booth (1998) showed that a rise in the incidence of breast cancer since the early 1980s, and its depiction as epidemic, can be treated as a social construction. They analyzed a variety of popular magazines and noted that many of the articles draw attention to the lifestyles of modern women, such as delaying first births and having careers. The authors also argued that the articles ascribe blame: 'Women are portrayed as victims of an insidious disease, but also as victims of their own behaviours, many of which are related to the control of their own fertility' (1998: 915).

This article concludes that, as a social category, the breast cancer epidemic is represented in popular magazines in a particular way—one that blames the victims and the lifestyles of women, particularly young women. This is in spite of the fact that fewer than 20 per cent of cases of breast cancer are in women under the age of 50. Lantz and Booth's study is fairly representative of a constructionist ontology in suggesting that the idea that young women's lifestyles cause breast cancer has been constructed as a social fact by popular magazine writers.

Similarly, Hallgrimsdottir *et al.* (2006: 266) argue that the media 'contributes to constructing, reproducing and deepening the social stigmas associated with working in the sex industry.' The authors compared media depictions of sex-trade workers in Victoria, BC, from 1980 to 2004 with how street prostitutes, escorts, and others viewed their own activities. Although the media portrayed these people as wicked and blameworthy in the earlier years, and as exploited, trapped, and innocent girls more recently, the sex workers themselves interpreted their experiences very differently. Although there was considerable heterogeneity in their experiences and attitudes towards their trade, many saw sex work as a largely mundane effort to earn a living. However, as marginalized and stigmatized individuals their voices are seldom heard—most people have their ideas about prostitution constructed for them by the media.

An alternative ontological position challenges the suggestion that things like an organization are external realities confronting social actors who have limited power to influence or change them. Strauss and colleagues (1973), for example, carried out research in a psychiatric hospital and proposed that its organization is best conceptualized as one of 'negotiated order.' Instead of viewing order as a pre-existing characteristic, they argued that it is worked at and created to some extent, and that the rules are far less extensive and less rigorously imposed than might be supposed from an objectivist account of organizations.

Indeed, Strauss and colleagues viewed rules more like general understandings than as commands (1973: 308). Precisely because relatively little of the spheres of action of doctors, nurses, and other personnel is specifically set down or prescribed, the social order of a hospital is an outcome of agreed-upon patterns of action that are themselves the products of negotiations among the different parties involved. For instance, the official rules may say that only a doctor can increase medication; however, some nurses, though it is never actually stated in the regulations, are routinely given this power. The social order is in a constant state of change because the hospital is 'a place where numerous agreements are continually being terminated or forgotten, but also as continually being established, renewed, reviewed, revoked, [and] revised. . . . In any pragmatic sense, this is the hospital *at the moment* [our emphasis]: this is its social order' (1973: 316–17). The authors argued that a preoccupation with the formal properties of organizations (rules, organizational charts, regulations, and roles) neglects the degree to which order in organizations has to be *accomplished* in everyday interaction. This *informal* organization arises because there cannot be rules for every possible contingency and the existing rules may be problematic, but this is not to say that the formal properties of organizations have *no* element of constraint on individual action.

Although Strauss and colleagues stressed the active role of individuals in the social construction of social reality, they did not push the argument to an extreme. For example, they did not claim that nurses can negotiate their roles to the point where they are allowed to operate on patients. But not all writers adopting a constructionist position are similarly prepared to acknowledge the existence or importance of an objective reality. It is precisely this split between viewing the social world as an objective reality, and seeing it as a subjective reality in a continuous state of flux, that Giddens sought to straddle in formulating his idea of structuration (recall Box 1.1).

The constructionist perspective that maintains that social reality can be negotiated also suggests that the concepts people employ to help them understand the natural and social world are social products whose meaning is constructed in and through social interaction. For example, a concept such as 'masculinity' is treated as a social construction. This implies that, rather than a distinct, timeless, and universal entity, the meaning of masculinity is built up through interaction. That meaning is likely to be ephemeral, in that it will vary over time and place. This tendency can be seen particularly well in discourse analysis, examined in Chapter 16. As Potter (1996: 98) observed: 'The world . . . is *constituted* in one way or another as people talk it, write it, and argue it.' This sense of constructionism frequently leads to an interest in how social phenomena are represented.

Relationship to social research

Questions of social ontology cannot be divorced from issues concerning the conduct of social research. Ontological assumptions and commitments affect how research questions are formulated and how the research is carried out. For example, if organizations are viewed as objective social entities that act on individuals, the researcher is likely to emphasize their formal properties. Alternatively, if the researcher is interested in the negotiated, changing nature of organizations, it is likely that research will focus on the active involvement of people in reality construction. In each case, a different research design is required.

General orientations: quantitative and qualitative research

Many writers on methodological issues distinguish between quantitative and qualitative research. The most basic distinction usually made is that quantitative research involves the use of numbers and statistics in the collection and analysis of data, while qualitative research utilizes mainly words and other non-numerical symbols. Although some writers see the distinction between the two types of research as fundamental, others see it as no longer useful or even 'false' (Layder 1993: 110). We're convinced, however, that although this issue has been vigorously debated, there is a meaningful difference between quantitative and qualitative research. This distinction will be employed in this book because it represents a useful means to classify different research methods and it is a helpful reference point for a range of issues in the practice of social research.

On the face of it, there seems to be little to the quantitative/qualitative difference other than quantitative researchers employ more formal and mathematical measurement and analysis techniques than qualitative researchers. But many sociologists and others suggest that the differences are deeper than merely the amount of quantification. For many writers, quantitative and qualitative research differ in their epistemological foundations and in other respects too. Indeed, examining the areas that were the focus of the last three sections—the connection linking theory and research, epistemological considerations, and ontological issues—quantitative and qualitative research can be seen as forming two distinctive *general orientations* to the conduct of social research. Table 1.1 outlines the differences between quantitative and qualitative research in terms of the three areas.

Thus, quantitative research:

- usually entails a *deductive* approach to the relationship between theory and research in which *theory testing* is a prime objective;
- incorporates the practices and norms of a natural science model and of positivism in particular; and
- generally embodies a view of society as being an external, objective reality.

By contrast, qualitative research:

- takes a predominantly *inductive* approach to the relationship between theory and research in which the *generation of theories and interpretations* is considered to be the main goal;
- rejects the use of the natural science and positivist models in social research, and replaces them

with methodologies that seek to determine how individuals interpret their social world; and
- embodies a view of social reality as a constantly shifting and emergent property of individuals' creations.

There is even more to the quantitative/qualitative distinction than this contrast suggests. In Chapters 3 and 8 the nature of quantitative and then qualitative research respectively will be outlined in greater detail. Then in Chapters 14 and 15 their contrasting features will be further explored, examining the effects of a commitment in quantitative research to a positivist epistemology and the rejection of that epistemology by qualitative researchers.

Finally, although it is useful to contrast the two general orientations, it is important not to hammer a wedge between them. For example, although quantitative research tends to be deductive and qualitative work is predominantly inductive, there are notable exceptions to that general tendency. It may seem perverse to introduce a basic set of distinctions and then suggest that they are problematic, but a recurring theme of this book is that discussing the nature of social research is just as complex as conducting the research itself. One can outline the typical philosophical assumptions and research practices of the two general orientations, but the full reality is messier than what our neat categories would suggest. Issues become more complicated the deeper one delves into them.

For example, we've seen that qualitative research is typically described as being concerned with the generation of theories rather than theory testing. However, there are many studies in which qualitative research tests rather than generates theories, like Hier's (2002) investigation of Ontario rave scenes with their all-night dancing and amphetamine use. Hier wanted to show how the regulation of raves was a contest between a city that feared increased drug use and supporters who eventually won the day by arguing that banning them would drive the drugs underground with even worse consequences. Similarly, although the Wilson (2002) study of the same topic is broadly interpretivist in epistemological orientation, with its examination of how ravers view their social situation, it includes some objectivist, rather than constructionist, overtones. For example, in exploring the effects of technology, including the Internet, on the scene, he was describing a world that is 'out there' and as having a formal, objective quality. It is thus another example of qualitative research that does not have *all* the features outlined in Table 1.1.

The point being made here is that quantitative and qualitative research represent different research orientations, and that the two approaches may be quite different in terms of the role of theory, epistemological issues, and ontological concerns. However, to reiterate, the distinction is not a hard-and-fast one: studies that have the broad characteristics of one research strategy may have some of the characteristics of the other. Also, many writers argue that the two can be combined within a single research project, and Chapter 15 examines that possibility.

Influences on the conduct of social research

You can now see how social research is influenced by a variety of factors. Figure 1.3 summarizes the influences examined so far, but has added three more—the impact of *values, politics,* and *practical considerations.*

Values

How might the values, personal beliefs, and feelings of researchers affect their work? Perhaps one would expect social scientists to be completely value-free and objective in their studies. Research that simply reflects the personal views of its practitioners would be biased and invalid, and thus unscientific. Durkheim (1858–1917) wrote that *social facts* are objects whose study requires that all 'preconceptions must be eradicated' (1938: 31). Since values are a form of preconception, his point implies that they should be suppressed when conducting research. But is that humanly possible? Values intrude in all phases of the research process, from the choice of a topic to the formulation of conclusions. This means that the social researcher is never working in a moral vacuum

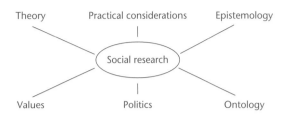

Figure 1.3 Influences on social research

but is instead influenced by a range of ethical presuppositions that have implications for the conduct of social research. This view is increasingly accepted among social researchers. Indeed, it is now recognized that values can intrude at any or all points in the process of social research, such as:

- choice of research area;
- formulation of the research question;
- choice of method;
- formulation of the research design and data collection techniques;
- data collection;
- analysis of data;
- interpretation of data; and
- conclusions.

There are, therefore, numerous points at which bias and the intrusion of values can occur during the course of research. For example, a researcher may develop an affection or sympathy for the people being studied. It is quite common, for instance, for researchers working within a qualitative research strategy, in particular when they use very intensive interviewing, to become so close to the people they are studying that they find it difficult to disentangle their role as social scientists from their concern for their subjects' well-being. As noted in Box 1.8, this possibility may be made worse by the tendency for sociologists to be sympathetic to underdogs.

Table 1.1   Fundamental differences between quantitative and qualitative research strategies

	Quantitative	Qualitative
Role of theory in research	Mainly deductive; testing of theory	Mainly inductive; generation of theory
Epistemological orientation	Natural science model; positivism	Interpretivism
Ontological orientation	Objectivism	Constructionism

Equally, social scientists may be repelled by those they study. In his research into an African society known as the Ik, a social anthropologist was appalled by what he saw: a loveless (and for him unlovable) group that left its young and very old to die (Turnbull 1973). Although he was able to point to the conditions lying behind these practices, he was very honest in his disgust for what he witnessed, particularly during his early time with them.

One way of dealing with the whole question of values and bias is to recognize that research cannot be value-free, and to try to ensure that values in the research process are acknowledged and made explicit. This is part of a larger process of *reflexivity* or self-reflection that researchers are encouraged to carry out. As Turnbull (1973: 13) put it at the beginning of his book on the Ik: 'The reader is entitled to know something of the aims, expectations, hopes, and attitudes that the writer brought to the field [in his case, Western values about the family], for these will surely influence not only how he sees things but even what he sees.' Researchers are increasingly prepared to forewarn readers of their biases and assumptions and to explain how these may have influenced their findings. There has been a growth since the mid-1970s in collections of inside reports of what doing a piece of research is really like, as against the generalities presented in social research methods textbooks (like this one). These collections frequently function as 'confessions' about personal biases and reveal the pride researchers take in telling readers how open they are in revealing them.

Still another approach is to argue for consciously value-laden research. For some writers on social research, a 'conscious partiality,' as Mies (1993: 68) called it, is celebrated. For example, Tastsoglou and Miedema (2003) clearly adopted a feminist, anti-racist approach in studying immigrant women in the Maritimes. Similarly, this perspective allowed Pratt and Valverde (2002) to refer to a large Canadian newspaper as a 'notorious tabloid' and 'obsessed' with what it called bogus refugees. It is also exemplified in Hallgrimsdottir *et al.*'s (2006) condemnation of the media's role in stigmatizing sex workers in BC. In fact, among some feminist researchers, doing research on women in an objective, value-neutral way would be considered undesirable (as well as difficult to achieve) because it would be incompatible with their values. Instead, many feminist researchers extol the virtues of a commitment to women that exposes the conditions of their disadvantage in a male-dominated society. Some feminist writers argue that only research on women intended *for* women is consistent with the wider political needs of women.

The significance of feminism in relation to values goes further than this, however. In particular,

Box 1.8   Taking sides in social research

Forty years ago, an interesting debate occurred between Becker and Gouldner, two prominent figures in American sociology. It raised many issues concerning the role of values in research; here the issue of taking sides in research will be considered. Becker (1967) argued that it is almost impossible to do research without being affected by personal sympathies. For example, much research is undertaken in the context of hierarchical relationships (police/criminal, managers/workers, doctors/patients, or teachers/students). Becker felt it would be difficult in such instances not to take sides, but claimed that the bigger dilemma involves deciding which side to take.

Becker recognized that within his field, the sociology of deviance, the sympathies of many practitioners lay with the underdogs in these hierarchical relationships, leading them at a minimum to seek to express or represent the subordinate's point of view. However, Becker argued, sociologists siding with the underdog are more likely to be accused of bias than those who identify with the more powerful. (There was greater respect for the powerful when Becker wrote than there is today.)

Gouldner (1968) countered that Becker exaggerated those issues, claiming that by no means must all research involve taking sides. He suggested that it is possible to take the point of view of a section of society seriously without sympathizing with that group. More recently, Liebling (2001) added that it is possible to see the merits of more than one side. Taking the case of prison research, she showed that not only is it possible to recognize the virtues of different perspectives, but one can do so without incurring the wrath of either side, in her case, prison officials and prisoners.

several feminist social researchers in the early 1980s proposed that quantitative research is incompatible with feminist ideals. For writers such as Oakley (1981), quantitative research is bound up with the male values of *control*, as seen in the researcher's control of the research subject/respondent and of the research context and situation. Moreover, the research process is seen as one-way, in which researchers extract information from those studied and give little or, more usually, nothing in return. For many feminists, such a strategy borders on exploitation and is incompatible with feminism's values of sisterhood and non-hierarchical relationships.

The antipathy towards quantitative research resulted in a preference for qualitative research among certain feminists. Not only was qualitative research seen as more consistent with the values of feminism, it was portrayed as more adaptable to those values. Feminist qualitative research came to be associated with an approach in which the investigator denied a value-neutral approach and related to the people being studied as human beings rather than research instruments. This stance demonstrates how values have implications for the process of social investigation. In more recent years, there has been a softening of the attitudes of feminists towards quantitative

research, especially when it is employed in conjunction with qualitative research (Oakley 1998). This issue will be revisited in Chapters 9, 15, and 16.

There are, then, different positions that can be taken in relation to values and value-free research. Fewer writers today subscribe to the position that the principle of objectivity can be put into practice fully. There is a greater awareness of the limits of objectivity, and some of the more categorical pronouncements on the subject, like those of Durkheim, have fallen into disfavour. At the same time, giving free rein to one's political beliefs and value positions can be problematic. Researchers today still have to fight the all too human propensity to demonize those whose values are different from their own, and struggle with the temptation to summarily reject research findings simply because the researcher's ideological or moral views are not compatible with their own.

Politics in social research

Considerations of how values and moral positions can affect social research draw attention to how *politics* may influence research. The following points illustrate how social research may be political.

Ethical issue 11.1

Ethics: an introduction

Ethical issues arise at every stage of social research and can affect the integrity of a specific research project as well as the discipline as a whole. Because they apply to so many decisions, ethical issues boxes have been placed in several different chapters. These boxes will include:

- some (in)famous cases in which obvious transgressions of ethical principles occurred, though it is important to recall that ethical concerns arise not only in such extreme cases;
- stances taken on ethics in social research;
- the significance and operation of four overlapping areas of ethical concern: informed consent, deception, harm to participants, and invasion of privacy. Each is relevant to defining the activities no researcher should engage in and in specifying how to treat the people that provide the data upon which the researcher is dependent.

But there are differences of opinion on what is and is not ethically acceptable; indeed, some of the disputes of the 1960s are being rehashed today. Even the professional ethical principles provided by the Canadian Sociology and Anthropology Association (current CSAA codes and guidelines can be found at www.csaa.ca/structure/code.htm) contain some ambiguity. Also, although the codes and guidelines of professional associations provide some direction, they often allow for a degree of autonomy with regard to ethical issues.

These debates about ethics are not easily resolved. But there is little disagreement that it is crucial is to be aware of the ethical issues involved in doing social research so that informed decisions can be made. If nothing else, readers of these boxes will become aware of the possible disapproval coming their way if they make certain choices as researchers.

- Social researchers sometimes *take sides*, as we have seen. This is precisely what many feminist researchers do when they focus on women's disadvantages and on the possibilities for improving the position of women. But taking sides occurs among other researchers as well. For example, some social scientists may promote a greater role for government in society and globally; others may endorse the merits of the free market.

- A related issue involves research *funding*. Much social research is funded by organizations such as private firms and government departments that may have a vested interest in the outcomes of the research. The very fact that these organizations fund some research projects but not others opens the door to political influence. Such organizations may seek to invest in studies that will be useful to them or supportive of their operations and world views. Frequently, they launch a call for researchers to tender bids for an investigation in a certain area. When social researchers participate in such exercises, they are participating in a political arena because their research may be designed to please the funding body. As a result, as Hughes (2000) observed in relation to research in the field of crime, an investigation of gun crimes among the 'underclass' is more likely to be looked upon favourably for funding than one concerned with state-related misdemeanours. Morgan (2000) pointed out that research funded by government is typically empirical and quantitative; it tends to be concerned with short-term costs and benefits of a policy or innovation; and it is generally uncritical in the sense that underlying government policies are not questioned, just the effectiveness of their implementation. Such features can be related to the fact that a funding agency itself may be involved in a political process of securing a continuous stream of government funding.

- Gaining *access* to research subjects and organizations is also a political process. Access is usually mediated by gatekeepers concerned not only about the researcher's motives but also about what the organization can gain from the investigation, what it will lose by participating in terms of staff time and other costs, and the potential risks to its image. Often, gatekeepers seek to influence how the investigation will take place: what kinds of questions can be asked; who can and cannot be a focus of study; the amount of time to be spent with each research participant; the interpretation of the findings; and the form the reports will take, even to the point of asking to approve drafts.

- Public institutions, such as police departments, schools, and hospitals, and most commercial firms, are concerned with how they are going to be represented in publications. Consequently, gaining access is almost always a matter of *negotiation* and as such inevitably turns into a political process. The results of this negotiation are often referred to as 'the research bargain' and it turns out that the term really should be plural. Once in the organization, researchers often discover layers of gatekeepers with whom a constant process of negotiation and renegotiation of what is and is not permissible transpires. For example, let's say permission to talk to the boys in a group home is given by the provincial government. Before research can begin, the head of the home has to be brought onside, then the staff, and then the actual adolescents. Frequently, one of the staff is then given the responsibility of dealing with the fieldworkers. A suspicion that they are really working for management then has to be overcome. And it is unwise to assume that simply because gatekeepers have given a researcher access, a smooth passage will ensue in subsequent dealings with the people to be studied. Perhaps the most powerful of the boys will turn out to be the key gatekeeper. Researchers may even find themselves used as pawns if subgroups attempt to enlist them in advancing a particular goal; and some research participants, because they doubt the utility of social research, may obstruct the research process. For example, some of Beagan's (2001) medical students refused to participate when they heard she was asking about gays and lesbians. Even a cooperating student wrote on the questionnaire about being sick of being asked about sexual preference.

- There may be pressure to restrict the *publication* of findings. Hughes (2000) cited a study of plea-bargaining in the British criminal justice system as a case in point. The researchers had uncovered what were deemed at the time to be disconcerting levels of informal plea-bargaining, concluding that the formal judicial process was being weakened. The English legal establishment sought to thwart the dissemination of the findings and was only persuaded to allow publication when a panel of academics confirmed the validity of the findings. Similarly, the editors of academic journals may refuse to publish pieces that do not conform to their own ideological or political preferences.

These are just a small number of ways in which politics intrudes in the research process.

Practical considerations

There are also a number of *practical issues* to be confronted in carrying out social research, many of which will be addressed in detail in later chapters. One important practical consideration is that the choice of research orientation, design, or method has to match the specific research question being investigated. For instance, if one is interested in measuring the impact of a number of possible causes of a social phenomenon, a quantitative strategy is probably appropriate. Alternatively, if the focus is on the world views of members of a certain social group, a qualitative research strategy—one sensitive to how participants interpret their social world—may be the way to go. If a researcher is interested in a topic on which no or little research has been done, the quantitative strategy may be difficult to employ because there is little prior literature from which to draw leads about its possible causes. A more qualitative, exploratory approach may be preferable because that type of investigation is typically associated with the generation rather than the testing of theory (see Table 1.1) and with a relatively unstructured approach to the research process.

Another dimension involves the nature of the topic and of the people being investigated. If a researcher wants to study individuals involved in illicit activities, for example, price fixing, shoplifting, or drug dealing, it is unlikely that a researcher could develop the rapport with them that is needed to conduct a social survey. It is not surprising, therefore, that researchers in these areas tend to use a qualitative strategy. On the other hand, it's unlikely that the hypothesis in Box 1.3 on the effects of societal religiosity on individual religious orthodoxy could have used a qualitative approach.

Although practical considerations may seem rather mundane and uninteresting compared with the lofty realm inhabited by the philosophical debates surrounding epistemology and ontology, they are important. All social research is a coming together of the ideal and the feasible. The nature of the topic, the type of people one may be investigating, and the related constraints on a researcher loom large in decisions about how best to proceed.

Research questions

The last practical consideration involves choosing a *research question*. Choosing a research question is in many ways like picking a destination before going hiking—the route to be taken and what you will experience along the way are largely determined by where you want to go. Similarly, what you stand to accomplish with a particular research study and how you will accomplish it are profoundly affected by your formulation of the research question.

What is a research question? A research question states the purpose of the study in the form of a question, which is very useful because a question may be more evocative and stimulating than a simple declarative sentence designed to do the same thing. A question arouses curiosity and challenges the researcher to find ways to answer it.

The process of formulating and assessing research questions is something of an art, but here are some general thoughts. Research often starts with the choice of a general area of interest, for example, male homosexuality. At this stage, a very general research question might be: How do people in general feel about gays? This broad research area has to be narrowed down, for example, to: How does the Canadian adult population react to the portrayal of gays on television dramas? But even that is too broad, so the next level of specification might be something like: Do straight, young men react differently than straight, young women to the portrayal of male gay romance on television program X? If so, can those differences be explained in terms of a more fluid sexual identity on the part of young women as compared to young men? Questions like the latter could be linked to larger theories of sex roles, sexual orientation acquisition, socialization, or the tolerance of difference in society.

A particular study cannot answer all the research questions that occur, but must select only a small number of them. This narrowing of the topic is not just a limit created by the time and cost of doing research. It is also due to the need for the project to have a clear focus.

As suggested above, the research question may change as the study progresses, for a number of reasons. The discovery of a new data source may change the focus a bit, as might some of the initial findings. For instance, if in the study of male homosexuality the researchers find that having a gay relative in one's immediate family makes a large difference in people's attitudes, the research question and the attendant methodology and theoretical orientation may be changed. The research question may also change because of limitations in time and other resources available to the researcher. Box 1.9 offers some tips in developing research questions.

Research questions in quantitative research are sometimes more specific than those in qualitative research. Indeed, some qualitative researchers advocate a very open approach with *no* research questions or only very broad ones. This is a very risky approach and can be a recipe for collecting masses of data without a clear sense of what to observe or what to ask interviewees. There is a growing tendency among qualitative researchers to take a somewhat more focused approach to their craft, as, for example, in Parnaby's (2003) study of Toronto's squeegee kids.

Research questions set realistic boundaries for research. Having none or having poorly formulated research questions can result in unfocused and substandard research. It does not matter how well designed a questionnaire is or how skilled the interviewers are; clear research questions are required to avoid going off in unnecessary directions and tangents. Research questions are crucial because they guide:

- the literature search;
- decisions about the kind of research design to employ;
- decisions about what data to collect and from whom;
- the analysis of the data; and
- the writing up of the findings.

Box 1.9   Considerations when developing research questions

Research questions should:

- be clear—they must be understandable to others;

- be researchable—they should allow for the development of a research design and the collection of data; this means that extremely abstract terms are not suitable;

- relate in some way to established theory and research—this means that there should be a literature to draw upon to show how the research questions may be approached. Even with a topic scarcely addressed by social scientists, there will probably be some relevant literature (for example, on related or parallel topics); making connections with theory and research also demonstrates how the research contributes to knowledge and understanding;

- be linked to each other—researchers should develop a single argument or at least a set of related arguments, which is hard to do with unrelated research questions;

- have the potential to make a contribution, however small, to the existing knowledge on the topic;

- be neither too broad (no research project can do justice to all aspects of a topic) nor too narrow (unable to make a significant contribution to an area of study).

If you are unsure about how to formulate research questions (or indeed about other aspects of research), look at journal articles or research monographs to see how other researchers have handled them.

Key Points

- Quantitative and qualitative research constitute different approaches to social investigation and carry with them important epistemological and ontological assumptions.

- Epistemological considerations loom large in the choice of a research strategy. To a great extent, the issues revolve around the desirability of employing a natural science model (and in particular positivism) versus using an interpretivist approach.

- Ontological considerations, such as objectivism versus constructionism, also constitute important dimensions of the quantitative/qualitative contrast.

- Theory can be something that precedes research and data gathering (the deductive method), or it may emerge out of it (induction).

- Feminist researchers have tended to prefer a qualitative approach, a situation that is changing now.

- Values can impinge on the research process in various ways. There are political dimensions to research that relate to values.

- The political dimensions of research are concerned with issues relating to the role and exercise of power at different stages of an investigation.

- Practical considerations can also affect decisions about research methods. Clear research questions improve the chances of success.

- Important ethical issues arise in collecting data and interacting with research participants.

- The main areas of ethical concern relate to informed consent, deception, harm to participants, and invasion of privacy.

Questions for Review

Theory and research

- If you were to conduct some social research, what would the topic be and what factors would influence your choice?

- Can you find, in your other courses, additional examples of middle range theories?

- What are the differences between inductive and deductive logic and why is the distinction important?

Epistemological considerations

- What is meant by each of the following terms positivism, realism, and interpretivism? Why is it important to understand each of them?

- How might a positivist and an interpretivist differ in conducting research on illegal drug use?

Ontological considerations

- What are the main differences between epistemological and ontological considerations?

- What do the terms 'objectivism' and 'constructionism' mean?

20   Part I

General research orientations: quantitative and qualitative research

- Outline the main differences between quantitative and qualitative research in terms of the relationship between theory and data, epistemological considerations, and ontological considerations.

- Under what circumstances might qualitative research be more concerned with testing theories and quantitative research with generating theories?

Influences on the conduct of social research

- What are some of the main influences on social research?

Politics in social research

- What is meant by the suggestion that politics play a role in social research?

- In what ways are politics manifested in social research?

Research questions

- Why are research questions so important in the overall research process?

- What are the main characteristics of good research questions?

Chapter overview

A research design is a framework for the collection and analysis of data. It must satisfy certain criteria and the form it takes depends on the research questions being asked. This chapter will discuss:

- reliability, replicability, and validity, which are criteria for assessing the quality of social research and which are important to consider when choosing a research design; the various kinds of validity—measurement validity, internal validity, and external validity—are illustrated;
- the suggestion that such criteria are relevant mainly to quantitative research, and that

alternative criteria should be employed for qualitative research;
- research ethics, which are an important consideration for any research design; and
- four prominent research designs:
  - experimental and related designs (such as the quasi-experiment);
  - cross-sectional designs, including survey research, its most common form;
  - longitudinal designs, such as panel and cohort studies; and
  - case study designs.

Introduction

Research designs are broad structures that guide the collection and analysis of data. A choice of research design involves decisions about what the researcher wants to accomplish with the study. Is one of the goals to describe the causal connections between variables? Will the study explore how a social phenomenon changes over time, and how it may be linked to other events and situations? Will it be important to search out the meanings the research subjects attach to certain things? Does the researcher want to generalize the findings to people and groups that were not part of the study? How these questions are answered will affect the choice of the research design.

Another important consideration in choosing a research design is the kind of explanation the researcher would like to make. Quantitative researchers often explain a phenomenon in terms of causes and effects expressed in terms of general

laws and principles. Such laws and principles are usually fairly general, and are meant to apply to people who were not part of the study. For example, a study may find that men are more likely to approve of pornography than women and explain that with a Darwinian theory of erotic attraction. This sort of explanation is supposed to apply to humanity in general, not just the people who participated in the study. This is referred to as the *nomothetic* approach to explanation.

Qualitative researchers, on the other hand, often seek a rich description of a person or group, although the description usually involves or implies proximate, specific causes that are not meant to explain other situations or the behaviour of people who were not part of the research. For instance, a qualitative analysis of a group of homeless teenagers may find that they avoid sleeping in the local homeless shelter because they value their privacy. That finding is not meant to apply to other homeless people or other shelters; it simply helps to explain why these particular teenagers act the way they do. These sorts of accounts are called *idiographic* explanations.

Once a design has been selected, a specific method for collecting data has to be chosen. There are many different ways of gathering data. One way is to use a preset instrument, such as a self-completion questionnaire or a structured interview schedule. Another is to utilize a less formalized method like *participant observation* in which the researcher takes part in the activities of a group of people, sometimes even living among them for a time.

Consider one of the research designs to be covered in this chapter—the case study. It entails a detailed exploration of a specific case, which could be a community, organization, person, or event. Once you've selected a case to investigate, how will you get data on it? Do you use participant observation? Do you observe from the sidelines? Do you conduct interviews? Do you examine documents? Do you administer questionnaires? In fact any or all of these methods for gathering data can be used.

Before we consider various research designs, some basic issues surrounding data gathering and assessing the quality of social research will be outlined.

Criteria for evaluating social research

Much of the discourse in the social sciences, in particular discussions of theories and causality, is expressed in terms of *variables*. A variable is simply a characteristic or attribute that varies, such as gender, income, fondness for mathematics, or athletic ability. Several of the criteria for evaluating research involve the measurement of variables. Three of the most prominent criteria are *reliability*, *replicability*, and *validity*. Each will be examined in greater detail in later chapters, but a brief treatment here will be helpful.

Reliability

Quantitative researchers are concerned with whether measures of social science concepts (such as poverty, racial prejudice, and religious orthodoxy) are *reliable*. Reliability refers to whether the same results would be received if a particular measurement technique were administered several times to the same research

subject. For example, if scores on a new intelligence test are unstable and fluctuate when administered to the same people on two or more occasions, or if different findings are produced when different psychologists use the test on the same people, that would mean that the test is unreliable.

Replicability

The idea of reliability is related to another criterion of research—*replicability*, which refers to whether others are able to repeat part or all of a study and get the same results. There are many reasons to do replications, such as a feeling that the results do not match prior evidence on the topic, or to simply check that the original research was carried out properly. For replication to take place, the initial researcher must spell out all research procedures in great detail.

Validity

A crucial criterion in the evaluation of social research is *validity*, which is concerned with the integrity of the conclusions generated by a piece of research. There are three main types of validity:

- *Measurement validity.* This type, sometimes referred to as *construct validity*, applies primarily to quantitative research and its measures of social concepts. Essentially, it refers to whether an indicator really measures what it is supposed to measure. The question, 'Do IQ tests really measure intelligence?' is asking whether IQ tests are a *valid* measure of intelligence. To take another example, in the study reported in Box 1.3, three concepts needed to be measured: national religiosity, religious orthodoxy, and family religious orientation. The question is, do the measures used by the researchers really gauge those concepts? If they do not, the study's findings are questionable. Moreover, measurement validity is related to reliability: if a measure of a concept is unstable and hence unreliable, it simply cannot be a valid measure of the concept in question.
- *Internal validity.* This form of validity relates to causality, dealt with in greater detail in Chapter 3. For example, in the study examined in Box 1.3, the authors concluded that a nation's religious environment affects the religious beliefs of its citizens.

Internal validity asks whether the religious environment really does influence people's religious beliefs. Could the cause be something else? In discussing issues of causality, it is common to refer to a proposed cause as an *independent variable* and the corresponding effect as the *dependent variable*. In this case, the 'religious environment of a nation' is the independent variable, and religious belief the dependent. Internal validity raises the issue of the degree of confidence one can have that the independent variable really does have an impact on the dependent variable.

- *External validity*. This kind of validity is concerned with two things. One is whether a study's findings are applicable to situations outside the research environment, namely, in everyday or natural social settings. Sometimes the research setting is so artificial or so different from real life that one may question whether the results actually tell us anything about the sorts of things people normally experience. The more the social scientist intervenes in natural settings or creates unnatural ones, such as a laboratory (or even just a special room to carry out interviews), the greater the chance that the findings will be externally *in*valid. Measurement validity and a reasonable level of internal validity cannot guarantee this form of external validity.

  Qualitative research tends to be high in this type of validity because it usually involves taking a *naturalistic* stance. Naturalism in this context refers to a style of research that seeks to minimize the use of artificial methods of data collection. It implies that the social world should be as undisturbed as possible when being studied (Hammersley and Atkinson 1995: 6). A naturalistic researcher collects data in naturally occurring situations and environments as opposed to artificial ones, for example, by living with people for months to observe their behaviour or by conducting intensive interviews.

  A second concern with external validity is whether the results of a study can be generalized beyond the people or cases analyzed by the researcher. The study in Box 1.2 asked 57 male, adolescent volunteers about their delinquency and if any of the currently popular sociological theories of delinquency could explain their behaviour. How far can the findings of this study be generalized? To other male adolescents who attended the same school? To all Canadian male adolescents? If the findings are fully externally valid, they can be applied to any population of interest. If they possess no external validity, their findings apply only to the 57 boys studied and to no one else. Usually, external validity falls somewhere between these extremes and it is in this context that the issue of how people are selected to participate in research becomes crucial. If a *representative sample* of people is selected (see Chapter 11), the researcher can be confident that the results of the study may be applied to the population from which the sample was drawn.

Relationship with the general research orientation

One striking feature of the discussion so far is that it seems to downplay qualitative research. Both reliability and measurement validity are essentially concerned with how adequately concepts have been measured, which is more of an issue in quantitative research. Internal validity is also something that is more pertinent to quantitative research. External validity has considerable relevance to both qualitative and quantitative work, but the representativeness of samples has a more obvious application to the latter, given the desire of quantitative researchers to generalize beyond the people or cases they are studying.

Some qualitative researchers even argue that applying the concepts of reliability and validity to their research is inappropriate. They propose that their studies be judged or evaluated according to different criteria. For example, Lincoln and Guba (1985) recommend *trustworthiness* as a criterion of how good a qualitative study is. Each aspect of trustworthiness has a parallel with the criteria mentioned earlier:

- *credibility*, which parallels measurement and internal validity—how believable are the findings? Did the investigator allow personal values to ruin any chance of intersubjectivity?
- *transferability*, which parallels external validity—do the findings apply to other people and other contexts?
- *dependability*, which parallels reliability—are the findings likely to be consistent over time?
- *confirmability*, which parallels replicability—would another investigator reach the same conclusions?

The distinctive features of qualitative research will be explored in depth in later chapters.

Research designs

Experimental design

True experiments are fairly rare in sociology, but they can be found in areas such as social psychology and studies of organizations. Researchers in social policy may also use them to assess the impact of reforms or new policies. But if experimental designs are uncommon, why discuss them at all? The chief reason is that *a true experiment is often used as a yardstick against which non-experimental research is measured.* Experimental research is frequently held up as a touchstone because experiments are, in theory at least, the best way to establish causality. In other words, experiments are strong on determining whether and to what degree a particular variable or set of variables affects the phenomenon being studied. To use the language introduced in this chapter, true experiments tend to be very high in internal validity.

Manipulation

If experiments are so strong in this respect, why do social researchers not make more use of them? The reason is simple: to conduct a true experiment, it is necessary to do something to people and observe the effects. To put the matter more formally, experiments *manipulate* an independent variable to determine its influence on a dependent variable. Typically, some subjects are allocated to a 'treatment' group in which the independent variable is changed or manipulated, while others are placed in a 'control' group where no manipulation takes place. The dependent variable is then observed and measured. The problem is that many of the independent variables of concern to social researchers cannot be manipulated. For example, some sociologists maintain that a country's national character is affected by whether the country came into existence through revolution (for example, Lipset 1990). In order to test this idea experimentally, revolution would have to be induced in some randomly selected areas to produce a new country, while in others no revolution would be fomented. The researcher would then compare the national characters of the revolutionary countries

with the non-revolutionary ones. Needless to say, such experimental manipulations would usually be impossible to bring about.

This example also illustrates a second reason why experiments are so rare in sociology—ethical concerns usually preclude them. To take a different example, suppose you are interested in the effect of nutrition on children's academic performance. In order to examine this issue experimentally, six-year-olds could be selected at random and placed in one of two groups. Those in the first group would be fed unhealthy foods for a month, while those in the second would be given nutritious diets. The experimenter would then test the two groups to see if they differed in academic ability. Although sound from a methodological standpoint, the ethical problems with such a study are obvious. In fact, ethical issues may arise even when the experimental manipulation is of very short duration (see Ethical issue 2.1).

Another reason why experiments are uncommon in sociology is that many of the things of interest to sociologists—gender roles, political preferences, the formation of social movements, and so on—have complex, long-term causes that cannot be easily simulated in experiments. Could the experimental method be used to explain the rise of second-wave feminism in the 1960s? Unfortunately not—experiments, for the most part, can only provide relatively simple, short-term manipulations of independent variables (see Brannigan 2004).

Before moving to a more complete discussion of experimental designs, it is important to introduce a basic distinction between *laboratory* and *field* experiments. The former take place in artificial settings, whereas the latter occur in real-life surroundings such as classrooms and factories. The Rosenthal and Jacobson (1968) study, described below, provides a well-known example of a field experiment.

Classic experimental design

Rosenthal and Jacobson (1968) tried to determine what effect teachers' expectations had on their students' academic performance. In addition to illustrating the classical experimental design, their study is a good example of research that gets a lot of attention, is then subject to intense methodological scrutiny (see Brannigan 2004: 80–9 for critiques), and ultimately provides the impetus for further research designed to improve on the original.

The research was conducted in a poor US school with many minority-group children enrolled. In the spring all students completed a test presented to them as a means of identifying 'spurters'—that is, students who were likely to experience a sudden increase in their academic performance. At the beginning of the following academic year, the teachers were given the names of the spurters in their class. In fact, a random 20 per cent of the schoolchildren had been identified as spurters. The test was re-administered eight months after the original one, allowing the authors to compare the so-called spurters with the other students on things such as IQ scores, reading ability, and intellectual curiosity. Since they believed that there was no initial difference in ability between the spurters and the others, any improvements were attributed to the fact that the teachers had been led to expect the spurters to perform better. The authors report that the teachers' expectations that the spurters would show superior academic performance

actually caused those students to do better than the others, presumably through the differential treatment they received from the teachers.

The Rosenthal and Jacobson study includes most of the essential features of what is known as the classical experimental design. Subjects (in this case, students) are randomly assigned to two groups. The experimental manipulation (different levels of the independent variable, here heightened teacher expectations) is given to what is known as the *experimental group* or *treatment group* (the spurters). The other group is not given the treatment and thus forms a *control group*. The dependent variable— academic performance—is measured before the experimental manipulation to make sure that the two groups really are, on average, equal at the start (see Figure 2.1). If they are equal, and because of random assignment they should be, the researchers can feel confident that any differences in student performance found between the two groups *after*

Ethical issue 2.1

An attempt to understand Nazi atrocities

Milgram (1963) was perplexed by the brutality that occurred in Nazi concentration camps during the Second World War and wanted a scientific explanation of how it came about. In particular, he wanted to know how a person could be led to cause extreme harm to an innocent human being, and whether being ordered to do so by an authority figure had anything to do with it. Milgram devised a laboratory experiment in which a supposedly reputable researcher (the authority figure) asked volunteers to act as 'teachers' who would punish 'learners' by giving them increasingly severe electric shocks for incorrect answers to questions. The shocks were not real, but the teachers/volunteers were not aware of this nor did they know that the howls of pain of the learners were simulated. Some teachers were further disadvantaged in that they could not see, only hear, the learners. In all instances, the teachers were told that shocking was part of the study and that they were not causing permanent harm to the learner, in spite of the increasingly shrill cries of pain. The experiment continued until the teacher/volunteer refused to administer more shocks. In the version of the study in which the teacher could not see the learner, a substantial majority (62 per cent) of the

subjects administered the highest shocks possible. Further, in one variant of the experiment, the subject did not have to administer the shock directly but could order another person (actually an accomplice of Milgram's) to shock the learner. In this instance more than 90 per cent of the subjects ordered the greatest shocks possible. Many of the participants were visibly upset as they carried out the experimenter's orders, but they still did what the authority figure told them to do.

Milgram saw these results as shedding light on the circumstances leading to the horrors of the concentration camp. Nonetheless, Milgram's study involved a number of ethical dilemmas. For one, deception was used on the experimental subjects— they were told that the experiment was about how people learn, not about how people come to commit cruel acts, and they were led to believe that the shocks were real. But could he have told the volunteers he wanted to see if they would act like Nazis? Would the experiment have worked? More importantly, can any insights arising out of this study justify the psychological discomfort that the subjects felt when they believed they were causing an innocent person to suffer?

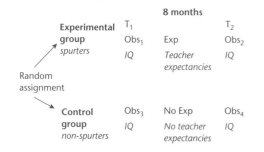

Figure 2.1 Classical experimental design

the manipulation is due to the treatment. Everything else about the two groups is presumed to be the same, leaving differences in teacher expectations as the only possible explanation for any differences that are found between the spurters and non-spurters.

To capture the essence of the classical experimental design, the following simple notation is used:

- **Obs:** an **obs**ervation made of the dependent variable. There may be more than two observations but, to simplify, the design shows the most common configuration: a *pre-test* and a *post-test*, here perhaps IQ test scores and reading levels before the experimental manipulation and after.
- **Exp:** the **exp**erimental treatment (independent variable), such as the creation of teacher expectancies. **No Exp** refers to the absence of an experimental treatment and represents the experience of the control group.
- **T:** the **t**iming of the observations made in relation to the dependent variable, such as when an IQ test is administered.

Classic experimental design and validity

What is the purpose of the control group? Surely it is what happens to the spurters (the experimental group) that really matters. But for a study to be a true experiment, it must control for (in other words, eliminate) rival explanations of a causal finding, leaving only teacher expectations as having created any differences in performance between the two groups. Of course, student performance is a complex phenomenon, with many causes, but the present study wanted to examine only one influence (teacher expectations) on it. The presence of a control group *and* the random assignment of subjects to the experimental and control groups

help to eliminate rival explanations for differences in academic performance, which in this case are any explanations other than different teacher expectations. By doing so, these procedures contribute to the study's internal validity. To see this, consider some threats to internal validity that would pose serious challenges to the study's conclusions if there were *no* control group or random assignment. The list of threats is taken from a book written by Cook and Campbell (1979). In each situation, the prospect of a rival interpretation of Rosenthal and Jacobson's findings is offered, but the presence of both a control group and random assignment greatly reduces the threat. As a result, confidence in the finding that teacher expectations influence student performance is enhanced.

- *History.* This refers to events that occurred other than the manipulation of teacher expectations that may have caused the spurters' scores to rise. The action of the school's principal to raise standards in the school is one such event. Without a control group, one cannot be sure if it was the teachers' expectations or the principal's actions that produced the increase in spurters' grades. With the control group there, one can say that history should have an effect on the control subjects too and therefore differences between the experimental and control groups can be attributed to the effect of teacher expectations alone.
- *Testing.* This threat refers to the possibility that subjects may become more experienced at taking a test or sensitized to the aims of the experiment as a result of the pre-test. The presence of a control group, which presumably would also experience the same things, diminishes this possibility.
- *Instrumentation.* This threat refers to the possibility that changes in the way a test is administered can account for an increase (or decrease) in scores between a pre-test and post-test; for example, the teachers knowing their students better or being more friendly the second time they give the test. Again, if there is a control group, this should affect the people in that group as well.
- *Mortality.* This relates to the problem of subjects leaving the experiment before it is over, found especially in studies that span a long period of time; here subjects may have moved to a different school, experienced a long-term illness, and so on. Since this problem is likely to afflict the control

group too, it probably did not make a difference to the results. However, experimenters should try to determine whether mortality has affected the experimental and control groups differently.

- *Maturation*. Quite simply, people change over time and the ways in which they change may have implications for the dependent variable. The spurters may have improved anyway as they got older, regardless of the effect of teacher expectancies. But the control group would also mature in this way, so maturation effects cannot explain the differences between it and the control group.

- *Selection*. When subjects are not assigned by a random process to the experimental and control group, variations between them in the post-test may be due to pre-existing differences between the two groups. For example, if all the best students were given the spurter label, their pre-existing academic ability rather than teacher expectations may have caused them to do better. However, since a random process of assignment to the experimental and control groups was employed here, that possibility is greatly reduced. With random assignment, roughly half of the top students would get the spurter designation, and about half would be placed in the non-spurter group, cancelling out the effect of pre-existing academic ability. However, even with the use of random assignment, if the number of people in each group is relatively small, there is still a risk of pre-existing differences between the experimental and control groups.

Even if research is deemed to be internally valid, that does not mean that questions cannot be raised about it. First, there is the question of measurement validity. In the case of the Rosenthal and Jacobson (1968) study, there are potentially two aspects to this. One is the question of whether academic performance is adequately measured. Measures like reading scores seem to possess *face validity*, in the sense that they appear to correspond to what they are supposed to be measuring. However, given the controversy surrounding IQ tests and what they measure, one may feel somewhat uneasy about how far gains in IQ test scores can be regarded as indicative of academic performance. Similarly, take another of the authors' measures, intellectual curiosity—is that a valid measure of academic performance? Does it really measure what it is supposed to measure?

Another question relating to measurement validity is whether the experimental manipulation really worked. In other words, did the identification of some schoolchildren as spurters adequately create the conditions needed for the hypothesis about teacher expectations to be tested? The study very much relies on the teachers being duped by the procedure for the duration of the experiment, but it is possible that as time went on some of them came to doubt or forget the 'information' about the spurters, thus contaminating the manipulation.

Second, is the research externally valid? The fact that the research is a field experiment that took place in a real school rather than a laboratory enhances this aspect of the Rosenthal and Jacobson research. Also, the fact that the students and the teachers seem to have been unaware that they were participating in an experiment may also have enhanced external validity, though at the same time this deception raises *ethical* concerns (see Ethical issue boxes 2.2 through 2.4).

Cook and Campbell (1979) identified five major threats to the external validity and hence the generalizability of findings derived from an experiment:

- *Interaction of selection and treatment*. This threat raises the question: To what social and psychological groups can a finding be generalized? Can it be generalized to a wide variety of individuals who differ in ethnicity, social class, religion, gender, and type of personality? In the case of the Rosenthal and Jacobson study, the students were largely from poorer groups and a large proportion from ethnic minorities. This may limit the generalizability of the findings.

- *Interaction of setting and treatment*. This threat relates to whether the results of a study can be applied to other settings, in Rosenthal and Jacobson's case to other schools. There is also the wider issue of whether expectation effects can also be discerned in non-educational settings.

- *Interaction of history and treatment*. This threat raises the question of whether the findings can be generalized to the past and into the future. The Rosenthal and Jacobson research was conducted 40 years ago. Would the findings still apply today? Also, their investigation was conducted at a particular juncture in the school year. Would the same results have been obtained if the research had been conducted at different points in the year?

- *Interaction effects of pre-testing*. As a result of being pre-tested, subjects in an experiment may become sensitized to the experimental treatment, affecting their responses as they become more test-wise. Consequently, the findings may not be generalizable to groups not pre-tested, and, of course, in the real world people are rarely pre-tested. This may have occurred in the Rosenthal and Jacobson research, since all students were pre-tested at the end of the previous academic year, so the students new to the school in the fall (when the teachers were told about spurters) presumably were not pre-tested.

- *Reactive effects of experimental arrangements*. People are frequently, if not invariably, aware of the fact that they are participating in an experiment. Their awareness may influence how they respond to the experimental treatment; for example, they may try to behave in a socially acceptable manner rather than sincerely and spontaneously, which could affect the generalizability of the findings. Since Rosenthal and Jacobson's subjects do not appear to have been aware that they were participating in an experiment, this problem is unlikely to have been significant. The issue of reactivity and its potentially damaging effects is a recurring theme in many types of social research.

A third issue relates to the question of replicability. Rosenthal and Jacobson laid out their procedures and measures, and anyone carrying out a replication

Ethical issue 2.2

Informed consent for experiments

Most researchers now adhere to the principle that potential research subjects should not only be asked for their consent before they are placed in an experiment, but they should also be informed of all the risks they would face if they were to participate. To assess those risks, prospective participants should be given a basic idea of what the study would entail. Homan (1991: 73) observed that implementing the principle of informed consent 'is easier said than done.' At least two major points stand out here.

- It is extremely difficult to present prospective participants with absolutely all the information required to make an informed decision about their involvement. In fact, relatively minor ethical transgressions probably pervade most social research, such as not giving all the details about the research for fear of contaminating people's answers to questions. On the other hand, Hessler *et al.*'s qualitative study of adolescent risk behaviour (2003) included a rather elaborate consent form.

- In ethnographic research, the researcher is likely to come into contact with a wide spectrum of people, and ensuring that absolutely everyone has the opportunity for informed consent is not practicable. Even when all research participants in a certain setting are aware that the ethnographer is a researcher, it is doubtful whether they are all similarly (let alone identically) informed about the nature of the research.

Most experiments involve deception because researchers want to limit participants' understanding of what the research is about so they will respond naturally and authentically in the experiment. For example, Goode (1996) placed four fake and slightly different dating advertisements in periodicals. He received nearly one thousand replies and was able to analyze how each advertisement led to different results because the people who replied believed that the advertisements were genuine.

As suggested in earlier discussions, it is rarely feasible or desirable to provide participants with a complete account of what the research is about. Could Milgram's subjects have been told that he wanted to know whether they would be willing to inflict severe pain and possibly death on an innocent person? Such information would have made the research useless.

Nonetheless, there are some important rules about deception. One is that it should be used only as a last resort, although most experimenters cannot avoid deception of some kind. Another is that if deception is used, it should be used as sparingly as possible. Finally, anyone deceived must be debriefed as quickly as possible; in particular, they should be told of the deception and why it was used. What may have happened had Milgram's subjects not been debriefed?

Ethical issue 2.3

Harm to participants

Research likely to harm participants is regarded by almost everyone as unacceptable. But what is 'harm'? Harm can mean a number of things, including: physical harm, loss of self-esteem, stress, and embarrassment. And what does 'likely' mean: a 1 per cent chance, a 10 per cent chance, a 50 per cent chance? Researchers should anticipate and guard against consequences for research participants that are expected to be harmful or disturbing. Still:

- In the Rosenthal and Jacobson (1968) study discussed earlier in this chapter, it is at least possible that the pupils not identified as spurters were adversely affected in their intellectual development by the greater attention given to the spurters. After all, teachers have limited time and energy, and time spent with the spurters meant time away from everyone else.

- In the Festinger *et al.* (1956) study of a doomsday/UFO cult, the researchers joined the group at a crucial time (close to the projected end of the world), thereby deluding group members into thinking that they had successfully recruited converts.

- In the Milgram experiment (1963) on obedience to authority, many of the participants experienced high levels of stress and anxiety after being incited to administer what they thought were electric shocks.

The issue of harm to participants is further addressed in ethical codes requiring that the identities and records of individuals remain confidential. This injunction means that when the findings are published, the individuals are not identifiable, although in rare instances, such as in work of a historical nature or in studies dealing with public figures, exceptions may be made. The study of an American town, 'Springdale' (a pseudonym for the real town), by Vidich and Bensman (1968) is instructive in this regard. Their book was uncomplimentary about the town and many of its leaders, and was written in what many people felt was a rather patronizing tone. To make matters worse, it was possible to identify individuals in the published account. The town's inhabitants responded with a Fourth of July Parade in which many of them wore badges citing their book

pseudonyms, and an effigy of Vidich was set up so that it was peering into manure. The townspeople also announced their refusal to cooperate in any more social research; they were clearly upset by the publication and to that extent were harmed by it.

One of the problems with the no-harm-to-participants principle is that it is not possible to identify all the circumstances in which harm is likely, though that fact should not be taken to mean that there is no point in seeking to protect research subjects. Kimmel (1988) noted in this connection the example of the 1939 Cambridge–Summerville Youth Study, an experiment conducted on 506 boys aged 5 to 13 who were identified either as likely to become delinquent or as having an average likelihood in that regard. The boys, equally divided in terms of this characteristic, were randomly assigned to either an experimental group to receive preventive counselling, or to a no-treatment control group. In the mid-1970s the boys (by then men) were examined and results were quite shocking. 'Treated subjects were more likely than controls to evidence signs of alcoholism and serious mental illness, died at a younger age, suffered from more stress-related diseases, tended to be employed in lower-prestige occupations, and were more likely to commit second crimes' (1988: 19).

In other words, the treatment may have brought about negative consequences, although given the complex and long-term nature of the causes of the characteristics measured, it seems likely that non-experimental factors contributed to the results. Nonetheless, the findings do illustrate the difficulty of anticipating harm to respondents. For another example, might a questionnaire on marital happiness lead a respondent to question and eventually leave a marriage? Could asking a grade eight boy in gym class about steroid use, something unknown to him, encourage experimentation with the drug? Some interviewees even find answering questions to be unsettling or find the cut and thrust of a focus group discussion stressful, especially if they inadvertently reveal more than they had intended. How should they be informed?

As mentioned, all ethical codes suggest that if there is any prospect of harm to participants, and if the risks of the research are greater than the risks of everyday life, informed consent is essential.

Ethical issue 2.4

Who defines harm?

Who makes the actual decision about what constitutes harm? It is probably the university or institutional ethics committee, which is normally made up of researchers and perhaps a layperson or two. As an aside, do the former have a conflict of interest as they too will eventually face a similar body, possibly made up of some of their co-members? How likely is it that the lay members will overrule the experts?

Pretend those two issues are well handled, though certainly the latter is often not. One rule of thumb when harm is expected is that it cannot outweigh the potential benefits of the research. But it is hard to measure both harm and benefit, and one's assessment of them ultimately involves value judgments as well as scientific decisions. Most social scientists are not curing cancer or ending racism. How much suffering or harm, if any, can be justified in social scientific research? That is a key ethical question facing researchers and the ethics committees that oversee their work.

'Pretend that these students are gifted, although they are not any more gifted, on average, than the students not on the list. We want to see whether you would treat such children differently, and whether differential treatment affects their academic performance'? Surely, that sort of approach would not have produced authentic behaviour on the part of the teachers, and the teachers may well have refused to participate under those conditions for ethical and practical reasons. Clearly, some form of deception was necessary for the experiment to work.

But deception raises ethical concerns—it is basically a form of lying. Ethical issue boxes 2.2 through 2.4 discuss the sorts of ethical dilemmas facing researchers in the social sciences.

The laboratory experiment

One of the main advantages of laboratory over field experiments is the researcher's greater control over the research environment. In particular, it is easier to randomly assign subjects to different experimental conditions in the laboratory than in a real-life situation, which enhances the internal validity of the study. For example, Walsh and colleagues (1999) could tell some randomly assigned university students in Eastern Canada that previous results on the mathematics test they were about to take showed that women perform less well than men on such tests. Other students, also randomly assigned, were not told this. The data showed that women scored lower than men when informed of this 'fact.' When told that the test was to compare Canadians and Americans, there was no gender difference. Without the chance to randomly assign subjects, there would always be some doubt that the treatment (being told that women score lower than men on the test) rather than a pre-existing difference between the two sets of subjects actually caused the women to do more poorly. Also, laboratory experiments are more easily replicated because they are less bound to a natural milieu that would be difficult to reproduce.

However, laboratory experiments like the one described in Box 2.1 also suffer from a number of limitations. First, the external validity is probably low, since the laboratory setting may not mirror real-world experiences and contexts, despite the fact that the subjects are very involved in most experiments and take them very seriously. In addition, the treatment effects may be unique to the people in the study; others may not react the same way. In

could obtain further information from them. Consequently, their research is replicable, although there has never been an exact replication. Clairborn (1969) conducted one of the earliest replications and followed a procedure very similar to Rosenthal and Jacobson's, although the study was carried out in three middle-class suburban schools, and the timing of the creation of teacher expectancies was different from the original study. Clairborn failed to replicate Rosenthal and Jacobson's findings, casting doubt on the external validity of the original research and suggesting that the first two threats to external validity referred to earlier in this chapter may limit the applicability of the findings.

Virtually all experiments in the social sciences involve deception of some kind. In the Rosenthal and Jacobson study, for example, the experimenters told the teachers that certain students were spurters, which simply was not true. But could the experiment have been carried out without any deception? For example, could the experimenters have told the teachers that they were testing the effects of teacher expectations on student achievement? Could they have given the teachers a list of students and said, technical terms, there may be an interaction of selection and treatment. In the case of Howell and Frost's (1989) study described in Box 2.1, for example, there are a number of difficulties. The subjects were students and not representative of the general population, if only for their youth, so their responses to the experimental treatment may have been distinctive. They were volunteers, who generally differ from non-volunteers (Rosnow and Rosenthal 1997: ch. 5); in addition, they were given incentives to participate, which may further separate them from others because not everyone will be equally motivated to earn the reward given to those who participate (see Ethical issue box 2.5). There was no effect of pre-testing because, as in many experiments, there was none. However, it is quite feasible that reactive effects occurred—the subjects knew they were in an experiment, which may have affected their behaviour.

Quasi-experiments

Quasi-experiments have certain characteristics of experimental designs but do not fulfill all the internal validity requirements. Several different types of quasi-experiments have been identified (Cook and Campbell 1979), but all of them cannot be covered here. A particularly interesting form is the case of

Box 2.1   A laboratory experiment

Howell and Frost (1989) were interested in whether 'charismatic' leadership of organizations is more effective than two other leadership approaches— 'considerate' and 'structuring.' They conducted a laboratory experiment to test a number of hypotheses, including one that individuals working under a charismatic leader will have higher task performance than those under a considerate leader (Howell and Frost 1989: 245). Course grades were enhanced by 3 per cent for the 144 students who volunteered for the experiment (what ethical issue does that raise?). They were randomly assigned to work on a simulated business task under one of the three types of leadership, all three of which were performed by two female actresses. In broad conformity with the hypotheses, subjects working under charismatic leaders generally scored higher in terms of measures of task performance than those working under other leaders, particularly the considerate leader.

Ethical issue 2.5

A monetary incentive

The participants in the Dinovitzer *et al.* (2003) study on educational attainment among immigrants were offered five dollars to participate. Probably no one answered the questionnaire simply for the small amount of money involved. Still, some ethics review boards do not allow subjects to be paid for their participation except to cover costs such as parking, etc. They do so to protect the poor from 'selling' themselves to researchers. Few would be critical of Beagan's (2001) offer to medical students for a chance at a $200 draw (which technically gets around the payment idea) for taking part in her study of discrimination. But would offering $10,000 for testing a promising drug with potentially dangerous side effects be acceptable? What about selling a kidney for research purposes? Fortunately, the risk of harm to participants in social scientific research is usually quite low, so that sort of question rarely has to be asked.

'natural experiments,' in which naturally occurring phenomena or changes brought about by people not doing research result in experiment-like conditions. When that occurs, researchers can gather data in a manner similar to the way it is done in experiments. For example, if an earthquake hit a particular city, but a city of comparable size and composition a few miles away was spared, the conditions for a natural experiment would be present. One could get a measure of the effects of the natural disaster on things like civic pride or attitudes toward local political leaders by comparing the two cities on those variables. (See Boxes 2.2 and 2.3 for further examples.) However, in natural experiments, it is usually impossible to randomly assign subjects to experimental and control groups. The absence of random assignment casts doubt on the study's internal validity, since the groups may not have been equivalent on all relevant characteristics before the independent variable was introduced. For instance, in the earthquake example, there may have been some pre-existing differences between the two cities before the earthquake struck that contributed to post-earthquake differences— perhaps the stricken city had a charismatic mayor and it was that, more than the earthquake, that contributed to the differences observed. However, the

Box 2.2   Quasi-experiments

A common type of quasi-experiment is to compare data taken before and after a policy shift by government or industry. For a hypothetical example, the number of car accidents before and after the lowering of a speed limit can be examined. If the number goes down after the speed limit has been lowered, the policy appears to be a success, but one cannot be sure because there is no control group not experiencing the change. Perhaps something other than lowering the speed limit caused the change, such as increased media coverage of car accidents.

In the case of the installation of cameras to detect speeding, if the cameras are placed only in randomly selected places and not in others, the research is changed from a quasi- to a real experiment. This provides experimental and control groups (camera and no camera) and the before and after structure needed to examine cause and effect.

Governments find it difficult, however, to subject some people to one condition and others to another. The prison system, schools, and other institutions controlled by governments are part of the real social world, and as such have to meet goals that are very different from those of experimental research. That makes it next to impossible for governments to randomly assign people to different conditions. Therefore, they usually have to make do with quasi-experimental evaluations of policy changes. A criminologist may want to randomly assign criminals to jail or home custody and then compare the two forms of detention, but the potential for some of the at-homes to re-commit crimes would be seen as too great a cost. Because minor criminals are more likely to get home custody than are more serious criminals, a fair test is not possible without random assignment. Similarly, when Canada abolished the death penalty, it was not meant as an experiment but as a policy decision. Data could be examined as if the change were part of a quasi-experiment, for example, by comparing the murder rate before and after capital punishment was abolished; but the legislation was definitely not set up for that purpose.

results of such studies are still compelling because they are real rather than artificial interventions in social life, making them high in external validity.

Quasi-experimental designs have been particularly prominent in *evaluation research* studies, which examine the effects of organizational innovation, such as a longer school day or greater worker autonomy in a plant (see Box 2.4). Sometimes the results are surprising. A quasi-experimental investigation on the effect of support for people who take care of the elderly (Demers 1996) showed that the extra support makes caregivers feel less depressed, but *more* burdened. She was not sure why—perhaps the help offered is seen as something else to be coordinated and managed. The situation Demers found herself in—not being sure of how to make sense of her findings—is actually quite common. It is one thing to come up with findings like hers, but another to explain them. The solution usually involves doing more research.

Significance of experimental design

As stated at the outset of this section, experiments are discussed in this book largely because a true experiment allows the researcher to establish the causal influence of a particular variable, which is something that researchers using other designs aspire to but may not fully achieve. As seen in the next section, cross-sectional designs of the kind associated with

Box 2.3   A natural (quasi-) experiment

The effect of television violence on children is one of the most contested areas of social research. St Helena in the South Atlantic provided a fascinating natural laboratory for the examination of various claims in that regard when television was introduced to the island for the first time in the mid-1990s. The findings—from video footage observing young children at play during school breaks, from diaries kept by about three hundred of the children, and from ratings by teachers—suggested that the introduction of TV was not followed by an increase in the number of aggressive acts observed (Charlton et al. 1998, 1999). The researchers suggest that in environments such as St Helena, where children are closely watched by the community and are expected to avoid violent or aggressive acts, television may have little effect on their behaviour.

survey research are frequently regarded as limited in that regard—they do not allow causality to be demonstrated unambiguously.

Logic of comparison

Before exploring such issues, it is important to draw attention to a significant general lesson that an examination of experiments reveals. A central feature of any experiment is a *comparison*: at the very least it compares the results obtained from an experimental group with those of a control group. In the case of the Howell and Frost (1989) experiment in Box 2.1, the research compared the effects of three different forms of leadership. The advantage of any kind of comparison like this is that it permits a better understanding of the phenomenon in question than would be possible by looking at it under one condition alone. The argument that charismatic leadership is an efficient, performance-enhancing form of leadership is much more persuasive when its effects can be compared to those associated with other forms of leadership. While the experimental design is typically associated with a quantitative research strategy, the specific logic of comparison provides lessons of broad applicability and relevance.

Cross-sectional design

The cross-sectional design is often connected in people's minds with questionnaires and structured interviewing. However, other data-gathering techniques may be used in cross-sectional research,

---

Box 2.4   Evaluation research

An example of evaluation research comes from the Pivot Legal Society in BC, which urged the repeal of Canadian prostitution laws. Based on interviews with 91 prostitutes, the society found, for example, that the law against communicating for the purpose of prostitution (prostitution itself is not illegal) is problematic. It forces prostitutes to make their arrangements in back alleys, where they are vulnerable to assault by their clients and others. It may also lead them to jump into cars before they have fully ascertained how safe they will be. Other groups objected to any change in the law, saying it will increase the numbers of prostitutes, make them more of a public nuisance, or even expose underage boys to their lure. Which side should win is a political and moral issue, but the validity of the claims regarding the social consequences of prospective changes in public policy is for evaluation research to resolve.

The essential question asked by such studies concerns whether the new policy initiative or organizational change achieved its goals. Ideally, the design would have one group that is exposed to the treatment, that is the new initiative, and a control group that is not. Since it is often not feasible or ethical to randomly assign research participants to the two groups, certainly not in the situation just described, such studies are usually quasi-experimental. For instance, data gathered from people before a change may be compared with data acquired after; the before becomes the control group, the after the experimental group. That approach has the added advantage that the two groups are basically the same, making random assignment unnecessary. Such a design could be used for the prostitution study if prostitution were ever legalized.

Experimental designs are fairly entrenched in evaluation research, but in recent years evaluations based on qualitative research have emerged. Although there are differences of opinion about how qualitative evaluation should be carried out, there is consensus on the importance of a full understanding of the context in which an intervention occurs and on hearing the diverse viewpoints of the stakeholders (Greene 2000). For example, Pawson and Tilley (1997) advocate a pluralistic methodology that examines not only the context but also the mechanisms that allow programs to work. Tilley (2000) later outlined an example of the approach in an evaluation of the use of closed-circuit television (CCTV) in parking lots. He observed that there are several ways in which CCTV deters car crime. For instance, it provides a direct deterrence to offenders (fewer people are willing to commit crimes if they think they will be filmed and caught), which encourages greater usage of car parks, which in turn increases personal surveillance, which itself deters crime. Examples of contexts relevant to the intervention are: time (such as when the car park fills up and empties during rush-hour periods, or slow times during the day); blind spots in car parks; and the availability of other nearby venues for offenders to commit car crimes. The kind of evaluation research advocated by Pawson and Tilley maps the different combinations of cause and context in relation to different outcomes.

including structured observation and analysis of official statistics or diaries. Each will be covered in later chapters, but in the meantime the basic structure of the cross-sectional design will be outlined here. In cross-sectional studies, observations are taken *at one point in time*—there are no before and after comparisons. Also, cross-sectional designs *do not involve any manipulations of the independent variable*—they are like snapshots taken of a group or phenomenon at one point in time.

A cross-sectional design entails the collection of data (usually quantitative) on more than one case. Researchers are interested in variation between different people, families, nation states, and so on, and variation can be established only when more than one case is examined. Usually, researchers employing this design select many cases, for a variety of reasons. First, a larger number makes it more likely to encounter variation in *all* of the variables of interest. Second, the requirements of certain statistical techniques are likely to require large sample sizes (see Chapter 11).

Data are collected on two or more variables which are then examined to detect patterns of association. This practice makes it difficult to show cause and effect because the independent and dependent variables are measured simultaneously, making any demonstration of temporal order (that the cause actually precedes the effect in time) hard to prove. All that can be said for certain is that the variables 'vary together.' As will be shown in Chapter 12, there are a number of ways for researchers to draw cautious inferences about causality, but they rarely have the credibility of the causal findings derived from an experimental design. As a result, cross-sectional research invariably lacks the internal validity that one finds in most experimental research. For example, there is a well-supported negative relationship between social class and serious forms of mental illness—more poor people are mentally ill than rich people. But there is also a debate about that relationship: Does being poor lead to stress and therefore to mental illness? Or does being mentally ill lead to difficulties in holding down a job and thus poverty? Or is it a bit of both?

To take another example, a study of 1000 men found that those who have two or more orgasms a week exhibit a 50 per cent reduced mortality risk compared with men who have on average fewer than one orgasm per week. It may be tempting to conclude that male orgasm leads to longer life expectancy, but it is also possible that the causal arrow points in the other direction: men who are ill (and thus at greater mortality risk) are less likely to be sexually active in the first place (Houghton 1998: 14). This finding and the preceding one are similar, showing what Blaxter (1990) called 'an ambiguity about the direction of causal influence.' There is only an *association* between the two variables—no clear causal link.

Reliability, replicability, and validity

How does cross-sectional research measure up in terms of the previously outlined criteria for evaluating quantitative research: reliability, replicability, and validity?

- The issues of reliability and measurement validity primarily relate to the quality of the measures employed to tap the concepts in which the researcher is interested, rather than to a research design. This will be covered in the next chapter.
- Replicability characterizes most cross-sectional research, so long as the researcher spells out the procedures for selecting respondents, administering research instruments (structured interview or self-completion questionnaire, etc.), and the analysis of data.
- Internal validity is typically weak. As just suggested, it is difficult to establish causal direction from the resulting data. Cross-sectional research designs can identify associations but cannot firmly establish causal connections.
- External validity is strong when the sample is a random one. When non-random methods of sampling are employed, external validity becomes questionable, an issue addressed in Chapter 11.

Variables that cannot be manipulated

As noted in the section on experimental design, in much (if not most) social research it is not possible to manipulate the variables of interest. This is why most quantitative social research employs a cross-sectional design rather than an experimental one. To more or less all intents and purposes, ethnicity, age, gender, and social backgrounds are 'givens' and not really amenable to the kind of manipulation necessary for a true experimental design (but see Box 2.5). For example, an experimenter with makeup and a fake accent can create a fictional man or a

Box 2.5   Manipulating non-manipulable variables: body weight, ethnicity, and race

A researcher was interested in how people respond to 'overweight' as against 'normal weight' people. She could have compared accounts told by people of different body weights or even directly observed responses of others to them. Instead, because she had gorged herself, filling her short frame to almost 100 kilograms, she conducted a personal experiment. She gradually slimmed down and at the same time looked for changes in the reactions of others as she did. Apparently, the effects of being fat were not as negative as anticipated, because she claimed that early on she 'had the most unbelievably good-looking man chat her up' (reported in Wilkinson and Whitworth 1998: 3). However, the experiment could be made less personal by showing pictures of individuals, first fat and then slim, and then asking respondents for their opinions of each.

Ethnicity too can be studied experimentally. Identical résumés could be sent out to prospective employers, but the names and birthplaces would vary. The researcher could then monitor the calls for personal interviews. This is a watered-down version of what Griffin (1961) did in the 1950s when he blackened his face and visible parts of his body and travelled around the American South as a person of colour, always keeping his eyes averted to show due deference to whites. He was treated as a black man in a number of ways, such as having to use segregated water fountains. Griffin's aim was to experience what it was like to be a black person in a period and region of racial segregation. While Griffin's study is interesting, it is doubtful that a brief sojourn as an African-American adequately captured the experience of being black in the American South at that time, a condition of subordination that was formed by many years of personal encounters and the knowledge that they would be ongoing.

woman—say, a Scot or a Swede—perhaps to see the effects on job offers, but the manipulation is limited to the external signs of gender and ethnicity, missing the more subjective and experiential aspects. Sometimes variables cannot be manipulated for ethical reasons, as Box 2.6 illustrates.

However, the very fact that certain variables are givens provides a clue as to how to make causal inferences in cross-sectional research. Many of the variables of interest can be assumed to be temporally prior to other variables. For example, in a relationship between ethnic status and alcohol consumption, the latter cannot be the independent variable because it occurs after ethnicity. Ethnicity still cannot be said with certainty to be the cause, however—just a possible cause. In other words, even though researchers are unable to manipulate things like ethnic status or gender, causal inferences can still be cautiously drawn from cross-sectional data.

The current discussion of the cross-sectional design places it firmly in the context of quantitative research. But qualitative research can also use a form of cross-sectional design. For example, Beardsworth and Keil (1992) carried out a study of the dietary beliefs and practices of vegetarians. They administered 'relatively unstructured interviews,' which were 'guided by an inventory of issues' with 76 vegetarians and vegans (1992: 261). The interviews were taped

Box 2.6   Sex offender treatment questioned: doing what is possible to create an experiment

Treating sex offenders in custody apparently has little effect on their re-offending after release. A group of 724 men serving time in a BC federal prison were analyzed and then divided into two groups depending on whether they took or did not take treatment. For ethical reasons there could be no random assignment and administering of the treatment to everyone in an experimental group, so the control group consisted of men incarcerated before the treatment was available. The experimental group was made up of those who chose to take the treatment. This was not a perfect assignment to groups because the people choosing treatment may have been more motivated to change than the people in the control group. In any case, the results showed equal re-offending in both groups, around 20 per cent. This statistic held for non-sexual crimes too—not very encouraging for the professionals who treat inmates.

Source: Adapted from Jane Armstrong, *Globe and Mail*, 31 March 2004.

and transcribed, yielding a large body of qualitative data.

The research was not preoccupied with quantitative criteria such as internal and external validity, replicability, measurement validity, and so on. In fact, the conversational interview style made the study more externally valid than research, using more formal instruments of data collection. The study was concerned with the factors that influence food selection, like vegetarianism. The very notion of an 'influence' carries a strong connotation of causality, suggesting that qualitative researchers are also interested in the investigation of causes and effects, albeit not using the language of quantitative research with its talk of independent and dependent variables. As well, the emphasis was much more on understanding the experience of something like vegetarianism than is often the case with quantitative research.

This qualitative research bears many similarities to the cross-sectional design in quantitative research. It entailed interviewing quite a large number of people and at a single point in time. And as with many quantitative studies using a cross-sectional design, the examination of people's past and current eating habits was based on the subjects' retrospective accounts of factors that affected their past and present behaviour.

Structure of cross-sectional designs

A cross-sectional design collects data on a series of variables (Obs_1 Obs_2 Obs_3 Obs_4 Obs_5 . . . $Obs n$) for different cases (which may be people, households, cities, nations, etc.) at a single point in time. The effect is to create a data set that comprises variables Obs_1 to $Obs n$ and cases $case_1$ to $case n$, as in Figure 2.2. Each cell in the matrix has data in it.

Obs_1	Obs_2	Obs_3	Obs_4	. . .	Obs_n
$Case_1$					
$Case_2$					
$Case_3$					
$Case_4$					
$Case_5$					
. . .					
$Case_n$					

Figure 2.2 The data rectangle in cross-sectional research

Longitudinal design(s)

With a longitudinal design, cases are examined at a particular time (T1) and again at a later time or times (T2, T3, and so on), but with no manipulation of an independent variable like there is in experiments (see Box 2.7). It thus allows insight into the time order of variables and is better able to deal with the problem of 'ambiguity about the direction of causal influence' that plagues cross-sectional designs. Because potential independent variables can be identified at T1, the researcher is in a better, if not perfect, position to infer that the effects identified at T2 or later occurred *after* changes occurred in the independent variables. In all other respects, the points made above about cross-sectional designs are the same as those for longitudinal designs. In spite of its heightened ability to show cause and effect, the longitudinal design is not frequently used in social research because of the additional time and cost involved.

Longitudinal studies can take different forms. For example, Goyder *et al.* (2003) examined how gender-influenced evaluations of occupational prestige had changed over 25 years. Some of the earlier male advantage had disappeared; indeed, some occupations showing a female incumbent were rated more highly than the same occupation with a male incumbent. Baer *et al.* (2001) did a 15-nation study examining whether membership in clubs and associations had changed over time. Kerr (2004) and Kerr and Michalski (2007) investigated hyperactivity in Canadian children as they got older and its sources in poverty and family structure.

There are two basic types of longitudinal design: the *panel study* and the *cohort study*. With the former, the same people, households, or other groups are studied on at least two different occasions. An example is the National Longitudinal Survey of Children and Youth (NLSCY), described in Box 2.8, in which the same children were studied in successive years. A panel study, especially one at the household level, needs rules for handling new entrants (for example, as a result of marriage or elderly relatives moving in) and exits (for example, as a result of marital break-up or children leaving home).

In a cohort study, people sharing the same experience, such as being born in the same year or graduating from a particular school at the same time, are studied over time, but the same people may not be

Box 2.7   Longitudinal research and the case study

Case study research frequently includes a longitudinal element. The researcher is often a participant observer in an organization or a member of a community for many months or years, or may conduct interviews with individuals over a lengthy period. Moreover, the researcher may be able to inject an additional longitudinal element by analyzing archival information and asking respondents to recall things that occurred before the study began, thus discovering some history.

A longitudinal element also occurs when a case that has been studied is returned to at a later time. A particularly interesting example of this occurred in 'Middletown,' a pseudonym for an American Midwest town first studied by Lynd and Lynd (1929) in 1924–5 and restudied in 1935 during the Depression to see what changes had occurred (Lynd and Lynd 1937). In 1977, the community was again restudied, this time in a post–Vietnam War setting (Bahr *et al.* 1983), using the same research instruments but with minor changes.

Box 2.8   The National Longitudinal Survey of Children and Youth

This panel study is a long-term effort to monitor Canadian children's development and well-being as they mature from infancy to adulthood. It began with a representative sample of children 11 years of age or younger in 1994–5 being interviewed, with follow-ups every two years. Statistics Canada collects the data, with direction provided by Human Resources Development Canada. The study hopes to follow the subjects until they are 25 years old, and to make a contribution to the development of policies that help children live healthy, active, and rewarding lives (see Michaud 2001). Researchers have now completed Cycle 7, which was conducted in 2006–7.

studied each time. For example, Walters (2004) used the 1982, 1986, 1992, and 1995 National Graduates Surveys to examine trends in the economic fortunes of Canadians graduating from post-secondary institutions. The same people were not selected for the sample each year, but the information was still useful in understanding each graduating cohort, as well as the similarities and differences between cohorts.

Panel and cohort studies share similar features. In social sciences like sociology, social policy, and human geography, both are usually in the form of repeated survey research using a self-completion questionnaire or structured interview. They have a similar design structure and are concerned both with illuminating social change and improving the understanding of causal influences.

Panel and cohort studies also share similar problems. First, there is the problem of sample attrition through death, moving, and so on, or through subjects choosing to withdraw at later stages of the research. For instance, the study by Dinovitzer *et al.* (2003) on the educational attainment of immigrant youth talked to only 65 per cent of those originally surveyed 19 years earlier. Comparing those who participated in the second round with those who were lost from the study, the authors found no significant differences. That comparison is a common practice and when no difference is found, the losses are treated as random and thus acceptable to ignore. The main problem with attrition is that those who leave the study may differ in some important respects from those who remain, so that the latter do not form a representative group. However, there is some evidence from panel studies that attrition declines with time (Berthoud 2000*a*); in other words, those who do not drop out after the first wave or two of data collection tend to stay on the panel.

Second, there are few guidelines for determining the best timing for further waves of data collection. Finally, there is evidence of a *panel conditioning* effect, whereby continued participation in a longitudinal study affects respondent behaviour. Menard (1991) cited a study of family caregiving in which 52 per cent of respondents indicated a change in how they cared for relatives as a result of their participation in the research.

It is easy to associate longitudinal designs more or less exclusively with quantitative research. However, qualitative research sometimes incorporates elements of a longitudinal design. This is especially noticeable in ethnographic research when the ethnographer is in a location for a lengthy period of time or when interviews are carried out on more than one occasion in order to address change. In an example of the latter, Smith *et al.* (2004) described a study of the experiences of citizenship for 110 young people. They were interviewed in depth in 1999 and then re-interviewed at two-year intervals to examine changes in their lifestyles, feelings, opinions, and ambitions in relation to citizenship issues. Only 64 young people participated in all three waves of data collection, illustrating the high level of sample attrition in this style of research.

Case study design

The basic case study design entails a detailed and intensive analysis of a single case. A case may be:

- a single community, as in Hughes's classic study of Drummondville, a textile town in Quebec (1943), and in Pratt and Valverde's (2002) research on Somalis in Toronto;
- a single family, like that found in Lewis's (1961) study of the Sánchez family in Mexico;
- a single organization, such as the automobile factory studied by Rinehart (1996), or a group within an organization, like the nurses in a Hamilton hospital researched by White (1990);
- a person, as in Nemni and Nemni's (2006) study of Pierre Trudeau; such research is characterized by use of the life history or biographical approach (see Chapter 10);
- a single event, like the fight against locating a home for recovering addicts in a Richmond, BC, neighbourhood (Huey 2003), or the Alberta election analyzed by Bell *et al.* (2007); or
- a state or province, as in Laplante's (2006) study of the rise of cohabitation in Quebec.

There is a tendency to associate case studies with qualitative research, such as Pratt and Valverde's (2002) study of the Toronto Somali community. Exponents of the case study design often favour methods like participant observation and unstructured interviewing, which are viewed as particularly helpful in generating an intensive, detailed examination of a case. However, case studies can also use quantitative methods, or some combination of quantitative and qualitative.

With a case study, the case is an object of interest *in its own right* and the researcher aims to provide an in-depth elucidation of it. Sometimes it is difficult to distinguish case studies from other research designs because almost any kind of research can be construed as a case study. Even research based on a national, random sample of Canadians could be considered a case study of Canada.

What distinguishes a true case study is the goal of finding and revealing the features of the case. Collecting in-depth, often qualitative data that may be unique to time and place is characteristic of this sort of research. Case studies are often idiographic in nature, seeking to provide a rich description of the subject matter, like Shalla's (2002) study of how Air Canada's customer and service agents became victims of airline restructuring.

When the predominant research orientation is qualitative, a case study tends to take an inductive approach to the relationship between theory and research. If a mainly quantitative strategy is adopted, the research is often deductive, guided by specific research questions derived from social theories.

Reliability, replicability, and validity of case studies

The question of how the case study fares on the research design issues of measurement validity, internal validity, external validity, reliability, and replicability depends in large part on whether the researcher feels these criteria are appropriate for their work. Writers of qualitative case study research tend to play down or ignore the salience of these factors (cf. Stake 1995). Those influenced by the quantitative research tradition see them as more significant, usually making efforts to develop case studies that meet the criteria.

One question that has generated a great deal of discussion concerns the *external validity* or *generalizability* of case study research. How can a single case possibly be representative of other cases? For example, would the findings from a study of the Toronto police department be generalizable to all large urban police departments in Canada? The answer, of course, is that the findings probably cannot be applied to other police departments. Usually, case study researchers do not delude themselves into thinking that it is possible to identify typical cases that can represent a class of objects, whether it is factories, mass media reporting, police services, or communities. In other words, they typically do *not* think that a case study is a sample of one.

Types of case

Yin (1984) distinguished three types of case, each of which relates to the issue of external validity:

- The *critical case*. Here the researcher has a clearly specified hypothesis, and a case is chosen on the grounds that it will allow a better understanding of the circumstances under which the hypothesis does or does not hold. The classic study by Festinger *et al.* (1956) of a doomsday/UFO cult is an example. The fact that the world did not end allowed the researchers to test propositions about how people respond to thwarted expectations. What did cult members do after quitting their jobs, leaving their homes, and waiting on a mountaintop, when nothing happened? Sneak down and move to another town? No, they decided that their faith had saved humankind and that their new role was to tell others of that miracle so more people could be converted to their religion.
- The *extreme*, even *unique*, *case* is a common focus in clinical studies. Margaret Mead's (1928) well-known (albeit controversial) study of growing up in Samoa seems to have been motivated by her belief that it represented a unique case and thus could challenge the then popular nature-over-nurture hypothesis. She reported that, unlike adolescents in most other societies, Samoan youth did not suffer a period of anxiety and stress in their teenage years. She explained this by their culture's strong, consistently enforced standards of conduct and morality. These factors were of interest because many readers thought they might contain lessons for Western youth.
- The *revelatory case*. The basis for the revelatory case exists 'when an investigator has an opportunity to observe and analyse a phenomenon previously inaccessible to scientific investigation' (Yin 1984: 44). This can happen when previously unavailable evidence becomes accessible, such as certain KGB files after the fall of the Soviet Union.

Cases may also be chosen for mundane reasons, such as being close and willing, and still provide an adequate context for certain research questions to be answered or for key social processes to be examined. To take a concrete example, Russell and Tyler's (2002) study of a Girl Heaven store in the UK (which caters to 3- to 13-year-old girls) was not motivated by it being critical, unique, or providing a context never before studied. It was selected for its capacity to illuminate the links between gender and consumption and the commodification of childhood in modern society. Indeed, often it is only at a very late stage in the research that the singularity and significance of the case becomes apparent (Radley and Chamberlain 2001).

As previously mentioned, one of the standard criticisms of the case study is that its findings cannot be generalized. Case study researchers argue strenuously that this is not the purpose of their craft. A valid picture of one case is more valuable than a potentially less valid picture of many. Their aim is to generate an intensive examination of a single case, which may or may not be used to engage in a theoretical analysis. Pratt and Valverde (2002) studied only Somalis and declared a hope that others would study other immigrant groups in other places. Their central concern was the richness of the data and the quality of the theoretical reasoning that the case allowed. As noted, sometimes case studies are primarily inductive, being used as information to generate theories. Other times they may be deductive in nature, providing data to assess theories.

Problems can arise when the research involves a comparison of more than one case. Dyer and Wilkins (1991), for example, argued that a multiple-case study approach leads to less attention being paid to the specific details of a particular case, and more to the ways in which multiple cases can be contrasted. Moreover, the need for comparison tends to result in the researcher acquiring an explicit focus at the outset, whereas it may be advantageous to adopt a more open-ended approach in many instances. These concerns about retaining contextual insight and a more unstructured research approach are associated with a qualitative research strategy. As illustrated in Boxes 2.9 and 2.10, comparative case study work is often quantitative in orientation.

The strength of comparative designs is that they highlight the similarities and differences between

Box 2.9 Comparative research: cross-cultural studies

Phenomena such as voting behaviour or crime victimization in two or more countries can be compared using the same research instruments, seeking similarities and differences and a deeper understanding of social reality in different national contexts. At the very least it supplies a replication. The research by Kelley and De Graaf (1997) referred to in Box 1.3 is an illustration of cross-cultural survey evidence collected in 15 nations.

Cross-cultural research has problems, apart from being more expensive than other approaches. When using existing data such as official statistics or survey evidence, the researcher must ensure that the variable categories and data-collection methods are comparable. When new data are being collected, the researcher must ensure that data-collection instruments (for example, questionnaires and interview schedules) are translated properly. Even when translation is carried out competently, there may still

be a problem with insensitivity to specific national and cultural milieus. For example, referring to the London 'tube,' the Toronto 'subway,' and the Montreal 'métro' is only a start because public transit experiences in the three cities may be very different in terms of ridership, safety, cleanliness, etc.

A strength of cross-cultural research is that it helps to illustrate how social scientific findings may be culturally specific. For example, Wilson's (2002) examination of Ontario raves made frequent comparisons to the earlier rave scene in Britain. However, the UK scene was primarily an outgrowth of working-class struggles, whereas Canadian raves appealed more to middle-class, culturally alienated youths. Similarly, Baer *et al.* (2001) found that joining clubs and voluntary organizations increased towards the end of the last century in the US, West Germany, and the Netherlands, was stable in Canada and 10 other countries, but decreased in Spain.

Box 2.10 Managing cross-cultural research

As its name implies, cross-cultural research entails the collection and/or analysis of data from two or more cultures. Possible models include:

1. A researcher, perhaps in conjunction with a research team, collects data in a number of countries. A related option is for a coordinator to recruit researchers in participating nations and to direct their investigations. The work is coordinated to ensure comparability of research questions, survey questions, and procedures for administering the research instruments.

Sometimes the foreign team leaders have considerable autonomy in deciding which cases they will study, provided that they meet predetermined criteria (for example, organizational level, size).

2. A lone researcher or small team replicates work done in a foreign country in his or her own country. For instance, a 2004 Ipsos-Reid survey for Canadian Blood Services found that 3.7 per cent of Canadians are blood donors, with the over-forty age group giving the most. This is less than half of the rate in Taiwan, and below the US rate of about 5 per cent.

cases, which can be used to assess or generate theories. They exhibit certain features similar to experiments and quasi-experiments, which also rely on the capacity to forge a comparison.

Bringing research orientation and design together

Finally, we can bring together the two general research orientations covered in Chapter 1 with the research

designs outlined in this chapter. Table 2.1 shows the typical form associated with each combination of research orientation and research design, along with a number of examples that either have been encountered so far or will be covered in later chapters. Table 2.1 also refers to research methods to be encountered in later chapters, but not referred to so far. The glossary provides a quick reference for unfamiliar terms.

The distinctions are not always perfect. In particular, in some qualitative research it is not obvious whether a study is an example of a longitudinal design

Table 2.1 Research strategy and research design

Research design	General Research Orientation	
	Quantitative	*Qualitative*
Experimental	Typical form: Most experiments involve quantitative comparisons between experimental and control groups on the dependent variable. Example: the Rosenthal and Jacobson (1968) study discussed in this chapter.	Experiments are not used in qualitative research, although they may inspire or be inspired by qualitative findings. For example, a qualitative study of the subjects who participated in the Milgram (1963) experiments would be enlightening.
Cross-sectional	Typical form: Survey research and structured observation on a sample at a single point in time are two forms; content analysis of a sample of documents is another. Sometimes there is a comparison, as in cross-cultural research. Example: Box 1.3.	Typical form: Qualitative interviews or focus groups at a single point in time are two forms; qualitative content analysis of a set of documents relating to a single period is another. Example: the Beardsworth and Keil (1992) study of vegetarianism discussed in this chapter.
Longitudinal	Typical form: Survey research on a sample on more than one occasion, as in panel and cohort studies is one form; content analysis of documents relating to different time periods is another. Example: Box 2.8.	Typical form: These include ethnographic research over a long period, qualitative interviewing on more than one occasion, or qualitative content analysis of documents relating to different time periods. Such research is longitudinal when the main purpose is to map change. Examples: the Lynd and Lynd (1929) study of 'Middletown' discussed in this chapter.
Case study	Typical form: Survey research is conducted on a single case with a view to revealing important features about its nature. Example: Bell *et al.* (2007) study of the 2004 Alberta provincial election.	Typical form: The intensive study is done by qualitative interviewing of a single case, which may be an organization, person, family, or community. Example: Box 1.6.

or a case study design. Life history studies, research that concentrates on a specific issue over time, and ethnography in which the researcher charts change in a single case, contain aspects of both designs. Such studies are perhaps better conceptualized as longitudinal case studies rather than as belonging to one category or another. A further point is that there is no typical form in the qualitative research orientation/experimental research design cell. Qualitative research in the context of true experiments is very unusual, with a quasi-experimental design being a more realistic alternative.

— Key Points

- There is an important distinction between a general research orientation (quantitative vs qualitative) and a research design.

- Reliability, replicability, and validity (measurement, internal, and external) are important criteria for evaluating the quality of social research.

- Four key research designs are experimental, cross-sectional, longitudinal, and case study.

- Threats to internal validity are of particular importance in non-experimental research.

- External validity (generalizability) is a concern with case studies.

- Ethics are always an issue in social research. Sometimes the boundaries between ethical and unethical practices are difficult to establish, although extreme violations are more easily discerned.

— Questions for Review

Criteria for the evaluation of social research

- What are the differences between reliability and validity, and why are both criteria important in social research?

- Give an example of each of the following: measurement validity, internal validity, and external validity.

- Why have some qualitative researchers sought to devise alternative criteria for reliability and validity to assess their investigations?

Research designs

- Which research design would be appropriate for examining the use of illegal drugs in a local high school?

- A researcher reasons that people who read broadsheet newspapers (wider than they are tall) are likely to be more knowledgeable about personal finance than readers of tabloid newspapers (taller than they are wide). One hundred people are interviewed about which type they read and their level of financial knowledge: 65 readers of tabloids and 35 of broadsheets. The latter are on average considerably more knowledgeable about personal finance than tabloid readers, so the researcher concludes that reading broadsheets enhances knowledge of personal finance. Assess that conclusion.

Experimental design

- 'Experiments are the best research design for establishing causal connections between variables.' Discuss.

- Following from the last question, if experiments are so useful and important, why are they not used more in disciplines like sociology or political science?

- What is a quasi-experiment?

Cross-sectional design

- What is meant by a cross-sectional research design?
- In what ways does the survey exemplify the cross-sectional research design?
- Assess the degree to which survey research can achieve internal validity.
- To what extent is the survey design exclusive to quantitative research?

Longitudinal design(s)

- Why might a longitudinal research design be superior to a cross-sectional one?
- What are the main differences between panel and cohort designs?

Case study design

- What is a case study?
- Is case study research exclusive to qualitative research?
- What are some of the principles by which cases might be selected?

Ethical principles

- How are ethical issues relevant to the conduct of social research?
- Does 'harm to participants' refer to physical harm alone?
- What are some difficulties with following this ethical principle?
- Why is the issue of informed consent so hotly debated?
- What are the main difficulties of following this ethical principle?
- Why is the privacy principle important?
- Why does deception matter?
- How helpful are studies like Milgram's electric-shock experiments for understanding ethical principles in social research?

The difficulties of ethical decision-making

- How easy is it to satisfy ethical criteria in social research?

Part II

Part II of this book is concerned with quantitative research. Chapter 3 sets the scene by exploring its main features. Chapter 4 focuses on structured interviews and questionnaires, two of the most widely used data-gathering techniques in quantitative research. Chapter 5 provides guidelines on how to ask questions using those instruments, while Chapter 6 discusses structured observation, a method that provides a systematic approach to the study of people in their natural surroundings. Chapter 7 examines other data sources, such as the information collected by other researchers and government agencies. These chapters provide the essential tools for doing quantitative research, from basic methodological principles to practical applications.

3 The Nature of Quantitative Research

Chapter overview

This chapter is concerned with quantitative research, an approach used by a large number of people in the social sciences. The emphasis in this chapter is on what quantitative research typically entails, though later in the chapter departures from this ideal type are outlined. This chapter explores:

- the main steps of quantitative research, presented as a linear succession of stages;

- the importance of measurement in quantitative research, and the ways in which measures are devised for concepts;
- procedures for checking the reliability and validity of those measures;
- the main goals of quantitative researchers: measurement, establishing causality, generalization, and replication; and
- some criticisms of quantitative research.

Introduction

In Chapter 1, quantitative research was outlined as a distinctive research strategy involving particular epistemological and ontological assumptions. It should be clear by now that much more than the presence of numbers distinguishes a quantitative from a qualitative research strategy. In very broad terms, quantitative research entails the collection of numerical data, a deductive relationship between theory and research, a predilection for the natural science approach to research (positivism in particular), and an objectivist conception of social reality. This chapter spells out the main steps in quantitative research, and outlines how some of its principal concerns, such as measurement validity, are addressed.

The main steps in quantitative research

Figure 3.1 outlines the main steps in quantitative research. This is very much an ideal account of the process: research is rarely as linear or as straightforward as the figure implies. However, it represents a useful starting point for coming to grips with the main facets of the quantitative approach.

Some of the steps were covered in the previous chapters. The fact that the model starts off with

1. Theory
2. Hypothesis
3. Research design
4. Devise measures of concepts
5. Select research site(s)
6. Select research subjects/respondents
7. Administer research instruments/collect data
8. Process data
9. Analyze data
10. Findings/conclusions
11. Write up findings/conclusions

Figure 3.1 The process of quantitative research

theory signifies a broadly deductive approach to the relationship between theory and research. Similarly, it is common for outlines of quantitative research to suggest that a hypothesis is deduced from a theory and is tested, another notion incorporated into Figure 3.1. However, a great deal of quantitative research does not specify a hypothesis beforehand; instead there may simply be a loosely defined set of concerns in relation to which the social researcher collects data. This was the case for Gazso-Windlej and McMullin's (2003) study of how time, resources, and patriarchy affect the continued unequal spousal sharing of domestic labour in Canada. The specification of testable hypotheses is more common in experimental research.

In step 3 a research design is selected, a topic explored in Chapter 2. This choice has implications for a variety of issues, such as the external validity of the findings and the ability to impute causality. Step 4 entails devising measures of concepts, a process often referred to as *operationalization*, a term derived from physics to refer to the operations performed to measure a concept such as temperature or velocity (Bridgman 1927). Further aspects of this issue are explored later in this chapter.

Box 3.1   Selecting research sites and sampling respondents: the Workforce Ageing in the New Economy (WANE) study

The WANE comparative study examines, among other things, age discrimination in hiring and forced early retirement in the IT sector. The project, which is being conducted through a consortium of researchers and private companies, involves research in four sites: Canada, the US, Australia, and the EU. It will eventually involve between 17 and 22 case studies in each locale. A large firm (100 or more employees) and a mid-sized firm will be selected in each country. The rest of the firms will be small (20 or fewer employees). In the small firms, all employees will be interviewed. In the mid- and large-sized firms the researchers will talk to a random sample of employees. The website www.wane.ca has more information about the project, but this brief description shows how researchers have to make decisions about selecting both research site(s) and respondents.

The next two steps are the selection of a research site or sites, and the selection of subjects/respondents. (Experimenters tend to call the people on whom they conduct research 'subjects,' whereas social survey researchers typically call them 'respondents.') In the study of delinquency among male adolescents described in Box 1.2, Teevan and Dryburgh (2000) first chose a particular school as a research site, one where the researchers had connections. Then they had to arrange for permission slips to be signed, which led to the investigators studying boys old enough to give their own permission. Finally, because of a less-than-eager response, all boys who were willing to participate became part of the study. In bigger studies, especially those in which the findings are expected to be applicable to some larger population, an elaborate sampling process (discussed in Chapter 11) is carried out to select people for the project, although such procedures are less likely to be used in experimental research. Box 3.1 provides another illustration of how practical decisions about research sites and the selection of respondents are made.

Step 7 is the administration of the research instruments. In experimental research, this usually means pre-testing subjects, manipulating the independent variable for the experimental group only, and post-testing. In cross-sectional research using survey research instruments, it involves interviewing the members of the sample with a structured interview schedule (a list of questions or statements to which the person being interviewed responds) or distributing a self-completion questionnaire. In research using structured observation, this step involves watching the setting of interest and the people in it, and then recording the types of behaviours observed.

Step 8 simply refers to the fact that the information collected must be systematically recorded so it can be analyzed. With some information this can be done in a relatively straightforward way. For example, for information relating to such things as people's ages, incomes, number of years spent at school, and so on, the information does not have to be transformed—the scores can simply be placed in a computer file. For other variables, processing the data entails *coding* the information—that is, transforming it into numbers to facilitate quantitative data analysis. This consideration leads into step 9—the analysis of the data. In this step, the researcher chooses among various statistical techniques to test for relationships between variables, tries to determine whether the measures are reliable, and so on.

Next, in step 10 the researcher must interpret the results of the analysis and it is at this stage that the 'findings' emerge. Here the researcher must consider the reasons why the research was done in the first place, in particular how the results may be used to answer the research question(s). If there is a hypothesis, is it supported? What are the implications of the findings for the theoretical ideas that were the background to the research? Do the findings support the theory? If not, should the theory be revised? Should it be abandoned entirely?

Then the research must be written up in step 11. Until it enters the public domain in some way, as a paper to be read at a conference, a report to the agency that funded the research, or as a book or journal article to be read by other researchers or students, it cannot have an impact beyond satisfying the researcher's personal curiosity. In writing up the findings and conclusions, the researcher is doing more than simply relaying results to others: readers must be convinced that the research conclusions are important and the findings robust. A significant part of doing research is convincing others of the relevance and validity of one's findings.

Once the findings have been published they become part of the stock of knowledge in their domain. Thus there is a feedback loop from step 11 back to step 1. The presence of both an element of deduction (steps 1 and 2) and induction (the feedback loop) is indicative of the positivist foundations of quantitative research. The emphasis on the translation of concepts into measures (step 4) is also a feature of positivism, and it is to that important phase of the research that we now turn. As will be seen, certain considerations follow from the need for measurement in quantitative research, in particular, finding valid and reliable ways to measure concepts.

Concepts and their measurement

What is a concept?

Concepts are ideas or mental representations of things. They are the building blocks of theory and represent the points around which social research is conducted. Just think of the numerous concepts that have already been mentioned so far in this book:

> emotional satisfaction, religious orthodoxy, religious orientation, hyperactivity, academic achievement, teacher expectations, charismatic leadership, crime, research ethics, and healthy lifestyle.

Each represents a label given to elements of the social world that seem to be significant and to have common features. As Bulmer succinctly put it, concepts 'are categories for the organisation of ideas and observations' (1984: 43). One item mentioned in Chapter 2 but missing from the list above is IQ. It has been omitted because it is not, strictly speaking, a concept. It is a *measure* of the concept of intelligence. This is a rare case for social science, a measure so well known that the measure and the concept are almost synonymous.

A concept can be an independent or a dependent variable. In other words, a concept can be presented as a possible cause of a certain aspect of the social world (independent), or it can represent something needing an explanation (dependent). Often the same concept is an independent variable in one context, but a dependent variable in another. The concept 'social mobility,' for example, can be used in either capacity: as a possible explanation of certain attitudes (are there differences between the downwardly mobile and others in their political attitudes?) or as something to be explained (why are some people upwardly mobile and others not?). Equally, concepts may be used for descriptive or comparative purposes. For instance, one may be interested in changes in the amount of social mobility in Canada over time, or in variations among comparable nations in their levels of social mobility.

Why measure?

There are three main reasons for the attention given to measurement in quantitative research:

- Measurement allows a delineation of *fine differences* between people in terms of the characteristic in question. This is very useful since, although it is often easy to distinguish between people in terms of extreme categories, finer distinctions are much more difficult to recognize. Clear variations in levels of job satisfaction—people who love their jobs and people who hate their jobs—are easy to see, but small differences are much more difficult to detect.

- Measurement gives a *consistent device* or yardstick for gauging such distinctions. This consistency relates both to time and to the people using the measure. A measure should not be influenced by when it is administered or by whom it is used. Saying that a measure should not be influenced by time means that the measure should generate consistent results *unless* the phenomenon or characteristic being measured has changed. For example, measures of worker morale used at different times should indicate the same level of morale unless the morale itself has changed. Similarly, those measures and the data they produce should be the same regardless of who is using them. Whether a measure actually possesses this consistency pertains to the issue of *reliability*, introduced in Chapter 2 and examined again later in this chapter.
- Measurement provides the basis for *estimates of the nature and strength of the relationship between concepts* (for example, through correlation analysis, which will be examined in Chapter 12).

Indicators

Concepts used in quantitative research are given two types of definition. One is a *nominal* definition, which describes in words what is meant by the concept, much like a dictionary definition. For example, a nominal definition of 'crime' might be: 'any violation of the *Criminal Code of Canada*.' How one measures a concept is referred to as the concept's *operational definition*, a term deriving from the idea of operationalization, discussed above. An operational definition spells out the operations the researcher will perform to measure the concept. For example, one way to measure the amount of crime is to use statistics provided by police forces; another is to ask a sample of people whether they have been victims of certain crimes.

To measure a concept it is necessary to have an indicator or indicators that stand for or represent the concept. Sometimes the term 'indicator' simply refers to a measure in the ordinary sense, for example, the total income reported on a tax return is an indicator of a person's wealth. However, sometimes it refers to an indirect measure of a concept that cannot be tapped easily or directly. For example, absenteeism may be used as an indirect measure of employee morale. Income declared for tax purposes may be a direct measure of personal income, but if used as an indicator of social class, it becomes an indirect measure.

There are a number of ways to devise indicators, for example:

- through questions that are part of a structured interview schedule or self-completion questionnaire. The questions can be concerned with the respondents' attitudes (for example, job satisfaction), their personal experiences (for example, stress), their behaviours (for example, leisure pursuits), and so on;
- by developing criteria for classifying observed behaviour (for example, pupil behaviour in a classroom);
- through the use of official statistics (for example, Statistics Canada);
- by developing classification schemes to analyze the content of written material (for example, Hallgrimsdottir *et al.*'s (2006) examination of how Victoria, BC, newspapers characterized sex trade workers at different times).

Indicators can be derived from a wide variety of sources and methods. Very often a researcher has to consider whether one indicator of a concept suffices. Rather than having just a single indicator, the researcher may seek several to tap a concept (see Boxes 3.2 and 3.4 for examples).

Using multiple-item measures in survey research

The main advantage in using a multiple-indicator measure of a concept is that there are potential problems in relying on just a single indicator:

- A single indicator may misclassify some individuals, due to the wording of the question or a misunderstanding of its meaning. But if there are a number of indicators and someone is misclassified through a particular question, it is possible that the other items will not have those sorts of problems and the person will be classified properly.
- One general, broad indicator may not capture all of the meaning in the underlying concept. Asking people how satisfied they are with their work, for

Box 3.2 A multiple-indicator measure of a concept

Christakis *et al.* (2008) did a study of University of Toronto medical students who were applying for a residency position in ophthalmology. One goal of the study was to determine how the medical students felt toward the issue of affirmative action. Another was to get an ethnic, racial, and gender breakdown of applicants to see whether a program of affirmative action was necessary. To measure attitudes towards affirmative action, respondents were given a series of statements on the role of gender and ethnicity in university admissions. They were asked to indicate whether they 'strongly agree, agree, neither agree nor disagree, disagree, or strongly disagree' with the statements. These sorts of attitude measures are called Likert items, though in some cases researchers use a seven-point rather than a five-point scale for responses. See Box 3.3 for a description of what a Likert scale entails. Examples of the statements used by Christakis *et al.* include:

- Admissions committees should be permitted to take race and ethnicity into account in their admissions process to achieve the educational benefits of a diverse student body.
- There should be quotas (fixed numbers or percentages of available places) for minority applicants.
- In Ontario some ethnic groups are being given an advantage in the admissions process.
- In Ontario some ethnic groups are being discriminated against in the admissions process.
- Sex plays a role in the admissions process.
- Sex should play a role in the admissions process.

The authors found that only 24 per cent of the medical students supported affirmative action and only 12 per cent were in favour of quotas for minority applicants, in spite of the fact that 62 per cent considered themselves to be members of an ethnic minority and 57 per cent were members of a visible minority. Given the attitudes of the students and their ethnic and racial breakdown, the researchers concluded that the ophthalmology program was not in need of an affirmative action program.

Box 3.3 Likert scales

The investigation of attitudes is a prominent area in survey research. One of the most common techniques for investigating attitudes is the Likert scale, named after Rensis Likert who developed the method. It is essentially a multiple-indicator measure of the intensity of feelings about a particular topic. In its most common format, it comprises a series of statements (known as 'items') on an issue or theme. Usually, each respondent is asked to indicate his or her level of agreement with the statement. The format for indicating level of agreement is normally a five-point scale from 'strongly agree' to 'strongly disagree,' but seven-point and other formats are used too. There is usually a middle position of 'neither agree nor disagree' or 'undecided' indicating neutrality on the issue. A respondent's reply on each item is scored and then the scores are aggregated to form an overall score. Variations on the typical format of agreement are scales referring to frequency (for example, 'never' through 'always') and evaluation (for example, 'very poor' to 'very good').

There are several points to remember in constructing a Likert scale. The following are particularly important:

- The items must be statements and not questions.
- The items must all relate to the same object (for example, a particular organization, the issue of unemployment, etc.).
- The items that make up the scale should be inter-related.
- It is useful to vary the phrasing so that some items imply a positive view of the phenomenon of interest and others a negative one. For example, in the 2007 Alberta Survey conducted by the Population Research Laboratory at the University of Alberta, attitudes towards body checking in minor hockey are measured using five-point Lickert items. One item reads: 'Body checking is the main cause of injuries for children in organized minor hockey.' A second is: 'Body checking is an essential part of the game of organized minor hockey.' The first implies a negative view of body checking, the second a more positive one.

Box 3.4   A multiple-indicator measure of another concept

In Kelley and De Graaf's (1997) research on religious beliefs, national religiosity and family religious orientation were each measured by a single indicator (see Box 1.3). However, religious orthodoxy was measured by four survey questions; answers to each of the four were given a value and then added together to form a religious belief score for each respondent. The questions were as follows:

- Please indicate which statement below comes closest to expressing what you believe about God:

  – I don't believe in God. (1)
  – I don't know whether there is a God and don't believe there is a way to find out. (2)
  – I don't believe in a personal God, but I do believe in a higher power of some kind. (3)
  – I find myself believing in God some of the time, but not at others. (4)
  – While I have doubts, I feel that I do believe in God. (5)
  – I know God really exists and I have no doubts about it. (6)

- Which best describes your beliefs about God?

  – I don't believe in God and I never have. (1)
  – I don't believe in God, but I used to. (2)
  – I believe in God now, but I didn't used to. (3)
  – I believe in God now and I always have. (4)

- How close do you feel to God most of the time?

  – Don't believe in God. (1)
  – Not close at all. (2)
  – Not very close. (3)
  – Somewhat close. (4)
  – Extremely close. (5)

- There is a God, one personally concerned with every human being.

  – Strongly agree. (5)
  – Agree. (4)
  – Neither agree nor disagree. (3)
  – Disagree. (2)
  – Strongly disagree. (1)

Notice the values attached to each answer. A person whose answers add up to 20 (6 + 4 + 5 + 5) has the highest level of religious belief possible on this measure, and a person with a sum of 4 (getting a 1 on each question) has the lowest.

instance, may miss the complexity of the situation. Someone saying 'not satisfied' may like some parts of their work, just as someone 'satisfied' can dislike a specific aspect. Alternatively, a more specific question may cover only one dimension of a particular concept. For example, to measure job satisfaction, is it sufficient to ask people how satisfied they are with their pay? Almost certainly the answer is no, because for most people there is more to job satisfaction than just satisfaction with pay. A single indicator like this misses things like satisfaction with benefits, with the work itself, and with other aspects of the work environment. But by asking a number of questions, the researcher can get access to a wider range of issues covered by the concept.

- One can make fine distinctions. Take the Christakis *et al.* (2008) measure of attitudes toward affirmative action as an example (see Box 3.2). If we were to use just one of the items as our measure, the scores for this variable could vary from 1 to 5 (since answers indicating strong disagreement are assigned a value of 1 and answers indicating strong agreement a value of 5). But with six indicators, the range is 6 (6 x 1) to 30 (6 x 5).

Dimensions of concepts

As suggested earlier, the concept of interest may have multiple facets or dimensions, often revealed in the theories and research associated with the concept. In developing a measure for a concept, its different aspects or components should be considered. Bryman and Cramer (2001) demonstrated this approach with reference to the concept of 'professionalism.' The idea is that people scoring high on one dimension of the concept (like respecting confidentiality) may not necessarily score high on other dimensions (like fiscal honesty or continuing education), so that for each respondent one can have a multidimensional 'profile.' Box 3.5 demonstrates the use of dimensions in connection with the concept of 'de-skilling' in the sociology of work.

However, in much quantitative research, there is a tendency to rely on a single indicator for each

Based on a reading of the literature on the topic
of de-skilling, Marshall *et al.* (1988) argued that
there are two important components or dimensions of the concept: 'skill as complexity and skill
as freedom,' which 'are central to the thesis that
work is being proletarianized through the de-skilling of tasks' (1988: 116). 'Skill as complexity' was
measured by a single interview question asking
respondents whether their current jobs require
more, less, or about the same amount of skill as
when they first started. 'Skill as freedom' was
measured by seven indicators treated separately
and not aggregated. The questions asked about
such things as whether respondents can reduce
the pace of the work done or initiate new tasks in
their work. Neither dimension offered significant
support for the de-skilling thesis.

concept. For some purposes, in particular when one
is measuring an uncomplicated variable such as age,
this is quite adequate. Some studies, like Kelley and
De Graaf's (1997; see Box 3.4), employ both single-
and multiple-indicator measures of concepts. What
is crucial is that measures be reliable and valid representations of the concepts they are supposed to be
gauging.

Reliability and measurement validity

Reliability

Reliability is concerned with the *consistency* of measures. There are at least three different meanings of
the term.

Stability over time

This pertains to whether the results of a measure
fluctuate as time progresses, assuming that what is
being measured is not changing. This means that
if one administers a measure to a group and then
re-administers it perhaps an hour later, there should
be little variation in the results. Most thermometers
have this kind of reliability.

The most obvious way of testing for the stability
of a measure is the *test–retest* method. This involves
administering a test or measure on one occasion

and then re-administering it to the same sample on
another occasion, that is:

$$T_1 \quad T_2$$
$$Obs_1 \quad Obs_2$$

One would expect to find a high correlation between
Obs_1 and Obs_2. For example, those who score high
on the first observation should also score high on
the second, and those who score low on the first
should score low on the second. Imagine a multiple-
indicator measure that is supposed to tap a concept
called 'designerism' (a preference for buying goods
and especially clothing with 'designer' labels). The
measure would be administered to a sample of
respondents and then later re-administered. If the
correlation between Obs_1 and Obs_2 is low, the measure
is unstable, implying that it cannot be relied upon.

However, there are a number of problems with
this approach to evaluating reliability. Respondents'
answers at T_1 may influence how they reply at T_2, for
instance if answering a question on designer goods
increases the respondents' interest in them. Yet giving
an answer at T_1 is not supposed to affect later measurements. Second, events may intervene between T_1
and T_2 that influence the degree of consistency. For
example, if a long span of time is involved, changes
in the economy or in respondents' personal financial
circumstances can influence their views about and
predilection for designer goods.

There are no clear solutions to these problems,
other than introducing a complex research design
and so turning the investigation of reliability into
a major project in its own right. Perhaps for these
reasons, many, if not most, research projects do not
include tests of stability over time.

When such tests are done, they may indicate there
is no problem, even when a substantial amount of
time has elapsed. Berthoud (2000*b*), for example,
was pleased that an index of illness achieved high
test–retest reliability despite the fact that the tests
were done a year apart.

Internal reliability (or internal consistency)

The key issue here is whether multiple measures
that are *administered in one sitting* are consistent—
in other words, whether respondents' scores on any
one indicator tend to be related to their scores on the
other indicators. For example, on a scale created to
measure attitudes toward liberal democracy, people

who agree with a statement that voting is an important right should also agree that freedom of speech is an important right.

Cronbach's alpha coefficient is a commonly used test of internal reliability. Its value varies from 1 (denoting perfect internal reliability) to 0 (denoting none). The figure .80 is typically employed to mark the minimum acceptable level of internal reliability, though many writers work with a lower figure. Berthoud (2000*b*: 169), for instance, wrote that a minimum level of .60 is 'good.' In the case of Kelley and De Graaf's (1997) measure of religious orthodoxy (see Box 3.4), which used four indicators, alpha ranged from .79 to .95 for each of the 15 national samples that made up the data. In a study of environmental values among Chinese- and Anglo-Canadians by Deng *et al.* (2006), the alphas ranged from .50 to .89 for various variables. The study of domestic labour by Gazso-Windlej and McMullin (2003) could only achieve alphas averaging .50 for its Likert-style items measuring gender ideology, although the study was only exploratory. The use of Cronbach's alpha has grown as a result of its incorporation into computer software for quantitative data analysis.

Another way of testing for internal reliability is the *split-half* method. Take the attitude toward affirmative action measure developed by Christakis *et al.* (2008) as an example (see Box 3.2). The six indicators would be divided into two halves of three, allocated on a random or an odd-numbered item/even-numbered item basis. The degree of correlation between the scores on the two halves for all respondents would then be calculated. If the six items are consistent, a respondent's score on the two groups of indicators should be similar, perhaps high on both, or low on both. A perfect positive correlation and therefore complete internal consistency would yield a correlation coefficient of 1; no correlation and therefore no internal consistency would produce a coefficient of 0. The meaning of correlation and correlation coefficients will be explored in much greater detail later on. The chief point at this stage is that the correlation coefficient establishes how closely respondents' scores on the two groups of indicators are related.

Inter-observer consistency

When subjective judgment is involved in activities like the recording of observations or the translation of data into categories, and where more than one 'observer' is involved in such activities, there is the possibility of a lack of consistency in their decisions. This can arise in a number of contexts. For example, this may be an issue if answers to open-ended questions have to be categorized, or in structured observation when observers have to decide how to classify subjects' behaviour. Is the person being studied 'afraid,' 'concerned,' or 'just thinking' when reading about the spread of yet another deadly new virus? Problems arise if all observers do not classify such behaviour in the same way. Cramer (1998: ch. 14) provides a very detailed treatment of the issue of inter-observer consistency and the techniques that can be used to maximize it.

Measurement validity

As noted in Chapter 2, measurement validity refers to whether an indicator (or set of indicators) devised to gauge a concept really measures that concept. When people argue about whether a person's IQ score really measures or reflects that person's level of intelligence, they are raising questions about the measurement validity of the IQ test in relation to the concept of intelligence. Whenever students and their teachers debate whether multiple-choice examinations provide an accurate measure of academic ability, they too are raising questions about measurement validity. Establishing face validity, concurrent validity, predictive validity, construct validity, and convergent validity shows that one has in fact measured what one wants to measure.

Face validity

At the very minimum, a researcher who develops a new measure should establish that it has *face validity*—that is, that it appears to reflect the content of the concept in question. Face validity can be established by asking those with expertise in a field to act as judges to determine whether, *on the face of it*, the measure seems to reflect the concept concerned. Face validity is, therefore, essentially an intuitive process.

Concurrent validity

The researcher can also seek to gauge the *concurrent validity* of the measure. Here the researcher employs a *criterion* relevant to the concept in question, one on which cases (for example, people) are known to differ. Assuming that as job satisfaction goes down, absenteeism goes up, to establish the concurrent validity of a new measure of job satisfaction, a researcher may look to see if people who are satisfied with their jobs are less likely than those who are not satisfied to be absent from work. If a lack of correspondence is found, such as no difference in absenteeism between those who are satisfied and those who are not, doubt is cast on whether the new measure is really gauging job satisfaction.

Construct validity

Some writers advocate that researchers estimate the *construct validity* of a measure, which involves seeing whether the concepts used in the research relate to each other in a way that is consistent with what their theories would predict. For example, a researcher may want to establish the construct validity of the new measure of job satisfaction. Drawing on a theory maintaining that job satisfaction is influenced by the stimulation that arises from performing a number of *different* activities, he or she may anticipate that people who do routine jobs are less satisfied with their jobs than those who have a greater chance for variety, complexity, and creativity. If these variables correlate in the expected way, then the measure in question has construct validity. On the other hand, some caution is required if the relationship is weak or non-existent, for example, if those who do routine jobs are just as satisfied as those with jobs involving a lot of variety. If so, the measures used may be invalid, or the deduction that is made from the theory may be misguided, or the theory itself may be in need of revision. Whatever the problem may be, it is probably best to seek another measure and try again.

Convergent validity

In the view of some methodologists, the validity of a measure ought to be gauged by comparing it to measures of the same concept developed through other methods. For example, if a questionnaire asks managers how much time they spend on various activities (such as attending meetings, touring their organization, informal discussions, and so on), its validity may be determined by directly observing the managers to see how much time is actually spent on those activities.

An interesting instance of convergent *in*validity is described in Box 3.6. Crime surveys were consciously devised to act as a check on official police statistics. The two sets of data are collected in quite different ways: official crime statistics are collected as part of the bureaucratic processing of offenders in the criminal justice system, whereas crime victimization surveys provide data from interviews with members of the general public. In the case reported in Box 3.6, a lack of convergent validity was found. This illustrates a problem with the convergent approach to testing validity—it is not easy to establish which of the two measures provides the more accurate picture. In the case of crime statistics, the two methods are really measuring somewhat different things. Victimization surveys measure the crimes people experience, as well as some things that may not be crimes; they also omit certain crimes, such as when a stolen item is presumed 'lost.' Police statistics, on the other hand, measure the crimes that people are willing to call the police about, plus the crimes the police themselves discover; and not all

Box 3.6 A case of convergent invalidity: crime statistics

Official police reports and national crime victimization studies often provide very different indications of the amount of crime in society. As part of the General Social Survey (GSS), Canadians are asked about their victimization experiences. It is widely known that the victimization data show more crime than the official police reports because many Canadians do not report their experiences with crime to the police, for a variety of reasons (such as the bother, the embarrassment, etc.). To take one example, for robbery the victimization rate reported in the surveys is almost three times the official rate. But for auto theft, the police data show 50 per cent more thefts, because the GSS does not gather data on the theft of company cars or cars taken from car dealerships (Silverman *et al.* 2000: 58). So there will probably always be a discrepancy between police statistics and victimization surveys on the amount of crime that exists. Another illustration of a lack of concurrence between two methods of data gathering pertains to murder rates. The police report 15 per cent more homicides in Canada than does the Mortality Database drawn from death certificates (Gabor *et al.* 2002); some officials in charge of the latter may be reluctant to classify certain deaths as homicides because doing so might upset the relatives of the victims.

Box 3.7   Developing a Likert scale: the case of attitudes to vegetarians

Noting that some non-vegetarians see vegetarian-ism as deviant and sometimes treat vegetarians with suspicion if not hostility, Chin *et al.* (2002) developed a scale to measure pro- or anti-vegetarian attitudes. It comprised 33 statements to which respondents were asked to indicate their strength of agreement or disagreement on a seven-point scale. The items were developed from the following: interviews with both vegetarians and non-vegetarians, a review of the literature on vegetarianism, field observations, brainstorming sessions within the team, and attitude scales that measure other forms of prejudice (for possible wording and presentation). The items were meant to tap four areas:

- forms of behaviour among vegetarians viewed as irritating, for example, 'Vegetarians preach too much about their beliefs and eating habits';

- disagreement with vegetarians' beliefs, for example, 'Vegetarians are overly concerned with animal rights';

- health-related aspects of being a vegetarian,

for example, 'Vegetarians are overly concerned about gaining weight'; and

- appropriate treatment of vegetarians, for example, 'It's okay to tease someone for being a vegetarian.'

The scale was tested on a sample of US under-graduates. Some items were dropped because of poor internal consistency with other items. Cron-bach's alpha for the remaining 21 items was .87.

The construct validity of the scale was also tested. Students completed other scales on variables thought to be associated with pro- or anti-vegetarian attitudes. For example, the authors hypothesized that people scoring high on an authoritarian attitude scale would be more likely to be anti-vegetarians. This was confirmed, although the relationship was weak. Worse, contrary to their hypothesis, their atti-tude-towards-vegetarianism score was not related to political conservatism measures. They had thought that liberals would be more tolerant of vegetarians. Thus their scale emerged as internally reliable but of slightly questionable construct validity.

crimes end up in official police statistics. In any case, the 'true' volume of crime at any one time is almost always a contested notion (Reiner 2000*a*).

Box 3.7 provides some more examples of the ways in which reliability and validity are assessed.

Reflections on reliability and validity

There are, then, a number of ways to investigate the merit of measures devised to represent social scien-tific concepts. However, the discussion of reliability and validity is potentially misleading because not all new measures of concepts are submitted to the rigours just described. In fact, many measures are simply used without their reliability and validity ever being tested. When a new multiple-indicator measure is devised, there may be an examination of face validity and a test for internal reliability, but in many cases no further testing takes place.

It should also be remembered that, although reli-ability and validity are analytically distinguishable, they are related: if a measure is not reliable, it cannot be valid. For example, a multiple-indicator measure lacking internal reliability is probably measuring two

or more different things and therefore is not a valid indicator of the single concept it is supposed to be measuring.

The main goals of quantitative researchers

Measurement

To understand the social order one must be able to go into the world and measure things like prejudice, the incidence of homelessness, attitudes towards the federal government, or the distribution of wealth in society. It would be awfully hard to make sense of such phenomena or to evaluate theories and inter-pretations of them without acquiring data on them, that is, without measuring them. It is not surprising then that there is a concern that such measurement be done properly, hence the focus on reliability and validity.

Establishing causality

Most quantitative research involves a search for causal explanations. Quantitative researchers are rarely satisfied with merely describing how things are—they are keen to find out *why* things are the way they are, an emphasis also found in the natural sciences. Researchers examining prejudice, for instance, may not only want to describe it, but also *explain* it, which means finding its causes. They may seek to explain prejudice in terms of personal characteristics (such as having a low level of education) or by way of social characteristics (such as the amount of social mobility in society, with higher levels possibly leading to less prejudice). In the resulting reports, prejudice is the dependent variable, the one to be explained, and level of education and social mobility are independent variables, the ones tested as possible causal influences on prejudice.

When an experimental design is employed, the independent variable is the variable that is manipulated, and there is little ambiguity about the direction of causal influence. However, with cross-sectional designs of the kind used in most social survey research, there is ambiguity about the direction of causal influence because the data on all variables are simultaneously collected, meaning one cannot say

with full confidence that a particular independent variable preceded the dependent one in time. To refer to independent and dependent variables in the context of cross-sectional designs, one must *infer* the temporal sequence of variables based on common sense or prior theory, as in the example concerning level of education and prejudice in the previous paragraph. However, there is always the risk that the inference is wrong, that the variable purported to be the cause did not precede the dependent variable in time (see Box 3.8).

An important criterion of good quantitative research is the level of confidence in the researcher's causal inferences. Research that exhibits the characteristics of an experimental design is often better able to establish causality than cross-sectional research since, as noted, with that design it is easier to demonstrate the direction of causal influence and to control for other independent variables. For their part, quantitative researchers who employ cross-sectional designs try to develop techniques that allow causal inferences to be made. Moreover, the rise of longitudinal research almost certainly reflects

Box 3.8   The case of displayed emotions in convenience stores

Following a review of the literature, Sutton and Rafaeli (1992) hypothesized a positive relationship between the display of positive emotions by staff to retail shoppers (smiling, friendly greeting, eye contact) and the level of retail sales. In other words, when retail staff are friendly and give time to shoppers, higher sales follow. Sutton and Rafaeli had data from 576 convenience stores in a US national retail chain. Structured observation of the retail workers provided data on the display of positive emotions, and quantitative sales data provided information for the other variable.

The hypothesis was not supported; indeed, stores in which retail workers are less inclined to smile, be friendly, and so on, have better sales. Sutton and Rafaeli (1992: 124) considered restating their hypothesis to make it seem that they had found what they had expected (see Ethical issue 15.1) but fortunately resisted the temptation. Instead, they conducted a qualitative investigation of four stores to help understand what was happening. They used a number of methods: unstructured observation of interactions between staff and customers; semi-structured

interviews with store managers; casual conversations with store managers, supervisors, executives, and others; and data gathered through posing as a customer. The qualitative investigation suggested that the relationship between the display of positive emotions and sales is indeed negative, but that sales are likely to be a cause rather than a consequence of the display of emotions. In stores with high levels of sales, staff are under greater pressure and encounter longer lineups at checkouts. Staff therefore have less time and inclination for the pleasantries associated with the display of positive emotions.

Thus, instead of the causal sequence being

More positive emotions → More retail sales

it is

More retail sales → Less positive emotions

This exercise also highlights the main difficulty associated with inferring causal direction from a cross-sectional research design.

a desire on the part of quantitative researchers to improve their ability to generate findings that permit a causal interpretation.

Generalization of findings to those not studied

In quantitative research, researchers usually want to generalize their findings beyond the confines of the particular context in which the research is conducted. Thus, if a study of prejudice involves people filling out a questionnaire, can the results apply to individuals other than those who actually participated in the study? Given that it is rarely feasible to send questionnaires to or interview whole populations (such as all members of a town, or the whole population of a country, or even everyone in an organization), those studied are only a *sample* of the larger population. A sample should be as representative of a population as possible in order for the researcher to have confidence that the results are not unique to the particular group upon whom the research is conducted, that is, the sample. This goal of generalization can be viewed as an attempt to develop law-like findings, an approach that has parallels in the natural sciences.

Probability sampling, explored in Chapter 11, is normally the first choice among researchers seeking a representative sample. This procedure largely eliminates bias by using a process of random selection. The use of a random selection process does not guarantee a representative sample, however, but it does make the selection of a representative sample much more likely. A related consideration is that even with a representative sample, of what population is it representative? The simple answer is that it is representative of the population from which it is selected and, strictly speaking, one cannot generalize beyond that population. This means that, if the population from which a sample is taken is all inhabitants of a particular town, city, or province, generalizations should be made only to the inhabitants of that town, city, or province. Nonetheless, it is very tempting to see the findings as having a more pervasive applicability, so that results from a sample selected from a city such as Vancouver or Toronto are thought to be relevant to similar cities. Even so, one should not make inferences beyond the population from which the sample is selected.

The concern with the generalizability of research findings is particularly strong among quantitative researchers using cross-sectional and longitudinal designs. Experimental researchers are concerned about generalizability too, as the discussion of external validity in Chapter 2 suggested, but people doing experiments usually give greater attention to internal validity than external validity.

Replication

The natural sciences are often depicted as wishing to reduce to a bare minimum the contaminating influence of the scientist's biases, values, characteristics, and expectations. Were biases pervasive, the claims of the natural sciences to provide a definitive picture of the world would be seriously undermined. Similarly, scientists also try to eliminate or minimize routine errors in the conduct of their research. To check on the influence of these potentially damaging problems, scientists believe that they should be able to replicate each other's research. If a scientist's findings cannot be reproduced after repeated tries, serious questions are raised about the validity of the findings. Likewise, researchers in the social sciences often regard the ability to replicate as an important criterion for doing good research. It is easy to see why: the possibility of the intrusion of the researcher's values would appear to be much greater when examining the social world than when a natural scientist investigates the natural order. Consequently, it is often regarded as important that the researcher spells out all research procedures clearly so that they can be replicated by others, even if the research does not end up being replicated.

Unfortunately, replication is not a high-status activity in the natural or social sciences, often being regarded as a pedestrian and uninspiring pursuit. Moreover, standard replications are not readily accepted for publication in many academic journals. Consequently, replications of research appear in print far less frequently than might be supposed. A further reason for the low incidence of published replications in the social sciences is that it is difficult to ensure that the conditions in a replication are precisely the same as those in the original study. So long as there is some ambiguity about whether the conditions relating to a replication are the same as those in the initial study, any differences in findings may be attributable to the design of the replication rather than to some deficiency in the original study. Nonetheless, it is crucial that the methods used in generating a set of findings are made explicit, so that it is *possible* to replicate a piece of research. Providing all the information needed to do a replication is often regarded as an important quality of quantitative research.

An example of the benefits of replication can be found in Goyder *et al.*'s (2003) study of occupational prestige conducted in the Kitchener–Waterloo area of Ontario. The authors replicated research done 25 years earlier (Guppy and Siltanen, 1977), taking great pains to insure that the methodologies of the two studies were as alike as possible. The replication not only provided a check for biases and routine errors; given that a quarter-century had passed since the original study, it also provided a measure of how much attitudes had changed with regard to the issue of occupational prestige and gender. As reported in Chapter 2, the authors concluded that the earlier male advantage in occupational prestige had disappeared by the time the replication was done. In fact in people-oriented jobs, women's prestige was higher than that for men in the more recent study. It should be noted that if the authors had not carefully

replicated the study, one would have no way of knowing whether actual social change was being observed, or whether the differences in the findings between the two studies were simply a by-product of using different methodologies.

Critiques of quantitative research

Every approach to research has its strengths and weaknesses. Over the years quantitative research, along with its epistemological and ontological foundations, has been the focus of criticism, particularly from exponents of qualitative research. The criticisms pertain to quantitative research as a general research strategy, and to specific methods and research designs with which quantitative research is associated.

Criticisms of quantitative research

To give a flavour of the critique of quantitative research, five criticisms are covered briefly here:

Box 3.9   Gap between stated and actual behaviour

A study of racial prejudice conducted many years ago by LaPiere (1934) illustrates that there may be a difference between what people say and what they actually do. LaPiere spent two years travelling with a young Chinese student and his wife, observing from a distance if they were refused entry at hotels and restaurants. Of 66 hotels approached, they were refused entry once; of 184 restaurants and diners, none refused entry.

LaPiere then allowed six months to elapse before sending questionnaires to the hotels and restaurants visited. One question asked: 'Will you accept members of the Chinese race as guests in your establishment?' Of the establishments that replied, 92 per cent of restaurants and 91 per cent of hotels said no. LaPiere's simple though striking study clearly illustrates a gap between reports of behaviour and actual behaviour. It should also be noted that the question asked was somewhat unclear, a feature not usually noted in connection with this widely cited study. 'Will you . . .?' can be interpreted as asking about the future or to state the establishment's policy. Why the more obvious formulation 'Do you . . .?' was

not used is not clear, though it is unlikely that this point had a significant bearing on the findings and their implications for survey research. On the other hand, the results may be just another example of the widespread difference between holding a prejudiced attitude and engaging in a discriminatory act. An experimental study of prejudice among college students (Frazer and Wiersma 2001) showed that in hypothetical situations the students hire black and white applicants of varying abilities equally, but a week later recall the black applicants as less intelligent than whites though both groups were equal. In the real world, peer pressure can make an unprejudiced person discriminate, to 'go along,' while a prejudiced person may not discriminate for fear of a lawsuit.

The gap is usually worst when predictions of future behaviour are involved. The Canadian Blood Services pointed out that 28 per cent of Canadians intend to give blood in any given year, but only 3.7 per cent actually do. Literally millions say that they intend to vote—many even revealing their preferences to pollsters—and then do not vote.

- *Quantitative researchers fail to distinguish people and social institutions from 'the world of nature.'* Some people object to the idea of treating the social world as if it were no different from the natural order. The critics argue that because people interpret the world around them, their actions and experiences cannot be studied using the methods employed in the natural sciences. They claim that science is only applicable to entities and processes lacking this sort of self-reflection, such as chemical elements, photosynthesis, and the circulation of blood. But many quantitative researchers maintain that humans (and other animals) really are part of the world of nature, and that it is simply wrong to think that our existence cannot be usefully analyzed using science. For instance, they would claim that consciousness itself is amendable to the scientific method, as are emotions, decision-making processes, and so on. The debate continues.

- *The measurement process produces an artificial and false sense of precision and accuracy.* For example, quantitative research presumes that different individuals responding to the same question on a survey are interpreting the key terms in the question the same way. For example, 'What is your social class?' can refer to current wealth to one person; to another it can mean ancestry, as in how many generations the family has been wealthy or poor. For many methodologists, respondents simply do not interpret such terms similarly. An often attempted solution to this problem is to use questions with fixed-choice answers—'Are you upper class, middle class, working class, etc.?'—but this approach merely provides 'a solution to the problem of meaning by simply ignoring it' (Cicourel 1964: 108). Quantitative social researchers counter that there are ways to test for shared meanings, although they would concede that this issue deserves more attention than it usually gets.

- *The reliance on instruments and procedures produces a disjuncture between research and everyday life.* This issue relates to the question of external validity. Many methods of quantitative research rely heavily on administering research instruments to subjects (such as structured interviews and self-completion questionnaires) or on controlling situations to determine causal

connections (as in experiments). However, as Cicourel (1982) asked, how do researchers know if survey respondents have the requisite knowledge to answer a question or whether they share a common sense of the importance of the topic in their everyday lives? If respondents answer a set of questions designed to measure attitudes toward federal–provincial relations, for example, is their level of interest in the topic sufficient to produce meaningful responses? Another issue, introduced in Chapter 2, is that experiments can produce only small, short-term manipulations of independent variables (Brannigan 2004), yet much of everyday life is affected by long-term, ongoing social processes.

- *The analysis of relationships between variables promotes a view of social life that is remote from everyday experience.* Blumer argued that studies that aim to bring out the relationships between variables omit 'the process of interpretation or definition that goes on in human groups' (1956: 685). This symbolic interactionist assessment incorporates the first and third criticisms above, that the meaning of events to individuals is ignored and that the connection to everyday contexts is missing. Quantitative researchers admit that can happen, but claim that their research does not preclude a search for how people interpret their everyday existence. For example, quantitative sociologists sometimes ask respondents what they think about social inequality, and try to link the responses with variables such as age, gender, class, ethnicity, and so on. Nonetheless, a more thorough and subject-centred search for meanings is usually undertaken by qualitative sociologists.

- *Quantitative researchers tend to assume an objectivist ontology.* As seen in Chapter 1, quantitative researchers often assume that a reality exists that may be independent of the observer or of individual consciousness. They may also see the social order as fixed or given—at least at a particular point in history—rather than created by individuals through negotiation, although the latter view is not universal among quantitative researchers. People on the quantitative side reply that it is not a mistake to assume that some things may exist and have certain characteristics in spite of how we perceive them. Again, the debate is ongoing.

Is it always like this? Reality and practice

One of the problems with characterizing any research orientation, design, or method is that to a certain extent each has to be presented in its pure form, a form that is rarely seen in actual research practice. The model of the process of quantitative research presented here is really a general *tendency* rather than a definitive description of all quantitative research. The gap between the ideal and actual can arise as a result of several factors. The failure to follow the procedures associated with good practice is not necessarily due to incompetence on the part of social researchers, though in some cases it is. More likely it is associated with matters of time, cost, and feasibility—in other words, the unavoidable pragmatic concerns of conducting research.

An illustration of how ideal and actual research practice may not be the same concerns reliability and validity. Analyses of published quantitative research in organization studies (Podsakoff and Dalton 1987) revealed that writers rarely report tests of the stability of their measures and even more rarely include evidence of measurement validity (only 3 per cent). The one exception is a large proportion of articles that use Cronbach's alpha, a measure of internal consistency for multiple-item measures, but for non-scale items the stability and validity of many measures in the field of organizations are unknown. This is not to say that the measures used are necessarily *un*stable and *in*valid, but that those features are simply unknown or not demonstrated. The reasons for these omissions are almost certainly the cost and time that would be required to pursue them. Researchers tend to be more concerned with theoretical and conceptual issues and less with the work required for thoroughly determining measurement quality. As Cicourel (1964) said, much measurement in sociology is 'measurement by fiat.'

These remarks on the lack of assessments to determine measurement quality should not be taken as a justification for students and researchers to neglect this aspect of their work. The aim here is merely to draw attention to some of the ways in which the practices described in this book are not always followed, and to suggest some reasons for those shortcomings.

A similar point can be made in relation to sampling. As noted, good research practice often requires *random* or *probability sampling*. However, a lot of research is based on inferior alternatives. Sometimes the use of non-probability samples is due to the impossibility or extreme difficulty of obtaining probability samples. Another reason is that the time and cost involved in securing a probability sample are too great relative to the level of resources available. An additional reason is that sometimes the opportunity to study a certain group arises and represents too good an opportunity to miss. Again, such considerations should not be viewed as a justification for ignoring the principles of sampling. The purpose here is to draw attention to the ways in which gaps between recommendations about good practice and actual research practice can arise.

Key Points

- Quantitative research can be characterized as a linear series of steps moving from theory to conclusions, but the process described in Figure 3.1 is an ideal from which there are many departures.

- Examining the reliability and validity of measures is important for assessing their quality.

- Quantitative research has the following key goals: measurement, the establishment of causality, generalization, and replication.

- Quantitative research has been criticized by qualitative researchers. These criticisms tend to revolve around rejecting the view that a natural science model is appropriate for studying the social world.

Questions for Review

The main steps in quantitative research

- What are the main steps in quantitative research?

- To what extent do the main steps follow a strict sequence?

- Do the steps suggest a deductive or inductive approach to the relationship between theory and research?

Concepts and their measurement

- Why is measurement important to a quantitative researcher?

- Why may multiple indicators of a concept be preferable to using a single indicator?

Reliability and validity

- Are some forms of reliability more important than others?

- 'Whereas validity presupposes reliability, reliability does not presuppose validity.' Discuss.

- What are the main criteria for evaluating measurement validity?

The main goals of quantitative researchers

- Outline the main goals of quantitative researchers. Why do quantitative researchers try to achieve them?

- Why is replication especially important to quantitative researchers, in spite of the tendency for replications in social research to be very rare?

The critique of quantitative research

- 'The crucial problem with quantitative research is its failure to adequately address the issue of meaning.' Discuss.

- 'The natural science model of research should not be used to study society.' Discuss.

4

Survey Research: Structured Interviewing and Questionnaires

Chapter overview

Survey research is one of the most commonly used data-gathering techniques in the social sciences. Surveys normally involve either structured interviews or written questionnaires that respondents fill out themselves. One of the strengths of survey research is that it allows for standardization in the asking of questions and the categorization of the answers given.

This chapter explores:

- the reasons for the widespread use of surveys, including a consideration of the importance of standardization to the process of measurement;
- the different ways to do survey research, such as using more than one interviewer, conducting interviews by telephone, or using the Internet or email to administer questionnaires;

- various prerequisites of structured interviewing, including: establishing rapport with the interviewee; asking questions exactly as they appear on the interview schedule; keeping to the question order as it appears on the schedule; and recording exactly what is said by interviewees;
- problems with survey research, including: the influence of the interviewer on respondents, and the possibility of systematic bias in answers (known as *response sets*);
- the advantages and disadvantages of the questionnaire compared to the structured interview;
- researcher-driven diaries as a form of survey research; and
- a feminist critique of structured interviews and questionnaires.

Introduction

Doing interviews and completing questionnaires are common occurrences in social life. There are job interviews, media interviews, and police interviews, and one is often asked to complete a questionnaire before getting medical treatment or after using a service of some kind. Research interviews and questionnaires share some common features with the everyday variety, although greater care is usually taken to elicit information that is valid and reliable. The information gathered can pertain to things such as the respondent's behaviour, attitudes, norms, beliefs, and values.

The structured interview

In a structured interview (sometimes called a standardized interview), the interviewer asks questions listed on an interview schedule, which is basically a formalized script that the interviewer must follow in detail. Interviewers are supposed to read out the questions exactly as they are stated, and in the same order as they are given in the schedule. All interviewees thus experience the same form of questioning and receive exactly the same interview stimulus. The goal is to allow interviewees' replies to be aggregated (added together to form group rates), and this can be achieved reliably only if those replies are in response to identical cues. Questions are usually very specific and offer the interviewee a fixed range of answers from which to choose.

The main reason why survey researchers use structured interviews is that they promote the standardization of both the asking of questions and the recording of answers. This feature has two closely related virtues: reducing error due to variation in the asking of questions, and greater accuracy and ease in processing respondents' answers.

Reducing error due to interviewer variability

Properly executed, standardization in both asking questions and recording answers means that variation in people's replies are due to 'true' or 'real' variation in the characteristic being measured rather than extraneous factors. Still, there is always a chance that some responses will be inaccurately measured, and there are a number of reasons for this. Some prominent sources of error in survey research are:

1. poorly worded questions;
2. interviewer error in asking a question;
3. misunderstanding on the part of the interviewee;
4. interviewee lapses in memory;
5. interviewer error in recording information;
6. mistakes in entering the data into a computer file; and
7. biases caused by the innate characteristics (such as gender or race) of the interviewers and the interviewees.

To take a simple illustration, a question on alcohol consumption among students will show that students vary in the amount of alcohol they consume. Most measurement will contain an element of error, so it is helpful to think of the measured variation in alcohol consumption as made up of two components: true variation and error. In other words: measured variation = true variation + variation due to error. The aim is to keep the error portion to a minimum (see Figure 4.1), since error reduces the validity of a measure. Standardization in the structured interview means that two sources of variation due to error—items 2 and 5 in the preceding list—are likely to be less pronounced.

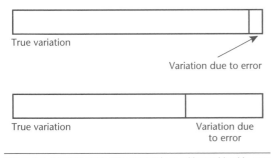

Figure 4.1 A variable with little error and one with considerable error

Variation due to error can come from several sources. One is *intra-interviewer variability*, whereby an interviewer is not consistent in asking questions or recording answers, either with different respondents or with the same respondent. For example, an interviewer may treat respondents differently depending on the respondents' personal characteristics or the interviewer's level of fatigue. Another source of error is *inter-interviewer variability*, which may occur when there is more than one interviewer (the usual case). If interviewers are not consistent with each other in the ways they ask questions and/or record answers measurement error can occur. Needless to say, these two sources of error are not mutually exclusive; they can coexist, compounding the problem even further.

Accuracy and ease of data processing

Like questionnaires, most structured interviews contain questions that are variously referred to as *closed*, *closed-ended*, *pre-coded*, or *fixed-choice*. With a closed question, the respondent is given a limited choice of possible answers from which to choose. Once an answer has been selected, the interviewer simply puts a tick on a form or does the equivalent using a keypad. The advantage is that the potential for interviewer variability is reduced: there is no problem with the interviewer not being able to write down everything that the respondent says, or with the interviewer misinterpreting the reply given. If an *open* or *open-ended* question is asked, the interviewer generally cannot write down everything said, may embellish what is said, or may misinterpret the response given.

However, the advantages of this type of question go further than this. An additional advantage is that closed questions greatly facilitate the processing of data. When an open question is asked, answers can be in the form of several sentences. These answers have to be examined and then categorized, so that each person's answer can be aggregated with other respondents' answers to the same question. A number is then allocated to each category of answer for quantitative analysis. This process is known as *coding* and will be examined in greater detail in Chapter 5. Not only is coding laborious, particularly if there are many open questions and/or respondents, but it also introduces the potential for another source of error—variability in the coding of answers.

If the rules for assigning answers to categories, collectively known as the *coding frame*, are flawed, any observed variation may not reflect the true variation in interviewees' replies but instead may result from the shortcomings of the coding frame. Also, there may be variation in the ways in which answers are categorized due to the administration of the interview schedule and/or the recording of responses. As with other forms of interviewing, this can come from two sources: *intra-coder variability*, whereby a coder varies over time in applying the rules for assigning answers to categories, and *inter-coder variability*, in which coders differ from each other in how to categorize the same answer. If either or both sources of variability emerge, at least part of the measured variation in interviewees' replies is caused by error rather than true variation.

The closed question sidesteps this problem neatly, because respondents allocate *themselves* to categories. The coding process is a simple matter of attaching a different number to each category of answer and entering the numbers into a computer database, as in: Strongly agree = 1, Agree = 2, etc. It is not surprising, therefore, that this type of question is often referred to as pre-coded because coding decisions are typically undertaken before any respondent has actually been asked questions. There is very little opportunity for interviewers or coders to differ in how they record answers. Of course, if any of the terms in the answers presented are misunderstood by respondents, or if the answers do not adequately cover the appropriate range of possibilities, the question cannot provide a valid measure. Nonetheless, when compared to open questions, closed questions reduce a potential source of error and are easier to process for quantitative analysis.

Dealing with interviewer effects

Some interviewer characteristics will affect the responses given. Sex and race are the key reactive issues that may have an impact, although their effects are mostly confined to sexual and racial issues and have less effect on other topics.

To illustrate, take the topic of whether jobs should be set aside for female applicants only. Here are some hypothetical results (percentage who approve): male talking to male interviewer, 37; male talking to female interviewer, 48; female talking to female interviewer, 58; female talking to male interviewer, 50. Something is wrong, but where? One might assume that some men are not being truthful with the female interviewer, and are instead offering a response that they think will please her. But maybe some men are not being candid with the male interviewer—a man may believe in employment equity, but knowing it is controversial he may hide his real views. Similarly, some of the women who say they agree may actually disagree. They may feel that the time for employment equity is past and that women should be hired strictly on their merits but keep that idea to themselves when talking to another woman so they don't appear to be deserting the feminist cause—sharing a common status does not always lead to candour.

What can be done? A first step is to train interviewers carefully to be professional, to stress that any answer is acceptable, and in the pilot study to see if any interviewers stand out in terms of getting responses that are very different from the others. The data collected by any one interviewer should be fairly similar to the data of the others. Researchers should check early for this problem and if found retrain the individual; as a last resort they may replace the interviewer. However, if the problem arises primarily from deeply felt biases on the part of respondents, there may be limits to what the researcher can do.

Interview contexts

In a traditional interview, an interviewer stands or sits in front of the respondent, asks a series of questions, and writes down or keys in the answers. However, there are several possible departures from this archetype.

More than one interviewer or interviewee

More than one interviewer is a very unusual situation in social research because of the considerable cost involved in dispatching two (or indeed more than two) people to interview someone. In the case of focus groups it is more common, but in that instance there is more than one interviewee too. However, it is very unusual for structured interviews to be conducted that way—it is almost always a specific individual who is the object of questioning by one interviewer. Indeed, it is usually advisable to *discourage* as far as possible the presence and intrusion of others during the course of the interview. Investigations in which more than one person is being interviewed tend to be conducted by qualitative researchers, though that is not always the case. For example, Pahl's (1990) study of patterns in the control of money among couples employed structured interviewing of the couples, and then of husbands and wives separately.

In person or by telephone?

While it is customary in academic social research not involving national samples to conduct research with face-to-face interviews, telephone interviewing is the norm in fields like market and government research. There are several advantages of telephone interviews over the face-to-face variety:

- They are far cheaper and quicker to administer. This arises because with in-person interviews, the interviewers have to spend a great deal of time travelling from one location to another to meet with respondents, a factor even more pronounced when a sample is geographically dispersed. Telephone interviews take time and hired interviewers have to be paid, but the cost of conducting a telephone interview is still lower than a comparable face-to-face one. Moreover, the general efficiency of telephone interviewing has been enhanced with the advent of computer-assisted telephone interviewing (CATI).

- The telephone interview is easier to supervise than the personal interview. This is a particular advantage when there are several interviewers calling from the same location at the same time. Interviewer errors, such as rephrasing questions or probing inappropriately, can be detected by supervisors. Face-to-face interviews can be tape-recorded so that data quality can be assessed, but the taping of interviews raises issues of confidentiality and so has to be treated cautiously.

- Telephone interviewing can also reduce bias arising from the characteristics of the interviewers or interviewees (for example, gender, class, and ethnicity). The remoteness of the interviewer in telephone interviewing removes this potential source of bias to a significant extent—the

interviewer's race and general appearance cannot be seen, although their gender is usually apparent.

On the other hand, telephone interviewing suffers from certain limitations when compared to the personal interview:

- People who do not have a telephone or otherwise cannot be contacted by telephone cannot be part of the study. Since this characteristic is most likely to be a feature of poorer households, the potential for sampling bias exists. Also, many people choose to be ex-directory (they have paid to have their telephone numbers *not* listed in a telephone book) or they use cell phones only and for that reason are not listed. This presents a problem if the researcher is using a directory to select respondents. A solution to the latter problem is *random digit dialling*. With this technique, a computer randomly selects telephone numbers within a predefined geographical area, a procedure used in the annual Alberta Survey conducted at the University of Alberta, as well as in the General Social Survey administered by Statistics Canada. This method can catch ex-directory households, though it cannot, of course, gain access to those without a telephone. In some areas laws prevent contacting cell phones in this way.

- Respondents with hearing impairments are likely to find telephone interviews more difficult than personal interviews.

- A telephone interview is unlikely to be sustainable beyond 20 to 25 minutes, whereas personal interviews can be conducted for longer periods of time (Frey 2004).

- There is some evidence that telephone interviews fare less well in asking about sensitive issues, such as drug and alcohol use, income, tax payments, and health. However, the evidence is not entirely consistent on this point, though it is probably sufficient to suggest that when many questions of this kind are to be used, a personal interview may be superior (Shuy 2002).

- Telephone interviewers cannot see the respondents. This means that they are not in a position to respond to signs of puzzlement or unease on their faces. In a personal interview, the interviewer may respond to such signs by restating the question or attempting to clarify the meaning of the question, though this has to be handled in a standardized way as far as possible. A further issue is that interviewers may be able to collect subsidiary information, such as whether the home in which the interview was conducted is in need of repair. That sort of information cannot be acquired when telephone interviews are employed.

- Frequently, a specific individual in a household or firm is the target of the research; for example, a person in a certain role or position, or someone with particular characteristics. It is probably more difficult to ascertain by telephone interview whether the correct person is replying.
- The telephone interviewer cannot employ visual aids such as show cards from which respondents select their replies (see Box 4.1). Similarly, diagrams or photographs cannot be used.

There is some evidence that the quality of data derived from telephone interviews is inferior to that of comparable face-to-face interviews. A series of experiments in the US using long questionnaires, reported by Holbrook *et al.* (2003), found that respondents interviewed by telephone are more likely to: express no opinion or give 'don't know' as an answer; give the same answer to a series of linked questions; express socially desirable answers; be apprehensive about the interview; and be dissatisfied with the time taken by the interviews (even though they were shorter than the face-to-face mode). Also, telephone interviewees tend to be less engaged in the interview process.

Computer-assisted interviewing

Today the use of computers in the interview process is common. There are two main formats for computer-assisted interviews: computer-assisted personal interviewing (CAPI) and computer-assisted telephone interviewing (CATI). The use of CAPI has been growing lately, mainly because of the increased portability and affordability of laptop computers and the availability of quality software packages.

With computer-assisted interviewing, the questions in the interview schedule appear on the screen. When an answer is given, the interviewer keys in the reply and proceeds to the next question. This process is very useful when *filter questions* are asked. Filter questions are used to determine whether it is appropriate to ask certain questions of a particular respondent. For example, some studies ask respondents to name the party they voted for in the last election, a question that presumes that the respondent did in fact vote in that election. But before they are asked about the party they voted for, a filter question would eliminate those who did not vote. In the 2006 Canadian Election Study (funded by Elections Canada), respondents were asked the filter question, 'Did you vote in the [2006] election?' Only those who said yes were then asked, 'Which party did you vote for?' Similarly, in a study of meals, there is no point in asking vegetarians lots of questions about eating meat—it is probably best to filter them out, that is, skip the questions about meat and go on to the next series of questions. Once the response to the filter question has been keyed in, the computer will automatically go to the next relevant question, eliminating inappropriate items where necessary. This removes the possibility of interviewers inadvertently asking meaningless questions or failing to ask some that should be asked. In this way, computer-assisted interviewing enhances the degree of control over the interview process and improves the standardization of the asking and recording of questions.

Computer-assisted interviewing may make it easier to perform other tasks as well. For example, sometimes it is beneficial to randomize the order in which certain items are presented to the respondent because the responses given may depend on the order in which the items are listed. Automatic randomization was used in the Goyder *et al.* (2003) study of occupational prestige done in southwestern Ontario. As the authors put it: 'The deck was electronically shuffled for each new respondent.' Another advantage of computer-assisted interviews is that if interviewers are out in the field all day, they can either take a disc with the saved data to the research office or send the data in electronically.

CAPI and CATI have not been incorporated into academic survey research to the same degree that they have in commercial survey research, although that picture is changing because of their many advantages. Many of the large datasets available for analysis now come from computer-assisted interviews conducted by large social research organizations.

Using online personal interviews

Although online interviews run a higher risk of respondent dropout, Mann and Stewart (2000:

138–9) have suggested that in fact it is possible to develop a relationship of mutual trust when using them. This can be accomplished by regularly sending messages to respondents reassuring them that their written utterances are helpful and significant, especially since interviewing through the Internet is still an unfamiliar experience for most people and takes longer than other forms. It is worth the trouble to do because online interviews make it easier for the researcher to go back to interviewees for further information or reflections, something difficult to do with face-to-face interviews.

A further issue for the online personal interviewer is whether to send all the questions at once or to conduct the interview on a question-followed-by-reply basis. The problem with sending all at once is that respondents may read through them and only reply to the most interesting ones. Asking one question at a time is likely to be more reliable. Nonetheless, Bampton and Cowton (2002) reported that conducting email interviews by sending questions in small batches takes the pressure off interviewees to make a quick reply, gives them the opportunity to provide considered replies (although there can be a loss of spontaneity), and gives the interviewers greater opportunity to respond to interviewee answers.

There is evidence that prospective online interviewees are more likely to agree to participate if agreement is solicited prior to sending the actual questions. Another way to encourage respondents to participate is for the researcher to use some form of self-disclosure, such as directions to a website that contains detailed contact information. It also helps to provide personal material about the researcher (like a picture), as well as information relevant to the research topic (Curasi 2001; O'Connor and Madge 2001, 2003). Such steps are necessary because unsolicited emails ('spam') are often seen as a nuisance and can result in an immediate refusal to take the message seriously.

Curasi (2001) conducted a comparison in which 24 interviews carried out through email correspondence were contrasted with 24 parallel face-to-face interviews. The interviews were concerned with shopping on the Internet. She found that:

- face-to-face is better than online for maintaining rapport with respondents;
- because greater commitment and motivation are required to complete an online interview, replies

are often more detailed than in face-to-face interviews; and
- online interviewees' answers tend to be more considered and grammatically correct because they have more time to ponder and tidy up answers. Whether this is a positive feature is debatable. There is the obvious advantage of a 'clean' transcript, but there may be some loss of spontaneity.

On the other hand, Curasi found that sometimes little detail comes from online interviews, perhaps because replies must be typed, not just spoken. The full significance of the difference between online and face-to-face interviewing is still being explored by researchers.

The webcam may offer further possibilities for online personal interviews, making the online interview similar to the telephone version, and quite comparable to an in-person interview because those involved in the exchange can see each other. However, one of the main advantages of the online interview is lost: respondents' answers need to be transcribed.

Conducting interviews

Know the interview schedule

Before interviewing anybody, an interviewer should have a thorough knowledge of the interview schedule. Interviewing can be stressful, and it is possible that under strain standard interview procedures can cause interviewers to get flustered and leave questions out or ask the wrong questions. All interviewers need to be fully trained to reduce interviewer variability in asking questions, a potential source of error.

Introducing the research

Prospective respondents have to be provided with a credible rationale for participating in the research, in particular for giving up their valuable time. This aspect of conducting interviews is of special significance at a time when response rates to survey research appear to be declining. The introductory rationale may be either spoken by the interviewer or printed for the respondent to read. It is usually spoken if interviewers 'cold call' potential respondents at their homes, either in person or by telephone. A written rationale is common to alert respondents that someone will be contacting them to request an interview. In many cases, respondents may be presented with both modes—for example, when they are sent a letter inviting them to participate in a study and are then called or spoken to in person.

Rapport

It is frequently suggested that it is important for the interviewer to establish *rapport* with the respondent. This means that a relationship must be forged fairly quickly to encourage respondents to participate in and persist with the interview. Unless an element of rapport is established, some respondents who have agreed to be interviewed may decide to terminate participation because of the time the interview is taking or perhaps because of the nature of the questions being asked. While this injunction essentially invites the interviewer to be friendly with respondents and to put them at ease, it is important that this not be stretched too far. Too much rapport can result in the interview going on too long and the respondent suddenly deciding that too much time is being spent on the activity. Also, the mood of friendliness can result in the respondents tailoring their answers to please the interviewer. The achievement of rapport between interviewer and respondent is therefore a delicate balancing act. Moreover, it is probably somewhat easier to achieve rapport in a face-to-face interview than over the telephone. In the latter situation the interviewer is unable to offer the visual cues of friendliness, like smiling or maintaining good eye contact, which are conducive to gaining and maintaining rapport.

Topics and issues to include in an introductory statement

There are several issues to include in an introductory statement to a prospective interviewee. The following are important considerations:

- Clearly identify yourself.
- Identify the auspices under which the research is being conducted (for example, a university, a government agency).

- Mention where any funding of the research came from (but see Ethical issue 4.1).
- If you are a student doing research for a thesis, make that fact clear.
- Indicate what the research is about in broad terms and why it is important, and give an indication of the kind of information to be collected.
- Indicate how the respondent has been selected (for example, by a random process, by convenience, because of special characteristics).
- Provide reassurance about the confidentiality of any information given by the respondent.
- Explain that participation is voluntary.
- Reassure respondents that they will not be identified or identifiable. This can usually be achieved by pointing out that when the data are aggregated or analyzed at the group level, individual participants cannot be identified.
- Provide the respondent with the opportunity to ask any questions (for example, provide a contact telephone number or email address). If in person, simply ask if the respondent has any questions.

These suggestions are also relevant to the covering letter that should accompany mailed questionnaires. The latter should also include a stamped, pre-addressed return envelope.

Ethical issue 4.1

Mentioning sponsorship

At one Ontario university, ethical rules prohibit including the name of the sponsor of the research in the cover letter. The rule is based on the consideration that people may feel pressured or coerced by reading, for example, that the research is sponsored by the Canadian Cancer Society. At another university, it is unethical *not* to supply that information as it is thought to be part of informed consent. For example, some people may not want the government to know anything about them, so if the federal Ministry of Fisheries is funding the study, they would want to be informed so they can choose not to participate. But listing the sponsor does not guarantee informed consent, because a sponsoring body (even a highly controversial one) may be virtually unknown to the general public. Ethical issues are never simple!

Asking questions

It was suggested earlier that one aim of the structured interview is to ensure that each respondent is asked exactly the same questions, thus removing a potential source of variation in replies that does not reflect 'true' variation. The structured interview is meant to reduce the likelihood of this occurring, but it cannot guarantee it will not occur because there is always the possibility that some interviewers will embellish or otherwise change a question when it is asked. There are many reasons why interviewers may vary the question wording, such as a reluctance to ask certain questions, perhaps because of embarrassment (Collins 1997). Therefore, training interviewers, paying them well, and monitoring them is very important.

Does it really matter? Do small variations to wording on the part of the interviewer make a significant difference to people's replies? While the impact of variation in wording obviously differs from context to context, and in any case is difficult to quantify exactly, three experiments suggested that even small variations in wording can affect replies (Collins 1997).

Recording answers

Interviewers should write down respondents' replies as exactly as possible. Not to do so can distort respondents' answers and introduce errors. Such errors are less likely to occur when the interviewer merely has to allocate respondents' replies to a category, as in a closed question, than in the case where answers to open questions are being written down (Fowler and Mangione 1990).

Question order

Interviewers should also be alerted to the importance of asking questions in their proper order. For one thing, varying the question order can result in certain questions being accidentally omitted, because the interviewer may forget to ask the ones that have been leapfrogged during the interview. Also, variation in question order can have an impact on replies. If some respondents have not been asked a question that they should have been asked, on unemployment, for example, and others have, their responses may reflect this. A source of variability and error may be introduced in a later question, for instance on the causes of increasing crime, with those previously asked about unemployment mentioning that as a cause of crime more often than those who were not asked about it.

Probing

A highly problematic area for researchers employing a structured interview method is *probing* respondents who need help with their answers. This may occur if respondents do not understand the question and then struggle to provide an adequate answer, or if they do not provide a complete answer and have to be probed for more information. For example, in the 2007 Alberta Survey, respondents were asked questions about AADAC (the Alberta Alcohol and Drug Abuse Commission). One open-ended question read: 'To the best of your knowledge, what does AADAC do?' The probe available for all interviewers is: 'What services does AADAC provide?' A potential problem with any probe is that some interviewers may be more inclined to use it than other interviewers, and the probe itself may affect the response given, which could lead to reliability problems. A bigger problem arises if different interviewers provide different probes, although proper organization and training should preclude that.

Some general tactics with regard to probes are as follows:

- If further information is required, usually in the context of an open-ended question, standardized probes should be employed, such as 'Can you say a little more about that?' or 'Are there any other reasons why you think that?'
- If, with a closed question, the respondent replies in a way that does not match one of the pre-designed answers, the interviewer should repeat the fixed-choice alternatives and make it apparent that the answer needs to be chosen from those provided.
- When the interviewer needs to know about something that requires quantification, such as the number of visits to a doctor in the last four weeks or the number of banks in which the respondent has accounts, but the respondent answers in general terms ('quite often' or 'I have several'), the interviewer needs to persist for a clearer answer. With fixed-response surveys, this will usually entail repeating the response options. The interviewer should not suggest an answer

on the basis of the respondent's reply since the respondent may not be comfortable with the idea of disagreeing with the interviewer.

In the course of a face-to-face interview, the interviewer may use 'show cards' (see Box 4.1) rather than reading out a series of fixed-choice alternatives. Sometimes called 'flash cards,' they display all the answers from which the respondent is to choose and are handed to the respondent at different points in the interview. Situations in which it may be beneficial to use show cards include the following:

- There is a very long list of possible answers; for example, respondents may be asked about which magazines they read most frequently. To read out a list of magazines would be tedious and it is probably better to hand the respondent a list from which to choose.
- Some people are not keen to divulge personal details such as their age or income. One way of reducing the impact of such questioning is to present respondents with age or income ranges with a letter or number attached to each (see Box 4.1). Such a procedure may be used with other sensitive topics such as sexual practices. This procedure will obviously not be appropriate if the research requires *exact* figures pertaining to sensitive topics.
- Sometimes, during the course of interviews, respondents are presented with statements or questions to which the same possible responses apply, for example: 'strongly agree, agree, neutral, disagree, and strongly disagree.' It is time-consuming and off-putting to read out all five possible answers over and over again. Also, it may be expecting too much of respondents to ask them to keep all possible answers in their heads for the entire batch of questions to which they apply. Providing a show card listing the possible responses is an obvious solution.

Prompting

Prompting occurs when the interviewer suggests a specific answer to a particular interviewee. It is very rare and should be used only as a last resort. An example of unacceptable prompting would be to ask an open-ended question, then suggest a

Box 4.1   Two show cards

Card 4 (Age)	Card 6 (for various items)
(a) Less than 20	(1) Strongly agree
(b) 20–29	(2) Agree
(c) 30–39	(3) Undecided
(d) 40–49	(4) Disagree
(e) 50–59	(5) Strongly disagree
(f) 60–69	
(g) 70 and over	

possible answer to a respondent who appears to be struggling to think of an appropriate reply. In all situations, interviewers should do what they can to allow respondents to come up with their own replies. Otherwise the data gathered will not be authentic— it may reveal more about the interviewer than the interviewee.

Leaving the interview

Do not forget common courtesies like thanking respondents for giving up their time. But the period immediately after the interview is one in which some care is necessary in that some respondents may try to engage the interviewer in a discussion about the purpose of the interview. Interviewers should have a standard response to that but should resist further elaboration because the respondents may communicate what they are told to others, which could bias the results if those told about the study later become interviewees themselves.

Training and supervision

As noted, interviewers must be properly trained to ensure that the research is carried out correctly. Fowler (1993) cited evidence to suggest that training periods shorter than one full day rarely create good interviewers. Researchers use various ways to determine whether an interviewer has been trained properly, including:

- checking individual interviewers' response rates;
- tape-recording at least a sample of interviews;
- examining completed schedules to determine whether any questions are being left out or if they are being completed properly; and

- making call-backs on a sample of respondents (usually about 10 per cent) to determine whether they were interviewed and to ask about interviewers' conduct.

Questionnaires

Questionnaires are essentially structured interviews without an interviewer. They can be delivered and retrieved in several different ways. Probably the most common way is by mail. That is how Anderson *et al.* (2006) studied family physicians in southwestern Ontario. Sometimes respondents deposit their completed questionnaires at a certain location, such as their supervisor's office if a study is being conducted in a business organization. Researchers may hand out questionnaires to students in a class and collect them there as well, as Smith and McVie (2003) did in their longitudinal cohort study on crime.

In many ways the questionnaire and structured interview are very similar. The obvious difference is that with questionnaires, respondents must read the questions themselves and record their own answers. Because there is no interviewer to administer it, the research instrument has to be especially easy to follow and the questions particularly easy to answer. As a result, questionnaires compared with structured interviews tend to:

- have fewer 'open' questions because 'closed' questions are easier to answer;
- have easy-to-follow designs to minimize the risk that a respondent will inadvertently omit a question or a part of one; and
- be shorter to reduce the risk of 'respondent fatigue,' since it is much easier for a tired respondent facing a long questionnaire to throw it out than it is for a tired interviewee to ask the interviewer to leave.

Advantages of the questionnaire over the structured interview

Cheaper, quicker, more convenient to administer
Interviewing is expensive, and the cheapness of the questionnaire is especially advantageous if a sample is geographically dispersed. This advantage is obviously less pronounced when compared to telephone interviews, but even there the mailed questionnaire enjoys cost advantages.

A thousand questionnaires can be sent through the post in one batch; a class of four hundred students can fill out questionnaires in one class period. Even with a team of telephone interviewers, it takes a long time to conduct personal interviews with samples of that size. However, it is important to remember that the questionnaires may not come back immediately (respondents usually fill them in at *their* convenience) and may take several weeks to be returned. Also, in many situations it is necessary to send out follow-up letters and/or duplicate questionnaires to those who fail to respond.

Absence of interviewer effects
It was already noted that interviewer characteristics may affect respondent answers. Obviously, since there is no interviewer present, those sorts of effects are not an issue with questionnaires. Similarly, with a questionnaire, no one is there to read the questions to the subject in the wrong order, to present them in different ways to different respondents, or to state the items with variable emphases from person to person, thus precluding the problems those practices can cause.

Probably of greater importance is the tendency for people to exhibit a social desirability bias when an interviewer is present, giving 'politically correct' rather than genuine responses. There is also a tendency for interview respondents to underreport activities that induce anxiety, or about which they are sensitive. By contrast, research summarized by Tourangeau and Smith (1996) strongly suggests that respondents tend to report more drug use and alcohol consumption and a higher number of sexual partners and abortions in questionnaires than in structured interviews.

Disadvantages of questionnaires versus structured interviews

Cannot explain the question
It is always important to ensure that the questions asked are clear and unambiguous, but this is especially so with questionnaires, since there is no interviewer to help respondents with questions they cannot understand. Also, as seen earlier in this chapter, great attention must be paid to ensure that the questionnaire is easy to complete; if instructions are unclear, questions may be inadvertently omitted.

Greater risk of missing data
Partially answered questionnaires are more common (because of a lack of probing or supervision) than partly completed interviews. It is also easier for respondents to decide not to answer a question when they are on their own than when they are with an interviewer. For example, questions that appear boring or irrelevant to the respondent are especially likely to be skipped. Questionnaire respondents are more likely than interview participants to become tired of answering questions that are not fully salient to them, and to abandon the project entirely. Put positively, when a research issue *is* important to the respondent, a high response rate is possible. This means that when the questions are highly relevant, a questionnaire may be a good choice, especially because of its much lower cost.

Cannot probe
There is no opportunity to probe respondents to elaborate an answer. However, this problem mainly applies to open questions, which are not used a great deal in questionnaire research.

Difficult to ask a lot of questions
As signalled above, because of the possibility of 'respondent fatigue,' long questionnaires are rarely feasible. They may result in a greater tendency for questionnaires not to be answered at all.

Difficult to ask other kinds of questions
It is also important to avoid asking more than a very small number of open questions, because respondents frequently do not want to write a lot. Questions with complex structures, such as filters, should be avoided as much as possible since some respondents find them difficult to follow.

Questionnaire can be read as a whole
Respondents are able to read the whole questionnaire even before answering the first question. When this occurs, none of the questions asked is truly independent of the others. It also means that one cannot be sure that questions have been answered in the correct order, raising the possibility of question order effects.

Not appropriate for some kinds of respondents
Respondents whose literacy is limited or whose facility with the language used is restricted may not be able to answer the questionnaire. The second of these difficulties cannot be entirely overcome when interviews are being employed, but the difficulties are likely to be greater with questionnaires.

One last problem: who filled out the questionnaire?
With mailed questionnaires, one can never be sure whether the designated respondent or someone else answered the questions. It is also impossible to have any control over other members of a household helping the respondent answer the questions. Similarly, if a questionnaire is sent to the manager of a firm, the task may simply be delegated to someone else. The same problem arises with structured interviews when they are administered by telephone.

Online social surveys

There has been a considerable growth in the number of surveys being administered online. It is uncertain whether the research instruments should be regarded as structured interviews or as questionnaires—in a sense they are both. So far as online social surveys are concerned, there is a crucial distinction between surveys administered by email (email surveys) and surveys administered via the web (web surveys). In the case of the former, the questionnaire is sent via email to a respondent, whereas with a web survey, the respondent is directed to a website in order to answer it. Sheehan and Hoy (1999) suggested that there has been a tendency for email surveys to be employed with 'smaller, more homogeneous groups of on-line user groups,' whereas web surveys have been used to study 'large groups of on-line users.'

Email surveys
With email surveys it is important to distinguish between embedded and attached questionnaires. In the case of the embedded questionnaire, the questions are to be found in the body of the email. There may be an introduction to the questionnaire followed by a graphic that partitions the introduction from the questionnaire itself. Respondents have to indicate their replies using simple notation, such as an 'X,' or they may be asked to delete alternatives that do not apply to them. If a question is open, they are asked to type in an answer. When finished, they simply hit the reply button to return the completed questionnaire. With an attached questionnaire, the questionnaire arrives as an attachment to an email

that introduces it. As with the embedded question-naire, respondents must select and/or type their answers. To return the questionnaire, it must be attached to a reply email, although respondents may also be given the opportunity to fax it back or to return it through the regular mail (Sheehan and Hoy 1999).

The chief advantage of the embedded question-naire is that it requires less computer expertise. Knowing how to read and then return an attachment requires a certain facility with handling online com-munication that is still not universally possessed. Also, the recipients' operating systems or software may present problems with reading attachments, while many respondents may refuse to open an attachment because of concerns about viruses. On the other hand, the limited formatting possible with most email software, such as using bold, variations in font size, indenting, and other features, makes the appearance of embedded questionnaires rather dull and featureless, although this limitation is rapidly changing. Furthermore, it is slightly easier for the respondent to type material into an attachment that uses well-known software such as Microsoft Word because if the questionnaire is embedded in an email the alignment of questions and answers may be lost.

Dommeyer and Moriarty (2000) compared the two forms of email survey in connection with an attitude study. The attached questionnaire was given a much wider range of embellishments in terms of appearance than was possible with the embedded one. Before conducting the survey, undergraduate students were asked about the relative appearance of the two formats. The attached questionnaire was deemed to be better-looking, easier to complete, clearer in appearance, and better organized. The two formats were then administered to two random samples of students, all active email users. The researchers found a much higher response rate with the embedded than with the attached questionnaire (37 per cent versus 8 per cent), but little difference in terms of speed of response or whether any questions are more likely to be omitted with one format rather than the other. Although Dommeyer and Moriarty (2000: 48) concluded 'the attached e-mail survey presents too many obstacles to the potential respon-dent,' it is important to appreciate that this study was conducted during what were still early days in the life of online surveys. It may be that as prospective respondents become more adept at using online communication methods and as virus-checking software improves in terms of accessibility and cost, the concerns that led to the lower response rate for the attached questionnaire will be less pronounced.

Web surveys

Web surveys invite prospective respondents to visit a website where the questionnaire can be found and completed online. The web survey has an important advantage over the email survey in that it can use a much wider variety of embellishments in terms of appearance (see Box 4.2). Plate 4.1 presents part of the questionnaire from the Gym Study from Chapter 12 in a web-survey format and answered in the same way as in Box 12.1. Common features include 'radio buttons' (whereby the respondent makes a choice between closed-question answers by clicking on a circle in which a dot appears—see question 8 in Plate 4.1) and pull-down menus of possible answers (see Plate 4.2). There are also greater possibilities to use colour. With open questions, the respondent is invited to type directly into a boxed area (for example, question 2 in Plate 4.1).

However, the advantages of the web survey are more than its appearance. The questionnaire can be designed so that when there is a filter question (for example, 'if yes, go to question 12; if no, go to question 14'), it skips automatically to the next appropriate question. The questionnaire can also be programmed so that only one question ever appears on the screen, or to allow the respondent to scroll down and look at all questions in advance. Finally, respondents' answers can be automatically pro-grammed to download into a database, thus elimi-nating the daunting task of coding a large number of questionnaires. There is a growing number of soft-ware packages designed to produce questionnaires with all the features just described.

Potential respondents need to be directed to the website containing the questionnaire. One way to do this is to email prospective respondents, as was done by Andrews et al. (2007) in their study of academic integrity (that is, cheating and plagiarism) in Cana-dian and American dental schools. It may be most efficient to send the email invitation to a person who can forward it to large numbers of potential participants. In the Andrews et al. study, it was sent to academic deans who then forwarded it to faculty members and students. Where a restriction on who may answer the questionnaire is needed, it may be

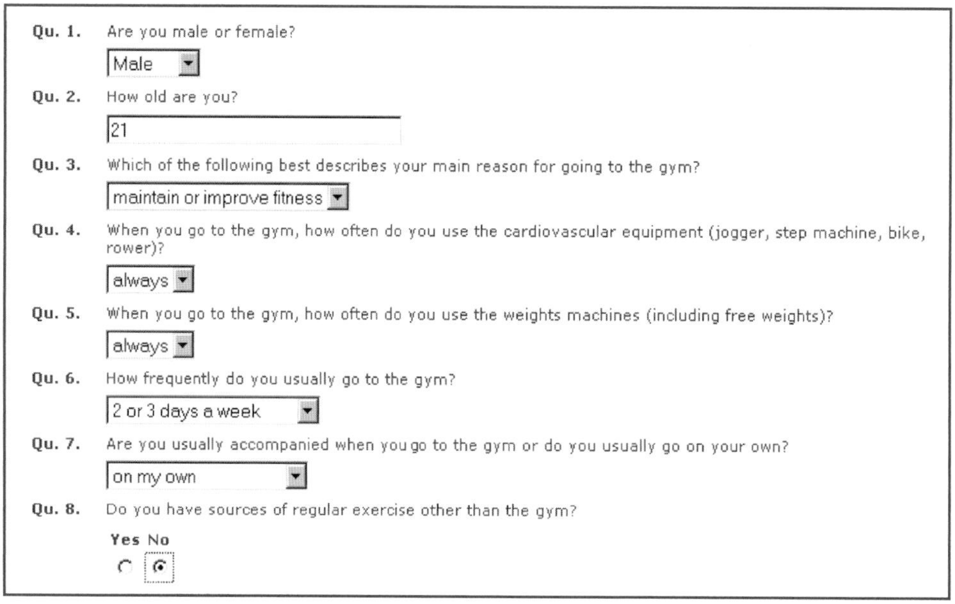

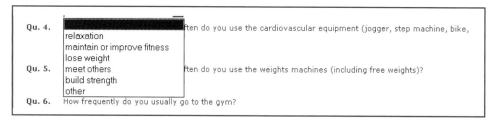

Plate 4.1 Gym study in web survey format

Plate 4.2 A pull-down menu for Qu. 3

necessary to set up a password system to filter out people for whom the questionnaire is not appropriate.

Researcher-driven diaries as a form of questionnaire

When the researcher is specifically interested in precise estimates of behaviour, the diary warrants serious consideration, though it is still a relatively underused method. Specifically, what Elliott (1997) called the *researcher-driven diary* can be used as a kind of questionnaire. The researcher asks diarists to record their perceptions, feelings, or actions with regard to certain matters shortly after the experience occurs. For example, the diary method has been used to study marital and family processes (Laurenceau and Bolger 2005). Hessler *et al.* (2003) used researcher-driven diaries in an email qualitative study of adolescent risk behaviour that resulted in

rich narratives of everyday life as perceived by adolescents. Sometimes, the collection of data in this manner is supplemented by a personal interview in which the diarist is asked questions about various things, such as what was meant by certain remarks.

Corti (1993) distinguished between 'structured diaries' and 'free text diaries.' Either can be employed by a quantitative researcher. The research on the domestic division of labour by Sullivan (1996) is an illustration of a structured diary. This type of diary has the general appearance of a questionnaire with largely closed questions. The kind of diary Sullivan used is often referred to as a 'time-use' diary because it is designed for diarists to record, more or less at the time of the actual behaviour, how long they engage in certain activities such as food preparation, childcare, eating, and so on. Sullivan also asked couples to record on a five-point scale the amount of enjoyment they derived from those kinds of activities.

Box 4.2   Advantages and disadvantages of online surveys compared to mailed questionnaires

This box summarizes the main advantages and dis-advantages of online surveys, both email and web varieties, compared to mailed questionnaires. All three share one disadvantage relative to personal and telephone interviews, namely that the researcher can never be certain of who is actually answering the questions.

Advantages

Low cost. Even though mailed questionnaires are cheap to administer, online surveys are even cheaper. There is no postage, paper, envelopes, and time taken to stuff covering letters and questionnaires into envelopes.

Faster response and processing. Online surveys can be returned considerably faster than mailed ques-tionnaires. Also, automatic skipping when using filter questions and an opportunity for immediate down-loading of replies into a database make this kind of survey quite attractive for researchers.

Fewer unanswered questions. There is evidence that online questionnaires are completed with fewer unanswered questions than mailed questionnaires.

Better response to open questions. Open questions are more likely to be answered online and to result in more detailed replies.

Disadvantages

Low response rate. Typically, response rates to online surveys are lower than those for comparable mailed questionnaires.

Restricted to online populations. Only people who are available online can reasonably be expected to participate in an online survey. This restriction should gradually ease over time but since the online population still differs in significant ways from the non-online population, it remains a difficulty.

Requires motivation. Because online survey respon-dents must pay for the connection and could be tying up their telephone lines, they may need a higher level of motivation than mailed questionnaire respondents. This suggests that the solicitation to participate must be especially persuasive.

Confidentiality and anonymity issues. It is normal for survey researchers to indicate that respondent replies will be kept anonymous. However, with email surveys, since the addresses of the respondents are known, they may find it difficult to believe that their replies really are anonymous.

Multiple replies. With web surveys, there is a risk that some people may mischievously complete the questionnaire more than once. There is much less risk of this with email surveys.

Source: Adapted from Cobanoglu *et al*. (2001); Kent and Lee (1999); Schaeffer and Dillman (1998); Sheehan and Hoy (1999); Tse (1998).

Such records of the time spent in different activi-ties are often regarded as more accurate than those done at the end of the day, perhaps because the events are less subject to memory problems. However, the method is more intrusive than answering a ques-tionnaire because it is a constant interruption and it may even change people's behaviour. For example, one can become preoccupied with the behaviours being researched and thus engage in them in a more thoughtful or premeditated way.

Sometimes diaries can be constructed as part of a larger structured interview. This is the approach taken in the 2005 Time Use study, which was part of the General Social Survey conducted for Statis-tics Canada. A 24-hour diary is produced by asking people what they were doing on a certain day. The first question is: 'On [diary day], at 4:00 am, what were you doing?' (Most people say 'sleeping,' and are then asked what time they got up.) 'And then, what did you do?' is asked repeatedly until the entire day is covered. Sometimes questions such as 'Where were you?' or 'Who was with you?' are asked as well.

An example of a free-text diary is provided in Coxon's (1994) study of how the risk of HIV/AIDS affects the sexual activities of gay men. One of several advantages of the diary method for this research is that it provided information on the time sequenc-ing of events (for example, which practice followed which) and context, information more difficult to glean from questionnaires. The method involved recording, for one week, the following information:

- location of the activity;
- nature and sequence of each separate sexual act (who did what to whom);
- whether drugs accompanied the practice;

- what activities—sexual or otherwise—preceded each item of sexual activity;
- whether any sexual aids were employed; and
- whether the diarist or his partner achieved orgasm.

Crook and Light (2002) employed time-use diaries within a free-text format. University students were asked to keep a diary for a week, divided into 15-minute intervals, of the different kinds of study and learning activity in which they engaged, where the activity took place, and the study resources used (for example, the library). The various activities were grouped into three types: classes, private study, and social study (that is, study with a peer). They were able to show the very different patterns and amounts of study typically undertaken during a day.

Using free-text recording of behaviour carries the same kinds of coding problems as those associated with open-ended interview questions—namely, the time-consuming nature of the exercise and the risk of introducing error while coding answers. However, the free-text approach is less likely to be problematic when, as in the case of Coxon's (1994) research, diarists are instructed about what is required and the behaviours of interest are specific and concrete. It would be much more difficult to code free-text entries relating to more general behaviours such as the domestic issues studied by Sullivan (1996).

Corti (1993) recommended that people doing research involving diaries should:

- provide explicit instructions for diarists;
- be clear about the time periods in which the behaviour of interest is to be assessed (for example, daytime, certain 24-hour periods, particular weeks), and indicate that in the diary template;
- supply a model of a completed section of a diary;
- provide brief checklists of 'items, events or behaviour' to jog the memory.

Advantages and disadvantages of the diary as a method of data collection

The studies illustrating the use of diaries suggest potential advantages:

- When fairly precise estimates of the frequency and/or amount of time spent in different forms of behaviour are required, the diary may provide

more valid and reliable data than questionnaires.
- When information about the sequencing of different types of behaviour is required, it is likely to perform better than questionnaires or interviews.
- Diaries are useful in producing data on behaviour that is personally sensitive, such as sexual activities.

On the other hand, diaries may suffer the following problems:

- They tend to be more expensive than personal interviews because of costs related to recruiting diarists and checking that diaries are being properly completed.
- Diaries can suffer from a process of attrition, as people tire of the task of completing them, which raises reliability issues.
- There is sometimes a failure to record details sufficiently quickly, which results in memory recall problems.

However, diary researchers such as Coxon and Sullivan argue that the data from diaries are more accurate than the information available from interviews or questionnaires dealing with the same topic.

Respondent problems

A number of problems with structured interviews, questionnaires, and diaries have been identified.

Response sets

This problem is especially relevant to multiple-indicator measures, where respondents reply to a battery of related questions or items. A response set occurs when people respond to a series of items, not according to how they actually feel about them but out of some other motive. Three of the most prominent types of response set involve the 'acquiescence,' 'social desirability,' and 'laziness or boredom' effects.

Acquiescence

Acquiescence refers to a tendency among some people to either agree or disagree with a set of questions or items, regardless of content, just to be 'cooperative' or to please the researcher. Imagine a respondent agreeing to both items from the 2007 Alberta Survey discussed in Chapter 3: 'Body checking is the main cause of injuries for children in organized minor hockey,' and 'Body checking is an essential part of the game of organized minor hockey.' Agreement with the first implies a negative view of body checking, while agreement with the second suggests the opposite. If someone agrees with both, at least one of those responses is probably not authentic. Therefore, researchers who employ this kind of multiple-item measure may use items that imply opposite positions to weed out those respondents who appear to have an acquiescence response set—one cannot agree with all the items or disagree with them all and still maintain a consistent attitude. Those who answer in that way may have to be removed from the study.

Social desirability

The social desirability effect refers to the idea that some respondents may provide replies that are not sincere or genuine, but which nonetheless make them appear to be respectable or likeable people. An answer perceived as socially undesirable is less likely to be given than one perceived as desirable. This phenomenon has been demonstrated in studies on mental health using psychiatric inventories of minor neuroses and anxieties—many respondents will not admit that they have those afflictions. The problem is compounded by the fact that some categories of people may be more truthful than others about certain issues. Women, for example, conceal their illnesses less than men do. On the other hand, men are more likely to be frank about certain sexual issues.

Laziness or boredom

Sometimes respondents will provide a series of answers just to get rid of the interviewer or to get the questionnaire over with. For example, when visiting a doctor's office for the first time, one often has to fill out a form that contains a long list of diseases, with a space provided for each one so patients can indicate whether they have ever suffered from them. Someone may begin by carefully reading the list and checking off 'No, No, No, …,' but may soon tire of the task and just tick 'No' for the remaining items without reading them closely. To avoid this sort of problem, researchers may have to devise a set of questions in which a person cannot give the same answer to all

items and be consistent or truthful, a tack similar to that used to test for acquiescent response set.

When these forms of response error go undetected, they represent sources of error in concept measurement. Some have suggested that the structured interview is particularly prone to them. Awareness of these potential problems has led to attempts to limit their impact, for example, by removing cases obviously affected by them, or by instructing interviewers to not become overly friendly with respondents and to avoid appearing judgmental about their replies.

The issue of meaning

Another issue survey researchers have to deal with involves the 'problem of meaning,' the fact that when humans communicate they not only draw on commonly held meanings but also create new ones. 'Meaning,' in this sense, is something worked at and achieved—not simply given. In structured interviewing this requires drawing attention to the presumption that interviewers and respondents have the same meanings for the terms employed in the interview questions and answer options, when in fact they may not. For example, respondents who say they 'hate' body piercing may use forceful language for everything, and so their 'hate' may be the same as a milder person's 'dislike.' Conversely, when a mild person says 'hate' in an interview or on a questionnaire, this may not have the same meaning as that assumed by a person prone to more colourful speech.

The feminist critique

Some feminist social researchers maintain that survey research methods involve an asymmetrical relationship between the researcher and the subject. According to this argument, the researcher extracts information from the research subject and gives nothing in return. For example, standard textbook advice of the kind provided in this chapter says that rapport should be established, but interviewers should guard against becoming too familiar with respondents. This often means that questions asked by participants (for example, about the topic of the study or about the research process) should be politely but firmly rebuffed on the grounds that they can bias the respondents' subsequent answers.

This is perfectly valid and appropriate advice according to the canons of structured interviewing, with its quest for standardization and for valid and reliable data. However, some feminists claim that such practices create a hierarchical relationship between the interviewer and respondent that can lead to exploitation. But as noted in Chapter 1, there has been some softening of attitudes towards the role of quantitative research among feminist researchers. Paying more attention to issues like privacy in the interview and providing special training in the handling of sensitive topics has contributed to changing outlooks toward this sort of research. Moreover, surveys in some countries have proven to be highly instructive about the frequency and causes of phenomena such as violence against women (cf. Walby and Myhill 2001). Such research, based on structured interviews, would seem to be consistent with the goals of most feminist researchers, and indeed of potentially great value for both women and men.

Key Points

- The structured interview is a research instrument used to standardize the wording and order of questions and the recording of answers, which minimizes interviewer-related error.

- Structured interviews can be administered in person, over the phone, or online.

- It is important for interviewers to keep to the wording and order of questions. Training in the asking of questions, recording of answers, and establishing rapport with respondents is essential.

- Questionnaires reduce some of the problems encountered in structured interviews. On the other hand, they have their own weaknesses.

- Online surveys can be categorized into two major types: web surveys and email surveys.

- The researcher-driven diary is an alternative to using questionnaires and interviews, especially when the research questions are concerned with specific behaviour rather than attitudes or opinions.

- Steps need to be taken to reduce response sets, a potential problem in structured interviews and questionnaires.

Questions for Review

The structured interview

- Why is it important to keep interviewer variability to a minimum?

- How successful is the structured interview in reducing interviewer variability?

- Why might a survey researcher prefer a structured interview to an unstructured one?

- Why do structured interview schedules typically include mainly closed questions?

Interview contexts

- In what circumstances is it preferable to conduct structured interviews with more than one interviewer?

- 'Given the lower cost of telephone interviews as against face-to-face interviews, the former are generally preferable.' Discuss.

Conducting interviews

- Prepare an opening statement for a school study of student shoplifting.

- To what extent is rapport an important ingredient of structured interviewing?

- What is the difference between probing and prompting? What danger does each pose?

Questionnaires

- What advantages do they have over structured interviews?

- What disadvantages do they have compared to structured interviews?

- What ethical issues are involved when professors ask their current students to fill out a questionnaire in class?

Online social surveys

- What is the significance of the distinction between email and web surveys?

- Are there circumstances in which embedded email questionnaires are more likely to be effective than attached questionnaires?

- What advantages do online surveys have over traditional research methods for collecting data?

- What disadvantages do they have in comparison with traditional research methods for collecting data?

Diaries as a form of questionnaire

- Are there circumstances when a diary approach is preferable to a questionnaire?

Problems with survey research

- What are response sets and why is it important to know about them?

- What are the main issues behind the feminist critique of survey research?

5 Asking Questions

Chapter overview

This chapter is concerned with the questions used in structured interviews and questionnaires, two data-gathering techniques discussed in Chapter 4. We will explore:

- issues involved in deciding whether to use open or closed questions;
- different kinds of questions that can be asked in structured interviews and questionnaires;
- rules to bear in mind when designing questions;

- optimal question order;
- how questionnaires can be designed to minimize error and to make answering easier for respondents;
- projection or vignette questions in which respondents are asked to reflect on a hypothetical scenario presented to them;
- the importance of pre-testing questions; and
- the use of questions taken from previous research.

Introduction

As suggested in Chapter 4, there is much more involved in survey research than an optimal phrasing of questions. However, question wording is a crucial concern and will be the focus of our attention here.

Open or closed questions?

One of the most significant considerations in survey research is whether to ask a question in an 'open' or 'closed' format, a distinction introduced in the last chapter.

With an open question, respondents can reply however they wish. With a closed question, they are presented with a set of fixed alternatives from which they have to choose an appropriate answer. All of the questions in Box 5.5 are of the closed kind. So too are the Likert scale items in Box 5.7. What, then, are some of the advantages and limitations of the two formats?

Open questions

Open questions present both advantages and disadvantages to a survey researcher. By and large,

however, problems associated with the processing of answers tend to limit their use, especially in quantitative research.

Advantages
Open questions have certain advantages over closed ones:

- Respondents can answer in their own terms, not just those chosen by the researchers.
- They allow unusual responses, replies that the survey researcher may not have contemplated and therefore may not have offered as a fixed-choice alternative.
- The questions do not suggest answers to respondents. That allows the participants' knowledge and understanding of issues to be tapped. The salience of particular issues for respondents can also be examined.
- They are useful for exploring new or changing areas.
- They can generate fixed-choice format answers, a point returned to later in this chapter.

Disadvantages

Open questions also present problems for a survey researcher:

- It is time-consuming to record the answers—interviewees are likely to talk longer with an open question than with a comparable closed question.
- The answers have to be 'coded,' which can also take a lot of time and effort. The next section outlines the nature of coding and provides the basics on how it is done.
- Because of the greater time and effort required, many prospective respondents are likely to be put off by the idea of having to write extensively, which may exacerbate the problem of low response rates with questionnaires.
- Because of the difficulty of writing down verbatim what respondents say, there may be inaccuracies in the recording of answers. One obvious solution is to use a tape recorder, but this can make some respondents nervous, and transcribing the answers to tape-recorded questions takes a long time. The problem of transcription is one continually faced by qualitative researchers using semi-structured and unstructured interviews (to be discussed in Chapter 10), but they solve it by speaking with only a small number of respondents, unlike the large numbers typical of survey research.

Coding

Coding is a key stage in quantitative research. Many forms of social science data are essentially unstructured and unorganized, including answers to open questions in interviews and questionnaires, and the content of newspaper articles. To make sense of the information one must go through it all, deriving themes or categories of behaviour to form the basis for codes (the labels or titles given to the themes or categories), for example 'hostile to outsiders,' or 'not hostile to outsiders.' Next, the researcher usually assigns numbers to the codes. This may be a largely arbitrary process, in the sense that the numbers themselves may simply be tags to allow the material to be stored quantitatively. One must then go through the information again to look for incidences of the theme or category, and to record the appropriate numbers on a computer spreadsheet. This approach is sometimes called *post-coding*. Post-coding can be an unreliable procedure because there may be inconsistencies in the judgments of different coders, which leads to both measurement error and lack of validity.

When Schuman and Presser (1981, see Box 5.3) asked an open question about the features of a job that people like, the answers were to be grouped into 11 codes: pay; feeling of accomplishment; control of work; pleasant work; security; opportunity for promotion; short hours; working conditions; benefits; satisfaction; other responses. Each of these 11 categories was assigned a number, such as: 1 for pay; 2 for feeling of accomplishment; 3 for control of work; and 4 for pleasant work.

Charles and Kerr (1988) conducted interviews with 200 women concerning the consumption of food in the home. Their interviews were of the semi-structured kind, and the questions were open-ended. Charles and Kerr were working with a qualitative research strategy, but for several of their questions they found it helpful to quantify respondents' answers. For example, one of their concepts was responsibility for meal preparation. It was divided into five categories of responsibility: self prepares all meals; self mainly, partner sometimes; either self or self and partner together equally; self mainly with help from partner and/or children sometimes; and other. See Box 5.1 for another example.

Box 5.1 Coding an open question

Foddy (1993) asked a small sample of his students, 'Your father's occupation is (was) . . .' and requested three details: nature of business, size of business, and whether owner or employee. The replies to the size of business question were particularly variable, and included the following: 'big,' 'small,' 'very large,' '3000 acres,' 'family,' 'multinational,' '200 people,' and 'Philips.' The problem here is obvious: these categories do not provide a useful measure of size. The problem has only partly to do with the difficulty of coding an open question; it is also due to a lack of specificity in the question. If Foddy had asked, 'How many employees are (were) there in your father's place of employment?' a more meaningful set of answers would have been forthcoming. Whether his students would have known this information is, of course, yet another issue. However, this illustrates some potential problems with asking an open question, particularly one that lacks a clear reference point.

Pre-coding, on the other hand, is a process in which the researcher designs a coding frame in advance of administering the survey instrument (as in Box 5.2). Closed questions in survey research are, by definition, pre-coded (as in Box 5.3). This means that respondents are asked to assign their answers to a category, with a number already set up by the researcher. In post-coding, the response or behaviour is elicited without knowledge of any classification scheme.

When coding, three basic principles need to be observed (Bryman and Cramer 2004):

- The categories must not overlap. If they do, the numbers assigned to them will not denote distinct behaviours or types of responses.
- The list of categories must be exhaustive and therefore cover all possibilities. If it does not, some material cannot be coded. This is why many classification schemes, such as those used to code open questions, include the category 'other.'
- There should be clear rules about how codes are to be applied, with examples of the kinds of answers that may be subsumed under a particular category. Such rules are meant to ensure that coders are consistent over time in how they assign the material to categories and, if more than one person is coding, that the various coders are consistent with each other. The term 'coding frame' is often employed to describe the lists of categories

that should be applied to unstructured data and the rules for their application. In content analysis and structured observation, the term 'coding manual' is often preferred.

Coding also occurs in qualitative research, but its role and significance are somewhat different.

Closed questions

The advantages and disadvantages of closed questions are in many respects implied in the considerations relating to open questions.

Advantages
Closed questions offer the following advantages to researchers.

- It is easy to process answers. For example, a questionnaire respondent or an interviewer using a structured interview schedule can place a tick on the form or can circle an answer to indicate the appropriate response. The mark can then be scanned by an optical reader (see Box 5.7 for an example). Similarly, responses may be recorded directly into a computer file by using a keyboard and the appropriate software.
- Closed questions enhance the comparability of answers. As mentioned, post-coding can be unreliable, even with inter- and intra-coder checks designed to insure that coders do not vary their coding conventions. Closed questions circumvent this problem.
- Some respondents may not be clear about what a question is getting at; the available answers may provide some clarification.
- Because interviewers and respondents are not expected to write extensively and instead to place ticks, circle answers, or enter the response using a keyboard, closed questions are easier and quicker to complete.
- As noted in Chapter 4, if interviewers cannot write down exactly what respondents say, a source of bias and hence of invalidity is introduced. Closed questions reduce this possibility, though there is still the potential problem that interviewers may have to *interpret* what is said to them in order to assign answers to a category, as when a person says 'beats me' when asked about what his or her income was in a particular year.

Box 5.2   Processing a closed question

Which party did you like the most [in the 2006 Canadian federal election campaign]?
[Interviewer: do not read list!]

1   Liberals
2   Conservatives
3   NDP
4   Bloc Québécois
5   Green Party
0   Another party, specify
97   None of them
d   Don't know
r   Refused

Source: *2006 Canadian Election Study—Post Election Survey* available at http://ces-eec.mcgill.ca/documents/post2006.pdf.

Box 5.3 A comparison of results for a closed and an open question

Schuman and Presser (1981) conducted an experiment to determine if responses to closed questions can be improved by asking the questions first as open questions and then developing categories of reply from respondents' answers. They asked a question about what people look for in work in both open and closed format. Different samples were used for each format. They found considerable disparities between the two sets of answers. They then revised the closed categories to reflect the answers they received to the open-ended question, and re-administered the questions to two large samples of Americans. The question (with revised response categories) and the answers they received are as follows:

'This next question is on the subject of work. People look for different things in a job. Which one of the following five things do you most prefer in a job? [closed question]. What would you most prefer in a job? [open question].'

Closed format		Open format	
Answer	%	*Answer*	%
Work that pays well	13.2	Pay	16.7
Work that gives a feeling of accomplishment	31.0	Feeling of accomplishment	14.5
Work where there is not too much supervision and you make most decisions yourself	11.7	Control of work	4.6
Work that is pleasant and people who are nice to work with	19.8	Pleasant work	14.5
Work that is steady with little chance of being laid off	20.3	Security	7.6
	96% of sample		57.9% of sample
		Opportunity for promotion	1.0
		Short hours/lots of free time	1.6
		Working conditions	3.1
		Benefits	2.3
		Satisfaction/liking a job	15.6
Other/dk/na	4.0	Other responses	18.3
	100%		100%

With the revised form of the closed question, Schuman and Presser found a much higher proportion of the sample whose answers to the open question corresponded with the closed categories. They argued that the new closed question was superior to its predecessor and also superior to the open question. However, it is still disconcerting that in only 58 per cent of the cases the answers given to the open question match the categories offered in the closed one. Also, the distributions are somewhat different: for example, twice as many respondents answer in terms of a feeling of accomplishment with the closed format than with the open one. Nonetheless, the experiment demonstrates the desirability of generating forced-choice answers from open questions.

Disadvantages
However, closed questions exhibit certain disadvantages:

- There may be a loss of spontaneity and authenticity in respondents' answers. There is always the possibility that replies relevant to the issue being investigated are not covered by the fixed answers provided. One solution is to use an open question to generate the categories (see Box 5.3). Also, it is often wise to include 'other' as a possible response category, and to allow respondents to elaborate on that choice.
- Care must be taken to ensure that the response categories do not overlap, for example, when the age categories offered are '20–30,' '30–40,' and '40–50.' Here the forced-choice answers are not mutually exclusive, so 30- and 40-year-old respondents do not know which category to select because they fit into two. Pre-tests and careful selection of categories usually eliminate this problem.
- It may be difficult to make forced-choice answers exhaustive. All possible answers should really be provided, but a common compromise is to list the most frequently used ones and then an 'other' category to avoid excessively long lists of possible answers. Should a particular 'other' response appear frequently in the pre-test, it can be added to the actual list.
- There may be differences among respondents in their interpretation of forced-choice answers, thus reducing validity. For example, the understanding of the word 'soon' in a question can vary immensely from person to person.
- Closed questions may irritate those respondents unable to find a category that they feel applies to them.
- In interviews, a large number of closed questions reduces conversation and gives the interview an impersonal feel, thus reducing rapport. On the other hand, closed questions may represent a welcome break from open ones.

Types of questions

Structured interviews and questionnaires generally contain several different types of question. There are various ways of classifying them, but here are the main forms:

- *Personal, factual questions.* These are questions that ask the respondent to provide personal information, such as his or her age, occupation, marital status, and income. This kind of question also includes questions about behaviour. Respondents often have to rely on their memories to answer these sorts of questions, as when they are asked about the frequency of their religious service attendance or how often they go out to see to a movie.
- *Factual questions about others.* These questions should be used only as a last resort because there may not only be problems of recall, as above, but respondents may have distorted or inaccurate knowledge of others' behaviours (Beardsworth and Keil 1997). It is better to interview the person directly than to rely on the second-hand accounts of others. However, if the researcher is interested in the respondent's own perceptions of how another acts or feels, questions on that topic are appropriate.
- *Factual questions about an entity or event.* Sometimes, those who are interviewed or who complete a questionnaire act as informants about something or some event with which they are familiar. Asking people about what they witnessed at a riot, such as how many people were there, whether the police took appropriate action, and the approximate ages of people engaged in looting, are examples. Although more defensible than the previous type of questions because the information may not be readily available from other sources, this sort of question may lead to problems because in everyday life people usually do not observe things carefully and systematically, and may have biases that affect their perceptions and recollections.
- *Questions about attitudes.* Questions about attitudes are very common in both structured interviews and questionnaire research. A five-point Likert scale (See Box 5.7 for an example) is one of the most frequently encountered formats for measuring attitudes.
- *Questions about beliefs.* Respondents are often asked about their social, political, moral, or religious beliefs. For example: 'Should Canada maintain its military presence in Afghanistan? Choose one: definitely yes, yes, unsure, no, definitely no.'

- *Questions about knowledge.* Questions can sometimes 'test' respondents' knowledge in an area. For example, the Dominion Institute often tests Canadians' knowledge of Canada and its history. A poll done in 2007 showed that 91 per cent of respondents knew who Canada's largest trading partner was, and 82 per cent could name the prime minister. But only 70 per cent could name the three oceans that border on Canada, and just 5 per cent could state four different rights or freedoms protected by the *Canadian Charter of Rights and Freedoms* (see www.dominion.ca/Dominion_Institute_Press_Release_Mock_Exam.pdf).

Most structured interview schedules and questionnaires include more than one type of question. When doing research, it is important to keep the various types in mind because:

- It helps to clarify what is being asked, albeit in rather general terms.
- It guards against asking questions in an inappropriate format. For example, a Likert scale may be unsuitable for asking certain factual questions about behaviour.
- When building scales, it is best not to mix different types of questions, as measurement validity may be threatened. For example, attitudes and beliefs sound similar and one may be tempted to mix them, but it is best to have separate scales for each one.

Rules for designing questions

Over the years, numerous rules have been devised in connection with the dos and don'ts of asking questions. In spite of this, mistakes persist. So here are three simple rules of thumb, followed by some more specific guidelines.

General rules of thumb

Keep the research questions in mind
The questions asked in a questionnaire or structured interview should be geared to answering your research questions. It is painful to find out too late that a particular research question was not addressed in your study. Focusing on the research questions also helps one avoid pursuing issues that are irrelevant, which would be a waste of your time as well as the respondents'.

What exactly do you want to know?
Rule of thumb number two relates to the first one. It is important to focus on exactly what you want to know. Consider the seemingly harmless question:

Do you have a car?

What is that question seeking to tap? Is it car ownership? If so, the question is inadequate, largely because of the ambiguity of the word 'have.' The question can be interpreted as: personally owning a car; having access to a car in a household; or being able to use a company car or a car for business. Thus, an answer of 'yes' may or may not be indicative of car ownership. To know whether a respondent owns a car, ask directly about it. Similarly, consider the question:

How many children do you have?

That may seem straightforward, but does 'children' include stepchildren? Adopted children? Grown children? Be as specific as possible. And if what you are trying to address is the standard of living of a person or household, the crucial issue may be how many children are living at home.

How would you answer it?
Rule of thumb number three is to put yourself in the position of the respondent. Ask yourself the question and try to work out a reply. If you do this, there is at least a possibility that the ambiguities inherent in the 'Do you have a car?' or 'How many children do you have?' type questions will become evident. You may remember that you have access to a car at work, or think about whether your partner's children from a previous relationship should be factored into your answer. Putting yourself in the position of the respondent can reveal the difficulty of answering the questions.

Specific rules when designing questions

Avoid ambiguous terms in questions
If possible, avoid terms such as 'often' and 'regularly' as measures of frequency. They are ambiguous;

different respondents will operate with different frames of reference when employing them. Sometimes it is unavoidable, but when it is possible to get a specific number from respondents, do so. Consider a question asked of people who have said that they own a cell phone:

How often do you use your cell phone?

Very often   _____
Quite often   _____
Not very often _____
Not at all   _____

This question suffers from the problem that, with the exception of 'not at all,' the terms in the response categories are ambiguous. Instead, ask about actual frequency, such as:

How often do you use your cell phone?
(Please tick whichever category comes closest to the number of times you use your cell phone.)

More than 10 times per day _____
5–9 times per day   _____
1–4 times per day   _____
A few times a week   _____
A few times a month   _____
Almost never   _____

Alternatively, one could simply ask respondents to estimate the number of times per day they use their cell phone.

It is also important to bear in mind that certain common words, such as 'dinner' and 'book,' mean different things to different people. For some, dinner is a light midday meal, whereas for others it is a substantial evening meal. Similarly, some people refer to magazines, catalogues or brochures as 'books,' while others work with a more restricted definition. In such cases, it is necessary to clearly define the terms that are being used.

Avoid long questions

Most methodologists agree that long questions are undesirable. In a structured interview, the interviewee can lose track of a long question, and when completing a questionnaire the respondent may be tempted to omit such questions or to skim them. However, Sudman and Bradburn (1982) have suggested that this advice is more applicable to attitude questions than to those asking about behaviour. They argued that when the focus is on behaviour, longer questions have certain positive features in interviews—for example, they are more likely to provide memory cues and facilitate recall because of the time taken to complete the question. However, by and large, it's best to keep questions short.

Avoid double-barrelled questions

How satisfied are you with your pay and working conditions?

The problem here is obvious: the respondent may be satisfied with one but not the other. Not only will the respondent be unclear about how to reply, but the answer provided may pertain to pay, to conditions, or to both. Similarly:

How frequently does your husband help with cooking and cleaning?

suffers from the same problem. A husband may provide extensive help with the cooking but be totally uninvolved in the cleaning, so that any stipulation of frequency of help is ambiguous.

The same rule applies to fixed-choice answers. In Box 5.3, one of Schuman and Presser's (1981) answers is:

Work that is pleasant and people who are nice to work with.

While there may well be symmetry between the two ideas in this answer—pleasant work and nice people—there is no *necessary* correspondence between these two things. Pleasant work may be important for someone who is indifferent to the issue of pleasant co-workers. A further instance of a double-barrelled question is provided in Box 5.4.

Avoid very general questions

It may be tempting to ask a very general question when what is needed is a response to a specific issue. The question:

How satisfied are you with your job?

seems harmless, but it lacks specificity. Does it refer to pay, working conditions, the nature of the work,

Box 5.4 Matching question and answers in closed questions (and some double-barrelled questions too)

A publisher inserted a feedback questionnaire within a novel's pages, including a series of Likert-style items regarding the book's quality. In each case, the respondent is asked to indicate whether the attribute being asked about is poor, acceptable, average, good, or excellent. However, in each case, the items are presented as questions. For example:

Was the writing elegant, seamless, imaginative?

One problem here is that, strictly speaking, the answer to this question should be 'yes' or 'no'. At most, respondents might have gradations of yes and no, such as definitely, to a large extent, to some extent, not at all. However, 'poor' or 'excellent' cannot be literal answers to this question. The questions would have been better presented as statements, such as:

Please indicate the quality of the book in each of the following categories:

The elegance of the writing:

Poor Acceptable Average Good Excellent

The seamlessness of the writing:

Poor Acceptable Average Good Excellent

How imaginative the writing is:

Very imaginative   Fairly imaginative
Fairly unimaginative   Very unimaginative

This also fixes the extra problem of the 'treble-barrelled' question because the original form actually asks about three attributes of the writing. The reader's views about the three qualities may vary.

It may be argued that the issue is a nit-picking one: someone reading the question obviously knows that he or she is being asked to rate the quality of the book in terms of each attribute. The problem is that the impact of a disjunction between question and answer is simply not known, so the publisher may well get the connection between question and answers wrong. Also, people whose first language is not the one used in the question will appreciate the extra care.

or all of these? Respondents are likely to vary in their interpretation of the question and this will be a source of error. A favourite general question comes from Karl Marx's *Enquête Ouvrière*, a questionnaire sent to 25 000 French socialists and others (though there is apparently no record of any being returned). The final (the one-hundredth!) question reads:

What is the general, physical, intellectual, and moral condition of men and women employed in your trade? (Bottomore and Rubel 1963: 218).

Avoid leading questions
Leading or loaded questions push respondents in a particular direction, although those participating in a study may rebut an implied answer (although not everyone feels comfortable doing so). A question like:

Would you agree to cutting taxes, even though welfare payments for the most needy sections of the population might be reduced?

is likely to make it difficult for some people to disagree, even if they think that taxes are too high. But once again, Marx is the source of a favourite leading question:

If you are paid piece rates, is the quality of the article made a pretext for fraudulent deductions from wages? (Bottomore and Rubel 1963: 215).

Avoid questions that actually ask two questions
The double-barrelled question is a clear instance of the transgression of this rule, but there are also more subtle versions of the problem. A question such as:

Which party did you vote for in the 2006 federal election?

provides an illustration. What if the respondent did not vote? The question is really two questions, which should be asked separately:

Did you vote in the 2006 federal election?

Yes _____
No _____

If YES, for which political party did you vote?

Another way in which more than one question can be asked is with a question like:

How effective have your different job search strategies been?

Very effective _____
Fairly effective _____
Not very effective _____
Not at all effective _____

The obvious difficulty is that a respondent may or may not use different job search strategies. Also, if respondents use more than one strategy, estimates of effectiveness may vary for each strategy. A mechanism is needed to assess the success of each strategy rather than forcing respondents to average out their sense of how successful the various strategies are.

Avoid questions that include negatives

The problem with questions with 'not' or similar formulations in them is that some respondents may miss the word 'not' and give an answer opposite to what was intended. There are occasions when it is impossible to avoid negatives in a question, but those like the following should be avoided as far as possible:

Do you agree with the view that university students should not have to take out loans to finance their education?

Instead, the question should be asked in a positive format: 'Some university students have to take out loans to finance their education. Is that fair?' Questions with double negatives are never appropriate, because it is difficult to know how to respond to them. Take the following example:

Would you rather not drink non-alcoholic beer?

It is difficult to know what a 'yes' or 'no' answer would actually mean in this case.

One context in which it is difficult to avoid using questions with negatives pertains to Likert-style items. Identifying respondents with response sets may require reversing the direction of some questions (more on this later in the chapter), making negatives difficult to avoid.

Minimize technical terms

Use simple, plain language and avoid jargon. Do not ask a question like:

Do you sometimes feel alienated from your work?

The problem here is that many respondents do not know the meaning of 'alienated,' and even if they do, they are likely to have different views on what it means. The same goes for acronyms and abbreviations—avoid them whenever possible. Consider the following question:

The influence of the CAUT on national politics has declined in recent years.

Strongly agree _____
Agree _____
Undecided _____
Disagree _____
Strongly disagree _____

The use of abbreviations such as CAUT (the Canadian Association of University Teachers) is a problem because many people are unfamiliar with what the initials stand for.

Does the respondent have the requisite knowledge?

There is little point to ask about matters unfamiliar to respondents. For example, it would not be useful to ask the general public questions about CAUT, because very few people have heard of the organization. Similarly, it is very doubtful that meaningful data about people's opinions on foreign affairs can be gained from respondents who do not follow international political issues.

Ensure symmetry between a closed question and its answers

A common mistake is for a question and its answers to be out of phase with each other, as in: 'Do you believe in God? Select one: strongly agree, agree, neither agree nor disagree, disagree, strongly disagree.'

It's not clear how the response categories relate to the question.

Ensure that the answers provided for a closed question are balanced

A fairly common error when asking closed questions is for the answers provided to be unbalanced. For example, imagine being given a series of options like:

Excellent _____
Good _____
Borderline _____
Poor _____

The response choices are weighted towards a favourable response. Excellent and Good are both positive; Borderline is a neutral or middle position; and Poor is a negative response. A second negative response choice such as Very poor is needed.

Memory problems

Do not overstretch people's memories. Although it would be nice to have accurate replies to a question about the number of times respondents have used their cell phones in the previous month, it is highly unlikely that most people can in fact recall such events accurately over such a long time (perhaps other than those who have not used their phones at all or only once or twice in the preceding month). It is for this reason that a suitable time frame should be used, such as per day in the case of cell phone use.

Don't know

One area of controversy when asking closed questions is whether to offer a 'don't know' or 'no opinion' option. The issue chiefly relates to questions concerning attitudes. The main argument for including a 'don't know' option is that *not* to include one risks forcing people to express views that they do not really hold. Many advocate offering survey respondents the 'don't know' option in the form of a filter question to remove those who do not hold an opinion on a topic. This means that the interviewer needs to ask two questions, the first being 'Do you have an opinion on this issue?', with the second question asked only of those who have an opinion.

The alternative argument in connection with 'don't know' is that making it an option allows some respondents to select it when they cannot be bothered to do the required thinking on the issue. A series of experiments conducted in the US found that many respondents who express a lack of opinion on a topic do in fact hold one (Krosnick *et al.* 2002). Respondents with lower levels of education are especially prone to selecting the 'don't know' option; and later questions in a questionnaire are more likely to elicit a 'don't know' response. The latter finding implies a kind of question order effect, a topic addressed in the next section; respondents may become increasingly tired or bored as the questioning proceeds and therefore more lazy in their answers. The researchers concluded that data quality is not enhanced by the inclusion of a 'don't know' option and that it may prevent some respondents from expressing an opinion that they probably hold. Consequently, these researchers would *not* offer a 'don't know' option unless absolutely necessary.

Question order

Quite a lot of research has been carried out on how asking questions at different points in an interview schedule affects people's responses. Few if any consistent effects of question order have been unveiled, with different results demonstrated on various occasions. Mayhew (2000) provided an interesting anecdote on question order in relation to a crime survey. The question 'Taking everything into account, would you say the police in this area do a good job or a poor job?' appeared twice by mistake for half of the respondents—once early on, but also later in the context of questions on contact with the police. Almost a quarter (22 per cent) gave a more positive rating the second time. Mayhew suggested that as the interview wore on, respondents became more sensitized to crime-related issues and more sympathetic to the pressures on the police. As nice as this explanation sounds, it cannot explain the 13 per cent who gave a lower rating. That is quite a reliability issue. Also, see Box 5.5.

However, it is difficult to draw general lessons from such research, at least in part because experiments in question order do not always reveal clear-cut effects, even in cases where effects might legitimately have been expected. Nonetheless, two general lessons have emerged:

- All respondents in a survey should receive questions in the same order.
- Researchers should be sensitive to the possible effects a question could have on subsequent questions.

Box 5.5   About question order

Imagine that there are two pollsters: one who wants the Liberals to look good, another who favours the Conservatives. The key question in both their surveys is: 'In the upcoming federal election, for which party do you intend to vote?' That question would be followed by an alphabetical list of the main political parties. Look at the two sets of Likert items that follow (assume there are five response options from 'strongly agree' to 'strongly disagree'), and imagine that the items immediately *preceded* the voting question. Try to determine whether (and how) these items would influence the voting question.

Set One:
1. It is essential to honour the Kyoto Protocol in order to protect the environment.
2. Tax cuts should wait until we clean up the environment.
3. Too many Canadian soldiers have died in Afghanistan.
4. A national daycare program would help most working families.

Set Two:
1. The recent reduction in the Goods and Services Tax helps everyone.
2. Canada's mounting debt is mortgaging the future of its children.
3. Canada's military presence in Afghanistan has helped the Afghan people, especially women and children.
4. The government should register criminals, not guns.

In case you do not follow politics closely, the first set would probably increase the number of people saying they would vote Liberal, the second would likely do the same for declarations of intent to vote Conservative. Although most pollsters avoid such blatant biases, sometimes more subtle influences on respondents go unnoticed. Also, did you notice the problem of response set? In any event, this is an interesting exercise because it illustrates the importance of question order in survey research—if a researcher really wanted to use these Likert items, it would be much better to place them *after* the voting question.

In addition, the following rules about question order are sometimes proposed:

- Early questions should be directly related to the announced research topic. This removes the possibility that respondents will be wondering at an early stage in the interview why they are being asked apparently irrelevant questions. This injunction also means that personal questions about age, social background, and so on should *not* be asked at the beginning of an interview.

- As far as possible, questions likely to be important or meaningful to respondents should be asked early in the interview, so that their interest and attention may be stimulated. This suggestion may conflict with the previous one if questions about the research topic are not of interest to respondents. In any case, questions relating to the research topic that may grab participants' attention should be asked at or close to the start of the interview.

- Potentially embarrassing questions or ones that may be a source of anxiety should be left, if at all possible, until later in the schedule, but not

to the very end. The respondent should not leave the interview or complete the questionnaire with misgivings or negative feelings about the research.

- With a long schedule or questionnaire, questions should be grouped logically and into related sections, and should not jump back and forth from one topic to another.

- Within each group of questions, general questions should precede specific ones. When a specific question comes first, the aspect of the general question covered by the specific one may be discounted in the minds of respondents, who feel they have already covered it. For example, if a question about how people feel about their salary precedes a general question about job satisfaction, some respondents may discount the issue of pay when responding about job satisfaction, having already answered it. Similarly, an item about whether abortion is morally acceptable in cases in which the mother's life is threatened may affect answers to a later, more general item such as: 'Abortion is a matter of individual personal choice.' Some who would otherwise disagree with that statement may have second thoughts about it because of the earlier item.

- It is sometimes recommended that questions dealing with opinions and attitudes precede questions about behaviour and knowledge. This is because questions that tap opinions and attitudes may be affected by the latter sorts of questions. For instance, if a husband reports that he does only 20 per cent of the housework, making that statement can affect how he responds when asked if housework should be shared equally between spouses.
- If a respondent provides an answer to a question to be asked later in the interview, the question should be repeated when the interviewer arrives at the spot at which it is normally asked. A different answer may be forthcoming at the latter juncture because of question order effects.

Designing the questionnaire

Clear presentation

Make sure that the layout is easy on the eye and that it facilitates answering all the questions applicable to the respondent. At the very least, a variety of print styles (for example, different fonts, print sizes, bold, italics, and capitals) can enhance the appearance *so long as they are used in a consistent manner*. This last point means, for example, using one style for general instructions, one for all headings, one for all specific instructions (like 'Go to question 7'), and so on. Mixing print styles, so that one style is sometimes used for both general instructions and then specific questions, can confuse respondents.

Vertical or horizontal closed answers?

Bearing in mind that most questions in a questionnaire are likely to be closed, one consideration is whether to arrange the fixed answers vertically or horizontally. Very often, the nature of the answers dictates a vertical arrangement because of sheer length. Many writers prefer a vertical format whenever possible because of the greater potential for confusion in horizontal format (for example, see Box 5.6). With the latter there is a risk, especially if the questionnaire is being answered in haste, that the required tick will be placed in the wrong space—for example, indicating Conservatives when NDP is the intended response. Also, a vertical format more clearly distinguishes questions from answers. To some extent, these potential problems can be reduced through the judicious use of spacing and print variation, but they represent significant considerations. A further reason why vertical alignments

---

Box 5.6   Closed question with a vertical or a horizontal format?

The following question is adapted from the *2006 Canadian Election Study—Post Election Survey*:

Which party did you like most in the 2006 Canadian federal election campaign?

1. Liberals _____
2. Conservatives _____
3. NDP _____
4. Bloc Québécois _____
5. Green Party _____
6. Another party, specify: _____
7. None of them _____
8. Don't know _____

Which party did you like most in the 2006 Canadian federal election campaign?

1. Liberals _____   2. Conservatives _____   3. NDP _____   4. Bloc Québécois _____
5. Green Party _____   6. Another party, specify: _____
7. None of them _____   8. Don't know _____

can be superior is that they are probably easier to code, especially when pre-codes appear on the questionnaire. However, when there is a battery of questions with identical answer formats, as in a Likert scale, a vertical format takes up too much space. One way of dealing with this is to use abbreviations with an accompanying explanation. An example is found in Box 5.7.

Identifying response sets in a Likert scale

One of the advantages of using closed questions is that they are pre-coded, which simplifies the data entry for computer analysis. However, some thought has to go into the scoring of the items, such as the ones presented in Box 5.7. One can, for example, score questions 3, 4, and 6 as follows:

Strongly agree = 5
Agree = 4
Undecided = 3
Disagree = 2
Strongly disagree = 1

Box 5.7   Formatting a Likert scale

In the next section you are presented with a set of statements. Please indicate your level of agreement or disagreement with each by indicating whether you:

Strongly Agree (sa), Agree (a), are Undecided (u), Disagree (d), or Strongly Disagree (sd).

(Please indicate your level of agreement by circling the appropriate response.)

3. My job is like a hobby to me.

    sa   a   u   d   sd

4. My job is usually interesting enough to keep me from getting bored.

    sa   a   u   d   sd

5. It seems that my friends are more interested in their jobs than I am in mine.

    sa   a   u   d   sd

6. I enjoy my work more than my leisure time.

    sa   a   u   d   sd

Using that setup, a high score for the items (a score of 5 or 4) indicates satisfaction with the job, and a low score (1 or 2) indicates an absence of job satisfaction. However, for question 5, the picture is different. Here, agreement indicates a *lack* of job satisfaction, and disagreement suggests satisfaction with one's job. One would have to reverse the scoring of this item, so that:

Strongly agree = 1
Agree = 2
Undecided = 3
Disagree = 4
Strongly disagree = 5

Now, with this reverse coding, for all four items the higher the score, the greater the job satisfaction. If one wanted to combine all four items to form a job satisfaction index, one could simply add the scores for the four items together.

A researcher may intentionally create a scale in which agreement with some items indicates high job satisfaction, but agreement with the others indicates low satisfaction. This is to identify people who exhibit *response sets*, mentioned in the last chapter. Under these conditions, if someone were to agree with all items or disagree with them all, the survey is unlikely to provide a valid assessment of job satisfaction for that person. One cannot agree with all items or disagree with them all and maintain a consistent attitude. If someone does that, they are not giving authentic answers and may have to be excluded from the study.

Clear instructions about how to respond

Always be clear about how respondents should indicate their replies to closed questions. Are they supposed to place a tick by the appropriate answer, or are they to underline it? Should they circle it? Is choosing more than one answer acceptable? If not, this should be indicated in the instructions, for example:

(Please choose the ONE answer that best represents your views by placing a tick in the appropriate box.)

If this is not made clear and some respondents choose more than one answer, their replies will have to be treated as if they had not answered. If choosing more than one category is acceptable, this too must be made clear, for example:

Practical Tip

Common mistakes when asking questions

Over the years, Bryman has read many projects and dissertations based on structured interviews and questionnaires. A number of mistakes recurred regularly, including:

- An excessive use of open questions. While a resistance to closed questions is understandable, open questions are likely to reduce the response rate and cause analysis problems. Keep the number to a minimum.

- An excessive use of yes/no questions. Sometimes students include lots of questions that provide just a yes/no form of response. This is usually the result of inadequate thinking and preparation. The world rarely fits into this kind of response. Take a question like:

  > Are you satisfied with opportunities for promotion in your firm?
  >
  > Yes _____   No _____

Such attitudes are complex, and most respondents are not simply 'satisfied' or 'not satisfied.' For one thing, people's feelings about such things vary in intensity. An improvement would be to rephrase the item as:

  > How satisfied are you with opportunities for promotion in your firm?
  >
  > Very satisfied _____
  > Satisfied _____
  > Neither satisfied nor dissatisfied _____
  > Dissatisfied _____
  > Very dissatisfied _____

This sort of answer also makes it possible to calculate some widely used statistics that are discussed in Chapter 12.

- Generally, do not let respondents choose more than one answer. While sometimes that is unavoidable, replies to such questions are often difficult to analyze.

- In spite of constant warnings about the problems of overlapping categories, students (and some professional researchers who should know better) still formulate response choices that are not mutually exclusive or omit some categories. For example:

  > How many times per week do you use public transport?
  >
  > 1–3 times _____
  > 3–6 times _____
  > 6–9 times _____
  > More than 10 times _____

Not only do respondents not know which to choose if the answer is 3 or 6 times, there is no answer for someone whose response is 10.

- Students sometimes do not make answers correspond to questions. For example:

  > Do you go to your gym or fitness centre regularly?
  >
  > Every day _____
  > 5–6 times per week _____
  > 2–4 times per week _____
  > Once per week _____
  > Once per month _____
  > Less than once per month _____

The problem here is that the answer to the question is logically either 'yes' or 'no.' However, the student quite sensibly wants to gain some idea of frequency (a good idea in light of the second point in this list). The problem is that the question and the response categories are out of kilter. A better question is:

  > How frequently do you go to your gym or fitness centre?
  >
  > Every day _____
  > 5–6 times per week _____
  > 2–4 times per week _____
  > Once per week _____
  > Once per month _____
  > Less than once per month _____

Box 5.8   A vignette to establish family obligations

Jim and Margaret Robinson are a married couple in their early forties. Jim's parents, who live several hundred miles away, have had a serious car accident and they need long-term daily help. Jim is their only son. He and his wife both could get transfers to work nearer his parents.

CARD E

(a) From the card, what should Jim and Margaret do?

Move to live near Jim's parents

Have Jim's parents move to live with them

Give Jim's parents money to help them pay for daily care

Let Jim's parents make their own arrangements

Do something else (specify)

Don't know

(b) In fact, Jim and Margaret are prepared to move and live near Jim's parents, but teachers at their children's school say that moving right now could have a bad effect on their children's education.

What should Jim and Margaret do? Should they move or should they stay?

Move

Stay

(c) Why do you think they should move/stay?

PROBE FULLY VERBATIM

(d) Jim and Margaret do go to live near Jim's parents. A year later Jim's mother dies and his father's condition gets worse so that he needs full-time care.

Should Jim or Margaret take an extended leave from work to take care of Jim's father?

IF YES: Who should, Jim or Margaret?

Yes, Jim should give up his job

Yes, Margaret should give up her job

No, neither should give up their jobs

Don't know/Depends

Source: Adapted from Finch (1987: 108).

(Please choose ALL answers that represent your views by placing a tick in the appropriate boxes. You may tick more than one box for each question—choose as many as apply to you.)

It is a common error for such instructions to be omitted and for respondents to be unsure about how to reply.

Keep question and answers together

This is a simple and obvious, though often transgressed, requirement. A question, or the question and the answers accompanying it, should not be split between two separate pages. A common error is for a question to appear at the bottom of a page and the responses on the next page. Doing this carries the risk of the respondent failing to answer the question, or paying insufficient attention to the question and giving a superficial answer (a problem that is especially likely when a series of questions with a common answer format is being used, as with a Likert scale).

Vignette questions

A form of closed question that is often used in examining people's ethical standards and beliefs is the vignette technique. It involves presenting respondents with one or more scenarios and asking them how they would respond if confronted with the circumstances depicted in the scenario. For example, Achille and Ogloff (1997) used vignettes of dying patients in their study of assisted suicide and found lethal injection less acceptable (79 per cent) than withdrawal of life support (90 per cent) among BC respondents. Box 5.8 describes a vignette employed in a study of family obligations. It sought to measure judgments about how family members should respond to relatives who are in need, and who in the family should do the responding.

The vignette was designed to tease out respondents' norms concerning several aspects of family obligations: the nature of the care (whether long- or short-term, and whether direct involvement or just the provision of resources would be appropriate); the significance of geographical propinquity; the dilemma of paid work and care; and the gender component of who should give up a job if necessary to oversee care. There is a gradual increase in the specificity of the situation facing Jim and Margaret as the vignette develops. At first the respondent is unaware of whether Jim and Margaret are prepared to move, then sees that they are. They do in fact move, which leads to whether one of them should become a full-time caregiver.

Many aspects of the issues being tapped by the series of questions can be accessed through attitude items, such as

> When a working couple decide that one of them should quit their job to care for ailing parents, the wife should be the one to give up her job.
>
> | | |
> |---|---|
> | Strongly agree | _____ |
> | Agree | _____ |
> | Undecided | _____ |
> | Disagree | _____ |
> | Strongly disagree | _____ |

The advantage of the vignette over such an attitude question is that it anchors the choice in a more realistic situation and thus reduces the possibility of an unreflective reply. Finch (1987) also argued that for a sensitive topic like this, some respondents may feel threatened and judged on their replies. The fact that the questions are about other people (and imaginary ones at that) creates a certain distance between the questioning and the respondent, and hence the chance for a more candid answer. One obvious requirement of the vignette technique is that scenarios must be believable.

Finch also pointed to some limits to this style of questioning. It is more or less impossible to establish what assumptions are being made about the characters in the scenario (such as their age, ethnicity, and number of children at home) and the significance of those assumptions for the validity and comparability of people's replies. It is also difficult to establish how far people's answers reflect their own normative views or indeed how they themselves would act when confronted with the kinds of choices revealed in the scenarios. Often how people say they would act in a particular situation is very different from how they would really act. People are not necessarily being dishonest—predicting behaviour, whether

Practical Tip

Getting help in designing questions

When designing questions, be empathetic—put yourself in the position of the people who will be answering them. This can be difficult, because some (if not all) of the questions may not apply to the person producing them—for example, to a young student doing a survey of retired people. However, try to think about how you would reply. This means concentrating not just on the questions themselves but also on links between the questions. For example, do filter questions work in the expected way?

Then try the questions out on some friends or classmates, as in a pilot study. Ask them to be critical and to consider how well the questions connect to each other. Also, look at the questionnaires and structured interview schedules experienced researchers have devised. They may not have asked questions on your topic, but how they have asked questions should give you an idea of what to do and what to avoid.

one's own or someone else's, is often more difficult than one would imagine. That is why experiments, structured observation, historical analysis, and other research techniques are so important. In spite of these reservations, the vignette technique can provide useful information, or at least a starting point for further research.

Pilot studies and pre-testing questions

It is always desirable to conduct a pilot study before collecting data from respondents, not just to ensure that individual questions operate well but also to check whether the research instrument as a whole is appropriate. Pilot studies may be particularly crucial in research based on questionnaires, since there is no interviewer present to clear up any confusion.

Here are some specific uses of pilot studies in survey research:

- If the study is going to employ mainly closed questions, open questions in pilot qualitative interviews can be used to generate the fixed-choice answers.
- Piloting an interview schedule can provide interviewers with some experience in using it and can give them greater confidence.

- If everyone (or virtually everyone) who answers a question gives the same answer, the resulting data are not likely to be useful. A pilot study allows such questions to be identified and modified into one with variable answers.
- In survey interviews, it may be possible to identify questions that make respondents feel uncomfortable and to detect any tendency for interest to flag at certain junctures.
- Questions that seem not to be understood (more likely to be realized in an interview than in a questionnaire context) or questions that are often not answered should become apparent. The problem of questions being skipped may be due to confusing or threatening phrasing, poorly worded instructions, or confusing positioning in the interview schedule or questionnaire (see Box 5.9). Whatever the cause, missing data are undesirable and a pilot study may be instrumental in identifying the problem.
- Pilot studies allow the researcher to determine the adequacy of the instructions given to the interviewers, or to respondents completing a questionnaire.
- It may be possible to consider how well the questions flow and whether it is necessary to move some of them around to improve that aspect of the study.

The pilot should not be carried out on people who may become members of the sample in the full study, since participating in the pilot study could affect how people respond in the study proper. Also, with small populations, the selecting out of a number of people could affect the representativeness of any subsequent sample. If this is an issue, do the pilot study on respondents who are not in that population, but are similar to those who are. Beagan (2002) did this in her study of medical students.

Using existing questions

One final observation regarding the asking of questions is to consider using questions employed by

---

Box 5.9   A bad questionnaire

How would you fix this questionnaire?

'Hello. I am taking a sociology course on research methods and would like to ask you some questions. Would that be OK?'

1. Were you ever scared that you were HIV-positive?

   Yes _____   No _____

For questions 2 to 6, please answer Agree or Disagree.

2. As a religious person, I feel sorry for AIDS victims.
3. I think victims of any disease deserve compassion.
4. I think the new legislation will be a boon to AIDS victims.
5. The government should not allocate more money to AIDS research.
6. People with AIDS and other sexual diseases should be quarantined.

   If agree, has your viewpoint changed since the 1980s when AIDS first widely emerged?

   Yes _____   No _____

Now there are just a few more questions.

7. If one were planned, would you fight having an AIDS hospice on your street?

   Yes _____   No _____

8. How does your spouse feel about AIDS victims?

   Compassionate _____   Sympathetic _____
   Concerned _____   Angry _____
   Don't know _____

9. Elizabeth Taylor has raised much money for AIDS research. Should people be doing more fundraising in this area?

   Yes _____   No _____

10. Do you know any AIDS victims? Yes _____ No _____

Finally I need a few facts for comparison purposes.

11. How old are you? _____
12. Did you graduate from high school?

    Yes _____   No _____

13. Did you ever have yourself tested for AIDS?

    Yes _____   No _____

Thank you for your cooperation.

other researchers for at least part of the question-naire or interview schedule. This may seem like stealing, but using existing questions means that the questions have in a sense already been piloted and investigated for their reliability and validity. A further advantage of using existing questions is that they allow comparisons with other research, showing whether change has occurred or whether location makes a difference in the findings. At the very least, examining questions used by others may provide ideas about how best to approach the research questions, even if a later decision is to modify them.

The use of existing questions is a common practice among researchers. For example, the researchers who developed the scale designed to measure attitudes to vegetarians (Box 3.7) used several existing questions devised for measuring other concepts in which they were interested, such as authoritarianism and politi-cal conservatism. These other measures had known levels of reliability and validity. Similarly, Walklate (2000: 194) described how in developing a survey instrument for victims of crime, she and her col-leagues used 'tried and tested questions taken from pre-existing criminal victimization surveys amended to take account of our own more localized concerns.'

Checklist of issues to consider for a structured interview schedule or questionnaire

☑ Is a clear and comprehensive introduction to the research provided for respondents?

☑ Can questions used by other researchers be used?

☑ Will the questions provide answers to all the research questions?

☑ Can any questions not strictly relevant to the research questions be dropped?

☑ Has the questionnaire been pre-tested with some appropriate respondents?

☑ If a structured interview schedule is used, are the instructions clear (for example, with filter questions, is it clear which question(s) should be omitted)?

☑ Are instructions about how to record responses clear (for example, whether to tick or circle; whether more than one response is allowable)?

☑ Has the number of open questions been limited?

☑ Can respondents indicate levels of intensity in their replies, rather than being forced into yes or no answers?

☑ Have questions and their answers been kept on the same page?

☑ Have sociodemographic questions been left until close to the end of the interview or questionnaire?

☑ Are questions relating to the research topic asked near the beginning of the interview or questionnaire?

☑ Have the following been avoided:

– Ambiguous terms in questions or response choices?

– Long questions?

– Double-barrelled questions?

– Very general questions?

– Leading questions?

– Questions that include negatives?

– Questions using technical terms?

☑ Do respondents have the requisite knowledge to answer the questions?

☑ Is there an appropriate match between ques-tions and response choices?

☑ Are the response choices properly balanced?

☑ Do any of the questions depend too much on respondent memory?

If using a Likert scale approach:

☑ Have some items that have to be reverse-scored been included, in order to identify response sets?

☑ Is there evidence that the items really do relate to the same underlying cluster of attitudes, so that the items can be aggregated?

☑ Are the response choices exhaustive and not overlapping?

— Key Points —

- While open questions undoubtedly have advantages in survey research, closed ones are typically preferable. They facilitate the asking of the questions, the recording of answers, and coding. This point applies especially to questionnaires.

- Open questions of the kind used in qualitative interviewing can have a useful role in formulating fixed-choice answers.

- Learning rules of question-asking allows one to avoid some serious problems.

- Question order is very important and some general rules should be followed.

- The visual presentation of closed questions and their general layout are important considerations in designing questionnaires.

- Always put yourself in the position of the respondent when devising questions.

- Ensure that the survey questions generate data appropriate to the research questions.

- A pilot study can clear up problems in question formulation.

— Questions for Review —

Open or closed questions?

- Why are closed questions preferred to open ones in survey research?

- What are the limitations of closed questions and how can each limitation be reduced?

Types of questions

- What are the main types of questions likely to be used in a structured interview or questionnaire?

Question order

- How strong is the evidence that question order can significantly affect answers?

Question layout

- Why is a vertical format for presenting answers to closed questions usually preferable to a horizontal format?

Vignette questions

- In what circumstances are vignette questions especially appropriate? Make one up to examine an addiction of your choice.

Pre-testing questions

- Why is it important to pre-test questions?

Using existing questions

- Why should one consider using questions devised by others?

6

Structured Observation

Chapter overview

Structured observation is a relatively underused method in social research. It entails the direct observation of behaviour, which is analyzed using categories that are devised before the observation begins. This chapter explores:

- the limitations of survey research for the study of behaviour;
- different forms of observation in social research;
- the potential of structured observation to contribute to our understanding of social behaviour;

- how to devise an observation schedule;
- different strategies for conducting structured observation;
- issues of reliability and validity in structured observation;
- field studies, in which a researcher intervenes in actual social life and records what happens as a consequence of the intervention;
- ethical issues in the above; and
- some criticisms of structured observation.

Introduction

Structured observation is a technique in which the researcher employs explicitly formulated rules for the observation, categorization, and recording of behaviour. One of its main advantages is that behaviour is observed directly, unlike in survey research where actions must be inferred from what the respondent reports. As noted in previous chapters, such inferences can be problematic—what people say and what they do may not be the same thing. Structured observation offers a possible solution to that problem.

Although structured observation may appear to be a logical alternative to survey research, it has not attracted a large following and tends to be used only in certain research settings such as classrooms, courts, and hospitals. One reason for this is that certain types of behaviour—such as criminal activity—are inherently difficult to observe. Another reason is that many social researchers want to generalize their findings, which means selecting large, random samples that provide information that can be extrapolated to some population of interest. Normally it is not feasible to adopt that sort of methodology in a structured observation study.

Problems with survey research

Chapter 4 dealt with several different aspects of survey research, including the problems typically associated with it. Box 6.1 summarizes some of the main elements. Also recall that practitioners have developed, with varying degrees of success, ways of dealing with these shortcomings or at least of reducing their impact.

So why not just observe behaviour directly?

An obvious solution to the problems identified in Box 6.1 is to observe people's behaviour directly rather than relying on research instruments like surveys. Structured observation (sometimes called 'systematic observation') is one way to do that. (See Box 6.2 for other types of observation research.) Using this method, the researcher formulates explicit rules outlining what behaviours are to be observed and how the observations are to be recorded. Each person in the study is observed for a predetermined period of time using the same rules. These rules are articulated in what is usually referred to as an *observation schedule*, which bears many similarities to a structured interview schedule. The resulting data resemble survey data in that the information collected on different aspects of behaviour can be treated as variables for analysis.

One of the classic schedules for the observation of small-group behaviour was developed by Bales (1951) (see Figure 6.1). Using Bales' observation schedule, it would be possible, for example, to compare leaders' and followers' styles in terms of such things as the relative emphasis on asking questions and answering them, on silence and talking, and so forth. Age and gender differences in tension reduction efforts,

---

Box 6.1   Problems with using survey research to investigate behaviour

- *Problems of meaning*. People may vary in their interpretations of key terms in a question. Does 'watching television' include having it on while making dinner or must one be concentrating on it?

- *Problems of memory*. Respondents may not remember certain aspects of their behaviour, or they may have false memories of it. For example, people may underestimate the number of alcoholic drinks they consume in a typical week.

- *Social desirability effect*. Respondents often give answers that they think will reflect well on them, perhaps the most important shortcoming of the method. This could mean, for example, overestimating amounts given to charity and underreporting traffic tickets.

- *Threatening or embarrassing questions*. These may lead to replies that are not fully truthful. For example, men who recently underwent surgery for prostate cancer may not want to admit to any incontinence.

- *Gap between stated and actual behaviour*. How people say they would behave and how they actually behave is often inconsistent (see Box 3.9). Husbands, for example, traditionally overestimate how much time they devote to housework. Perrucci et al. (2000) found two quite different pictures of racial relations on a predominantly white university campus—what they called 'front stage' and 'back stage.' The latter only became fully apparent when direct observation supplemented questionnaires, and showed less acceptance of racial minorities.

Box 6.2   Other types of observation research

- *Participant observation*. This is one of the best-known methods of social science research, especially in sociology and anthropology. It is primarily qualitative and entails the relatively prolonged immersion of the observer in a social setting (for example, a group, organization, or community). The main goal is usually to elicit the meanings the people being observed attribute to their environment and behaviour. Participant observers vary considerably in how much they participate in the social settings in which they locate themselves. Chapter 8 offers a more detailed treatment.

- *Non-participant observation*. This term applies to a situation in which the observer does not participate in what is going on in the social setting, other than to observe it. Bell (2007) conducted this sort of observation on western-Canadian separatists. It can be called 'unobtrusive observation' if the people observed are unaware that they are being viewed and analyzed. It may involve structured or unstructured observation (see below). Bell's observation was unstructured, but the people he was studying knew he was observing and analyzing them.

- *Unstructured observation*. As its name implies, unstructured observation does not use formalized rules for making observations or for recording the information gained. Instead, the aim is to record, in as much detail as possible, the behaviour of participants, and then develop a narrative account (story) of that behaviour. Most participant observation is unstructured.

1	Helps, rewards, affirms others
2	Tension release, jokes, shows satisfaction
3	Agrees, concurs, complies
4	Gives direction
5	Gives opinion, evaluation
6	Gives orientation, repeats, clarifies
7	Asks orientation, for repetition/clarification
8	Asks opinions
9	Asks for direction, possible ways of action
10	Disagrees, withholds help
11	Shows tension, withdraws
12	Shows antagonism, deflates, defends self

Sum of 13: Balancing task areas (neutral affect)

6 + 7 Communication

5 + 8 Evaluation

4 + 9 Decision

Sum of 13: Balancing socioemotional reactions

(−) (+)

10 + 3 (Dis)agreement

11 + 2 Tension (reduction)

12 + 1 (Dis)integration

Adapted from Bales (1951)

Figure 6.1 Small group interaction process

categories 1 and 12, could be explored. It could also be used to compare different leadership styles. For example, is there less tension and thus less need for tension relief in an 'authoritarian' or in a 'shared' leadership style? A scheme like this could help leadership trainees improve on their leadership abilities.

One might want to code what is happening every 15 seconds. The coding for a 12-minute period might then look like Figure 6.2. Notice how questions tend to be followed by answers and negative affect by smoothing positive affect (sum of 13). Two

types of leaders often emerge, a task specialist and a socioemotional leader, the latter being more responsible for group members' feelings.

The observation schedule

Devising a schedule for recording observations is clearly a crucial step in a structured observation project. The considerations are very similar to those involved in producing a structured interview schedule. For example:

- A clear focus is necessary, meaning that the research problem needs to be clearly stated. The observer must know exactly who is to be observed and which of their many behaviours are to be recorded.
- As with the production of a closed question for a structured interview schedule, the categories of behaviour must be both mutually exclusive (that is, not overlapping) and exhaustive (everything must have a category). What if someone knocks on the door to ask about emptying the trash can while the study is underway? Perhaps the best approach is to have a category of behaviour coded 'other' or 'interruption.' Pilot studies help to reveal possible problems associated with a lack of exhaustiveness.
- The classification scheme must be easy to use. Complex systems listing many types of behaviour may be unworkable. Much like interviewers using a structured interview schedule, observers need to be trained, but even with training it is easy for an observer to become flustered or confused if faced with too many options.
- A problem can arise if the observation schedule requires too much interpretation on the part of the observer. For example, in Bales' scheme it can be difficult to distinguish between a Category 10, *withholds help*, and a Category 11, *withdraws*. If

7	7	6	6	6	7	6	6	8	5	10	2
5	8	5	12	1	9	9	4	4	5	4	4
10	11	12	12	2	1	1	11	2	8	8	5
5	10	10	2	1	3	2	1	3	6	2	1

Figure 6.2 Coding sheet for imaginary study of small group

Note: Each cell represents a 15-second interval and each row is 3 minutes.

interpretation is needed, clear guidelines and considerable training and experience are required.

Strategies for observing behaviour

There are different ways to observe and record behaviours:

- One can record in terms of *incidents*. This means waiting for something to happen and then recording what follows from it. Essentially, this is what LaPiere (1934, Box 3.9) did as he waited for a Chinese couple to negotiate entry to a hotel or restaurant and then noted whether they were allowed in or not.
- One can observe and record a wide variety of behaviours, in either short or long periods of time. In the research reported in Box 2.3, children in St Helena were videotaped over a two-week period during their morning, lunch, and afternoon breaks. The tapes were then coded using 'the Playground Behaviour Observation Schedule, an instrument for recording the occurrence of 23 behaviours (e.g., games; fantasy play; character imitation; anti-social and pro-social behaviour) and their behaviour groupings (i.e., whether the behaviour was undertaken by an individual, a pair, by 3 to 5 children, or 6 or more). . . . A separate schedule was completed for each 30-second segment' (Charlton *et al.* 1998: 7).
- *Time sampling* is another approach to the observation of behaviour. In the Rosenhan study described later in this chapter, the hospital observers could be in the ward at 9 a.m. for an hour, at the nurses' desk at 11 a.m. for 15 minutes, and in the chapel at 3 p.m. for 5 minutes, etc., taking notes on what occurred (using the observation schedule).

Issues of reliability and validity

Compared with interviews and questionnaires, structured observation 'provides (*a*) more reliable information about events; (*b*) greater precision regarding their timing, duration, and frequency; (*c*) greater accuracy in the time ordering of variables; and (*d*) more accurate and economical reconstruction of large-scale social episodes' (McCall 1984: 277). This is a very strong endorsement, but there are issues of reliability and validity to consider. Some of them are similar to those faced by any researcher seeking to develop measures in social research (especially survey research), while others are specific to structured observation.

Reliability

One thing practitioners of structured observation have been concerned with is *inter-observer consistency*. Essentially, this entails considering how closely two or more observers of the same behaviour agree on how to code it (see Boxes 6.3 and 6.4).

A second consideration is *intra-observer consistency*—the degree of consistency in the application

---

Box 6.3   A study of shoplifting

Buckle and Farrington (1994) reported a replication of a study of department store shoplifting. Customers were selected at random as they entered the store and were followed by two observers until they left. The observers recorded such details as: cost of items bought; gender, race, and estimated age; and shopping behaviour. In the original study of 486 people, 9 people shoplifted; in the replication it was 6 out of 502. Most shoplifting was of small items of relatively little monetary value, and most shoplifters purchased other goods and then walked out with the stolen materials. In each instance shoplifters were likely to be male, but they were under 25 years of age in the first study and over 55 in the replication. Does this discrepancy mean that the study should be redone? Are larger sample sizes needed?

Box 6.4   Cohen's kappa

Cohen's kappa is a measure of the level of agreement between two people's coding decisions that takes into consideration agreement that can occur by chance. It can be applied to any coding. Much like Cronbach's alpha (see Chapter 3), the coefficient varies from 0 to 1. The closer it is to 1, the higher the agreement and the better the inter-observer consistency. As a rough rule of thumb, a coefficient over .75 is considered 'very good'; from .6 to .75, 'good'; 'fair' ranges from .4 up to .59.

Box 6.5   Reactive effects in social research in general

Webb *et al.* wrote about 'reactive measurement effect' (1966: 13). It occurs whenever a subject's knowledge of participating in research leads to a change in their behaviour, thus confounding the investigator's data. Response sets, social desirability, and political correctness can cause reactive effects. If a respondent reacts to the characteristics of the interviewers (such as their gender or ethnicity), that is another example of a reactive effect. Here are a few more:

- *The guinea pig effect* — awareness of being tested. The classic studies were done at the Hawthorne Works (located near Chicago) in the 1920s (see Roethlisberger and Dickson, 1939). A series of quasi-experiments showed that each time working conditions improved (such as through improved lighting), productivity went up, at least temporarily. But it also went up after working conditions deteriorated! It appeared that performance improved simply because the workers were being observed and analyzed, not because of the experimental manipulation itself — this is the so-called 'Hawthorne effect.' A well-known general problem in experimental studies is that some individuals seek out cues about the aims of the research, and then adjust what they say and do to make it consistent with what they believe to be the purpose of the study. That is a problem, even if such subjects are mistaken about the aims of the research.

- *Role selection*. Webb *et al.* argued that participants may be tempted to adopt a particular kind of role in research. Some people with no strong opinion on an item may develop one when asked, feeling they should be knowledgeable. Even telling them how important they are to the research can encourage some 'expertise.' Other, fairly opinionated individuals may back off a bit, scared by the tape recorder perhaps, or not wanting to come on too strongly to a stranger.

- *Researcher presence as a change agent*. The very fact that the researcher is present may itself cause things to be different. For example, the fact that there is an observer sitting in a classroom means a chair is being used that may otherwise have been unoccupied, which results in changes in space and privacy to those at close hand. When Whyte (1955) in his study of Cornerville joined one of the bowling teams, he in effect removed one of his subjects from that role and turned that person into a rival on an opposing team.

- *Trying to help or to be nice to the researcher*. Too often it is assumed that research participants are passive. But even in experiments this is not true. They may also be trying to please. An old saying holds that if you ask friends to do push-ups, they will say 'what?' or 'why?' But subjects in an experiment (especially students, the usual pool from which subjects are drawn) will say 'where?'! In fact, subjects generally try to do what they think they are supposed to do, although a few are deliberately mean and do the opposite. Some even ask 'Was I good?' at the end of the experiment. But such behaviour can be problematic if it affects the phenomenon being studied.

- Different researchers may elicit different reactions and may get the data they want by communicating, often unconsciously, their expectations. This is why experiments are supposed to be double blind so no one knows the hypothesis being tested (single blind means that just the subject is in the dark). Here, hiring others to collect the data can help.

Reactive effects are likely to occur in any research in which participants know they are the focus of investigation. Webb *et al.* called for greater use of what they called *unobtrusive measures* or non-reactive methods in which participants are not aware of the fact that they are being studied. Records can be checked, for instance, at hospitals and courts, removing the reactivity, but for ethical reasons permission must first be obtained, and getting such permission may be difficult or impossible.

Alternatively, the usual tools of social research can be used. A confidentiality guarantee and reminders of it may help, as can anonymous questionnaires and telephone (rather than in-person) interviews, although these have their own downsides. It also helps to phrase questions so they are as non-threatening and non-judgmental as possible, for example: 'Many people did not have time to vote in the referendum or could not make up their minds. Did you vote?' To allow more men to admit fear of being out late at night, do not ask how afraid they are. Use a vignette: 'John does not like to walk alone at night in his neighbourhood. There is a lot of crime there, and police officers are rarely if ever seen. Is John almost of the observation schedule by a single observer over time. This is clearly a difficult undertaking because of the capacity for people to behave differently depending on the context. Reliability may also be threatened because of the effects of such factors as observer fatigue and lapses in attention. This should not be exaggerated, however, because observers can be trained to get highly reliable results using complex coding schedules. The procedures for assessing intra-observer reliability across all possibilities are broadly similar to those applied to the issue of inter-observer consistency.

Validity

Measurement validity relates to the question of whether an indicator is measuring what it is supposed to measure, even when it is administered properly. The validity of any measure can also be affected by error that arises from faulty administration.

The first of these issues simply means that in structured observation it is necessary to attend to the same kinds of issues concerning the checking of validity (assessing face validity, concurrent validity, and so on) encountered in interviews and questionnaires. The second aspect of validity—error in implementation—relates to two matters in particular.

- Is the observation schedule administered as directed? This is the equivalent of ensuring that structured interviewers follow instructions exactly as indicated. Variability between observers or over time makes the measure unreliable and therefore invalid. Observers should have a thorough understanding of how the observation schedule is to be implemented.
- Do people change their behaviour because they know they are being observed? If they do, that

would constitute one of several kinds of 'reactive effects' that can occur in various forms of research (see Box 6.5). If people adjust the way they behave because they know they are being observed (perhaps because they want to be viewed in a favourable way by the observer), their behaviour would have to be considered atypical or not authentic. However, as McCall (1984) noted, there is evidence that participants become accustomed to being observed and that the researcher becomes less intrusive the longer he or she is in the field. This of course applies less to sensitive areas like sexual or deviant behaviour.

Field experiments as a form of structured observation

A field experiment is a study in which a researcher directly intervenes in a natural setting to observe the consequence of that intervention. That's what LaPiere (1934) did when he arranged for a Chinese couple to seek entry to hotels and restaurants in order to observe the effects (although his study was an imperfect experiment because there was no control group of non-Chinese people). Unlike most structured observation, in a field experiment participants do not know they are being studied.

Another famous field experiment was done by Rosenhan (1973). He was one of eight researchers who posed as patients and were admitted to mental hospitals in the US. Each pseudo-patient was instructed to claim 'hearing voices,' which resulted in diagnoses of schizophrenia. As soon as they were admitted, the pseudo-patients were instructed to cease exhibiting any symptoms. In spite of the fact that they were all 'sane,' it took many of them quite a long time to be released. The length of hospitalization varied between 7 and 52 days, with an average of 19 days. In four of the hospitals, pseudo-patients approached psychiatrists and nurses with a request for release, and recorded the nature of the response: 71 per cent of psychiatrists moved on with their heads averted and 88 per cent of nurses did likewise. To Rosenhan this indicated that a mental patient becomes powerless and depersonalized. This study is highly

Checklist for structured observation research

- ☑ Are the research questions stated clearly?
- ☑ Does the observation schedule indicate precisely the kinds of behaviour to be observed?
- ☑ Have observation categories been designed to minimize the need for observers to interpret what is going on?
- ☑ Has any overlap in the categories of behaviour been eliminated?

- ☑ Are the categories of behaviour exhaustive?
- ☑ Do the different categories of behaviour allow an answer to the research questions?
- ☑ Has a pilot study using the observation schedule been conducted?
- ☑ Are the coding instructions clear?
- ☑ Is it easy to log the behaviour while it is happening?

Ethical issue 6.1

Ethics of covert observation

In spite of the widespread condemnation of violations of informed consent and the view that covert observation is especially vulnerable to unethical practice in this regard, studies using this method still appear periodically. The defence is usually that the benefits outweigh the risk or harm. Virtually all codes of ethics allow covert research as a last resort, but often state that it should be avoided 'as far as possible.' Those who use this method argue that it is needed to prevent research participants from changing their behaviour because they know they are being studied. Still, where informed consent has not been obtained prior to the research, permission to use the data gathered should be obtained post-hoc. That is a general rule, but it is often broken in dealing with dangerous subjects, like pimps and other criminals. Where such permission has not been obtained, it is absolutely crucial to maintain the anonymity of the people observed.

One difficulty with the arguments justifying the use of covert methods is the assumption that it is impossible to obtain the data using other means. Covert observers sometimes base their judgments on the *anticipated* difficulty of gaining access to a setting rather than the actual experience of being denied entry. For example, Homan justified his use of covert participant observation of a religious sect on the grounds that sociologists are viewed very negatively by group members and therefore: 'It seemed probable that the prevalence of such a perception would prejudice the effectiveness of a fieldworker declaring an identity as sociologist' (Homan and Bulmer 1982: 107).

One of the most famous cases of controversial covert research is Humphreys' *Tearoom Trade* (1970), made less offensive and then partially replicated in Canada many years later by Desroches (1990). The researchers (Humphreys himself and police acting for Desroches) observed homosexual encounters in public toilets ('tearooms'), taking the role of 'watch queen'—someone who watches out for possible intruders while men meet and engage in sexual activity. Such 'voyeurism' was offensive to some critics.

As part of his research, Humphreys recorded the participants' car licence numbers. He was then able to track down their names and addresses, thus further invading their privacy, and ended up with a sample of 100 active tearoom-trade participants. To reduce the risk of being recognized, Humphreys waited a year before contacting his respondents, and also changed his hairstyle. After this deception, he then conducted an interview survey (Desroches did not do this) of a sample of the men about their health issues (a ruse), including some questions about marital sex. He neither told them he knew about their activity nor did he debrief them when finished, which is generally considered to be unethical.

controversial, in part because of its use of *deception* (see Ethical issue 6.1). Also, in this sort of research, employing an observation schedule is limited because excessive use will blow the observer's cover. The most that can usually be done is limited coding.

Criticisms of structured observation

Some problems with structured observation have already been mentioned in the discussion of its reliability, validity, and generalizability. Other criticisms include the following:

- There is a risk of imposing an inappropriate observation schedule on the setting observed, a risk especially great in settings about which little is known. This point is similar to the problem of a closed question whose answer categories may not be appropriate. One solution is for the structured observation to be preceded by a period

of unstructured observation, so that appropriate variables and categories can be specified in advance.

- Because it concentrates on directly observable behaviour, structured observation is less able to get at the *intentions* behind behaviour. When intentions are of interest, observers must impute them. Essentially, the problem is that structured observation does not readily allow the observer to get a grasp of the *meanings* people attach to their behaviours, which according to Weber is crucial in understanding human thought and action. In a similar vein, things like the context of the behaviour or what is going on in the larger world may be given insufficient attention as factors that may be affecting the observed behaviour.

- There is a tendency for structured observation to generate many small bits of data. The problem can then be one of finding general themes that illustrate the bigger picture that lies behind them. This is compounded by the previous criticism

---

Ethical issue 6.2

Random response technique

This technique was originally designed for interview situations in which the respondent is asked about controversial or illegal activities. One impetus for developing it was to protect both respondents and researchers so police could not examine the data and then bring researchers into court as witnesses. (Can some harm be anticipated here, as when the still-free criminals repeat their crimes?)

The process involves respondents flipping a coin but not revealing the results. About half of them should get a head, half a tail. All respondents are then instructed: 'For the following question, if you have a head you must say yes, regardless of whether it is true or not. With tails you should answer the question truthfully.' Then comes the question: 'Have you ever used cocaine?' Even if no one used it, about 50 per cent should say yes because they got a head.

Assume 60 per cent of respondents say yes. The excess over the 50 per cent (heads who had to say yes) can be used to calculate how many people used cocaine. Here the excess is 10 per

cent, which presumably came from people who got a tail and have used the drug. But that figure must be doubled to get the percentage in the sample who used cocaine because one would expect the same number of cocaine users in the heads condition.

One of the authors of this book did this as a class exercise and had students raise their hands to say yes or no. When the behaviour in question was shoplifting after the age of 16, the data revealed 80 per cent 'yes,' meaning a 60 per cent (30 per cent plus another 30 per cent) shoplifting rate. The results were different when the topic was post-puberty homosexual behaviour, which came out at only 50 per cent yes. Here there are several possibilities: no one had engaged in the activity; a few had, but because heads and tails rarely come out exactly 50–50, they were concealed in the fluctuation; students getting heads may have been too afraid that their classmates would think a raised hand was an admission and not a head; or perhaps people engaging in this behaviour did not want to give any indication that they had done so.

that observers may not know the meanings the actors attach to their behaviours.

On the other hand ...

It is clear from the previous section that there are limitations to structured observation. However, it also has to be remembered that when overt behaviour is the focus of analysis and issues of meaning are less salient, structured observation is almost certainly more accurate and effective than getting people to report their behaviour in a survey. Structured observation may work best when accompanied by another method, especially one that can probe for the reasons people have for their behaviours (see Ethical issue 6.2).

Key Points

- Structured observation is an alternative to survey-based measures of behaviour.

- It involves explicit rules for recording behaviour.

- Structured observation has generally been applied to a narrow range of behaviours, such as that occurring in schools, courts, and hospitals.

- It shares with survey research many common problems concerning reliability, validity, and generalizability.

- Reactive effects have to be taken into account, but should not be exaggerated.

- The field experiment is a form of structured observation, but can involve ethical difficulties.

- Problems with structured observation include determining the meaning people give to their behaviour, and ensuring that the framework for recording the observations is valid.

Questions for Review

Observing behaviour

- What are the chief characteristics of structured observation?

- To what extent does it provide a better approach to the study of behaviour than questionnaires or structured interviews?

The observation schedule

- 'An observation schedule is much like a questionnaire or structured interview except that it was not designed for asking questions.' Discuss.

- With a partner, devise an observation schedule for a place with which you are familiar, such as a popular student hangout. Ask others with whom you normally interact how well they think the schedule matches what goes on, and if it missed anything.

Strategies for observing behaviour

- What are the main ways to record behaviour in structured observation?

Issues of reliability and validity

- How do the considerations of reliability and validity in structured observation mirror those encountered in the asking of questions in survey research?

- What are reactive effects and how can they be problematic in structured observation research?

Field experiments as a form of structured observation

- What are field experiments and what ethical concerns do they pose?

Criticisms of structured observation

- 'The chief problem with structured observation is that it does not reveal the intentions that lie behind behaviour.' Discuss.

7 Other Sources of Data

Chapter overview

This chapter examines sources of data not considered in previous chapters, including personal documents, state records, and data collected by other researchers. It will discuss:

- personal documents in both written form (such as diaries and letters) and visual form (such as photographs);
- official government documents;
- official documents from private sources;
- mass media outputs, such as radio or television scripts;
- virtual outputs, such as Internet resources;

- the criteria for evaluating each of the above sources;
- secondary analysis—the use of data collected by other researchers or government agencies;
- the advantages and disadvantages of secondary analysis;
- the growing recognition in recent years of the usefulness of official statistics, following a period in which such statistics were criticized; and
- the notion that official statistics are an *unobtrusive measure*, insofar as research participants are unaware of being studied and therefore act naturally.

Introduction

This chapter is concerned with a fairly heterogeneous set of data sources, such as letters, diaries, autobiographies, newspapers, television shows, websites, and photographs. They are collectively referred to here as 'documents,' for ease of presentation. With sources such as these, the search for relevant data can often be a highly protracted process. Moreover, once they have been collected, considerable interpretative skill is required to ascertain the meaning of the materials uncovered.

Documents in this chapter are materials that:

- can be read (though the term 'read' is defined loosely here when it comes to visual materials like photographs); and
- were *not* produced specifically for the purpose of social research.

Documents are important because they provide an unobtrusive measure. They are non-reactive, thus removing a common threat to the validity of the data.

In discussing the different kinds of documents used in social science, Scott (1990) distinguished between personal and official documents, and further classified the latter in terms of private and state documents. These distinctions are used in much of the discussion that follows. Scott also enumerated four criteria for assessing the quality of documents (1990: 6):

- *Authenticity*. Is the evidence genuine and of unquestionable origin?
- *Credibility*. Is the evidence free from error and distortion?

- *Representativeness.* Is the evidence typical of what it is supposed to represent (for example, social life at a particular time and place), and if not, is the extent of its uniqueness known?
- *Meaning.* Is the evidence clear and comprehensible?

This is an extremely rigorous set of criteria against which documents should be gauged, and frequent reference to them is made in the discussion.

Personal documents

Diaries, letters, and autobiographies

Diaries and letters are often used by historians, but they have been given less attention by other social researchers (see Box 7.1). Whereas a letter is a form of communication with other people, diarists presumably write for themselves. When written for wider consumption, diaries are difficult to distinguish from another kind of personal document—the autobiography. Used with a life history or biographical method, diaries, letters, and autobiographies (whether solicited or unsolicited) can either be the primary source of data, or adjuncts to other sources such as life story interviews. However, as noted, it is with unsolicited documents that this chapter is primarily concerned.

The distinction between biographies and autobiographies can sometimes break down, and Walt Disney provides a case in point. The first biography of Disney, written by his daughter, Diane Disney Miller (1956), would almost certainly have included information from Mr Disney himself. Moreover, several people have noted the 'sameness' about subsequent biographies, a feature attributable to tight control by the Walt Disney Corporation of the primary materials in their Disney archive (letters, notes of meetings, and so on) out of which the biographies were fashioned. As a result, although Walt Disney never wrote an autobiography in the conventional meaning of the term, his hand, and subsequently that of the company, can be seen in the biographies written.

In evaluating personal documents, the *authenticity* criterion is clearly of considerable importance. Is the purported author of the letter or diary the real author? In the case of autobiographies, this has become a growing problem in recent years as a result of the increasing use of 'ghost' writers. But the same is potentially true of other documents. For example, in the case of Augustus Lamb (Box 7.1), Dickinson (1993: 126–7) noted that there are 'only three letters existing from Augustus himself (which one cannot be certain were written in Augustus's own hand, since the use of amanuenses was not uncommon).' This raises the question of how far Augustus was in fact the author of the letters, especially in the light of his apparent learning difficulties.

Turning to the issue of *credibility*, Scott (1990) observed that there are at least two major concerns with respect to personal documents: the factual accuracy of the reports and whether they do in fact depict the true feelings of the writer (see Box 7.2). The case

---

Box 7.1   Using historical personal documents: the case of Augustus Lamb

Dickinson (1993) provided an interesting account of the use of historical personal documents in the case of Augustus Lamb (1807–36), the only child of Lady Caroline Lamb and William Lamb, the second Viscount Melbourne. It is possible that the boy suffered from epilepsy throughout his short life, though he seems to have had other medical problems as well. Dickinson was drawn to him because of her interest in nineteenth-century reactions to non-institutionalized people with mental handicaps. In fact, Dickinson doubted whether the term 'mental handicap' was applicable to Augustus, and suggested the somewhat milder description of 'learning difficulties.' At the same time, she showed the problems that people around him experienced in coming to terms with his conditions, in large part because of their difficulty in finding words to describe him that were consistent with his high social status.

The chief sources of data are 'letters from family and friends; letters to, about and (rarely) from Augustus' (1993: 122). Other sources included the record of the post-mortem examination of Augustus and extracts from the diary of his resident tutor and physician for the years 1817–21. Despite the many sources, Dickinson still could not conclude with certainty that she gave a definitive portrayal of what the boy was like.

of Augustus Lamb, in which clear differences were found in people's views of him and his condition, suggests that a definitive, factually accurate account is at the very least problematic. Scott recommended a strategy of healthy skepticism regarding the sincerity with which the writer reports his or her feelings. Famous people may be fully aware that their letters or diaries will be of considerable interest to others and may have one eye firmly fixed on the degree to which they truly reveal themselves in their writings. In another context, adolescents may write their diaries knowing that a parent could 'accidentally' read their words. Finally, what is *not* said can be of great importance. In a particularly poignant illustration of this, Sugiman (2004) suggested that the Japanese-Canadian women interned during the Second World War often did not write down their experiences, thus shielding their children from that painful episode in their family histories.

Representativeness is clearly a major concern in assessing these materials. Since literacy was far lower in the past, letters, diaries, and autobiographies were likely to be the preserve of a small class of wealthy, literate people. Moreover, because boys were often more likely to receive an education than girls, the voices of women tended to be underrepresented in these documents. Some researchers argue that women are also less likely to have had the self-confidence to write diaries and autobiographies. Therefore, such historical documents are likely to be biased in terms of their applicability to the society as a whole.

A further problem is the selective survival of documents like letters. Why do any survive at all, and what proportion are damaged, lost, or thrown away? One does not know, for example, how representative suicide notes are of the thoughts and feelings of all suicide victims. Quite aside from the fact that only a relatively small percentage of suicide victims leave notes, some of those few notes that are written may be destroyed by family members, especially if they contain accusations against them.

Finally, the question of meaning is often rendered problematic by things like damage to letters and diaries and the use by authors of abbreviations or codes that are difficult to decipher. Also, as Scott (1990) observed, letter writers leave much unsaid in their communications because they share with their recipients common values and assumptions that are taken for granted and thus not stated.

Sometimes researchers have to search long and hard for new or surprising materials in diaries. Not so in the case of the diaries of former Canadian prime minister William Lyon Mackenzie King. When the King diaries were first released to the public in the 1970s, they caused a sensation (see Box 7.3).

Visual objects

There is a growing interest in the visual in social research, with photographs the most obvious manifestation of this trend. Rather than being thought of as incidental to the research process, photographs and other visual objects are becoming key objects of interest (see Box 7.4). One of the main ways in which photographs may be of interest to social research is in terms of what they reveal about families. As Scott (1990) observed, many family photographs are taken as a record of ceremonial occasions such as weddings and graduations, and of recurring events such as reunions and holidays. Scott distinguished three types of home photograph: *idealization*, a formal pose—for example, the wedding photograph or a photograph of the family in its finery; *natural portrayal*, which entails capturing actions as they happen, though there may be a contrived component to the photograph; and *demystification*, depicting a subject in an atypical (and often embarrassing)

Box 7.2   Letters: a dying art in hard copy

The potential of letters in historical and social research is limited to a certain time period. As Scott (1990) observed, letter writing became a common activity only after the introduction of an official postal service in the nineteenth century. The emergence of the telephone in the twentieth century reduced letter writing, and it is likely that the growth of email communication, especially insofar as emails are not kept in electronic or printed form, is likely to mean that the role of letters for historical purposes will continue to decline.

On the other hand, there is growing interest in email in its own right. For example, Sharf (1999) reported how, while conducting research into rhetoric about breast cancer, she joined a listserv (a managed list of email addresses around a specific theme) devoted to breast cancer and gradually realized that electronic communications had considerable potential for her research.

Box 7.3   The Mackenzie King Diaries

William Lyon Mackenzie King was prime minister of Canada for 21 years. He first took office in 1921, and served in that capacity, with a few interregna, until 1948. He was an avid diarist for most of his life, recording his thoughts and feelings about both personal issues and national and international events. Judging by the content of the diaries, he did not intend to have them read by members of the public. The diaries reveal his political views in considerable detail, but also a side of the man that shocked many people when the transcripts were released. King believed strongly in psychic phenomena and spiritualism—he attended séances, consulted mediums, and believed that he was in communication with various deceased persons, including Franklin Delano Roosevelt and his own mother. He also believed

that he could commune with his deceased dog Pat. (While King's spiritualism may be considered odd today, the practice was quite common when he was a young man in the late-nineteenth and early-twentieth centuries.) Sensationalism aside, the King diaries are a valuable primary source of information for a significant portion of Canadian and world history.

An aspect of the King diaries that is often neglected pertains to the ethics of their publication. Is it a violation of privacy rights to publish or quote from someone's diary, especially if the person is deceased and cannot raise objections? Mackenzie King's diaries are now available online through the National Archives of Canada at: http://www.collectionscanada.gc.ca/databases/king/index-e.html.

situation. Scott suggested a need to be aware of these different types in order to avoid being deceived by the superficial appearance of images. One must probe beneath the surface. He wrote:

> There is a great deal that photographs do not tell us about their world. Hirsch [1981: 42] argued, for example, that 'The prim poses and solemn faces which we associate with Victorian photography conceal the reality of child labour,

women factory workers, whose long hours often brought about the neglect of their infants, nannies sedating their charges with rum, and mistresses diverting middle class fathers' (Scott 1990: 195).

As Scott argued, this means not only that the photograph must not be taken at face value when used as a research source, but it is also necessary to have considerable knowledge of the social context in order to get its full meaning. Sutton (1992) makes a similar

Box 7.4   Photographs in social research

Photographs can play a variety of roles in social research. They can be used in qualitative research, as well as in questionnaires and as prompts in connection with an experiment. Three prominent roles photographs can play are:

- *Illustrative*. Photographs may illustrate points and therefore enliven what might otherwise be a rather dry discussion of findings. In some classic reports by anthropologists, photographs played such a role.

- *As data*. Photographs may be data in their own right. When produced for research purposes, they become essentially part of the researcher's field notes. When based on extant photographs, they may become the main source of data about the

field in which the researcher is interested, as in the work of Blaikie (2001) and Sutton (1992, see Box 7.5).

- *As prompts*. Photographs may be used as prompts to entice people to talk about what they see in them. Both research-created photographs and previously existing ones may be used in this way. Sometimes, research participants may volunteer their own photographs. For example, Riches and Dawson (1998) found in their interviews with bereaved parents of deceased children that the parents often showed them pictures of their late children (just as they were previously shown to neighbours and friends) in an effort to handle their grief.

point in Box 7.5. In fact, one may wonder whether photographs in such situations can be of any use to a researcher. At the same time, the interpretations of the researcher should not be accepted uncritically either. For example, was life in Victorian times always bleak and miserable? Were there never any moments of human warmth or compassion? Or fun?

Scott saw the issue of *representativeness* as a particular problem for the analyst of photographs. As he suggested, photographs that survive the passage of time—for example, in archives—are very unlikely to be representative; instead, they may have been subject to selective retention. The example provided in Box 7.5 of photographs of visits to Disney theme parks suggests that the process of discarding photographs may be systematic rather than random. The other problem relates to the issue of what is *not* photographed, as suggested by Sutton's idea that unhappy events at Disney theme parks may not be photographed at all. An awareness of what is not photographed can reveal the 'mentality' of the person(s) behind the camera. It is clear that the question of representativeness is much more fundamental than the issue of what survives, because it points to how the selective survival of photographs may be part of a reality that family members (or others) deliberately seek to fashion. As in Sutton's

example, that very manufactured reality may then become a focus of interest for the social researcher.

The real problem for the user of photographs is recognizing the different ways in which the image may be comprehended. Blaikie (2001) found some fascinating photographs in the local museums of the Northern Isles of Orkney and Shetland provided by local photographers and donated family albums. As Blaikie observed, in the images themselves and the ways in which they are represented by the museums, the 'apparently raw "reality" of island culture has already been appropriated and ordered' (2001: 347). For example, the image of a crofter standing by his home can suggest respectability or poverty. Was the photographer providing a social commentary, or depicting a disappearing way of life, or merely providing an image with no obvious subtext? Any or a combination of these different narratives may be applicable. While acknowledging the diversity of interpretations that can be bestowed on the images he examined, Blaikie argued that they provide a perspective on the emergence of modernity and the sense of the loss of a way of life. Coming to this kind of understanding requires being sensitive to the contextual nature of images and the variety of interpretations that can be made about them.

Box 7.5   Photographs of the Magic Kingdom

Sutton (1992) noted a paradox about people's visits to Disney theme parks. On the one hand, the Magic Kingdom is supposed to be 'the happiest place on Earth' with employees ('cast members') being trained to enhance that experience. However, it is clear that some people do not enjoy themselves while visiting. Time spent waiting in lines, in particular, is a gripe for visitors ('guests') (Bryman 1995). Nonetheless, people expect their visit to be momentous and therefore take photographs that support their assumption that the Disney theme parks are happy places. When they return home, they 'discard photographs that remind them of unpleasant experiences and keep those that remind them of pleasant experiences' (Sutton 1992: 283). In other words, positive feelings are a post-visit reconstruction substantially aided by one's photographs. Thus the photographs provide not accurate recollections of a visit but distorted ones.

Government documents

The state is a source of much information of potential significance for social researchers. It produces a great deal of quantitative statistical information. For example, Bell *et al.* (2007) used both government voting records as well as census information to assess the issue of one-party dominance in Alberta. The state is also the source of a great deal of textual material of potential interest, such as official reports. For example, in his study of the issues surrounding synthetic bovine growth hormone, Jones (2000) used transcripts of the Canadian senate inquiry on the topic. Briefly, Monsanto, the manufacturer, lost the battle to have it accepted for use; health groups claimed that the hormone was unnecessary and worse, that it posed a health risk both to cows and to humans who drink their milk. Similar materials, but in a different context, were employed by Abraham (1994) in his research on the medical drug Opren. The research was concerned with the role of self-interest and values in scientists' evaluations of the safety of medicines. The author described his sources as 'publicly available transcripts of the testimonies of scientists, including many employed in the manufacture of *Opren*, Parliamentary debates, questions and answers in *Hansard*, and leaflets, letters, consultation papers and other documentation disposed by the [drug regulatory authority]' (Abraham 1994: 720). His research showed inconsistencies in the scientists' testimonies, suggesting that self-interest can play an important role in such situations. He also used his findings to argue that an 'objective' scientific ethos, influential in the sociology of science, has limited applicability in areas in which self-interest arises.

In terms of Scott's (1990) four criteria, such materials can certainly be seen as authentic and as having meaning (in the sense of being clear and comprehensible to the researcher), but the two other standards require somewhat greater consideration. The question of credibility raises the issue of whether the documentary source is biased. This is exactly the point of Abraham's (1994) research—such documents can be interesting precisely because of the bias they reveal. Equally, this point suggests that caution is necessary in attempting to treat them as depictions of reality.

Official documents from private sources

This is a very heterogeneous group of sources, but a common one is company documents. Companies (and indeed organizations generally) produce many documents, some of which are in the public domain, such as annual reports, press releases, advertisements, and public relations material in printed form and on the World Wide Web. Other documents may not be accessible to the public, such as company newsletters, organizational charts, minutes of meetings, memos, internal and external correspondence, and manuals for new recruits. This kind of material is often used by organizational ethnographers in their investigations, but the difficulty of gaining access to it means that many other researchers have to rely on public domain documents. Even if the researcher is an insider with access to an organization, certain private documents may still remain unavailable.

Private documents also need to be evaluated using Scott's four criteria. As with the materials considered in the previous section, documents deriving from private sources like companies are likely to

be authentic and meaningful (in the sense of being clear and comprehensible to the researcher), though this is not to suggest that the analyst of documents should be complacent. Issues of credibility and representativeness are still likely to require scrutiny.

People who write documents generally want to convey a particular point of view. An interesting illustration of this observation is provided by a study of career development issues in a major retail company (Forster 1994). Forster analyzed company documentation as well as interviews and a questionnaire. Because he was able to interview many of the authors of the documents, 'both the accuracy of the documents and their authorship could be validated by the individuals who had produced them' (1994: 155). In other words, the authenticity of the documents was confirmed and apparently the credibility as well. However, Forster also said that the documents revealed divergent interpretations of key events and processes:

> One of the clearest themes to emerge was the apparently incompatible interpretations of the same events and processes among the three sub-groups within the company—senior executives, HQ personnel staff, and regional personnel managers. . . . These documents were not produced deliberately to distort or obscure events or processes being described, but their effect was to do precisely this (1994: 160).

Members of the different groupings expressed, in the documents, perspectives that reflected their positions in the organization. Consequently, although the authors of the documents could confirm their contents, those contents could not be regarded as 'free from error and distortion,' as Scott put it. This shows how documents may not be objective accounts of a state of affairs. They have to be analyzed critically and compared with other sources of data. As Forster's case suggests, the different stances taken by the authors of documents can be used to develop insights into the processes and factors that lie behind their creation.

Issues of representativeness are also important. Did Forster have access to a total set of documents? It could be that some had been destroyed or that he was not allowed access to certain sensitive ones. This is not to say that such documents necessarily exist but that a healthy skepticism is often warranted.

Mass media outputs

Newspapers, magazines, television programs, films, and other mass media are potential sources for social scientific analysis. Parnaby's (2003) study of how Toronto tried to deal with its squeegee kids, for example, examined 200 newspaper articles appearing from 1995 until 2000, mostly in the *Toronto Star*, *Sun*, and *Globe and Mail*—what he deemed a popular, a mass, and a quality newspaper. Similarly, Hier's (2002) study of the ecstacy panic surrounding raves in Toronto looked at hard-copy newspaper stories in all four major Toronto newspapers (2002). And Hallgrimsdottir *et al.* (2006) looked at how Victoria, BC, newspapers characterized sex trade workers in that province.

Films, television shows, and magazines provide similar potential for research, as the example in Box 7.6 suggests. Coté and Allahar (1994), for example, concluded in their examination of magazines aimed at adolescents that these 'teenzines' turn adolescents into uncritical consumers at the same time as they divert them from protesting against their lack of adult privileges.

Authenticity issues are sometimes difficult to ascertain in the case of mass media outputs. While the outputs can usually be deemed to be genuine, the authorship of articles is often unclear (for example, editorials, some magazine articles), so that it is difficult to know whether the account was written by someone in a position to provide an accurate version. Credibility is frequently an issue, but in fact, as the examples used in this section show, it is often the uncovering of error or distortion that is the objective of the analysis. Representativeness may not be an issue for analyses of newspaper or magazine articles, since many publications take a consistent tone or ideological bent. Finally, the evidence is usually clear and comprehensible but may require considerable awareness of contextual factors, such as Giulianotti's need to be aware of the symbolic significance of sheep to Aberdeen football supporters (see Box 7.6).

Virtual outputs and the Internet as objects of analysis

A certain word has been avoided in this chapter so far—text. It has traditionally been employed as a synonym for 'written document,' but in recent years the word has been applied to an increasingly wide range of phenomena, including theme parks, technologies, paintings, buildings, virtual documents, and a wide range of other objects. Contemporary writers and researchers use such 'texts' as materials out of which a 'reading' can be fashioned.

The relative newness of the Internet means that websites and web pages as potential sources of data are still fairly underused by social researchers, although Wilson's look at Toronto's rave scene did use Internet newsgroups (2002). However, the vastness of the Internet and its growing accessibility make it a likely source of documents for both quantitative and qualitative data analysis. Hier (2000), for example, examined a Toronto-based racial supremacy website and found that it allows people to be exposed to its ideas in a relatively anonymous way, without, for example, subscribing to a hard-copy newsletter. He feared that ordinary citizens might become susceptible to its messages.

The use of images in websites can also be quite revealing. Crook and Light (2002) analyzed the photographs in 10 university prospectuses. The authors noted that the images that accompany departmental entries often include photographs of students apparently studying; however, they are rarely shown in the

---

Box 7.6   Aberdeen football 'fanzines'

Giulianotti (1997) wrote about the fan[maga]zines that emerged in connection with Aberdeen's football club, one of the teams that were the focus of his ethnographic research. He showed how the fanzines help to create a sense of identity among supporters, especially during a period of the sport's decline. He showed, for example, that 'the fanzines combine the more traditional sense of cultural differences from the rest of Scotland with the North-East's self-deprecating, often self-defeating humour' (1997: 231). An illustration of this tendency concerns sheep. Rival fans insist that Aberdeen supporters have an interest in this creature that extends beyond its potential as a provider of food and wool. This is revealed in the repetitive chant of rival supporters: 'Sheep-shagging bastards, you're only [etc.] . . .' (1997: 220). This allegation of bestiality is turned by the supporters upon themselves in their fanzines, so that a sheep is frequently used in cartoons and stories about sheep are common.

typical contexts of formal university learning, such as at lectures or alone in their rooms. Instead, they are usually shown in 'social' forms of learning where they are active, engaged, and frequently out of doors. The authors argued that these less typical learning contexts are chosen because they are more seductive.

In addition, other forms of Internet-based communications (such as listservs, discussion groups, and chat rooms) have been used as objects of analysis. For their study of online social support groups, Nettleton *et al.* (2002) examined the interactions between people who use those sorts of virtual communications. In a study of the use of email in two organizations, Brown and Lightfoot (2002) found that online communication is strongly influenced by pre-existing, non-online forms of communication (such as written memos), meaning that previous ways of working are not fully displaced. In addition, they noted that email is often employed as a means of establishing who is responsible (and not responsible) for certain actions.

There is clearly a huge potential with Internet documents, but Scott's criteria need to be kept in mind. First, authenticity: anyone can set up a website, so matters such as financial predictions may be given by someone who is not an authority. Second, credibility: are there possible distortions? For example, some websites encourage people to buy or sell particular stocks held by the website authors, so it may be the case that their value has been exaggerated. Third, given the constant flux of the Internet, it is doubtful whether one can ever know how representative websites on a certain topic are. As Ho *et al.* (2002) pointed out, new websites are continually appearing,

others disappearing, still others being modified. Searching on the Internet is like trying to hit a target that not only continually moves, but is also in a constant state of metamorphosis. In a related vein, any one search engine provides access to only a portion of the web, and there is evidence that even the combined use of several search engines gives access to just under a half of the total population of websites, and there is no way of knowing if they are a biased sample. Finally, websites are notorious for a kind of 'webspeak,' so it can be difficult to comprehend what is being said without some insider knowledge.

Researchers basing their investigations on websites need to recognize these limitations as well as the opportunities available. Scott's suggestions invite consideration of why a website was constructed; in other words, why is it there at all? Is it there for commercial reasons? Political reasons? In other words, be no less skeptical about websites than about any

Practical Tip

Referring to websites

There is a growing practice in academic work that when referring to websites, the date they were consulted should be included. This convention is very much associated with the fact that websites often disappear and frequently change, so that if subsequent researchers want to follow up any findings, or even to check on them, they may find that they are no longer there or that they have changed. Citing the date(s) the site was visited may help to relieve any anxieties about such problems.

Checklist for evaluating documents

Have the following questions been answered?

 Who produced the document?

 Why was the document produced?

Was the person or group who produced the document in a position to write authoritatively about the subject?

Is the material genuine?

Did the person or group have an axe to grind or a particular slant?

 Is the document typical of its kind, and if not, is it possible to establish how atypical it is and in what ways?

 Is the meaning of the document clear?

 Can the events or accounts presented in the document be corroborated?

 Are there different interpretations of the document from the one you offer, and if so what are they? Have you discounted them? If so, why?

other kind of document. Employing both traditional printed documents and website materials can provide a basis for cross-validating sources.

Introduction to secondary analysis

Survey research and structured observation can be extremely time-consuming and expensive to conduct, and are usually well beyond the means of most students. This is where *secondary analysis* comes in. Large amounts of quantitative data already exist, collected by individual social scientists and by organizations such as government departments and university-affiliated research centres (see Box 7.7). The latter include the Institute for Social Research

at York University, the Population Research Laboratory at the University of Alberta, and the Institute of Urban Studies at the University of Winnipeg. Many make raw statistical data available on topics such as income, fertility, crime, unemployment and a host of other social and political issues. Using secondary data rather than collecting new information has the additional advantage of not bothering an already over-surveyed public. For this reason, secondary analysis should be considered not just by students but by all social researchers. Indeed, some granting agencies require applicants proposing to collect new data to demonstrate that relevant data are not already available in an archive. On the other hand, the use of official statistics for social research has been controversial, and aspects of that debate are addressed later in this chapter.

Box 7.7   Existing data sets

Many important studies have been conducted through a secondary analysis of existing data. Some high-quality data sets used by researchers in Canada are:

1. The National Longitudinal Survey of Children and Youth, which contains data on young people up to age 25; used by Brannigan *et al.* (2002) and Kerr (2004).
2. The National Population Health Survey, begun in 1994–5 and planned to continue for 20 years; it examines health and health care in Canada.
3. National Graduates Surveys, which ask graduates two years after finishing their post-secondary education about their employment; used by Walters (2004).
4. The Longitudinal Immigration Data Base (IMDB) developed by Citizenship and Immigration Canada and Statistics Canada to provide data for studying immigrants' long-term earnings; used by Li (2003).
5. The Canadian National Election surveys, which provide data for all federal elections from 1965 to the present; they are available through the Inter-University Consortium for Political and Social Research; scores of publications have been produced using these surveys, for example, Gidengil *et al.* (2006).

These are only a few data sets, included here for illustrative purposes.

Advantages of secondary analysis

There are several reasons for considering secondary analysis as a serious alternative to collecting new data. Its advantages have been enumerated by Dale *et al.* (1988).

- *Cost and time.* As noted at the outset, it offers good-quality data (like those sources listed in Box 7.7) for a tiny fraction of the cost involved in collecting new data.
- *High-quality data.* Most of the data sets employed for secondary analysis are of extremely high quality. First, the sampling procedures have been rigorous, in most cases resulting in samples that are as close to being representative as is reasonably possible. Although those responsible for these studies suffer the same problems of non-response as anybody else, well-established procedures are usually in place for following up non-respondents and thereby keeping this problem to a minimum. Second, the samples are often national in scope or at least cover a wide variety of regions, which is a highly desirable but costly feature. Third, many data sets have been generated by highly experienced researchers and, in the case of some of the large data sets, gathered by social research organizations with strong control procedures to check on data quality.
- *Opportunity for longitudinal analysis.* Secondary analysis can provide an opportunity for longitudinal research, another valuable feature.

Box 7.8   General Social Survey features

INTRODUCTION

In 1985, Statistics Canada initiated the General Social Survey (GSS), which covers major topics such as the health of Canadians and their level of social support. The GSS has two principal objectives: first, to gather data regularly on Canadian social trends; and second, to provide information on specific policy issues of current interest. The GSS is a continuing research project with a survey cycle each year. Each cycle classifies subjects by age, sex, education, and income. Core content areas, however, cannot be treated adequately in each survey cycle. Instead, they are usually covered every five years. The content by cycle is as follows:

Cycle	Year	Topics
1	1985	Health, Social Support
2	1986	Time Use, Social Mobility, Language
3	1988	Personal Risk, Victim Services
4	1989	Education and Work
5	1990	Family and Friends
6	1991	Health (Various Topics)
7	1992	Time Use, Culture, Sport and Unpaid Activities
8	1993	Personal Risk, Alcohol and Drug Use
9	1994	Education, Work, Transition into Retirement
10	1995	Family Effects of Tobacco Smoke
11	1996	Social Support, Tobacco Use
12	1998	Time Use
13	1999	Victimization, Spousal Violence, Senior Abuse, and Public Perceptions of Alternatives to Imprisonment
14	2000	Access to and Use of Information Communication Technology
15	2001	Family History
16	2002	Social Support and Aging
17	2003	Social Contact with Family, Friends, and Neighbours; Involvement in Formal Organizations; Political Activities and Volunteer Work; Values and Attitudes; Trust in Public Institutions
18	2004	Criminal Victimization
19	2005	Replication of Time-use Study
20	2006	Family Life in Canada

COLLECTION METHODS

Telephone interviewing is the major form of data collection due to its low cost, ease of monitoring interviewers, and data quality. The sample size for each cycle of the GSS is approximately 10 000 households, generally one person per household.

AVAILABILITY

The GSS provides a series of publications that present national and regional summary data, primarily in the form of tables and charts, along with initial analyses and findings. Public-use microdata files, together with supporting documentation, are available for secondary analyses. These files contain individual records, screened to ensure confidentiality.

Source: Statistics Canada (www.statcan.ca/english/Dli/Data/Ftp/gss.htm), accessed on 29 April 2008.

Sometimes, as with the General Social Survey (GSS) (see Box 7.8), a panel design (in which the same subjects are examined at different times) has been employed to chart trends over time. Similarly, because certain interview questions are recycled and asked of different samples each year, shifting opinions or changes in behaviour can be identified. See Box 7.9 for an example of the creative use of longitudinal secondary data.

- *Subgroup analysis*. When large samples are the source of data (as in the GSS) there is an opportunity to study subgroups. In a sample of 100 people, for example, one may find only three seniors over age 85. No quantitative researcher wants to talk about those three seniors, as in 'only 33 per cent of the aged are in good health.' That is one person. With a national sample of 2000, the numbers are increased twentyfold to 60. With this number, which is still small, estimates of seniors' health are more meaningful. It is impossible to get numbers like those in a small study unless the groups in question are the specific focus of the research.

Myles and Hou (2004) used a 20 per cent sample of 1996 census data to study 18 000 blacks and similar numbers of Chinese and South Asian respondents in their investigation of the spatial assimilation of new racial minority immigrants in Toronto. They found a traditional pattern for blacks and South Asians: when they come to Canada they move into ethnic enclaves, and then as they become more affluent they disperse into the wider society. Chinese immigrants were different. They bought houses earlier than the other two groups and chose to stay in or form new Chinese communities. Box 7.10 provides a further example of subgroup analysis.

- *Opportunity for cross-cultural (international) analysis*. It is easy to forget that many findings may not apply to countries other than the ones in which the research was conducted. Cross-cultural research can address that issue. The research on religiosity described in Box 3.4 by Kelley and De

---

Box 7.9   Labour market outcomes of different fields of study: an example of secondary analysis

Walters (2004) was interested in Canadian post-secondary education and specifically whether incomes for graduates with highly specialized technical skills was greater than that for people with liberal arts backgrounds. Pooling national graduate surveys from 1982, 1986, 1990, and 1995, he found that fine arts graduates made the least money after graduation, followed by those in the humanities and the social sciences respectively; engineering, math, and business graduates all made more than people in the first three groups. But he found that the gap was generally consistent, that the liberal arts are not losing ground to more technical areas. His work was not applied research, but it probably has some policy implications, such as in the areas of paying back student loans and variable tuition. A study like this allows an important topic to be illuminated using a relatively large, representative sample that would be beyond the reach of most individual researchers.

Box 7.10   The labour force participation of women in mid-life: an example of secondary analysis

Ginn and Arber (1995) were interested in the declining labour force participation of married women in the 15 or so years before they reached pensionable age. To explore some of the factors behind this tendency, national surveys for 1988, 1989, and 1990 were pooled to provide a sample of more than 11 000 women aged 40 to 64 and living in private households. The authors were especially interested in the relative importance of women's personal characteristics (such as their age, health, and social class) and the characteristics of their households (the number of children, whether the husband was employed and if so, his income). One of the most significant variables for women of all mid-life ages is whether their partner is employed; if their partner is not in paid employment, they tend not to be working either. The authors also noted the significance of not having information on certain issues: 'The correlation between partners' non-employment may be due to several factors, which cannot be distinguished with these data; husbands and wives may synchronise their retirement in order to avoid the wife being employed when the husband is at home, or their joint non-employment may reflect the [similar] local labour market conditions faced by couples' (1995: 90).

Graaf (1997) provides an example of using cross-cultural secondary data. The authors describe the process as follows:

> Data are from the 1991 'Religion' module of the International Social Survey Programme (ISSP) . . . a module containing exactly the same questions, answer categories, and sequencing for all countries surveyed. . . . The samples are all large, representative national samples of adults. The most common procedure is to hold face-to-face interviews . . . followed by a leave-behind self-completion questionnaire containing the ISSP module . . . (1997: 642).

Kelley and De Graaf's results were based on a secondary analysis of data from 15 nations. Opportunities for such cross-cultural analysis appear to be increasing. For example, common core questions may be used in national surveys conducted in several countries. Both the US and Britain have the equivalent of our GSS. This allowed Grabb and Curtis (2004) to create a body of literature comparing the US and Canada, revealing cross-national regional differences where national differences were widely expected.

- *More time for data analysis.* Precisely because data collection is time-consuming, the analysis of the data is often rushed. It is easy to perceive data collection as the difficult phase and to view the analysis as relatively straightforward, but this is not the case. Working out what to make of the data requires considerable thought and often a preparedness to learn unfamiliar statistical techniques. While secondary analysis invariably entails a lot of data management—partly to get to know the data and partly to get it into a proper form (see later in this chapter)—the analysis phase should not be underestimated. Freed from having to collect fresh data means that data analysis can be better planned and executed.
- *Reanalysis can offer new interpretations.* It is easy to think that once a set of data has been analyzed, the data have in some sense been drained of all insight. In fact, data can be analyzed in so many different ways that it is very unusual for all possible analyses to be undertaken. For example, a secondary analyst may look at relationships between variables not previously considered, prompting a reconsideration of the relevance of the data (see Box 7.11). Also, new methods of

quantitative data analysis, offering the prospect of a rather different interpretation of the data, are continuously emerging. As awareness of such techniques spreads, and their potential relevance is recognized, researchers can apply them to existing data sets.
- *The wider obligations of the social researcher.* For all types of social research, research participants give up some of their time, usually for no reward. It is not unreasonable that the public should expect the data they provide to be mined to the fullest. Indeed, much social research is chronically underanalyzed because primary researchers often want to look at data only with respect to *their* research questions, or they lose interest in their existing data as they imagine a new set of research questions that requires new data. Making data available for secondary analysis enhances the chance of a fuller use.

Limitations of secondary analysis

The foregoing list of benefits sounds almost too good to be true. But there are some drawbacks to analyzing data gathered by others:

- *Lack of familiarity with data.* With data collected by others, a period of familiarization is necessary to come to grips with a wide variety of variables, the ways in which they were coded, and various

Box 7.11   Secondary analysis and new research questions

Secondary analysis can involve topics that in all likelihood were not envisaged by those responsible for the data collection. In a secondary analysis of data on dietary choices, attitudes, and practices, Beardsworth et al. (2002) added gender as a focus, one not examined in previous analyses. The analysis showed that women are more likely than men to adopt a 'virtuous' pattern of eating, one that is in keeping with Western ethical and nutritional principles. The article also showed that adherence to these principles has a negative side in that it may be related to feelings of guilt, irregular eating patterns, and concerns about body shape. This work serves as an example of a profitable extension of prior research using existing data.

aspects of their organization. This period can be quite substantial with large data sets.

- *Complexity of the data.* Some of the best-known data sets employed for secondary analysis, such as the GSS, are very large both in the number of cases and the number of variables they contain. Sometimes, the sheer volume of data can present problems and again, a period of acclimatization may be required. Also, some of the most prominent data sets employed for secondary analysis are *hierarchical*, meaning that the data are collected and presented at the level of both the household and the individual (and sometimes other levels). Different data may apply to each level. Thus, at the household level, data on such variables as number of cars may appear, while at the individual level, data on income and occupation are found. The secondary analyst must decide which level of analysis to use; if the decision is to analyze individual-level data, the individual-level data must then be extracted from the data set.

- The *ecological fallacy.* This can be a problem if data gathered by region or neighbourhood (such as census data) are used to make statements about *individuals*. The term comes from the common practice of acquiring data for a geographical area, such as the crime rate in a particular neighbourhood. Coleman and Moynihan (1996) provide an example of this fallacy as it relates to the relationship between ethnicity and crime. They observed that findings showing a higher incidence of crime in neighbourhoods with high concentrations of ethnic minorities have been used to imply that members of such minority groups are more likely to commit crimes. However, *individual* data are needed to examine this hypothesis, which may or may not be true. For example, it may not be the members of the minority groups who are responsible for the high levels of offending, but their non-minority neighbours. Similarly, people could be coming from adjoining neighbourhoods to commit crimes on victims they perceive as more vulnerable. Group data cannot evaluate these possibilities. To avoid the ecological fallacy, the unit of analysis (for example, the individual, the group, the neighbourhood) of the data must be the same as the unit of analysis of the statement or hypothesis. For example, if one wants to test the hypothesis that people in group X are more likely to commit crimes than people not in group X, one needs data on *individuals*, not neighbourhoods or regions.

- *No control over data quality.* The point has been made on several occasions that secondary analysis offers the opportunity for students and others to examine data of far higher quality than they could collect themselves. However, this point applies mainly to reputable data sets such as the GSS and others. With lesser-known data sets, more caution may be necessary with regard to data quality, although certain fundamental checks on quality are usually made by the archives in which the data are deposited.

- *Absence of key variables.* Because secondary analysis entails the analysis of data collected by others for their own purposes, one or more of the secondary analysts' key variables may not be present, or may be measured differently in different years. In the study described in Box 7.9, for example, Walters (2004) had this problem so he had to modify the original data. Similarly, analysts may want to see if a known relationship between two variables holds even when other variables are taken into account, but those other variables may not be in the data set. Considering more than one independent variable at a time is a form of *multivariate analysis*, an area to be touched on in Chapter 12.

Official statistics

Agencies of the state are often required to keep a running record of their activities. For example, in Canada the police compile data that are used to calculate the crime rate, and Statistics Canada collects data that are used to estimate the level of unemployment. These are just two sets of statistics that can be subsumed under the general category of 'official statistics.'

The use of official statistics for social research has been controversial for many years. Still, official statistics offer the social researcher certain advantages over some other forms of quantitative data, such as data based on surveys:

- The data are often based on populations, not samples, allowing a complete picture to be obtained.
- Since the people who are the source of the data are not being asked questions as part of a

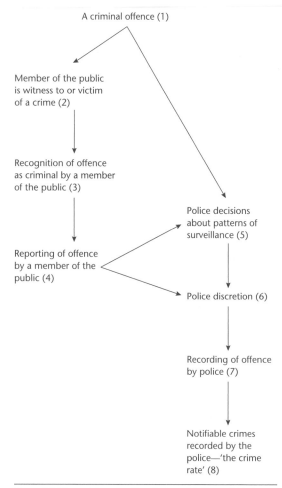

Figure 7.1 The social construction of crime statistics—eight steps
Source: Adapted from a figure in Beardsworth *et al.* (n.d.).

record only those individuals who are processed by the agencies that have the responsibility for compiling the statistics. Crime and other forms of deviance have been a particular focus of attention and concern among critics of the use of official statistics. Figure 7.1 illustrates, in connection with crime and the crime rate, some of the factors of concern.

Taking a criminal offence as the starting point (step 1), consider the factors that affect its becoming part of the crime rate. To be included in the crime rate, a victim or a witness has to be aware of it (step 2). Would you notice that $5 is missing from your wallet? A crime has to be recognized as such before it can be reported to the police (step 3). Did you lose that money or was it stolen? Next, if it is recognized as a criminal offence, the victim or the witness still must choose to bring the crime to the notice of the police (step 4). But sometimes that does not happen. Male victims of sexual assault, for instance, rarely report their experiences. So far this means that if a criminal act goes unnoticed, or is noticed but not recognized as criminal, or is noticed and recognized as criminal but is not reported to the police, it does not enter the official statistics.

Even if the crime is reported it may not become part of the crime statistics, because the police have considerable discretion about whether to proceed officially and may choose to let a suspect off with a warning (step 6). The police may be influenced by such factors as: the severity of the crime, the perpetrator's previous record, the perpetrator's demeanour or suggestions of contrition, even the victim's demeanour (do argumentative drunks get as much attention as sober victims?), the officer's volume of work at the time, or how close it is to quitting time.

Alternatively, a crime may be observed by the police during their patterns of surveillance, itself a product of decisions about how best to deploy police officers (step 5). Once again, the crime may not become part of the crime rate because no police are available to witness it. Overall, this means that only after the police exercise discretion in such a way as to lead them to seek a prosecution (step 6) is the offence recorded (step 7) and becomes a part of the crime rate (step 8).

The general implication of this process for the crime rate and for criminal statistics is that a substantial amount of crime goes unrecorded, frequently referred to as 'the dark figure' (Silverman

research project, the problem of *reactivity* is less pronounced than when data are collected by interview or questionnaire.

- There is a greater prospect of analyzing the data both longitudinally and cross-culturally. Because the data are compiled over many years, it is possible to chart trends over time and perhaps to relate them to broader social changes. As well, official statistics from different nations can be compared for a specific area of activity. Durkheim's ([1897] 1952) famous study of suicide, for example, was the result of a comparative analysis of official statistics from several countries.

However, as mentioned earlier in this book, official statistics can be very misleading because they *et al.* 2000). Other official statistics suffer from the same problem. As noted previously, suicide statistics almost certainly fail to include many cases. Deciding whether the deceased was involved in an accident or committed suicide can be difficult in the absence of a suicide note. Moreover, those responsible for concluding whether a death is a suicide or not may come under considerable pressure not to record it as such, possibly because of the potential stigma or because of religious taboos.

To push the point even further, the deficiencies of official statistics extend beyond things like crime and suicide. For example, official levels of unemployment may misrepresent the 'real' level of unemployment. People who have given up trying to get jobs are often missed in the statistics, while those who form part of the 'underground or informal economy' (thus not really unemployed) are included in the unemployment statistics. In addition, definitions of terms such as 'unemployment' or 'socioeconomic class' used by those responsible for compiling official statistics may not be the same as those used by social researchers.

Reliability and validity

Issues of reliability and validity loom large in the official statistics just discussed. Reliability is jeopardized when definitions and policies regarding the phenomena to be counted vary over time. For example, local governments may decide to place more police services into surveillance of a certain crime, such as drug use, prostitution, or driving while intoxicated, thus 'increasing' these rates. Moreover, as part of such crackdowns, police officers may be less likely to use their discretion and thus not let perpetrators off with a warning. Zero tolerance programs have the same result. This illustrates how variations over time in levels of particular crimes may not be due to variations in levels of transgression, but may result from variations in the propensity to expend resources on surveillance and to proceed with prosecution. For one final point, a further factor that can impair the reliability of crime statistics is 'fiddling' by police officers (see Box 7.12). To the extent that such factors operate, the reliability of the crime data is adversely affected and, as a result, validity is impaired.

Problems with official statistics extend to the examination of variables associated with crime.

Box 7.12 Fiddling the crime figures

An article in *The Times* [of London] (Leake 1998) reported growing evidence that senior police officers frequently massage crime statistics. The author argued that many officers deliberately 'lose' crimes in order to make their detection rates look better. As a result, official crime rates are often lower than they should be. The article cited the following methods of suppressing crimes:

- classifying multiple offences as a single incident;
- excluding common assaults from the figures for violent crime when people are not seriously injured; and
- excluding drug offences in which people were only cautioned.

These methods of reducing the official crime rate adversely affect its reliability and thus its validity as a crime statistic, but they also hurt longitudinal analyses. Variations over time in the propensity to massage the data make meaningful comparisons of different time periods very problematic.

Variations in criminal activity among ethnic groups or social classes may be a product of such factors as: variations in the likelihood of members of the public reporting a crime when the perpetrator is of one ethnic group or class rather than another (are First Nations people more often noticed and reported?); variations in the surveillance activities of the police so that areas with a high concentration of members of one ethnic group or class rather than others are more likely to be the focus of activity (do patrols favour some neighbourhoods more than others?); variations between ethnic groups or social classes in the propensity of police officers to exercise discretion; and problems for the police in learning about and investigating certain crimes that are related to ethnicity or class (for example, white-collar crime). With regard to suicide, variations among ethnic groups in suicide rates may be partly due to how much power each group has to pressure officials like coroners not to treat a death as a suicide. Also, religious groups view suicide differently and this affects the probability of leaving suicide notes, which in turn affects official statistics.

Condemning and resurrecting official statistics

In the 1960s there was a torrent of criticism of official statistics, especially those connected with crime. In fact, so entrenched was the belief in many quarters that official statistics were of dubious value to social researchers that it was recommended that they instead investigate the organizational processes that produce such deficient official data. An effect of this view was to consign official statistics to the sidelines of social research; although some work continued, it was sensitive to the fact that official statistics are not tailored to the needs of social researchers.

An important article by Bulmer (1980) questioned the relative neglect of official statistics and marked a turning point in the views of many towards this source of data (Levitas and Guy 1996). For one thing, Bulmer argued that the critique of official statistics had largely revolved around statistics relating to crime and deviance. Both are subject to special well-known problems, making it wrong to generalize these problems to the full range of official statistics. Moreover, the flaws in many of the official statistics not concerned with crime and deviance are probably no worse than the errors that occur in measurement deriving from methods such as surveys, if only for the latter's higher non-response rates. Indeed, some forms of official statistics, such as those relating to births, marriages, and deaths, are probably very accurate by almost any set of criteria. All social measurement is prone to error; what is crucial is taking steps to keep that error to a minimum.

Today, the wholesale rejection of official statistics by social researchers has been tempered. While there is widespread recognition and acknowledgment that problems remain with certain forms of official statistics, each type should be evaluated on its own merits.

Official statistics as an unobtrusive measure

One of the most compelling and frequently cited bases for the continued use of official statistics is that they are an *unobtrusive measure* (sometimes called an 'unobtrusive method') (Lee 2000). An unobtrusive measure removes the observer from the behaviour being studied. There are three main types (Webb *et al.* 1966):

1. *Physical traces.* These are the 'signs left behind by a group' and include such things as graffiti and trash, or a paper trail of financial transactions.
2. *Archive materials.* This category includes documents and other information collected by governmental and non-governmental organizations.
3. *Simple observation.* This refers to 'situations in which the observer has no control over the behaviour . . . in question, and plays an unobserved, passive, and non-intrusive role in the research situation' (1966: 112).

Official statistics belong in Category 2, as does the example given in Box 7.13. Structured observation of the kind covered in Chapter 6 typically does not

---

Box 7.13   Using unobtrusive measures: the case of New York taxi drivers

Following his informal observation of the behaviour of New York taxi drivers ('cabbies'), Camerer (1997) tested two theories about the relationship between the number of hours a driver works and average hourly earnings. One theory—the law of supply—predicted that cabbies would want to work more when their average hourly earnings are high (for example, during bad weather or on weekdays when more businesspeople are around). The second theory—daily income targeting—suggests that cabbies set an income target for the day and once that target is attained they stop work for the day. On good days (when hourly income is higher) this theory simply means that they will go home earlier.

Camerer obtained taximeter readings from the New York Taxi and Limousine Commission. The data allowed 3000 observations of cabbies' behaviour for 1988, 1990, and 1994. Tips were not recorded, so a guess had to be made about them. The data provided unequivocal support for the daily income targeting theory. However, further analysis revealed a difference between newer and more experienced drivers: the former behaved very much in line with income targeting theory, but the experienced drivers were more varied and their overall behaviour was closer to that predicted by the law of supply theory. Overall, if cabbies were to obey the law of supply, mean incomes would rise by around 15 per cent.

fall into Category 3, because the observer is usually known to those being observed.

It is important to realize that Webb *et al.* did not want unobtrusive methods to supplant conventional methods. They sought greater 'triangulation' in social research, with conventional (reactive) and unobtrusive (non-reactive) methods employed in conjunction with each other. For example, they wrote that their inventory of unobtrusive methods 'demonstrates ways in which the investigator may shore up reactive infirmities of the interview and questionnaire' (1966: 174).

Key Points

- Documents (as the term is used here) provide many different kinds of information, and can take the form of personal documents, official documents from state or private sources, and output from the mass media.

- Such materials can be the focus of both quantitative and qualitative inquiry.

- Documents may be in printed, visual, digital, or any other retrievable format.

- For many researchers, just about anything can be 'read' as a text.

- Criteria for evaluating the quality of documents include authenticity, credibility, representativeness, and meaning. Their relevance varies somewhat according to the kind of document being assessed.

- Secondary analyses allow researchers to conduct their inquiries without having to collect new data.

- Very often, secondary analysis involves the use of high-quality data sets taken from large, representative samples.

- Secondary analysis presents a few disadvantages, such as the absence of theoretically important variables.

- The analysis of official statistics, especially those relating to crime and deviance, can be a controversial form of secondary analysis because of reliability and validity concerns.

- The problems associated with official data relating to crime and deviance should not be generalized to all official statistics. Many forms of official statistics are less prone to the kinds of errors detectable in crime and deviance data.

- Official statistics represent a form of unobtrusive measure and enjoy certain advantages (especially lack of reactivity) because of that.

Questions for Review

- What is meant by a 'document'?

- Should there be a fifth criterion for assessing documents? If so, what should it be?

Personal documents

- List the different kinds of personal documents, and rank how each fares in terms of Scott's four criteria.

- What is the role of personal documents in a life history method?

- What uses can family photographs have in social research?

- Go online and take a look at the King diaries. What themes would you use to analyze them if you were to do a study of King's life?

Official government documents

- How might official government documents be biased?

- How do such documents fare in terms of Scott's criteria?

Official documents deriving from private sources

- What kinds of documents may be considered private official documents?

- How do such documents fare in terms of Scott's criteria?

Mass media outputs

- How might mass media outputs be biased?

- How do they fare in terms of Scott's criteria?

Virtual outputs

- Can anything be treated as a text?

- Do Internet documents and other virtual outputs raise special problems in satisfying Scott's criteria?

Other researchers' data

- What is secondary analysis?

- Outline the main advantages and limitations of secondary analysis.

- Examine recent issues of a Canadian sociology journal such as the *Canadian Journal of Sociology*. Locate an article that uses secondary analysis. How well do the advantages and limitations just outlined fit with this article?

Official statistics

- What reliability and validity issues do official statistics pose?

- What other unobtrusive measures can be used in secondary analysis?

Part III

Part III of this book is concerned with qualitative research. Chapter 8 explores its main features, while Chapter 9 deals with ethnography and participant observation, two important ways of collecting qualitative data. Chapter 10 is concerned with qualitative interviewing and focus groups. The discussion provides both the background knowledge needed to understand this sort of research, as well as some practical instructions on how to conduct it.

8

The Nature of Qualitative Research

Chapter overview

Qualitative research uses mainly words and images rather than numbers in its data analysis. Those using this strategy tend to produce inductivist, constructionist, and interpretivist studies, but qualitative researchers do not always subscribe to all three of those perspectives. This chapter will consider:

- the main steps in qualitative research (although they are not followed as closely as the stages of quantitative research);
- the relationship between theory and research in qualitative studies;
- the role of concepts in qualitative research;

- whether reliability and validity are appropriate criteria for qualitative researchers, and if alternative criteria more tailored to qualitative research are necessary;
- the main goals of qualitative researchers: seeing through the eyes of research participants; rich description; presentation of context; and concepts and theories as outcomes of the research process;
- some common criticisms of qualitative research; and
- the main contrasts between qualitative and quantitative research.

Introduction

As noted, qualitative research is concerned primarily with words and images rather than numbers. Several other distinguishing features are also significant:

- It usually involves an *inductive* view of the relationship between theory and research—qualitative researchers usually start with field research, and then develop theories and concepts from it.
- It is normally *interpretivist*, which involves understanding the social world by seeking out other people's interpretations of it.
- Qualitative writers are often *constructionist*, in the sense that they hold that social life is an outcome of the interactions and negotiations between individuals, rather than a fixed structure to which individuals must conform and adapt.
- It involves a *naturalistic* approach in that qualitative researchers maintain that the social world should be as undisturbed as possible when being studied.

Although qualitative research tends to share these features, there can also be important differences between the approaches and subject matter adopted by qualitative researchers. For example, the following are different kinds of qualitative research:

- *Ethnography/participant observation.* These are two very similar approaches to qualitative data collection. In both, a researcher is immersed in a social setting for some time, observing and listening to people with a view to gaining an appreciation of their culture. It has been employed in such social research classics as Whyte's (1955) study of street corner life in a slum community, and Gans's (1962) research on residents in the throes of urban redevelopment.
- *Qualitative interviewing.* This is a very broad term that describes in-depth, semi-structured or unstructured interviewing. Qualitative

researchers conducting ethnographic or participant observation research typically also engage in a substantial amount of qualitative interviewing.

- *Focus groups.* Several people are interviewed together, often using a semi-structured format.
- Language-based approaches such as *discourse* and *conversation analysis.*
- Qualitative analysis of *texts* and *documents.*

Each of these approaches will be examined in detail in later chapters. Quite often, a multi-method approach is employed when doing qualitative studies. For example, an ethnographer may conduct qualitative interviews, and analyze texts and documents as well.

The main steps in qualitative research

The sequence outlined in Figure 8.1 provides a representation of the qualitative research process. To illustrate the steps, a published study by Foster (1995) on crime in a housing estate in east London (previously encountered in Box 1.6) is used.

- *Step 1. General research question(s).* It is frequently assumed that communities with public housing and high levels of crime tend to have low levels of social control. But Foster (1995) argued that little is known about how informal social control operates in such communities and what its significance is for crime. Foster formulated a set of general concerns about public housing and criminality, and the possible role of social control among residents. She noted that some writers suggest that the level of crime is attributable to flaws in the design of public housing, not just to the tenants and the people in the neighbourhood.
- *Step 2. Selecting relevant site(s) and subjects.* The research was conducted in a community (with the fictitious name 'Riverside') that had a high level of crime and the housing features frequently associated with it. Relevant research participants, mainly the residents, were identified.
- *Step 3. Collection of data.* Foster described her research as 'ethnographic.' She spent 18 months 'getting involved in as many aspects of life there as possible from attending tenant meetings, the mothers and toddlers' group, and activities for young people, to socializing with some of the

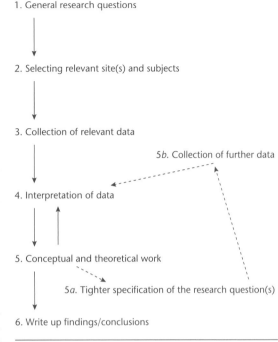

Figure 8.1 An outline of the main steps of qualitative research

residents in the local pub' (1995: 566). Foster also reported 'extended interviews' with 45 residents of Riverside (and a few more from a contiguous area) and 25 'officials' such as police and housing officers. Foster's account of her research methods suggests two types of data: fieldwork notes based on her ethnographic observation of life in the community, and detailed notes of her interviews.

- *Step 4. Interpretation of data.* One of the key findings to emerge from the data is that, in spite of its high crime rate, crime is not perceived as a major problem by Riverside residents. For example, she quoted from an interview with an elderly tenant: 'They used to say that they couldn't let the [apartments] here . . . but I mean as far as muggings or anything like that you don't hear of nothing like that even now' (Foster 1995: 568). Instead, housing problems loom larger in the minds of residents than crime. She also found 'hidden economy' crimes (such as hiding income from welfare inspectors) to be quite common, and that much of the crime in the complex is tolerated by residents. Finally, she observed that, contrary to expectations about places like Riverside, there was clear evidence of informal social control mechanisms such as shaming practices that reduce or prevent crime.

- *Step 5. Conceptual and theoretical work.* No new concepts emerged from Foster's research, but her findings enabled her to tie together some of the elements outlined under step 1. For example, she wrote:

> Crime then need not be damaging *per se* providing other factors cushion its impact. On Riverside these included support networks in which tenants felt that someone was watching out for their properties and provided links with people to whom they could turn if they were in trouble. Consequently while generalized fears about crime remained prevalent, familiarity and support went some way to reducing the potential for hostile encounters (1995: 580).

It is this step, coupled with the interpretation of data, which formed the study's findings.

- *Steps 5a. Tighter specification of the research question(s),* and *5b. Collection of further data.* There is no specific evidence in Foster's account that she collected further data after making early interpretations of the information she had gathered. However, when this does occur, there can be an interplay between interpretation and theorizing on the one hand, and data collection on the other. For instance, once a particular interpretation is made, further data may be required to determine whether the interpretation is valid. Such a strategy is frequently referred to as *iterative*. Foster did write at one point that some residents and officials were interviewed twice and in some cases even three times in the course of her research. This raises the possibility that she was re-interviewing certain individuals in light of her emerging ideas.

- *Step 6. Writing up findings/conclusions.* In any form of research, an audience has to be convinced about the credibility and significance of the interpretations offered. Researchers are more than just conduits for the things they see and the words they hear. Foster made clear to her audience that her findings have implications for policies regarding public housing and crime, and for understanding the links between housing, communities, and crime. A key point to emerge from her work, which she emphasized throughout

the article and hammered home in her concluding section, is that being an insider to Riverside allowed her to see that a community regarded by outsiders as having a high propensity towards crime is not necessarily viewed that way by the members of the community themselves.

An important part of qualitative research concerns how the theory and concepts of the study relate to the research data. It is to that issue that our discussion now turns.

Theory and concepts in qualitative research

Most qualitative researchers treat theory as something that emerges out of the collection and analysis of data. As will be seen in Chapter 13, practitioners of *grounded theory*—a much-used approach to the analysis of qualitative data—stress the importance of using data to *develop* theoretical ideas. But some qualitative researchers argue that qualitative data can and should have an important role in *testing* theories as well. Silverman (1993) maintains that qualitative researchers have become increasingly interested in testing theories; indeed, there is no reason why qualitative research cannot be employed to test theories specified in advance of data collection. Besides, much qualitative research entails the testing of theories in the iterative process described above. In Figure 8.1, the loop back from step 5a 'tighter specification of the research question(s)' to step 5b 'collection of further data' implies that a theoretical position may emerge in the course of research that spurs the collection of further data to test it. This oscillation between testing emerging theories and collecting data is a definitive feature of grounded theory. However, it is presented as a dashed line in Figure 8.1 because it is not always carried out—the generation of theory rather than theory testing still tends to be the preferred approach.

Unlike the situation in quantitative research, most qualitative researchers do not consider the measurement of concepts to be a central part of their work, although concepts are still very much a part of the landscape. Also, the way in which concepts are developed and employed is often rather different. Blumer's (1954) distinction between 'definitive' and 'sensitizing' concepts captures part of that difference. Blumer argued that fine nuances in the form a concept can assume and alternative ways of viewing its manifestations may be lost in the process of operationalization. Instead, Blumer recommended that social researchers view their concepts as 'sensitizing,' as providing 'a general sense of reference and guidance in approaching empirical instances' (1954: 7). For Blumer, concepts should provide a very general idea of what to look for, and act as a means for uncovering the variety of forms the phenomenon covered by the concept can assume.

But Blumer's distinction is not without its problems. It is not clear how far a very general formulation of a concept can serve as a useful guide to empirical inquiry. If it is too general, it will fail to provide a useful starting point because its guidelines are too broad. If it is too narrow, it is likely to repeat some of the difficulties he identified with 'definitive' concepts. However, his view of concepts is important in that it illustrates the value of starting out with a broad definition of a concept, and then narrowing it down during the course of data collection (for an example, see Box 8.1).

Reliability and validity in qualitative research

In Chapters 2 and 3 it was noted that reliability and validity are important criteria for establishing and assessing the quality of quantitative research. But many qualitative writers argue that these criteria are not directly applicable to their work. For example, since measurement is not a major concern among qualitative researchers, the issue of measurement validity seems to have little bearing on their investigations. As foreshadowed briefly in Chapter 2, different stances have been taken by qualitative researchers on these issues.

Adapting reliability and validity for qualitative research

One approach to reliability and validity in qualitative research is to adopt most of the core ideas used in quantitative research without making any special adjustments. Mason (1996), for example, uses terms

---

Box 8.1   The emergence of a concept in qualitative research: the case of emotional labour

Hochschild's (1983) idea of emotional labour—labour that 'requires one to induce or suppress feelings in order to sustain the outward countenance that produces the proper state of mind in others' (1983: 7)—has become a very influential concept in the sociology of work and in the developing area of the sociology of emotions. She gathered data on emotional labour by looking at how airline workers manage to keep smiling at some of their truly obnoxious customers. Somewhat ironically for a predominantly qualitative study, Hochschild's initial conceptualization emerged from a questionnaire she had developed on a related topic. To develop the idea of emotional labour Hochschild gained access to Delta Airlines, and in the course of her investigations:

- watched training sessions for flight attendants and had many conversations with both trainees and experienced attendants;

- interviewed various airline personnel, such as managers and advertising agents;

- examined Delta advertisements that spanned a 30-year period;

- observed the flight attendant recruitment process at Pan American Airways, since she had not been allowed to do this at Delta; and

- conducted 'open-ended interviews lasting three to five hours each with thirty flight attendants in the San Francisco Bay Area' (1983: 15).

For a contrasting occupational group also involved in emotional labour, she interviewed five debt collectors. Her book explored such topics as the human costs of emotional labour and the issue of gender in relation to it. It is clear that Hochschild's concept of emotional labour began with a somewhat imprecise idea that emerged out of a specific concern, which was gradually developed to address its wider significance. The concept has been picked up by other qualitative researchers in the sociology of work. For example, Leidner (1993) did an ethnographic study of a McDonald's restaurant and an insurance company to investigate how organizations seek to 'routinize' the display of emotional labour.

like reliability, validity, and generalizability (external validity) in the sense they are employed in quantitative research. For instance, she considers validity to be concerned with whether 'you are observing, identifying, or "measuring" what you say you are' (1996: 24).

Others have used terms similar to those employed in quantitative research, but invested them with somewhat different meanings. LeCompte and Goetz (1982), for instance, discussed the following:

- *External reliability*, by which they meant the degree to which a study can be replicated. This is a difficult criterion to meet in qualitative research since, as LeCompte and Goetz recognized, it is impossible to 'freeze' the social setting and circumstances of an initial study to make it replicable in the usual sense of the term (see Chapter 3). However, they pointed to several strategies that can be introduced to satisfy the requirements of external reliability. For example, they suggested that a qualitative researcher replicating ethnographic research needs to adopt a similar social role to that adopted by the original researcher in order to increase chances of seeing and hearing the same things that were observed in the original research.
- *Internal reliability*, which refers to whether, when there is more than one observer, members of the research team agree about what they see and hear. This is similar to the notion of *inter-observer consistency* (see Chapter 3).
- *Internal validity*, meaning whether there is a good match between the researchers' observations and the theoretical ideas they develop. LeCompte and Goetz argued that internal validity tends to be a strength of qualitative research, particularly ethnographic research, because the prolonged participation in the social life of a group allows the researcher to ensure a high level of congruence among theories, concepts, and observations.
- *External validity*, which refers to the degree to which findings can be generalized across social settings. LeCompte and Goetz argued that, unlike internal validity, external validity represents a problem for qualitative researchers because of their tendency to employ case studies and small samples, which make it difficult to know whether the findings of the study can be applied to other people or other locations.

Alternative criteria for evaluating qualitative research

Another position in relation to reliability and validity in qualitative research is sometimes taken. Some writers suggest that qualitative studies should be judged or evaluated according to criteria that are quite different from those used in quantitative research. Lincoln and Guba (1985) and Guba and Lincoln (1994), for instance, proposed that it is necessary to assess the quality of qualitative research in new ways and with new terms. They proposed two primary criteria for assessing a qualitative study: *trustworthiness* and *authenticity*.

Trustworthiness is made up of four criteria, each of which has an equivalent criterion in quantitative research:

- *credibility*, which parallels internal validity;
- *transferability*, which parallels external validity;
- *dependability*, which parallels reliability; and
- *confirmability*, which parallels objectivity.

Let's consider these terms in more depth.

Credibility
The idea of credibility is tied in with the notion that different people may interpret the social world in different ways. Since there can be several possible accounts of an aspect of social reality, the researcher has to ensure that the interpretations presented in the study ring true to the people observed. The establishment of credibility entails both following proper research procedures *and* submitting the findings to the people studied for confirmation that the account is in agreement with how they see their world. The researcher is, after all, describing their reality. This technique is referred to as *respondent validation* or *member validation*.

The aim of respondent or member validation is to seek corroboration or criticisms of the researcher's observations and interpretations. It can take several different forms:

- Each research participant may be provided with an account of what he or she said to the researcher or others, and a description of the behaviours observed. For example, Bloor (1997) reported that after he carried out observations of ear, nose, and throat (ENT) consultants concerning their assessment of patients, he submitted a report to each consultant on his or her practices and asked for feedback. Bloor said that for his research on therapeutic communities, he conducted taped group discussions with community members to gauge reactions to draft research reports.

- The researcher may show pre-publication versions of articles, books, etc., to those who were the subject of the investigation. Skeggs (1994), for example, asked the young working-class women who were the focus of her ethnography to comment on draft chapters (see Box 9.11 for further details).

In each case, the goal is to seek confirmation that the researcher's findings and impressions are congruent with those on whom the research was conducted, and to seek out areas in which there is a lack of correspondence and the reasons for it. However, the idea is not without its practical difficulties:

- Respondent validation may lead to defensive reactions from some research participants and even to demands for censorship.
- Bloor (1997: 45) observed that because some research participants develop relationships of 'fondness and mutual regard' with the researcher, there may be a reluctance to be critical of the study.
- It is highly questionable whether research participants can validate all of a researcher's analysis, since it will include inferences made for an audience of social science peers, including concepts and theories and the appropriate social science context necessary for publication. Hobbs (1993), for example, gave some of his scholarly publications to his informants, but they could make little sense of what he had written. Similarly, Skeggs (1994: 86) reported: 'Can't understand a bloody word it says was the most common response.'

Transferability

Because qualitative research typically entails an in-depth, intensive study of a small number of people, qualitative findings tend to flow out of the context in which the observations are made. As Lincoln and Guba (1985: 316) put it, whether the findings 'hold in some other context, or even in the same context at some other time, is an empirical issue.' Rather than

trying to come up with findings that can definitely be applied to other times, places, and people, qualitative researchers are encouraged to produce what Geertz (1973) called *thick description*—rich, detailed accounts of a group's culture or people's experiences. Lincoln and Guba argued that thick description provides others with a database for making judgments about the possible transferability of findings to other milieus.

Dependability

As a parallel to reliability in quantitative research, Lincoln and Guba proposed the idea of dependability, and argued that to establish it researchers should adopt an 'auditing' approach. This entails ensuring that complete records are kept of all phases of the research process—problem formulation, selection of research participants, fieldwork notes, interview transcripts, data analysis decisions, and so on—and that the records be accessible. Peers would then act as auditors, possibly during the course of the research, and certainly at the end, to establish whether proper procedures had been followed and to assess the degree to which the study's theoretical inferences can be justified. Auditing has not, however, become a popular approach to enhancing the dependability of qualitative research. A rare example is a study of behaviour at an American 'swap meet,' where second-hand goods are bought and sold (Belk *et al.* 1988). A team of three researchers collected data over four days through observation, interviews, photography, and video records. The researchers conducted several trustworthiness tests, such as respondent validation. In addition to that, they submitted their draft manuscript and the entire data set to three peers, whose task 'was to criticize the project for lack of sufficient data for drawing its conclusions, if they saw such a void' (1988: 456). This study also highlights problems associated with auditing. One is that it is very demanding for the auditors, because qualitative research generates extremely large data sets. That may be the major reason why auditing has not become a widely used approach to validation.

Confirmability

Although objectivity is a difficult if not impossible standard to live up to in social research, confirmability is concerned with ensuring that the researcher has acted in good faith. In other words, it should be apparent that personal values or theoretical inclinations did not blatantly sway the conduct of the research and the findings derived from it. Lincoln and Guba suggest that establishing confirmability should be one of the objectives of auditors.

Overview of the issue of criteria

There is a recognition—albeit to varying degrees—that a simple application of the quantitative researcher's notions of reliability and validity to qualitative research is not feasible, but writers vary in the degree to which they propose an overhaul of those criteria. Most qualitative researchers bolster their accounts through some of the strategies advocated by Lincoln and Guba, such as thick description and respondent validation exercises.

To some extent, traditional quantitative research criteria have made something of a comeback. One reason is that rejecting notions like reliability and validity can be taken by some constituencies (such as funding bodies) as indicating a lack of scientific rigour, not a desirable impression to create. Consequently, there has been some increased concern with those issues. Armstrong *et al.* (1997), for example,

---

Box 8.2   Reliability for qualitative researchers

Gladney *et al.* (2003) reported an exercise in which two multi-disciplinary teams of researchers were asked to analyze qualitative interviews conducted with 80 Texas school students on three topics: violence on television, the reasons for violence among some young people, and the reasons why some young people are not violent. One group of raters read transcripts of the interviews; the other group listened to the audiotaped recordings. Despite the different media, there was remarkable consistency between the two groups in the themes identified. For example, in response to the question 'Why are some young people violent?', Group One identified the following themes: family/parental influence; peer influence; social influence; media influence; and coping. Group Two's themes were: the way they were raised; media influence; appearance; anger, revenge, protection; and peer influence. These procedures show how a concern for reliability can be found in qualitative research.

---

reported the results of an 'inter-rater reliability' exercise in which six experienced researchers analyzed a transcript of a focus group session conducted with sufferers of cystic fibrosis (CF). These 'raters' were asked to find prominent themes in the transcript, one of the main ways of analyzing qualitative data. The six tended to identify similar themes, but differed in how the themes were 'packaged.' For example, one theme identified by all six was 'visibility': CF sufferers feel disadvantaged relative to other disabled groups because the public are more inclined to be sympathetic towards those whose disabilities are more visible. However, two analysts linked it with stigma and one to managing invisibility. In any case, this study illustrates how a concern for issues like reliability can be found among qualitative researchers. A similar exercise is described in Box 8.2.

The main goals of qualitative researchers

Seeing through the eyes of the people being studied

Many qualitative researchers try to view the social world through the eyes of the people they study. Hiller and DiLuzio (2004) took this so far as to analyze the interview experience itself from the perspective of the interviewees. Studying internal migrants in Canada, they examined what interviewees get out of the process and found, for example, that they like meeting someone who values them and validates their life experiences.

Qualitative researchers maintain that '(1) . . . face-to-face interaction is the fullest condition of participating in the mind of another human being, and (2) . . . you must participate in the mind of another human being (in sociological terms, "take the role of the other") to acquire social knowledge' (Lofland and Lofland 1995: 16). This tendency reveals itself in frequent references to *empathy*. Here are some examples:

- Armstrong carried out research on British soccer hooliganism through participant observation. He described his work as located in '*Verstehende* sociology—trying to think oneself into the situations of the people one is interested in . . . in this case the "hooligan." This approach involves recognizing social phenomena as due not to any single or simply identifiable cause and attempting to make sense from the [multi-causal] social actors' viewpoint' (Armstrong 1993: 5–6).

- For their research on teenaged girls and violence, Burman *et al.* (2001: 447) 'sought to ground the study in young women's experiences of violence, hearing their accounts, and privileging their subjective views.'

This predilection for seeing through the eyes of the people studied is often accompanied by the closely related goal of probing beneath surface appearances. After all, by taking the position of those under study, the prospect is raised that they may view things differently from what an outsider with little direct contact would expect. This insight is revealed in:

- Foster's (1995) research on crime in a housing complex in east London (discussed earlier in this chapter) that indicated that the residents do not see crime as a serious problem where they live;
- Taylor's (1993: 8) study of intravenous female drug users, which showed that they are not 'pathetic, inadequate individuals' but 'rational, active people making decisions based on the contingencies of both their drug-using careers and their roles and status in society';
- Armstrong's (1993: 11) finding that, contrary to the popular view, hooligans are not a highly organized group led by clearly identifiable ringleaders;
- Atkinson's (2004) ethnography of tattooing, which rejected the view that it is a form of pathological self-injury, and instead saw it as a prosocial and regulated act of communication; and
- Hallgrimsdottir *et al.*'s (2006) study of sex trade workers which revealed that, contrary to media depictions, prostitutes often hold rather mundane views about their occupation, such as seeing it as a way to make a living.

On the other hand, sometimes qualitative research confirms popular notions of a particular group. For example, Bell's (2007) work with the western-Canadian separatist movement found that the media depictions of the movement as very right-wing were essentially correct.

The empathetic stance of seeing the world through the eyes of one's research participants is not without practical problems. For example: the problem of how far the researcher should go to develop a sense of empathy, such as whether to participate in illegal or dangerous activities; and the possibility that the researcher will be able to see through the eyes of only some of the people in a social scene but not others, such as people of another gender or culture. These and other practical difficulties will be addressed in later chapters.

Description and the emphasis on context

Qualitative researchers are much more inclined than quantitative social scientists to provide a lot of descriptive detail when reporting their research. However, they are not exclusively concerned with description. They are also engaged in explanation. For example, Skeggs (1997) tried to answer the question, 'Why do women who are clearly not just victims of some ideological conspiracy, consent to a system of class and gender oppression which appears to offer few rewards and little benefit?' (1997: 22).

Nonetheless, many qualitative studies do provide a detailed account of what goes on in the setting being investigated. On the surface, some of this detail may appear irrelevant, and, indeed, there is a risk of becoming too embroiled in descriptive detail. Lofland and Lofland (1995: 164–5), for example, warned against the sin of what they call 'descriptive excess' in qualitative research, whereby the amount of detail overwhelms or inhibits the analysis of the data.

One of the main reasons why qualitative researchers are keen to provide considerable descriptive detail is that it permits a contextual understanding of social behaviour. This implies that one cannot understand the behaviour of members of a social group without some knowledge of the specific environment in which they operate. Behaviour that may appear odd or irrational may make perfect sense when understood in the context within which it takes place. The emphasis on context in qualitative research goes back to many of the classic studies in social anthropology, which often demonstrated how a particular practice, such as a magical ritual that accompanies the sowing of seeds, makes little sense unless it is understood as part of the society's belief system. The provision of descriptive detail is also a manifestation of the naturalism that pervades qualitative research, that is, the belief that the social world should be studied as it actually is (as opposed to using contrived settings such as formal interviews or experiments).

Emphasis on process

Qualitative research tends to view social life in terms of processes. This tendency reveals itself in a number of different ways but the main one is in the concern with showing how events and patterns unfold over time. Qualitative evidence often conveys a strong sense of change and flux. As Pettigrew (1997: 338) put it, process is 'a sequence of individual and collective events, actions, and activities unfolding over time in context.' Qualitative research using participant observation is particularly well suited to the study of process. Ethnographers are typically immersed in a social setting for a long time—frequently years. Consequently, they are able to observe how events develop over time and how the different elements of a social system (such as values, beliefs, and behaviour) interconnect. Such findings can inject a sense of process by presenting social life as interdependent streams of actions and events (see Box 8.3).

Box 8.3   Process in youth shelters

Karabanow (2002) described his experiences in street shelters for homeless and runaway youth. As a participant observer, he could monitor routine activities there and describe the shelter culture. In addition to observation, he carried out in-depth interviews with three levels of shelter workers and used agency archival materials. As a result, he was able to highlight dramatic transformations in the shelters' external environment and internal operations over a period of years that provided the basis for his analysis of the evolution of their organizational processes. This example shows the development of a sense of process in at least two ways. First, through observation of the shelters over time, so that developments and interconnections between events could be brought out. Second, by connecting these events with historical and other data, which showed how the shelters were affected by the larger society.

A sense of process can also be arrived at through semi-structured and unstructured interviewing in which participants are asked to reflect on the activities leading up to or following an event. McKee and Bell (1985: 388), for example, used a 'largely unstructured, conversational interview style' with 45 couples in which the husband was unemployed to show how accommodations to the husband's unemployment were made over time by both husbands and wives. The various accommodations were not an immediate effect of unemployment but were gradual and incremental responses over time. The life history approach is another form of qualitative research that can be used to show process. One of the best-known studies of this kind is Lewis's (1961) classic study of a poor Mexican family. Lewis carried out extended taped interviews with family members to reconstruct their life histories.

Flexibility and limited structure

Many qualitative researchers are disdainful of approaches that impose a predetermined set of assumptions on the social world. This position relates to the preference for seeing the world through the eyes of the people being studied. After all, a structured method of data collection is bound to be the product of an *investigator's* prior ruminations, expectations, and decisions about the nature of a social reality the researcher may not have even encountered before. That limits the degree to which he or she can genuinely adopt the world view of those being studied, and can lead to serious misunderstandings. Keeping structure to a minimum is supposed to enhance the opportunity to genuinely reveal the perspectives of the people being observed. This approach allows aspects of people's social world that are particularly important to them to come to light; often such things do not even cross the mind of a researcher using a more structured method. For that reason, qualitative research tries to avoid limiting areas of inquiry, and usually involves asking fairly general rather than specific research questions (see step 1 in Figure 8.1).

Ethnography, with its emphasis on participant observation, is particularly well suited to an unstructured approach. It allows researchers to submerge themselves in a social setting with a fairly general research idea in mind and then gradually narrow down the topic after making a number of observations.

Another advantage of the unstructured nature of most qualitative inquiry is that it offers the prospect of flexibility. The researcher can change the direction of the investigation much more easily than in quantitative research, which tends to have a built-in momentum once the data collection is underway. If one sends out hundreds of postal questionnaires and realizes after getting some back that an issue has been left out, it is not easy to rectify the situation. Structured interviewing and structured observation can involve some flexibility, but the requirement that interviews be as comparable as possible limits it. O'Reilly (2000) wrote that her research on British people on the Costa del Sol (in Spain) shifted in two ways over the duration of her participant observation: from an emphasis on the elderly to expatriates of all ages; and from a focus on permanent residents to less-permanent populations such as tourists. These changes occurred because the elderly and permanent migrants were not as distinctive as she had supposed. See Box 8.4 for a further illustration of how the unstructured data collection style of qualitative research can suggest alternative avenues of inquiry or ways of thinking.

Critiques of qualitative research

Just as quantitative research has been criticized by people in the qualitative tradition, the latter has been taken to task by quantitative social scientists. Some of the more common criticisms of qualitative research are discussed below.

Qualitative research is too subjective

Quantitative researchers sometimes criticize qualitative research for being too impressionistic and subjective. By these criticisms they usually mean that qualitative findings rely too much on the researchers' values and opinions about what is significant and important. A related problem is that the close personal relationships that many researchers strike up with the people they study can lead to bias. Also, because qualitative research often begins in a relatively open-ended way and entails a gradual narrowing-down of the research questions or problems, the reader of the research reports is given few clues as to why one area was the chosen focus rather than another. By contrast, quantitative researchers typically discuss problem formulation explicitly, usually justifying the topic of their research in terms of gaps in the existing literature or potential contributions to key theoretical ideas.

Difficult to replicate

Some quantitative researchers argue that the problem of subjectivity is made worse by the difficulty of replicating a qualitative study, although replication in the social sciences is rarely done, regardless of the research methods used. Because it is unstructured

---

Box 8.4   Emerging concepts

Along with some colleagues, Bryman undertook an evaluation of new staff appraisal schemes in four universities. The research entailed collecting both quantitative and qualitative data, the former deriving from large numbers of interviews with appraisers, appraisees, senior managers, and many others. In the course of conducting the interviews and analyzing the data, they became increasingly aware of a cynicism in many of those interviewed. For some it was a belief that nothing of any significance happens as a result of an appraisal meeting; for others it was a feeling that the appraisal process is not very meaningful. As one of the interviewees said: 'It's like going through the motions of it [appraisal]. It's just get it over with and signed and dated and filed and that's the end of it' (Bryman et al. 1994: 180).

On the basis of these findings it was suggested that the attitudes towards appraisal and the behaviour of those involved in it are characterized by 'procedural compliance,' a term coined by the researchers. They defined it as 'a response to an organizational innovation in which the technical requirements of the innovation . . . are broadly adhered to, but where there are substantial reservations about its efficacy and only partial commitment to it' (1994: 178).

Ethical issue 8.1

Qualitative research and ethics committees

Van den Hoonaard (2001) suggested that it is often harder to get ethics approval for qualitative research than for quantitative studies. Qualitative research is often seen as less scientific, and ethics committees may prefer the epistemology of quantitative research, with its derived hypotheses and specific plans. This can be a fatal problem because if the ethics committee rejects the research proposal, the work can neither be funded nor carried out.

On strictly ethical grounds, qualitative research has been faulted for difficulties with confidentiality. In particular, there is a fear that the rich detail and small number of subjects may lead to violations of confidentiality. Also, unlike in quantitative research where data are usually collected one on one, here a whole group may be watched, including some who may not have wanted the attention. One ethics committee suggested that a researcher go ahead with her work, but to turn her head when someone who had not previously signed a consent form entered her field of vision.

and relies on the qualitative researcher's ingenuity, it is almost impossible to conduct a true replication of qualitative work. What is observed and heard and also what the researcher decides to concentrate upon are often at the whim of the researcher; different researchers may choose to observe different things and as a result they may come up with different findings. Also, the responses of the people being observed or interviewed are likely to be affected by the characteristics of the researcher (personality, age, gender, and so on). The difficulties that qualitative social scientists experience when they revisit ground previously trodden on by another researcher (often referred to as a 'restudy') do not inspire confidence in the replicability of qualitative research (Bryman 1994).

Problems of generalization

It is often suggested that the scope of qualitative findings is restricted. When participant observation is used or when unstructured interviews are conducted with a small number of individuals in one organization or locality, many argue that it is impossible to know if the findings can be applied to other people or other settings. Can just one or two cases be representative of some larger population? For example, can one really treat Karabanow's (2002) study of two shelters for homeless youth (Box 8.4) as generalizable to all youth shelters? In the case of research based on interviews rather than participation, are those who were interviewed representative of some larger population? Do the interview findings from sex trade workers in Victoria (Hallgrimsdottir *et al.* 2006), for example, apply to prostitutes in Toronto? Are the prostitutes from three Western provinces in the Nixon *et al.* (2002) study representative of those found in other regions of the country?

The answer to these questions in most qualitative research studies is 'probably not.' But a case study is not a sample of one drawn from a known population. The people interviewed in qualitative research are not necessarily meant to be representative of some larger group. In fact with some sorts of people, such as prostitutes, it may be impossible to enumerate the population in any precise manner, which makes the selection of a representative sample impracticable.

Usually, the purpose of qualitative research is not the production of generalizable knowledge. The research normally stands on its own, providing an in-depth analysis of a person or a small group of people, something that quantitative research rarely does. Also, qualitative research can contribute to the creation of generalizable knowledge insofar as it produces theories or concepts that can be assessed using other research methods. For instance, Williams (2000) argued that qualitative researchers are often in a position to produce generalizations regarding the people or events studied (a group of drug users, a group of soccer hooligans, a strike) that 'can be seen to be instances of a broader set of recognisable features' (2000: 215). In addition, Williams argued that when generating findings relating to the hooligans who follow a certain soccer club, a researcher will often draw comparisons with the findings of other researchers relating to comparable groups. Indeed, the researcher may also draw comparisons and linkages with followers of other professional sports teams or to violent groups not linked to sport. However, such generalizations will always be limited and somewhat more tentative than those associated with the statistical generalizations associated with quantitative research.

Lack of transparency

A further criticism often made of qualitative research, but one perhaps less influenced by quantitative research criteria, is that qualitative research frequently lacks transparency in terms of how the research was conducted. It is sometimes difficult to establish what the researchers actually did and how they arrived at their conclusions. For example, qualitative research reports are sometimes unclear about such matters as how people were chosen for observation or interview. This deficiency contrasts sharply with the often detailed accounts of sampling procedures in reports of quantitative research.

Is it always like this?

There can be departures from the qualitative research practices described above. One of the main differences is that qualitative research is sometimes a lot more focused than is implied by the suggestion that the researcher begins with general research questions, and then narrows them down as theories and concepts emerge in the data collection process. There is no reason why qualitative research cannot be employed to investigate a specific research problem. For example, Hammersley *et al.* wanted to examine the contention that 'external examinations lead to

lecturing and note-taking on the part of secondary-school teachers and instrumental attitudes among their pupils' (1985: 58). This claim was evaluated by comparing two schools that varied considerably in the emphasis they placed on examinations.

A related way in which qualitative research may differ from the standard model is in the amount of structure and formality used in collecting and analyzing the data. As will be seen in Chapter 16, techniques such as conversation analysis entail the application of a highly codified method for studying talk. Moreover, the growing use of computer-assisted qualitative data analysis software is leading to greater transparency in the procedures used for analyzing qualitative data, which may in turn lead to greater standardization in qualitative data analysis.

Some contrasts between quantitative and qualitative research

Several writers have contrasted quantitative and qualitative research with tables that highlight their differences (for example, Hammersley 1992*b*). Table 8.1 attempts to draw out the chief contrasts. As with any summary of a large body of material, the table outlines general tendencies. The full picture is more nuanced—there are exceptions to these general points, as will be seen in Chapters 14 and 15.

- *Numbers vs. Words.* Quantitative researchers place great store in precise, numerical measurements of

Table 8.1   Common contrasts between quantitative and qualitative research

Numbers	Words
Point of view of researcher	Points of view of research participants
Researcher distant	Researcher close
Theory testing	Theory development
Structured	Unstructured
Generalizable knowledge	Contextual understanding
Hard, reliable data	Rich, deep data
Macro	Micro
Behaviour	Meaning
Artificial settings	Natural settings

social phenomena, and use those measurements to calculate statistics to understand social life; qualitative researchers use mainly words in their analyses of society.

- *Point of view of researcher vs. Points of view of participants.* In quantitative research, investigators are in the driver's seat; their concerns structure the investigation. In qualitative research, the perspective of those being studied—what they see as important and significant—provides the point of orientation.

- *Researcher is distant vs. Researcher is close.* In quantitative research, researchers tend to be less involved with their subjects and in some cases, as in research based on mailed questionnaires, they may have no direct contact at all. Often this distance is regarded as desirable by quantitative researchers, because they want to be as objective as possible and feel their objectivity would be compromised if they were to become too involved with the people they study. Qualitative researchers seek involvement with the people being investigated so that they can see the world through their eyes.

- *Theory and concepts tested in research vs. Theory and concepts developed from data.* Before data collection begins, quantitative researchers typically have a theory in mind that they want to test. In qualitative research, concepts and theories develop as the data are collected.

- *Structured vs. Unstructured.* Quantitative research is typically highly structured to maximize validity and reliability; in qualitative research, the approach is less structured in order to allow the researcher to get a sense of the meanings people derive from their everyday lives, and to permit the development and elaboration of concepts and theories as the data are collected.

- *Generalizable knowledge vs. Contextual understanding.* Whereas quantitative researchers want their findings to be applicable to some larger population, qualitative researchers seek an understanding of the behaviour, values, and beliefs of the people in their study. Qualitative findings usually arise out of the context these people find themselves in, and the insights gained may or may not apply to other people.

- *Hard, reliable data vs. Rich, deep data.* Quantitative data are often depicted as 'hard' in the sense of being robust and unambiguous, owing to the greater precision offered by their measurement techniques. Qualitative researchers claim, by contrast, that their contextual approach and their often-prolonged involvement in a setting engender rich, nuanced, and very detailed information.

- *Macro vs. Micro.* Quantitative researchers are often involved in uncovering large-scale social trends and connections between variables; as noted above, their research is generally designed to be applicable to large populations. Qualitative researchers are usually concerned with in-depth analyses of small-scale aspects of social reality, such as personal interaction.

- *Behaviour vs. Meaning.* It is sometimes suggested that the quantitative researcher focuses more on people's behaviour, and the qualitative researcher more on the meaning of that behaviour for the actor.

- *Artificial settings vs. Natural settings.* Whereas quantitative research is conducted in a contrived context, such as an experiment or a formal interview setting, qualitative researchers investigate people in their natural environments, such as at social gatherings or in the workplace.

— Key Points —

- Qualitative research does not lend itself to a clear set of linear steps. It tends to be a more open-ended research strategy than is typically the case with quantitative research.

- In qualitative research, theories and concepts are outcomes of the research process.

- There is considerable unease about the direct application of reliability and validity criteria to qualitative research. Indeed, some writers prefer alternative criteria.

- Most qualitative researchers try to see the social world through the eyes of their research participants.

— Questions for Review —

The main steps in qualitative research

- Does a research question in qualitative research have the same significance and characteristics as one in quantitative research?

Theory and concepts in qualitative research

- Is the approach to theory in qualitative research inductive or deductive?

- What is the difference between definitive and sensitizing concepts?

Reliability and validity in qualitative research

- How have some writers adapted the notions of reliability and validity to qualitative research?

- Why have some writers sought alternative criteria for evaluating qualitative research?

- How far do Lincoln and Guba's criteria stray from quantitative criteria?

- What is respondent validation?

The main goals of qualitative researchers

- How do the main goals of qualitative researchers differ from those of quantitative researchers?

The critique of qualitative research

- What are some of the main criticisms of qualitative research?

- To what extent do they reflect the concerns of quantitative researchers?

- Can qualitative research be used to test hypotheses?

Some contrasts between quantitative and qualitative research

- 'The difference between quantitative and qualitative research revolves entirely around the concern with numbers in the former and with words in the latter.' To what extent do you agree with this statement? Why?

9 Ethnography and Participant Observation

Chapter overview

Ethnography and participant observation require the extended involvement of a researcher in the social life of the people being studied. This chapter explores:

- the problems of gaining access to different settings and suggestions about how to overcome them;
- whether a covert research role is practicable and acceptable;
- the role of key informants;
- the different roles ethnographers can assume in the course of their fieldwork;
- the function of field notes and the forms they can take;
- the role of visual materials in ethnography;
- bringing an ethnographic study to an end; and
- the controversy over feminist ethnography.

Introduction

Discussions about *participant observation* have been fairly standard in textbooks on social research. However, for some time, writers on research methods have preferred the term '*ethnography.*' In both, a researcher is immersed in a group of people for an extended period of time (sometimes for years), observing behaviour, listening to what is said in conversations, and asking questions. Typically, participant observers and ethnographers gather further data through documents and interviews, especially on issues not directly observable or about which they are unclear. Desroches (1990), for example, added interviews with 15 investigating officers to his hidden video-equipment recordings of sexual activities in public washrooms.

The terms 'participant observation' and 'ethnography' are essentially synonymous, although here ethnography will be used in a more inclusive way and will include participant observation, which will refer more specifically to the observational component of this kind of research.

This chapter outlines some of the main decisions ethnographers must make, along with some of the many contingencies they face. However, given the diversity of experiences that confronts ethnographers and the variety of ways in which they deal with them, it is difficult to generalize about this kind of research or to provide specific recommendations

> ### Practical Tip
>
> **Micro-ethnography**
>
> In doing research for an undergraduate project or master's thesis, it is generally not feasible to conduct a full-scale ethnography, if only because of time limitations. Nevertheless, it may be possible to carry out a form of micro-ethnography (Wolcott 1990), involving a focus on one specific aspect of a group. For example, if a student is interested in call centres, one possibility would be to focus on how staff manage to interact and discuss work problems with one another in spite of continuously receiving calls and being monitored. A shorter period of time (from a couple of weeks to a few months) can be spent in the organization—either on a full-time or a part-time basis—to achieve this more limited goal.

	Open/public setting	Closed setting
Overt role	*Type 1*	*Type 2*
	• Wilson's (2002) study of Toronto raves	• Karabanow's (2002) study of two Canadian youth shelters (Box 8.3)
	• Totten's (2001) study of youth gang members (Box 9.6)	• Clancey's (2001) study of scientists in the Arctic (Box 9.10)
Covert role	*Type 3*	*Type 4*
	• Desroches's (1990) updates on homosexual activities in public washrooms	• Lauder's (2003) discussion of covert research on the Heritage Front

Figure 9.1 Four types of ethnography

Box 9.1   Perils of covert observation: field notes in the lavatory

Ditton's (1977) research in a bakery provides an interesting case of the practical difficulties of taking notes during covert observation, as well as an illustration of an ethnographer who shifted positions from covert to overt observer at least in part because of those difficulties:

> Right from the start, I found it impossible to keep everything that I wanted to remember in my head until the end of the working day . . . and so had to take rough notes as I was going along. But I was stuck 'on the line,' and had nowhere to retire to privately to jot things down [except the washroom]. [Eventually] . . . my frequent requests for 'time out' after interesting happenings or conversations in the bakehouse and the amount of time I was spending in the lavatory began to get noticed. I had to pacify some genuinely concerned work-mates . . . and 'come out' as an observer—albeit in a limited way. I eventually began to scribble notes more openly, but still not in front of people when they were talking. When questioned about this, as I was occasionally, I coyly said that I was writing things down that occurred to me about 'my studies' (Ditton 1977: 5).

about it. The following comment makes this point well:

> Every field situation *is* different and initial luck in meeting good informants, being in the right place at the right time, and striking the right

note in relationships may be just as important as skill in technique. Indeed . . . many unsuccessful episodes are due as much to bad luck as to bad judgement (Sarsby 1984: 96).

However, this statement should not be taken to mean that forethought and an awareness of alternative approaches are irrelevant. It is with those issues that the rest of this chapter is concerned. Issues to do with the conduct of interviews by ethnographers are reserved for Chapter 10.

Access

One of the most important and yet most difficult steps in ethnography is gaining access to the social setting one wants to research. How to gain access depends on several things, one of which is whether the setting is relatively open (public) or closed (private or restricted) (see Lofland and Lofland 1995). Closed settings generally include organizations of various kinds, such as firms, schools, cults, and social movements. The open setting refers to areas where anyone can gain access, such as libraries, parks, and sidewalks, but even there it can be quite difficult to make observations and talk to people. 'Open' does not necessarily involve easy access to people.

Overt versus covert ethnography

One way to ease the access problem is to assume a *covert* role—in other words, not disclosing that you are a researcher. Getting access can be very problematic, and the adoption of a covert role removes some of the difficulties. These two distinctions—the open versus closed setting, and the overt versus covert role—suggest a fourfold distinction in forms of ethnography (see Figure 9.1); an example of recent Canadian work is given for each of the four types.

Three points should be noted about Figure 9.1. First, the open versus closed setting distinction is not hard and fast. Sometimes gaining access to 'open' groups can have an almost formal quality—such as having to answer a gang leader's questions about your goals. Also, 'closed' organizations and social movements sometimes create contexts that have a public character—such as meetings arranged for members or prospective recruits. Bell (2007), for example, attended many western-Canadian separatist meetings and rallies that were open to the public, and was able to get a lot of information on the movement and its leaders that way.

Second, the overt versus covert distinction can vary from context to context even within the same research project. For instance, although ethnographers may seek access through an overt route, there may be many people with whom they come into contact who are unaware of their status as a researcher. Atkinson

(1981: 135) noted in connection with his research on the training of doctors in a medical school that although he was 'an "open" observer with regard to doctors and students,' he was 'a "disguised" observer with regard to the patients.' Also, some ethnographers move between the two roles (see Box 9.1).

Another interesting case is provided by Glucksmann (1994), who in the 1970s left her academic post to work on a factory assembly line in order to shed light on the reasons why feminism appeared not to be relevant to working-class women. In a sense, she was a covert observer, but her motives for the research were primarily political, not academic. At the time she was undertaking the research she had no intention of writing the book that subsequently was published under a pseudonym. Was she an overt or a covert observer (or neither or both)? Whichever description applies, this is an interesting case of what might be termed 'retrospective ethnography,' which involves using observations that were gathered before one decided to do a study.

A third point with regard to Figure 9.1 is that the preferred choice is that of an overt role. There are

Ethical issue 9.1

Stances on ethics

Writers on research ethics take different positions on ethical issues, including the following:

- *Moral universalism.* This is the view that ethical precepts should never be broken. It is rarely adhered to—it is difficult if not impossible to conduct research without committing at least a minor ethical violation. For example, although informed consent is normally required before the research begins, Van Maanen (1991*b*) wrote up his experiences as a ride operator in Disneyland many years after he had been employed there for school vacation jobs. He never went back and got permission from the people he described in the study, but that would have been very difficult to do.

- *Situation ethics.* Goode (1996) argued for deception in research to be considered on a case-by-case basis, a 'principled relativism' based on 'the end justifies the means.' Some writers argue that without some breaking of ethical rules, one could never gain knowledge about terrorists, cults, drug gangs, white-collar criminals, etc., which often

require some kind of disguised observation. Some social reformers might add that exposing the sins of the powerful would be another acceptable use of deception, but that argument opens the door to its use in other situations. For example, is it acceptable to engage in deception to expose the sins of the underclass and the less powerful? Is lying to a priest to uncover pedophilia more acceptable than lying to an animal rights activist to reveal a plan to destroy a mink coat factory?

- *Ethical transgression is pervasive.* Virtually all research involves practices that are at least ethically questionable. For instance, this occurs whenever all participants are not given absolutely all the details of the research. Punch (1994: 91), for example, observed that 'some dissimulation is intrinsic to social life and, therefore, to fieldwork.' He quoted Gans (1962: 44) in support: 'If the researcher is completely honest with people about his activities, they will try to hide actions and attitudes they consider undesirable, and so will be dishonest. Consequently, the researcher must be dishonest to get honest data.'

several reasons for this. As Box 9.2 reveals, this has to do with practical and ethical considerations, with the latter being more important. Because of the ethical problems that beset covert research (and indeed some of the practical difficulties), the bulk of the discussion of access issues that follows focuses on ethnographers doing their research overtly (see Ethical issue 9.1).

Access to closed settings

Gaining access to most organizations requires strategic planning, hard work, and sometimes luck. In selecting a case study for an ethnographic investigation, the researcher may employ several criteria, each determined by the research area of interest. One may choose a certain case or setting because of its 'fit' with the research questions, but there are no guarantees of access. Sometimes, sheer perseverance pays off. Leidner (1993) was determined that McDonald's be one of the organizations in which she conducted ethnographic research on the routinization of service work. She wrote:

> The company was a pioneer and exemplar of routinized interaction, and since it was locally based, it seemed like the perfect place to start.

McDonald's had other ideas, however, and only after tenacious pestering and persuasion did I overcome corporate employees' polite demurrals, couched in terms of protecting proprietary information and the company's image (1993: 234–5).

This kind of determination is necessary for any instance in which a specific organization is the target, such as a particular religious sect or social movement. Rejection can mean having to seek a completely different research topic.

However, with many research questions, several potential cases are likely to be suitable. Organizational researchers have developed a range of tactics, some of which may seem rather unsystematic but are still worth considering:

- Use friends, contacts, and colleagues to help gain access; as long as the organization is relevant to the research question, the route should not matter.
- If possible, get someone in the organization to vouch for you and the value of the research. Such people are considered 'sponsors.' If permission is granted at a lower level of the hierarchy, clearance from top management or senior executives may

---

Box 9.2   The covert role in ethnography

Advantages

- *Easier access*. Adopting a covert role can help with access problems; no special permission to gain entry to a social setting or organization may be needed.

- *Less reactivity*. Because participants do not know they are being observed by a researcher, they will speak and act more naturally than they would otherwise.

Disadvantages

- *The problem of taking notes*. It is difficult and sometimes impossible to take notes without revealing that research is being conducted. But notes are very important to an ethnographer, and it is too risky to rely on memory alone.

- *The problem of not being able to use other methods*. If the researcher is in a covert role, it is dangerous to steer conversations in a certain direction for fear of detection and it is essentially impossible to engage in interviewing.

- *Anxiety*. Ethnography is frequently a stressful research method and the worries about detection can add to those anxieties. Moreover, if the ethnographer is found out, the whole research project may be jeopardized. In extreme cases, such as covert research on gangs, being found out could even put the researcher's life at risk.

- *Ethical problems*. Covert observation transgresses two important ethical tenets: deception of participants and failure to get informed consent. It can also involve a violation of privacy. Indeed, many writers think covert investigations can harm the practice of research, with innocent researchers being tarred with the same brush as outed covert observers, who are considered snoops or voyeurs (or worse). On the other hand, in some situations, like investigating the neo-Nazi Heritage Front, Lauder (2003) concluded that covert participant observation may be justified.

still be needed. People from whom permission must be granted in order to get access are sometimes called 'gatekeepers.'

- Offer something in return, for example, a *final report* (if you provide a working draft people may ask you to make changes that you do not consider acceptable). However, this strategy carries a risk of making the researcher a cheap consultant. Some writers on research methodology do not recommend offering something in return, although among researchers on formal organizations, it is commonplace.
- Provide a clear explanation of your aims and methods. Suggest a meeting to deal with the worries and concerns of the participants and provide an explanation of what will happen in terms easily understood by people who are not familiar with social research.
- Be prepared to negotiate—almost no one gets complete access.
- Be frank about the amount of people's time likely to be needed. This issue is relevant when seeking access to commercial organizations and to many not-for-profit ones too.

Access to open settings

Gaining access to people in open settings is similar in many ways to getting into closed settings. For instance, sometimes ethnographers have their paths smoothed by 'sponsors' and 'gatekeepers.' In seeking entrance to a group of soccer hooligans, Giulianotti (1995; see Box 9.3) sought out someone who could adopt both roles for him. Later, he was able to draw upon existing acquaintances to ease his entrée into a second group. In seeking access to female intravenous drug users, Taylor (1993) contacted a drug counsellor who introduced her to some local users and accompanied her on her first few research visits. A 'research bargain' (Becker 1970) was struck in which Taylor agreed in return to see any of the counsellor's clients who preferred to discuss issues with a woman.

'Hanging around' is another common access strategy. An example of the difficulties that await the researcher using this approach is found in one of Whyte's (1955) early field encounters in Boston's North End in his classic case study *Street Corner Society*. The following incident occurred in a hotel bar:

> I looked around me again and now noticed a threesome: one man and two women. It occurred to me that here was a maldistribution of females that I might be able to rectify. I approached the group and opened with something like this: 'Pardon me. Would you mind if I join you?' There was a moment of silence while the man stared at

Box 9.3   Access to soccer hooligans

Giulianotti (1995) sought access to two groups of soccer hooligans. Access to one was reasonably smooth in that he was a close friend of 3 of the 47 men caught by the police engaging in unruly behaviour at a soccer game. He had also gone to school and socialized with many of them, and in terms of 'age, attire, and argot' his personal characteristics were similar to those he was studying. Gradually his contacts grew and eventually he 'began socializing freely with the gang at [soccer] matches, travelling to and from matches within the main grouping' (1995: 4).

Access to the other group of supporters was much more difficult for three reasons: absence of prior acquaintanceships; his background and accent; and a high level of negative newspaper publicity about them at the time he was seeking access, which made the hooligans wary of people writing about them. Giulianotti sought out a sponsor who could ease his entry into the group. After some abortive attempts, he was finally introduced to someone at a game and this contact gave him access to more supporters. Eventually, he was able to negotiate access to the group as a whole by striking a 'research bargain': he would provide details of what rival fans thought of them. Giulianotti described his overall research strategy as:

> regularly introducing myself to new research acquaintances; renegotiating association with familiar casuals; talking with them, drinking with them, and going to matches with them; generally participating with them in a variety of social situations; but disengaging myself from . . . participating in violence, within and outside of [soccer] match contexts (1995: 3).

me. He then offered to throw me downstairs. I assured him that this would not be necessary and demonstrated as much by walking right out of there without any assistance (1955: 289).

Wolf (1991) employed a hanging-around strategy to gain access to Canadian outlaw bikers. On one occasion he met a group of them at a motorcycle shop and expressed an interest in hanging out with them. But he tried to move too quickly in seeking information about them and was forced to abandon his plans. Eventually, a hanging-around strategy resulted in him being approached by the leader of a biker group (Rebels MC), who acted as his sponsor. To bring this off, Wolf ensured that he was properly attired in biker garb. Attention to dress and demeanour can be a very important consideration when seeking access to either public or closed settings.

As these anecdotes suggest, gaining access to social settings is a crucial first step in ethnographic research. But it is also fraught with difficulties and in certain cases with danger—for example, when the research is on groups engaged in violent or criminal activities. One must exercise caution in choosing an access strategy.

Ongoing access

Access problems do not end after initial contact and entrée to the group. Maintaining access is in many ways an ongoing activity and is likely to prove a persistent problem in closed contexts like organizations.

- People will be suspicious, perhaps seeing the researcher as an instrument of top management (it is very common for members of organizations to believe that researchers are placed there to check up on them). When Sharpe (2000: 366) began research on prostitution in a red light area, she was quickly depicted as being 'anything from a social worker to a newspaper reporter with hidden cameras and microphones.' When conducting her research on the British on the Costa del Sol, O'Reilly (2000) was suspected of being a tax inspector.
- Group members will worry that what they say or do may get back to bosses or colleagues. Van Maanen (1991a) noted that when conducting ethnographic research among police officers, one is likely to observe activities that are deeply

discrediting and even illegal. Credibility is established by the researcher using discretion in those sorts of situations.

- If the people being studied have concerns or suspicions about the researcher, they may appear to go along with the research but in fact sabotage it, engage in deceptions, provide misinformation, or not allow access to 'back regions' (Goffman 1956).

There are three ways to smooth the path of ongoing access:

- Play up your credentials—talk about your past work, your experience, your knowledge of the group, and your understanding of its problems.
- Do not give people a reason to dislike you—be non-judgmental when hearing about informal activities or about the organization; make sure information given does not get back to others, whether bosses or peers.
- Play a role—this may involve constructing a 'front' using demeanour and dress, and by offering plausible explanations of why you are there, helping out occasionally with work, or offering advice. Be consistent—the various aspects of your role should complement each other.

Similar considerations apply to research in public settings:

- Make sure a plan exists for how people's suspicions can be allayed. Giulianotti (see Box 9.3) simply said that he was doing research on soccer fans for a book.
- Be prepared for tests of either competence or credibility. Taylor (1993) reported that at a meeting at a drop-in centre, 'proper cups' for tea were put out. Afterwards, Taylor was told that, if she had crooked her 'wee finger' as the leader of the centre had done, her informant 'would have put [Taylor] down in such a way that you'd never want to speak to us again' (1993: 15). When doing research on gang members in a poor community, Horowitz wrote that she was frequently told 'confidential' stories (which turned out to be fictional) to see if she could keep a secret (Gerson and Horowitz 2002; see Box 9.7).
- Be prepared for changes in circumstances. Both Giulianotti (Box 9.3) and Armstrong (1993) found that sudden newspaper exposés of soccer

hooliganism and evidence of police infiltration led to worries that they were not what they said they were.

Key informants

One aspect of having sponsors or gatekeepers who smooth access for the ethnographer is that they may become *key informants* in the course of the field-work. The ethnographer relies on informants a lot, but certain ones may become particularly important by developing an understanding of the research and directing the ethnographer to situations, events, or people likely to be helpful to the investigation. Whyte's (1955) study is again an extreme example of this development. He reported Doc (a key infor-mant) as saying to him at one point: 'You tell me what you want to see, and we'll arrange it. When you want some information, I'll ask for it, and you listen. When you want to find out their philosophy of life, I'll start an argument and get it for you. If there's something else you want to get, I'll stage an act for you' (1955: 292). Doc was also helpful in warning Whyte that he was asking too many questions, when he told him to 'go easy on that "who," "what," "why," "when," "where" stuff' (1955: 303). Taylor (1993) said that in her participant observation of 50 female drug users, intensive interviews were carried out with 26 women, 8 of whom were key informants.

Key informants can clearly be of great help to the ethnographer and frequently provide a support that helps with the stress of fieldwork. However, it also needs to be borne in mind that using them can be risky. An ethnographer may develop an undue reliance on key informants, and rather than seeing social reality through the eyes of all or several group members, may instead be seeing it only through the eyes of the key informants.

In addition, ethnographers encounter many others who will act as informants whose accounts may be solicited or unsolicited by the researcher. Some researchers prefer the latter, because of greater spontaneity and naturalism. Very often, research par-ticipants develop a sense of the events or encounters the ethnographer wants to see. Armstrong (1993) said that he would sometimes get tip-offs while doing research on hooligans in a club called 'Blades.'

> I often travelled on the same coach as Ray [an informant]; he would then sit with me at matches and in pubs . . . giving me background information. Sometimes he would start conversations with Blades about incidents which he knew I wanted to know about and afterwards would ask 'Did you get all that down then?' . . . There was never one particular informant; rather, there were many Blades . . . who were part of the core and would always welcome a beer and a chat about 'It,' or tell me who I 'ought to 'ave a word wi' ' (Armstrong 1993: 24–5).

Such unsolicited sources of information are highly attractive to the ethnographer because of their relative spontaneity, although, as Hammersley and Atkinson (1995: 130–1) observed, they may on occa-sion be staged for the ethnographer's benefit.

Solicited accounts can occur in two ways: by interview (see Chapter 10) or by casual question-ing during conversations (though in ethnographic research the boundary between an interview and a conversation is by no means clear). When the eth-nographer needs specific information on an issue not amenable to direct observation or that is not cropping up during 'natural' conversations, solicited accounts are likely to be the only way forward.

Roles for ethnographers

Related to the issue of ongoing access is the question of the role an ethnographer adopts in relation to the social setting and its members. Often the various roles in fieldwork are arrayed on a continuum from complete involvement to complete detachment (see Figure 9.2). It should also be noted that the full gamut of roles may be employed at different times in the course of a single ethnographic project, and for different purposes.

For example, the participant observer can be a:

● *Complete participant:* a fully functioning member of a social setting but whose true identity is unknown to members, thus a covert observer,

Figure 9.2 Classification of participant observer roles (Gold 1958)

Box 9.4   What is 'going native'?

Although the term 'going native' has vaguely racist overtones, it is commonly used in ethnography in a non-pejorative way. It refers to losing one's sense of being a researcher and becoming wrapped up in the world view of the people one is studying. The prolonged immersion of ethnographers in the lives of the people they study, coupled with a commitment to see the social world through their eyes, lie behind the risk of this happening. Going native is a potential problem for several reasons but especially because the ethnographer may find it difficult to maintain a social scientific perspective on the collection and analysis of data. As Hobbs (1988: 6) wrote of his own fieldwork, he: 'often had to remind himself that [he] was not in a pub to enjoy [himself] but to conduct an academic inquiry, and repeatedly woke up the following morning with an incredible hangover, facing the dilemma of whether to bring it up or write it up.' He may have been on the brink of going native.

A related issue for him concerned illegal activity. Hobbs admitted that he engaged in some.

A refusal, or worse still an inquiry concerning the legal status of the 'parcel,' would provoke an abrupt conclusion to the relationship. Consequently, I was willing to skirt the boundaries of criminality on several occasions, and I considered it crucial to be willingly involved in 'normal' business transactions, legal or otherwise. I was pursuing an interactive, inductive study of an entrepreneurial culture, and in order to do so I had to display entrepreneurial skills myself. . . . [My] status as an insider meant that I was afforded a great deal of trust by my informants, and I was allowed access to settings, detailed conversations, and information that might not otherwise have been available (1988: 7, 15).

like Humphreys in the tearoom (Ethical issue 6.1). The ethnographer is engaged in regular interaction with people and participates in their daily lives but assumes the researcher's role in private to write down notes once the situation has unfolded.

- *Participant-as-observer:* same as above but members of the social setting are aware that the ethnographer is studying them. All the research referred to in Figure 9.1 involving an overt role—whether in open or closed settings—is of this kind, as is Giulianotti's research (see Box 9.3).
- *Observer-as-participant:* the researcher is mainly an interviewer and observer, but participates only marginally in the group's activities. This was Bell's (2007) role in his study of western-Canadian separatists. Ethnographic research on the police is often like this, since the opportunities for genuine participation are few because of legal and safety limitations. Norris (1993) described how as an observer-as-participant, he concentrated on gathering two types of data: 'naturally occurring inter-officer talk' and 'detailed descriptions of how officers handled "live" incidents' (1993: 126). See also Box 9.4 for a further illustration. (Some critics question whether research based on this role is genuine ethnography, but as noted,

sometimes there is no alternative to minimal involvement.)

Box 9.5   Not going native

It should not be assumed that the risk of going native is inevitable in ethnography nor indeed that it is the only risk in participant observers' relations to the social situations in which they find themselves. Lee-Treweek (2000) carried out research on auxiliary caregivers in two homes for the elderly. She described how in one she had an almost completely opposite reaction to going native. She disliked the home and found the staff unappealing because of their lack of sympathy for and their uncaring approach to the elderly people for whom they were responsible. Nonetheless, she felt she 'was gathering good data, despite [her] feelings of being an outsider' (2000: 120). Similarly, although Bell (2007) spent over a year observing western-Canadian separatists, at no point was he ever tempted to become one of the group. The lesson here is that going native is not inevitable and that in the final report, one must be careful to let neither liking nor distaste for the people studied colour the results.

- *Complete observer*: the final possibility is no inter-action with the people observed. Most writers do not include this as a form of ethnography since by definition there is little or no involvement or par-ticipation. There may be less *reactivity* (behaving unnaturally because of being observed) because the researcher is more distant from the people being studied; but there is also greatly reduced potential for *understanding* because the person conducting the study does not ask questions or try in other ways to get into the heads of the people who are being researched.

Each role carries its own advantages and risks; some of these are discussed in Box 9.2 in the case of covert ethnography. The participant-as-observer role carries the risk of over-identification and hence of 'going native' (see Boxes 9.4 and 9.5), but at the same time it offers an opportunity to get close to people. The observer-as-participant role carries the risk of not understanding the social setting and its people sufficiently and therefore making incorrect

inferences. In an interesting variant of this problem, Hessler *et al.* (2003) cautioned observers (in their case regarding adolescent risk behaviour) against the temptation to act as counsellors to respondents. See also Boxes 9.6, 9.7, and 9.8.

Gans (1968) would add that even if it were pos-sible, adopting a single ethnographic role over the entire course of a project is probably undesirable. There would be a lack of flexibility in handling situ-ations and people, and the risks of excessive involve-ment (and hence going native) or of too much detachment would loom large.

Active or passive?

A further issue is concerned with how active or passive to be. Even when the ethnographer is in an observer-as-participant role, sometimes there is a compulsion to engage in the group's activities. In most studies, involvement in the group's actions, at least for a time, is unavoidable. For example, Fine's (1996) research on the work of chefs in restaurants was carried out largely with semi-structured inter-views. In spite of this limited participation, he found himself involved in washing up in the kitchens to

Box 9.6   Legal, ethical, and clinical implications of doing fieldwork with violent gang members

In his ethnographic research, Totten (2001) was interested in how youth gang members inter-preted the violence they perpetrated against their girlfriends, and how they accounted for their racist and homophobic activities. One underlying factor he uncovered was their mental construc-tion of masculinity, which was rather limited. Most had lived on the street, were themselves victims of severe child abuse and neglect, and had wit-nessed their mothers being beaten. They saw their own violence as affirming their masculinity.

That was the sociology, but what about the welfare of the people being studied? Here the researcher had to act in some instances. By law, he had to report any abuse suffered by children under the age of 16, whether by gang members or their victims. Second, those deemed at risk of suicide had to be referred to mental health provid-ers. Finally, some of the gang members were on probation or living in treatment facilities, so the authorities there also had to be informed. Totten handled the confidentiality issue by studying only those boys who agreed to these limits.

Box 9.7   Narrowing the focus of an ethnography

Gerson and Horowitz (2002) started their work on young people in a very poor community in Chicago by asking some very general research questions, such as 'what is really going on' in such groups and communities? How do people make sense of their social worlds? In the early stages of her research, Horowitz used these general research questions to guide her data collection but 'began to focus on specifying the sociological issues only after some time in the field' (2002: 202).

She found a great deal of variety in the behav-iour, ambitions, orientations, patterns of interac-tion, and attitudes towards street life among the young people she observed. Horowitz began to ask questions about how well the world of these young people fit with two prominent models used to explain the worlds of the poor. She concluded that neither model 'account[ed] for young people's creativity or for the struggles they mounted and the choices that they made in the face of great obstacles' (2002: 202).

help out during busy periods. Similarly, if one is researching bouncers, the participant observer is not going to have the luxury of deciding whether to become involved in fights, since involvement comes with the territory (Winlow *et al.* 2001).

Sometimes, ethnographers feel they have no choice about getting involved because a failure to participate may suggest a lack of commitment to the group. In such situations, standing back could lead to a loss of credibility in the eyes of the people studied. This situation can arise especially when the activities are illegal or dangerous. On the other hand, many writers counsel against active participation in criminal or dangerous activities (see Box 9.6). Both Armstrong (1993) and Giulianotti (1995; see Box 9.3) refused to fight while doing their research into soccer hooliganism. The latter wrote: 'My own rules are that I will not get involved in fighting or become a go-between for the two gangs in organizing fights' (1995: 10). That is an illustration of why it is not a good idea to do covert research on criminals or those involved in dangerous actions—it is much more difficult for someone in such a role to decline to participate in group activities (see Box 9.4).

Box 9.8   Virtual participant observation

Kanayama (2003) was interested in the nature of an Internet community formed by a group of Japanese senior citizens, one that included 120 members by 1991. Kanayama described her 10-month study as follows:

> I had participated in this group as a technical volunteer supporter for two years to help senior members use PCs and the Internet and . . . took a position as a non-active participant. . . . Many members, including representatives of the group, knew of [my] personal background. I also conducted in-depth interviews with six female and seven male members . . . by telephone (2003: 274).

She found that members of this virtual community operated well with the medium and could construct real social relationships in cyberspace, and were thus able to provide a supportive environment for each other.

Field notes

Because of the frailties of human memory, ethnographers must jot down their observations. These should be fairly detailed summaries of events and behaviour and the researcher's initial reflections on them. The notes need to specify key dimensions of whatever is observed or heard. Here are some general principles:

- Write down notes, however brief, as quickly as possible after seeing or hearing something interesting.
- Write up full field notes at the end of the day at the very latest and include such details as location, the people involved, what prompted the exchange or event, and date and time of the day.
- Some may prefer using a tape recorder, but that creates the problem of having to transcribe a lot of speech.
- Notes must be vivid, clear, and complete. If in doubt, write it down.

Obviously, it is good to take notes straightaway, that is, as soon as something significant happens. However, wandering around with a notebook and pencil in hand and continually scribbling notes can make the people being observed feel self-conscious. It may be necessary, therefore, to take small amounts of time away from the group to write down your observations, but that should be done without making the participants anxious or suspicious (see Box 9.1).

To some extent, strategies for taking field notes are affected by the degree to which the ethnographer enters the field with clearly delineated research questions. As noted in Chapter 8, most qualitative research begins with general research questions, but there is considerable variation in their specificity. Obviously, when there is a clear focus to a research question, ethnographers have to orient their observations to it. At the same time, they have to maintain a fairly open mind so that flexibility in the themes explored in the study—a strength of qualitative research—is not eroded.

In the context of her research on female drug users, Taylor (1993: 15) explained that in her early days in the field she tended to listen rather than talk because she 'did not know what questions [she] wanted to ask.' Armstrong (1993: 12) wrote in connection with his research on soccer hooliganism that his research 'began without a focus' and that as a result 'he decided to record everything.' Therefore a typical Saturday would mean 30 pages of hand-written notes. Such open-endedness usually cannot last long, because trying to record the details of absolutely everything is quickly tiring. Eventually the ethnographer begins to narrow down the focus of the research, sometimes by relating the emerging findings to the social-scientific literature on the topic. This approach is implied by the sequence suggested in Figure 8.1.

For most ethnographers, the main equipment needed for observation is a notepad and pen (for example, Armstrong 1993: 28). A tape recorder may be useful but, as suggested earlier, it is likely to radically increase the amount of transcription and may be more obtrusive than writing notes. Also, after a period of time participants usually grow accustomed to the presence of the researcher, but speaking into a tape recorder can rekindle fears about participating. In some gatherings it may be difficult to use a tape recorder because of the extraneous noise. Photography can be an additional source of data and pictures help to stir the ethnographer's memory, but in some kinds of research (especially involving crime and deviance) photography may not be feasible.

Types of field notes

Some writers have found it useful to classify the types of field notes generated in the process of conducting ethnography. The following classification is based on categories suggested by Lofland and Lofland (1995) and Sanjek (1990):

- *Mental notes:* particularly useful when it is inappropriate to be seen taking written notes; however, they should be put into writing at the earliest opportunity.
- *Jotted notes (also called scratch or rough notes):* very brief notes to jog one's memory about events that should be written up more fully later. Lofland and Lofland (1995: 90) referred to these as being made up of 'little phrases, quotes, key words, and the like.' They need to be written inconspicuously, preferably out of sight, since taking detailed notes in front of people may be off-putting for research participants.
- *Full field notes:* the main data source in ethnographic research. They should be written as soon

as possible, usually at the end of the day. Provide as much detail as possible about events, people, conversations, etc. At first, a particular quote from a person being studied or an account of an event that you witnessed may not seem to be that important. But later, once some kind of interpretive structure has been developed, its significance may become apparent. Without good notes, valuable data may be lost. Write down, in brackets, initial ideas about your interpretations, impressions, and feelings.

It is worth adding that in field notes the ethnographer's presence is frequently evident. This can be seen in Whyte's description of almost being thrown down the stairs reported earlier. However, in the finished work the ethnographer is sometimes written out of the picture. Field notes, except for brief passages, are primarily for the researcher's own use (Coffey 1999), whereas the written ethnography is for public consumption and has to be presented as a credible account of the social setting and culture in question. To put the ethnographer in the text too much risks making the account look like a description of his or her activities rather than those of the group purportedly under study. This issue will be addressed in further detail in Chapter 17.

Analytic memos

Most of the previous discussion focused on the mechanics of note taking. But content is even more important. There can be notes on the setting, the people, methodological problems encountered, etc. There can also be *analytic memos* that record not what the researchers see, but some initial thoughts on what it all means. They are written to oneself to help bridge the gap between the data and the concepts, interpretations, and theories that are developed to make sense of what is being observed. The memos should be dated and reviewed regularly. They should be kept separate from notes on actual observations because they are not data but comments on them.

The rise of visual ethnography

The use of visual materials in social research is by no means new. For example, for many years cultural anthropologists have used photographs in their portrayals of traditional societies. However, there is a clear sense that their use in social research has entered a new phase, one that can be discerned in books in this area, such as *Visual Ethnography* by Pink (2001).

A distinction can be made between the use of visual materials that existed before the research began and those produced more or less exclusively for research purposes. The former were featured in Chapter 7. This chapter emphasizes research-driven visual images, mainly photographs but also video recordings and other visual media. It is worth noting that although the term 'visual ethnography' is increasingly popular, it is sometimes used in a way that does not imply the kind of sustained immersion in a social setting that has been discussed in this chapter.

There are a number of ways in which visual materials have been employed by qualitative researchers:

1. as *aides mémoires* in the course of fieldwork, where they essentially become components of the ethnographer's field notes;
2. as sources of data in their own right; and
3. as prompts for discussion by research participants.

Pink (2001) drew an important distinction between two positions on visual materials. The traditional framework is a *realist* one in which the material simply captures an event or setting that then becomes a 'fact' for the ethnographer to interpret along with other data. The image and what it represents is presented as unproblematic, as a window on reality. This has been the dominant frame within which visual resources have been produced and analyzed. In contrast, Pink also drew attention to a position that she called *reflexive*. This entails an awareness of and sensitivity to the ways in which the researcher had an impact on what the visuals reveal. This sensitivity requires a grasp of the ways in which the researcher's age, gender, social background, academic proclivities, etc., may influence what is depicted and how it is presented.

Additionally, this approach to the visual is frequently collaborative in the sense that research participants may be involved in decisions about what visuals should be taken and how they are to be interpreted. Further, there is the recognition that the images may be viewed by different people in different ways. In Pink's research on Spanish bullfighters, enthusiasts interpreted the images she took of bullfights in terms of bullfighter performance.

Plate 9.1 *The Bullfighter's Braid*

Other viewers of the images might employ a different interpretive frame, such as one to do with animal rights and cruelty.

Plate 9.1 presents an image, referred to as *The Bullfighter's Braid*, from Pink's research. It depicts a female bullfighter and appealed to many connoisseurs of the sport who saw in it different artistic and other meanings. For Pink, it held additional significance in terms of her interests in gender and the broader discipline of social anthropology (see Pink 2001: 101 and http://sunsite.ualberta.ca/reflexive-frames/1_rprf/_E/gal_pink_1.html for more information about this photograph). Further examples of the use of visual resources in ethnographic contexts are described in Boxes 9.9 and 9.10.

Visual materials have great potential for ethnographers and qualitative researchers in general. For example, in her research on Niketown in Chicago, Peñaloza (1999) was interested in what she dubbed 'spectacular consumption,' that is, turning what would otherwise be a mundane consumption event (purchasing sportswear) into a spectacle through the use of sporting images, sounds, and atmosphere. In

Box 9.9   Photographs in a study of hospital wards

Radley and Taylor (2003a, 2003b) were interested in the role played by the physical setting of a hospital ward in patient recovery. Nine patients in a ward were asked to take photographs on the ward a few days after their surgery. Each patient was supplied with a camera and asked to take up to 12 photographs of things that were personally significant in the hospital. The only constraint was not to include people in their photographs (because of hospital restrictions). The researchers stayed with the patients while they took their photographs. Patients were interviewed a day after the photos were developed, and again a month or so later at home. On each occasion, patients were asked about all the photographs and which ones best expressed their stay in hospital. This approach to interviewing, namely, asking people to discuss

photographs and their meaning and significance, is often referred to as *photo-elicitation* or *photo-voice*.

Most of the images taken appear very mundane and neither striking nor interesting. However, the photographs took on considerable significance in the interviewees' narratives on the positive and negative aspects of their stays. As the authors expressed it: 'The camera engaged the patients with the hospital setting in a critical way. This meant that the photographic prints also became part of the passage . . . from hospital to home, something we have found to be important in how patients manage their recovery.'

Source: www.lboro.ac.uk/departments/ss/visualising_ ethnography/hospital.html, accessed 6 June 2008.

Box 9.10   Visual ethnography?

Clancey (2001) described a study in the Canadian High Arctic that used the extreme environment there to see how scientists might someday live and work on Mars. The research used a variety of methods and techniques, including ethnography (to understand how scientists like to work and live), photography, and time-lapse videos. He found this combination applicable to other multidisciplinary field expeditions that are spread over a large terrain.

exploring the role of the environment in creating a sense of spectacular consumption, an approach that included photography was very appropriate because spectacle is largely a visual phenomenon.

Visual research methods require researchers to 'read' images while being sensitive to the context in which they were generated, the potential for multiple meanings among researchers, study participants and others, and the potential for the researcher to influence the image and its presentation. In addition, researchers usually include non-visual research methods, such as interviews, in their investigations. This leads to the question of the relative significance of words versus images in the analysis of data and the presentation of findings. Since words are the

traditional medium, it is easy to slip into seeing the visual as less important, which is not always justified. Finally, visual research methods raise certain ethical issues, such as invasion of privacy and anonymity.

The end

Knowing when to stop is not an easy or straightforward matter in ethnography. Because of its unstructured nature and the absence of specific hypotheses for testing (other than those that may emerge during data collection and analysis), there is a tendency for ethnographic research to lack an obvious end point. It may be that there is an almost natural end to the research, such as investigations into the waning Toronto rave scene, but this is a fairly rare occurrence. Sometimes the rhythms of the ethnographer's occupational career or personal and family life necessitate withdrawal from the field. Such factors include: the end of a period of sabbatical leave; the need to write up and submit a doctoral thesis by a certain date; or funding for research being exhausted. Taylor (1993) wrote that one factor contributing to her departure from the field was the lengthy illness of her youngest son.

Also relevant is the fact that ethnographic research can be highly stressful for many reasons: the nature of the topic, which may place the fieldworker

Box 9.11   A feminist ethnography

Skeggs's (1997) longitudinal ethnographic study of 83 white, working-class women was 'based on research conducted over a total period of 12 years including 3 years' full-time, in-the-field participant observation. It began when the women enrolled in a "caring" course at a local college and it followed their trajectories through the labour market, education, and the family' (1997: 1).

The elements of a distinctively feminist ethnography can be seen in the following comments:

- 'This ethnography was politically motivated to provide space for the articulations and experiences of the marginalized' (1997: 23).
- The 'study was concerned to show how young women's experience of structure (their class and gender positioning) and institutions (education

and the media) frame and inform their responses and how this process informs constructions of their own subjectivity' (1994: 74). This comment, like the previous one, reflects a commitment to documenting women's lives and allowing their experiences to come through, while also pointing to the significance of context.

Skeggs felt that her relationship with the women was not exploitative. For example, she wrote that the research enabled the women's 'sense of self-worth' to be 'enhanced by being given the opportunity to be valued, knowledgeable, and interesting.' She claimed she was able to 'provide a mouthpiece against injustices' and to listen 'to disclosures of violence, child abuse, and sexual harassment' (1994: 81)

---

in tense situations (as in research on crime); the marginality of the researcher in the social setting and the constant need to manage a front; and the often prolonged absence from one's normal life. Ethnographers may simply feel that they have had enough.

An important reason for bringing fieldwork to a close is that reasonable answers to the research questions have been formulated. The ethnographer may even feel a strong sense of *déjà vu* towards the end of data collection if new data simply reiterate what has already been discovered. In the language of grounded theory, all the researcher's categories may become thoroughly *saturated*, although Glaser and Strauss's (1967) approach suggests that one should be certain that there are no new questions to be asked and no new comparisons to be made.

In sum, the reasons for bringing ethnographic research to a close can involve a wide range of factors, from the personal to matters of research design. Whatever the reason, disengagement has to be *managed*. For one thing, this means that promises must not be forgotten (for example, was a report promised as a condition of entry?). It also means that ethnographers must provide good explanations for their departure. Members of a social setting may know that the researcher is a temporary fixture, but over a long period of time, especially if there was genuine participation in activities within that

setting, people may forget that the ethnographer's presence is not permanent, so farewells may have to be arranged. Also, the ethnographer's *ethical* commitments must not be forgotten, such as the need to ensure that persons and settings are made anonymous—unless, of course, as sometimes happens, there has been an agreement that the social setting can be disclosed (as often occurs in the study of religious sects and cults).

Can there be a feminist ethnography?

This heading is in fact the title of a widely cited article by Stacey (1988) that rebuts the view that there can be a distinctively feminist ethnography. Reinharz (1992) saw feminist ethnography as important to feminism because:

- it documents women's lives and activities, which previously were seen as marginal and subsidiary to men's;
- it understands women from their perspective, so that research that 'trivializes females' activities and thoughts, or interprets them from the standpoint of men in the society or of the male researcher' (1992: 52) is rejected; and
- it understands women in context.

Similarly, Skeggs (2001: 430) observed that ethnography 'with its emphasis on experiences and the words, voice and lives of the participants' has been viewed by many feminist researchers as well suited to the goals of feminism.

Such commitments and practices go only part of the way. Of great significance to feminist researchers is whether the ethnography allows for a non-exploitative relationship between the researcher and the researched. One of the main elements of such a strategy is for the ethnographer not to treat the relationship as a one-way process of extracting information from others, but one in which the researcher can provide something in return. Skeggs's (1994, 1997) ethnographic research on young women represents one such attempt to create a non-exploitative relationship with the people being studied (see Box 9.11).

Stacey (1988), however, argued on the basis of her fieldwork experience that the various situations she encountered as a feminist ethnographer placed her 'in situations of inauthenticity, dissimilitude, and potential, perhaps inevitable betrayal, situations that I now believe are inherent in fieldwork method. For no matter how welcome, even enjoyable the fieldworker's presence may appear to "natives," fieldwork represents an intrusion and intervention into a system of relationships, a system of relationships that the researcher is far freer to leave' (1988: 23). Stacey also argued that when the research is written up, it is the feminist ethnographer's interpretations and judgments that come through and have authority, not those of the women who were studied. Skeggs responded to this by acknowledging that in the case of her own study her academic career was undoubtedly enhanced by the research, but added that Stacey's views present women research participants as victims. Skeggs maintained that:

> The young women were not prepared to be exploited; just as they were able to resist most things which did not promise economic or cultural reward, they were able to resist me. . . . They enjoyed the research. It provided resources for developing a sense of their self-worth. More importantly, the feminism of the research provided a framework [for them to see] . . . that their individual problems are part of a wider structure and not their personal fault (1994: 88).

Similarly, Reinharz (1992: 74–5) argued that, although ethnographic fieldwork relationships may sometimes seem manipulative, a clear undercurrent of reciprocity often lies beneath them. The researcher may offer help or advice to her research participants, or she may exhibit reciprocity by giving a public airing to normally marginalized voices (although the ethnographer is always the mouthpiece for such voices and may be imposing a particular 'spin' on them).

It is clear that the question of whether there is or can be a feminist ethnography is a matter of ongoing debate. The fact that female researchers are in careers that place them in a fairly desirable socioeconomic position while their subjects are often taken from more disadvantaged sectors of society is an issue that is not easily resolved. Nor, for that matter, is this issue easily dealt with by male researchers, who also tend to study the socially marginalized.

Key Points

- The ethnographer is typically a participant observer who also uses interviews and documents.

- The ethnographer may adopt an overt or covert role, but the latter carries great ethical difficulties.

- The method of access to a social setting depends in part on whether it is open (public) or closed (private or restricted).

- Key informants frequently play an important role in ethnography, but care is needed to ensure that their impact on the research is not excessive.

- Field notes are important memory aids for the ethnographer.

- Visual materials such as photographs and videos have attracted considerable interest among ethnographers in recent years, not just as adjuncts to data collection but as objects of interest in their own right.

- Ethnography conducted from a feminist standpoint has become a popular way to do this sort of research, although there have been debates about whether there can be a feminist ethnography as such.

— Questions for Review —

- To what extent can ethnography rely solely on observation?

Access

- 'Covert ethnography can make it easier to gain access to certain settings and therefore has much to recommend it.' Discuss.

- Does the problem of access end as soon as the researcher has gained entry to a particular setting?

- What is the role of key informants in ethnographic research? Is there anything to be concerned about when using them?

Roles for ethnographers

- What is meant by 'going native'?

- Should ethnographers be active or passive in their research settings? Explain.

Field notes

- Why are field notes important for ethnographers?

- Why is it useful to distinguish between different types of field notes?

The rise of visual ethnography

- How can visual materials be used in ethnography?

- Do photographs provide unproblematic images of reality? Discuss.

The end

- How does one decide when to bring an ethnographic study to a close?

Can there be a feminist ethnography?

- What are the main features of feminist ethnography?

- Assess Stacey's argument about whether feminist ethnography is possible, taking Skeggs's research or that of any other feminist ethnographer into consideration.

10 Interviewing in Qualitative Research

Chapter overview

This chapter is concerned with interviews in qualitative research. Two types are discussed: unstructured and semi-structured interviews. This chapter is concerned mainly with interviews with individuals, but the focus group method is also examined. The highlights of this chapter include:

- the differences between structured and qualitative interviewing;
- the main characteristics of and differences between unstructured and semi-structured interviewing;
- how to devise and use an interview guide for semi-structured interviewing;
- the different kinds of questions that can be placed in an interview guide;
- the importance of recording and transcribing qualitative interviews;

- the potential uses and pitfalls of online interviewing;
- how focus groups should be conducted, including such issues as the number and size of the groups, how to select participants, and how direct the questioning should be;
- issues concerning the interactions between participants in focus group discussions;
- some practical difficulties with focus group sessions, such as the possible loss of control over the proceedings and the potential for unwanted group effects;
- the significance of qualitative interviewing and focus groups in feminist research; and
- the advantages and disadvantages of qualitative interviewing relative to ethnography.

Introduction

The interview is probably the most widely used method in qualitative research. Ethnography usually involves a substantial amount of qualitative interviewing, and this undoubtedly contributes to its widespread use. But one can conduct qualitative interviews without doing a full-blown ethnographic study. In fact the flexibility of the qualitative interview and its economy of time and effort relative to ethnography make it an attractive option for many researchers. Although interviewing, transcribing interviews, and the analysis of transcripts are all very time-consuming, they can be more readily accommodated into researchers' personal lives than spending extended periods of time with their research subjects.

The two main types of qualitative interview are the unstructured and the semi-structured interview. A variety of specialized interview forms fall under those two headings and will be explored below, including focus groups, oral history interviews, and life history interviews.

Differences between structured and qualitative research interviews

Qualitative interviewing is quite different from interviewing in quantitative research:

- In quantitative research, the approach is highly structured to maximize reliability and validity in measuring key concepts. The researcher usually has a clearly specified set of research questions that the interview is designed to answer. Qualitative interviewing, on the other hand, is much less structured and tends to be more open-ended. It also allows a greater freedom to modify and add research ideas once the investigation has begun.

- There is greater interest in the interviewee's perspectives and concerns in qualitative interviewing; in quantitative research, the interview is driven mainly by the research agenda of the person conducting the study.
- In qualitative interviewing, going off on tangents is often encouraged. The investigator can ask unplanned questions that follow up on interviewees' replies, and the researcher may vary the order and even the wording of questions—doing so may provide insight into what the interviewee sees as relevant and important. In quantitative research, departing from the interview schedule is usually regarded as a nuisance and discouraged because it diverges from the specific research plan and may affect reliability and validity.
- Qualitative interviewing tends to be flexible, responding to the direction in which interviewees take the interview and perhaps adjusting the

emphases in the research as a result of the issues that emerge during the interview. By contrast, structured interviews are typically inflexible, because of a need to standardize the interactions with all interviewees.

- In qualitative interviewing, the researcher wants rich, detailed answers; in structured interviewing the interview is normally designed to generate specific answers that can be coded and processed quickly.
- In qualitative interviewing, it is not uncommon for the interviewee to be interviewed more than once (see Box 10.1 for an example). In structured interviewing, unless the research is longitudinal in character, the person is usually interviewed only once.

Unstructured and semi-structured interviewing

As noted, the two major types of qualitative interviewing are:

- The *unstructured interview:* here the researcher uses at most an *aide mémoire*, a small set of self-prompts to investigate certain topics. There may be just a single question asked by the interviewer

Box 10.1   Unstructured interviewing

Malbon (1999: 33) described his strategy for interviewing 'clubbers' (people who frequent nightclubs) as follows:

> interviews were very much 'conversational' in style, although all interviews were taped. The first interview was designed . . . to put the clubber at ease while also explaining fully and clearly in what ways I was hoping for help; to begin to sketch in details of the clubbers clubbing preferences, motivations and histories; and to decide how to approach the night(s) out that I would be spending with the clubber. . . . The main content of the second [more relaxed] interview consisted of comments, discussion, and questions about the club visits . . . and the nature of the night out as an experience. . . . [D]iscussion occasionally diversified . . . to cover wider aspects of the clubbers' lives.

Box 10.2 Semi-structured interviewing

Lupton (1996) investigated Australian food preferences using 33 semi-structured interviews conducted by four female interviewers (including herself). She wrote:

> Interviewees were asked to talk about their favourite and most detested foods; whether they thought there was such a thing as 'masculine' or 'feminine' foods or dishes; which types of foods they considered 'healthy' or 'good for you' and which not; . . . whether they liked to try new foods; which foods they had tasted first as an adult; whether there had been any changes in the types of food they had eaten over their lifetime; whether they associated different types of food with particular times, places or people; . . . whether they ate certain foods when in certain moods and whether they had any rituals around food (1996: 156, 158).

and the interviewee is allowed to respond freely, with the interviewer pursuing points that seem worthy of follow-up. Unstructured interviewing tends to be similar in character to a conversation.

- The *semi-structured interview*: the researcher has a list of questions or fairly specific topics to be covered, often referred to as an interview guide, but the interviewee still has a great deal of leeway in how to reply (see Box 10.2 for an illustration). Questions may not follow the exact order on the guide and some questions not included on the list may be asked as the interviewer picks up on things said by interviewees. Nonetheless, all of the questions are usually asked and a similar wording is used from interviewee to interviewee. Box 10.3 provides an example of these features, while Box 10.4 gives an example of the qualitative interviewing typical of life history research.

In semi- and unstructured interviews, the process is designed to bring out how the *interviewees themselves* interpret and make sense of issues and events. Bell (2007), for example, wanted to understand what western-Canadian separatists thought of Canadian federalism and the federal party system. Tastsoglou and Miedema (2003) sought to understand the meaning of community from the perspective of immigrant women, and Smith (2008) examined the meanings of pain for professional wrestlers. This is rather different than testing the *researcher's* hypotheses or theories about such matters, which is what is normally done in quantitative studies. Once again, recall that qualitative research is not just quantitative research without the numbers.

There is a growing tendency for semi-structured and unstructured interviews to be referred to collectively as *in-depth interviews* or *qualitative interviews*, although the semi- and unstructured types can produce very different results. The choice of one type rather than the other is affected by a variety of factors.

- Researchers who feel that using even the most rudimentary interview guide hinders genuine access to the world views of members of a social setting are likely to favour an unstructured interview. But even here it is rarely completely unstructured—the researcher usually has at least a general topic that is to be discussed.
- If the researcher is beginning the investigation with a fairly clear rather than a general focus, it is likely that the interviews will be semi-structured, so that the more specific issues can be addressed.
- To ensure a modicum of comparability of interviewing style if more than one person is to carry out the fieldwork, semi-structured interviewing may be preferred.
- Multiple-case study research generally needs some structure to ensure cross-case comparability, such as in the Workforce Ageing in the New Economy project mentioned in Box 3.1.

Preparing an interview guide

An interview guide is much shorter and less detailed than a structured interview schedule. In fact, it is often simply a brief list of memory prompts for areas to be covered in unstructured interviewing and a somewhat more elaborate list of issues to be addressed or questions to be asked in semi-structured interviewing. What is crucial is that the actual questioning is flexible, allowing interviewers to pursue leads offered by research participants as they begin to open up and reveal their view of the social world.

In preparing for qualitative interviews, Lofland and Lofland (1995: 78) suggested asking the question 'Just what about this thing is puzzling me?' This

Box 10.3 Flexibility in semi-structured interviewing

Like Lupton (see Box 10.2), Beardsworth and Keil (1992) were interested in food-related issues, particularly in vegetarianism. They carried out 73 'relatively unstructured interviews':

> guided by an inventory of issues to be covered in each session. As the interview program progressed, interviewees themselves raised additional or complementary issues, and these formed an integral part of the study's findings. In other words, the interview program was not based upon a set of relatively rigid pre-determined questions and prompts. Rather, the open-ended, discursive nature of the interviews permitted an iterative refinement, whereby lines of thought identified by earlier interviewees could be taken up and presented to later ones (Beardsworth and Keil 1992: 261–2).

Box 10.4   Life history interviews

One special form of interview associated with qualitative research is the life history interview. It is often combined with various kinds of personal documents like diaries, photographs, and letters. Subjects are invited to look back in detail across their entire life course, and to report their experiences and how they understood their world. While there has been a trickle of studies using this approach over the years (not including biographies of prominent figures), until fairly recently it was not popular. It was only rarely used because of the belief that a single life story is of limited generalizability, but generalization is usually not what is intended. Valuable insights may be gained from a life history regardless of whether other people have had the same experiences as the person described in the work. It also has the advantage of illustrating *process*—how events unfold and interrelate in people's lives over long periods of time.

An example of the life history interview approach is provided by Lewis (1961) in his research on the Sánchez family and their experiences in a Mexican slum:

> I asked hundreds of questions of [the five members of the Sánchez family]. . . . While I used a directive approach to the interviews, I encouraged free association, and I was a good listener. I attempted to cover systematically a wide range of subjects: their earliest memories, their dreams, their hopes, fears, joys, and sufferings; their jobs; their relationship with friends, relatives, employers; their sex life; their concepts of justice, religion, and politics; their knowledge of geography and history; in short, their total view of the world. Many of my questions stimulated them to express themselves on subjects that they might otherwise never have thought about (1961: xxi).

Miller (2000) points out that there has been a resurgence of interest in the method in recent years, one associated with the growing popularity of 'narrative interviews' in which the person studied 'tells a story' rather than responds to interviewer questions. The growing use of such interviews has come to be associated less and less with the study of a single life (or indeed just one or two lives) and is increasingly applied to several lives in a single project. M. Atkinson (2002, 2004), for example, conducted narrative interviews with women tattoo enthusiasts.

P. Atkinson (2004) observed that the duration of life story interviews varies considerably from study to study, but that it usually takes two or three sessions lasting 60 to 90 minutes each. He provided a catalogue of questions that can be asked, and divided them into the following groups (1990: 43–53):

- Birth and family of origin, for example, 'How would you describe your parents?'

- Cultural traditions, for example, 'Was your family different from others in town?'

- Social factors, for example, 'What were some of your struggles as a child?'

- Education, for example, 'What are your best memories of school?'

- Love and work, for example, 'How did you end up in the work you do or did?'

- Inner and spiritual life, for example, 'What are the stresses of being an adult?'

- Major life themes, for example, 'What were the crucial decisions in your life?'

- Vision of the future, for example, 'Is your life fulfilled yet?'

- Closure questions, for example, 'Have you given a fair picture of yourself?'

One variant of the life history interview is the *oral history* interview, a technique often used by historians. It is usually somewhat more specific in tone than the interviews described above in that the subjects may be asked to reflect on certain historical events or eras they have lived through. The emphasis is often on how the individual's life was affected by those things. The information gathered is sometimes combined with other sources of data, such as documents.

The chief problem with the oral history interview (which it shares with the life history interview) is the possibility of bias caused by memory lapses and distortions. Sugiman (2004) pointed out in her work on Japanese-Canadian women interned during the Second World War that memory is a social and even political act, involving recall, forgetting, transforming, and shaping of recollections. On the other hand, oral history testimonies can provide a voice to groups that are typically marginalized in historical research (true of life history interviews in general), either because of their lack of power or because they are regarded as unimportant.

can be applied to each of the research questions generated or it may be a mechanism for generating research questions. They suggested that puzzlement may be stimulated by various activities: random thoughts in different contexts (written down as quickly as possible); discussions with colleagues, friends, and relatives; and, of course, reading the existing literature on the topic. The formulation of the research question(s) should not be so specific that alternative avenues of inquiry that arise during fieldwork are closed. Such premature closure of the research focus would be inconsistent with qualitative research's prime purpose—to explore the world view of the people being studied, rather than testing the researcher's own ideas about that world.

The interview guide should:

- create a certain amount of order, so that questions flow reasonably well, but still allow the order of the questions to be changed and the impromptu asking of different questions;
- include questions or topics that address the research questions (without being too specific);
- use language that is comprehensible and familiar to those being studied;
- not ask leading questions, that is, questions that imply a 'correct' or socially acceptable answer (for example, 'Have you ever done something really stupid like take crack?'); and
- include prompts to remind the researcher to record basic information about the participant (name, age, gender, etc.) as well as more specific information that is relevant to the research questions (position in company, number of years employed, number of years involved in a group, etc.); such information is useful for putting people's comments into context.

There are also some practical details to attend to before the interview.

- Become familiar with the research setting, which is often the everyday surroundings of the interviewees. This will help to put their comments in context.
- Get a reliable tape recorder. Qualitative researchers (with the possible exception of ethnographers and people doing participant observation research) nearly always record and then transcribe their interviews. This is important for the

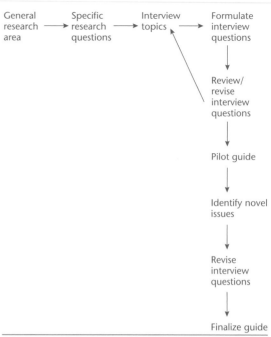

Figure 10.1 Formulating questions for an interview guide for social research

detailed analysis required in qualitative research, and to ensure that the interviewees' answers are captured in their own terms. It is too easy to lose words and phrases if note taking is used.
- Make sure as far as possible that the interview takes place in a setting that is quiet (so there is little or no noise to affect the quality of the recording) and private (so the interviewee does not worry about being overheard).
- Prepare for the interview by cultivating the traits of a quality interviewer suggested by Kvale (1996) (see Box 10.5).

After the interview, make notes about:

- how the interview went (was interviewee talkative, cooperative, nervous, etc.?);
- where the interview took place;
- any other feelings about the interview (did it open up new avenues of interest?); and
- the setting (noisy/quiet, many/few other people in the vicinity).

The steps to be taken to formulate questions for an interview guide in qualitative research are presented in Figure 10.1.

Box 10.5   Kvale's ten traits of an effective interviewer (plus three others)

Kvale (1996) proposed ten characteristics of a successful interviewer:

- *Knowledgeable:* is thoroughly familiar with the topic of the interview.

- *Structuring:* gives interviewee purpose of interview; asks if interviewee has questions.

- *Clear:* asks simple, easy, and short questions; no jargon.

- *Gentle:* lets people finish; gives them time to think; tolerates pauses.

- *Sensitive:* listens attentively to what is said and how it is said; is empathetic.

- *Open:* responds to what is important to the interviewee; is flexible.

- *Steering:* knows what needs to be found out.

- *Critical:* is prepared to challenge what is said, for example, when there is an inconsistency in interviewees' replies.

- *Remembering:* relates what is said to what has previously been said.

- *Interpreting:* clarifies and extends meanings of interviewees' statements but without imposing meaning on them.

To Kvale's list, please add the following:

- *Balanced:* does not talk too much, which can make interviewees passive, and does not talk too little, which can cause interviewees to feel their talk is not along the right lines.

- *Ethically sensitive:* for example, ensures the interviewee that all answers will be treated confidentially.

- *Non-judgmental:* does not communicate (even subtly) a moral judgment about what the interviewee has said or done; negative judgments may cause the participant to withhold information that may be useful to the study; positive judgments may result in the interviewee trying to please the interviewer rather than providing authentic commentary.

Kinds of questions

The kinds of questions asked in qualitative interviews are highly variable; Kvale (1996) suggested nine. Most interviews contain virtually all of them, although interviews that rely on lists of topics are likely to follow a somewhat looser format. Kvale's nine types are as follows:

- *Introducing questions:* 'Please tell me about when your interest in X first began?'; 'Have you ever …?'; 'Why did you go to …?'

- *Follow-up questions:* getting the interviewee to elaborate on an answer, such as 'What do you mean by that …?'; even, 'Yeesss?' Kvale suggested repeating significant words in an answer to stimulate further explanation. See Box 10.6 for an example.

- *Probing questions:* following up what has been said through direct questioning, such as 'Can you say some more about that?'; 'You said earlier that you prefer not to do X. Can you say what kinds of things have put you off it?'; 'In what ways do you find X disturbing?'

- *Specifying questions:* 'What did you do then?'; 'How did (name) react to what you said?'; 'What effect did (event) have on you?' See Box 10.6 for an example.

- *Direct questions:* 'Do you find it easy to keep smiling when serving customers?'; 'Are you happy with the way you and your husband decide how money should be spent?' Such questions are perhaps best left until later in the interview, in order not to influence the direction of the interview too much.

- *Indirect questions:* 'What do most people around here think of the ways that management treats its staff?' but only after asking 'How do you feel?' in order to get at the individual's own view first.

- *Structuring questions:* 'I would now like to move on to a different topic.'

- *Silence:* allow pauses to signal to the interviewee an opportunity to reflect and amplify an answer; do not pause so long that it embarrasses the interviewee.

- *Interpreting questions:* 'Do you mean that your leadership role had to change from one of encouraging others, to a more directive one?'; 'Is it fair to say that you don't mind being friendly towards customers most of the time, but when they are unpleasant or demanding you find it more difficult?'

As this list suggests, one of the main ingredients of the interview is listening—being attentive to what the interviewee is saying or not saying. It means that the interviewer is active without being intrusive—a difficult balance. But the interviewer cannot just sit back and relax, even if the interview is being recorded. In fact, an interviewer must be attuned and responsive not just to what the interviewee is saying and not saying but also to what the interviewee is doing. This is important because things like body language can indicate that the interviewee is becoming uneasy with a line of questioning. An ethically sensitive interviewer does not place undue pressure on an interviewee and is prepared to cut short any line of questioning that is clearly a source of anxiety.

It is also likely that the kinds of questions asked will vary in the different stages of a qualitative interview. Charmaz (2002) distinguished three types of questions in this connection. Note: the past and factual come first, then feelings, and finally questions of process and summing up.

- *Initial open-ended questions:* Examples are: 'What events led to . . .?'; 'What was your life like prior to . . .?'; 'Is this organization typical of others you have worked in?'
- *Intermediate questions:* 'How did you feel about . . . when you first learned about it?'; 'What immediate impact did . . . have on your life'; 'What do you like most/least about working here?'
- *Ending questions:* 'How have your views about . . . changed?'; 'What advice would you give to someone who is undergoing a similar experience . . .?'; 'If you had to do it over, would you choose to work for this organization?'

Most questions are likely to be of the intermediate kind and, in practice, some overlapping of categories is likely. Nonetheless, these are useful distinctions to bear in mind.

Remember as well that interviews include different kinds of topics, such as:

- values—of the interviewee, of the group, of the organization;
- beliefs—of the interviewee, of individual others, of the group;

Box 10.6   Using a semi-structured interview: research on female offenders

Two factors seem to have been instrumental in Davies' (2000) decision to use semi-structured interviewing with female offenders. First, she felt that her research questions—'exploring the types of crimes individuals engaged in and details of the ways in which they conducted them' (2000: 85)—were an important factor in her decision. A second factor was the consistency of semi-structured interviewing with the principles of feminist research 'because such interviews seek not to be exploitative but to be appreciative of the position of women' (2000: 86). Davies interviewed female offenders both in prison, which necessitated a lengthy series of negotiations about access, and in the community. Women in the latter were selected by already willing interviewees putting her in touch with others. She described her interview strategy as follows: 'Most important is to listen, then prompt and encourage when appropriate without "leading," and to steer the discussion back on track if it appears to be heading down a less promising avenue' (2000: 91). At one point, as a follow-up question, she repeated the interviewee's

words, a tactic mentioned by Kvale (1996), and then followed up the reply with what Kvale called a probing question (Davies is PD):

PD: You mentioned security tags and foil?
F: It depended on the shops—some shops we would just. . . when we just started out we didn't know about the foil so we used ter take in a pair of wire clippers, take them off, and dump them in the changing room but they made one hell of a crack—have you heard wire being cut? It made a hell of a bang so we just used ter take them off and shove them anywhere—yer know what I meant—somewhere they wouldn't be found like in a pocket of someone else's coat and . . . then we found out about the foil an we started doing that.
PD: How did you find out about that? (2000: 91).

Interviews were transcribed and written up within a day or two of their taking place so that any particular nuances or impressions would not be forgotten.

- behaviour—of the interviewee, of others;
- formal and informal roles—of the interviewee, of others;
- relationships—of the interviewee, of others;
- places and locales;
- emotions—particularly of the interviewee, but also of others;
- encounters; and
- stories.

Try to vary the type of question asked (as suggested by Kvale's nine types outlined above) and the different topics just listed, where appropriate. Vague questions or questions that are too general are usually best avoided. Mason (2002) counselled against using them, arguing that they merely force interviewees to puzzle over them or to ask for clarification.

Vignette questions can be used to ground interviewees' ideas and accounts of behaviour in particular situations (Barter and Renold 1999). By presenting interviewees with concrete and realistic scenarios, the researcher can elicit a sense of how certain contexts mould behaviour. Hughes (1998) employed the technique in a study of perceptions of HIV risk among intravenous drug users. Context is important for this topic because the drug users' willingness to engage in risky behaviour is influenced by situational factors. Scenarios were produced that presented risk behaviour, and respondents were asked about the kinds of behaviour they felt the drug users *should* engage in (such as using prophylactics when having sex) and then how they felt the hypothetical users *would* behave (when, for example, there is an opportunity for unprotected sex). Hughes argued that a scenario approach is particularly valuable with

---

Box 10.7   Part of the transcript of a semi-structured interview

Interviewer: OK. What were your views or feelings about the presentation of different cultures, as shown in, for example, Jungle Cruise or It's a Small World at the Magic Kingdom or in World Showcase at Epcot?

Wife: Well, I thought the different countries at Epcot were wonderful, but I need to say more than that, don't I?

Husband: They were very good and some were better than others, but that was down to the host countries themselves really, as I suppose each of the countries represented would have been responsible for their own part, so that's nothing to do with Disney, I wouldn't have thought. I mean some of the landmarks were hard to recognize for what they were supposed to be, but some were very well done. Britain was OK, but there was only a pub and a Welsh shop there really, whereas some of the other pavilions, as I think they were called, were good ambassadors for the countries they represented. China, for example, had an excellent 360-degree film showing parts of China and I found that very interesting.

Interviewer: Did you think there was anything lacking about the content?

Husband: Well I did notice that there weren't many black people at World Showcase, particularly the American Adventure. Now whether we were there on an unusual day in that respect I don't know, but we saw plenty of black Americans in the Magic Kingdom and other places, but very few if any in that World Showcase. And there was certainly little mention of black history in the American Adventure presentation, so maybe they felt alienated by that, I don't know, but they were noticeable by their absence.

Interviewer: So did you think there were any special emphases?

Husband: Well, thinking about it now, because I hadn't really given this any consideration before you started asking about it, but thinking about it now, it was only really representative of the developed world, you know, Britain, America, Japan, world leaders many of them in technology, and there was nothing of the Third World there. Maybe that's their own fault, maybe they were asked to participate and didn't, but now that I think about it, that does come to me. What do you think, love?

Wife: Well, like you, I hadn't thought of it like that before, but I agree with you.

sensitive topics and for eliciting a range of responses to different contexts.

Using an interview guide: an example

Box 10.7 is taken from a study of visitors to Disney theme parks (Bryman 1999). The interview is with a man in his sixties and his wife who is two years younger. They had visited Walt Disney World, and were very enthusiastic about the visit.

The sequence begins with the interviewer asking what is considered a 'direct question,' in terms of the nine question types suggested by Kvale (1996). The replies are very bland and do little more than reflect the interviewees' positive feelings about their visit to Disney World. The wife acknowledges this when she says, '. . . but I need to say more than that, don't I?' Interviewees frequently know that they are expected to be expansive in their answers. This sequence occurred about halfway through the interview, so the interviewees were primed by then into realizing that more details were expected. There is a tinge of embarrassment that the answer is so brief and not illuminating. The husband's answer is more expansive but not particularly enlightening.

Then the first of two important prompts by the interviewer follows. The husband's response is more interesting in that he now begins to answer in terms of the possibility that black people are underrepresented at attractions like the American Adventure, which tells the story of America via a debate between Mark Twain and Benjamin Franklin. The second prompt yields further useful reflection, this time that Third World countries are underrepresented in World Showcase in the Epcot Centre. The couple are clearly aware that the prompting has made them provide

these reflections when they say: 'Well, thinking about it now, because I hadn't really given this any consideration before you started asking about it.' This is the whole point of prompting—to get the interviewee to think more about the topic and to provide an opportunity for a more detailed response. It is not a leading question, since the interviewees were not being asked 'Do you think that the Disney company fails to recognize the significance of black history (or ignores the Third World) in its presentation of different cultures?' There is no doubt that the prompts elicit the more informative replies, which is precisely their role.

Recording and transcription

The point has been made several times that in qualitative research the interview is usually audio-recorded and then transcribed (not just listened to) whenever possible. Qualitative researchers are frequently interested not only in what people say but also in the way they say it. If this aspect is to be fully woven into an analysis, the complete series of exchanges in an interview must be available. Also, because interviewers are supposed to be highly alert to what is being said—following up interesting points made, prompting and probing where necessary, drawing attention to any inconsistencies in the interviewee's answers—it is best if they do not have to concentrate on writing down what is said as well. Also, recording interviews allows scrutiny by other researchers, who can evaluate the original analysis or even conduct a secondary analysis, which can help to counter accusations that the findings were influenced by the researcher's values or biases. In addition, recording allows the data to be reused in ways other than those intended by the original researcher—for example, to be analyzed using new theoretical ideas or analytic strategies.

As with just about everything in social research, there is a cost (other than the financial one of buying recording equipment and tapes or disks) in that the use of a recorder can upset respondents, who may become self-conscious or alarmed at the prospect of their words being preserved in that way. Most people will allow their interview to be recorded, though it is not uncommon for a small number to refuse. When that happens, the interview can be conducted by taking notes (as can interviews in which the tape recorder malfunctions). Among those who do agree to be recorded, some will still be fearful and as a

Practical Tip

Transcribing interviews

A student doing research for a thesis may not have the resources to pay for professional transcription, and unless he or she is an accurate touch typist, it can take a lot longer than the usual estimate of five to six hours per hour of speech, although using a transcription device with a foot-operated stop-start mechanism makes the task much easier. The important thing is to allow sufficient time for transcription and to be realistic about how many interviews can be transcribed in the time available.

result their interviews may not be as informative as they otherwise would be.

Another consideration is that transcribing a recorded interview takes a lot of time—five to six hours of transcription for every hour of speech. There is some debate over whether the interviewer should do it (more familiar with what was actually said) or an outside person (less time-consuming) (Rafaeli *et al.* 1997: 14). Furthermore, transcription yields vast amounts of text that then must be read. Beardsworth and Keil (1992: 262) reported that their 73 interviews on vegetarianism (see Box 10.3) generated 'several hundred thousand words of transcript material.' It is clear that, while transcription has the advantage of keeping the interviewee's (and interviewer's) words intact, it does so by piling up the text to be analyzed. It is no wonder that writers like Lofland and Lofland (1995) advise that the analysis of qualitative data not be left until all the interviews have been completed and transcribed. Insights may be gained by examining the content of early interviews, and it may be useful to pursue those points in greater detail in later interviews—there are good grounds for making analysis an ongoing activity (see Box 10.3 for an example). Also, to wait until all interviews have been completed may make the task of transcription seem overwhelming.

Practical Tip

Transcribing sections of an interview

Quite often whole interviews or at least large portions of them are not useful, perhaps because interviewees are reticent or their comments are not as relevant to the research topic as originally thought. There seems little point in transcribing such material. For example, Gerson and Horowitz (2002: 211) found some of their qualitative interviews 'uninspiring and uninteresting.' Therefore, one suggestion is to listen to the interviews closely once or twice before transcription begins, and then only transcribe those portions that seem useful or relevant. The same applies to focus group research, which is often more difficult and time-consuming to transcribe because of the number of speakers involved. The downside is that you may miss things, or certain things may emerge as significant only later on. If that happens, one would have to go back to the tapes to get the needed material.

It is easy to view transcription as a relatively unproblematic conversion of the spoken word into written form. However, given the importance of transcripts in qualitative research, the issue should not be taken lightly. Transcribers need to be trained in much the same way that interviewers are. Moreover, even among experienced transcribers errors occur. Poland (1995) provided some fascinating examples of the mistakes in transcription that can result from many different factors such as mishearing, fatigue, or carelessness. For example, one transcript contained the following passage:

> I think unless we want to become like other countries, where people have, you know, democratic freedoms . . .

But the actual words on the audiotape were:

> I think unless we want to become like other countries, where people have no democratic freedoms . . . (1995: 294)

Clearly, steps need to be taken to check on the quality of transcription.

In qualitative research, there is often a large amount of variation in the time that interviews take. For example, in Wilson's rave study (2002), the interviews lasted between 45 minutes and 4 hours. It should not be assumed that shorter interviews are necessarily inferior to longer, with the exception of those marked by interviewee non-cooperation or anxiety about being recorded. Indeed, when a long interview contains very little of significance it may not be worth the time and cost of transcription. Thankfully, such occasions are relatively unusual. If people do agree to be interviewed, they usually do so in a cooperative way and loosen up after initial anxiety about the microphone. As a result, even short interviews are often quite revealing.

Flexibility in the interview

A further point is the need for a flexible approach to interviewing. This advice involves more than being responsive to what interviewees say and following up on the interesting points they make. Flexibility is also important in such areas as varying the order of the questions and clearing up inconsistencies in answers. It is important in other respects too, such as coping with audio recording equipment breakdown and refusals by interviewees to allow a recording to take place.

A further issue that interviewers often confront is that as soon as they switch off their recording equipment, the interviewee may continue to ruminate on the topic of interest. It is usually not feasible to switch the machine back on again, so try to keep it on for as long as possible. If that fails, take some notes either while the person is talking or as soon as possible after the interview. Such 'unsolicited accounts' can often be the source of revealing information. This is certainly what Parker, in his study of organizations, found with 'unrecorded comments prefixed with a silent or explicit "well, if you want to know what I really think." . . . Needless to say, a visit to the toilet to write up as much as I could remember followed almost immediately' (2000: 236).

Focus groups: an introduction

Most people think of an interview as involving an interviewer and one interviewee. The focus group technique, however, involves speaking with more than one (usually at least four) interviewees at the same time. Essentially it is a group interview in which the interviewees can speak to and interact with one another.

Most focus group researchers work within a qualitative research tradition. They try to provide a fairly unstructured setting in which the person who runs the focus group, usually called the *moderator* or *facilitator,* guides each session but does not intrude. The distinguishing features of focus groups include:

- The technique allows the researcher to develop an understanding of *why* people feel the way they do. In an individual interview, the interviewee is often asked about their reasons for holding a particular view, but the focus group approach allows people to probe each other's reasons for holding it. This can be more informative and revealing than the question-followed-by-answer method of ordinary interviews. For one thing, an individual may answer in a certain way, but after hearing others may want to qualify or modify their views. Alternatively, some may want to voice agreement with something that they probably would not have thought of without hearing the views of

others. These possibilities permit focus groups to elicit a wide variety of perspectives on an issue.

- In conventional one-to-one interviewing, interviewees are rarely challenged; they may say things that are inconsistent with earlier replies or that patently cannot be true, but interviewers are often reluctant to point out such deficiencies. In a focus group, individuals often argue with each other and challenge each other's views. Arguing means the researcher may get more realistic accounts of what people think, because they are forced to defend and possibly revise their views.

- The focus group offers an opportunity to study how individuals collectively make sense of a phenomenon and construct meanings of it. It is a central tenet of theoretical positions like symbolic interactionism that meanings and understandings are not derived by individuals in isolation. Instead, they develop out of interactions and discussions with others. In this sense, focus groups reflect the processes through which meaning is constructed in everyday life, which allows them to be more naturalistic than individual interviews (Wilkinson 1998). On the other hand, it is unclear whether these new meanings persist beyond the focus group session.

Conducting focus groups

A number of practical aspects of conducting a focus group are considered below.

How many groups?

How many focus groups are needed? Table 10.1 provides some data on this, and on some other aspects of focus groups (cf. Deacon *et al.* 1999). As it suggests, there is a good deal of variation in the numbers of groups used, but generally they range from 10 to 15.

It is unlikely that just one group is sufficient, since the responses may not be typical of other groups. Nonetheless, there are good reasons for limiting the number of groups (besides saving time and resources). When the moderator can anticipate fairly accurately what the next group is going to say, enough groups have participated. This notion is similar to *theoretical saturation* discussed in Chapter 9.

One factor that can affect the number of groups is whether the researcher thinks that the range of views is likely to be affected by sociodemographic factors, such as age, gender, or social class. Many focus group researchers like to ensure that different demographic groups are included, which results in a large number of groups being studied. In connection with the research described in Box 10.9, Kitzinger (1994) wrote that a large number of groups is preferred in order to capture as much diversity in perspectives as possible. On the other hand, more groups increase the complexity of the analysis. For example, Schlesinger *et al.* (1992: 29; see Table 10.1 and Box 10.8) reported that their 14 tape-recorded

hour-long sessions produced more than 1400 pages of transcription for analysis.

Size of groups and selecting participants

How large should the groups be? Morgan (1998*a*) suggested 6 to 10 members. To control for the problem of 'no-shows,' over-recruiting is sometimes done (for example, Wilkinson 1999*a*: 188). Morgan recommended small groups when the participants are likely to have a lot to say, as often occurs when they are emotionally involved with the topic, when

---

Box 10.8   Asking about violence

Researchers usually want to inject some structure into their focus group sessions. An example of this is the research conducted by Schlesinger *et al.* (1992; see Table 10.1) on women viewing a film that featured varying levels of violence. For a rape scene, the reactions of the groups were gleaned through 'guiding questions' under five main headings, the first three of which had several more specific elements:

- Initially, participants were given the opportunity to discuss the film in terms of things like its purpose, its realism, and the storyline.

- The questioning then moved to reactions to the characters such as the woman who was raped, the three rapists, the female lawyer, and the male lawyers.

- Participants were then asked about their reactions to certain scenes, such as: the rape; the female

lawyer's decision to support the case after initially not supporting it; and winning the case.

- Participants were asked for their reactions to the inclusion of the rape scene.

- Finally, they were asked to give an assessment of the film's value, in particular whether the fact that it was American made a difference to their reactions.

While the research by Schlesinger and colleagues examined a lot of specific topics, initial questions were designed to generate relatively open-ended reactions. Such a general approach to questioning is fairly common in focus group research. It allows the investigator to address the research questions, ensures that there is some comparability between sessions, and permits participants to raise issues that *they* see as significant.

Box 10.9   Focus group in action: AIDS in the Media Research Project

Focus groups were part of Kitzinger's research on the representation of AIDS in the mass media. The focus groups were concerned with how 'media messages are explored by audiences and how understandings of AIDS are constructed. We were interested not solely in what people thought but in how they thought and why they thought as they did (Kitzinger 1994: 104).'

Details of the groups are given in Table 10.1. Since one goal of the research was to emphasize the role of interaction in the construction of meaning, it was important to provide a platform for doing that. Accordingly, 'instead of working with isolated individuals, or

collections of individuals drawn together simply for the purposes of the research, we elected to work with pre-existing groups—people who already lived, worked or socialized together' (Kitzinger 1993: 272). As a result, the groups were made up of collections of people such as a team of civil engineers working on the same site, six members of a retirement club, intravenous drug users, and so on. The sessions themselves are described as having been 'conducted in a relaxed fashion with minimal intervention from the facilitator—at least at first' (Kitzinger 1994: 106). Each session lasted approximately two hours and was tape-recorded.

Table 10.1 Composition of groups in focus group research

Authors	Frohlich *et al.* (2002)	Kitzinger (1993, 1994)	Lupton (1996)	Macnaghten and Jacobs (1997)	Miraftab (2000)	Schlesinger *et al.* (1992)
Area of research	A contextual understanding of pre-adoles-cent smoking behaviour	Audience responses to media mes-sages about AIDS	Responses to diet and health controversies	Understanding and identifi-cation with sustainable development	Housing experiences of Kurdish and Somali refugees in Vancouver	Responses of women to watching violence
Number of groups	Not specified	52	12	8 (each group had 2 sessions)	Not specified	14
Size range of groups	Probably 12	Not specified but appears to be 3–9 or 10	3–5	6–10	10–15	5–9
Average (mean) size of groups	na	6.75	4.1	approximately 8	na	6.6
Criteria (if any) for inclusion	4 groups out of 32 Quebec communities	No, but groups made up of specific groups (e.g., retirement club members, male prosti-tutes)	Gender	Age, ethnicity, gender, occupation/ retired, rural/ urban location	None, except being recent immigrant	Experience of violence, Scottish/ English, ethnicity, class
Natural groups	No	Yes	Yes	No	No	Some

the topic is controversial or complex, or when exploring personal interpretations. Larger groups are appropriate when the researcher wants 'to hear numerous brief suggestions' (1998a: 75).

Most topics do not require a particular kind of participant, but the topic should be relevant to those taking part. A wide range of people is often required, but they may be put into separate groups on the basis of age, gender, education, having or not having had a certain experience, and so on. The aim is to look for any variation in how the different groups discuss the matter at hand. For example, to examine responses of women to viewing violence, Schlesinger *et al.* (1992) showed 14 groups (see Table 10.1) four levels of mass-media violence: incidental violence, moderate violence, marital violence, and an extremely vivid sexual assault scene. The authors concluded:

Having a particular experience or a particular background does significantly affect the

interpretation of a given text. The four programs screened are obviously open to various readings. However, on the evidence, *how* they are read is fundamentally affected by various socio-cultural factors and by lived experience (1992: 168; emphases in original).

A slight variation on this approach is Kitzinger's (1994) study of reactions to media representations of AIDS (see Box 10.9 and Table 10.1). Her groups were made up of people in a variety of different situations. Some were what she called 'general population groups' (for example, a team of civil engineers working on the same site) but others were made up of those who might have a special interest in AIDS (for example, male prostitutes or intravenous drug users). Increasingly, focus group practitioners try to discern patterns of variation by putting together groups with particular attributes.

A further issue in selecting group participants is whether to select people who are unknown to each other, or to use natural groups (for example, friends, co-workers, or students in the same class). Some researchers prefer to exclude people who know each other, fearing that pre-existing styles of interaction or status differences may contaminate the session. Others prefer to select natural groups whenever possible. Holbrook and Jackson (1996) reported that, for their research on shopping centres, they initially tried to secure participants unknown to each other, but this strategy attracted no takers. They then sought out participants in various social clubs. Their new view was defended by arguing that, because their research questions concerned shopping in relation to the construction of identity and how it relates to people's sense of place, recruiting people who knew each other would be a highly appropriate strategy. Opting to recruit people from natural groups is not always feasible, however, because of the difficulties in getting everyone in the group to participate. Morgan (1998*a*) revealed another downside—because people in natural groups know each other, they may have taken-for-granted assumptions that they feel do not need to be explained or justified. He suggested that if it is important that such assumptions are made explicit, groups of strangers are better.

Asking questions and level of moderator involvement

There are different questioning strategies and approaches to moderating focus group sessions. Most lie between a rather open-ended style and a more structured one. For example, Macnaghten and Jacobs' (1997) middle-of-the road approach to question structuring can be seen in the following passage in which a group of working women reveal a cynicism about government and experts regarding the reality of environmental problems (in this passage 'F' is 'female' and 'Mod' is moderator):

> *F:* They only tell us what they want us to know. And that's just the end of that, so we are left with a fog in your brain, so you just think—what have I to worry about? I don't know what they're on about.
> *Mod:* So why do Government only tell us what they want us to hear?
> *F:* To keep your confidence going. (All together)
> *Mod:* So if someone provides an indicator which says the economy is improving you won't believe it?
> *F:* They've been saying it for about 10 years, but where? I can't see anything!
> *F:* Every time there's an election they say the economy is improving (1997: 18).

In this passage, there is an emphasis on the topic to be addressed but also a capacity to pick up on what the group says.

How involved should the moderator/facilitator be? This question is similar to the considerations about how unstructured the interview should be. There is a tendency for researchers to use a fairly small number of very general questions to guide the focus group session. Obviously, if the discussion goes completely off topic it may be necessary to refocus the participants' attention, but even then it is necessary to be careful, because what may appear to be digressions may reveal something of significance. More direction is probably needed if the research questions are not being addressed by participants or if a particularly meaningful point made by one participant is not followed up by the others.

Both intervention and non-intervention carry risks. The style of questioning and moderating depends on the nature of the research topic; if it is embarrassing, for example, it may require more direction from the moderator. The level of interest and knowledge among participants can make a difference as well. A low level of participant interest or knowledge may require a somewhat more structured approach. If in doubt, the best advice is to err on the side of minimal intervention.

Recording and transcription

Recording the focus group session is even more important than it is in other forms of qualitative research. Writing down not only exactly what people say but also who says it is too difficult. In an individual interview one may be able to ask a respondent to 'hold on' while writing something down, but doing this in an interview involving several people speaking rapidly is not feasible and would probably break the flow of the discussion.

Transcribing focus group sessions is also more complicated and hence more time-consuming than it is with other forms of interview. Sometimes people's voices are hard to distinguish, making it difficult to determine who is speaking. Also, people sometimes talk over each other, which can make transcription even more problematic. Therefore, a very high-quality recording device, one capable of picking up even faint voices from many directions, is a necessity. Focus group transcripts always seem to have more missing bits, due to lack of audibility, than transcripts from other sorts of interview.

Group interaction in focus group sessions

Kitzinger (1994) observed that reports of focus group research frequently do not take group interaction into account. This is surprising, given that such interaction is a distinguishing feature of focus groups. Wilkinson reviewed over 200 focus group studies, published between 1946 and 1996, and concluded: 'Focus group data is most commonly presented as if it were one-to-one interview data, with interactions between group participants rarely reported, let alone analyzed' (1998: 112).

In the context of her research on the coverage of AIDS in the mass media, Kitzinger (1994) drew attention to two types of interaction in focus groups: complementary and argumentative interactions. The former allow collective interpretations and understandings to develop, with each participant building on the preceding remark, as in the following passage taken from Morgan and Spanish's (1985: 414) research on heart attack victims:

No. 1: But I think maybe what we're saying here is that there's no one cause of heart attacks, there's no one type of person, there's probably umpteen different types of heart attacks and causes coming from maybe smoking, maybe obesity, maybe stress, maybe design fault, hereditary,

overwork, change in life style. Any of these things in themselves could be . . .
No. 2: And when you start putting them in combination [unclear].
No. 3: Yeah, you may be really magnifying each one of these particular things.
No. 2: Yeah, and depending on how, and in each person that magnification is different. Some people can take a little stress without doing any damage, some people can take a little smoking, a little drinking, a little obesity, without doing any damage. But you take a little of each of these and put them together and you're starting to increase the chances of damage. And any one of these that takes a magnitude leap increases the chances.

This sequence brings out the emerging consensus around the question of who has heart attacks and why. No. 1 summarizes several factors that have been discussed; No. 2 then introduces the possible significance of some of these factors existing in combination; No. 3 agrees about the importance of combinations of factors; and No. 2 summarizes the position of the group on the salience of combinations of factors, raising at the same time the possibility that for each person there may be unique combinations of factors that are responsible for heart attacks.

However, as Kitzinger (1994) suggested, argumentative interactions in focus groups can be equally revealing, and moderators can play an important role in identifying differences of opinion and exploring with participants the factors that lie behind them. Disagreement can provide participants with a chance to revise their opinions or to think about why they hold them. By way of illustration, a passage from Schlesinger *et al.* (1992; see Table 10.1) is presented. The group is made up of women with no experience of violence. The debate is concerned with a rape scene in a film:

Speaker 1: I think . . . that they could've explained it. They could easily leave [out] that rape scene.
Speaker 2: But it's like that other film we watched. You don't realize the full impact, like, the one we were watching, the first one, until you've got the reconstruction.
Speaker 3: Yeah, but I think with that sort of film, it would cause more damage than it would good, I mean, if someone had been raped, would you like to have [to] sit through that again?

The debate then continued to consider the significance of the scene for men:

> *Speaker 1:* Men would sit down and think, 'Well, she asked for it. She was enjoying it and look, the men around enjoyed it (1992: 51–2).'

One factor that seems to be behind the unease of some of the women about the inclusion of the rape scene is that some men may enjoy it rather than find it repulsive, and identify with the onlookers depicted in the film. This interpretation came about because of earlier disagreement within the group, which allowed a fuller account of women's reactions to the scene to be forged.

In sum, as Kitzinger (1994) argued, drawing attention to patterns of interaction within focus groups allows a researcher to determine how group participants view the issues at hand. The posing of questions by focus group members as well as the agreement and disagreement among them help to bring out this knowledge. The resolution of disagreements also forces participants to justify why they hold the views they do.

Limitations of focus groups

Focus groups are particularly useful in illustrating how meaning is jointly constructed. What, then, are their chief limitations?

- The researcher probably has less control over the proceedings compared to individual interviews. As seen, not all writers on focus groups perceive this as a problem and indeed feminist researchers often see it as an advantage. However, the question of control raises issues about the extent to which a researcher can allow the participants to 'take over' the discussion. There is clearly a delicate balance to be struck over how involved moderators should be and how far a set of prompts or questions should influence the conversation. What is not clear is the degree to which it is appropriate to surrender control, especially when there is a set of research questions to be answered.
- An unwieldy amount of data is sometimes produced. For example, Bloor *et al.* (2001) suggested that one focus group session can take up to eight hours to transcribe, somewhat longer than an equivalent personal interview, because of variations in voice pitch and the need to take account of who says what. Also, focus group recordings are particularly prone to inaudible comments from those far away from the microphone, which affect transcription.
- The data may be difficult to analyze. Developing a strategy of analysis that incorporates both the themes found in the discussion and patterns of interaction is not easy.
- They are difficult to arrange, both in terms of achieving the initial agreement to participate and getting people to show up. Very small payments, such as book tokens, are sometimes made to induce participation, but nonetheless it is common for people not to turn up.
- Group effects may be a problem. This includes the obvious issue of dealing with reticent individuals and with those who hog the stage. Krueger (1998) suggested that the people running the focus group should make it clear to participants that other people's views are definitely required; for example, he suggested saying something like 'That's one point of view. Does anyone have another point of view?' (1998: 59). As for those who do not speak very much, it is recommended that they be actively encouraged to say something.

In another context, it would be interesting to know how far agreement among focus group participants is more frequently encountered than disagreement, perhaps due to group pressure to conform. Related to that is the fact that participants in a group setting may be more prone to expressing socially acceptable views than in individual interviews. Morgan (2002) cited a study in which group interviews with boys on the topic of relationships with girls were compared with individual interviews with boys on the same subject. Alone, the boys express a degree of sensitivity not present in the group context, where more macho views tend to be forthcoming. This suggests that in groups the boys were trying to impress each other or avoid embarrassment, and were influenced by peer pressure. However, this does not make the group interview data tainted, because it may be the gulf between privately and publicly held views that is of interest.

- Madriz (2000) proposed that there are circumstances when individual interviews are more appropriate. One is when participants are likely to disagree profoundly with each other, a second when participants are not comfortable in each other's presence (for example, people in hierarchical relationships). Finally, because of the potential for focus groups to cause discomfort among participants (such as when intimate details of private lives need to be revealed), an individual interview or even a questionnaire may be better.

Online interviews and focus groups

Conducting qualitative interviews and focus groups online has become increasingly common as more and more members of the general public gain familiarity with the Internet. At the time of writing, online focus groups appear to have attracted greater attention than online personal interviews, perhaps because of their practical advantages. For example, with focus groups, a great deal of time and administrative effort can be saved by working online, whereas there is less to be gained in that regard with online personal interviews (unless a great deal of travel is avoided by going online).

Doing this sort of research online has its pros and cons. Selecting participants may be difficult, since everyone taking part must have access to the necessary hardware and software. Carefully selected websites, online bulletin boards, and chat rooms are potential sources of recruitment.

Online qualitative interviews

Markham (1998) conducted Internet interviews that followed a period of 'lurking' (reading but not participating) in computer-mediated communication forums like chat rooms. The asking and answering of questions were in real time, rather than what might occur via email, where a question might be answered hours or days later. She used an interview guide, with the interviews lasting for about one to four hours. Such interviews are a challenge for both interviewer and interviewee because neither party can pick up on visual cues (puzzlement, anxiety) or auditory cues (sighs, groans).

One of Markham's interests lay in the reality of online experiences. This can be seen in the following brief sequence (Markham is Annette):

Annette: How real are your experiences in the Internet?
Sherie: How real are experiences off the Internet? (1998: 115)

Markham noted how her notion of 'real' was different from that of her interviewees. For Markham, 'real' carried a connotation of genuineness and authenticity, but for her interviewees it had more to do with distinguishing experiences that occur offline (real) from those online (not real). It is likely that these distinctions between life online and life offline will become less significant as everyday life is increasingly conducted on the Internet.

Kendall (1999: 62) came up with similar findings. She spent three years as an online participant observer, along with conducting face-to-face interviews and attending gatherings in person. She was interested in issues to do with identity and the online presentation of self, and found that the participants gave higher status to actual experiences (real) over virtual ones (online and not real).

Online focus groups

Mann and Stewart (2000) suggested that an online focus group have between six and eight people. Larger groups make it difficult for some people to participate, especially those with limited keyboard skills. Also, moderating the session can be more difficult with larger numbers, and as Adrienssens and Cadman (1999) have suggested, large groups can present administrative problems.

Before starting an online focus group session, moderators are advised to send out a welcome message introducing the research and laying out some of the ground rules for the discussion. There is evidence that participants respond more positively if the researchers reveal something about themselves (Curasi 2001). This can be done in the opening message or by creating links to a personal website.

In online focus groups, participants make contributions more or less immediately after the previous one (whether from the moderator or other participants). As all are simultaneously online, contributions can be responded to as soon as they are typed (and with some forms of software, the contributions can be seen as they are being typed). As Mann and Stewart (2000) observed, because several

Box 10.10 An online focus group study

O'Connor and Madge (2001, 2003; see also Madge and O'Connor 2002) employed conferencing software in a virtual focus group study that examined the use of an online information website for parents. Initially, the researchers set up a web survey on the use of the website. When respondents sent in their questionnaires, they were thanked for their participation and asked via email whether they were prepared to be interviewed in-depth. Of the 155 respondents who returned the questionnaires, 16 agreed to be interviewed. Interviewees were sent the software to install on their computers. The researchers tried to ensure that each group was asked more or less the same questions. For each session, the researchers introduced themselves and asked participants to do likewise. In addition, they placed descriptions and photographs of themselves on a website to which participants were directed. An important part of the process of building rapport was the fact that both of the researchers were mothers. One of the findings was that the greater anonymity afforded by the Internet gives participants greater confidence in asking embarrassing questions, a finding that has implications for online focus groups in general. This can be seen in the following excerpt:

> *Amy:* I feel better asking BW [Babyworld] than my health visitor as they're not going to see how bad I am at housekeeping!!!

Kerry: I feel the same. Like the HV [health visitor] is judging even though she says she isn't
Kerry: Although my HV has been a lifeline as I suffer from PND [post-natal depression]
Amy: Also, there are some things that are so little that you don't want to feel like you're wasting anyone's time. Asking the HV or GP might get in the way of something mroe important, whereas sending an e-mail, the person can answer it when convenient.
Amy: My HV is very good, but her voice does sound patronising. I'msure she doesn't mean it, but it does get to me . . .
Kerry: Being anon means that you don't get embarrassed asking about a little point or something personal (O'Connor and Madge 2001: 10.4).

This extract reveals a good flow without intervention by the researchers. It contains several mistakes (for example, 'I'msure'), but they are retained to preserve the authenticity of the interaction. Another plus is that the researchers do not have to transcribe the material because it is already in textual form. Also, the fact that participants appear to relish the anonymity of the Internet has implications for online focus groups because participants may find it easier to ask naïve questions or make potentially embarrassing comments than they do in face-to-face focus groups.

---

participants can type in a response to something at the same time, the convention of taking turns in regular conversations is largely sidelined.

Online focus groups are unlikely to replace their face-to-face counterparts but instead are likely to be used for certain kinds of research topics and/or samples. As regards the latter, dispersed or inaccessible people are especially suitable for online focus group research; slow typists are not. As Sweet (2001) pointed out, appropriate topics for online research are likely to be those involving sensitive issues or ones about Internet use itself (see, for example, Box 10.10).

While much research on the Internet treats the technology as a given, recent studies examine how it is *interpreted* by users. Hine (2000: 9), for instance, presented the Internet 'as a product of culture . . . shaped by the ways in which it is marketed, taught,

and used.' Box 10.11 summarizes the main advantages and disadvantages of doing focus groups and personal interviews online compared to administering them in person. The two methods are combined because the tally of advantages and disadvantages applies more or less equally well to both of them.

Feminism and interviewing in qualitative research

Unstructured and semi-structured interviewing are prominent in feminist research. The popularity of qualitative research is attributable in part to the view that it allows many of the goals of feminism to be realized. One writer has observed: 'Whilst several brave women in the 1980s defended quantitative

Box 10.11   Advantages and disadvantages of conducting focus groups and individual interviews online compared to face-to-face settings

Advantages

- Online interviews and focus groups are extremely cheap to conduct compared to comparable face-to-face equivalents.

- Interviewees or focus group participants who would otherwise be inaccessible (for example, in another country) or reluctant to participate (for example, senior executives or other very busy people) are more easily brought into the study.

- Interviewees and focus group participants are able to read and reread their statements (and in focus groups, those of the other participants as well).

- The interviews do not have to be audio recorded, thus eliminating interviewee apprehension about that and avoiding the time-consuming and expensive process of transcription.

- The transcripts of the interviews are more accurate because mishearing and not hearing do not arise. This is a particular advantage with focus group discussions.

- Participants can employ pseudonyms to conceal their identity, making it easier for them to discuss embarrassing issues or to divulge potentially unpopular views.

- In focus groups, shy or quiet people may find it easier to participate and overbearing participants are less likely to predominate, though variations in keyboard skills may militate against equal participation.

- Participants are less likely to be influenced by factors like the age, ethnicity, or appearance (and possibly even gender if pseudonyms are used) of the other participants in a focus group.

- Similarly, interviewees and focus group participants are less likely to be affected by the characteristics of interviewers or moderators, and the latter are less likely to be affected by the participants' characteristics, thus reducing reactivity.

- When interviewees and participants are online at home, they are essentially being provided with an 'anonymous, safe and non-threatening environment' (O'Connor and Madge 2002: 11.2), one that may be especially helpful to vulnerable groups.

- Similarly, researchers do not have to enter what may be unsafe environments to reach the people studied.

---

methods, it is nonetheless still the case that not just qualitative methods, but the in-depth face-to-face interview has become the paradigmatic "feminist method'" (Kelly *et al.* 1994: 34). Feminist researchers advocate a framework for conducting interviews that establishes:

- a high level of rapport between interviewer and interviewee;
- a high degree of reciprocity on the part of the interviewer;
- the perspective of the woman being interviewed; and
- a non-hierarchical relationship.

However, as noted in previous chapters, while the adherence to a set of principles for interviewing in feminist research continues, it has been tempered with a growing recognition of the potential of quantitative research (and the structured interview) to achieve feminist goals.

A dilemma arises when feminist researchers have to decide what to do if their own 'understandings and interpretations of women's accounts would either not be shared by some of the research participants, and/or represent a challenge or threat to their perceptions, choices, and coping strategies' (Kelly *et al.* 1994: 37). It is the first type of situation that is examined here, at least in part because its implications go beyond feminism to the tricky question of how far a commitment to seeing through the eyes of those being studied can or should be stretched. Two examples are relevant. Reinharz (1992: 28–9) cited a study by Andersen in which 20 'corporate wives' came across in their interviews as happy with their lot and supportive of feminism only in relation to employment discrimination. Andersen interpreted their responses as indicating a 'false

Box 10.11 . . . Continued

Disadvantages

- Online focus groups and interviews take longer.

- Only people with access to online facilities and who are comfortable using them are likely to participate.

- It is more difficult for the interviewer to establish rapport with interviewees. This is less of a problem when the topic is of greater interest to participants.

- Probing is more difficult, though not impossible. Curasi (2001) reported some success in eliciting further information from respondents, but it is easier for them to ignore or forget about these requests.

- There is less spontaneity in responding since interviewees can reflect on their answers much more than is possible in a face-to-face situation. However, this can be construed as an advantage in some respects since interviewees are likely to give more considered replies.

- There is a tendency for non-response to be higher in online personal interviews.

- The researcher cannot be certain that the people who are interviewed are who they say they are

(though this issue may apply on occasion to face-to-face interviews as well).

- Online interviews and focus groups require considerable commitment from interviewees and participants if they have to install software onto their computers and remain online for extended periods of time. This is especially problematic if they have to pay for the software (though reimbursement may be possible), and if participation blocks their telephone lines.

- The interviewer/moderator may not be aware that the interviewee/participant is distracted by something and in such circumstances will continue to ask questions as if they have the person's full attention.

- Online connections may be lost and long breakdowns may ensue, which can break the flow of the discussion.

- Interviewers cannot capitalize upon body language that might suggest puzzlement or in the case of focus groups a waning desire to contribute to the discussion.

Source: Adapted from Adrianssens and Cadman (1999); Bampton and Cowton (2002); Clapper and Massey (1996); Curasi (2001); Mann and Stewart (2000); O'Connor and Madge (2001); Sweet (2001); Tse (1999).

---

consciousness'—in other words, she concluded that they did not really understand how gender relations work. When Andersen wrote an article based on her findings, the women wrote a letter rejecting her account, affirming that women can be fulfilled as wives and mothers. A similar situation confronted Millen (1997) when she interviewed 32 female scientists using semi-structured, in-depth individual interviewing. As Millen (1997: 5.6, 5.9) put it:

> From my external, academically privileged vantage point, it is clear that sexism pervades these professions, and that men are assumed from the start by other scientists, to be competent scientists of status whilst women have to prove themselves, overcome the barrier of their difference before they are accepted. These women, on the other hand, do not generally view their interactions in terms of gendered social

systems. There is therefore a tension between their characterisation of their experience and my interpretation of it . . .

Two important issues arise from these two accounts. First, how can such a situation come about? If researchers are genuinely committed to seeing through the eyes of others, the 'tension' to which Millen referred should not have developed. However, it did, and this suggests that qualitative researchers are more affected by their own perspectives and research questions than would be expected from textbook accounts of the qualitative research process. Second, given that feminist research is often concerned with the wider political goal of emancipation, a tension between participants' world views and the researcher's position raises moral questions about the appropriateness of imposing an interpretation not shared by the research participants themselves. Such an imposition can hardly be regarded as consistent with the principle of a non-hierarchical relationship in interviews.

These issues have a significance that extends beyond feminism. Any qualitative researcher—whether feminist or non-feminist—may have to make a decision about what to do when they strongly disagree with the views of the people being studied.

The focus group as a feminist method

The use of focus groups by feminist researchers has grown considerably in recent years and Wilkinson (1998, 1999*b*) has argued for its great potential in this regard. Three aspects of the method stand out in terms of their compatibility with the ethics and politics of feminism.

- Focus group research is less artificial than many other methods because it features group interaction, which is a normal part of social life. Moreover, the tendency to recruit participants from naturally occurring groups reinforces its realistic qualities, since people are able to discuss matters in situations that are quite normal for them. As a result, there is greater opportunity to derive understandings that resonate with the 'lived experience' of women. However, not all writers accept the contention that focus groups are more natural

than individual interviews. Even when pre-existing groups are used, gathering people to discuss a certain topic (such as a television program) is not inherently naturalistic, the critics claim, because the interaction is so unusual and contrived. In real life one is rarely asked to discuss, in a group, an issue not of one's choosing.

- Feminist researchers have expressed a preference for methods that study the individual within a social context. The tendency for most methods to treat the individual as an isolated entity devoid of a social context is disliked by many feminist researchers, who prefer to analyze 'the self as relational or as socially constructed' (Wilkinson 1999*b*: 229–30).

- As noted previously, feminist researchers are suspicious of research methods that exploit participants and create a power relationship between the researcher and the respondent. Wilkinson observed that the risk of this occurring is greatly reduced in focus groups because the participants are able to take control of the discussion. Indeed, they may even subvert the goals the researcher had for the session. As a result, participants' points of view are much more likely to be revealed in a focus group than in a traditional interview.

Wilkinson did not argue that focus groups, or indeed any method, are inherently feminist. Her

Box 10.12 Focus group: a model of women-centred research

A recent qualitative study (Graham *et al.*, 2004) used focus groups to investigate factors that promote or inhibit women's sexual arousal. The purpose of the study was to develop a questionnaire on the topic for women. One already existed for men, but rather than adapting it for women with minor changes, the researchers 'wanted to hear from women themselves' (2004: 528). The study focused on several themes, including 'feelings about one's body; concern about reputation; unwanted pregnancy/contraception; feeling desired versus feeling used by a partner' (2004: 527), and involved nine groups of women that varied on a number of characteristics such as age, race, education, and sexual orientation.

In Canada, recent feminist research using focus groups includes Ristock (2001), Little (2001), and Wachholz and Miedema (2000). Ristock examined how 70 feminist counsellors responded to clients

reporting abuse in a lesbian relationship, and revealed how even feminist models and therapies for heterosexual violence may need revision in such instances. Little looked at Ontario single mothers on welfare after they had experienced reduced support services and enhanced measures to force job seeking. Specifically, she conducted a secondary analysis of 200 focus group interviews done by Ontario Workfare Watch. As a result, she was able to dispel some of the myths about these women and to underscore some of the ways they were forced to cope, including not eating and moving in with abusive ex-partners. Finally, Wachholz and Miedema examined how immigrant women feel about the police intervention that follows official reports of spousal abuse. The 'solution' often brings with it the harm of extra economic hardships for immigrant women already faced with socioeconomic vulnerability.

Ethical issue 10.1

Ethics in research on prostitution

O'Connell Davidson and Layder (1994) discussed a small-scale ethnographic research on a prostitute, Desiree [a pseudonym], and her clients. While Desiree and the women who served as her receptionists by welcoming clients were fully aware of O'Connell Davidson's status, the clients were not. Both researchers acknowledged an invasion of client privacy and a lack of informed consent, but were 'untroubled' by the intrusion because the clients were anonymous to O'Connell Davidson and she was not 'in a position to secure, store or disclose information that could harm them' (1994: 214). The fact that there was no harm to participants was regarded as the litmus test of the ethical status of the research. They offered a further defence by saying that ethical transgression is pervasive: 'Virtually all social research is intrusive and exploitative to some degree' (1994: 215). There was an acknowledged commitment to

and sympathy for Desiree and her receptionists, but these sentiments did not extend to her clients:

> I have . . . no personal liking and no real sympathy for them. I have a professional obligation to preserve their anonymity and to ensure that they are not harmed by my research, but I feel no qualms about being less than frank with them, and no obligation to allow them to choose whether or not their actions are recorded (1994: 215).

In other words, rights of informed consent and of not being deceived are differentially distributed in society, according to these authors. In such circumstances, researchers set themselves up as the judge of which individuals or groups 'deserve' ethical treatment. This view has far-reaching implications and is more common than one might think.

point is simply that focus groups have considerable potential for feminist research. A key point is that they allow the voices of highly marginalized women to be heard. Madriz (2000: 843), for example, writes that for lower-socioeconomic-class women of colour, focus groups constitute a relatively rare opportunity for them to 'empower themselves by making sense of their experience of vulnerability and subjugation.'

Qualitative interviewing (without immersion in a social setting) versus ethnography

The aim of this section is to compare the merits and limitations of interviewing in qualitative research (without immersion in a social setting) with those of ethnography. They are probably the two most prominent methods of data collection in qualitative research, so there is some value in assessing their relative strengths.

Advantages of ethnography compared to qualitative interviewing

Seeing through others' eyes
As noted in Chapters 1 and 8, this is one of the main purposes of qualitative research, but on the face of

it the ethnographer would seem to be better placed for gaining a foothold on social reality in this way. Their prolonged immersion in a social setting probably makes them better equipped to see as others see. Ethnographers are not only in much closer contact with people for a longer period of time, they also participate in many of the same kinds of activity as those being studied. Research that relies on interviewing alone, on the other hand, is likely to entail more fleeting contacts, although qualitative research interviews can last many hours and re-interviewing is not unusual.

Learning the native language
Becker and Geer (1957) argued that the ethnographer is like a social anthropologist visiting a distant land: to understand a culture the language must be learned. Usually, however, it is not the formal language that must be understood, but the 'argot'—the special uses of words and slang—that are important for penetrating a group's culture. Such an understanding is arrived at through a prolonged observation of language use. See Chapter 16 for more on language analysis.

Things taken for granted
The interview relies primarily on verbal accounts of the interviewee's world, so certain things that

interviewees take for granted may not be mentioned. For example, an interviewer may never ask a street prostitute about her relationship with the police, and she may never talk about it in the interview. But an ethnographer may learn by being on the scene that street prostitutes have to deal with police surveillance on a regular basis, and that it is an important part of their activities.

Deviant and hidden activities

Much of what is known about criminal and deviant subcultures has been gleaned from ethnography. There are certain things, including drug taking, violence, shoplifting, illegal commerce, and hooliganism, which interviewees are reluctant to talk about in a one-on-one interview. Similarly, ethnographers have uncovered information about people's resistance at work (such as work-to-rule practices and industrial sabotage) and about groups that support a deviant ideology, such as white supremacists. Ethnographers are more likely to be able to infiltrate the social worlds of people who are wary of talking to outsiders.

Sensitivity to context and flexibility

The ethnographer's extensive contact with a social setting allows the context of people's behaviour to be mapped out fully. The ethnographer interacts with people in a variety of different situations so that links between behaviour and context can be forged.

Naturalistic emphasis

Ethnography can be more naturalistic because the researcher confronts members of a social setting in their natural environments. Interviewing, which usually interrupts the normal flow of events even when it is at its most informal, is often less naturalistic. It is no surprise that when referring to naturalism as a tradition in qualitative research, Gubrium and Holstein (1997) referred mostly to ethnography.

Advantages of qualitative interviewing in comparison to ethnography

Issues resistant to observation

Many issues are simply not open to observation, so asking people about them may be the only way to get information about them. For example, consider domestic violence. Would it be feasible for a researcher to hang around in people's homes, waiting for the violence to unfold? Here reactivity

would impinge in a big way, since perpetrators try to hide their violence as much as they can.

Reconstruction of events and future plans

A reconstruction of past events and future behaviour cannot be accomplished through observation alone. Qualitative research frequently entails a reconstruction of events by asking interviewees to think back about how a series of previous activities may have created a current situation. Beardsworth and Keil (see Box 10.3) employed the symbolic interactionist notion of *career* to understand how people become vegetarians. Indeed, most qualitative studies ask about events that occurred before the study began; for example, questions can be asked about the early family experiences of gang members, recent immigrants, and prostitutes. Some call this 'retrospective interviewing.' See Box 10.13 for a further example.

Reactive effects

The issue of reactive effects is by no means straightforward. As with structured observation (see Chapter 6), it can be anticipated that the presence of an ethnographer will result in reactive effects—as mentioned at several points in this book, people's awareness that they are being observed can make them behave unnaturally (although ethnographers, like researchers using structured observation, typically find that people become accustomed to their presence and begin to behave more naturally the longer they are around). Ethnography also suffers from the related problem of observers disturbing the very situation being studied because conversations and interactions occur, both with and about the observer, that otherwise would not have happened.

Less intrusive in people's lives

Ethnography can be costly in that the researcher is likely to take up more of the participants' time than would be the case with interviews alone. Interviews in qualitative research can sometimes be very long, and as noted, re-interviewing is not uncommon, but their impact is probably still less than the effect of having to deal with ethnographers on a regular basis. Ethnography can be especially intrusive in terms of people's time when it occurs in organizational settings, for example, when the rhythm of work is disrupted.

Longitudinal research easier

Interviewing can be carried out within a longitudinal research design somewhat more easily because

Box 10.13 Information through interviews: research on prostitution

McKeganey and Barnard (1996) discussed their strategies for conducting research into prostitutes and their clients. Their approach was largely that of observer-as-participant (see Figure 9.2), in that their research was based primarily on interviews with prostitutes and their clients, as well as some (frequently accidental) observation of interactions and overheard conversations. The interviews they conducted were especially important in gaining information on such areas as: how the prostitutes had moved into this line of work; permitted and prohibited sex acts; links with drug use; experience of violence; and the management of identity. In the following passage, a prostitute reconstructs her movement into prostitution:

I was 14 and I'd run away from home. I ended up down in London where I met a pimp. . . . He'd got me a place to stay, buying me things and everything and I ended up sleeping with him as well. . . . One night we got really drunk and stoned and he brought someone in. . . .

[Then] after it happened I thought it was bad, I didn't like it but at least I was getting paid for it. I'd been abused by my granddad when I was 11 and it didn't seem a million miles from that anyway (1996: 25).

One area of particular concern to McKeganey and Barnard was the spread of HIV/AIDS infection and its implications for prostitutes and their work. This area was specifically addressed in the interviews. For example:

I've got a couple of punters who'll say 'I'll give you so and so if you'll do it without [a condom].' But never, I always use a condom for anal sex, oral sex and even for hand jobs; there's no way I'll let them come anywhere near me (1996: 66).

You still get the bam-pots [idiots] asking for sex without. I had one the other night—I said, 'where have you been living—on a desert island?' (1996: 66).

repeat interviews may be easier to organize than repeat visits to the ethnographer's research settings.

Ethnography can be used for longitudinal studies, but there are limits to the time that ethnographers can spend away from their normal lives—normally not more than two or three years—which limits the extent to which an ethnographic study can be longitudinal. When the research is being conducted on an episodic basis, a longer time period may be feasible.

Ethical issue 10.2

Lack of informed consent

McKeganey and Barnard's (1996; see Box 10.13) research was on negotiations between prostitutes and clients over the use of condoms in light of the threat of HIV/AIDS infection. Had they been asked, some prostitutes may have agreed to wear hidden 'wires' to record these discussions, but clients would not have been party to such agreements, so ethical principles of informed consent and invasion of privacy would have been transgressed. As a result, the researchers relied on interviews with the prostitutes about these negotiations.

Armstrong's (1993) research on soccer hooliganism, referred to several times in Chapters 8 and 9, entailed six years of participant observation, but since soccer hooligans are not engaged full-time in this activity, the research did not require the researcher's continued absence from work and other personal commitments.

Greater breadth of coverage

Interviewing may allow access to a wider variety of people and situations. In ethnographic work, the researcher is invariably limited to a fairly restricted range of people, incidents, and localities. Observation of a large organization, for example, often means that knowledge of the organization beyond the confines of the area studied is unlikely to be very extensive.

Specific focus

As noted in Chapter 8, qualitative research sometimes begins with a specific focus, and indeed Silverman (1993) was critical of the notion that it should be regarded as an open-ended form of research. Qualitative interviewing seems to be better suited for dealing with a specific issue, since an interview can address a particular matter in detail. Research by Bryman *et al.* (1996) had a very specific focus, in line with its funding—namely, conceptions of leadership among police officers. Because of its clear focus, it was more appropriate to conduct the research using semi-structured interviewing than ethnography, since issues to do with leadership do not emerge naturally on a regular basis.

Overview

When Becker and Geer (1957: 28) proclaimed half a century ago that the 'most complete form of the sociological datum . . . is the form in which the participant observer gathers it,' Trow (1957: 33) reprimanded them for making such a universal claim. He argued that 'the problem under investigation properly dictates the methods of investigation.' The latter view is very much the one taken in this book. Specific research methods are appropriate for some issues but not others. The discussion of the merits and limitations of ethnography versus qualitative interviews is meant to draw attention to some of the factors to take into account if given an opportunity to use one method or the other. The points raised can also be used to evaluate existing research.

Checklist of issues to consider in qualitative interviewing

☑ Have you thought about how you will present yourself in the interview, such as how you will be dressed?

☑ Is there a clear and comprehensive way of introducing the research to interviewees?

☑ Does the interview guide clearly relate to the research questions?

☑ Has a pilot test been done with some appropriate respondents and are the interviewers fully trained?

☑ Does the interview guide contain a good mixture of different kinds of questions, such as probing, specifying, and direct questions?

☑ Do the interviews allow novel or unexpected themes and issues to arise?

☑ Is the language in the questions free of jargon?

☑ Are the questions relevant to the people being interviewed?

☑ Have the questions been designed to elicit in-depth responses so that interviewees are not tempted to answer simply 'yes' or 'no'?

☑ Do the questions offer a real prospect of seeing the world from the interviewees' point of view rather than imposing a frame of reference on them?

☑ Has the setting in which the interviews will take place been checked out? Has the recording equipment been pre-tested and a dry run undertaken? Have all aids to be used (for example, visual aids, segments of film, case studies) been pre-tested?

☑ Is there a plan in place if the interviewee does not turn up for the interview?

For a focus group:

☑ What is planned if not all participants turn up for the session?

☑ Have the questions been designed to encourage group interaction and discussion?

☑ Is there a strategy for dealing with silences and for particular participants who are reluctant to speak?

☑ Is there a strategy for dealing with participants who speak too much and 'hog' the discussion?

☑ Is there a strategy to follow if the discussion goes off on a tangent?

— Key Points —

- Interviewing in qualitative research is typically unstructured or semi-structured.

- Qualitative interviewing is meant to be flexible and to seek out the world views of research participants.

- If an interview guide is used, it should allow some flexibility in the asking of questions.

- The qualitative interview should be recorded and then transcribed.

- Qualitative interviews can be conducted online.

- The focus group allows the researcher to explore the joint production of meaning.

- There are several issues concerning the recruitment of focus group participants—in particular, whether to use natural groups.

- The focus group moderator generally tries to give free rein to the discussion. However, there may be contexts where it is necessary to ask specific questions.

- Group interaction is an important aspect of focus groups.

- The growing use of the Internet offers significant opportunities for gaining access to potential focus group participants.

- A qualitative interview is a popular method of data collection in feminist studies and some writers view focus groups as well suited to a feminist standpoint.

- Whether to use ethnography or qualitative interviews alone depends in large part on the research questions to be addressed. Still, ethnographers usually conduct some interviews in their investigations.

— Questions for Review —

Differences between structured interviews and qualitative interviews

- How does qualitative interviewing differ from structured interviewing?

Unstructured and semi-structured interviewing

- What are the differences between unstructured and semi-structured interviewing?

- Can semi-structured interviewing compromise the flexibility of qualitative research?

- What are the differences between life history and oral history interviews?

- What considerations need to be borne in mind when preparing an interview guide?

- What kinds of question can be put in an interview guide?

- What skills does the interviewer need to develop for qualitative interviewing?

- Why is it important to record and transcribe qualitative interviews?

- What role can vignette questions play in qualitative interviewing?

Introduction to focus groups

- What advantages can the focus group method offer compared to an individual qualitative interview?

Conducting focus groups

- Are there any circumstances in which it is a good idea to select participants who know each other?

Group interaction in focus group sessions

- Why is it important to examine group interaction when analyzing focus group data?

Limitations of focus groups

- How can group effects and the loss of control over the discussion damage a focus group study?

Qualitative research using online personal interviews

- Can online personal interviews really be personal interviews? To what extent does the absence of direct contact mean that the online interview cannot be a true interview?

Qualitative research using online focus groups

- Is the role of the moderator in online focus groups different from that in the face-to-face variety?

Feminist research and interviewing in qualitative research

- Why is the qualitative interview so prominent among feminist researchers?
- What dilemmas are posed for feminist researchers using qualitative interviewing?
- What dilemmas are posed for feminist researchers using focus groups?

Qualitative interviewing alone versus ethnography

- Outline the advantages and disadvantages of qualitative interviewing (without immersion in a social setting) compared to ethnography.
- Is one method more in tune with the research needs of qualitative researchers than the other?

Part IV

Chapter 11 presents some of the main issues involved in choosing a sample. It also includes a bit of statistics, the topic of Chapter 12, to wet your feet. Chapter 12 walks you through the basic procedures used to calculate statistics using SPSS computer software—a very widely used package of programs. Different approaches to qualitative data analysis are discussed in Chapter 13, which also offers advice on how that sort of analysis can be conducted using NVivo software.

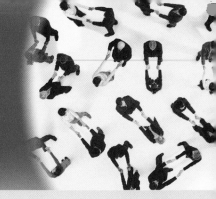

11 Sampling

Chapter overview

Sampling principles are not exclusively the concern of survey and other quantitative researchers; they are also relevant to the qualitative work you read about in the last three chapters. In fact this chapter discusses sampling as it is done in both quantitative and qualitative studies. Putting these topics together here reflects our view that these two approaches, despite their differences, share certain goals and can complement each other, a point that will be addressed in greater depth in later chapters. This chapter explores:

- the role of sampling in relation to the overall process of doing research;
- why generalizable findings (that is, findings that can be applied to some larger population) require a representative sample;
- the idea of a *probability sample*—one using a random selection process;

- the main types of probability sample: simple random; systematic; stratified random; and the multi-stage cluster sample;
- the main issues involved in deciding sample size;
- different types of non-probability sampling, including quota sampling, which is widely used in market research;
- potential sources of sampling error in survey research;
- sampling in structured observation research, where times and contexts are sampled;
- sampling strategies in ethnography, in particular *theoretical sampling*, which is associated with the grounded theory approach to qualitative data analysis;
- sampling in content analysis; and
- raising response rates.

Introduction

This chapter is concerned with selecting individuals and other units of analysis for research. The key terms used in sampling are explained in Box 11.1. We'll begin with a discussion of sampling in studies involving structured interviews or questionnaires. The techniques used for other methods of quantitative research are then discussed, followed by sampling in qualitative research. Finally, ways to increase response rates are considered.

Let's assume that you are wondering about the attitudes of your fellow students on certain matters, or perhaps about their behaviours or backgrounds. To examine any of these areas, structured interviews

or mailed questionnaires would be appropriate. However, let's say that there are around 30 000 students at your university. It would cost a great deal of money to send questionnaires to all 30 000, and the time and energy required to interview them all would be prohibitive. It is almost certain that a *sample* of students would have to suffice. As a matter of fact, the need to sample is almost universal in quantitative research.

But for student projects, would any sample suffice? Would it be all right to stand in a busy location on campus and then interview anyone who agreed to speak with you? Alternatively, would it be appropriate to give questionnaires to everyone in your classes?

The answer to these questions is yes if your goal is simply to get some experience in data gathering and analysis, or to conduct a pilot study. However, if the object is to get a *representative sample*, one that can be used to make inferences about all 30 000 students, the answer is no. Why? There are various reasons, but the following stand out:

- The first approach depends heavily on the avail-ability of students during the times you are seeking them out. Not all students are likely to be available at any one time—some are at work, others skipped classes that day, many will have a timetable different from yours. Some students may have no need to be where you are. The sample will exclude such people.

- The decisions about whom to approach may be influenced by judgments about how friendly or cooperative prospective respondents appear to be. Gender, race, age, and many other factors may have an impact on who is approached and who is ignored.

- The problem with the second strategy is that anyone not taking a course with you is omitted. How many music or engineering majors take sociology, for instance?

In other words, using these sampling methods, decisions about whom to sample are influenced by personal judgments and by prospective respondents' availability, both of which are non-universal criteria. Such limitations mean, in the language of survey sampling, that the sample is *biased*—it does not represent the population from which it is selected.

Box 11.1   Basic terms and concepts in sampling

- *Element* or *unit*—a single case in the population, which in the social sciences is usually a person. However, not only people are sampled—the researcher may want to sample from a universe of nations, cities, regions, schools, firms, etc. Finch and Hayes (1994), for example, based part of their research on a random sample of wills of deceased people.

- *Population*—all cases about which one seeks knowledge, or all cases to which a researcher's conclusions are meant to apply. For example, if one is studying voting behaviour, the population may be all people in a particular jurisdiction who are eligible to vote. If the topic is hyperactivity among young children, the population may be all children aged 2 to 11. 'Population' is defined differently here compared to the everyday use of the term.

- *Sampling frame*—the list of elements from which the sample will be selected.

- *Sample*—the elements selected for investigation, a subset of the population. The method of selec-tion may involve probability or non-probability sampling (see below).

- *Representative sample*—a sample that is a micro-cosm of the population, one that 're-presents' its essential characteristics. A sample like this is most likely to be selected when a probability sampling process is used (see next).

- *Probability sample*—a sample selected using a random process such that each unit in the popu-lation has a known chance of being selected. The aim of probability sampling is to keep sampling error (see below) to a minimum.

- *Non-probability sample*—a sample selected using a non-random method. Essentially, this implies that some units in the population are more likely to be selected than others.

- *Sampling error*—errors of estimation that occur if there is a difference between the characteristics of a sample and those of the population from which it was selected. Sampling error can occur even if a random method is used. For example, if 45 per cent of a national probability sample is in favour of more public funding for the arts, but the actual figure in the population is 49 per cent, some sampling error has taken place.

- *Non-response*—occurs whenever some unit selected for the sample refuses to participate in the study, cannot be contacted, or for some other reason does not supply the required data.

- *Census*—if an attempt is made to collect data from all elements in the population rather than from a sample, the data are a census. The phrase 'the census' typically refers to the enumeration of all (or nearly all) members of the population of a nation state—that is, a national census.

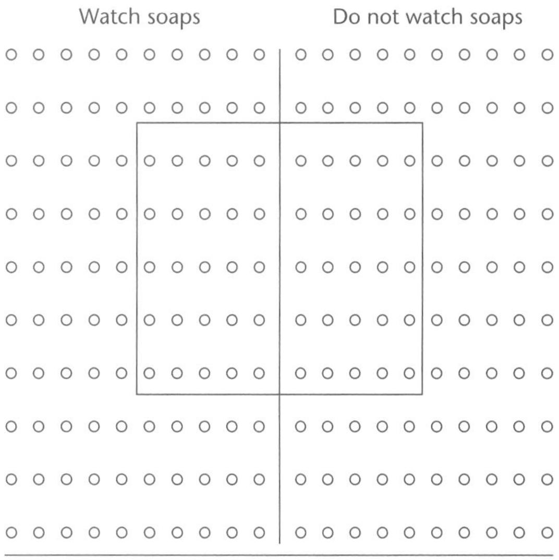

Watch soaps   Do not watch soaps

Figure 11.1 A sample with no sampling error

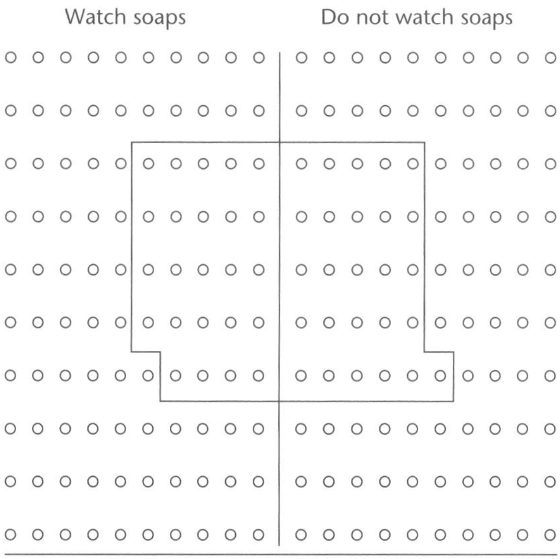

Watch soaps   Do not watch soaps

Figure 11.2 A sample with very little sampling error

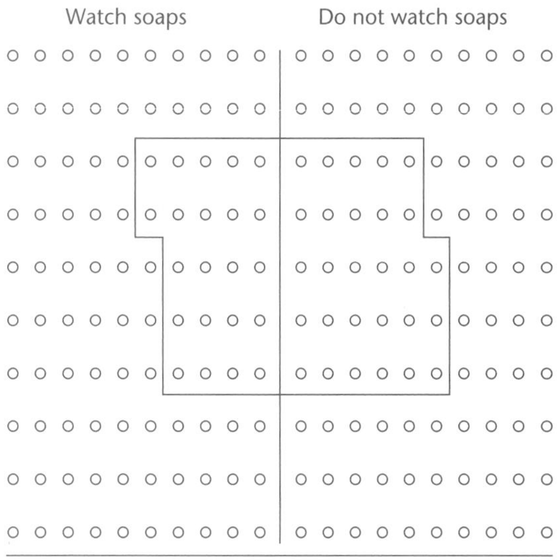

Watch soaps   Do not watch soaps

Figure 11.3 A sample with some sampling error

Watch soaps   Do not watch soaps

Figure 11.4 A sample with a lot of sampling error

While it is incredibly difficult to remove bias altogether and to get a truly representative sample, steps should be taken to keep bias to a minimum.

Three sources of bias can be identified:

- *Not using a random method to pick the sample.* Essentially, a random method is one in which each element has the same chance of being selected, like numbers from a lottery cage (although in some circumstances that principle may be violated for technical reasons, for example, to get a sufficiently large number of people from a small subgroup into the sample). As illustrated above, if a random method is not used, there is a good possibility that human judgment will affect the selection process, making some members of the population more likely to be selected than others. This source of bias is eliminated through the use of probability sampling, described later in this chapter.

- *The sampling frame or list of potential subjects is inadequate.* If the sampling frame excludes cases or is otherwise inaccurate, the sample derived from it cannot represent the population, even if a random sampling method is employed.

- *Some people in the sample refuse to participate or cannot be contacted—in other words, there is non-response.* The problem with non-response is that those who agree to participate may differ from those who refuse or cannot be reached in ways relevant to the subject matter being investigated. If that is the case, the sample may not be representative. For example, if one is studying rates of criminal victimization and those who have been victims of violent crime decline to participate, that would skew the results.

If the data are available, a researcher can check how non-respondents differ from the population. It is often possible to do this in terms of characteristics such as gender or age, or, in the case of a sample of university students, whether non-respondents reflect the entire student body in terms of faculty of registration. However, it is usually impossible to check characteristics that go beyond basic demographic categories, such as attitudes towards separatism and patterns of smoking behaviour, because population data are generally not available on these topics.

Sampling error

To appreciate the significance of sampling error for achieving a representative sample, consider Figures 11.1 through 11.4. Imagine a population of 200 people and a sample of 50. Imagine as well that the topic is whether people watch soap operas, with the population equally divided between those who do (100) and those who do not (100). If the sample is representative, the sample of 50 should also be equally split in terms of this variable (see Figure 11.1). If there is a small amount of sampling error, so that there is one person too many who does not watch soap operas and one too few who does, it would look like Figure 11.2. Figure 11.3 shows a more serious overrepresentation in the sample of people who do not watch soaps. This time there are three too many who do not watch them and three too few who do. In Figure 11.4 there is a very serious overrepresentation of people who do not watch soaps; there are 35 people in the sample who do not watch them, which is much larger than the 25 that would be there if the sample were perfectly representative.

Ethical issue 11.1

The whole truth, and nothing but the truth?

Pretend you are interviewing senior citizens for your honours thesis. It has taken much longer than you thought and time is running out. You have just had three refusals in a row. Then you knock on the door of an elderly man, and before you can say anything he says, 'I guess you are from the census, come on in.' Your questions are harmless, even easier than those in the census. Do you say nothing and accept his invitation to enter?

It is important to appreciate that it is impossible to completely eliminate sampling error. Even with a well-crafted probability sample, a degree of sampling error is likely to creep in, just as in flipping a coin 100 times is likely to yield more 49Heads/51Tails and 51Heads/49Tails results *combined* than 50Heads/50Tails outcomes, even though the latter is the most probable single result. Ask your instructor for this course to take a minute to do an experiment in your class with 20 flips, and see the surprisingly large number of outcomes that are *not* 10Heads/10Tails. However, probability sampling stands a better chance than non-probability sampling of minimizing sampling error, so it is very unlikely that the sample characteristics will end up looking like Figure 11.4 when it is used. Moreover, probability sampling allows the researcher to employ tests of statistical significance that permit inferences to be made about the population from which the sample was selected, with a known probability of error. This will be addressed in Chapter 12.

Types of probability sample

Imagine a study on the social variables related to alcohol consumption, to be done at a university that has 9000 full-time students. This hypothetical example will be used in the illustrations that follow.

Simple random sample

The simple random sample is the most basic form of probability sample. With it, each unit of the population has an equal probability of inclusion in the sample. Suppose there is enough money to interview 450 students at the university. This means that the probability of inclusion in the sample is

$$\frac{450}{9000}, \text{ that is, 1 in 20.}$$

This is known as the *sampling ratio* and is expressed as

$$n/N$$

where n is the sample size and N is the population size.

The key steps in devising a simple random sample are as follows:

1. Define the population. Here it is all full-time students at the university, N or 9000.
2. Select or devise a comprehensive sampling frame. Virtually all universities have an office that keeps student records; assume that you have access to the list of full-time students for this year. As an aside, what ethical issue arises in you having access to such a list? But certainly it is not feasible to write to every student asking permission to view the list in order to devise a random sample. It would be just as easy to send everyone the questionnaire.
3. Decide sample size (n), here 450.
4. List all the students in the population and assign them consecutive numbers from 1 to N, here 1 to 9000.
5. Using a table of random numbers, or a computer program that can generate random numbers, select n (450) different random numbers from 1 to N (9000).
6. The students who match the n (450) random numbers constitute the sample. Two points are striking about this process. First, there is almost no opportunity for bias. Students are not selected on subjective criteria like looking friendly and approachable as in the non-random method discussed earlier. Their selection is entirely random. Second, the process is not dependent on students being available. They do not have to be walking in the interviewer's proximity to be included in the sample. The process of selection is done without their knowledge. Not until contacted by an interviewer do they know they will be asked to be part of a social survey.

Step 5 mentions the possible use of a table of random numbers, found in the back of many statistics books or generated by computer software. The tables are usually made up of columns of five-digit numbers, such as:

09188	08358
90045	28306
73189	53840
75768	91757
54016	89415

The first thing to notice is that, since these are five-digit numbers and the population size is 9000 (a four-digit number), none of the random numbers seems appropriate, except for 09188 and 08358, although the former is larger than the largest possible case number for this study. The answer is to take just four digits in each number, for example, the last four, yielding the following:

9188	8358
0045	8306
3189	3840
5768	1757
4016	9415

Still, two of the resulting numbers—9188 and 9415—exceed 9000; no student has that case number. The solution is simple: ignore these numbers and go on to the next ones. This means that the student assigned the number 45 will be the first to be included in the sample; the student assigned the number 3189 next; the student assigned 5768 next; and so on.

Not wanting to interview the same person twice, ignore any random number that appears more than once and continue down the list. This procedure produces a sample known as a simple random sample *without replacement*: no number is placed back in (replaced after having been selected) for a second chance at inclusion. Virtually all simple random samples in social research are like this and so the qualifier 'without replacement' is usually omitted. Strictly speaking, without replacement means the result is not a true simple random sample, as those chosen later have a greater chance of being selected than those selected earlier. Notice the first person chosen has one chance in 9000 of being included. Removing that person means person two has one chance in the remaining 8999. The last person chosen will have one chance out of the 8551 people remaining; 1/8551 is greater than the first chosen person's chance of being selected of 1/9000. Generally researchers overlook this problem, a small one compared with others in sampling.

Systematic sample

A systematic sample is selected directly from the sampling frame, without using random numbers.

In the present case, 1 student in 20 is to be selected (450/9000). That 1 in 20 figure is called the *sampling interval*. A *random start* begins the process, which in this case can be achieved by selecting at random a number from 1 to 20, possibly by using the last two digits in a table of random numbers. With the 10 random numbers above, the first relevant one is 54016, since it is the first one where the last two digits yield a number in the desired range (1–20), namely 16. This means that the 16th student in the sampling frame is the first one to be included in the sample. Thereafter, take every 20th student on the list; the sequence of case numbers would be: 16, 36, 56, 76, 96, 116, etc. Who is the last person in the sample? Case number 8996.

In systematic sampling, it is important to ensure that there is no inherent ordering or pattern in the sampling frame, a feature called *periodicity*. For example, imagine that the sampling frame was set up such that case 1 was male, case 2 female, case 3 male, case 4 female, and so on for all cases. In the example above, that would yield a sample of 450 females and 0 males, in all likelihood a very unrepresentative sample. If there is any pattern to the list, arrange the cases in random order or choose a different sampling method.

Note that with systematic sampling, not every possible combination of cases has an equal chance of being selected. Once that first case number (here 16) is chosen, every case number in the sample must end in six, and no even-numbered prefixes will qualify, such as 26, 86, or 166.

Stratified random sampling

In the imaginary study of university students discussed earlier, the student's discipline may be relevant to what you will be researching. Generating a simple random sample or a systematic sample *may* yield one in which, for example, the proportion of kinesiology students in the sample is the same as that in the student population, but usually it is not an exact match. Thus, if there are 1800 students majoring in kinesiology, using a sampling ratio of 1 in 20 should produce 90 students in the sample from this faculty. However, because of sampling error, there may be, say, 85 or 93.

So long as data are available on each student's faculty of registration, it is possible to ensure that students are exactly represented in terms of their faculty membership by using stratified random sampling. In the language of sampling, this means stratifying the population (that is, dividing it into subgroups) by a criterion (in this case faculty), and selecting either a simple random sample or a systematic sample from each of the resulting strata. In the present example, five faculties mean five strata, with the sample in each stratum being one-twentieth of the total for each faculty, as in Table 11.1, which also shows a hypothetical outcome of a simple random sample, one that does not exactly mirror the population.

Table 11.1 The advantages of stratified sampling

Faculty	Population	Stratified sample	Hypothetical simple random or systematic sample
Humanities	1800	90	85
Social sciences	1200	60	70
Pure sciences	2000	100	120
Applied sciences	1800	90	84
Engineering	2200	110	91
TOTAL	9000	450	450

The advantage of stratified sampling is clear: it ensures that the sample is distributed in the same way as the population in terms of the stratifying criterion. Using a simple random or systematic sampling approach *may* result in a distribution like that of the stratified sample, but it is unlikely. On the other hand, this strategy requires that the relevant criteria for stratifying be known in advance of the research, which is not always the case.

Two more points are relevant here. Stratified sampling is feasible only when it is relatively easy to identify and allocate units to strata. Five strata based on physical activity level, from 'competitive athletes' at one end to 'couch potatoes' at the other, would be very hard to set up, because it would require an initial study just to get the population data on activity level needed to create these strata. Second, more than one stratifying criterion can be used at the same time. In our example, one could stratify by faculty and gender, or faculty, gender, and whether students are undergraduates or postgraduates, etc., so long as the criteria are easy to use and relevant to the research question. But as mentioned, such stratifying is practicable only when data on the relevant stratifying criteria are available for the population. At your school, is there an accessible list of female, undergraduate, engineering students?

Multi-stage cluster sampling

In the previous example, the students to be interviewed attend a single university so there would not be a lot of travel for interviewers. However, imagine a *national* sample of students. The travel involved would add a great deal to the time and cost of doing the research. This kind of problem can occur not only for national populations but even for a large city. Another problem with large populations is a lack of an adequate sampling frame. Is there a list somewhere of all students registered at Canadian universities? No. Without a sampling frame, one cannot select a simple random or systematic sample.

One way to deal with these problems is to employ *cluster sampling*. With cluster sampling, the primary sampling unit (the first stage of the sampling procedure) is not the individuals or units of the population to be studied, but an aggregate of them, known as a *cluster*. Imagine a nationally representative sample of 5000 students. Using simple random or systematic sampling (if that were practicable) would

yield a geographically dispersed sample, and mean a great deal of travel for interviewers. One solution is to sample universities and then students from each of the sampled universities, with a probability sample at each stage. For example, one could randomly sample 10 universities from the entire population of universities, yielding 10 clusters, and then interview 500 randomly selected students at each of the 10 universities selected.

Suppose the result of sampling 10 universities is the following:

- Alberta
- McGill
- Simon Fraser
- Winnipeg
- Dalhousie
- Guelph
- Brandon
- University of Western Ontario
- Nipissing
- Toronto

This list is fine, but interviewers would still be involved in a great deal of travel because the 10 universities are far from each other. And note the absence of universities in Saskatchewan, Newfoundland, and Prince Edward Island. An alternative solution to the one just presented is to group all universities by region (assuming that the topic of interest does not vary significantly by region); for example, Maritimes, Quebec, Ontario, Prairies, and BC, and then randomly sample two regions. Five universities can be sampled from each of the two lists of universities, and then 500 students from each of the 10 universities. These are the stages:

- group universities by region and sample two regions; then
- sample 5 universities from each of the two regions; then
- sample 500 students from each of the 10 universities.

Cluster sampling is a multi-stage approach involving clusters first and then subunits within clusters. If the clusters are not created judiciously the chances of having an unrepresentative sample may increase, but if done properly cluster sampling can be very effective. With large populations, it is very economical compared to simple random or systematic sampling when doing in-person interviews, although less money is saved by using the technique with telephone interview research since phone charges are now so low.

In addition to reducing costs, cluster sampling solves the second problem: no adequate sampling

Box 11.2   An example of a multi-stage cluster sample

To study the influence of social class on voting in Canada, suppose the goal is to get 2000 interviews from a random selection of Canadian adults eligible to vote. This may involve:

• Sampling the 308 federal ridings

– These are stratified by population size (not all ridings have the same number of people in them) into large, average, and small ridings; whether the riding is mostly rural or mostly urban; and dependence on federal transfer payments (high and low).

– One hundred ridings are then randomly sampled.

• Sampling polling districts

– Two polling districts are randomly chosen from each sampled riding.

• Sampling addresses

– Ten addresses from each sampled polling district are systematically sampled.

• Sampling individuals

– One person at each address is chosen according to some pre-defined random method.

---

frame. The student study described above does not require a list of all university students in Canada, something that would be rather hard to come by. With cluster sampling, no such list is ever required.

Quite often, cluster sampling also entails stratification. One could, for example, stratify universities in terms of whether they are 'new,' those receiving their charters after the great university expansion of the 1960s, or 'old.' In each of the two selected regions, group universities along the old/new university criterion first and then select universities from each of the strata.

Box 11.2 provides an example of a multi-stage cluster sample. It entails four stages: the sampling of parliamentary constituencies, the sampling of polling districts, the sampling of addresses, and the sampling of individuals.

The advantage of multi-stage cluster sampling should be clear by now: it allows interviews to be far more geographically concentrated than is the case for simple random or systematic sampling, and no population sampling frame is required. However, even when a very rigorous sampling strategy is employed, sampling error cannot be eliminated completely, as the example in Box 11.3 shows.

The qualities of a probability sample

Many researchers prefer probability samples because they allow one to make inferences from the sample to the population from which it was selected. In other words, with probability samples, the sample findings can be generalized to the population. This is not to say that the sample and population characteristics are exactly the same, but one can be used to estimate the other with a known probability of error. In the example of alcohol consumption in the sample of 450 students, the mean number of units consumed by the sample ($\overline{X}$) was used to estimate the population mean (μ) with a known margin of error. Greek letters are used to denote population characteristics, the Latin alphabet (the one used to write in English) for sample characteristics.

To expand on this point it is necessary to use some basic statistical ideas. These are presented in Box 11.4 and can be skipped if just a broad idea of sampling procedures is required.

Sample size

One question asked more than any other is 'How large should a sample be?' or 'Is the sample large enough?' The decision about sample size is not straightforward, as we will see below. Also, the quest for the perfect sample is usually constrained by the practical considerations of cost and time, which is frequently a disappointment to those who pose such questions.

Absolute and relative sample size

One of the most basic considerations, and possibly the most surprising, is that contrary to common expectation, it is the *absolute* size of a sample that is important, not the proportion of the population that it comprises. This means that a national probability sample of 1000 Canadians has about as much validity as a national probability sample of 1000 Americans, even though the latter involves a much larger population.

Increasing the size of a sample increases the precision of the estimates derived from it; for instance, a larger sample size means that the 95 per cent confidence interval referred to in Box 11.3 is narrowed. However, a large sample cannot *guarantee* precision, so it is probably better to say that increasing the size of a sample *probably* increases the precision of the estimates it can create. In other words, as sample size

---

Box 11.3   Generalizing from a random sample to the population

If an average of 9.7 units of alcohol is consumed in the previous seven days by respondents in a probability sample, would a similar figure be found in the population? The answer is complex but it is sketched out here and in Box 11.4. Assume for the sake of illustration that it would be possible to take an infinite number of random samples of the same size from a population. Not all of the resulting sample means would be perfect estimates of the population mean. One can never know the population figure with 100 per cent certainty, but one can imagine another study with a sample mean of 9.6 units, another with 9.8, and so on. These outcomes, as long as there are enough of them and the sample size is sufficiently high, will take the form of a bell-shaped curve known as a normal distribution (see Figure 11.5) with the

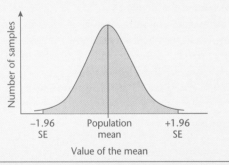

Figure 11.5 A distribution of sample means

sample means clustering around the population mean. Of the sample means not exactly at the population mean, half will be below the population mean and the other half will be above it. Moving to the left or to the right (away from the population mean), the curve tails off, reflecting the smaller and smaller number of samples generating means that depart considerably from the population mean. The variation of sample means around the population mean is the *sampling error* and is measured using a statistic known as the *standard error of the mean*. This is an estimate of the amount that a sample mean is likely to differ from the population mean.

This consideration is important because sampling theory tells us that about 95 per cent of all sample means lie within (+ or –) 1.96 standard errors of the population mean (see Box 11.4). In other words, one can be 95 per cent confident that one's sample mean lies within 1.96 standard errors of the population mean.

To illustrate further, if a sample has been selected according to probability sampling principles, we can be 95 per cent certain that the population mean lies between: a) [the sample mean]—[1.96 times the standard error of the mean]; and b) [the sample mean] + [1.96 times the standard error of the mean]. This is known as the 95 per cent confidence interval. If the mean level of alcohol consumption in the previous seven days in our sample of 450 students is 9.7 units and the standard error of the mean is 1.3, one can be 95 per cent certain that the population mean lies between

$$9.7 - (1.96 \times 1.3)$$

and

$$9.7 + (1.96 \times 1.3)$$

that is, between 7.152 and 12.248 units of alcohol.

Under certain conditions, in a stratified sample the standard error of the mean is smaller than in other probability samples. In other words, stratification may inject an extra increment of precision into the probability sampling process (for example, stratifying by university when levels of alcohol consumption vary widely between universities), since a possible source of sampling error is eliminated.

By contrast, a sample without stratification may exhibit a larger standard error of the mean than a comparable sample with stratification. This occurs because a possible source of variability between students is disregarded.

Box 11.4   Sampling distributions

Assume a population of five cases (scores = 6, 8, 10, 12, 14) from which a random sample of two cases is selected. The five scores sum to 50 and therefore the mean of the population is 50/5, or 10. Taking all possible random samples of two cases with replacement (meaning that after a case is chosen it goes back into the pool, so that two 6's or two 14's are possible), and calculating the means of each sample of size two, the following results:

Value of First Observation in Sample

		6	8	10	12	14
	6	6	7	8	9	10
Value of	8	7	8	9	10	11
Second Observation	10	8	9	10	11	12
in Sample	12	9	10	11	12	13
	14	10	11	12	13	14

Thus the 7, where 6 and 8 meet, is the mean of 6 + 8/2 = 7; the 13 is where 12 and 14 meet, 12 + 14/2 = 13. Now count the number of the sample means in the table; there are 25. There is only one mean of 14, in the bottom right corner, but five means of 10, on the diagonal. Thus five of the 25 sample means, or 20 per cent of them, have a value of 10, *the same as the population mean*. Sample means of 9 and 11 are the next most frequent at 32 per cent (a combined total of 8 of 25 means). With 8 and 12, another 24 per cent (6 of 25) are now counted. So sample means of 8, 9, 10, 11, and 12 represent 76 per cent of all possible sample means. The sample means furthest from the population mean, the 6 and 14 (in each corner) are the rarest, at 4 per cent (1 of 25) each.

Those percentages are really probabilities. The probability of getting a sample mean of 7 is 2 chances in 25, or as more usually expressed, 8 chances in 100 or 8 per cent.

The logic of a confidence interval should now be more apparent. A researcher normally takes only one sample, but most random sample results stay close to the population value. In our example, 76 per cent of the sample means are within (+/–) 2 units of the population mean. When plotted, that is not exactly the bell curve shown in Box 11.3, but you can see the broad outline. Including more and more cases in the sample shapes the lines into a normal curve.

With a real sample, an extension can be created on each side of the sample mean to make it more likely to be correct than if the sample mean by itself were used. The extension for a 95 per cent confidence interval is equal to 1.96 times the standard error of the mean. (In Box 11.3 the sample mean was 9.7, and the extensions were +/– [1.96 × 1.3] or +/– 2.548). The extensions around the sample mean create what is called an interval. There is only a 5 per cent chance that the interval does not include the population mean for a 95 per cent confidence interval.

SAMPLE

Mean	Frequency	%
14	1	4
13	2	8
12	3	12
11	4	16
10	5	20
9	4	16
8	3	12
7	2	8
6	1	4
	$\sum$ 25	100

This is basically how athletes using banned substances are caught. They provide one bio-sample (actually two, but one is a backup). The authorities have the data that would parallel the table above, although it is much more sophisticated. But pretend the above works. Assume the population mean value for testosterone, for example, is 10. Athlete X comes in at 14. While that is a possible (non-drugged) outcome, it is rare. So if the doping committee is willing to be wrong 4 per cent of the time (how often an honest 14 occurs), the athlete can be accused. With a reputation at stake, a 4 per cent chance of error is too high. That is why the tests allow for only much less likely errors.

increases, sampling error tends to decrease. Common sample sizes are 100 (minimum) and then 400, 900, 1600, and 2500. These sample size increases cut the sampling error in half, then by one-third, then by one-fourth, and then by one-fifth respectively. (You can ignore this, but if it helps, this is because square roots are involved in the denominator of the calculation; thus the original square root of 10 for a sample of 100 becomes 20, 30, 40, and 50 [the square root of 2500], yielding the one-half, one-third, one-quarter, and one-fifth.) Notice how the increases in precision become less pronounced (going from 100 to 400 cuts sampling error in half, but 400 to 900 reduces it by only one-third) and thus the rate of decline in the standard error of the mean declines. Considerations of sample size are likely to be profoundly affected by matters of time and cost at such a juncture, since striving for smaller and smaller increments of precision becomes an increasingly uneconomic proposition, as ever-larger samples become less and less cost efficient.

Fowler (1993) warned against a simple acceptance of this size criterion and argued that it is not normal for researchers to be able to specify in advance 'a desired level of precision' (1993: 34). Moreover, since sampling error is only one component of any error entailed in an estimate, the notion of a desired level of precision is not realistic. Instead, to the extent that this notion affects decisions about sample size, it usually does so in a general rather than calculated way. It is usually cost that ultimately determines sample size.

Non-response

Considerations about sampling error do not end with issues of sample size. The problem of low *response rates* should be borne in mind as well.

What is a response rate? Invariably, some people in the sample will refuse to participate or will be unable to do so. The response rate is the percentage of the sample that participates in the study. Beagan's (2001) research on medical students made three attempts to get the people chosen for the sample to participate, which resulted in a 59 per cent response rate. However, its calculation is more complicated than this. First, not everyone who agrees to be interviewed or who fills out a questionnaire is included. If a large number of questions are not answered by a respondent or if it is clear that the interview or questionnaire was not taken seriously, some researchers exclude such a person and then take only

the number of usable interviews or questionnaires as the numerator. Similarly, not everyone in a sample turns out to be a suitable or appropriate respondent or can be contacted. Thus the response rate could be calculated as follows:

$$\frac{\text{number of usable questionnaires}}{\text{total sample} - \text{unsuitable or uncontactable members of the sample}} \times 100$$

Those who are chosen for the sample but do not participate must be examined, from whatever data exist on them, to see if they are different from those who do participate. Are the people who cannot be contacted richer and on vacation? Are they ill and in hospital? Such differences may be important (depending on the research topic) and may have to be taken into account in the analysis.

Given that 100 per cent response rates will not occur, sample size will have to be adjusted. For example, if the aim is for 450 students and a prediction, based on other surveys, is for an 80 per cent rate of response, it may be advisable to sample 575 individuals, on the grounds that approximately 115 (20 per cent) will be non-respondents, leaving 460 and still room for some additional refusals.

The issue of refusal to participate is of particular significance because many researchers are experiencing declining response rates to social surveys. In the US, estimates put it at about 30 per cent. However, Smith (1995) showed that things like the subject matter of the research, the type of respondent, and the level of effort expended on improving the number of cooperating respondents affect response rates.

Another issue in connection with non-response is that of how far researchers should go to boost response rates. Later in the chapter, a number of steps that can improve response rates to mailed questionnaires (which are particularly prone to poor response rates) are discussed. However, boosting response rates can be expensive. Teitler *et al.* (2003) presented a discussion of the steps taken to increase the response rate of a US sample that was hard to reach, namely both unwed parents of newly born children. They found that although increasing the sample from an initial 68 per cent to 80 per cent of all couples meant that the final sample more closely resembled the population from which the sample had been taken, diminishing returns set in. However, this does not mean that steps should not be taken to improve response rates. For example, following up on people who do not respond to a mailed questionnaire usually results in an improved response rate, at little additional cost.

Heterogeneity of the population

Yet another consideration is the heterogeneity of the population from which the sample is to be taken. When a population is heterogeneous with regard to characteristics relevant to the topic under study, like a whole country or city normally is, the samples drawn are likely to be highly varied. When it is relatively homogeneous, such as a population of students or of members of a particular occupation, the amount of variation is less. Generally, the greater the heterogeneity of a population, the larger a sample should be in order to maximize the chances that all groups are adequately represented.

Kind of analysis

Finally, researchers should bear in mind the *kind of analysis* intended. An example is a contingency table showing the relationship between two variables. In a 2 × 2 table there are four cells into which the cases can fall, let's say gender (M/F) × whether the person voted in the last election (Y/N). Suppose there were only 10 males and 10 females in the sample, and that 50 per cent of the men and 50 per cent of the women voted, showing no relationship between gender and voting. But suppose the sample by chance included one more woman who voted and one more man who did not. Now the figures are 40 per cent of men voted versus 60 per cent of women, quite a difference. To prevent such a small change in the sample from having a major impact on the estimate, a larger sample is required. One would probably want to have at least 50 males and 50 females. Because the population is approximately half male and half female, this is easy to achieve. But what if the variable is religion? Fifty Roman Catholics (or 50 Anglicans) are easy to find in any random sample of 1000, but what about 50 Jehovah's Witnesses or 50 Hindus? One strategy to achieve statistically meaningful results is to randomly over-sample some of these small groups, as Dinovitzer *et al.* (2003) did to guarantee sufficient social class variation. Similarly, the Canadian National Election Study usually over-samples the less populous provinces (such as Prince Edward Island) in order to make interprovincial comparisons. This shows how sample size depends in part on the analysis to be conducted.

Types of non-probability sampling

Non-probability sampling includes all forms of sampling that are not conducted according to the canons of probability sampling outlined earlier. It covers a wide range of different types of sampling strategy, at least one of which—the quota sample—is claimed by some practitioners to be almost as good as a probability sample. This section covers three main non-probability samples: the convenience sample; the snowball sample; and the quota sample.

Convenience sampling

A convenience sample is one that is used simply because the elements are readily available to the researcher. Imagine a professor in a faculty of education who is interested in the qualities teachers want in their principals, and who administers

---

Practical Tip

Sample size and probability sampling for students

For most quantitative researchers sample size does matter, the bigger the sample the more representative it is likely to be (provided the sample is randomly selected), regardless of the size of the population from which it is drawn. However, students have to do their research with very limited resources and a truly random sample may not be feasible. The crucial point is to be clear about your sampling decisions and to justify what you have done. Explain the difficulties that you would have encountered in generating a random sample. Explain why you really could not increase your sample size. But above all, do not make claims about your sample that are not warranted. Do not claim that it is representative or that you have a random sample unless that is true. Also, there may be good features about your sample—the range of people included, the good response rate, the high level of honesty displayed. Make sure to play up these positive features at the same time as being honest about its limitations. This is what professional researchers do.

a questionnaire to several of her classes because of the convenience. (Recall, however, the ethical question of asking people dependent on a grade from the researcher to participate in research.) Imagine further that all of the students in her classes are teachers taking a part-time master's degree in education. The chances are that the researcher will receive all or almost all of the questionnaires back, thus achieving a high response rate. However, the use of that sampling strategy makes it impossible to generalize the findings to teachers as a whole—the very fact they are taking this degree program marks them off as different from teachers in general.

This is not to suggest that convenience samples should never be used. In fact they are used more often than one might think. Beagan's (2001) study of one class at a medical school and MacKinnon and Luke's (2002) study of cultural change involved small convenience samples. Convenience samples are also good for pilot studies. Pretend that the education professor is developing a battery of questions to measure the leadership preferences of teachers. Since it is highly desirable to pre-test such a research instrument before actually using it, administering it to a group that is not part of the main study is a legitimate way of doing some preliminary

analysis of such issues as whether respondents will reply honestly to questions on sensitive topics, and whether the questions are clear and comprehensible. A convenience sample may also be used to test newly created scales for reliability and to generate ideas for further research. Box 11.5 contains an example of a convenience sample.

Snowball sampling

Snowball sampling is a form of convenience sample, but worth distinguishing because it has attracted quite a lot of attention over the years. With this approach, the researcher makes initial contact with a small group of people who are relevant to the research topic and then uses them to establish contacts with others. Tastsoglou and Miedema (2003) used an approach like this to create a sample of immigrant women in the Maritimes. Box 11.6 describes the generation of a snowball sample of marijuana users for what is often regarded as a classic study of drug use.

Becker's comment on creating a snowball sample is interesting: 'The sample is, of course, in no sense "random"; [indeed] it would not be possible to draw a random sample, since no one knows the nature of

Box 11.5   A convenience sample

Suppose you want to study university undergraduates to find out the extent of their part-time employment while at school. To save time and effort you conduct the study at your school, which makes the sample a convenience one because it rules out all other universities in Canada. You could use probability sampling to get participants from your university, but you think the problem not important enough to justify the cost. Instead you choose five faculties, and within each, one or two of the specific degree programs offered by the faculty. Assume the final result is anthropology, visual arts, chemistry, electrical engineering, French, kinesiology, media studies, and psychology. This choice of subjects is designed to maximize variety in the type of degree program and to provide similar numbers of males and females (since in particular degree programs one gender frequently predominates). Questionnaires can then be given to students in first-, second-, third-, and fourth-year courses.

These procedures represent a good attempt to generate a varied sample. It is a convenience sample, because the choice of university, faculty, degree program, and course is done purposively rather than randomly. Because of the way the questionnaires are administered (in class), there is a very high response rate. On the other hand, absentees from classes do not get a chance to fill out a questionnaire. An important question is whether absence from class is connected in some way to part-time working, the latter variable being the focus of your study. In other words, is absence higher among students who work part-time, perhaps because they are working at the time of the class? Are some students too tired to go to class because of their part-time work? If so, you will probably underestimate the proportion of students who work part-time. Also, because you have selected a convenience sample, you must say so in your research report, acknowledging that the results cannot be generalized to Canadian students as a whole or even to the student population at your university.

Box 11.6 A snowball sample of marijuana users

Becker (1963: 45–6) reported on how he generated a sample of marijuana users:

> I had been a professional dance musician . . . and my first interviews were with people I had met in the music business. I asked them to put me in contact with other [marijuana] users who would be willing to discuss their experiences with me. . . . Although in the end half of the fifty interviews were conducted with musicians, the other half covered a wide range of people, including labourers, machinists, and people in the professions.

the universe from which it would have to be drawn' (Becker 1963: 46). What Becker is saying here is that there is no accessible sampling frame for the population from which the sample is to be taken. The difficulty of creating such a sampling frame means that a non-probability approach is the only feasible one. Moreover, even if one could create a sampling frame of marijuana users or, say, British visitors to Disney theme parks, it would almost certainly become obsolete very soon, because those populations are constantly changing. People become and cease being marijuana users all the time, while new theme park visitors arrive every minute.

The problem with snowball sampling is that it is very unlikely to be representative of the population, though, as just suggested, the very notion of a population is problematic in some circumstances. However, by and large, snowball sampling is used not within a quantitative research strategy, but within a qualitative one: both Becker's work on marijuana users and Bryman's studies on theme parks used a qualitative research framework, and concerns about the ability to generalize do not loom large in qualitative research. Indeed, Tastsoglou and Miedema (2003) warned the reader not to generalize from their 40 women to all immigrant women in the Maritimes, much less to those in the rest of Canada. This is not to suggest that snowball sampling is entirely irrelevant to quantitative research: when the researcher needs to focus upon relationships between people, tracing connections through snowball sampling can be a better approach than

conventional probability sampling. Statistically small groups—such as gay francophone lawyers in New Brunswick, for example—are researchable with a snowball approach. Taking a random sample from that population would not be feasible.

Quota sampling

While quota sampling is infrequently used in academic social research, it is used intensively in commercial research such as market research, and in political opinion polling in some countries. The aim of quota sampling is to produce a sample that reflects a population in terms of the relative proportions of people in different categories, such as those pertaining to gender, ethnicity, age, socioeconomic status, and region of residence, and often in combinations of these categories. However, unlike a stratified sample, the sampling of individuals is not carried out randomly, since the final selection of people is left up to the interviewer. Information about the stratification of the Canadian population or about certain regions can be obtained from sources like the census and from surveys based on probability samples such as the General Social Survey.

Once the categories and the number of people to be interviewed within each category (known as *quotas*) have been decided, interviewers merely have to select people who fit these categories. The quotas are typically interrelated. In a manner similar to stratified sampling, the population may be divided into strata in terms of, for example, gender, employment, and age all at once (see Table 11.2). Census data can identify the number of people who should be in each subgroup; thus the numbers to be interviewed in each subgroup reflect the population. Interviewers can then seek out individuals who fit the subgroup quotas. Accordingly, an interviewer may be told to find and interview five 25- to 44-year-old unemployed females at an assigned location, such as a mall. Interviewers usually ask people who are available to them about those characteristics (though gender will presumably be self-evident) in order to determine their suitability for a particular subgroup. Once a subgroup quota (or a combination of subgroup quotas) is achieved, the interviewer is no longer concerned to locate individuals for that subgroup and moves on to another.

Many Canadians have been approached in a mall by a person toting a clipboard and interview

Table 11.2 Strata for gender, age, and employment

Older, female, unemployed (5%)	Younger, female, unemployed (4%)
Older, female, employed (17%)	Younger, female, employed (20%)
Older, female, other (7%)	Younger, female, other (1%)
Older, male, unemployed (3%)	Younger, male, unemployed (6%)
Older, male, employed (15%)	Younger, male, employed (15%)
Older, male, other (6%)	Younger, male, other (1%)

schedule and asked about their age, occupation, and so on, before being asked a series of questions about a product. That person is almost certainly an interviewer with a quota sample to fill. Sometimes, she will decide not to interview you because the quota for your group is already filled or you are in a group with no quota, students for example, who are often declared ineligible for inclusion.

A number of criticisms are frequently levelled at quota samples:

- The proponents of probability sampling argue that because the choice of respondent is left to the interviewer, a quota sample is not likely to be representative. As noted earlier, in their choice of people to approach, interviewers may be unduly influenced by their perceptions of how friendly people are or by whether the people make eye contact with the interviewer (unlike many who look at the ground and shuffle past as quickly as possible, not wanting to be bothered).
- People who are in an interviewer's vicinity at interview times, therefore available to be approached, may not be typical. There is a risk, for example, that people not in full-time paid work may be overrepresented, especially in malls, making the sample unrepresentative.
- Judgments about eligibility may sometimes be incorrect, for instance regarding the respondent's age, and even more so for social class. For example, someone who is actually eligible to be interviewed,

but is younger than he or she looks, is not asked, because the quota of the older group is filled. In such a case, an element of bias is being introduced.
- It is not appropriate to calculate a standard error term from a quota sample; in fact most statistical estimates are meaningless unless random sampling has been used.

All of this makes the quota sample a poor bet if one's goal is to make accurate inferences with confidence about some larger population. That is why it is not favoured by academic social researchers. It does have some arguments in its favour, however:

- It is undoubtedly cheaper than a comparable probability sample. There is generally no travelling involved and it is easier to manage. It is unnecessary to keep track of people who need to be re-contacted or to keep track of refusals. Still, patterns of refusal should be reported. For example, if it becomes apparent that most men (but not women) do not want to take part, this can signal a gender bias in the results.
- When speed is of the essence, a quota sample is invaluable. Newspapers frequently need to know something about how voters feel about a topic or how they intend to vote. Alternatively, a sudden major news event may require a more or less instant picture of people's views or responses. Again, a quota sample is much faster.
- As with convenience sampling, it is useful for conducting tests on new measures or research instruments, or in exploratory work from which new theoretical ideas may be generated.

Structured observation and sampling

Just like survey research, structured observation necessitates decisions about sampling. However, the issues are not limited to how to sample *people*. Several other sampling issues may be involved:

- If the structured observation is to take place in public areas, such areas have no sampling frames (lists of people who frequent them). It would be very difficult, for example, to get a complete list of people who walk along a particular street, or of men who frequent certain 'tearooms.' One can, however, choose the people by use of a table of random numbers, for example, the 3rd, then 7th, then 18th person seen in the public area. That same table can be used to establish random samples of time, place, or activity.

- Time sampling involves an observer recording whatever is happening at a particular time, for example, in a pub every 15 minutes after a random start time. This can be done on one person or on several individuals at once and the 15-minute figure can be varied using a table of random numbers. It may be necessary that individuals watched on more than one day not be observed at the same time of the day; the observation periods may have to be randomly selected. For example, it would be an error to observe a certain pupil in a school classroom always at the end of the day when most students are tired. Being tired can give a false impression of that pupil's behaviour.

Time sampling should be combined with the next strategy:

- a list of places can be randomly sampled, for example, in a pub near the phone, at the bar, by the pool table, outside where the smokers congregate, the washroom area, and the booths; and
- 'behaviour sampling,' whereby an entire group is watched and the observer records a particular kind of behaviour, may be conducted. Thus in that same pub, one can observe the nth pick-up (second then fifth, etc.) that occurs once the previous one has been observed, that n taken from a random number table.

Considerations relating to probability sampling derive largely from concerns about external validity. For example, if a structured observation study is conducted over a relatively short span of time, issues of the stability or representativeness of the findings over longer periods are likely to arise. If the research is conducted in schools, for example, observations conducted towards the end of the school year, when examinations are likely to loom large in the thinking of both teachers and students, may produce different results compared to those made at a different point in the academic year. Consequently, consideration has to be given to the question of the timing of the observations. Furthermore, how are the sites in which structured observation is to take place selected? Are they representative? Clearly, a random

sampling procedure for the selection of schools can assuage any worries in this connection. However, in view of the difficulty of securing access to settings such as schools and business organizations, it may be that the organizations to which access is secured are not representative.

Limits to generalization

An important point, often not fully appreciated, is that even when a sample is selected using probability sampling, any findings can be generalized *only* to the population from which the sample is taken. This is an obvious point, but it is easy to think that findings from a study have a broader applicability. If the study is based on a random sample of adult Calgarians, for example, its findings cannot be generalized to the whole province of Alberta, much less to other regions of Canada. The opinions of Calgarians may be very different from those of Edmontonians or people who live in Lethbridge, and even more different from the opinions of Montrealers' or residents of St John's.

One issue rarely discussed in this context, and almost impossible to assess, is whether there is a time limit on the findings generated. Quite aside from the fact that findings cannot (or at least should not) be generalized beyond the population sampled, is there a point at which one should say, 'Well, those findings applied *then*, but do they apply *now*?' To take a simple example: no one should assume that the findings of a 1980 study of university students' budgeting and personal finance habits apply to today's students. Ever-increasing costs have changed how students finance their education, including perhaps a greater reliance on part-time work, parents, and loans. But even when there is no definable or recognizable source of relevant change, there is still the possibility (or even likelihood) that the findings are time-specific. Changes over time are a major reason why it is important to conduct replications.

Sampling problems

There is some evidence that compared to random samples, quota samples are often biased. They underrepresent people in lower social strata, people who work in the private sector and manufacturing, and people at the extremes of income; and they overrepresent women in households with children and people from larger households (Butcher 1994). On the other hand, probability samples may be biased too—for example, they may underrepresent men and employed people (Marsh and Scarbrough 1990); such people may be both harder to contact and busier, thus less willing to participate.

Other errors with respect to sampling (see Figure 11.6) include:

- *Sampling error*, discussed earlier in this chapter and defined in Box 11.1, arises because it is rare to end up with a perfectly representative sample, even when probability sampling is employed.
- *Sampling-related error* arises from activities or events related to the sampling process. Examples are an inaccurate sampling frame and non-response; each reduces the generalizability or the external validity of findings.

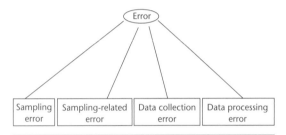

Figure 11.6 Four sources of error in research

Qualitative sampling

The sampling of informants in ethnographic research is often a combination of convenience sampling and snowball sampling, and usually involves taking information from whatever sources are available. Ethnographers often face opposition, or at least indifference, to their research and are relieved to glean information or views from whoever is prepared to divulge such details. This seems to have been the essence of Taylor's (1993) strategy; her female drug users were

> eventually obtained by a mix of 'snowballing techniques' . . . and my almost continuous presence in the area. . . . Rather than ask to be introduced or given names of others I could contact, when I met a woman I would spend as much time with her as she would allow,

participating in her daily round, and through this come to meet others in her social circle. My continued presence in the area also led other women drug users to approach me when I was alone. . . . In addition, the drug worker in the area would mention my presence and interest to women with whom he came in contact and facilitate introductions where possible (1993: 16).

Ethnographers who take on a role that is closer to that of observer-as-participant rely somewhat more on formally asking for the names of other people who may have relevant information and who can be contacted.

Whichever strategy is adopted, the question is whether either results in a representative sample of informants. Probability sampling is almost never used in ethnographic research and is rarely employed even in qualitative research based on interviews. In many cases, it is not feasible to select a probability sample because it is difficult and often impossible to map 'the population' from which a random sample may be taken. Instead, ethnographers have to ensure that they gain access to as wide a range of individuals as possible, so that many different perspectives and ranges of activity can be analyzed.

Theoretical sampling

An alternative strategy is *theoretical sampling*, advocated by Strauss and Corbin (1998). In their view, because of its reliance on statistical rather than theoretical criteria, probability sampling is not appropriate to qualitative research. Theoretical sampling is meant to be an alternative strategy and 'done in order to discover categories and their properties and to suggest the interrelationships into a theory. Statistical sampling is done to obtain accurate evidence on distributions of people among categories to be used in descriptions and verifications' (Glaser and Strauss 1967: 62).

What is theoretical sampling? In theoretical sampling, the researcher simultaneously collects and analyzes the data, decides what data to collect next and where to find them, and develops a theory in the process. Data collection is influenced by the emerging theory, whether substantive or formal. It is an ongoing process rather than a distinct and single stage of the research, unlike probability sampling.

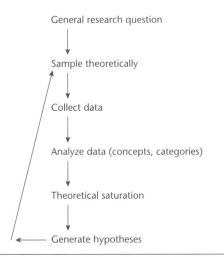

General research question

↓

Sample theoretically

↓

Collect data

↓

Analyze data (concepts, categories)

↓

Theoretical saturation

↓

Generate hypotheses

Figure 11.7 The process of theoretical sampling

For Charmaz (2000: 519), theoretical sampling is a 'defining property of grounded theory' and is concerned with the refinement of ideas, rather than boosting sample size.

Moreover, theoretical sampling can involve not only people, but also settings and events. This can be seen in a more recent definition: 'Data gathering driven by concepts derived from the evolving theory and based on the concept of "making comparisons," whose purpose is to go to places, people, or events that will maximize opportunities to discover variations among concepts and to identify categories in terms of their properties and dimensions' (Strauss and Corbin 1998: 201).

Figure 11.7 outlines the main steps in theoretical sampling. Data collection (observing, interviewing, and collecting documents) continues until the point of *theoretical saturation* is reached. The key is to carry on until a category has been saturated with data. 'This means, until (a) no new or relevant data seem to be emerging regarding a category, (b) the category is well developed in terms of its properties and dimensions demonstrating variation, and (c) the relationships among categories are well established and validated' (Strauss and Corbin 1998: 212). In the language of grounded theory, a category operates at a somewhat higher level of abstraction than a concept in that it may group together several concepts that have common features denoted by the category.

Saturation means that previous interviews/observations have both formed the basis for the creation of a category and confirmed its importance. There

is no longer a need to collect data in relation to that category. Instead, the researcher should move on and generate hypotheses out of the categories that are building up, and then collect data related to those hypotheses.

Not just people

As pointed out in the last section, ethnographic sampling is not just about people but also about other things. Time and context may be sampled. Attending to time means that the ethnographer must make sure that people or events are observed at different times of the day and different days of the week, to avoid drawing inferences valid only for mornings, or for weekdays rather than weekends, for example.

Because behaviour is influenced by contextual factors, it is also important to observe in a variety of locations. For instance, soccer hooliganism is not a full-time occupation. To understand the hooligans' culture and world view, writers like Armstrong (1993) and Giulianotti (1995) had to ensure that they interacted with them in a variety of contexts in addition to soccer stadiums, such as pubs where they engaged in general socializing. Rosenhan in his study of psychiatric hospitals had to do the same (see Chapter 6).

Content analysis sampling

There are several phases in the selection of a sample for content analysis. Applying content analysis to the mass media is explored here but the basic principles have broader applications.

Sampling media

Many studies of the mass media specify a research problem in the form of 'examining the representation of X in the mass media.' The X may be things like trade unions, women, food scares, crime, or drunk driving. But which mass media to choose—newspapers, television, radio, or chat rooms? And, if newspapers, will it be tabloids, broadsheets, or both? Will it include Sunday papers, free newspapers? Will feature articles and letters to the editor be included? Beharrell's (1993) study of the reporting and representation of AIDS/HIV concentrated on national

Table 11.3 Comparing the strengths of different ways of contacting members of the chosen sample

	Mode of survey administration				
	Face-to-face interview	Telephone interview	Posted questionnaire	Email	Web
Resource issues					
Is the cost of the mode of administration relatively low?	✓	✓✓	✓✓✓	✓✓✓	✓ (unless access to low-cost software)
Is the speed of the mode of administration relatively fast?	✓	✓✓✓	✓✓✓	✓✓✓	✓✓✓
Is the cost of handling a dispersed sample relatively low?	✓ (✓✓ if clustered)	✓✓✓	✓✓✓	✓✓✓	✓✓✓
Sampling-related issues					
Does the mode of administration tend to produce a good response rate?	✓✓✓	✓✓	✓	✓	✓
Is the researcher able to control who responds (that is, the person targeted is the one who answers)?	✓✓✓	✓✓✓	✓✓	✓✓	✓✓
Is the mode of administration accessible to all sample members?	✓✓✓	✓✓	✓✓✓	✓ (because of need for respondents to be accessible online)	✓ (because of need for respondents to be accessible online)
Is the mode of administration less likely to result in non-response to some questions?	✓✓✓	✓✓✓	✓✓	✓✓	✓✓

Notes: Number of ticks indicates the strength of the mode of administration of a questionnaire in relation to each issue. More ticks correspond to more advantages in relation to each issue. A single tick implies that the mode of administering a questionnaire does not fare well in this area. Two ticks imply that it is acceptable and three ticks that it does very well. This table was influenced by Czaja and Blair (1996).

newspapers over three years and ended up with over 4000 news items.

Sampling dates

Sometimes, the decision about dates is dictated by when the phenomenon of interest occurs. For example, the time for studying the growing presence of squeegee kids in Toronto was dictated by their initial proliferation and then their legislated disappearance (Parnaby 2003). One could hardly examine the issue prior to their spread nor continue after their removal. Similarly, the time to study western-Canadian separatism (Bell 2007) was when the movement was active, not when it was in a dormant phase. With a research question that entails an ongoing general phenomenon like crime,

the matter of dates is more open. In such cases probability sampling can be used for sampling dates, for example, by generating a systematic sample by randomly selecting one day and then selecting every nth day thereafter.

The time span analyzed in content analysis depends on the research questions, and often the key decision is when to stop selecting cases. For example, if Jagger (1998) had wanted to look for long-term changes in how men and women represent themselves in dating advertisements (see Box 16.1), she would have had to examine the columns of earlier years. She could have taken comparable samples from 10 and 20 years earlier or gone back even further. Warde (1997) was interested in changes in representations of food (what should be eaten and how it should be eaten) in food columns in five of the most widely read women's weekly magazines. He looked at two years, 20 years apart, and within each year at the February, May, August, and November issues to ensure that seasonal factors did not overly influence the findings. (If he had selected magazines just from November, there might have been a preoccupation with Christmas fare, while findings from a summer issue might have been affected by the greater availability of certain foods, such as particular types of fruit.) The choice of the years and months to analyze was somewhat arbitrary, however.

Reducing non-response

There is little consistent evidence on whether response rates are lower using telephone as compared to in-person interviews (see Table 11.3). However, there is a general *belief* that telephone interviews achieve slightly lower response rates than personal interviews (Shuy 2002; Frey 2004). Developments in telephone communications such as the growing use of call screening and cell phones have certainly had an adverse effect on telephone survey responses.

Interviewers in both types of study play an important role in maximizing the response rate for a survey study. The following points should be borne in mind:

- Interviewers should be prepared to keep calling back if interviewees are out or unavailable. This requires taking into account people's likely work and leisure habits—for example, there is no point in daytime calling for people who work during the day. People living alone may be reluctant to answer the door, especially after dark.
- Be optimistic; a better response rate may result from presuming that people will agree to be interviewed than by assuming that they will refuse.
- Reassure people that you are not a salesperson. Because of the unethical tactics of organizations whose representatives say they are doing market or social research, many people have become very suspicious of people saying they would 'just like to ask a few questions.'
- When conducting in-person interviews, dress in a way that is acceptable to a wide spectrum of people.
- Make it clear that you are happy to find an interview time to suit the respondent.

Practical Tip

Response rates

Response rates are important because the lower the response rate, the more likely it is that questions will be raised about the representativeness of the sample. Mailed questionnaires in particular are often associated with low response rates and as Mangione's classification illustrates, according to some authorities a response rate below 50 per cent is not acceptable. Then again, a great deal of published research achieves only a low response rate, so do not despair. The key point is to recognize and acknowledge its possible negative implications. Many students find mailed and other forms of questionnaire attractive because of their low cost and quick administration. Do not be put off using such techniques just because of the prospect of a low response rate. There are other considerations.

Also, response rates are usually an issue only with randomly selected samples. Samples not selected with probability methods are not expected to be representative of a population even if everyone selected participates. But here again, it is necessary to acknowledge the limitations of the sample.

Improving response rates to mailed questionnaires

Mangione (1995: 60–1) provided the following classification of response rates to mailed questionnaires:

Over 85%	excellent
70–85%	very good
60–69%	acceptable
50–59%	barely acceptable
Below 50%	not acceptable

Because of the tendency for mailed questionnaires to generate lower response rates than structured interviews (and the implications this has for the validity of findings), a great deal of thought and research has gone into improving response rates for the former. The following steps are frequently suggested:

- Write a good covering letter explaining the reasons for the research, why it is important, and why the recipient has been selected; provide guarantees of confidentiality.

- Make it personal by having the respondent's name and address in the covering letter, and by ensuring that each letter is individually signed. Writing the cover letter to 'Occupant' loses most people. The downside of the personal approach is it may raise concerns: How did they know about me and will my responses really be confidential? The researcher should try to deal with these potential fears in the letter.
- The mailed questionnaires should always be accompanied by a stamped return envelope, or at the very least, return postage.
- Do not allow the questionnaire to appear unnecessarily bulky. Some researchers reduce the size of the questionnaire to fit a booklet format. As with structured interviewing, begin with questions most likely to be of interest to the respondent.
- Follow up individuals who do not reply at first, possibly with two or three further mailings. The importance of reminders cannot be overstated—they do work. One approach is to send out a reminder letter to non-respondents two weeks after the initial mailing, reasserting the nature and aims of the survey and suggesting that the person contact a member of the research team to obtain a replacement copy of the questionnaire should the original one have been lost. Then, two weeks after that, all continuing non-respondents should be sent another letter along with a further copy of the questionnaire. These reminders have a demonstrable effect on the response rate. Some writers argue for even more than two mailings of reminder letters. If a response rate is worryingly low, further mailings are certainly desirable.
- Providing monetary incentives increases the response rate but can be deemed unethical. They are more effective if the money comes with the questionnaire than if it is promised after its return. Apparently, respondents typically do not take the money and discard the questionnaire. The evidence also suggests that quite small amounts of money have a positive impact on the response rate, but that larger amounts do not necessarily improve the response rate any further.

Virtual sampling issues

A major limitation of online surveys is that not everyone is online and has the technical ability to handle questionnaires in either email or web formats.

Certain other features of online communications also make such surveys problematic, such as:

- many people have more than one email address;
- many people use more than one Internet Service Provider (ISP);
- a household may have one computer but several users;
- Internet users are a biased sample of the population in that they tend to be better educated, wealthier, younger, and not representative in ethnic terms (Couper 2000); and
- few sampling frames exist for the general online population and most of these are likely to be expensive to acquire since they are controlled by ISPs or may be confidential.

Such issues make surveys using probability samples difficult to do. This is not to say that online surveys should not be considered. For example, in many organizations, most if not all non-manual workers are likely to be online and familiar with using email and the Internet. Most university students are that way too (Couper 2000).

The chief problem with virtual sampling strategies is that the representativeness of the sample is almost always in question. On the other hand, given the paucity of knowledge and understanding of online behaviour, one could argue that some information about these areas is a lot better than none at all, provided the limitations of the findings in terms of their generalizability are appreciated.

There is growing evidence that online surveys typically generate lower response rates than mailed questionnaires (Tse 1998; Sheehan 2001). In the early years, response rates for email surveys were quite encouraging (Sheehan and Hoy 1999), but more recently they have been declining and are at lower levels than those for most mailed questionnaires (Sheehan 2001), though there are exceptions. Two factors may account for the decline: the novelty of email surveys in the early years has worn off and there is now a growing antipathy towards unsolicited emails. However, various researchers have used the following strategies in an effort to boost response rates:

1. Contact prospective respondents before sending them a questionnaire. This is regarded as basic 'netiquette.'

2. As with mailed questionnaires, follow up non-respondents at least once.

Overview

Online surveys are still in their infancy and have potential if only for their low cost. There is evidence that having a web survey or email option can boost response rates to mailed questionnaires (Yun and Trumbo 2000). Several problems have been identified with web and email surveys but it is too early to dismiss these forms of data gathering because methodologists are only beginning to come to grips with the approach and may gradually develop ways of overcoming its limitations. Moreover, as pointed out previously, as more and more people and organizations go online, some of the problems are bound to diminish.

One last point

Sampling decisions are the last step for most researchers before going into the field, so this is a good time to review the ethical principles presented previously. They are included here for your perusal (see Ethical issue 11.2).

Ethical issue 11.2

A final checklist of ethical issues to consider before going into the field to collect data

- Have you submitted your project to your institution's research ethics board? If only certain types of research need to be submitted for formal approval, is your research exempt or does it require clearance?

- Have you ensured that there is no prospect of serious harm coming to participants?

- Does your research conform to the principle of informed consent, so that research participants understand:

  – what the research is about?
  – the purposes of the research?
  – who is sponsoring it?
  – the nature of the participant's involvement in the research?
  – how long their participation is going to take?
  – that participation is voluntary?
  – that they can withdraw from the study at any time, even after the research starts?
  – what is going to happen to the data (for example, how kept, when destroyed)?

- Are you sure that the privacy of the people involved in your research will not be violated and that the confidentiality of the data will be maintained?

- If deception is involved, have you ensured that research participants will be debriefed in a timely matter, that is, that they will get an explanation of the true purposes of the study as soon as possible?

- After the data have been collected, have you ensured that the names of research participants and/or organizations involved will be made unidentifiable? Does the strategy for archiving data in electronic form comply with data protection legislation?

Key Points

- Probability sampling is a mechanism for reducing bias in sample selection.

- Become familiar with key technical terms in sampling such as representative sample, random sample, non-response, population, and sampling error.

- Randomly selected samples are important because they permit generalizations to the population of interest.

- Sampling error generally decreases as sample size increases.

- Under certain circumstances, quota samples can be an alternative to random samples, but they have some deficiencies.

- Convenience samples can provide useful data, but it is crucial to be aware of their limited generalizability.

- Sampling and sampling-related error are just two sources of error in social survey research.

- Sampling considerations in qualitative research differ from those addressed in quantitative research, in that issues of representativeness are less important.

- Sampling in qualitative research may be done on people, places, times, and even behaviours.

- Response rates vary by the medium of communication and most can be improved by persistent follow-up procedures.

Questions for Review

- What do each of the following terms mean: population; non-probability sampling; sampling frame; and representative sample?

- What are the goals of sampling?

- What are the main areas of potential bias in sampling?

Sampling error

- What is the significance of sampling error for achieving a representative sample?

Probability sampling

- What is probability sampling and why is it important?

- What are the main types of probability sample?

- How does a stratified random sample offer greater precision than a simple random sample?

- To conduct an interview survey of 500 people in Winnipeg, what type of probability sample would be best and why?

- A researcher positions herself on a street corner and asks every fifth person who walks by to be interviewed until she has a sample of 250. List some of the kinds of people to whom she should not generalize her results.

Sample size

- What factors should be taken into account in deciding the size needed for a probability sample?

- 'Non-response makes even most probability samples non-representative and thus not really worth the extra cost.' Discuss.

Non-probability samples

- Which form of non-probability sample is probably least useful and which the most useful?

- What circumstances make snowball sampling appropriate?

- 'Both quota samples and true random samples generate representative samples, with little difference between them. This accounts for the widespread use of quota samples in market research.' Discuss.

Limits to generalization

- 'The problem of generalization to a population involves more than getting a representative sample.' Discuss.

Qualitative sampling

- What is theoretical sampling?

- What is theoretical saturation and how does it relate to theoretical sampling?

Reducing non-response

- Realistically, what can you do to improve the response rate to a mailed questionnaire?

12 Quantitative Data Analysis

Chapter overview

In this chapter, some of the most basic and frequently used methods for analyzing quantitative data are presented. To illustrate them, an imaginary data set on attendance at a gym is attached, the kind of data set that could be generated from a small research project feasible for most undergraduates.

The chapter explores:

- the importance of anticipating questions of analysis early in the research process, before all the data have been collected;

- the different kinds of variables generated in quantitative research; knowing how to distinguish them is crucial in deciding which statistic to use;
- methods for analyzing a single variable (*univariate analysis*);
- methods for analyzing relationships between two variables (*bivariate analysis*);
- analysis of relationships among three or more variables (*multivariate analysis*); and
- SPSS software procedures for doing all three types of analysis.

Introduction

In this chapter, some basic techniques for analyzing quantitative data are examined. Following that, a widely used statistical software package (SPSS for Windows) is introduced. The formulas that underpin the software are not presented in order to keep the discussion focused on methodological rather than statistical issues. One chapter cannot do justice to these topics; readers are advised to consult books that provide more detailed and advanced treatments (for example, Healey 2009; Agresti and Finlay 2008).

Before beginning this exposition of techniques, a warning is in order. The biggest mistake in quantitative research is to think that data analysis decisions can wait until after the data have been collected. Data analysis does occur after that stage, but one should be fully aware of what techniques will be used before data collection begins—for example, the questionnaire, observation schedule, and coding frame should be designed with the data analysis in mind. The two main reasons for this are:

- The statistical techniques that can be used depend on how a variable is measured. If it is not measured appropriately, it may be impossible to conduct certain types of data analysis.
- The size and nature of the sample also imposes limitations on the kinds of techniques that are suitable for the data set.

A small research project

The discussion of quantitative data analysis provided here is based on an imaginary piece of research carried out by an undergraduate for her honours thesis on leisure in modern society. She chose that topic because of her enthusiasm for gyms and workout facilities, and her interest in how and why such venues are used. She had a hunch that they may be indicative of a 'civilizing process' and used this theory as a framework for her findings (Rojek 1995:

50–6). She was also interested in issues relating to gender and body image, and suspected that men and women differ in their reasons for going to a gym and in their activities there.

She secured the permission of a gym close to her home to contact a sample of its members by post. The gym had 1200 members and she decided to take a simple random sample of 10 per cent of them (that is, 120 members). She sent out mailed questionnaires to members of the sample with a covering letter testifying to the gym's support for her research. One thing she wanted to know is how much time people spend on each of the three main classes of activity in the gym: cardiovascular equipment, weights, and other activities (for example,

stretching exercises). She defined each of these carefully in the covering letter and asked members of the sample to note down how long they spent on each of the three activities on their next visit. They were then requested to return the questionnaires to her in a prepaid reply envelope. She ended up with 90 questionnaires out of the 120—a response rate of 75 per cent.

The entire questionnaire ran to four pages; 12 of the questions along with the responses of a fictional respondent are provided in Box 12.1. Questions 1, 3, 4, 5, 6, 7, 8, and 9 were pre-coded; the respondent simply had to circle the appropriate code. With the others, specific figures were requested, which were later transferred to the code column.

Box 12.1   Part of a completed questionnaire on use of a gym

Questionnaire

Code

1. Are you male or female? (please tick)

   Male ✓   Female ____

   ① 2

2. How old are you?

   21 Years

3. Which of the following best describes your main reason for going to the gym? (please circle one code only)

Relaxation	____	1
Maintain or improve fitness	____	②
Lose weight	✓	3
Meet others	____	4
Build strength	____	5
Other (please specify)	____	6

4. When you go to the gym, how often do you use the cardiovascular equipment (treadmill, step machine, bike, rower)?

   (please tick)

Always	✓	①
Usually	____	2
Rarely	____	3
Never	____	4

5. When you go to the gym, how often do you use the weights? (please tick)

Always	✓	①
Usually	____	2
Rarely	____	3
Never	____	4

continued on next page

Box 12.1   . . . Continued

6. Generally, how frequently do you go to the gym? (please tick)

Every day	_____	1
4–6 days a week	_____	2
2 or 3 days a week	✓	③
Once a week	_____	4
2 or 3 times a month	_____	5
Once a month	_____	6
Less than once a month	_____	7

7. Do you usually go with someone else to the gym or usually on your own?
(please circle one code only)

On my own	✓	①
With a friend	_____	2
With a partner/spouse	_____	3

8. Do you have sources of regular exercise other than the gym?

Yes _____ No ✓   1 ②

If you have answered No to this question, please proceed to question 10.

9. If you have replied Yes to question 9, please indicate the main source of regular
exercise in the last six months from this list. (please circle one code only)

Sport	_____	1
Cycling on the road	_____	2
Jogging	_____	3
Long walks	_____	4
Other (please specify)	_____	5

10. During your last visit to the gym, how many minutes did you spend on the
cardiovascular equipment (treadmill, step machine, bike, rower)?

33 Minutes   33

11. During your last visit to the gym, how many minutes did you spend on weights?

17 Minutes   17

12. During your last visit to the gym, how many minutes did you spend on other
activities (e.g., stretching exercises)?

5 Minutes   5

Missing data

The data for all 90 respondents are presented in Box 12.2. Each of the 12 questions is designated initially as a numbered variable (var00001, var00002, etc.); the number corresponds to the question number in Box 12.1 (that is, var00001 is question 1, var00002 is question 2, etc.). An important issue in data analysis is how to handle the 'missing data' that arise when respondents do not reply to a question—by accident, because they do not want to answer the question, or because the question does not apply to them. For example, respondent 24 failed to answer question 2 on age. This was coded as 999, a number chosen because it cannot be mistaken

Box 12.2 Gym survey data

Case	var00001	var00002	var00003	var00004	var00005	var00006	var00007	var00008	var00009	var00010	var00011	var00012
1	1	21	2	1	1	3	1	2	8	33	17	5
2	2	44	1	3	1	4	3	1	2	10	23	10
3	2	19	3	1	2	2	1	1	1	27	18	12
4	2	27	3	2	1	2	1	2	8	30	17	3
5	1	57	2	1	3	2	3	1	4	22	0	15
6	2	27	3	1	1	3	1	1	3	34	17	0
7	1	39	5	2	1	5	1	1	5	17	48	10
8	2	36	3	1	2	2	2	1	1	25	18	7
9	1	37	2	1	1	3	1	2	8	34	15	0
10	2	51	2	2	2	4	3	2	8	16	18	11
11	1	24	5	2	1	3	1	1	1	0	42	16
12	2	29	2	1	2	3	1	2	8	34	22	12
13	1	20	5	1	1	2	1	2	8	22	31	7
14	2	22	2	1	3	4	2	1	3	37	14	12
15	2	46	3	1	1	5	2	2	8	26	9	4
16	2	41	3	1	2	2	3	1	4	22	7	10
17	1	25	5	1	1	3	1	1	1	21	29	4
18	2	46	3	1	2	4	2	1	4	18	8	11
19	1	30	3	1	1	5	1	2	8	23	9	6
20	1	25	5	2	1	3	1	1	1	23	19	0
21	2	24	2	1	1	3	2	1	2	20	7	6
22	2	39	1	2	3	5	1	2	8	17	0	9
23	1	44	3	1	1	3	2	1	2	22	8	5
24	1	999	1	2	2	4	2	1	4	15	10	4
25	2	18	3	1	2	3	1	2	1	18	7	10
26	1	41	3	1	1	3	1	2	8	34	10	4
27	2	38	2	1	2	5	3	1	2	24	14	10
28	1	25	2	1	1	2	1	2	8	48	22	7
29	1	41	5	2	1	3	1	1	2	17	27	0
30	2	30	3	1	1	2	2	2	8	32	13	10
31	2	29	3	1	3	2	1	2	8	31	0	7
32	2	42	1	2	2	4	2	1	4	17	14	6
33	1	31	2	1	1	2	1	2	8	49	21	2
34	2	25	3	1	1	2	3	2	8	30	17	15
35	1	46	3	1	1	3	1	1	3	32	10	5
36	1	24	5	2	1	4	1	1	2	0	36	11
37	2	34	3	1	1	3	2	1	4	27	14	12
38	2	50	2	1	2	2	3	2	8	28	8	6
39	1	28	5	1	1	3	2	1	1	26	22	8
40	2	30	3	1	1	2	1	1	4	21	9	12
41	1	27	2	1	1	2	1	1	3	64	15	8
42	2	27	2	1	2	4	2	1	4	22	10	7
43	1	36	5	1	1	3	2	2	8	21	24	0
44	2	43	3	1	1	4	1	2	8	25	13	8
45	1	34	2	1	1	3	2	1	1	45	15	6
46	2	27	3	1	1	2	1	1	4	33	10	9
47	2	38	2	1	3	4	2	2	8	23	0	16
48	1	28	2	1	1	3	3	1	2	38	13	5
49	1	44	5	1	1	2	1	2	8	27	19	7

Box 12.2   . . . Continued

Case	var00001	var00002	var00003	var00004	var00005	var00006	var00007	var00008	var00009	var00010	var00011	var00012
50	2	31	3	1	2	3	2	2	8	32	11	5
51	2	23	2	1	1	4	2	1	1	33	18	8
52	1	45	3	1	1	3	1	1	2	26	10	7
53	2	34	3	1	2	2	3	2	8	36	8	12
54	1	27	3	1	1	2	3	1	3	42	13	6
55	2	40	3	1	1	2	2	1	4	26	9	10
56	2	24	2	1	1	2	1	1	2	22	10	9
57	1	37	2	1	1	5	2	2	8	21	11	0
58	1	22	5	1	1	4	1	1	1	23	17	6
59	2	31	3	1	2	3	1	1	4	40	16	12
60	1	37	2	1	1	2	3	2	8	54	12	3
61	2	33	1	2	2	4	2	2	8	17	10	5
62	1	23	5	1	1	3	1	1	1	41	27	8
63	1	28	3	1	1	3	3	2	8	27	11	8
64	2	29	2	1	2	5	2	1	2	24	9	9
65	2	43	3	1	1	2	1	2	8	36	17	12
66	1	28	5	1	1	3	1	1	1	22	15	4
67	1	48	2	1	1	5	1	1	4	25	11	7
68	2	32	2	2	2	4	2	2	8	27	13	11
69	1	28	5	1	1	2	2	2	8	15	23	7
70	2	23	2	1	1	5	1	1	4	14	11	5
71	2	43	2	1	2	5	1	2	8	18	7	3
72	1	28	2	1	1	4	3	1	2	34	18	8
73	2	23	3	1	1	2	1	2	8	37	17	17
74	2	36	1	2	2	4	2	1	4	18	12	4
75	1	50	2	1	1	3	1	1	2	28	14	3
76	1	37	3	1	1	2	2	2	8	26	14	9
77	2	41	3	1	1	2	1	1	4	24	11	4
78	1	26	5	2	1	5	1	1	1	23	19	8
79	2	28	3	1	1	4	1	2	8	27	12	4
80	2	35	2	1	1	3	1	1	1	28	14	0
81	1	28	5	1	1	2	1	1	2	20	24	12
82	2	36	2	1	1	3	2	2	8	26	9	14
83	2	29	3	1	1	4	1	1	4	23	13	4
84	1	34	1	2	2	4	2	1	8	24	12	3
85	1	53	2	1	1	3	3	1	1	32	17	6
86	2	30	3	1	1	4	1	2	8	24	10	9
87	1	43	2	1	1	2	1	1	2	24	14	10
88	2	26	5	2	1	4	1	1	1	16	23	7
89	2	44	1	1	1	4	2	2	8	27	18	6
90	1	45	1	2	2	3	3	2	8	20	14	5

for a person's age. Also, question 9 has a large number of 8s, because for this variable an 8 means 'not applicable'—many people did not answer this question, having been filtered out by the previous one (that is, they do not have other sources of regular exercise). Everyone answered questions 10, 11, and 12, so there are no missing data for those variables. Were there some, it would be necessary to code the missing data with a number that cannot also be a true figure, like 999, which is also easy to remember. The various missing data codes are stored in the information for each variable so they cannot be read by the computer as anything other than missing data.

Getting started in SPSS

Introduction

SPSS for Windows is the most widely used package of computer software for this kind of analysis, probably because it is relatively straightforward to use. SPSS, short for *Statistical Package for the Social Sciences*, has been in existence since the mid-1960s and over the years has undergone many revisions, particularly since the arrival of personal computers. The version used in preparing this section is SPSS 16. From this point on, when referring to SPSS for Windows in the text, it is called simply SPSS. The gym survey is used to illustrate how the software is used.

SPSS operations are presented in **bold**, for example, **Analyze**. Names given to variables are in ***bold italics***, for example, ***gender*** and ***reasons***. Labels given to values or to variables are also in bold but are not italicized, for example, **reasons for visiting** and **male**. Box 12.3 presents a list of basic operations in SPSS. One further element in the presentation is that a right-pointing arrow means 'left click once with the mouse' to make selections.

To start, double click on the SPSS icon on the computer screen. If there is no icon, click the **Start**

Box 12.3   Basic operations in SPSS for Windows

- The SPSS **Data Editor**. This is the mode in which data may be entered and subsequently edited and defined. It is made up of two screens: **Data View** and **Variable View**. Move between these two views by selecting the appropriate tab at the bottom left of the screen.

- **Data View**. This is the spreadsheet into which the data are entered. When starting up SPSS, the Data View appears.

- **Variable View**. This is another spreadsheet, but this one displays information about each of the variables (such as the variable name, the variable labels and value labels) and allows that information to be changed (see below).

- **Output**. After a statistical analysis or the production of a graph (sometimes called a 'chart' in SPSS), the output is deposited here. The Output window superimposes itself over the Data Editor after an analysis has been performed or a graph has been generated.

- **Variable Name**. This is the name given to a variable, for example, ***gender***. Until given a name, the variable is referred to as var00001, var00002, etc. Once given a name, the name appears in the column for that variable in the Data View window. It is generated from the Data View.

- **Variable Label**. This is a label attached to a particular variable, and is optional. It is usually longer and therefore more explanatory than the variable name. Spaces can be used, for example, **reasons for visiting**. The label appears in any output generated and comes from the Variable View.

- **Value Label**. This is a label attached to the code used when entering the data. Thus, for var00001, one can attach the label **male** to 1 and **female** to 2. In output, such as a frequency table or chart, the labels for each value are presented, making the interpretation of output easier than if the code were used. It is generated from the Variable View.

- **Missing Values**. If data for a particular variable are missing, one must specify how missing values are coded so the computer can omit them from the calculations. Missing values are generated from the Variable View.

- **Analyze**. This is the button on the menu bar along the top of the Data Editor from which (via a drop-down menu) the method of analysis is selected. Note that whenever an item on a menu appears with a right-pointing arrow after it, a further sub-menu is available.

- **Graphs**. This is the button at the top of the Data Editor used to get access to the **Chart Builder** (via a drop-down menu), which can be used to create various graphs and charts.

- **Chart Builder**. This feature is used to make charts and graphs. A very useful tutorial is available by clicking **Help → Tutorial → Creating and Editing Charts**.

- **Chart Editor**. A graph can be edited with the Chart Editor. To activate this editor, double-click anywhere in the graph. A small Chart Editor window appears along with a version of the main graph and stays until the Chart Editor is exited. Using the Chart Editor, various changes and enhancements to the graph can be made.

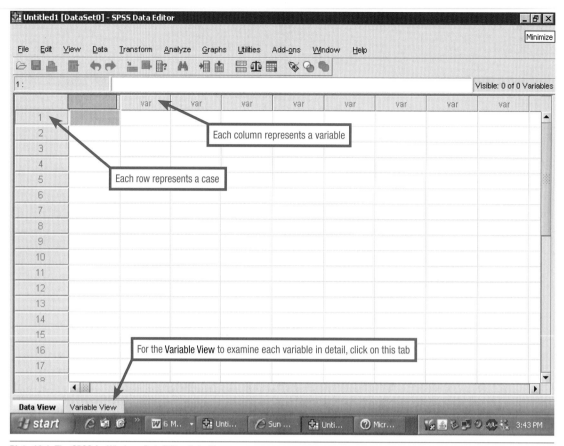

Plate 12.1 The SPSS for Windows Data Editor **Data View**

button in the bottom left-hand corner of the screen and select SPSS from the menu of programs. A series of follow-on menus appear: select SPSS **16.0**. If after SPSS loads an opening dialogue box with the title 'What do you want to do?' and a list of options appears, disable it. It is not important in the following exposition, so → **Cancel**, which gives you the SPSS **Data Editor**, made up of two components: **Data View** and **Variable View**. Move between these two by selecting the appropriate tab at the bottom left of the screen. The **Data View** provides a spreadsheet grid into which data are entered. The columns represent *variables*—in our example, information about characteristics of each person in the gym study sample, like *gender* and *age*. Until data are entered, each column simply has **var** as its heading. The rows represent *cases*, which can be people (as in this example) or other units of analysis. Each block in the grid is referred to as a 'cell.' Note also that when the data are in the SPSS spreadsheet, they look different, for example, 1 is 1.00 (although that can be adjusted if necessary).

Entering data in the Data View

To input the data into the **Data View**, make sure that the top left-hand cell in the grid is highlighted (Plate 12.1). If it is not, simply click once in that cell. Then type the appropriate number in that cell—that is, 1. This number goes directly into that cell and into the box beneath the toolbar. As an alternative to using the mouse, many people find it easier to use the arrow keys on their keyboard to move from cell to cell. If a mistake is made, simply click once in the cell in question, type in the correct value, and click once more in that cell. The last piece of data goes into the bottom right-hand cell of what will be a perfect rectangle of data. Plate 12.2 shows the **Data View** with the data from the gym survey entered (though only part of the data set is visible, in that only the

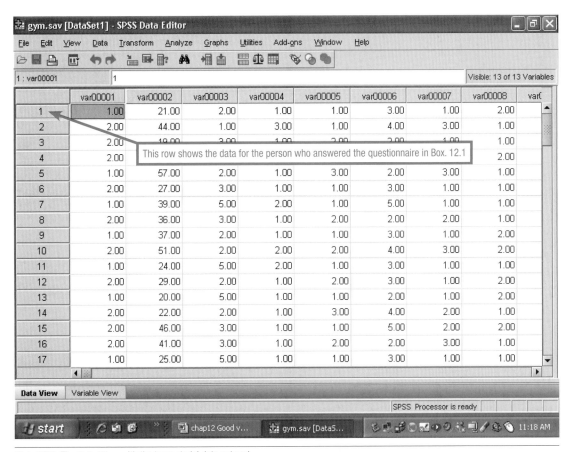

Plate 12.2 The **Data View** with the 'gym study' data entered

first 17 respondents and 8 of the 12 variables are visible). The first row of data contains the coded answers (provided by the first respondent) from the completed questionnaire in Box 12.1.

To proceed further, SPSS works in the following typical sequence for defining variables and analyzing data.

1. Make a selection from the menu bar at the top of the screen, for example, → **Analyze**.
2. From the menu that will appear, make a selection, for example, → **Descriptive Statistics**.
3. This will bring up another menu where you provide more information, such as the operation to be performed—for example, **Frequencies**.
4. This will bring up a *dialogue box* in which you provide further information, such as the variables to be analyzed.
5. Very often, further information is needed; → a button that brings up a *sub-dialogue box*.

6. Provide the information in the sub-dialogue box and then go back to the dialogue box. Sometimes, a further sub-dialogue box is required before going back to the dialogue box.

When finished going through the entire procedure, → OK. The toolbar beneath the menu bar allows shortcut access to certain SPSS operations.

Defining variables: variable names, missing values, variable labels, and value labels

Once finished entering the data, prepare the variables. The following steps explain how this is done:

1. → the **Variable View** tab at the bottom left of the **Data Editor** (opens the window shown in Plate 12.3).
2. To provide a variable name, click on the current variable name (for example, **var00003**) and type

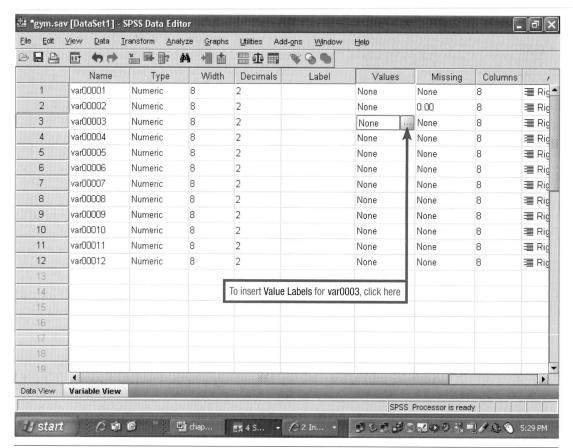

Plate 12.3 The Data Editor **Variable View**

a name for it (for example, *reasons*). The name cannot include spaces. This name is the identification needed for instructing the computer to perform an analysis with this variable. It is arbitrary and can be anything, but choose a name that indicates what the variable is measuring.

3. Give the variable a more detailed designation, known in SPSS as a **variable label**. To do this, → the cell in the **Label** column for this variable. Then type in the variable label (for example, **reasons for visiting**). This label will appear on your output, just like a designer label appears on clothes. If no variable label is specified, the variable name is used for the output.

4. Provide 'value labels' for the values of the variables, where appropriate. The procedure generally applies to variables that are not interval/ratio. The latter do not need value labels (unless you are grouping them in some way). To assign value labels, → in the cell in the **Values** column for the variable in question. A small button

with three dots on it appears. → the button. The **Value Labels** dialogue box appears (Plate 12.4). → the box to the right of **Value:** and begin to define the value labels. To do this, enter the value (for example, 1) in the area to the right of **Value:** and then type in the value label (for example, **relaxation**) in the area to the right

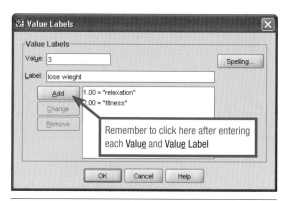

Plate 12.4 The **Value Labels** dialogue box

of **Label:**. Then ➔ **Add**. Do this for each value. When finished ➔ OK. A variable name for question one on the questionnaire could be ***gender***, the variable label 'gender of respondent,' and the value labels, 1 'male' and 2 'female.' The computer reads only numbers (male is 1, female 2) so the value labels are optional, but if omitted the data will tell you about the 1s and 2s instead of males and females.

5. Designate missing values. In the case of ***reasons***, missing data are given a value of 0. To assign the missing value, ➔ the cell for this variable in the **Missing** column. Again, ➔ the button that has three dots on it. This will generate the **Missing Values** dialogue box (Plate 12.5). In the **Missing Values** dialogue box, enter the missing value (0) below **Discrete missing value**s and then ➔ OK.

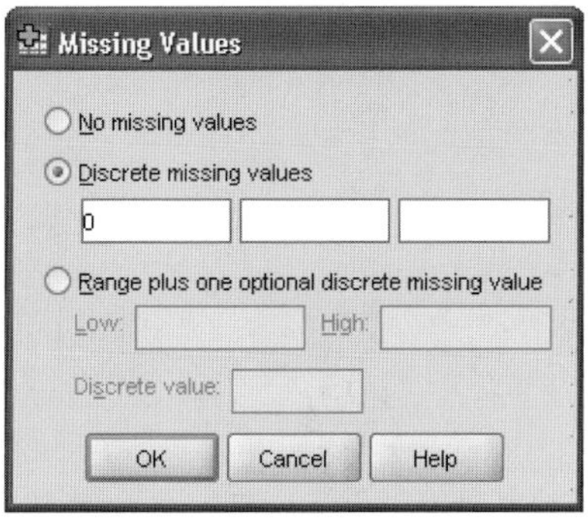

Plate 12.5 The **Missing Values** dialogue box

To simplify the following presentation, ***reasons*** is the only variable for which a variable label and missing values are defined.

Saving the data

To save the data for future use, make sure that the **Data Editor** is the active window. Then,

➔ **File** ➔ Save **As**...

The **Save Data As** dialogue box then appears. It needs a name for the data, which is placed after **File <u>n</u>ame:** and a place to save the data—for example, onto a portable disk or the hard drive of your computer. To select the destination drive, ➔ the downward pointing arrow to the right of the box by **Save <u>in</u>**. Then choose the drive on which to save the data and ➔ <u>S</u>ave.

This procedure saves the data *and* any work done on it—for example, value labels and missing values specifications. If doing more work on the data, such as creating a new variable, the data must be saved again or the new work will be lost. SPSS gives a choice of renaming the data, in which case there will be two data files (one with the original data and one with the revised data), or keeping the same name. In the latter case the original file is lost but its name retained and now applied to the modified file.

Retrieving data

To retrieve a data file, ➔ **<u>F</u>ile** ➔ **<u>O</u>pen** ➔ Data... The **Open Data** dialogue box will appear. Go to the location in which the data are deposited to retrieve the file containing the data and then ➔ **<u>O</u>pen**.

Now at last, analysis of the data that has been entered can begin!

Types of variables

Look at the different questions and notice that some of them call for answers in terms of real numbers: questions 2 (***age***), and 10, 11, and 12. Questions 1 (***gender***) and 8 yield either/or answers, which are called dichotomies (only two possible responses). The rest of the questions take the form of lists of categories, but there are also differences among them. Some of the answers can be rank ordered: see questions 4, 5, and 6. Thus one can say for question 6 that the category 'every day' implies greater frequency than '4–6 days a week,' which in turn is a greater frequency than '2 or 3 days a week,' and so on. Compare this to questions 3, 7, and 9 where the categories can*not* be rank ordered. One cannot say in the case of question 3 that 'relaxation' is more or less of something than 'maintain or improve fitness' is.

This discussion illustrates that different types of variables can be generated in the course of research. The four main types are distinguished by looking at the relationship between the categories of the variable *as manifested by any one individual*. The four are:

● *Nominal variables*. These variables, also known as *categorical variables*, are composed of categories that have no relationship to one another except to say that they are *different*. Religion is an example. The categories may be, for example, Roman Catholic, Protestant, Jewish, Muslim,

Box 12.4   Computing a new variable

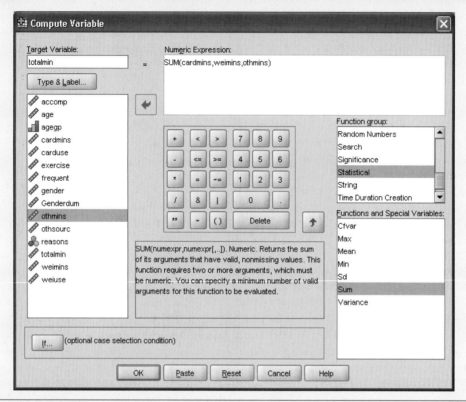

Plate 12.6 The **Compute Variable** dialogue box

A person's total amount of time spent in the gym is made up of three variables: ***cardmins***, ***weimins***, and ***othmins*** (questions 10, 11, and 12 respectively). Adding them up gives the total number of minutes spent on activities in the gym, and a new variable ***totalmin*** can be created for that purpose. To do this, take the following steps:

1. → **Transform** → **Compute Variable**. . . [opens the Compute Variable dialogue box shown in Plate 12.6]
2. under Target Variable: type **totalmin**
3. under **Function group**, select **Statistical**; under Functions and Special Variables, select **Sum**; then click on the button with an upward-pointing arrowhead to send it into the box underneath **Numeric Expression:**
4. from the list of variables at the left, → ***cardmins*** → adjacent button [puts ***cardmins*** in box after SUM]; → ***weimins*** → button [puts ***weimins*** in box after ***cardmins***]; → ***othmins*** → button [puts ***othmins*** in box after ***weimins***]; be sure to put commas (but not spaces) between the variable names, and to delete any '?' that remain in the Numeric Expression box.
5. → OK

The new variable ***totalmin*** is created and appears in the **Data Editor**.

Hindu, Other, and No Religion. Two research participants are either in the same category or they are in different categories, the only kind of comparison possible. This means that the order of the categories is arbitrary: it could have begun with No Religion and ended with Roman Catholic. Switching the order has no implications for how the data are interpreted.

- *Ordinal variables.* With these variables not only are the categories different, but they can be rank ordered. That means that 'greater than' ($>$) and 'less than' ($<$) statements can be made about the categories and the people in them. For example, for question 5 'always' indicates greater frequency than 'usually,' which indicates more frequency than 'rarely,' etc. Note also that it would be illogical to re-order them as, say: always, never, sometimes, usually.

- The distance or amount of difference between the categories, however, may not be equal across the range. Thus the difference between the category 'always' and 'usually' is probably not the same as the difference between 'usually' and 'rarely,' and so on. This is because no unit of measurement is used for this question. These ordinal variables are those in prose with a comparative 'er' or superlative 'est' attached to them, as in slim, slimmer, and slimmest.

- *Interval/ratio variables.* These are variables where a unit of measurement exists and thus the distances or amount of difference between the categories can be made identical across the range of categories. These involve numbers such as 1, 2, and 16. In the case of variables var00010 to var00012, the unit is the minute and the distance between the categories is a one-minute interval. Thus, a person who spends 32 minutes on cardiovascular equipment is spending one minute more than someone who spends 31. That difference is the same as the difference between someone who spends 8 minutes and another who spends 9 minutes on the equipment. At the interval/ratio level of measurement, one can say that two scores are equal or not equal (like the nominal level), for example, $32 \neq 31$; that they have greater or lesser values (like the ordinal level), for example, $32>31$, $8<9$; and specify the distance or amount of difference between them, for example, $32-31 = 1$.

Ratio variables are interval variables with a fixed and non-arbitrary zero point, as in wind speed of 0 kilometres per hour. Since many social science variables exhibit this quality (for example, income, age, years of school completed), they are not being distinguished here. But to understand, take two incomes: $30K and $45K. They are nominally unequal and the first is $<$ the second, in fact $15K less. But with that real 0, one can also say the first is 2/3 of the second (or the second is 1.5 times the first). The first income to the second income also has a 2:3 *ratio*. This is the highest level of measurement, one allowing the widest range of analysis techniques including addition, subtraction, multiplication, and division. See Box 12.4 for a description of how to create a new interval/ratio variable.

The four main types of variable and illustrations from the gym survey are provided in Table 12.1. Strictly speaking, items that have Likert-style response categories (see Box 3.3) produce ordinal variables. However, many writers argue that they

Table 12.1 Types of variable

Type	Description	Examples in gym study	Variable Name in SPSS
Nominal	Variables whose categories cannot be rank ordered; also known as categorical	var00001 var00003 var00007 var00008 var00009	gender reasons accomp othsourc exercise
Ordinal	Variables whose categories can be rank ordered but the distances between the categories are not equal across the range	var00004 var00005 var00006	carduse weiuse frequent
Interval/ratio	Variables where the distances between the categories are identical across the range	var00002 var00010 var00011 var00012	age cardmins weimins othmins

can be treated as though they produce interval/ratio variables because of the relatively large number of categories they generate. For a brief discussion of this issue, see Bryman and Cramer (2001: 58–9). See Box 12.5 for the opposite issue, reducing an interval/ratio level variable to an ordinal or even a nominal variable. Figure 12.1 provides guidance about how to identify variables of each type.

Univariate analysis

Univariate analysis refers to the examination of one variable at a time and in this section, several common approaches are outlined.

Frequency tables

A frequency table provides the number and percentage of people belonging to each of the categories

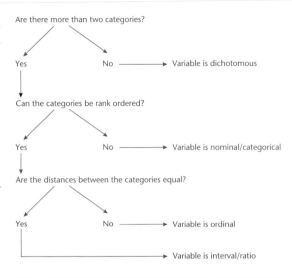

Figure 12.1 Deciding how to categorize a variable

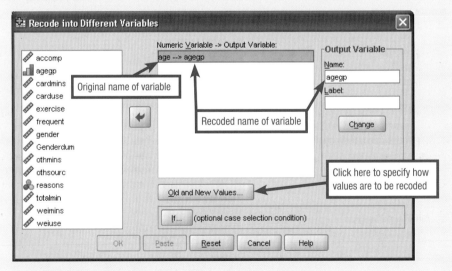

Box 12.5   Recoding variables

Sometimes one needs to recode variables—for example, to group scores together, as was done to produce a table like Table 12.3 for an interval/ratio variable (var00002, now given the variable name **age**). SPSS offers two choices: change **age**, or keep **age** as it is and create a new variable. This latter option is appropriate here, because you may need the data for **age** in its original form for some other analysis. We will preserve the original variable and create a new one, **agegp**, for age groups, with five age categories, as in Table 12.3.

1. → **Transform** → **Recode into Different Variables** [opens Recode into Different Variables dialogue box shown in Plate 12.7]

Plate 12.7 The **Recode into Different Variables** dialogue box

Box 12.5 . . . Continued

2. ➔ *age* ➔ adjacent button [puts age in Numeric Variable ➔ Output Variable: box] ➔ box beneath Output Variable Name: and type *agegp* ➔ **Change** [puts *agegp* in the Numeric Variable ➔ Output Variable: box] ➔ **Old and New Values** . . . [opens Recode into Different Variables: Old and New Values sub-dialogue box shown in Plate 12.8]

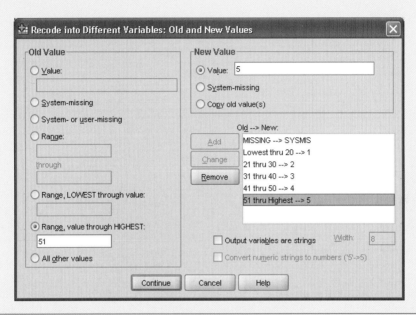

Plate 12.8 The **Recode into Different Variables: Old and New Values** sub-dialogue box

3. ➔ the circle by **System-** or **user-missing**, and by **System-missing** under New Value, if there are missing values for a variable (which is the case for this variable), then ➔ **Add**
4. ➔ circle by **Range: LOWEST through value** and type 20 in the box ➔ circle by **Value:** in New Value and type 1 ➔ **Add** [the new value appears in the Old ➔ New: box]
5. ➔ first circle by **Range:** and type 21, and in box after 'through' type 30 ➔ circle by **Value:** in New Value and type 2 ➔ **Add**
6. ➔ first circle by **Range:** and type 31 and in box after 'through' type 40 ➔circle by **Value:** in New Value and type 3 ➔ **Add**
7. ➔ first circle by **Range:** and type 41, and in box after 'through' type 50 ➔ circle by **Value:** in New Value and type 4 ➔ **Add**
8. ➔ circle by **Range: value through HIGHEST** and type 51 in the box ➔circle by **Value:** in New Value and type 5 ➔ **Add** ➔ **Continue** [closes the Recode into Different Variables: Old and New Values sub-dialogue box shown in Plate 12.8 and returns to the Recode into Different Variables shown in Plate 12.7]
9. ➔ OK

The new variable *agegp* is created and appears in the **Data View**. To generate value labels for the five age bands and a variable label, repeat the approach described earlier in the text for those procedures.

Table 12.2 Frequency table showing reasons for visiting the gym

Reasons for visiting

		Frequency	Per cent	Valid per cent	Cumulative per cent
Valid	relaxation	9	10.0	10.0	10.0
	fitness	31	34.4	34.4	44.4
	lose weight	33	36.7	36.7	81.1
	build strength	17	18.9	18.9	100.0
	TOTAL	90	100.0	100.0	

of the variable in question and can be created for all three variable types. An example of a frequency table for a nominal variable is provided for var00003 (*reasons*) in Table 12.2. The table shows, for example, that 33 members of the sample go the gym to lose weight and that they represent 37 per cent (percentages are often rounded in frequency tables) of the entire sample. This is calculated by the simple formula: n in category/TOTAL N.

When an interval/ratio variable (like people's ages) is put in frequency table format, some of the categories may be combined in some way. When doing so, take care to ensure that the categories created do not overlap (for example: 20–30, 30–40, 40–50, etc. would be unacceptable). This violates the *mutually exclusive rule* (required for telling whether two cases are equal or not equal), meaning that no

one should be able to fall into two (or more) categories. Where does a 30-year-old go, into the first or second category? Also recall from coding, the *exhaustive rule*: everyone must have a category, even if it is one for missing data or not applicable (see Box 12.6).

An example of a frequency table for an interval/ratio variable, var00002 (*age*) is shown in Table 12.3. Not to group people in terms of age ranges would mean 34 different categories, which is too many to meaningfully describe. By creating 5 categories, the distribution of ages is easier to comprehend. Notice that the sample totals 89 and that the 'Valid Per cent' column is based on a total of 89 rather than 90. This is because this variable contains one missing value (from respondent 24). Use the 'Valid Per cent' column to cite percentages because the 'Per cent' column includes missing values in the calculations.

Table 12.3 Frequency table showing ages of gym members

Ages of gym visitors

		Frequency	Per cent	Valid per cent	Cumulative per cent
Valid	20 and below	3	3.3	3.4	3.4
	21-30	39	43.3	43.8	47.2
	31-40	23	25.6	25.8	73.0
	41-50	21	23.3	23.6	96.6
	51 and over	3	3.3	3.4	100.0
	TOTAL	89	98.9	100.0	
Missing	System	1	1.1		
TOTAL		90	100.0		

Box 12.6   Losing information

When one groups an interval/ratio variable like var00002 (*age*), into categories (for example, 20 and under; 21–30; 31–40; 41–50; 51 and over), it is transformed into an ordinal variable. No longer can the data be added as is possible at the interval/ratio level. Where feasible, researchers avoid moving down to a lower level of measurement, because that involves losing information. Dinovitzer *et al.* (2003), however, did transform years of education, a ratio variable, into a four-level ordinal variable. In effect, they were saying, for example, that those with one to eight years of education are basically similar and that differentiating a person with four years from one with five is not necessary. They are all 'low.'

If variables contain data that have only two categories (such as in male and female for the variable *gender*) they are often called dichotomous variables. Ordinal variables can also be dichotomous (for example, mild versus severe depression) but this is infrequent, since finer gradations are usually more meaningful.

Sometimes researchers, especially students, have no choice but to move to a lower level of measurement, that is, to give up some information. This may arise because they just do not have enough cases for the detail they want. For example, examine the following data. Note how in some instances (for example, in the West Secede variable) where most people strongly disagree and only a few agree, feel neutral, or disagree, there could be too few people in the latter three categories to perform certain statistical analyses. In such instances, one can collapse the data into a dichotomy (two parts); for example, for this variable any level of agreement versus any level of disagreement. Sometimes the data are combined into three, four, or more categories. When collapsing categories, be sure your decisions make conceptual and theoretical sense. For instance, for the NAFTA variable it would not be advisable to combine the people in the neutral category with those in the agree or disagree categories.

	Gun-control (%)	Pro-choice (%)	NAFTA (%)	West Secede (%)
Strongly agree	36	45	21	12
Agree	17	23	10	4
Neutral	2	1	40	2
Disagree	18	10	6	8
Strongly Disagree	27	21	23	74

Diagrams

Diagrams are sometimes used to display quantitative data. With nominal or ordinal variables, the *bar chart* and the *pie chart* are two of the easiest to use. A bar chart of the data in Table 12.2 is presented in Figure 12.2. The height of each bar represents the number of people in each category. This figure and the next two were produced with SPSS for Windows.

Another way of displaying the same data is in a pie chart, like the one in Figure 12.3. This also shows the size of the different categories but more clearly brings out the size of each relative to the total sample. The percentage that each slice represents of the whole sample is also given in this diagram.

To display an interval/ratio variable, like var00002 (*age*), a *histogram* is likely to be employed. Figure

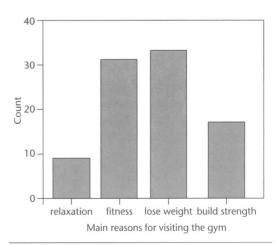

Figure 12.2 Bar chart showing main reasons for visiting the gym (SPSS output)

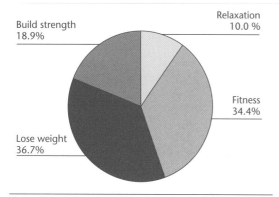

Figure 12.3 Pie chart showing main reasons for visiting the gym (SPSS output)

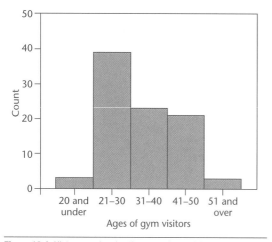

Figure 12.4 Histogram showing the ages of gym visitors (SPSS output)

12.4 uses the same data and categories as Table 12.3. As with the bar chart, the bars represent the relative size of each of the age bands but in a histogram, there is no space between the bars. This is to distinguish histograms, produced for interval/ratio variables, from bar charts, which are used with nominal and ordinal variables.

This is a good point to continue with SPSS for Windows. The discussion begins with a general introduction followed by instructions on how to generate the charts discussed above. Then we move back to forms of analysis, with SPSS instructions for generating them interspersed in the text as appropriate. Learning new software requires some perseverance, but it is worth the effort. It would take far longer to perform calculations by hand (even on our small sample of 90) than to learn the software. With more advanced techniques and larger samples, the time saved is even more substantial. Imagine calculating the mean age of 2500 people by hand!

Data analysis with SPSS

Generating a frequency table

To produce a frequency table like the one in Table 12.2:

1. → <u>A</u>nalyze → <u>D</u>escriptive Statistics → <u>F</u>requencies. . . [opens the **Frequencies** dialogue box shown in Plate 12.9].
2. → *reasons* → adjacent button [puts *reasons* into **Variable(s):** box]
3. → OK
4. The table then appears in the **Output Viewer** (see Plate 12.10)

Note that in the **Frequencies** dialogue box, the variable name appears. If you would prefer to work with variable labels (which provide more information on what the variable measures), go into the **Data Editor**, → **Edit** → **Options** → **General**, and in the top left-hand corner you can select variable labels to be used. Similarly, if you prefer that the variables be arranged in alphabetical order, you can specify that there.

Generating a bar chart

To produce a bar chart like the one in Figure 12.2:

1. → **Graphs** → **Chart Builder. . .** [opens **Chart Builder** dialogue box]
2. → **Gallery** → **Bar** , and drag the type of bar chart you want into the 'canvas,' the large area above the Gallery [see plate 12.11]
3. drag *reasons* into the X-axis box at the bottom of the canvas
4. → OK

As mentioned earlier, for some useful details on this procedure, do the tutorial available in the **Data Editor** at **Help** → **Tutorial** → **Creating and Editing Charts**.

Generating a pie chart

To produce a pie chart like the one in Figure 12.3:

1. → **Graphs** → **Chart Builder. . .** [opens **Chart Builder** dialogue box]

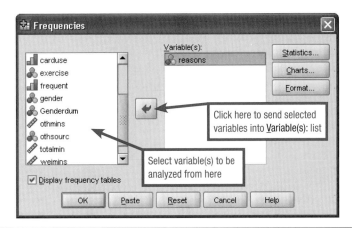

Plate 12.9 The **Frequencies** dialogue box

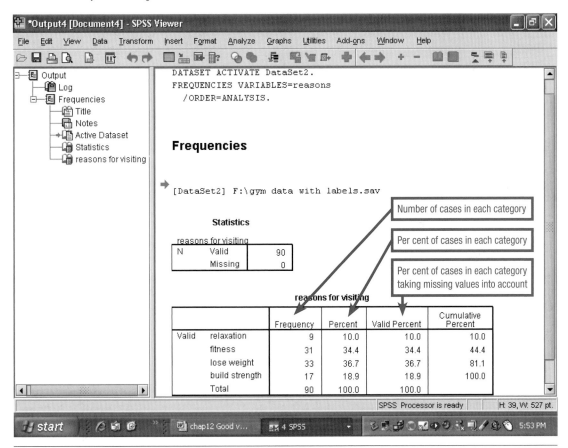

Plate 12.10 The **Output Viewer**

2. → **Gallery** → **Pie/Polar,** and drag the pie chart into the 'canvas,' the large area above the Gallery.

3. right-click **reasons** in the Variables: list and choose nominal

4. drag **reasons** into the 'Slice by?' drop zone at the bottom of the canvas

5. → OK

6. *double-click* anywhere in the chart to bring up the **Chart Editor** (Plate 12.12). The graph

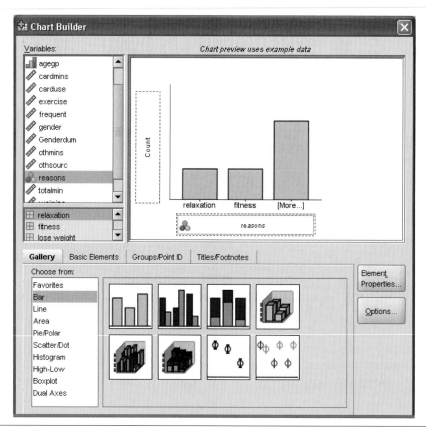

Plate 12.11 The **Chart Builder** dialogue box

appears in the **Chart Editor → Elements → Show data labels**. This will place the percentage in each category in the appropriate slices of the pie [see Plate 12.13].

The chart is in colour, but if you only have access to a monochrome printer, you can change the pie chart into patterns, which allows the slices to be clearer. Get into the **Chart Editor**, which allows all figures to be edited, **→ Edit → Properties → Variables**. By **reasons for visiting** (the variable label) select **Style: Colour**, and change that to **Style: Patterns → Apply**. This procedure applies to all charts. Once again, for some useful details on this procedure, do the tutorial available in the **Data Editor** at **Help → Tutorial → Creating and Editing Charts**.

Generating a histogram

Producing a histogram like the one in Figure 12.4 is just as simple except that it requires defining the ages to be grouped (or using the newly created

agegp variable). Create a histogram for *agegp* using the **Chart Builder → Gallery → Histogram**. (Make sure that **agegp** is defined as a scale [interval/ratio] variable by right-clicking on it in the Variables: list while in the **Chart Builder**.) There are other ways to present interval/ratio data, like measures of central tendency and dispersion, which are discussed below.

Printing output

To print all the output in the SPSS **Viewer**, make sure that the **Viewer** is the active window and then **→ File → Print. . .** The **Print** dialogue box appears and then **→ OK**. To print just some of the output, hold down the Ctrl button on the keyboard and click once on the parts of the output you want to print. The easiest way to do this is to select the elements from the output summary in the left-hand segment of the SPSS **Viewer** shown in Plate 12.10. Then bring up the **Print** dialogue box. When the **Print** dialogue

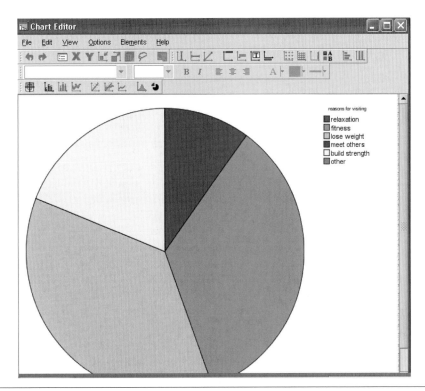

Plate 12.12 The **Chart Editor**

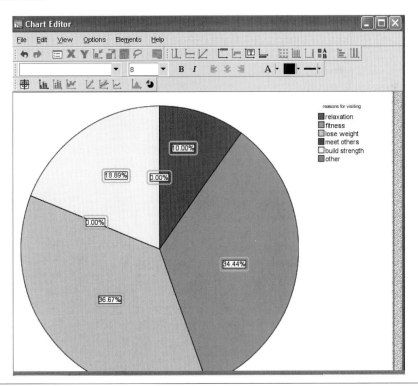

Plate 12.13 The **Chart Editor** showing pie chart percentages

box appears, make sure **Selected Output** under **Print Range** is selected.

More univariate analysis and spss

Measures of central tendency

Measures of central tendency provide, in one number, a typical or 'average' score for a distribution or group of scores. Three measures of central tendency are commonly used: the mode, the median, and the mean. Whether a particular one can be used depends on the level of measurement.

- *Mode.* This is the value that occurs most frequently in a distribution. The mode for var00002 (*age*) is 28—there are more 28s than any other score. The mode can be used with all types of variable but it is most applicable to nominal data.
- *Median.* This is the mid-point in a distribution of scores, derived by arraying all the scores in order (typically from the lowest to the highest), and then finding the middle one. If there is an even number of values, the median is calculated by taking the mean of the two middle numbers in the distribution. In the case of var00002, the median is 31. The median can be used with both interval/ratio and ordinal variables. It cannot be used with nominal data because those sorts of scores cannot be rank ordered.
- *Mean.* This is the average as understood in everyday use—that is, the sum of all numbers in a distribution, divided by the number of scores. The mean for var00002 is 33.6, meaning that the average age in our sample of gym visitors is about 34. This is slightly higher than the median because a few considerably older members (especially respondents 5 and 10) inflate it. The mean is vulnerable to such *outliers* (extreme values at either end of the distribution), which exert considerable upward or downward pressure on the mean. In such instances, the median is recommended, as it is not affected in this way. (Some researchers exclude outliers and then calculate the mean, noting the removal in the text.)

One final point: as mentioned, SPSS reads numbers only. It can calculate a 'mean' for a variable like *gender* by adding up all of the 1s (males) and 2s (females). A mean of 1.5 means equal numbers of each. What does an average of 1.6 mean? It signifies more females than males, but strictly speaking such calculations should not be done with this sort of variable.

Measures of dispersion

The amount of variation in a sample can be just as important as its typical value. Two in-class tests can have the same mean of 60 per cent, but on one most people get between 50 and 70, while for the other the grades are evenly dispersed from the low 20s to 100 per cent. (In testing it is said that the first test does not discriminate; the brightest and least bright students get fairly close marks.) In the gym study, is there more or less variability in the amount of time spent on cardiovascular equipment compared with weights?

The most obvious way of measuring dispersion is by calculating the *range*. This is simply the difference between the maximum and the minimum value in a distribution of interval/ratio scores. (It can be applied to an ordinal variable too, but is more definitional there [for example, a range from working class to upper class] than descriptive.) The range is 64 minutes for the cardiovascular machines and 48 minutes for the weights. This suggests that there is more variability in the amount of time spent on the former, probably because some people spend almost no time on cardiovascular equipment. However, like the mean, the range is influenced by outliers, such as respondent 41, who spent 64 minutes on the cardio equipment.

Another measure of dispersion is the *standard deviation*, which is a measure of variation around the mean. It is calculated by taking the difference between each value in a distribution and the mean, squaring it, dividing the total of these differences by the number of values, and then taking the square root. The standard deviation for var00010 (**cardmins**) is 9.9 minutes and for var00011 (**weimins**) it is 8 minutes. This indicates that not only is the average amount of time spent on the cardiovascular equipment higher than for the weights, there is more deviation from the mean too. The standard deviation is also affected by outliers, which are sometimes excluded.

Generating the arithmetic mean, median, standard deviation, and range

SPSS uses the following typical sequence for analyzing data.

1. Make a selection from the menu bar at the top of the screen, for example → **Analyze** → **Descriptive Statistics** → **Descriptives**.
2. This brings up a *dialogue box* for telling SPSS what is needed, for example, the specific variables to be analyzed.
3. Very often, SPSS needs further information; → a button to bring up a *sub-dialogue box*.
4. Provide the information in the sub-dialogue box and then go back to the dialogue box. Sometimes,

a further sub-dialogue box appears; when finished, go back to the dialogue box.

When finished with the entire procedure, → OK.

To produce the mean, median, standard deviation, and the range for an interval/ratio variable like *age*, follow these steps:

1. → **Analyze** → **Descriptive Statistics** → **Explore . . .** [opens the **Explore** dialogue box]
2. → *age* → the button to the left of **Dependent List:** [puts *age* in the **Dependent List:** box] → **Statistics** under **Display** → OK
3. The output also includes the 95 per cent confidence interval for the mean, which is based on the standard error of the mean. The output is in Table 12.4.

Table 12.4 Explore output for age (SPSS output)

Explore

Case Processing Summary

	Cases					
	Valid		Missing		Total	
	N	Per cent	N	Per cent	N	Per cent
AGE	89	98.9%	1	1.1%	90	100.0%

Descriptives

			Statistic	Std. Error
AGE	Mean		33.5955	.9420
	95% Confidence	Lower bound	31.7235	
	Interval for mean	Upper bound	35.4675	
	5% Trimmed mean		33.3159	
	Median		31.0000	
	Variance		78.971	
	Std. Deviation		8.8866	
	Minimum		18.00	
	Maximum		57.00	
	Range		39.00	
	Interquartile Range		14.0000	
	Skewness		.446	.255
	Kurtosis		−.645	.506

	Nominal	Ordinal	Interval/ratio
Nominal	Contingency table + chi-square (χ^2) + Cramér's V	Contingency table + chi-square (χ^2) + Cramér's V	Contingency table + chi-square (χ^2) + Cramér's V. If the interval/ratio variable can be identified as the dependent variable, compare means with eta.
Ordinal	Contingency table + chi-square (χ^2) + Cramér's V	Kendall's tau-b	Kendall's tau-b
Interval/ratio	Contingency table + chi-square (χ^2) + Cramér's V. If the interval/ratio variable can be identified as the dependent variable, compare means with eta.	Kendall's tau-b	Pearson's r

Figure 12.5 Methods of bivariate analysis, one variable on top, other variable on side

Bivariate analysis

Bivariate analysis examines whether there is a relationship between two variables. Several techniques are available for examining relationships, but their use depends on the level of measurement of the two variables being analyzed. Figure 12.5 details the main types of bivariate analysis according to the types of variable involved.

Contingency tables

Contingency tables are probably the most flexible of all methods of analyzing relationships in that they can be employed in relation to any pair of variables, from nominal to interval/ratio. They are not, however, the most efficient method, especially for interval/ratio data, which is the reason why the method is not recommended in all of the cells in Figure 12.5. A contingency table is like a frequency table but it allows two variables to be simultaneously analyzed so that relationships between them can be examined. It is normal for contingency tables to include percentages, since they make the tables easier to interpret. Table 12.5 examines the relationship between gender and reasons for visiting the gym using our survey data. Gender is the presumed independent variable and for that reason becomes the column variable, a preference among most researchers. 'Reasons' is the presumed dependent or row variable (but see Box 12.7). In this case, gender is assumed to influence reasons for going to the gym; reasons for going to the gym cannot influence gender. The percentages are *column percentages*, that is, those for *the independent variable*. The number in each cell is calculated as a percentage of the total

number in its column. Thus, to take the top left-hand cell, the 3 men who go to the gym for relaxation out of 42 men in total, make 3/42 or 7 per cent of the men in the sample. The procedure for generating a contingency table with SPSS is described below.

Contingency tables are generated to look for patterns of association. In this case, there are clear gender differences in reasons for visiting the gym. As our student anticipated, females are much more likely than men to go to the gym to lose weight. They are also somewhat more likely to go to the gym for relaxation. By contrast, men are much more likely to go to the gym to build strength. There is little gender difference in terms of fitness as a reason. The next section outlines how to generate a contingency table using SPSS. That is immediately followed by the alternatives available in SPSS to analyze those tables; the options depend on the type of variables involved in the bivariate relationship.

Table 12.5 Contingency table showing the relationship between gender and reasons for visiting the gym

	Gender			
	Male		Female	
Reasons	*No.*	*%*	*No.*	*%*
Relaxation	3	7	6	13
Fitness	15	36	16	33
Lose weight	8	19	25	52
Build strength	16	38	1	2
Total	42	100	48	100

Note: χ^2 = 22.726 p < .0001, Cramér's V =.50.

Box 12.7   Relationships not causality

An important point to bear in mind about analyzing relationships between variables is that it is *relationships* and not *causes* that they uncover. One problem associated with this issue is that the *direction* of causation cannot be determined simply by establishing that a relationship exists between two variables. Indeed, there are cases when what appears to be a causal influence working in one direction actually works in the other way. An example of this problem of causal direction was presented in Chapter 3, where Sutton and Rafaeli (1988) expected to find that a display of positive emotions (for example, smiling or friendliness) by retail checkout staff caused increased sales. In fact, the relationship is in the opposite direction: levels of retail sales exert a causal influence on the display of emotions: the more sales, the busier the staff, and the less time and inclination they have to smile!

Sometimes, one may feel confident in inferring a causal direction—for example, in the relationship between age and voting behaviour. It is impossible for the way people vote to influence their age; so, if the two variables are related, age is the independent variable. It is not uncommon for researchers, when analyzing their data, to draw inferences about causal direction based on assumptions like this. However, even if the direction of causation is properly attributed, the relationship may be spurious or non-causal, that is, caused by a third variable.

Generating a contingency table

To generate a contingency table, like Table 12.5, follow this procedure:

1. → **Analyze** → **Descriptive Statistics** → **Crosstabs. . .** [opens the **Crosstabs** dialogue box shown in Plate 12.14]
2. → *reasons* → button by **Row(s):** [*reasons* appears in the **Row(s):** box] → *gender* → button by **Column(s):** [*gender* appears in the **Column(s):** box] → **Cells** [opens **Crosstabs: Cell Display** sub-dialogue box shown in Plate 12.15]
3. Make sure **Observed** in the **Counts** box is selected. Make sure **Column** under **Percentages** is selected. If either of these was not selected, simply click at the relevant point. → **Continue** [closes **Crosstabs: Cell Display** sub-dialogue box and return to the **Crosstabs** dialogue box shown in Plate 12.14]

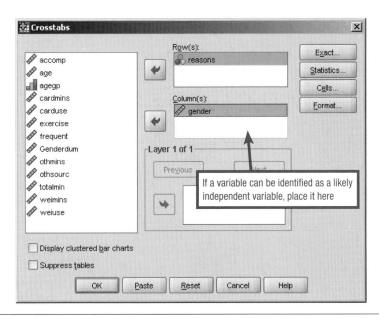

Plate 12.14 The **Crosstabs** dialogue box

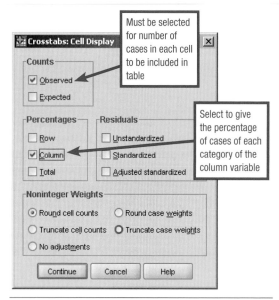

Plate 12.15 The **Crosstabs: Cell Display** sub-dialogue box

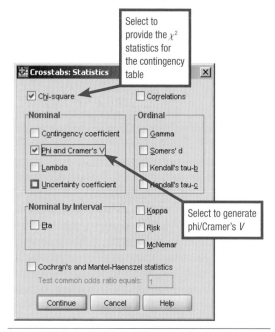

Plate 12.16 The **Crosstabs: Statistics** sub-dialogue box

4. → **Statistics. . .** [opens the **Crosstabs: Statistics** sub-dialogue box shown in Plate 12.16]. For example suppose Cramér's *V* is needed (because of having two nominal variables). → **Chi**-square → **Phi and Cramér's *V*** → **Continue** [closes **Crosstabs: Statistics** sub-dialogue box and returns to the **Crosstabs** dialogue box shown in Plate 12.14]

5. → OK

The resulting output is in Table 12.6. Cramér's *V* is just one of the available statistics.

Pearson's *r*

Pearson's *r* is a statistic for examining relationships between two interval/ratio variables. Its chief features are:

- the coefficient has values from 0 (which indicates there is no relationship whatever between the two variables) to +1 or −1 (the first indicating a perfect positive relationship, the second a perfect negative);
- the closer a positive coefficient is to 1, the stronger the relationship; the closer it is to zero, the weaker the relationship;
- similarly, the closer a negative coefficient is to −1, the stronger the relationship; the closer it is to zero, the weaker the relationship;
- the sign of the coefficient (positive or negative) indicates the *direction* of a relationship. Negative means that as one variable is going up, the other is going down; it does not matter which is which. Positive means the two are going in the same direction, either both up or both down.

To be able to use Pearson's *r*, the relationship between the two variables must be broadly *linear*—that is, when plotted on a scatter diagram, the values of the two variables approximate a straight line (even though they may be scattered as in Figure 12.9) and do not curve. To check on this requires a scatter diagram.

Generating scatter diagrams

The production of scatter diagrams, known as *scatterplots* in SPSS, is illustrated in the relationship between *age* and *cardmins*. If one variable can be identified as likely to be the independent variable, it is by convention placed on the *X*-axis, the horizontal axis. Since *age* is bound to be the independent variable, follow these steps:

1. → **Graphs** → **Chart Builder** → **Gallery** → **Scatter/Dot**
2. drag the Simple Scatter diagram into the canvas
3. drag *age* into the **X-Axis?** box at the bottom of the canvas

Table 12.6 Contingency table for **reasons for visiting** by *gender* (SPSS output)

Crosstabs

Case Processing Summary

	Cases					
	Valid		Missing		Total	
	N	Per cent	N	Per cent	N	Per cent
reasons for visiting * GENDER	90	100.0%	0	.0%	90	100.0%

reasons for visiting * GENDER crosstabulation

			GENDER		
			male	female	Total
reasons for visiting	relaxation	Count	3	6	9
		% within GENDER	7.1%	12.5%	10.0%
	fitness	Count	15	16	31
		% within GENDER	35.7%	33.3%	34.4%
	lose weight	Count	8	25	33
		% within GENDER	19.0%	52.1%	36.7%
	build strength	Count	16	1	17
		% within GENDER	38.1%	2.1%	18.9%
Total		Count	42	48	90
		% within GENDER	100.0%	100.0%	100.0%

Chi-Square Tests

This is the χ^2 value referred to in the text

	Value	df	Asymp. Sig. [(2-sided)]
Pearson Chi-Square	22.726[a]	3	.000
Likelihood Ratio	25.805	3	.000
Linear-by-Linear Association	9.716	1	.002
N of Valid Cases	90		

[a] 2 cells (25.0%) have expected count less than 5. The minimum expected count is 4.20.

Since this is not a 2 × 2 table, interpret Cramér's V

Symmetric Measures

		Value	Approx. Sig.
Nominal by Nominal	Phi	.503	.000
	Cramer's V	.503	.000
N of Valid Cases		90	

Shows level of statistical significance of computed value of Cramér's V

Shows strength of relationship

[a] Not assuming the null hypothesis.
[b] Using the asymptotic standard error assuming the null hypothesis.

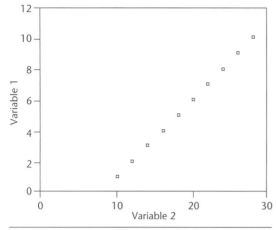

Figure 12.6 Scatter diagram showing a perfect positive relationship

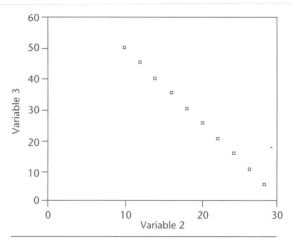

Figure 12.7 Scatter diagram showing a perfect negative relationship

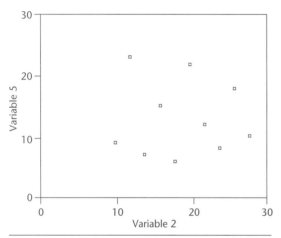

Figure 12.8 Scatter diagram showing two variables that are not related

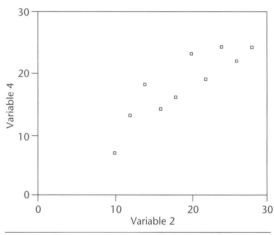

Figure 12.9 Scatter diagram showing a strong positive relationship

4. drag *cardmins* into the **Y-Axis?** box at the left side of the canvas

5. → OK

To illustrate these features consider Box 12.8, which gives imaginary data for five variables, and the scatter diagrams in Figures 12.6 to 12.9, which look at the relationship between pairs of interval/ratio variables. The scatter diagram for variables 1 and 2 is presented in Figure 12.6 and shows a perfect positive relationship, which yields a Pearson's *r* correlation of +1. This means that, as one variable increases, the other variable increases, and the value of one variable perfectly predicts the value of the other. If the correlation is below 1, at least one other variable is affecting the relationship between them, possibly affecting variable 1 as well as variable 2.

The scatter diagram for variables 2 and 3 (Figure 12.7) shows a perfect negative relationship, which yields a Pearson's *r* correlation of −1. This means that, as one variable increases the other variable decreases, and that the values of one variable perfectly predict the values of the other. In both this and the prior instance, the line could be extended beyond the data to make predictions of what would happen to either variable if the other moved beyond the range shown, although it is risky to go beyond what is known. Also, social data usually exhibit so many exceptions that few cases fall exactly on the line, so general rather than specific predictions are usually offered.

No apparent pattern in the scatter diagram, as in the relationship between variables 2 and 5 (Figure 12.8) means no or virtually no correlation between the variables. The correlation is close to zero, at

Box 12.8 Imaginary data from five variables to show different types of relationship

Variables

1	2	3	4	5
1	10	50	7	9
2	12	45	13	23
3	14	40	18	7
4	16	35	14	15
5	18	30	16	6
6	20	25	23	22
7	22	20	19	12
8	24	15	24	8
9	26	10	22	18
10	28	5	24	10

−.041. This means that the variation in the dependent variable is probably associated with variables other than the one used in this analysis.

If a relationship is strong, a clear patterning to the variables is evident. This is the case with variables 2 and 4, whose scatter diagram appears in Figure 12.9. There is clearly a positive relationship and in fact

the Pearson's *r* is .88 (usually, positive correlations are presented without the + sign). This means that the variation in the two variables is very closely connected, but that there is also some influence of other variables.

Going back to the gym survey, the correlation between *age* (var00002) and the amount of time spent on weights *weimins* (var00011) is −.27, a weak negative relationship. This suggests a tendency for older people to spend less time on such equipment, but also that other variables influence that time.

Generating Pearson's *r*

To produce Pearson's *r*, in particular the correlation between *age*, *weimins*, and *cardmins*, follow these steps:

1. → **Analyze** → **Correlate** → **Bivariate. . .** [opens **Bivariate Correlations** dialogue box shown in Plate 12.17]
2. → *age* → button → *cardmins* → button → *weimins* → button [*age*, *cardmins*, and *weimins* should now be in the **Variables:** box] → **Pearson** [if not already selected] → OK

The resulting output is in Table 12.7.

To produce Kendall's tau-b, follow the same procedures but instead of selecting **Pearson**, → **Kendall's tau-b**. Somer's d and Kendall's tau-c are other options, but for clarity are not explained here.

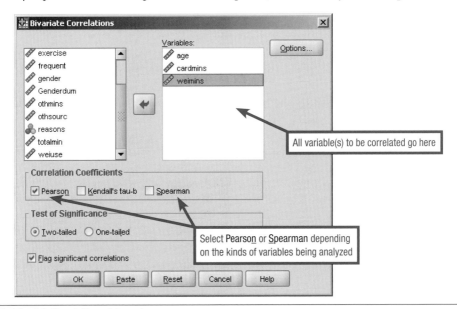

Plate 12.17 The **Bivariate Correlations** dialogue box

Table 12.7 Correlations output for age, weimins, and cardmins (SPSS output)

Correlations

Correlations

> Correlations of $p < 0.05$ are 'flagged' with asterisks

		AGE	WEIMINS	CARDMINS
AGE	Pearson Correlation	1.000	−.273 **	−.109
	Sig. (2-tailed)	.	.010	.311
	N	89	89	89
WEIMINS	Pearson Correlation	−.273 **	1.000	−.161
	Sig. (2-tailed)	.010	.	.130
	N	89	90	90
CARDMINS	Pearson Correlation	−.109	−.161	1.000
	Sig. (2-tailed)	.311	.130	.
	N	89	90	90

** Correlation is significant at the 0.01 level (2-tailed).

> Shows strength of relationship as indicated by Pearson's r

> Shows number of cases, less any cases for which there are missing data for either or both variables

> Shows level of statistical significance of computed value of Pearson's r

Generating Kendall's tau-b

Kendall's tau-b is designed for pairs of ordinal variables, but is also used, as suggested by Figure 12.5, when one variable is ordinal and the other is interval/ratio. (Notice the general rule of how data can be moved down a level, interval to ordinal, but not up.) It is exactly the same as Pearson's r in terms of possible outcomes in that the computed value of Kendall's tau-b can be positive or negative, and varies from 0 to ±1. In the gym study there are three ordinal variables: var00004 (*carduse*), var00005 (*weiuse*), and var00006 (*frequent*; see Table 12.1). Using Kendall's tau-b to calculate the correlation between the first two variables—frequency of use of the cardiovascular and weights equipment—it turns out to be very low. A slightly stronger relationship is found between var00006 (frequency of going to the gym) and var00010 (*cardmins*, the amount of time spent on the cardiovascular equipment): close to .4. The SPSS procedure is the same as described above for Pearson's r. Note too that Spearman's rho, another option, can be used if relating two ordinal variables (but it can only accommodate a small number of ties, that is, cases with the same rank on a variable). It ranges from −1, a perfect negative relationship, to +1, a perfect positive relationship. For example, look at the participation rank (A) and popularity rank (B) of a group of seven people.

Person	Mary	John	Bill	Sally	Kim	Susan	Joe
A	1	2	3	4	5	6	7
B	1	2	3	4	5	6	7

Spearman's rho is 1.0; knowing a person's participation rank perfectly predicts the popularity rank. It is called rank-order correlation to remind you of its ordinal character and to distinguish it from Pearson's r.

Generating Cramér's V

Cramér's V is suitable for examining the strength of a relationship between two nominal variables (see Figure 12.5). Its coefficient ranges from 0 to 1. It is always positive because nominal categories cannot be rank-ordered; its values cannot go up or down.

The value of Cramér's V for the analysis presented in Table 12.6 is .503, a moderate relationship. Cramér's V is usually reported with a contingency table and a chi-square test (see below). It is not normally presented on its own. The procedure for generating

Table 12.8 Comparing subgroup means: time spent on cardiovascular equipment by reasons for going to the gym

	Reasons				
Time	Relaxation	Fitness	Lose weight	Build strength	Total
Mean number of minutes spent on cardiovascular equipment	18.33	30.55	28.36	19.65	26.47
n	9	31	33	17	90

it with SPSS is to click **Statistics** in the **Crosstabs** window, and select it (see Plates 12.14 and 12.16).

Comparing means and eta

There are may other bivariate statistics but we will present just one more. To examine the relationship between an interval/ratio variable and a nominal variable (if the latter can be construed as the independent variable), one can compare the means of the interval/ratio variable for each subgroup of the nominal variable. As an example, consider Table 12.8, which presents the mean number of minutes spent on cardiovascular equipment (var00010, **cardmins**) for each of the four categories of reasons for going to the gym (var00003, **reasons**). The four means shown suggest that people who go to the gym for fitness or to lose weight spend considerably more time on this equipment than people who go to the gym to relax or to build strength.

The statistic eta can be calculated with these variables; it expresses the level of association between them. Since one variable is nominal (meaning no

rank ordering), its values are always positive. The eta for the data in Table 12.8 is .48, a moderate relationship between the two variables.

To produce a table like Table 12.8, follow these steps:

1. → **Analyze** → **Compare Means** → **Means. . .** [opens the **Means** dialogue box shown in Plate 12.18]
2. → **cardmins** →button to the left of **Dependent List:** → **reasons** → button to the left of **Independent List:** → **Options** [opens the **Means: Options** sub-dialogue box]
3. → **Anova table and eta** underneath **Statistics for First Layer** → **Continue** [closes the **Means: Options** sub-dialogue box and returns to the **Means** dialogue box shown in Plate 12.18] → OK

Amount of explained variance

Squaring eta, Kendall's tau-b, Spearman's rho, and Pearson's *r* yields a further useful statistic: how much of the variation in one variable can be explained or

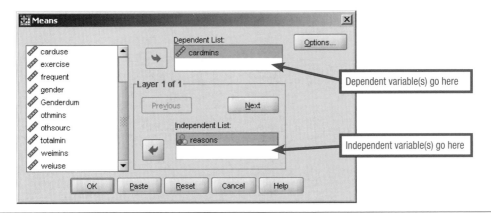

Plate 12.18 The Means dialogue box

Box 12.9   What is the level of statistical significance?

If one rejects a null hypothesis, there is always a chance that the rejected null is actually true. (Null hypotheses typically state that there is no relationship in the population between two variables, or that two or more populations are the same on some characteristic.) The amount of risk associated with rejecting a true null hypothesis is called the level of statistical significance. The maximum acceptable risk in the social sciences is 5 chances in 100. This means that, in 100 samples, about 5 of them would exhibit a relationship when there is not one in the population. (We have to say 'about' 5 because this is based on probabilities, not certainties.) Any one sample of the 100 samples may be one of those five, but the risk is fairly small. This significance level is denoted by $p = .05$ (p means probability).

A significance level of $p = .1$ means that about 10 in 100 samples would show a relationship where none exists in the population. Therefore, one would have less confidence in generalizing with that level of significance than with $p = .05$. If one wants a more stringent test than the latter p-level provides, perhaps because of concerns about the use that may be made of the results, one can choose the $p = .01$ level. This means that the risk is 1 in 100 that the results could have arisen by chance alone (that is, due to sampling error). Therefore, even if the results, following administration of a test, are statistically significant at the $p = .05$ level, but not the $p = .01$ level, the null hypothesis should not be rejected. In what instances would this be appropriate?

predicted by the other variable. Thus, if r is -.27, r^2 is .0729. This can be expressed as a percentage by multiplying r^2 by 100, yielding 7.29 per cent. This means that about 7 per cent of the variation in the use of cardiovascular equipment can be predicted by age. This also shows that a strong correlation like .7 explains only 49 per cent of the variance. For nominal data, squaring Cramér's V (.50 in Table 12.6) provides an approximation of this, meaning that about 25 per cent of the variation in reasons for visiting the gym is attributable to gender.

Statistical significance and inferential statistics

One difficulty with working on sample data is a lingering worry about whether the findings are generalizable to the population from which the sample was drawn. As seen in Chapter 11, there is always the possibility of *sampling error*, even when probability sampling procedures are followed (as in the gym survey). If this happens, the sample is to some degree unrepresentative of the wider population. To make matters worse, there is no feasible way of finding out for sure how extensive the sampling error is, as no one has the time or money to study every case in the population—that is why sampling is done in the first place. This is where various tests of *statistical significance* come in.

What is a test of statistical significance? It provides an indication of the risk we are taking when we use a particular sample statistic to estimate a population characteristic (see Box 12.9). For example, the mean age of the people in the gym sample is 33.6 years. Using the concept of the standard error of the mean, the 95 per cent confidence interval for the population mean extends from 31.72 to 35.47 years of age. The risk that this range does not contain the population mean is 5 per cent. Chapter 11 (see Box 11.3), in the discussion of the standard error of the mean, revealed some of the ideas behind statistical significance. The rest of this section looks at tests for determining the degree of confidence for measures of relationships between variables. All of the tests have a common structure.

- *Set up a null hypothesis.* This is an hypothesis to be disproved; it often states that there is no association between two variables or that two populations do not differ on some characteristic. For example, it could state that there is no relationship between gender and visiting the gym in the population. Rejecting that gives indirect support to the *research hypothesis* that there *is* a relationship in the population.
- *Establish an acceptable level of statistical significance.* This is essentially the level of risk associated with rejecting the null hypothesis (implying that there *is* a relationship in the population) when it

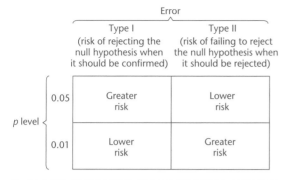

Figure 12.10 Type I and Type II errors

should not be rejected (when there is no relationship in the population). Levels of statistical significance are expressed as probability levels—that is, the probability of rejecting the null hypothesis when it is in fact true. The convention among most social researchers is that an acceptable level of statistical significance is $p \leq .05$, meaning that there are at most 5 chances in 100 that the sample shows a relationship not also found in the population. This risk level varies, depending on the circumstances. Five errors in 100 are too high for testing a drug for its efficacy, especially a drug with side effects. Probably p would be set at .00001, accepting only one chance in 100 000 of an error.

- *Determine the statistical significance of the findings* (that is, use a statistical test, for example, chi-square).
- If the findings are statistically significant at the .05 level—so that the risk of getting a relationship as strong as the one found, when there is *no* relationship in the population, is no higher than 5 in 100—*reject* the null hypothesis. The results are unlikely to have occurred by *chance* alone.

There are in fact two possible types of error when inferring statistical significance, known as Type I and Type II errors (see Figure 12.10). A Type I error occurs when a true null hypothesis is rejected. This means that the results arose by chance; one erroneously concluded that there is a relationship in the population when in fact there is none. The level of significance is the probability of making a Type I error, so a $p = .05$ level of significance means being more likely to make a Type I error than a $p = .01$ level of significance.

There is a second type of error—not rejecting the null hypothesis when it should be rejected. This is

called a Type II error. One is more likely to make this error when the significance level is .01 than when it is .05, because using .01 makes it less likely that the null will be rejected. The two types of error cannot be minimized at the same time; if one lessens the chances of making a Type I error, one increases the chances of a Type II error, and vice versa. Researchers usually make the conservative choice of minimizing the Type I error, as this means more often failing to reject the null and thus less acceptance of the research hypothesis.

If an analysis reveals a statistically significant finding, this does not mean that the finding is important. It simply means that the results are probably not due to chance alone. For example, a study may find a correlation between time spent jogging per week and the amount of money spent on running shoes. While the finding may be statistically significant, is it important? And recall that statistical significance gets easier to achieve as sample size goes up. Also, it is important to appreciate that tests of statistical significance can only be conducted on probability samples.

Correlation and statistical significance

Examining the statistical significance of a correlation from a randomly selected sample provides information about the likelihood of the correlation existing in the population. With a Pearson's r of $-.62$ in the sample, what is the likelihood that there is no relationship between the two variables in the population? How likely is a $-.62$ to arise by chance alone, that is, due to sampling error?

Whether a correlation coefficient is statistically significant or not is affected by two factors:

- the size of the computed coefficient; and
- the size of the sample.

This second factor may appear surprising, but it is true for all statistics. The larger a sample, the more likely it is that a computed correlation coefficient is statistically significant. Thus, even though the correlation between age and the amount of time spent on weight machines in the gym survey is just $-.27$, a fairly weak relationship, it is statistically significant at the $p = .01$ level. This means that there is only one chance in 100 that there is no relationship between age and weights in the population. Because

Table 12.9 How chi-square is affected by increasing the size of N and not affected by changes to column headings

	A			B			C		
Self-esteem	Contact sports	Non-contact sports	No sports	Contact sports	Non-contact sports	No sports	Contact sports	Non-contact sports	No sports
H	7	3	10	14	6	20	24	26	50
M	5	10	15	10	20	30	10	20	30
L	12	13	25	24	26	50	14	6	20
	$\chi^2 = 1.93$, not sig.			$\chi^2 = 5.08, p < .05$			$\chi^2 = 5.08, p < .05$		

the question of whether a correlation coefficient is statistically significant depends so much on the sample size, it is important always to examine *both* the correlation coefficient *and* the significance level. This is true for any calculated statistic.

This treatment of correlation and statistical significance applies to both Pearson's *r* and Kendall's tau-b. A similar interpretation can also be applied to Cramér's *V* and the chi-square test.

The chi-square test

The chi-square (χ^2) test is applied to contingency tables like Table 12.5. It is a measure of confidence that a relationship between two variables in a sample would also be found in the population. The test works by calculating for each cell in the table an expected frequency—that is, one that would occur on the basis of chance alone. Think of the days of the week and crime: one might expect that 14.29 per cent (1/7) of all crimes would occur on each day of the week. That is what would be *expected* if there were no relationship between day of the week and crime. The data say otherwise; more crimes are committed on Friday and Saturday. The chi-square value, which in Table 12.6 is 22.726, is calculated by taking the differences between the actual and expected values for each cell in the table and then summing those differences (it is slightly more complicated than this, but the details need not be of concern here). The chi-square value means nothing by itself and can be meaningfully interpreted only in relation to its associated level of statistical significance, which in this case is $p < .0001$. This means that there is less than one chance in 10 000 of rejecting a true

null hypothesis (that is, inferring that there *is* a relationship in the population when none exists). One can be extremely confident that there is a relationship between gender and reasons for visiting the gym among all gym members, since the chance of obtaining a sample that shows the sample relationship when there is no relationship among all gym members is less than 1 in 10 000.

But a chi-square value is also affected by the number of cases. While one wants a large chi-square to reject a null hypothesis, a larger N makes this easier to achieve. This is why it is necessary to look at the data and not just at the final statistic. Examine Table 12.9, which shows level of self-esteem for three categories of people (those who engage in contact sports, those who engage in non-contact sports, and those who do not do any sports at all). Because the independent variable is nominal, chi-square is more appropriate than Kendall's tau-b. Note the information in the bottom row of the table.

The first two parts of Table 12.9, A and B, show that just by doubling the size of the sample, the results change from being very likely due to chance in A (thus the null hypothesis of no relationship cannot be rejected) to less than 5 chances in 100 that they occurred by chance in B, and thus a rejection of the null. This is problematic because it suggests that one could collect more and more data until the null can be rejected. Now look at the last part of the table, C. Why was it included? When the data from B for high and low self-esteem are switched around in C, which in most instances should mean something, chi-square stays the same. This illustrates how statistical significance pertains only to whether the results may have resulted from chance alone, and says nothing

Figure 12.11 A spurious relationship

about practical significance or importance. There is a big practical difference between a situation in which half the respondents at all levels of sports participation have low self-esteem and one in which half have high self-esteem, but that makes no difference to the level of statistical significance—it remains the same in each situation. The practical implications of a finding go beyond its level of statistical significance.

Comparing means and statistical significance

A test of statistical significance called analysis of variance can be applied to the comparison of means in Table 12.8. This procedure entails treating the total amount of variation in the dependent variable—amount of time spent on cardiovascular equipment—as made up of two types: variation *within* each of the four subgroups that make up the independent variable, and variation *between* them. The latter is often called the *explained variance* (explained by the group one is in) and the former the *error variance*. A test of statistical significance for the comparison of means entails relating the two types of variance to form what is known as an *F* statistic, which expresses the amount of explained variance in relation to the amount of error variance. In the case of the data in Table 12.8, the resulting *F* statistic is statistically significant at the $p < .001$ level. This finding suggests that there is less than one chance in 1000 that there is no relationship between the two variables among all gym members. SPSS produces information regarding the *F* statistic and its statistical significance if the procedures described earlier for eta are followed.

Multivariate analysis

Multivariate analysis entails the simultaneous analysis of three or more variables, and can only be introduced here. It is sometimes called *elaboration* as it is more complicated and creates a more valuable picture than bivariate analysis—one rarely finds an adequate explanation of a particular phenomenon

by looking at only one possible cause. It is recommended that readers examine a textbook on quantitative data analysis for more information on the techniques (for example, Healey 2009, Agresti and Finlay 2008). There are three main contexts within which multivariate analysis is employed. Each is explained below.

Is the relationship spurious?

To establish a relationship between two variables, not only must there be logical and temporal evidence of a relationship but the relationship must be shown to be *non-spurious*. A spurious relationship exists when there appears to be a relationship between two variables, but the relationship is not real: it is being produced because each variable is itself related to a third variable. Think about the positive relationship between the number of fire engines at a fire and the fire damage: the more engines, the greater the devastation. Does this mean that the number of fire engines present *causes* the amount of fire damage? Of course not. The size of the fire accounts for both the number of engines responding and the damage. Variation in the two variables (number of fire engines and amount of damage) is being caused by a third factor, the size of the fire.

Consider a social science example. Assume there is a positive relationship between income and voting behaviour such that the more income a person has, the more likely he or she is to vote for a conservative party. But can this relationship be explained by age (see Figure 12.11)? The older one is, the more likely one is to have a higher salary; and the older one is, the more conservative one tends to be. If age is producing the apparent relationship between income and voting behaviour, that relationship is spurious.

Is there an intervening variable?

An intervening variable suggests that the relationship between the original two variables is not a direct one. Assume there is a positive relationship between income and self-esteem; for example, that the higher one's income, the more positive one feels about oneself. But maybe there is more to it than that. Maybe income affects one's overall level of physical vibrancy (richer people tend to be healthier, more physically fit, and smoke less than poorer people), which in turn affects self-esteem: income → physical vibrancy ➔ level of self esteem. If this is true, what should happen to the relationship between income and self-esteem if physical vibrancy is controlled? (Controlling in this instance would involve, for example, taking only people who had high levels of physical vibrancy, and seeing whether there is still a positive relationship between income and self-esteem among them.) If physical vibrancy were an intervening variable, that would weaken or eliminate entirely the original association between income and self-esteem. Also, note the 'control' word? Yes, the purpose is to make cross-sectional research more like an experiment where random assignment makes all other things equal or controlled.

Is there an interaction?

If the relationship between two variables holds for some groups or situations but not for others, an interaction exists. The word interaction is used in a statistical sense here, one that is different from its everyday meaning. In statistical terms, if the effect of one independent variable varies at different levels of a second independent variable, there is an interaction. In the gym study, for example, is the relationship between *age* and whether visitors have other sources of regular exercise (var00008, *othsourc*) different for men and women? Table 12.10 shows the relationship between age and other sources of exercise and includes both men and women. (Age has been broken down into just three age bands to make the table easier to read.) The table suggests that

the 31-to-40 age group is less likely to have other sources of regular exercise than the 30-and-under and 41-and-over age groups. However, Table 12.11, which breaks the relationship down by gender, suggests that the pattern for males and females is somewhat different. Among males, the pattern shown in Table 12.10 is very pronounced (the 31-to-41 age group is less likely to have other sources of exercise than the other two age groups), but for females the likelihood of having other sources of exercise declines with age. We can say that the relationship between age and having other sources of exercise is moderated by gender. Another way to put this is that there is an interaction between age and gender.

Generating a contingency table with three variables

To create a table like Table 12.11, do as follows:

1. ➔ **Analyze** ➔ **Descriptive Statistics** ➔ **Crosstabs. . .** [opens the **Crosstabs** dialogue box shown in Plate 12.14]
2. ➔ *othsourc* ➔ button by **Row(s):** [*othsourc* appears in the **Row(s):** box]
3. ➔ *age3* [this is the name given to the newly created variable with *age* recoded into three categories] ➔ button by **Column(s):** [*age3* appears in the **Column(s):** box] ➔ *gender* ➔ button beneath **Previous** [*gender* appears in the box underneath **Layer 1 of 1**] ➔ **Cells** [opens **Crosstabs: Cell Display** sub-dialogue box shown in Plate 12.15]
4. Make sure **Observed** in the **Counts** box has been selected. Make sure **Column** under **Percentages** has been selected. If either has not, simply click at the relevant point. ➔ **Continue** [closes **Crosstabs: Cell Display** sub-dialogue box and returns to the **Crosstabs** dialogue box shown in Plate 12.14]
5. ➔ **OK**

The resulting table looks somewhat different from Table 12.11 in that *gender* appears as a row rather than as a column variable.

Other uses for multivariate analysis

Multivariate analysis can also be used to determine how much of the variation in the dependent variable is explained or predicted by the independent

Table 12.10 Contingency table showing the relationship between age and whether gym visitors have other sources of regular exercise (percentages)

	Age		
Other source of exercise	30 and under	31–40	41 and over
Other source	64	43	58
No other source	36	57	42
n	42	23	24

Table 12.11 Contingency table showing the relationship between age and whether gym visitors have other sources of regular exercise for males and females (percentages)

	Gender					
	Male			Female		
Other source of exercise	30 and under	31–40	41 and over	30 and under	31–40	41 and over
Other source	70	33	75	59	50	42
No other source	30	67	25	41	50	58
n	20	9	12	22	14	12

variables. It also provides a test to find out which, if any, of the independent variables are significant predictors after controlling for the others. These uses will be illustrated by examining *multiple linear regression*. Our brief discussion of this topic will also acquaint you with some key concepts in multivariate analysis.

Consider the variable **weimins**, the number minutes spent on weights. What might cause that to vary? One relevant factor might be **age**. Perhaps the older people get, the less likely they are to work out using weights. To test this idea, we could perform a bivariate regression with **weimins** as the dependent variable and **age** as the independent variable. To perform a bivariate regression in SPSS:

1. → **Analyze** → **Regression** → **Linear**. This will produce the **Linear Regression** dialogue box shown in plate 12.19.
2. → *weimins* → button to put it in the **Dependent:** box.
3. → *age* → button to put it in the **Independent(s):** box.
4. → **OK**. [The output appears in Table 12.12]

The first part of Table 12.12 shows an R Square value of .074. That indicates that **age** by itself explains 7.4 per cent of the variation in **weimins**, which is not very much. The value of R Square tends to be somewhat inflated, especially if the sample size is small (which is true in our example) or the

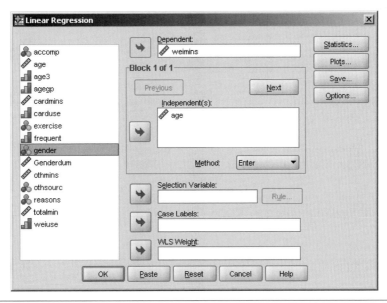

Plate 12.19 The **Linear Regression** dialogue box

Table 12.12 SPSS output showing results of bivariate regression

Model summary

Model	R	R Square	Adjusted R Square	Std. error of the estimate
1	.273[a]	.074	.064	7.72123

[a] Predictors: (Constant), age

ANOVA[b]

Model		Sum of squares	df	Mean square	F	Sig.
1	Regression	417.236	1	417.236	6.999	.010[a]
	Residual	5186.719	87	59.617		
	Total	5603.955	88			

[a] Predictors: (Constant), age
[b] Dependent variable: weimins

Coefficientsª

Model		Unstandardized coefficients		Standardized coefficients	t	Sig.
		B	Std. error	Beta		
1	(Constant)	23.209	3.218		7.213	.000
	age	−.245	.093	−.273	−2.645	.010

[a] Dependent variable: weimins

number of independent variables is large (Agresti and Finlay 1997: 435). A more realistic estimate is the Adjusted R Square, which in our case has a value of .064 or 6.4 per cent.

The ANOVA section of the output indicates a significance or p-value of .010, which is the significance level of the model as a whole. Our model at this point is made up of only one independent variable (*age*). The final section of the output, 'Coefficients,' has two subsections: 'Unstandardized coefficients' and 'Standardized coefficients.' The unstandardized coefficient for *age* is −.245, which represents the estimated change in the dependent variable for each unit change in the independent variable. In our example, the model predicts that for each one-year increase in age, the time spent on weights decreases by .245 minutes. The standardized coefficient of −.273 indicates that for every standard deviation increase in age, the time spent on weights decreases by .273 standard deviation units. Standardized coefficients (sometimes called *beta weights*) are useful in comparing the effect of independent variables that may be measured in different units—the higher the standardized

coefficient, the more important the independent variable is considered to be. Finally, the significance level for *age* is shown to be .010, which indicates that the probability that the association between *age* and *weimins* is due to chance alone is 1 in 100, suggesting that it's a pretty safe bet that there is a relationship between those two variables in the population.

As mentioned, one rarely if ever encounters a good explanation for something by invoking just a single cause or independent variable. Let's see what happens if we put a second independent variable—*gender*—into the model. Normally, the variables used in linear regression have to be at the interval/ratio level of measurement, but a special procedure allows us to use nominal variables like *gender* as well. Such variables have to be converted to indicator or 'dummy' variables, a process that goes beyond the purposes of our discussion here. Assume that the dummy variable we have created is called *gender2*, and that we have labelled it 'Gender dummy variable.'

It is quite simple to add a second independent variable to the model using SPSS. Once you are in the **Linear Regression** dialogue box (described

Table 12.13 Multiple Regression Output with *gender* (recoded) in the model

Model summary

Model	R	R Square	Adjusted R Square	Std. error of the estimate
1	.478[a]	.228	.210	7.09088

[a] Predictors: (Constant), Gender dummy variable, age

ANOVA[b]

Model		Sum of squares	df	Mean square	F	Sig.
1	Regression	1279.830	2	639.915	12.727	.000[a]
	Residual	4324.125	86	50.281		
	Total	5603.955	88			

[a] Predictors: (Constant), Gender dummy variable, age
[b] Dependent variable: weimins

Coefficients[a]

Model		Unstandardized coefficients		Standardized coefficients		
		B	Std. error	Beta	t	Sig.
1	(Constant)	20.831	3.010		6.920	.000
	age	−.260	.085	−.289	−3.053	.003
	Gender dummy variable	6.251	1.509	.393	4.142	.000

[a] Dependent variable: weimins

above and shown in Plate 12.19), just click on *gender2* (or whatever variable you would like to add), then click the arrow button to put the variable in the **Independent(s)**: box along with *age*.

Table 12.13 shows the output generated after *gender2* was added to the model. The 'Model Summary' shows that the R Square value has increased to .228 (or that 22.8 per cent of the variation in *weimins* can be explained or predicted by the new model), and that the more conservative Adjusted R Square has risen to .210 (or 21.0 per cent). This indicates that by adding *gender2* we have produced a much better model, although the majority of the variation in *weimins* is still unaccounted for. The ANOVA significance level is .000, which indicates that the findings for the new model as a whole (which includes both *age* and *gender2* as independent variables) have a probability of less than 1 in 1000 of being due to chance alone.

The 'Coefficients' sections show an unstandardized coefficient of −.260 for *age*, which means that, controlling for *gender2*, for each one year increase

in *age*, the model predicts a decline of .260 minutes spent on weights. The standardized coefficient for *age* is −.289, indicating a decrease of .289 standard deviation units in *weimins* for each standard deviation increase in *age* (controlling for *gender2*). The significance level for *age* is .003, which means that *age* remains significant even when *gender2* is held constant. Had the significance level exceeded .050, we would have had to consider dropping *age* from the model.

The 'Coefficients' section shows an unstandardized coefficient of 6.251 for *gender2*. Because of how this dummy variable was coded, the coefficient means that, holding *age* constant, the model estimates that the average time men spend on weights is 6.251 minutes greater than that spent by women. The standardized coefficient of .393 tells us that according to the model, the average time men spend on weights is .393 standard deviation units higher than that of women (controlling for *age*). Also, *gender2* has a p-value of .000, indicating that the association observed between it and *weimins* (after controlling for *age*) has a probability of less than 1 in 1000 of being due to chance alone. Had the significance level been greater than .050, we would have had good reason to exclude *gender2* from the model. But with these results, it stays in.

Checklist on doing and writing up quantitative data analysis

☑ Have missing data codes been specified for all variables?

☑ Are the statistical techniques used appropriate for the level of measurement (that is, nominal, ordinal, or interval/ratio)?

☑ Are the most appropriate and powerful techniques for answering the research questions used?

☑ If the sample is not randomly selected, are inferences about a population avoided (or at least if included, their limitations outlined)?

☑ If the data come from a cross-sectional design, have unsustainable inferences about causality been resisted?

☑ Does the analysis go beyond univariate to include bivariate and even multivariate analyses?

☑ Are the research questions answered, and only the analyses relevant to them presented?

Key Points

- Think about data analysis before designing research instruments.

- Know the difference between nominal, ordinal, and interval/ratio variables. Techniques of data analysis are applicable to some types of variable and not others.

- Become familiar with computer software like SPSS.

- Do not confuse statistical significance with importance or practical significance.

Questions for Review

- What are missing data and how do they arise?

Getting started in SPSS

- Outline differences among variable names, variable labels, and value labels.

- In what circumstances is it appropriate to recode a variable?

- In what circumstances is it appropriate to create a new variable?

Types of variables

- Make sure to know the differences among the three types of variable outlined in this chapter: nominal, ordinal, and interval/ratio.

- Why is it important to be able to distinguish among them?

- Imagine answers to the following questions in an interview survey. What kind of variable would each generate: nominal, ordinal, or interval/ratio?

1. Do you enjoy going shopping?

   Yes ____

   Unsure ____

   No ____

2. How many times have you shopped in the last month? Please write the number here ____.

3. For what items do you most enjoy shopping? Please tick one only.

   Clothes (including shoes) ____

   Food ____

   Things for the house ____

   Presents or gifts ____

   Entertainment (CDs, videos, etc.) ____

4. How important is it to you to buy clothes with designer labels?

   Very important ____

   Fairly important ____

   Not very important ____

   Not at all important ____

Univariate analysis

- What is an outlier and how does having one affect the mean and the range?

- In conjunction with which measure of central tendency is the standard deviation usually reported: the mean, the median, or the mode?

Bivariate analysis

- Can one infer causality from bivariate analysis?

- Why are percentages crucial when presenting contingency tables?

- In what circumstances does one use each of the following: Pearson's *r*, Kendall's tau-b, Cramér's *V*, Spearman's rho, eta?

Data analysis with SPSS

- Using the gym survey data, create:

  - a frequency table for the variable *exercise*;
  - a bar chart and pie chart for *exercise* and compare their usefulness;
  - a histogram for *cardmins*;
  - measures of central tendency and dispersion for *cardmins*;
  - a contingency table and Cramér's *V* for *gender* and *exercise*;
  - a scatter diagram for *age* and *cardmins*;

– Pearson's r for *age* and *cardmins*;
– Kendall's tau-b for *carduse* and *weiuse*; and
– a difference of means analysis for reasons for visiting and *totalmin*.

Statistical significance

- What does statistical significance mean and how does it differ from importance or practical significance?

- What is a significance level?

- What does the chi-square test achieve?

- What does it mean to say that an eta of .42 is statistically significant at p < .05?

Multivariate analysis

- What are the uses of multivariate analyses?

- What is a spurious relationship?

- What is an intervening variable?

- What is a statistical interaction?

- How do multivariate analyses improve on bivariate (two-variable) analyses?

13 Qualtitative Data Analysis

Chapter overview

Because qualitative data from interviews or participant observation typically take the form of a large body of unstructured textual material, their analysis is not straightforward. Moreover, unlike in quantitative research, clear-cut rules about how to conduct qualitative data analysis have not been developed. In this chapter, some general approaches to qualitative data management are examined, including *coding*, its main feature. The most significant recent development in qualitative research is computer software for these procedures. This software, often referred to as computer-assisted qualitative data analysis software (CAQDAS), removes many if not most of the clerical tasks associated with the manual coding and retrieving of data. There is no industry leader among the different programs (in the sense that SPSS holds this position among quantitative data analysis software). This chapter introduces a relatively new entrant that is having a big impact—QSR NVivo (the version discussed in this chapter is NVivo 7).

This chapter will discuss:

- *grounded theory* as a general strategy of qualitative data analysis; its main features, processes, and outcomes are presented along with some criticisms;
- *coding* as a key process in grounded theory and in qualitative data analysis more generally; there is an extended discussion of what it entails and some of its limitations;
- how to set up research materials for analysis with NVivo;
- how to code using NVivo, how to retrieve coded text, and how to create memos;
- some of the debates about the desirability of using CAQDAS;
- the criticism that coding tends to fragment data; and
- the idea of *narrative analysis,* an approach that is gaining a following because it reduces that fragmentation.

Introduction

Because of its reliance on prose in the form of field notes, interview transcripts, or other documents, qualitative research rapidly generates a large, cumbersome database. Miles (1979) described qualitative data as an 'attractive nuisance'—attractive because of its richness but also a nuisance because that very richness can lead to a failure to examine its wider scientific significance.

Finding a path through that thicket of prose is not an easy matter, and can be baffling to many researchers confronting such data for the first time. 'What do I do with it now?' is a common refrain. In large part this is because there are few well-established and widely accepted rules for the analysis of qualitative data. Although learning the techniques of quantitative data analysis in a statistics course may seem painful at the time, it does provide an unambiguous set of rules about how to handle data. Results must be interpreted, but at least there are relatively clear rules for getting to that point. Analytic procedures for qualitative data analysis have not reached that degree of codification, and many argue that that would be undesirable anyway (cf. Bryman and Burgess 1994*b*). What *can* be provided are broad guidelines (Okely 1994), which is what this chapter provides.

It has two main sections:

- *General strategies of qualitative data analysis:* analytic induction and grounded theory.
- *Basic operations in qualitative data analysis:* coding and narrative analysis, the latter differing in style from both grounded theory and the secondary analysis of qualitative data. The chapter includes an outline of the use of computer software in qualitative data analysis.

General strategies of qualitative data analysis

Analytic induction

One difference between qualitative and quantitative data analysis is that, with the latter, analysis occurs after all the data have been collected. Qualitative analysis, on the other hand, is often *iterative* (as noted in Chapter 8), meaning that analysis takes place after some of the data have been collected and then the implications of that analysis shape further data collection.

Analytic induction is an example of a type of qualitative research that uses an iterative process. It begins with a rough definition of a research question, proceeds to a hypothetical answer, and then data are collected. What makes it unique is that analytic induction seeks universal explanations of phenomena that permit no exception. If a case inconsistent with the hypothesis is encountered, the analyst either redefines the hypothesis to exclude the deviant or negative case or reformulates the hypothesis and proceeds with further data collection. With each new deviant case found, the analyst must choose again between reformulation and redefinition. Data collection continues until no new inconsistent piece of evidence is found. It is, in effect, a special case of grounded theory, one that holds 100 per cent of the time. But it is also rare, as the requirement to be able to explain all cases means that the explanation may become too broad to be useful. While analytic induction is an extremely rigorous method of analysis, it is not favoured by current qualitative researchers, and indeed most of the examples used in textbooks to illustrate analytic induction are not recent. A Canadian exception is research by Whitehead and Carpenter (1999) on unsafe sexual behaviour in the military, an environment, they claim, in which condoms are thought of by some as protection from disease rather than a method of contraception. They found that the greater the social and cultural distance between sex partners, the greater the likelihood of condom use.

One further problem with analytic induction is that it does not provide useful guidelines (unlike grounded theory) on the number of cases required before the absence of negative cases can be assumed and the validity of the hypothetical explanation (whether reformulated or not) can be confirmed.

Grounded theory

In its most recent incarnation, grounded theory is defined as 'theory that was derived from data, systematically gathered and analyzed through the research process' (Strauss and Corbin 1998: 12). Its two central features are its development of theory out of data, and an iterative or recursive approach in which, as seen above, data collection and analysis proceed in tandem, repeatedly referring back to each other.

Grounded theory is by far the most widely used framework for analyzing qualitative data. There is, however, considerable controversy about what grounded theory entails (Charmaz 2000). For example, it is vague on certain points, such as the difference between concepts and categories (see later in this chapter). The term 'categories' is increasingly being used rather than 'concepts,' but inconsistent use of key terms is not helpful to practitioners of the craft or to people trying to understand the overall process.

Against such a background, writing about the essence of grounded theory is not easy. As well, grounded theory cannot be described here in all its facets; instead, its main features are outlined, beginning with a distinction between *tools* and *outcomes* in grounded theory.

Tools of grounded theory
Some of the tools of grounded theory have been referred to in previous chapters.

- *Theoretical saturation*—reaching a point at which there is no more point in reviewing old data or collecting new information to see how it fits with concepts or categories; new data are no longer illuminating.

- *Constant comparison*—a process of maintaining a close connection between data and conceptualization, so that the correspondence between concepts and categories with their indicators is not lost. More specifically, attention to the procedure of constant comparison enjoins the researcher to continually compare phenomena being coded under a certain category so that a theoretical elaboration of that category can emerge. Glaser and Strauss (1967) advised writing a *memo* (see later in this chapter) on the category after a few phenomena have been coded. It also entails being sensitive to contrasts between emerging categories.
- *Coding*—the key process in grounded theory, whereby data are broken down into component parts and given names. It begins soon after the initial collection of data. As Charmaz put it: 'Unlike quantitative research that requires data to fit into *preconceived* standardized codes, the researcher's interpretations of data shape his or her emergent codes in grounded theory' (emphasis in original) (2000: 515). In grounded theory, different types or levels of coding are recognized, which are discussed below.

Coding in grounded theory

Coding in grounded theory entails reviewing transcripts and/or field notes and giving labels (names) to items that share a similar theme, seem to be of potential theoretical significance, and/or appear to be particularly salient within the social worlds of those being studied. As Charmaz (1983: 186) put it: 'Codes . . . serve as shorthand devices to *label, separate, compile,* and *organize* data' (emphases in original). This coding is a somewhat different process from coding quantitative data, such as social survey data. While in quantitative analysis coding is more or less a way of managing data that have already been at least broadly categorized, in grounded theory and other approaches to qualitative data analysis, coding is somewhat more tentative and less fixed, and may be in a constant state of revision and fluidity. The data are treated as potential indicators of concepts, and the indicators are repeatedly compared to see with which concepts they fit best. Ad hoc compromises may have to be made when two researchers are doing the coding (Tastsoglou and Miedema 2003). Also, in qualitative research, coding is an important first step in the generation of theory, whereas

quantitative analysis often involves testing a *pre-existing* theory.

Strauss and Corbin, drawing on their grounded theory approach, distinguished among three types of coding:

- *Open coding*—'the process of breaking down, examining, comparing, conceptualizing, and categorizing data' (1990: 61); this process stays very close to the data and yields the concepts later grouped and turned into categories. Noting various emotions, like anger, jealousy, or affection, is an example.
- *Axial coding*—'a set of procedures whereby data are put back together in new ways after open coding, by making connections between categories' (1990: 96). This is done by linking codes to contexts, consequences, patterns of interaction, and apparent causes. The category of emotion above could be linked to the contexts in which it is expressed, as in times of hardship or loss.
- *Selective coding*—'the procedure of selecting the core category, systematically relating it to other categories, validating those relationships, and filling in categories that need further refinement and development' (1990: 116). A core category is the focus around which other categories are integrated, what Strauss and Corbin called the storyline that frames the account. 'Adaptation' could turn out to be the core category in our example.

The three types of coding are really different levels of coding and each relates to a different point in the elaboration of categories in grounded theory. Not all grounded theory practitioners operate with this threefold distinction; indeed the notion of axial coding has been especially controversial because it is sometimes perceived as closing off the coding process too quickly. Charmaz (2004) preferred to distinguish between open or initial coding and selective or focused coding. The former tends to be very detailed and may even result in a code per line of text. It is crucial at this stage of the research to be open-minded and to generate as many new ideas and hence codes as necessary to organize the data. Selective or focused coding entails emphasizing the most common codes and those seen as most revealing about the data. Combining the initial codes generates new codes. The data are then re-explored and re-evaluated in terms of the selected codes. Pidgeon and Henwood (2004: 638) provided a useful example in their study of 60 mother-daughter relationships:

> The initial coding led to the development of a long and varied, but highly unwieldy, list of instances under the label 'Relational Closeness.' . . . [A] closer reading and comparison of the individual instances indicated a much more mixed view of the emotional intensity of the relationships, ranging from a welcome but painful sense of gratitude and debt to a stance of hypersensitivity and a desire to flee from a relationship which involved 'confinement' or 'smothering.' . . . [T]his subdivision was retained and coded through their respective labels 'Closeness' and 'Overcloseness.'

Coding thus involves a movement from generating codes that stay very close to the data, to more selective and abstract ways of conceptualizing the phenomenon of interest.

Outcomes of grounded theory

The following are the products of different phases of grounded theory.

- *Concepts*—are the 'building blocks of theory' (Strauss and Corbin 1998: 101) and refer to labels given to discrete phenomena; they are produced through *open coding*.

- *Categories*—at a higher level of abstraction than concepts, a category subsumes two or more concepts. An especially crucial category may become a *core category* (see Box 13.1).
- *Properties*—attributes or aspects of a category.
- *Hypotheses*—initial hunches about relationships between concepts.
- *Theory*—according to Strauss and Corbin (1998: 22): 'a set of well-developed categories . . . that are systematically interrelated through statements of relationship to form a theoretical framework that explains some relevant social . . . or other phenomenon.' In grounded theory there are two levels of theory: *substantive theory* and *formal theory*. The former relates to theory in a certain *empirical* instance, for example, racial prejudice in a hospital setting (see Box 14.1). A formal theory is at a higher level of abstraction and has applicability to several substantive areas, such as prejudice generally and in a number of different spheres. The generation of formal theory requires data collection in contrasting settings.

The different elements are portrayed in Figure 13.1. As with any diagram, it is only an approximation, but particularly so in this instance because there can be different approaches to grounded theory. Also, it is difficult to get across diagrammatically the iterative nature of grounded

---

Box 13.1   Categories in grounded theory

Orona's (1997) study of sufferers of Alzheimer's disease and their relatives exemplifies many features of grounded theory. She began with an interest in the decision-making process that leads relatives to place Alzheimer sufferers in a home. She gradually realized from coding her interview transcripts that this process is not as crucial a feature for relatives as she had anticipated, mainly because many of them simply feel they have no other choice. Instead, she was slowly taken by the significance for relatives of the 'identity loss' sufferers are deemed to experience. This gradually became her core category. She conducted further interviews to flesh this notion out and reread existing transcripts in light of it. The link between indicators and category can be seen in relatives' references to the sufferer as 'gone,' 'different,' 'not the same person,' and as a 'stranger.' Orona was able to unearth four major themes that emerged

around the process of identity loss. The theme of 'temporality' was particularly significant in Orona's emerging theoretical reflections and is revealed in such comments in transcripts as:

> At the beginning . . .
>
> It got much worse later on.
>
> More and more, he was leaning on me.
>
> Before she would never have been like that.
>
> She used to love coffee (Orona 1997: 179–80).

In other words, such comments allowed the category 'temporality' to be built up. The issue of temporality was significant in Orona's emerging analysis, because it related to the core category of identity loss. Relatives seek to help sufferers maintain their identities. Gradually, however, crucial events mean that the relatives can no longer deny the sufferers' identity loss.

theory—in particular the recursive relation-ship between data collection and analysis (this is depicted in the diagram by arrows pointing in both directions). The figure implies the following:

- The researcher begins with a general research question (step 1).
- Relevant people and/or incidents are theoretically sampled (step 2).
- Relevant data are collected (step 3).
- Data are coded (step 4), which may, at the level of open coding, generate concepts (step 4a).
- There is a constant movement backwards and forwards among the first four steps, so that early coding suggests a need for new data, which results in a need to theoretically sample, and so on.
- Through a constant comparison of indicators and concepts (step 5) categories are generated (step 5a). It is crucial to ensure a fit between indicators and concepts.
- Categories are saturated during the coding process (step 6).
- Relationships between categories are explored (step 7) in such a way that hypotheses about connections between categories emerge (step 7a).
- Further data are collected via theoretical sampling (steps 8 and 9).
- The collection of data is likely to be governed by the theoretical saturation principle (step 10) and by the testing of the emerging hypotheses (step 11), which lead to a specification of substantive theory (step 11a). See Box 13.2 for an illustration.
- The substantive theory is explored using grounded theory processes in a different setting from that in which it was generated (step 12), so that formal theory can be generated (step 12a). A formal theory relates to more abstract categories not specifically examined in the research conducted.

Step 12 is relatively unusual in grounded theory, because researchers typically concentrate on a certain setting.

Concepts and categories are the key elements in grounded theory. Indeed, it is sometimes suggested that grounded theory is better for generating categories than producing theories. In part, this is because studies claiming to use the approach often fail to generate grounded theory as such. Concepts and categories are nonetheless at the heart of the approach, and key processes such as coding,

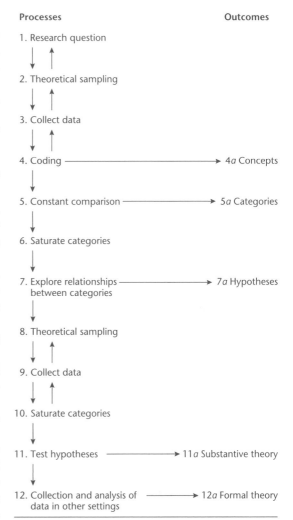

Figure 13.1 Processes and outcomes in grounded theory

theoretical sampling, and theoretical saturation are designed to guide their generation. Again, Box 13.2 provides an illustration of a study that incorporates some key features of grounded theory.

Sometimes people claim to have used the grounded theory approach when in fact they have not (Charmaz 2000), such as when a researcher has simply based a theory on data. But grounded theory is more than that. Other researchers appear to have used just one or two features of grounded theory, but refer to having used the approach without qualification (Locke 1996).

Memos

One aid to conducting grounded theory is the *memo*, a note researchers write for themselves or colleagues concerning concepts and categories. Memos serve as reminders about what is meant by the terms used and provide building blocks for reflection. Memos are potentially very helpful to researchers in helping to crystallize ideas and to not lose track of thoughts on various topics. An illustration of a memo is provided in Box 13.3.

Criticisms of grounded theory
Grounded theory has limitations:

- Some question whether researchers can fully suspend awareness of existing theories or concepts until the late stages of analysis when their theories are supposed to emerge. Most social researchers are sensitive to the conceptual armoury of their disciplines and it seems unlikely that this awareness can be put aside. Indeed, today it is rarely accepted that theory-neutral observation is possible. It is generally agreed that what is 'seen,' even in research, is conditioned by what is already known about the social world being studied (in terms of both social scientific conceptualizations and everyday ones). Also, many writers view this situation as desirable in that their investigations can build upon the work of others.
- There are practical difficulties with grounded theory. The time to transcribe recordings of interviews, for example, can make it difficult for researchers, especially with tight deadlines, to carry out a genuine grounded theory analysis, with its requisite constant interplay of data collection and conceptualization.
- It is doubtful whether grounded theory in many instances really results in *theory*. As previously suggested, it provides a rigorous approach to the generation of concepts, but it is often difficult to see what theory, in the sense of an *explanation* of something, is put forward. Moreover, in spite of frequent lip-service paid to generating formal theory, most grounded theories pertain to the specific social phenomenon being examined and not to a broader range of phenomena.
- Grounded theory often invites researchers to code the data into discrete chunks. However, in the eyes of some, this kind of fragmentation results in a loss of context and narrative flow (Coffey and Atkinson 1996), a point returned to later.

Nonetheless, grounded theory today probably represents the most influential general strategy for conducting qualitative data analysis, though to what extent for the approach is followed varies from study to study. What can be said is that many of its core processes, such as coding, memos, and the very idea of allowing theoretical ideas to emerge out of the

Box 13.2 Grounded theory in action

The research by Charmaz (1997) is concerned with the identity dilemmas of men who have chronic (but not terminal) illnesses. She outlined clearly the chief steps in her analysis:

- Interviews with men and a small number of women.
- Exploring the transcripts for gender differences.
- Searching for themes in the men's interviews and published personal accounts (for example, autobiographies). An example is the theme of 'accommodation to uncertainty,' as men find ways of dealing with the unpredictable paths of their illnesses.
- Building 'analytic categories from men's definitions of and taken-for-granted assumptions about their situations' (1997: 39). Of particular significance in her work is the idea of 'identity dilemmas'—that

is, the ways in which men approach and possibly resolve the assault on their traditionally masculine self-images. She showed that men often use strategies to re-establish earlier selves, so that for many audiences their identity (at least in their own eyes) can be preserved.

- Further interviews designed to refine the categories.
- Rereading personal accounts of chronic illness with a particular focus on gender.
- Reading a new group of personal accounts.
- Making 'comparisons with women on selected key points' (1997: 39).

Charmaz provided a substantive theory that helps to explain the importance of notions of masculinity for carving out an identity for chronically ill men.

Box 13.3   A memo

In their research into the bus industry, Bryman *et al.* (1996) noticed that the managers frequently mentioned that their companies still followed officially discontinued rules and practices. They often referred to the idea of 'inheriting' characteristics that now held them back in trying to meet the new competitive environment they faced. 'Inheritance' is what Strauss (1987) called an *in vivo code*—one that derives from the language of people in the social context being studied—rather than a *sociologically constructed code*, which is a label created by the researcher. The following memo outlines the concept of inheritance, provides some illustrative quotations, and suggests some properties of the concept.

Memo for inheritance

Inheritance: many of our interviewees suggest that they have inherited certain company traits and traditions that would not be of their choosing. The key point about this inheritance is that our interviewees see it as hindering their ability to respond to a changing environment.
Inherited features include:

- expensive and often inappropriate fleets of vehicles and depots;
- the survival of attitudes and behaviour

patterns, particularly among bus drivers, seen as inappropriate to the new environment (for example, lack of concern for customer service) and which hinder service innovation; and

- high wages from the earlier era; means that new competitors can more easily enter the market while paying drivers lower wages.

Sample comments:

'I suppose another major weakness is that we are very tied by conditions and practices we've inherited' (Commercial Director, Company G).

'We have what we've inherited and we now have a massive surplus of double decks. . . . We have to go on operating those' (Managing Director, Company B).

Managing Director of Company E said the company had inherited staff steeped in old attitudes: 'We don't have a staff where the message is "the customer is number one."'

Inheriting surplus capacity: such as too many buses or wrong size.

data, have been very influential. Indeed, it is striking that one of the main developments in qualitative data analysis in recent years—the use of computer software—has implicitly promoted many of these processes, because the software programs have often been written with grounded theory in mind (Lonkila 1995).

Basic operations in qualitative data analysis

Coding is the starting point for most forms of qualitative data analysis (although some writers prefer to call it *indexing* rather than coding). The principles involved have been well developed by writers concerned with grounded theory and other perspectives. Some of their considerations in developing codes (cf. Lofland and Lofland 1995) are:

- Of what general category is this datum an instance?
- What does this datum represent?
- What is this datum about?
- What question does this datum suggest?
- What sort of answer to that question does this datum imply?
- What is happening here?
- What are people doing?
- What do people say they are doing?
- What kind of event is going on?

Steps and considerations in coding

The following considerations are helpful in preparing for and doing coding:

- *Code as soon as possible (that is, as data are being collected), like grounded theory suggests.* This may sharpen an understanding of the data and help with theoretical sampling. Also, it can help to alleviate the feeling of being swamped by the data. At the very least, begin transcription of any recorded interviews at a relatively early stage.

- *Read through the initial set of transcripts, field notes, documents, etc., without taking any notes or considering an interpretation*; perhaps at the end jot down a few general notes about what seems especially interesting, important, or significant.
- *Do it again.* Read through the data again, but this time make marginal notes about significant remarks or observations, as many as possible. Initially, they will be very basic—perhaps keywords used by respondents or themes in the data. This is *coding*—generating terms that will help in interpreting the data.
- *Do not worry about generating what seem to be too many codes*—at least in the early stages of analysis; some will be fruitful, others not. The important thing is to be as inventive and imaginative as possible; tidying up can be done later. Remember that any one datum can, and often should, be coded in more than one way. An outburst of anger, for example, can be seen as an emotion, a cause of stress, or the beginning of a new level of integration. Charmaz (2004) recommended, as a first stage in coding for grounded theory, 'line by line coding,' whereby virtually every line in a transcript or other source of data has a code attached to it. She argued that this process means that the qualitative researcher does not lose contact with the data and the perspectives and interpretations of those being studied. While this process almost always results in a proliferation of codes, this should not be alarming. What the qualitative researcher needs to do is ask questions about what these codes have in common so that they can be combined into higher-order and more abstract codes.
- *Review the codes, possibly in relation to the transcripts.* Are two or more words or phrases being used to describe the same phenomenon? If so, remove one of them. Do some of the codes relate to concepts and categories in the existing literature? If so, is it sensible to use those instead? Are there connections between the codes? Is there evidence that respondents believe that one thing tends to be associated with or caused by something else?
- *Consider more general theoretical ideas in relation to codes and data.* At this point, generate some general theoretical ideas about the data. Try to outline connections between concepts and any developing categories. Consider in more detail how they relate to the existing literature. Develop hypotheses about the linkages being made and go back to the data to see if they can be confirmed.
- *Finally, keep coding in perspective.* It is only one part (albeit an important part) of the analysis. It is a mechanism for thinking about the meaning of the data *and* for reducing the data to a manageable size. The larger task of interpretation awaits, including forging interconnections between codes, reflecting on the overall importance of the findings for the research literature, and pondering the significance of the coded material for the lives of those studied.

Turning data into fragments

The coding of such materials as interview transcripts typically entails writing marginal notes on them and gradually refining those notes into codes and then cutting and pasting (sometimes in the literal sense of using scissors and paste). It entails cutting up transcripts into chunks of data (and of course carefully identifying the origins of the chunk with, for example, name, position, date) for later data retrieval. Word-processing programs can accomplish this but CAQDAS software is increasingly being used to perform these tasks.

CAQDAS has been a growth area in terms of both the proliferation of programs and the number of people using them. Most of the best-known programs allow analysts to code text and later retrieve it, tasks that were once done manually. For example, the software can search for all chunks of text relating to a code, and then cut and paste them together. Human input is still crucial, however. CAQDAS does not and cannot help with decisions about the codes or the coding of textual materials, or with the interpretation of findings. This situation is similar to the use of quantitative data analysis software like SPSS where someone must still choose the variables to be analyzed and the specific techniques of analysis, and then make sense of the results. Each form of software requires creativity. CAQDAS differs from SPSS largely in terms of the type of data that can be used with it.

There is no CAQDAS industry leader, but NUD*IST (Non-numerical Unstructured Data Indexing Searching and Theorizing) is a package that most researchers would at least know by name, and was the software used by Tastsoglou and Miedema (2003). It became very popular in the 1990s and has been improved with the emergence of QSR NUD*IST Vivo, known as NVivo. This software is the one featured in this chapter, and draws upon many features in NUD*IST so that if your access is only to NUD*IST, much of the chapter is still applicable.

To use or not to use CAQDAS? With a very small data set, it is probably not worth the time and trouble navigating around new software. Catterall and Maclaran (1997) have argued that CAQDAS is not very suitable for focus group data because the code and retrieve function tends to hide the communication process typical of focus groups. On the other hand, learning new software provides useful skills that may be needed on a future occasion. It is likely to be too expensive for personal purchase, though there are student and educational discounts. Demonstration copies of some of the main packages can be downloaded from the distributor's Internet site; they are full working programs but require purchase for actual use. This chapter provides an introduction to NVivo using qualitative data from a study of visitors to Disney theme parks.

There is no one correct approach to coding data. As suggested earlier, grounded theory conceives of different types of code. Coffey and Atkinson (1996) pointed to three different levels of coding, applied below to a passage from an interview first appearing in Box 10.7.

- First there is a very basic coding, which, in the passage in Box 10.7, can be liking or disliking the visit to a Disney theme park. However, such a coding scheme is unlikely to provide anything but a superficial analysis.
- A second level comprises a deeper awareness of the content of what is said and is organized around the focus of the research. An example is countries 'well-represented' and 'missing.'
- A third level moves slightly away from a close association with what the respondent says to a concern with broader analytic themes. This is how the passage in Box 10.7 was coded in terms of such features as whether a response: is fully enthusiastic ('uncritical enthusiasm') or is not critical of the Disney Corporation ('not critical of Disney'); reveals comments made about typical visitors ('visitors' ethnicity'); or makes critical comments ('aesthetic critique,' 'ethnicity critique,' 'nationality critique'). Interestingly, the passage also reveals the potential for a code employed by Coffey and Atkinson (1996: 43–5), the use of a 'contrastive rhetoric' which occurs when a person makes a point about something by comparing it to something else. This feature occurred when the husband made a point about the representation of British culture, which he regarded as poor, compared to that of China, which he regarded as good.

As Coffey and Atkinson (1996) observed, following Strauss and Corbin's account (1990) of grounded theory, codes should not be thought of purely as mechanisms for the fragmentation and retrieval of text. They can do more than simply manage the data gathered. For example, an examination of the interconnections between codes may reveal that some are dimensions of a broader phenomenon. For example, 'ethnicity critique' came to be seen as a dimension of 'ideology critique,' along with 'class critique' and 'gender critique.' In this way, a map of the more general or formal properties of concepts being developed can be started.

Learning NVivo

This exposition of NVivo and its functions addresses just its most basic features; tutorials have been included in the program to assist learners and are recommended for more in-depth instruction. In the following account, as in Chapter 12, → signifies 'click once with the left-hand button of your mouse.'

On opening NVivo, a welcome screen is presented (Plate 13.1). The screen shows any existing NVivo projects and is the springboard for either opening one of the existing projects or starting a new one. If you are starting a new project, as in the example that follows, → **File** → **New Project**. The **New Project** dialogue box appears and you are asked to provide a **Title** for your project. For this exercise, the title 'Disney Project1' was chosen. You are also asked to give a **Description** of the project, though this is an optional feature. When you have done this, → OK.

You then need to import the documents you want to code. In this case, they will be interview transcripts from the project on visitors to Disney theme parks, referred to earlier. Other kinds of documents

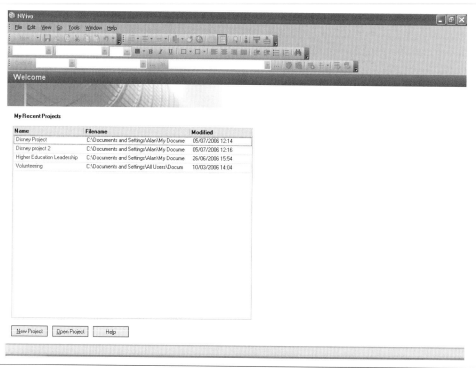

Plate 13.1 The opening screen

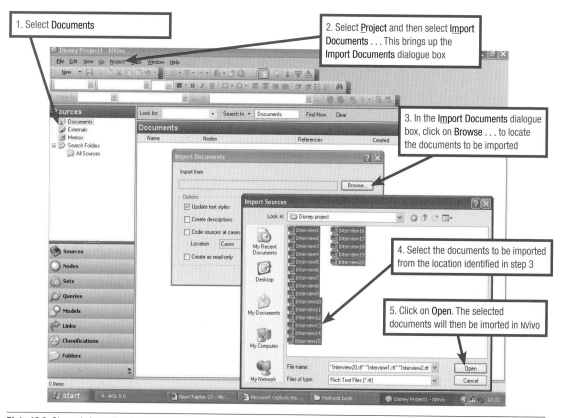

Plate 13.2 Stages in importing documents into NVivo

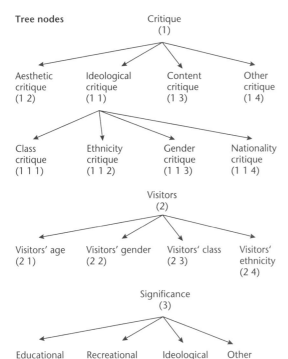

Tree nodes

Critique
(1)

| Aesthetic critique (1 2) | Ideological critique (1 1) | Content critique (1 3) | Other critique (1 4) |

| Class critique (1 1 1) | Ethnicity critique (1 1 2) | Gender critique (1 1 3) | Nationality critique (1 1 4) |

Visitors
(2)

| Visitors' age (2 1) | Visitors' gender (2 2) | Visitors' class (2 3) | Visitors' ethnicity (2 4) |

Significance
(3)

| Educational significance (3 1) | Recreational significance (3 2) | Ideological significance (3 3) | Other significance (3 4) |

Free nodes

Uncritical enthusiasm
Not critical of Disney

Figure 13.2 Nodes used in the Disney Project

Box 13.4   What is a node?

NVivo's help system in earlier releases defined coding as 'the process of marking passages of text in a project's documents with *nodes*' (emphasis added). Nodes are, therefore, the route by which coding is undertaken. In the latest release, a node is defined as 'a collection of references about a specific theme, place, person or other area of interest.' When a document has been coded, the node incorporates references to those portions of documents in which the code appears. Once established, nodes can be changed or deleted. Nodes can take different forms, but only two are covered in this chapter. First, there are *tree nodes*, in which nodes are held in a tree-like structure, implying connections between them. Hence there can be groups (trees) of related nodes. The other type covered here is *free nodes,* which are independent of any tree.

---

can be imported such as fieldwork notes. Earlier versions of NVivo could not import documents in Microsoft Word format (.doc), so Word documents had to be converted to rich text format (.rtf). This is not the case with NVivo 7, the release used here. It can accept documents in both rich text and Word formats. To import the documents, → **Documents** (below **Sources**) → **Project** → **Import Documents** … [opens the **Import Documents** dialogue box] → **Browse** to locate the documents that are to be imported → select the documents to be imported → **Open** (see Plate 13.2 for the series of steps). The documents will then be visible in the Documents **List View**. Once the documents have been imported, they can be read and edited. All you need to do is double-click on the yellow icon to the left of each interview in the **List View**.

Coding

As noted, coding data is one of the key processes in qualitative data analysis. For NVivo, coding is accomplished through nodes (see Box 13.4).

There are several ways of coding in NVivo. The approach taken in the Disney Project was to:

1. Read through the interviews both in printed form and in the Document viewer (Plate 13.3).
2. Work out some codes that seem relevant to the documents.
3. Go back into the documents and code them using NVivo.

An alternative strategy is to code while browsing the documents.

Creating nodes
The nodes used in our example are presented in Figure 13.2. Notice that there are two *free nodes* and three groups of *tree nodes*. With the latter, each node point—the equivalent of a code—has a unique number. These numbers have been inserted in Figure 13.2. The nodes and their associated numbers can be created in the following way.

CREATING A FREE NODE
1. While in **Navigation View** [this is the term used to describe the general screen shown in Plate 13.2] → **Nodes**
2. → **Free Nodes**.

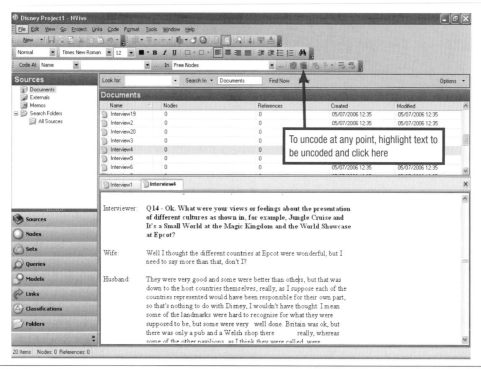

Plate 13.3 The document viewer

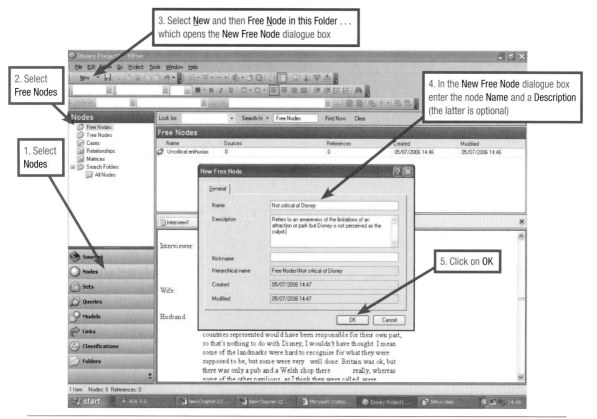

Plate 13.4 Stages in creating a free node

3. → **New** → **Free Node in This Folder** [opens the **New Free Node** dialogue box shown in Plate 13.4].

4. Enter the node **Name** [*not critical of Disney*] and a **Description** (the latter is optional)

5. → OK

To create a tree node, the initial process is exactly the same as with a free node. In the following example, we will create the tree node *Class Critique*, which is a branch of the tree node *Ideological Critique*, which is itself a branch of the tree node *Critique* (see Figure 13.2). The following steps will generate this node.

1. While in the **Navigation View** → **Nodes**

2. → **Tree Nodes**

3. → **New** → **Tree Node in This Folder** ... [opens the **New Tree Node** dialogue box—see Plate 13.5]

4. Enter the node **Name** [*Critique*] and a **Description** (the latter is optional). This node will form the initial root of the tree node.

5. → OK

6. → *Critique* in the Tree Node viewer

7. → **New** → **Tree Node in This Folder** ... [opens the **New Tree Node** dialogue box]

8. Enter the node **Name** [*Ideological Critique*] and a **Description** (the latter is optional). This node will form a branch of the tree node. See Plate 13.5.

9. → OK

10. → *Ideological Critique* in the Tree Node viewer

11. → **New** → **Tree Node in This Folder** ... [opens the **New Tree Node** dialogue box]

12. Enter the node **Name** [*Class Critique*] and a **Description** (the latter is optional). This node will form a branch of the tree node *Ideological Critique*.

13. → OK

Applying nodes in the coding process

Coding is carried out by applying nodes to segments of text. Once some nodes have been set up (and remember they can be added or altered at any time), when you are in the viewer you can highlight the area of the document that you want to code and then right-click while holding the cursor over the highlighted text. Then, → **Code** → **Code Selection at New Mode**. This opens the **New Code** dialogue box. The default is that it allows you to create a free node,

but if you → **Select** … you have the opportunity to create a tree node and to locate it appropriately within a tree structure.

One of the easiest ways of encoding in NVivo 7 is to drag and drop text into a node (see Plate 13.6). To do this, highlight the text to be coded and then, holding down the left-hand button, drag the text over to the appropriate mode.

An alternative is to highlight the text to be coded, right-click over the highlighted text, → **Code** → **Code Selection at Existing Nodes**, which opens the **Select Project Items** dialogue box (see Plate 13.7). Tick the node(s) you want to use. If you do not see the node(s) you need, → the yellow folder 🗀 that you need. To find a node within a tree, → the ⊞ sign next to a tree node. Thus, in the example in Plate 13.7, the tick by *Uncritical enthusiasm* will code the highlighted text at that node. If you also wanted to code it as a tree node, you would need to → yellow folder 🗀 at **Tree Nodes** and then find the appropriate root node or a branch of it by → the ⊞ sign. To *uncode* at any point, simply highlight the passage to be uncoded, and → the button with a red cross in it (see Plate 13.3). Alternatively, you can right-click on the highlighted text and select **Uncode**.

These instructions apply to the application of both free nodes and tree nodes.

Coding stripes

It is helpful to see the areas of text coded and the nodes applied to them. NVivo has a very useful aid to this called *coding stripes*. Selecting it produces multi-coloured stripes that represent portions of coded text and the nodes that have been used. Overlapping codes do not represent a problem at all.

To activate this facility, → **View** and then → **Coding Stripes** → **Show Nodes Recently Coding Item**. Plate 13.8 shows these stripes. Notice that some segments have been coded at two or more nodes—such as *visitors ethnicity* and *ethnicity critique*. All the nodes that have been used are clearly displayed.

Searching text

Once the data are coded, however preliminary that may be, you will probably want to conduct searches of your data. For example, you may want to retrieve all occurrences of a particular node. NVivo allows you to trawl through all you documents so that you can get all text that was coded at a particular node.

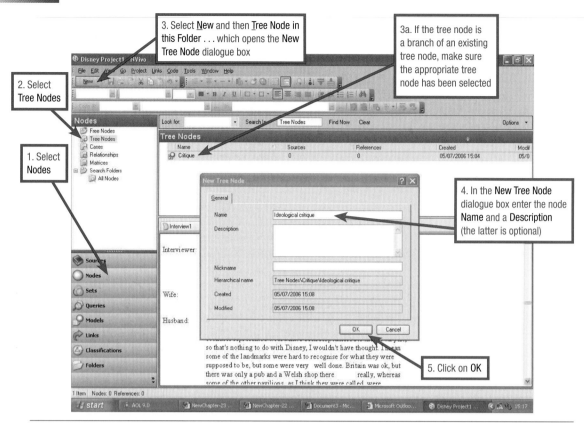

Plate 13.5 Stages in creating a tree node

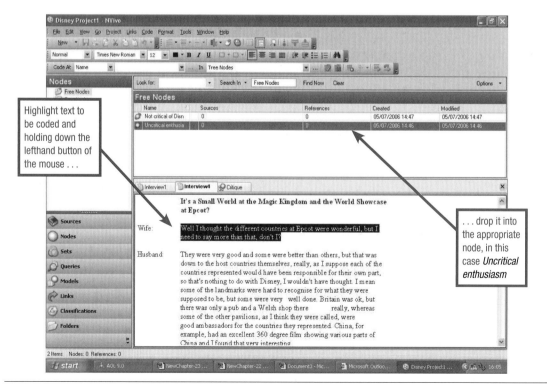

Plate 13.6 Using drag and drop to code

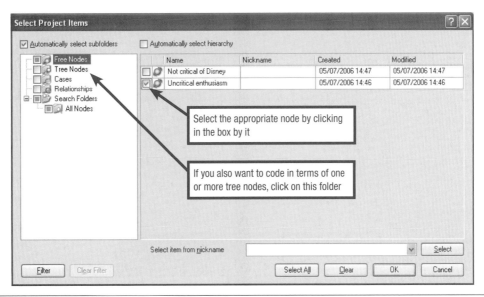

Plate 13.7 Coding in NVivo

To search for occurrences of a single node
These steps describe how to conduct a search for sequences of text that have been coded in terms of the node *ethnicity critique*. The stages are outlined in Plate 13.9.

1. While in the **Navigation View** ➔ **Nodes** [this opens the list of node folders in the top left-hand pane of Plate 13.9]
2. ➔ 🖼 at **Tree Nodes** [this generates a list of all three nodes, as in Plate 13.9]
3. ➔ on the ⊞ sign to the left of *Critique* [this brings up a list of all branches of the node *Critique*]
4. ➔ on the ⊞ to the left of *Ideological critique* [this brings up a list of all branches of the node *Ideological critique*]
5. ➔ the icon to the left of *Nationality critique* (see Plate 13.10)
6. All instances of coded text at the node *Nationality critique* will appear at the bottom of the screen, as in Plate 13.10.

To search for text coded in terms of a free node, the process is simpler in that you need to ➔ the **Free Nodes** folder rather than the **Tree Nodes** folder and then ➔ the icon to the left of the appropriate tree node.

To search for the intersection of two nodes
These steps describe how to conduct a search for sequences of text that have been coded at two nodes:

aesthetic critique and *not critical of Disney*. This type of search is known as a 'Boolean search.' It will locate text coded in terms of the two nodes together (that is, where they intersect) and ignore where each appears singly. The following steps are required:

1. In the **Navigation View** ➔ **Queries** to the bottom left
2. ➔ **New** on the toolbar in the top left
3. ➔ **Coding Query in This Folder** [opens the **Coding Query** dialogue box in Plate 13.11]
4. ➔ **Coding Criteria** tab
5. ➔ **Advanced tab**
6. In the **Define more criteria:** panel, ➔ **Coded by** from the drop-down menu
7. ➔ **Select …** You then need to choose the two nodes to be analyzed
8. ➔ Once the nodes have been selected, ➔ **Add to List**
9. ➔ **AND** from the drop-down menu
10. ➔ **Run**

To search for specific text
NVivo can also perform searches for specific words or phrases, often referred to as 'strings' in computer jargon. For example, to search for *Magic Kingdom*, the following steps are appropriate:

1. On the menu bar at the top, ➔ **Edit**
2. ➔ **Find** … [opens the **Find Content** dialogue box in Plate 13.12]

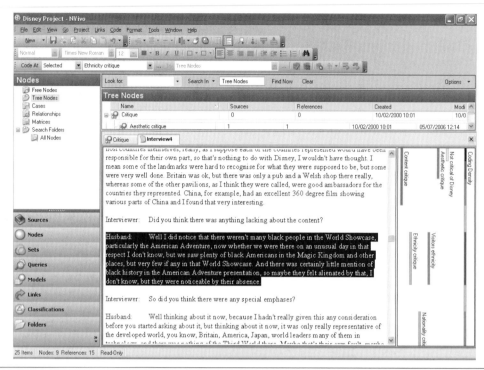

Plate 13.8 Coding stripes

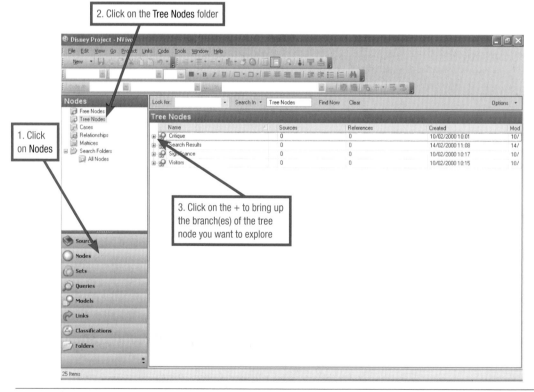

Plate 13.9 Stages in retrieving text from a tree node

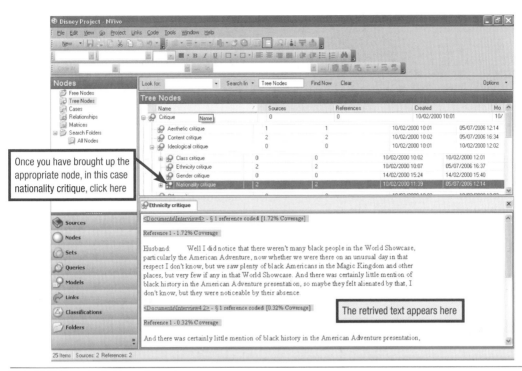

Plate 13.10 Retrieving text from a tree node

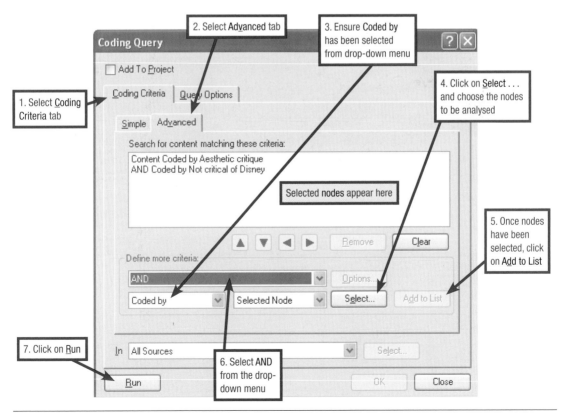

Plate 13.11 The **Coding Query** dialogue box (searching for the intersection of two nodes)

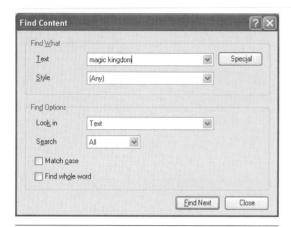

Plate 13.12 The **Find Content** dialogue box

3. Insert **Magic Kingdom** to the right of **Text**
4. To the right of **Look in**, make sure that **Text** has been selected
5. → **Find Next**

Text searching can be useful for locating possible *in vivo* codes. They require going back to the documents to conduct *in vivo* coding.

Output

To find the results of coding at a particular node, → the **Nodes** button in the bottom left. This will bring up your node structure. Find the node you are interested in and double-click on that node. This will bring up all text coded at that node along with information about which interview(s) the text comes from.

Memos

Earlier it was noted that one feature of the grounded theory approach to qualitative data analysis is the use of memos in which ideas and illustrations are stored. Memos can be easily created in NVivo. The following steps, which are outlined in Plate 13.13, should be followed:

1. In the **Navigation View** → **Sources**
2. Under **Sources** → **Memos**
3. → **New**
4. → **Memo in This Folder** … [opens up **New Memo** dialogue box shown in Plate 13.14]
5. After Name, type in a name for the document (for example, **gender critique memo**). You can

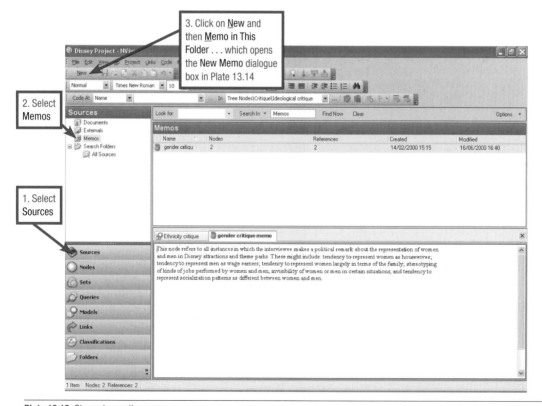

Plate 13.13 Stages in creating a memo

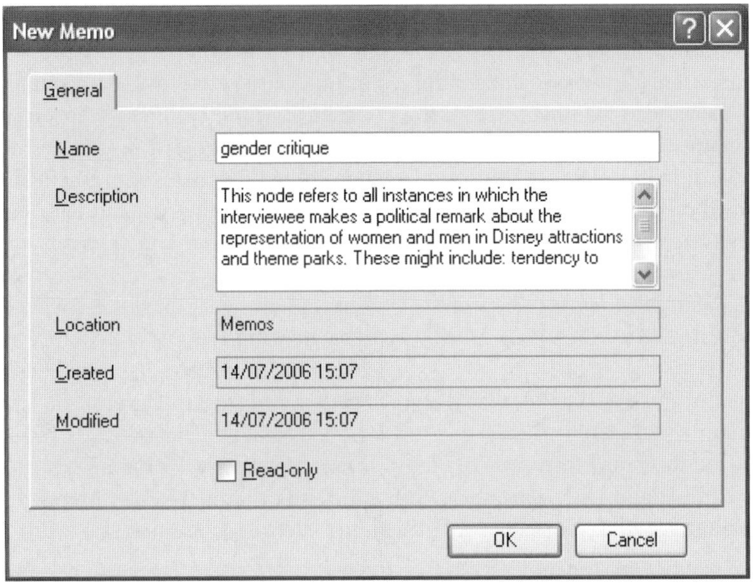

Plate 13.14 The **New Memo** dialogue box

also provide a brief description of the document in the window to the right of Description, as in Plate 13.13.

6. → OK

Saving and retrieving an NVivo project

When you are finished working on the data, it must be saved for future use. To do this, on the menu bar at the top, → **File** → **Save Project**. This will save all the work you have done. You will then be given the opportunity to exit NVivo or to create or open a project without worrying about losing all your hard work. You might also consider backing up the project. To do this, you will need to exit the project you are working on by → **File** → **Close Project**. This will take you to the Welcome screen. → **File** → **Copy Project**. The **Copy Project** dialogue box will then be opened. This will allow you to specify the project you want to copy and where you want the copy to be stored—for example, on a flash memory drive.

Opening an existing NVivo project

To retrieve a project you have created, at the Welcome screen, → **File** → **Open Project**. This opens the **Open Project** dialogue box. Select the project you want to work on. Then → **Open**.

You can also open a NUD*IST project, or one designed with an earlier release of NVivo, by selecting the appropriate project type from the drop-down menu to the right of **Files of type**.

General thoughts on using NVivo

A short discussion like this can provide only the most basic features of the software and a brief impression of what it is like. Doubtless, some readers will decide it is not for them and that the tried-and-tested scissors-and-paste method or perhaps a modified Word search can do the trick. On the other hand, the software warrants serious consideration because of its power and flexibility.

Problems with coding

One of the most common criticisms of coding qualitative data is the possibility of losing the context of what is said. (For a general critique of qualitative data analysis packages see Box 13.5.) By plucking chunks of text out of the context in which they appear, such as a particular interview transcript, the social setting can be lost. A second criticism is that it results in a fragmentation of the data, causing the narrative flow of the data to be lost (Coffey and Atkinson 1996). Sensitivity to this issue has been heightened since the late 1980s by a growing interest in narrative analysis (see later in this chapter). Riessman (1993: vi) became concerned about fragmentation when coding themes in her structured interview study on divorce and gender:

Some [interviewees] developed long accounts of what had happened in their marriages to justify their divorces. I did not realize these were narratives until I struggled to code them. Applying traditional qualitative methods, I searched the texts for common thematic elements. But some individuals knotted together several themes into long accounts that had coherence and sequence, defying easy categorization. I found myself not wanting to fragment the long accounts into distinct thematic categories.

Riessman's account is interesting because it suggests several possibilities: that the coding method can fragment the data; that some forms of data may be unsuitable for coding; and that researchers can produce narrative analysis, since what she provided in this passage is precisely a narrative. Interest in narrative analysis certainly shows signs of growing and in large part this trend parallels the rebirth of interest in the life history approach (see Box 10.4). Nonetheless, coding is unlikely to become less prominent because of several factors: its widespread acceptance in the research community; not all analysts are interested in research questions that lend themselves to narratives; the powerful influence of grounded theory and its associated techniques; and the growing use and acceptance of computer software for qualitative data analysis, which frequently invites a coding approach.

Regardless of analytical strategy, it is unacceptable to simply say: 'This is what my subjects said and did, isn't that incredibly interesting?' Interpretation and theorizing are necessary. But many researchers

Box 13.5   Lack of agreement about the utility of CAQDAS

Unlike the almost universal use of computer software in quantitative data analysis, among qualitative data analysts the use of software is often avoided, for several reasons.

- Some writers are concerned that the ease with which coded text can be quantified with qualitative data analysis packages means that qualitative research will be colonized by the reliability and validity criteria of quantitative research (Hesse-Biber 1995).

- Others feel that CAQDAS reinforces and even exaggerates the tendency towards a fragmentation of the textual materials (Weaver and Atkinson 1995), destroying the natural flow of interview transcripts and field notes. An awareness of context is crucial to many qualitative researchers and the prospect of this being sidelined is not attractive.

- Stanley and Temple (1995) suggested that most of the coding and retrieval features needed for qualitative data analysis, such as search, cut, and paste already exist in word-processing software. Using Word for Windows, for example, would not only save money but also reduce the time spent in learning new software.

- Coffey et al. (1996) argued that the style of qualitative data analysis in most CAQDAS presumes a certain style of analysis—one based on coding and retrieving text—that owes a great deal to grounded theory. Coffey et al. argued that the emergence of grounded theory as a new standard is inconsistent with a key strength of qualitative research: its flexibility.

On the other hand, several writers have sought to extol the virtues of such packages on a variety of grounds:

- CAQDAS like NVivo invites thought about 'trees' of interrelated ideas, a useful feature in that it urges the analyst to consider possible connections between variables.

- Quantitative researchers often criticize the tendency towards 'anecdotalism' found in much qualitative research—that is, the tendency to use quotations from interview transcripts or field notes but with little sense of their frequency or prevalence, that is, their generalizability. CAQDAS offers the opportunity to count the frequency with which a form of behaviour occurs or a viewpoint is expressed in interviews.

- CAQDAS enhances the transparency of qualitative data analysis. How qualitative data were analyzed is often unclear in published reports (Bryman and Burgess 1994b). CAQDAS may force researchers to be more explicit and reflective about the process of analysis, and may indirectly encourage replication, a feature often lacking in qualitative analysis.

are wary of that—they worry that they may fail to do justice to what they have seen and heard or that they may contaminate their subjects' words and behaviour. That is a risk, but it has to be balanced against the fact that findings acquire significance in an intellectual community only when they have been subject to reflection. The researcher is not there as a mere note taker or recorder.

Narrative analysis

Narrative analysis is a term that covers a wide variety of approaches concerned with the search for and analysis of stories that people tell to understand their lives and the world around them. As noted, it has become particularly prominent in connection with the life history or biographical approach. However, as Box 13.6 shows, narrative analysis is not exclusively concerned with telling life histories. As Roberts (2002) observed, the term 'narrative analysis' is often used to refer to both the approach—one that examines the recounting of lives and events—and to the stories that people tell in recounting their lives. While there is little consensus on what narrative analysis entails, at the very least it entails a sensitivity to: the connections in people's accounts of past, present, and future events and states of affairs; people's sense of their place within those events and situations; the stories they generate about them; and the significance of context for the unfolding of events and people's sense of their role within them. It is the way people organize and forge connections between events and the sense they make of those connections that provide the raw material of narrative analysis. Riessman (2004b) helpfully distinguished four models of narrative analysis:

- *Thematic analysis*—examines what is said rather than how it is said.
- *Structural analysis*—places emphasis on the way a story is related. Issues of content do not disappear but attention is focused on the use of narrative mechanisms for increasing the persuasiveness of a story.
- *Interactional analysis*—looks at the dialogue between the teller of a story and the listener. Especially prominent is the co-construction of meaning by the two parties, though content and form are by no means marginalized.
- *Performative analysis*—analyzes narrative as a performance; explores the use of words and gestures to get a story across. This model of narrative analysis includes an examination of audience responses to the narrative.

With narrative analysis, attention shifts from 'What actually happened?' to 'How do people make sense of what happened?' Proponents of narrative analysis argue that most approaches to the collection and analysis of data neglect the fact that people perceive their lives in terms of continuity and process, and that attempts to understand social life not attuned to that neglect the perspective of those being studied. Life history research is an obvious location for the application of a narrative analysis, but its use can be much broader. For example, narrative analysis can relate not just to the lifespan but also to accounts of shorter episodes and their interconnections.

Some researchers apply narrative analysis to interviews. For example, in her account of her 'click moment' as a narrative researcher, Riessman described how she applied narrative analysis to conventional interview transcript material, and then began to uncover the stories her interviewees were telling her. In this case, Riessman was applying a narrative approach to materials gathered in a conventional way for conventional purposes. Other researchers start out with the intention of conducting a narrative analysis and deliberately ask people to recount stories (for example, Miller 2000). While stories can arise out of answers to questions not designed to elicit a narrative, certain kinds of

---

Box 13.6   Tattoo narratives

As part of a three-year participant observation study of tattoos, Atkinson (2002, 2004) elicited tattoo narratives from the women he interviewed. The great increase in the numbers of women getting tattoos has firmly challenged the older masculinity explanations for men who engage in that behaviour. Drawing upon feminist theories about bodies, he found that these women are not misfits, and instead they use tattoos to signify their 'established' or 'outsider' constructions of femininity. Ideas about femininity, including conformity to and resistance against cultural norms, are crucial in explaining women's tattooing.

question are especially likely to produce stories. Riessman (2004a) suggested that remarks like 'tell me what happened' followed with 'and then what happened?' are much more likely to provide a narrative account than 'when did X happen?' While some narrative researchers prefer to start people off by asking them to tell their story about an event, Riessman argued that it is usually necessary to keep asking follow-up questions to stimulate the flow of details and impressions. For example, in her study of divorce, she often asked: 'Can you remember a time when . . .?' and then followed it up with 'What happened that makes you remember that particular moment in your marriage?'

Coffey and Atkinson (1996) argued that a narrative should be viewed in terms of the functions that the narrative serves for the teller. The aim of narrative interviews is to elicit interviewees' reconstructed accounts of connections between events and links between events and contexts (see Box 13.7 for an example). Miller (2000) proposed that narrative interviews in life story or biographical research are far more concerned with eliciting the interviewee's reflections and interpretations, as revealed in the telling of the story of his or her life or family, than with the facts of the matter.

Box 13.7 provides an example of narrative analysis beyond the life story approach. In this case, the author explored competing narratives in accounting for the failed implementation of an information technology system in a hospital.

Narrative analysis, then, is an approach to the analysis of qualitative data that examines the stories that people use to explain events. It can be applied to data that have been acquired through a variety of research methods (notably semi-structured and unstructured interviewing and participant observation), but it has also become an interviewing approach in its own right. Also, as will be seen in connection with the writing of ethnographic research (see section on 'Writing up ethnography' in Chapter 17), there is growing recognition of ethnography as a narrative designed to tell a story about a way of life.

Narrative analysis has been criticized. Bury (2001), while noting the increased interest in *illness narratives* (stories people tell about an illness they or others have experienced, and its impact on people's lives), argued that there has been a tendency for narrative researchers to treat the stories they are told uncritically. For example, he suggested that the frequent reference in illness narratives to coping with and 'normalizing' chronic illness may in large part be an attempt to convince the audience (for example, an interviewer or the reader of a book about someone's struggle with illness) of competence, which

---

Box 13.7 An example of organizational narratives in a hospital

Brown (1998) examined the competing narratives involved in the aftermath of the introduction of new information technology (IT) in a hospital. The implementation was largely seen as unsuccessful because of the absence of clear clinical benefits and because of cost overruns. Drawing on his unstructured and semi-structured interviews with key actors, Brown presented three contrasting narratives: the ward narrative, the laboratory team's narrative, and the implementation team's narrative.

The three narratives provide a very clear sense of the organization as a political arena in which groups and individuals contest the legitimacy of each other's interpretations of events. Thus, while the three groups had similar (but not the same) motivations for participating in the IT initiative, mainly in terms of the espousal of an ethic of patient care, they had rather different latent motivations and different interpretations of what went wrong (Brown 1998: 49).

In terms of the former, whereas the ward narrative implied a latent motivation to save doctors' and nurses' time, the laboratory team emphasized the importance of retaining the existing IT systems. The implementation team stressed the possible advantages for their own careers, in large part by the increased dependence on their skills. In terms of the contrasting narratives of what went wrong, the ward narrative looked at the failure of the implementation team to coordinate the initiative and meet deadlines, and the laboratory team emphasized the tendency for the implementation team not to listen or communicate. For their part, the implementation team's diagnosis pointed to the ward staff failing to communicate their needs, a lack of cooperation from the laboratory staff, and poorly written software.

may have more to do with wanting to be seen as a fully functioning member of society than a realistic account of coming to terms with a medical condition. However, as Bury recognized, the social conditions that prompt such narratives and the form the narratives take are themselves revealing. In drawing attention to the motives that lie behind illness narratives, he was not seeking to undermine narrative analysis but to draw attention to what narratives are supposed to reveal to the researcher.

Key Points

- The collection of qualitative data frequently results in the accumulation of a large volume of information.

- Qualitative data analysis is not governed by codified rules to the same extent as quantitative data analysis.

- There are different approaches to qualitative data analysis; grounded theory is probably the most prominent.

- Coding is a key process in most qualitative data analysis strategies, but it may fragment and decontextualize the information.

- Narrative analysis emphasizes the stories that people tell in the course of interactions with a qualitative researcher; it has become a distinct strategy in its own right for producing and analyzing qualitative data.

Questions for Review

- What is meant by suggesting that qualitative data are an 'attractive nuisance'?

General strategies of qualitative data analysis

- What are the main components of analytic induction?

- What are the main features of grounded theory?

- What is the role of coding in grounded theory and what are the different types of coding?

- What is the role of memos in grounded theory?

- Charmaz wrote that theoretical sampling 'represents a defining property of grounded theory' (2000: 519). Why do you think she feels this way?

- What are some of the main criticisms of grounded theory?

Basic operations in qualitative data analysis

- Is coding associated solely with grounded theory?

- What are the main steps in coding?

- To what extent does coding result in the fragmentation of data?

Learning NVivo

- What is a node?

- What is the difference between a free node and a tree node?

- What is *in vivo* coding?

- Do nodes have to be set up in advance?

- How does one search for a single node or the intersection of two nodes?

- Why is it useful to display coding stripes?

- How does one search for specific text?

Narrative analysis

- To what extent does narrative analysis provide a solution to data fragmentation?

- How does the emphasis on stories in narrative analysis provide a distinctive approach to the production and analysis of qualitative data?

- Can narrative analysis be applied to all kinds of qualitative interviews?

Part V

Part V explores areas that transcend the quantitative/qualitative divide. Chapter 14 invites readers to reconsider the distinction between those two approaches to social research. This may seem like an odd thing to do, since this book has been organized around the differences between them. However, the aim is to show that the distinction is not a hard-and-fast one. Chapter 15 considers the different ways in which quantitative and qualitative research can be combined. Such combinations are referred to as *multi-strategy research*. Chapter 16 examines content analysis, the study of media and other text, and applies qualitative strategies to it, including conversation analysis and discourse analysis, and explores some quantitative aspects of that form of research as well. Chapter 17 looks at issues relating to the writing-up of social research, and discusses some features of good writing in both quantitative and qualitative research. Chapter 18 offers advice to students faced with the often daunting prospect of writing a senior research paper or honours thesis. It is also helpful to those who have to do smaller projects as part of their coursework requirements.

These chapters draw together certain issues from previous parts of the book, probing them in greater depth and making connections between them.

14

Breaking Down the Quantitative/ Qualitative Divide

Chapter overview

This chapter is concerned with how far the quantitative/qualitative distinction should be taken. It shows that, while there are many differences between the two research strategies, there is also much that unites them. One way this can be seen is by combining quantitative and qualitative research, the focus of the next chapter. The present chapter is concerned with points of overlap between them. It examines:

- aspects of qualitative research that can contain elements of the natural science model;

- aspects of quantitative research that can contain elements of interpretivism;
- how research methods are more independent of epistemological and ontological assumptions than is sometimes supposed;
- ways in which the quantitative/qualitative contrast may break down;
- studies in which qualitative research is used to analyze quantitative research and vice versa; and
- the use of quantification in qualitative research.

Introduction

With the emphasis placed thus far on the distinction between quantitative and qualitative research, it may appear perverse at this stage to raise the prospect that the differences between these two perspectives may be overblown. But the dichotomy has been maintained to this point for two simple reasons:

- There *are* differences between quantitative and qualitative research strategies.
- It is a useful means of organizing research methods and approaches to data analysis.

As seen in earlier chapters, certain epistemological and ontological positions may be associated with particular research methods—for example, a natural science epistemology is often paired with social survey research, and an interpretivist epistemology with qualitative interviewing. However, the connections posited in Chapter 1 between epistemology and ontology, on the one hand, and

research method, on the other, are best thought of as tendencies rather than definitive connections. Thus, one cannot say that the use of a structured interview or self-completion questionnaire *necessarily* implies a commitment to a natural science model, or that ethnographic research *must* mean an interpretivist epistemology.

Research methods are much more free-floating than is sometimes supposed. A method of data collection like participant observation can be employed such that it is in tune with constructionism, but equally it can be used in a manner that reveals an objectivist orientation. Also, it is easy to underestimate the significance of practical considerations in how social research is conducted. Conducting a study of drug dealers by mailed questionnaire is not impossible, but for practical reasons it is unlikely to succeed. The rest of the chapter demonstrates why the contrast between quantitative and qualitative research should not be overstated.

The natural science model and qualitative research

One of the chief difficulties in linking issues of epistemology with research methods is the frequent characterization of the natural sciences as inherently *positivist* in orientation. But the term 'positivism' is often used in a polemical way, usually as a negative and unhelpful criticism of another's work. Moreover, qualitative research frequently exhibits features associated with a natural science model. This tendency is revealed in several ways:

- *Empiricist overtones.* Although empiricism (see Chapter 1) is typically associated with quantitative research, many qualitative researchers place a similar emphasis on the importance of direct contact with social reality. For example, they frequently stress the importance of direct experience with social settings, and advocate understanding social reality via that contact. The very idea that theory is to be grounded in data (recall Chapter 8) is central to empiricism. It is unsurprising, therefore, that some writers claim to detect 'covert positivism' in qualitative research.

  Another example of empiricist overtones is the suggestion that social reality must be studied from the vantage point of the research participants. Yet the only way to gain access to those interpretations is through extended contact with the people being studied, implying that their meanings are accessible to the senses of the researchers. The empiricism of qualitative research is perhaps most notable in conversation analysis (examined in Chapter 16), an approach that takes precise transcriptions of talk as its starting point and applies rules of analysis to them. The analyst is actively discouraged from engaging in speculations about intention or context; in other words, the empiricist notion that one should not stray too far from the data is strictly upheld.

- *A specific problem focus.* As noted, qualitative research can investigate quite specific, tightly defined research questions of the kind normally associated with the natural science model.

- *Hypothesis- and theory-testing.* Following from the last point, qualitative researchers typically test hypotheses or theories generated in the course of conducting their research, as in analytic induction or grounded theory. This is well within the bounds of a natural science model even if, in practice, the natural sciences tend to be deductive. Also, there is no reason why hypothesis or theory testing in qualitative social research cannot be done with previously specified hypotheses or theories. In fact it has already been done on many occasions. For example, Wilson's qualitative study of raves (2002) used theory as a departure point. The research by Festinger *et al.* (1956) on a doomsday cult used participant observation, a qualitative technique, to test a theory about how people respond when a belief they zealously endorse is disconfirmed. The authors argued that it is possible to imagine a number of conditions that, if met, would result in the belief being held *more* fervently after its disconfirmation. They thought that the cult would provide an ideal opportunity for testing their ideas. The researchers and hired observers pretended to be converts and joined the group, thereby gaining access to first-hand observations to test the theory. Cult

---

Box 14.1 Critical realist ethnography

Porter (1993, 2002) used a critical realist stance in his ethnographic study of a large Irish hospital where he spent three months as a staff nurse. His interest was in racism in this setting and one of his hypotheses was that the hospital setting would affect how the racism was expressed. Porter found that racism exists in the form of racist remarks made behind the backs of members of racial minorities. It does not, however, intrude into work relationships, because of the greater weight given to people's achievements and performance (such as qualifications and medical skills) than to 'race' when judging members of professions. In part, this is due to how black or Asian doctors emphasize their knowledge and qualifications during their interactions with whites so that their professional credentials are confirmed. In terms of critical realism, one possible structural mechanism (racism) is countered by the operation of another structural mechanism (professional ideology). Only on rare occasions does tension between the two surface, as when a minority doctor conducted a religious observance on his knees in the middle of a hospital unit (Porter 2002).

members decided that their faith had saved the world and they went on to proselytize for their group, thus substantiating the theory.

- *Realism*. Porter's (1993) critical realist ethnography (see Box 14.1) demonstrates how ethnography can be based on an epistemological position derived from the natural sciences. It also relates to the previous point in providing a further illustration of hypothesis-testing in qualitative research.

In addition, some qualitative researchers include explicitly quantitative elements in their research. Miller (2000), for example, engaging in what he called *neo-positivism*, made theoretically based predictions about people's lives using the life history method. Another illustration is Charmaz's (2000) suggestion that in spite of the differences that developed between Glaser (1992) and Strauss (for example, Strauss and Corbin 1998)—who were major proponents of grounded theory—both maintained that an objective, external reality exists, a position taken in the natural science model. Each posited a social world beyond the researcher and maintained that it is the job of the social investigator to reveal its nature and functioning.

Quantitative research and interpretivism

Qualitative research would seem to have a near-monopoly on the ability to study meaning. Its proponents imply that only qualitative research allows the social world to be seen through the eyes of the people studied. But this contention seems rather at odds with the widespread study of *attitudes* in social surveys based on interviews and questionnaires. For example, there is a huge literature on political attitudes, and many indexes and scales have been designed to measure them (see Robinson *et al.* 1999). The widespread inclusion of questions about attitudes in social surveys suggests that quantitative researchers are interested in matters of meaning too.

It may be objected that survey questions do not really tap issues of meaning because they are based on categories devised by the designers of the interview schedule or questionnaire and not by the subjects themselves. Two points are relevant here. First, the notion that qualitative research is better at gaining access to the point of view of those being studied is generally *assumed rather than demonstrated*.

Qualitative researchers frequently claim to have tapped into participants' world views because of their extensive participation in the daily life of those they study, the length of time they spend in the setting being studied, or the lengthy and intensive interviews conducted. However, the explicit demonstration that interpretative understanding has been accomplished—for example, through any respondent validation (see Chapter 8)—is rarely undertaken. Second, if the design of attitude questions is based on prior questioning that seeks to bring out the range of possible attitudinal positions on an issue, attitudinal questions can certainly provide access to meaning.

Also, the practice in much survey research of asking respondents the reasons for their actions implies that quantitative researchers are frequently concerned with uncovering meaning. For example, in the research on delinquency in Box 1.2, the boys were asked to give the reasons for their actions in their own words and then to choose the sociological theories that came closest to explaining them. Examples such as these point to the possibility that the gulf between quantitative and qualitative research is not as wide as is sometimes supposed.

Quantitative research and constructionism

It was noted in Chapter 1 that a keynote in qualitative analysis is constructionism, how people build up images or representations of the social world. Qualitative content analysis plays an important role in developing an understanding of how people construct their visions of reality, in the same way discourse analysis (Chapter 16) does using newspaper reports and television programs.

Lantz and Booth's (1998) research on the social construction of breast cancer provides an example. As Box 1.7 makes clear, much of their understanding of the representation of breast cancer came from a qualitative content analysis, but they employed a quantitative content analysis as well. The latter was used to determine that 80 per cent of the women in photographs attached to breast cancer articles were under age 50, and that 85 per cent of the anecdotes and case stories related to women in this age group. This emphasis on younger women helped to create the impression that they were the most at risk. But in reality, fewer than 20 per cent of new cases of breast cancer are in women under 50, and the mean age at diagnosis is 65. This inconsistency allowed Lantz and Booth to uncover how the media draw a connection between youthful lifestyles (working outside of the home, postponing parenthood, greater sexuality) and breast cancer, one consistent with the 'blame the victim' theme that the articles convey. The quantitative content analysis of articles on breast cancer played an important part in revealing the social construction of beliefs about the disease. More generally, this example shows how quantitative research can play a significant role in constructionist research.

Research methods and epistemological and ontological considerations

To review the argument so far:

- there can be differences between quantitative and qualitative researchers in their epistemological and ontological positions; *but*
- research strategies and epistemological and ontological assumptions do not necessarily go hand in hand. There is a *tendency* for quantitative and qualitative research to be associated with the epistemological and ontological positions outlined in Table 1.1, but the relationship is not perfect.

Nonetheless, some writers mistakenly suggest that research methods carry with them a full cluster of epistemological and ontological commitments. For example, it is sometimes assumed that to choose a questionnaire as a research option also means selecting a natural science model and an objectivist world view. Similarly, the use of participant observation is often taken to imply a commitment to interpretivism and constructionism. But as seen, there is no perfect correspondence between research strategies and matters of epistemology and ontology. Any notion that a method inherently carries certain wider assumptions about knowledge and the nature of social reality is bound to break down.

Research methods are much more 'free-floating' in terms of epistemology and ontology than is often supposed. This can be seen in studies on social research itself. For example, Platt's (1986) historical research on American sociology suggested that the alleged connection between conservative functionalist theory, itself often associated with positivism, and the social survey is greatly exaggerated. Her research suggested that 'the two originated independently, and that leading functionalists had no special propensity to use surveys and leading surveyors no special propensity for functionalism' (1986: 527). Moreover, Platt's general conclusion on the use of research methods in American sociology between 1920 and 1960 is very revealing:

> Research methods may on the level of theory, when theory is consciously involved at all, reflect intellectual . . . *post hoc* justifications rather than . . . carefully chosen fundamental assumptions. Frequently methodological choices are steered by considerations of a practical nature . . . and are just slogans and aspirations . . . (1996: 275).

Again, even when there are discernible links between research methods and assumptions about knowledge, the connections are not absolute.

Further evidence of the autonomy of research methods is the fact that both quantitative and qualitative approaches may be employed within a single piece of research. This will be the focus of Chapter 15.

Problems with the quantitative/ qualitative contrast

The contrasts between quantitative and qualitative research drawn in Chapter 8 suggest a sharp distinction between the two (see, in particular, Table 8.1). Here is a more nuanced view.

Behaviour versus meaning

A distinction is sometimes drawn between a quantitative focus on behaviour and a qualitative focus on meanings. But as suggested, quantitative research frequently attempts to study meanings in the form of attitudes. In fact in the social sciences in general in recent decades there has been increasing recognition of the importance of examining not only what people do, but also how they think and make sense of the world. Since the 1970s there has been a 'cognitive revolution' in psychology in which people's thoughts and feelings have been the topic of extensive research. The use of rational choice theory and game theory in economics, political science, and sociology assumes that it is important to examine how people think and make choices. Many different perspectives in the social sciences now acknowledge the importance of meanings and interpretations in understanding social pheneomena.

Looking at the other side of the divide, qualitative research frequently, if not invariably, examines *behaviour*, albeit in context. Qualitative researchers often want to interpret people's behaviour in terms of the norms, values, and culture of the group or community in question. In other words, quantitative and qualitative researchers are typically interested in both what people do and what they think, although they may go about the investigation of these areas in different ways. The degree to which the behaviour versus meaning contrast coincides with quantitative and qualitative research should not be overstated.

Theory and concepts tested in research versus those emerging from the data

A related point concerns the characterization of quantitative research as driven by theory testing. While experimental investigations probably fit this model well, survey-based studies are often more exploratory than this view implies. Although concepts have to be measured, the nature of their interconnections and specific hypotheses are frequently not specified in advance. There are so many questions asked and so many possible correlations and ways of organizing the findings that many hypotheses are designed *after* the data collection has taken place. The analysis of quantitative social survey data is often more exploratory than is generally appreciated and consequently offers opportunities for generating theories.

The common depiction of quantitative research as solely an exercise in theory testing also fails to appreciate the degree to which findings frequently suggest new departures and theoretical contributions. Reflecting on his career in social survey research, Glock (1988: 45–6) provided the following example from his research on American church involvement. He found that women, older persons, the poor, and those without families are more religiously active than people not in those categories. These results, he pointed out, may mean that such people have more time on their hands to become involved. Alternatively (or in addition), these people may be compensating for their being deprived relative to their counterparts, a conflict view that Marx would have preferred. He could not rule out either explanation with his data so he collected *new* data to test them, thus allowing his original quantitative data to lead to new research ideas. Quantitative research commonly follows that path.

Numbers versus words

Even this most basic distinction between quantitative and qualitative research has problems. Qualitative researchers sometimes undertake a limited amount of quantification of their data in an attempt to uncover the generality of the phenomena being described. While observing doctor–patient interactions in public and private oncology clinics, for example, Silverman (1985) quantified some of his data to show that patients in private clinics have a greater influence over what goes on in the consultations. Still, Silverman warned that such quantification should reflect the research participants' own ways of understanding their social world.

Also, it has often been noted that qualitative researchers engage in 'quasi-quantification' through the use of terms like 'many,' 'often,' and 'some' (see later in this chapter). All that is happening in cases of the kind described by Silverman is that the researcher is injecting greater precision into such estimates of frequency.

Artificial versus natural

The artificial/natural contrast can similarly be criticized. It is often assumed that because much quantitative research employs research instruments (such as questionnaires) that offer only limited and indirect indicators of people's lives, it provides an artificial account of how the social world operates. Qualitative research is often viewed as more naturalistic in that it allows the researcher to observe people in their natural surroundings and settings, behaving as they normally do. Ethnographic research in particular would seem to exhibit this quality, because the participant observer studies people in their normal social worlds and contexts—in other words, as they go about everyday activities. However, when qualitative research is based on interviews (such as semi-structured and unstructured interviewing and focus groups), the depiction 'natural' is less applicable. Interviews still have to be arranged and interviewees have to be taken away from activities they would otherwise be engaged in, even when the interviewing style is of the more conversational kind. Little is known about interviewees' reactions to and feelings about being interviewed.

Phoenix (1994) reported on the responses of interviewees to in-depth interviews in connection with two studies—one concerned with mothers under the age of 20 and the other with the social identities of young people. While many of her interviewees apparently quite enjoyed being interviewed, it is equally clear that they were conscious of the fact that they had been engaged in interviews rather than conversations. This is revealed in the replies quoted by Phoenix for some of the interviewees: one young black woman is reported as saying that she liked the interview, and added: 'I had the chance to explain how I feel about certain things and I don't really get the opportunity to do that much.' Another interviewee said it was a 'good interview' and added: 'I have never talked so much about myself for a long time, too busy talking about kids and their problems' (1994: 61). While such qualitative interviews are clearly valuable in allowing the perspectives of people whose voices are normally silent to surface, they do not fit the definition of 'naturalistic' used by critics of quantitative social science. Thus it is inaccurate to conclude that artificiality is a problem only in quantitative research.

As noted in Chapter 10, focus group research is often described as more natural than qualitative interviewing because it resembles the way people discuss issues in real life. Natural groups are often used to emphasize this element. However, whether this is how focus group participants view the nature of their interactions is unclear. In particular, since people in focus groups are often paid strangers who have travelled some distance to discuss topics they rarely if ever talk about, it is clear that the naturalism of this sort of research is more assumed than demonstrated.

In participant observation, the researcher can be a source of interference, thus making the research situation less natural than it may appear to be. It is difficult to estimate the degree to which this reactivity has an impact on the research findings, but once again the naturalism of such studies is often assumed rather than demonstrated. When the ethnographer also engages in interviewing (as opposed to casual conversations), the naturalistic quality is

definitely compromised, although in all likelihood the research is still less artificial than would be the case if quantitative methods were used.

These observations cast doubt on the rigidity of the quantitative/qualitative contrast. Once again, this is not to suggest that the contrast is unhelpful, but that it should not be exaggerated. Students should not view quantitative and qualitative research as two absolutely divergent research strategies.

The mutual analysis of quantitative and qualitative research

The barriers between quantitative and qualitative research are also undermined when one approach is used to analyze the other.

A qualitative research approach to quantitative research

There has been a growing interest in examining quantitative research using some of the methods associated with qualitative research. In part, this trend is an extension of the growing interest among qualitative researchers in ethnography. The attention to quantitative research is very much a part of this trend because it reveals that the written account of research constitutes both the formal presentation of findings and an attempt to persuade the reader of the credibility of those findings. This is true of the natural sciences too; for example, research by Gilbert and Mulkay (1984) showed how scientists, when writing up their findings, took pains to demonstrate how proper procedures were followed. Gilbert and Mulkay learned from interviewing scientists that the research process was also influenced by the scientists' personal biographies.

One way in which a qualitative approach to quantitative studies is done is through what Gephart (1988: 9) called *ethnostatistics*, 'the study of the construction, interpretation, and display of statistics in quantitative social research.' Gephart showed that there are a number of ways in which ethnostatistics can be conducted, but just one—understanding statistics as rhetoric—is presented here. The very use of statistics can be regarded as a rhetorical device because quantification means that social research can look more like natural science and achieve greater legitimacy and credibility by virtue of that association. The chief point is that the nature of quantitative research can be illuminated through qualitative research.

A quantitative research approach to qualitative research

In Chapter 16, Hodson's (1996) content analysis of workplace ethnographies will be discussed (see Box 16.7). Essentially, Hodson applied a quantitative content analysis to qualitative research. This form of research, sometimes called a *meta-ethnography*, may have potential in other areas of social research in which ethnography has been a popular method, such as the study of social movements, religious sects, and cults. Hodson's research is one solution to the problem of making comparisons between ethnographic studies in a given area. One downside is that it largely ignores contextual factors in order to explore relationships between variables abstracted from the ethnographies.

Certain key issues need to be resolved when conducting analyses of this kind. One relates to conducting the literature search for suitable studies. Hodson chose to analyze just books, rather than articles, because of the limited amount of information usually included in the latter. Even then, criteria for the inclusion of a book needed to be stipulated. Hodson employed three: '(a) the book had to be based on ethnographic methods of observation over a period of at least 6 months, (b) the observations had to be in a single organization, and (c) the book had to focus on at least one clearly identified group of workers . . .' (Hodson 1999: 22). The application of these criteria resulted in the exclusion of 279 out of 365 books uncovered. A second crucial area involved the coding of the studies. Hodson stressed the importance of having considerable knowledge of the subject area, adopting clear coding rules, and pilot testing the coding schedule. In addition, he recommended checking the *reliability* of coding by having 10 per cent of the documents coded by two people. The process of coding was time-consuming; each book-length ethnography took 40 or more hours to code.

This approach has many attractions, not the least of which is that it compensates for the fact that no single researcher can conduct investigations in such a varied set of organizations. Also, it means that more in-depth data can be used than is typically gathered by quantitative researchers. The method also allows hypotheses derived from established theories to be tested, such as the 'technological implications' approach, which sees technology as having an impact on the experience of work (Hodson 1996). However, the loss of a sense of social context is likely to be unattractive to many qualitative researchers.

Of particular significance is his remark that 'the fundamental contribution of the systematic analysis of documentary accounts is that it creates an analytic link between the in-depth accounts of professional observers and the statistical methods of quantitative researchers' (Hodson 1999: 68). In other words, the application of quantitative methods to qualitative research may provide a meeting ground for the two research strategies.

Quantification in qualitative research

As noted in Chapter 8, the numbers versus words contrast is perhaps the most basic difference between quantitative and qualitative research. However, as mentioned above, in most instances there is quantification in qualitative research. Quite aside from the issue of combining quantitative and qualitative research, three observations are worth making about quantification in the analysis and writing-up of qualitative data.

Thematic analysis

In Chapter 8, it was observed that a very common approach to qualitative data analysis is a search for themes in transcripts or field notes. The choice of themes, however, is often determined by how often certain incidents, words, phrases, and so on that denote a theme recur. This process may also account for the prominence given to some themes over others. In other words, a kind of implicit quantification probably influences both the identification of themes and the elevation of some over others.

Quasi-quantification in qualitative research

As noted, qualitative researchers engage in 'quasi-quantification' through the use of terms such as 'many,' 'frequently,' 'rarely,' and 'some,' which by definition are based on the relative frequency of the phenomenon of interest. However, as expressions of quantities, they are imprecise, and it is often difficult to discern why they are being used at all. A limited use of actual numbers, when appropriate, can support the point better.

Combating anecdotalism through limited quantification

One of the criticisms often levelled against qualitative research is the anecdotal nature of the evidence provided, which gives the reader little guidance as to their generalizability. The widespread use of brief sequences of conversation, snippets from interview transcripts, and accounts of encounters between people provides little sense of the prevalence of what such items of evidence are supposed to indicate. There is also the related risk that a particularly striking statement or an unexpected activity may be given more significance by the researcher than is warranted.

At least partly in response to these problems, qualitative researchers sometimes undertake a limited amount of quantification of their data. Gabriel's (1998) research collected 377 stories about organizational culture in the course of 126 interviews in five organizations. He identified different types of stories and noted the frequency of each type. For instance, there were: 108 comic stories (which were usually a mechanism for the disparagement of others); 82 epic stories (survival against the odds); 53 tragic stories (undeserved misfortune); and 40 gripes (personal injustices). The stories could have been presented as anecdotes, but the use of such simple counting conveyed a clearer sense of their relative prevalence.

This sort of approach can counter the criticism that qualitative data are too anecdotal and that they do not provide readers with a sense of the *extent* to which certain beliefs or behaviours occur. Their greater precision is also superior to the estimates of frequency that must be inferred from quasi-quantification terms like 'some' or 'many.' Moreover, there may be greater use of quantification in qualitative research in the future as a result of the growing use of software programs for qualitative data analysis. Most of the major software programs allow the analyst to produce simple counts for such things as the use of a particular word or the incidence of a coded theme. In many cases, they can also produce simple cross-tabulations—for example, showing whether men or women more often use the passive voice.

Key Points

- It is important not to exaggerate the differences between quantitative and qualitative research.

- Connections between epistemology and ontology on the one hand, and research methods on the other, are not fixed or absolute.

- Qualitative research can exhibit features normally associated with a natural science model.

- Quantitative research can incorporate an interpretivist stance.

- The artificial/natural contrast used to distinguish quantitative and qualitative research is often exaggerated.

- A quantitative research approach can be used to analyze qualitative data, and qualitative research methods can be used to analyze the rhetoric of quantitative researchers.

- Some qualitative researchers employ quantification in their work.

Questions for Review

The natural science model and qualitative research

- How can some qualitative research use a natural science model?

Quantitative research and interpretivism

- How can some quantitative research exhibit characteristics of interpretivism?

Quantitative research and constructionism

- How can some quantitative research be constructivist?

Research methods and epistemological and ontological considerations

- How closely tied are research methods with epistemological and ontological positions?

Problems with the quantitative/qualitative contrast

- Outline some of the ways in which the quantitative/qualitative contrast is not as hard-and-fast as often supposed.

The mutual analysis of quantitative and qualitative research

- What are some implications of Gilbert and Mulkay's (1984) research (on how scientists write up their findings) for the qualitative analysis of quantitative research?

- Assess the significance of ethnostatistics.

- Assess the significance of Hodson's (1996, 1999) research on workplace ethnographies.

Quantification in qualitative research

- To what extent is quantification a feature of qualitative research? Should there be more quantification in qualitative studies?

15 Combining Quantitative and Qualitative Research

Chapter overview

This chapter is about research that combines quantitative and qualitative approaches to inquiry. While using both in the same study may seem like a logical thing to do, there are sometimes practical difficulties, and it is not without controversy. This chapter explores:

- arguments against the combination of quantitative and qualitative research;

- two versions of the debate on combining quantitative and qualitative research, one concentrating on methods of research and the other on epistemological issues;
- different ways in which multi-strategy research has been carried out; and
- the claim that multi-strategy research is not inherently superior to research employing just a single research strategy.

Introduction

So far this book has emphasized the strengths and weaknesses of methods associated with quantitative and qualitative research. One possible response to this is to combine the two to allow their various strengths to be capitalized on and their weaknesses compensated for. Indeed, the amount of combined research has been increasing since the early 1980s. However, not all research methodologists would agree that such integration is either desirable or feasible. In discussing the combination of quantitative and qualitative research, this chapter looks at three main issues:

- the arguments against integrating quantitative and qualitative research;
- the different ways in which quantitative and qualitative research have been combined; and
- whether a combined research strategy is necessarily superior to investigations relying on just one strategy.

This chapter uses the term *multi-strategy research* for work that integrates quantitative and qualitative approaches. It should not be confused with the

use of several quantitative methods within a single study, or the integration of more than one qualitative method. For example, there is research that combines structured interviewing with structured observation, and some that combines ethnography with semi-structured interviewing. In the current discussion, multi-strategy research refers only to studies that combine qualitative and quantitative research in the same project.

The argument against multi-strategy research

The argument against multi-strategy research tends to be based on the following assumptions:

- that particular research methods are associated with certain epistemological and ontological positions; and
- that quantitative and qualitative research are inherently incompatible on epistemological and ontological grounds.

These two positions are briefly reviewed below.

The embedded methods argument

This first position, outlined in Chapter 14, implies that research methods are permanently rooted in epistemological and ontological commitments. This point is illustrated in statements such as the following:

> every research tool or procedure is inextricably embedded in commitments to particular versions of . . . knowing th[e] world. To use a questionnaire . . . to take the role of participant observer, to select a random sample . . . and so on, is to be involved in conceptions of the world which allow [the use] of these instruments (Hughes 1990: 11).

According to this view, a decision to employ, for example, participant observation is not simply a choice about data collection but a commitment to an epistemological position that is consistent with interpretivism and incompatible with positivism or a natural science model in general.

This view has led some writers to argue that multi-strategy research is not feasible. An ethnographer may collect questionnaire data about a slice of social life not amenable to participant observation, but this does not represent an integration of quantitative and qualitative research because the epistemological positions of the two methods are irreconcilable. The chief difficulty with this kind of argument is that, as noted in Chapter 14, the idea of research methods carrying with them fixed epistemological and ontological implications is very difficult to sustain.

The paradigm argument

The paradigm argument is closely related to the previous one. It conceives of quantitative and qualitative research as *paradigms*. A paradigm is a set of beliefs and assumptions about how the world works and how knowledge of it is to be gained. Kuhn (1970) popularized the term in his portrayal of natural science as going through periods of revolution, whereby 'normal' science (science carried out in terms of the prevailing paradigm) is increasingly challenged by new findings inconsistent with the assumptions and established findings in the discipline. The increasing frequency of such anomalies eventually gives way to a crisis, which in turn occasions a revolution. The period of revolution is resolved when a new paradigm gains acceptance and a period of the new 'normal' science sets in. An important feature of paradigms is that they are incommensurable, that is, inconsistent with each other because of their divergent assumptions and methods. Disciplines in which no paradigm has emerged as pre-eminent, such as sociology and other social sciences, are deemed 'pre-paradigmatic.'

The paradigm argument maintains that quantitative and qualitative research are based on paradigms in which epistemological assumptions, values, and methods are inextricably intertwined and which are incompatible with each other (Morgan 1998*b*). Therefore, when researchers combine participant observation with a questionnaire, they are not really combining quantitative and qualitative research, since the paradigms are incompatible: the integration is only at a superficial level and within a single paradigm.

The problem with the paradigm argument is that it rests, as does the embedded methods claim, on an interconnection of method and epistemology that has not been demonstrated. Moreover, while Kuhn (1970) certainly argued that paradigms are incommensurable, it is by no means clear that quantitative research and qualitative research are in fact separate paradigms. As suggested in Chapter 14, there are areas of overlap and commonality between them.

Two positions in the debate about quantitative and qualitative research

There are two opposing arguments regarding the issue of whether quantitative and qualitative research can be combined.

- An *epistemological argument*, as in the embedded methods and paradigm positions discussed above, which sees quantitative and qualitative research as grounded in incompatible epistemological principles (and ontological ones too, but these tend to be given less attention). According to this version, multi-strategy research is not possible in principle.
- A *technical argument*, in which research methods are perceived as being independent of any specific

epistemological position. According to this view, a research method from one research strategy can be pressed into the service of another—quantitative and qualitative methods can be fused. This is the position taken by most researchers whose work is mentioned in the next section.

The technical argument views the two research strategies as compatible, and multi-strategy research as both feasible and desirable. It is in that spirit that the chapter now turns to a discussion of the ways in which quantitative and qualitative research can be combined.

Approaches to multi-strategy research

Hammersley (1996) proposed three approaches to multi-strategy research:

- *Triangulation*—the use of quantitative research to corroborate qualitative research findings or vice versa.
- *Facilitation*—the use of one research strategy to aid research using another.
- *Complementarity*—the use of two different research strategies so that diverse aspects of an investigation can be combined.

The logic of triangulation

Triangulation entails using more than one method in the study of social phenomena. The term has been employed somewhat more broadly by Denzin (1970: 310) to refer to an approach that uses 'multiple observers, theoretical perspectives, sources of data, and methodologies,' but the emphasis has tended to be on methods of investigation and sources of data. One of the reasons for the advocacy by Webb *et al.* (1966) of greater use of unobtrusive methods is their potential for triangulation (see Box 6.5). Triangulation can operate within and across research strategies. It was originally conceptualized by Webb *et al.* (1966) as a way of developing additional measures, resulting in greater confidence in findings, and was very much associated with a quantitative research strategy. However, triangulation can also take place within qualitative research. In fact, ethnographers often check their observations with interview questions to look for possible misunderstandings. Bloor

(1997) reported that he tackled the process of death certification in two ways: interviews with clinicians responsible for certifying causes of deaths, and asking the same people to complete dummy death certificates based on case summaries he had prepared. Increasingly, triangulation refers to a process of cross-checking findings deriving from both quantitative and qualitative research (Deacon *et al.* 1998).

An illustration of a triangulation approach is Hughes *et al.*'s (1997) study of the consumption of 'designer drinks' (fortified wines and strong white ciders) by young people. The authors used two main research methods:

- a qualitative method: eight focus groups with 56 children and young adults. Each discussion lasted around two hours.
- a quantitative method: a survey administered in two parts to a multi-stage cluster sample of 824 12–17-year-olds. The first part was an interview, and the second was a questionnaire (to elicit more sensitive information).

The results achieved with the two research strategies were mutually reinforcing. The qualitative findings showed age differences in attitudes towards designer drinks and other forms of alcoholic drink: the youngest people (12–13-year-olds) tended to adopt a generally experimental approach; the 14- and 15-year-olds thought of drinking as a means of having fun and losing inhibitions, and felt that designer drinks met their needs well; the oldest group (16- and 17-year-olds) were mainly concerned with appearing mature and establishing relationships with the other sex, and tended to think of designer drinks as targeted at immature, younger drinkers. These connections with age were confirmed by the quantitative evidence, which also corroborated the suggestion from the qualitative evidence that consuming designer drinks was largely associated with a desire to get drunk.

In this research, two features are worth noting: the use of a triangulation strategy seems to have been planned by the researchers, and the two sets of results are broadly consistent. However, researchers may use different research strategies for different purposes, but in the course of doing so discover that they have generated quantitative and qualitative findings on related issues, and that they can treat such overlapping findings as a triangulation exercise.

Whether planned or unplanned, when a triangulation exercise is undertaken, the possibility of a failure to corroborate findings always exists. This raises the issue of how to deal with inconsistent results. Arbitrarily favouring one set of findings over another is not an ideal approach to reconciling conflicting findings deriving from a triangulation exercise. Usually, further research is required to resolve the matter.

Deacon and colleagues (1998) gathered data through several quantitative and qualitative research methods but had not intended a triangulation exercise. The analysis of their data revealed an inconsistency: the quantitative data suggested a broad consensus between journalists and social scientists on the reporting of social scientific research in the media, but the qualitative findings suggested a greater collision of approaches and values between them. Rather than opt for one set of findings over the other the data were re-examined, revealing that a major component of the discrepancy is the tendency for social scientists, when answering survey questions about coverage of their research, to reply with relief that it is not as bad as expected. However, in interviews, social scientists tend to make much more of what Deacon *et al.* called 'war stories'—that is, memorable and often highly wounding encounters with the media. Thus, in general, the questionnaires revealed that social scientists are relatively pleased with the reporting of their research, but, when encouraged to reflect on specific problems in the past, their replies were more negative.

Another example of triangulation can be found in Fenton *et al.*'s (1998) study of the same topic. It employed both quantitative and qualitative methods:

1. content analysis of news and current affairs coverage (local and national newspapers, TV, and radio);
2. mailed questionnaires covering 674 social scientists' views about media coverage and their own practices;
3. mailed questionnaires from 123 social scientists who, as identified in the content analysis, received media coverage;
4. semi-structured interviews with 20 social scientists who, as identified in the content analysis, received coverage;
5. semi-structured interviews with 34 journalists identified in the content analysis;
6. semi-structured interviews with 27 representatives of funding bodies and government;
7. tracking of journalists at three conferences; and
8. focus group analysis of audience reception of media items (13 focus groups).

Qualitative research facilitates quantitative research

There are several ways qualitative research can guide quantitative research:

- *Providing hypotheses.* Because of its tendency toward an unstructured, open-ended approach to data collection, qualitative research is often a source of hypotheses that can be tested using a quantitative strategy. An example is Phelan's (1987) research in which she conducted qualitative interviews and conversations with family members attending a treatment program for incest. After a considerable amount of qualitative data had been collected, she became aware of differences in the meaning of incest for biological fathers compared with stepfathers. Quantifiable data were collected through interviews with family counsellors that supported her hypothesis that 'the process of incest in structurally different families may vary' (Phelan 1987: 39). Similarly, Bell's (2007) study of western-Canadian separatism started out as a qualitative investigation involving attendance at separatist events and hanging out with separatists. A hypothesis emerged from the data gathered that support for separatism was associated with a neo-liberal ideology and a partisan dislike for the ruling federal Liberal Party, a view that was later substantiated in a multiple regression analysis using survey data.
- *Aiding measurement.* The in-depth knowledge of social contexts acquired through qualitative research can be used to inform the design of survey questions for structured interviewing and self-completion questionnaires. Johnson and colleagues (2003) used data from unstructured interviews to develop highly structured questions for later interviews with adolescent smokers. Walklate (2000) explained that for her research on fear of crime and safety issues in high-crime areas, a survey using traditional questions about victimization was used. However, the questions were

amended to reflect the local context following six months of interviews, ethnography, and examination of local newspapers. Similarly, the survey questions used in Bell's (2007) analysis of western-Canadian separatism were generated in part from his experiences in gathering qualitative data.

Quantitative research facilitates qualitative research

One way in which quantitative research can prepare the ground for qualitative work is through the selection of people to be interviewed. This can occur in several ways. In the case of Fenton *et al.*'s (1998) research on the reporting of social science research in the mass media, discussed above, a media content analysis (method 1) was used as a source of data. However, it also served as a means of identifying journalists who had reported relevant research (method 5). In addition, replies to questions in the general survey of social scientists (method 2) were used to help identify two groups of social scientists, those with high and those with low levels of media coverage of their research, who were then interviewed with a semi-structured approach (method 4). Similarly, Jamieson (2000) administered a questionnaire to a sample of young men on their criminal activity. On the basis of their replies, qualitative interviews were conducted with equal numbers of young men in each of three categories: those who did not offend; those who had offended but not recently; and persistent offenders.

Filling in the gaps

This approach to multi-strategy research occurs when the researcher cannot rely on either a quantitative or a qualitative method alone. For example, ethnographers may employ structured interviewing or possibly a self-completion questionnaire, because not everything they need to know is accessible through direct observation, or because of the difficulty of gaining access to certain groups of people.

Morgan's (1998*b*) approach to multi-strategy research is based on two criteria:

- The priority decision. Is a qualitative or quantitative method the principal data-gathering tool?
- The sequence decision. Which method is used first?

Figure 15.1 Morgan's classification of approaches to multi-strategy research

These criteria yield four possible types (see Figure 15.1).

One difficulty with Morgan's scheme is that it may be difficult to know whether quantitative or qualitative research had priority, and which one came first in the sequence. Sometimes research uses both strategies and several methods, but no single one is dominant.

Static and process features

One of the contrasts suggested by Table 8.1 is that quantitative research tends to bring out a static picture of social life and qualitative research shows more about process. While the term 'static' is often viewed in a negative light, in fact it uncovers the regularities that allow the analysis of process. A multi-strategy research approach offers the prospect of being able to combine both. An illustration is provided by MacKinnon and Luke's (2002) study of cultural change from 1981 to 1995. Their main method of data collection was survey research, but to complete the picture they also examined census and public opinion data, as well as newspaper articles on historical events. They found reduced homophobia and anti-Semitism but also reduced sympathy for First Nations over that time period. They cautioned that their small sample (70) and what were essentially 'good guesses' meant that their conclusions, 'like the interpretations of an ethnographer . . . are subject to alternative interpretations by others' (2002: 332).

Researcher and participant perspectives

Sometimes, researchers want to gather two kinds of data: qualitative data that show the general perspectives of their subjects, and quantitative data for exploring specific issues. For example, Milkman (1997) was interested in the meaning of industrial work and in particular whether factory conditions had changed since the 1950s, when they were portrayed very negatively. She employed semi-structured interviews and focus groups with GM car-production workers to find out. She was also interested in a 'buyout' plan that the company's management introduced in the mid-1980s after it had initiated a variety of changes to work practices. The plan gave workers the opportunity to give up their jobs for a substantial cash payment. In 1988 and again in 1991, Milkman carried out a questionnaire survey of workers who had taken up the company's buyout offer. The surveys inquired about the reasons for taking the buyout, how those taking it had fared since leaving General Motors, how they felt about their current employment, and differences among social groups (in particular ethnic groups) in current earnings relative to those at General Motors.

The problem of generality

As noted in Chapter 14, one problem in qualitative research is the tendency for findings to be presented in an anecdotal fashion without sufficient evidence of how typical the findings are, and without showing how the group being researched compares with some larger population. Partly to counter this criticism, Tastsoglou and Miedema (2003) used quantitative national data on women's volunteering to compare their admittedly non-random sample of immigrant women with the Canadian population, and found that the immigrant women actually volunteered more than the national average.

Qualitative research may help to interpret the relationship between variables

One of the problems that frequently confront quantitative researchers is how to explain relationships between variables. One strategy is to look for what is called an intervening variable, one that is influenced by the independent variable but in turn has an effect on the dependent variable. For example, in a relationship between ethnicity and occupation, education may be an intervening variable:

ethnicity ➔ education ➔ occupation

This sequence implies that the variable ethnicity has an impact on education (for example, ethnic groups differ in their levels of education), which in turn has implications for the jobs that people in different ethnic groups attain. Qualitative work could be done examining how different ethnic groups perceive the issue of education, which could lead to a fuller understanding of education as an intervening variable. It could also provide leads that point to a different theoretical perspective on the general topic of ethnicity, education, and occupation.

Another illustration is provided by research on HIV-related risk behaviour among drug injectors. Data from structured interviews with 503 injectors revealed that 'females report significantly higher levels of needle sharing, sexual activity, and AIDS awareness than their male counterparts. Furthermore, women who are co-habiting with sexual partners who are themselves injectors, are particularly likely to report high levels of risk behaviour and also AIDS awareness' (Barnard and Frischer 1995: 357). What produces this relationship between gender, risk behaviour, and co-habitation? Semi-structured interviews with 73 injectors revealed that the relationship between these variables 'can be explained by the tendency for women to be in sexual relationships with men who themselves inject and with whom they are unlikely to use condoms' (1995: 360). Here qualitative data were used to shed light on relationships among variables derived from quantitative research.

Studying different aspects of a phenomenon

There is a tendency to think of quantitative research as most suited to the investigation of 'macro' phenomena (such as social mobility and social stratification) and qualitative research as more appropriate for 'micro' issues (such as interactions between wait staff and their customers). The macro/micro distinction can also be discerned in Table 8.1. In the example shown in Box 15.1, Wajcman and Martin (2002) used quantitative methods in the form of a questionnaire survey to explore career patterns of male and female managers. However, they also carried out qualitative, semi-structured interviews to explore how managers *made sense* of their career patterns in terms of their identity. The choice of methods was therefore determined by what the research question asked.

Another illustration of the use of multi-strategy research to study different aspects of a phenomenon are the family-obligations studies conducted by

Box 15.1   Combining survey research and qualitative interviewing in a study of managers

Wajcman and Martin (2002) conducted survey research using a questionnaire on male and female managers (470 in total) in six Australian companies and conducted semi-structured interviews with 136 managers in each company. The survey evidence showed that male and female managers are generally more similar than different in terms of career orientations and attitudes. Contrary to what many had anticipated, women's career experiences and orientations were *not* found to be distinctive. They then examined the qualitative interviews in terms of narratives of identity and found that both male and female managers depict their careers in 'market' terms (they respond to the requirements of the managerial labour market by developing their skills and experience). But whereas for men narratives of career mesh seamlessly with narratives of domestic life, for women there is a disjuncture. Female managers find it harder to reconcile managerial identities with domestic ones and more often have to opt for one or the other. In this way, choices about career and family are still gendered. This research shows how a multi-strategy approach can reveal much more than could have been gleaned through one method alone.

Finch (1985) and Mason (1994). This research was concerned with the distribution within families of the obligation to care for relatives. It comprised two main data collection elements: a survey of a sample of nearly 1000 people by structured interview, and semi-structured interviewing with 88 people. A major component of the survey interviewing was the use of the vignette technique described in Box 5.8. Mason described the purpose of integrating quantitative and qualitative research as follows:

> From the beginning . . . we were using the two parts of our study to ask different sets of questions about family obligations. Not only were we employing different methods to generate different types of data, but we also anticipated that these would tell us about different aspects of family obligations. . . . [O]ur view was that an understanding of kin obligations *in practice* would require an analysis of the relationship between the two data sets and the social processes they expressed (Mason 1994: 90–1).

What were the sets of research questions to which Mason referred? The survey was designed to provide information about the degree to which there is a consensus about '"the proper thing to do" for relatives in a variety of circumstances' (Mason 1994: 90). Through the semi-structured interviews, Finch and Mason tried 'to discover what people actually did in practice for their own relatives, and also the processes by which they came to do it and make sense of it: did a sense of obligation or responsibility have a role in the process? How did people in practice work out what to do for their kin, or ask of their kin?' (Mason 1994: 90).

In multi-strategy research, then, the different methods may be geared to addressing different kinds of research questions. The research on the reporting of social science research in the British mass media by Fenton *et al.* (1998), discussed earlier, is a further example of a project designed to use quantitative and qualitative research to answer different questions, for example:

- Questions about coverage, such as: How much coverage is there of social science research? What gets covered? Where? (method 1).
- Questions about the production of media items, such as: What kinds of attributes do journalists look for when thinking about whether to write an item on social science research? (methods 5 and 7).
- Questions about social scientists' attitudes to media reports of research in general (method 2) and to the reporting of their own research (methods 3 and 4). Method 4 was designed to allow the findings derived from method 3 to be elaborated and more fully understood.
- Questions about reception, such as: How do readers/viewers interpret media reporting of social science research? (method 8).
- Questions about the communication environment, such as: What are the policies of universities, government departments, and funding bodies concerning the media reporting of research? (method 6).

Box 15.2   Research methods used in a study of gender and organization

Halford *et al.* (1997) conducted research on the role and significance of gender in organizational contexts in two contrasting British labour markets, an economically buoyant new town experiencing problems of recruitment, and a larger metropolitan area suffering from manufacturing decline and high unemployment. They examined contrasting organizations in each of these areas: local government organizations, a bank, and a hospital. In other words, their design was comparative in terms of both area (contracting and expanding economically) and type of organization.

Three sources of data were employed. First, key informants supplied overall views on gender and career-related issues in all of the organizations and provided documentary materials. Second, a mailed questionnaire surveyed nearly 1000 employees, with a response rate of around 50 per cent. The questionnaire 'was designed to provide broad descriptive information about employees, careers, and [employees'] attitudes to their organization and to opportunities for women in particular' (Halford *et al.* 1997: 56). This material was used 'to describe broad patterns of response across a range of areas, such as occupational mobility, for different subgroups of the sample . . . or attitudes to the organization.' Third, between 25 and 35 employees in each of the three sectors were interviewed using a semi-structured interview as 'a filter for choosing people to interview in-depth' (1997: 56). The researchers said that they 'frequently found the information provided by in-depth interviews more revealing' (1997: 59).

This form of multi-strategy research entails making decisions about which kinds of research question are best answered using a quantitative method and which by a qualitative method. (Box 15.2 provides another example.) It is also concerned with how best to interweave the different elements, especially since, as suggested in the context of the discussion about triangulation, the outcomes of mixing methods are not always predictable.

Solving a puzzle

The outcomes of research are, as suggested, not easy to anticipate. Although people sometimes cynically claim that social scientists find what they want to find, or that they just convey the obvious, the capacity of research to provide puzzling surprises should never be underestimated. When this occurs, employing a research method associated with a strategy not initially used can be helpful. One context in which this may occur is when qualitative research is used as a salvage operation if an anticipated set of results from a quantitative investigation fails to materialize (Weinholtz *et al.* 1995). The study discussed in Box 15.1 provides an illustration of this.

Like unplanned triangulation, this category of multi-strategy research is more or less impossible to plan in advance. It essentially provides the quantitative researcher with an alternative to reconstructing the hypothesis (see Ethical issue 15.1) or filing the results away (and probably never looking at them again) when the findings are inconsistent with the hypotheses.

Reflections on multi-strategy research

There can be little doubt that multi-strategy research is becoming more frequent. Two particularly significant factors in this development are:

- a growing preparedness to view research methods as techniques of data collection unencumbered by epistemological and ontological baggage; and
- a softening in the attitude towards quantitative research among feminist researchers, who previously had been highly resistant to its use (see Chapter 8 for a discussion of this point).

Other factors are relevant, but these two are especially important. An example of their operation can be found in research on audience reception of media and cultural texts, which is studied mainly using qualitative research methods (in particular, focus groups). Some researchers in this area have called for a rethinking of the field's attitude to quantitative research. Lingering unease among some qualitative researchers in this area, particularly regarding the reliability and generalizability of findings, has led to calls for researchers to consider the use of quantitative research in tandem with qualitative methods (for example, Schrøder 1999).

However, multi-strategy research is not necessarily superior to one-method or one-strategy research. Four points must be borne in mind in this regard:

- Multi-strategy research must be competently designed and conducted. Poorly conducted research yields suspect findings, no matter how many methods are employed.
- Multi-strategy research must be appropriate for the research questions asked. There is no point in collecting additional kinds of data on the assumption that 'more is better.'
- Multiple methods are likely to take considerably more time and financial resources than research relying on just one approach, and can even dilute the research effort in the various areas if resources are thinly spread.
- Not all researchers have the skills and training to carry out both quantitative and qualitative research, and their 'trained incapacities' may act as a barrier to integrating the different forms of research.

Multi-strategy research is not a panacea. It may provide a better understanding of a phenomenon than if just one method is used. It may enhance confidence in the findings, and it may even improve the chances of access to research settings. Milkman (1997: 192), for example, suggested in her research on a General Motors factory that her promise of 'hard,' quantitative data facilitated her entry to the plant even though she had no experience with this method. But the general point remains: multi-strategy research, while offering great potential in many instances, is subject to constraints similar to those in research relying on a single strategy.

Ethical issue 15.1

Revising the hypothesis to fit the data in positivist research

Assume that your reading of the literature leads you to the hypothesis that boys who are victims of sexual assault are less likely to report it than are victimized girls. But suppose the analysis of your data reveals the counterintuitive opposite. What do you do? One unethical path would be to pretend that you always expected the boys to report it more, perhaps due to recent publicity on sexual abuse in private schools and churches. The review of the literature can then be rewritten to reflect this expectation. Another unethical option would be to pretend the study was an inductive one in which the hypothesis was developed after the data were gathered.

An ethical solution would be to leave the literature and hypothesis intact and then in the discussion explain why you think the hypothesis was not supported. The hypothesis could then be revised, for example, to maintain that in 'normal' times of little publicity on child sexual assault, the usual pattern of girls reporting more than boys should reappear. You would then outline how the new hypothesis could be tested with further research.

— Key Points

- While there has been growth in the amount of multi-strategy research, not all writers support its use.
- The view that there are epistemological and ontological impediments to the combination of quantitative and qualitative research is a barrier to multi-strategy research.
- There are several different ways of combining quantitative and qualitative research; some can be planned in advance, others cannot.

Questions for Review

- What is multi-strategy research?

The argument against multi-strategy research

- What are the strengths and weaknesses of the embedded methods and paradigm arguments against multi-strategy research?

Opposing arguments about combining quantitative and qualitative research

- What are the epistemological and technical arguments regarding the prospect of combining quantitative and qualitative research? What are their implications for multi-strategy research?

Approaches to multi-strategy research

- What are the chief ways in which quantitative and qualitative research have been combined?

- What is the logic of triangulation?

- Traditionally, qualitative research is depicted as having a preparatory role in relation to quantitative research. To what extent do the different forms of multi-strategy research reflect this view?

Reflections on multi-strategy research

- Why has multi-strategy research become more prominent?

- Is multi-strategy research necessarily superior to single-strategy research?

16 Content Analysis

Chapter overview

Content analysis involves the examination of various documents and texts, which may be printed, visual, aural, or virtual. It can be quantitative, coding data into predetermined categories in a systematic and easily replicable manner, or qualitative, seeking to uncover deeper meanings in the materials. This chapter considers:

- the kinds of research question content analysis can answer;
- the features of the documents or texts that are commonly analyzed;
- how to code, a key part of content analysis;
- semiotics and hermeneutics;
- active and passive audiences;
- conversation analysis, and its roots in ethno-methodology;
- the assumptions and analytic strategies of discourse analysis;
- the advantages and disadvantages of content analysis.

Introduction

Suppose you are interested in how newspapers cover crime. You come up with the following questions:

- Do certain newspapers report more crimes than others?
- How much crime is reported? Where in the paper do crime stories appear—front page, inside pages?
- Do columnists as well as reporters write about crime?
- Are some crimes given more attention, perhaps in more detail or accompanied by pictures?
- Do more crime stories appear during the week or on weekends?
- What sorts of crime predominates in newspaper articles: crimes against the person; property crime; crimes in which society is the victim?

Most content analysis of the media is likely to entail several research questions, generally revolving around: *who* (does the reporting); *what* (gets reported); *where* (does the issue get reported); *why* (does the issue get reported); and *when* (it gets reported)—the same five *W*'s of any news report. But researchers are also interested in omissions in coverage. For example, interviews with the family of the accused are rare; such inattention is itself notable, revealing what is and is not important to writers and publishers.

Another issue frequently encountered in content analysis is the change in the coverage of an issue over time. For example, Miller and Reilly (1995) studied newspaper coverage of a 'food scare' about salmonella in eggs, and found a massive amount of newspaper coverage for about 20 days following government statements about a particularly controversial incident. In the subsequent 12 months, however, the amount of coverage was sharply lower and it petered out further over the next 4 years, in spite of public health evidence that the incidence of salmonella poisoning was increasing. Apparently what was lacking was another 'headlining' incident.

Such content analyses yield a quantitative description of the characteristics of a communication. Those using content analysis claim to be objective and systematic, which means that rules for the assignment of the raw material to categories are clearly specified in advance. Researchers try to create transparency in the coding procedures so that personal biases intrude as little as possible. The coding rules in question may, of course, reflect the researcher's interests and concerns and therefore be a product of subjective bias, but once formulated, the rules can be (or should be capable of being) applied without bias.

Content analysis can be applied to unstructured information, such as transcripts of semi- and unstructured interviews, and even qualitative case studies of organizations (for example, Hodson 1996). Although until recently content analysis has been used mainly to examine printed texts and documents, other sorts of materials may also be analyzed, for example:

- visual images in women's and men's magazines, to look at how messages about bodily appearance are gendered (Malkin *et al.* 1999);
- websites;
- gender roles in animated cartoons (Thompson and Zerbinos 1995); and
- lyrics of popular songs, to look for changes in the representation of women (Marcic 2002).

What things are to be counted?

Obviously, decisions about what should be counted in a content analysis are determined by specific research questions. In quantitative studies of this kind, what is to be counted is usually specified in advance to guide both the selection of the media to be analyzed and the coding schedule to be used. The following are frequently a focus of attention.

Words

Counting the frequency of certain words is often the first step in content analysis. Jagger's (1998) study of dating advertisements (see Box 16.1), for example, counted the words 'slim' and 'non-smoker' to uncover the characteristics deemed desirable in a date. This enumeration can reveal emphasis, style, and even the overplaying of certain events. For example, Dunning *et al.* (1988) noted a tendency for the British press to sensationalize disturbances at soccer matches. The use of such emotive words as 'hooligan' and 'lout,' along with inferences about 'war,' are examples; less dramatic terms like 'fan' and 'hard-fought contest' would have encouraged different emotions among readers.

A variation on the search for the occurrence of certain words is the examination of the pairing of keywords. The growing availability of the written news media in electronic form, such as on websites

---

Box 16.1 Finding love

Jagger (1998) reported a content analysis of 1094 dating advertisements in four newspapers with a general readership. The sample was chosen over two four-week periods. Three research questions drove the study:

- What is 'the relative significance of monetary resources and lifestyle choices as identity markers and desirable attributes for men and women'?

- How do men and women vary in how they market themselves and describe their preferred (or ideal) partners in terms of the body?

- How much are 'traditional stereotypes of masculinity and femininity . . . still in operation' (1998: 799)?

Jagger noted the tendency for a considerable percentage of both men and women to market themselves in terms of their lifestyle choices. She also found that women are far more likely than men to stress the importance of economic and other resources in a preferred partner. There is also a somewhat greater propensity for women to market themselves in terms of physical appearance. As an aside, men are just as likely to market themselves as 'slim,' suggesting certain preferences in body shape are not exclusive to one gender. More generally, her results pointed to the significance of the body in identity construction in modern society for both men and women. In a later publication, Jagger (2001) reported the findings from a qualitative content analysis of a sub-sample of the 1094 advertisements.

and CD-ROM, greatly facilitates this search. Hier (2002) found 'rave' and 'drug use' linked, giving an appearance of a greater urgency to control raves. Parnaby (2003), on the other hand, noted how 'squeegee kids' and 'homelessness' were not paired, thus encouraging a simple solution to a complex problem. The examination of such accompanying keywords can be a starting point for a more in-depth analysis.

Subjects and themes

Frequently in a content analysis the researcher wants to code text in terms of certain subjects and themes, thus requiring a more interpretative approach. At this point, the analyst is searching not just for the obvious or *manifest* content, but also for some of the underlying or *latent* content as well. This occurs if the researcher wants to probe beneath the surface to ask deeper questions about what is happening. In the reports on crime, for example, who is blamed for the incident—the accused, as expected, or is the victim also blamed? Is the occupation of the accused or the victim stated? If not, is it implied in other material, like the address or the picture? Why in reports of a man being mugged do you think that his marital status is sometimes included? In seeking to answer these sorts of questions, what began as a quantitative content analysis may develop into a qualitative study.

Value positions

A further level of interpretation is likely when the researcher seeks to demonstrate that a certain value position has been taken in the texts being analyzed. For example, the researcher may want to establish whether journalists who write about crime are sympathetic or hostile to the criminal. Is there something to show that the blame is on the accused, with the implication that punishment is the solution? Or is the focus on social conditions and thus less blame

placed on the criminal? If there are no manifest indications of such value positions, can inferences be made from the latent content?

Another way in which value positions are revealed in content analysis is through the coding of ideologies, beliefs, and principles. Jagger (1998) coded dating advertisements in terms of whether stereotypical categories of masculinity and femininity are employed when advertisers describe themselves (see Box 16.1). She found that women are more likely than men to advertise themselves in terms of their physical appearance, whereas men are more likely to advertise themselves in terms of their employment. It seems that each knows its audience.

Coding

As the foregoing has implied, coding is a crucial part of content analysis. There are two main elements to a content analysis coding scheme: designing a coding schedule and creating a coding manual. To illustrate, imagine a student is interested in crime reports in a local newspaper. To simplify, assume the study is limited to crimes where the victim is a person rather than an organization, and that it considers just these variables:

1. nature of the offence;
2. gender of perpetrator;
3. occupation of perpetrator;
4. age of perpetrator;
5. gender of victim;
6. occupation of victim;
7. age of victim;
8. victim precipitation; and
9. position of news item in the paper.

Content analysts are normally interested in a much larger number of variables than this, but this simple illustration can help to get across how a coding schedule and coding manual operate.

Case number	Day	Month	Nature of offence I	Gender of perpetrator	Occupation of perpetrator	Age of perpetrator	Gender of victim	Occupation of victim	Age of victim	Depiction of victim	Nature of offence II

Figure 16.1 Coding schedule

Nature of offence I

01. Violence against the person
02. Sexual offences
03. Robbery
04. Burglary in a dwelling
05. Burglary other than in a dwelling
06. Theft from a person
07. Theft of bicycle
08. Theft from shops
09. Theft from vehicle
10. Theft of motor vehicle
11. Other theft and handling stolen goods
12. Fraud and forgery
13. Drug offences
14. Other offences

Gender of perpetrator

1. Male
2. Female
3. Unknown

Occupation of perpetrator

01. Professionals, administrators, officials and managers in large establishments; large proprietors
02. Lower-grade professionals, administrators, and officials; higher-grade technicians; managers in small business and industrial establishments; supervisors of non-manual employees
03. Routine non-manual employees in administration and commerce
04. Personal service workers
05. Small proprietors, artisans, etc., with employees
06. Small proprietors, artisans, etc., without employees
07. Farmers and smallholders; self-employed fishermen
08. Lower-grade technicians, supervisors of manual workers
09. Skilled manual workers
10. Semi-skilled and unskilled manual workers (not in agriculture)

11. Agricultural workers
12. Other
13. Unemployed
14. Homemaker
15. Student
16. Retired
17. Unknown

Age of perpetrator

Record age (−1 if unknown)

Gender of victim

1. Male
2. Female
3. Unknown

Occupation of victim

Same as for occupation of perpetrator
If not applicable, code as 99

Age of victim

Record age (−1 if unknown)

Depiction of victim

1. Victim responsible for crime
2. Victim partly responsible for crime
3. Victim not at all responsible for crime
4. Not applicable

Nature of offence II (code if second offence mentioned in relation to the same incident; code 0 if no second offence)
Same as for Nature of offence I

Position of news item

1. Front page
2. Inside
3. Back page

Figure 16.2 Coding manual

Coding schedule

The coding schedule is a form onto which the data are entered (see Figure 16.1). The schedule shown has been simplified to facilitate the discussion. Each of the columns in Figure 16.1 is a dimension (indicated by the column heading) to be coded. The blank cells on the coding form are the places in which codes are to be written. One row is used for each media item coded. The codes can then be transferred to a computer data file for analysis with a software package like SPSS.

Coding manual

On the face of it, the coding schedule in Figure 16.1 seems bare, providing little information about what is to be done or where. This is where the coding manual comes in. It is a set of instructions to coders that includes all possible categories for each dimension being coded. It provides: a list of all the dimensions; the different categories subsumed under each dimension; the numbers (that is, *codes*) that correspond to each category; and guidance to coders on what should be taken into account in coding a

Case number	Day	Month	Nature of offence I	Gender of perpetrator	Occupation of perpetrator	Age of perpetrator	Gender of victim	Occupation of victim	Age of victim	Depiction of victim	Nature of offence II	Position of news item
001	24	11	01	1	10	26	1	16	68	2	00	2

Figure 16.3 Completed coding schedule

Case number	Day	Month	Nature of offence I	Gender of perpetrator	Occupation of perpetrator	Age of perpetrator	Gender of victim	Occupation of victim	Age of victim	Depiction of victim	Nature of offence II	Position of news item
002	25	12	06	1	13	34	2	16	86	3	01	2

Figure 16.4 Completed coding schedule with errors

particular dimension. Figure 16.2 provides a coding manual that corresponds with the coding schedule in Figure 16.1.

Our coding manual includes the occupation of both the perpetrator and the victim of the crime, using a simple social-class scheme. The offences are categorized in the manner used by the police in recording crimes. Their statistics have been criticized for reliability and validity (recall Chapter 7), so a comparison between police data and the reporting of crime in local newspapers is a possible research topic. Finer distinctions can be used, but since the student may not be planning to examine a large sample of news items, broader categories are preferable. Note also that the coding schedule and manual permit two offences to be recorded for any incident. If there are more than two, the student has to make a judgment concerning the two most significant offences.

The coding manual is crucial because it provides a complete listing of all categories for each dimension being coded, and guidance about how to interpret the dimensions. It is on the basis of these lists that a coding schedule of the kind presented in Figure 16.1 is made. Detailed rules about how to code should be formulated, because both inter-coder and intra-coder reliability is always a concern (see below).

Here is a news report of a fictional road rage incident. Two male motorists, one a retired school-teacher aged 68, the other a 26-year-old assembly-line worker, got into an argument and the worker punched the retired man, causing him to fall, hit his head, and suffer a concussion. There was no second offence. The coding of the incident would

then appear as in Figure 16.3 and the data would be entered into a computer program such as SPSS.

Suppose a second article, appearing the next day, described how an unemployed 34-year-old female took an 86-year-old woman's purse, and then knocked her down. The code is provided in Figure 16.4 but with a few errors. Can you spot them? Forms like these would be completed for each news item within the chosen period(s) of study.

Potential pitfalls in devising coding schemes

The potential dangers in devising a content analysis coding scheme are similar to those involved in designing structured interview and observation schedules. Points to recall include:

- *Mutually exclusive categories.* There should be no overlap in the categories supplied for each dimension. If the categories are not mutually exclusive, coders will not know how to code an item that fits into more than one category.
- *Exhaustive.* Every possible dimension should have a category.
- *Clear instructions.* Coders should be clear about what factors to take into account when assigning codes. Sometimes these have to be very elaborate. In quantitative content analysis, coders generally have little or no discretion in how to code the units of analysis.
- *A clear unit of analysis.* For example, in the imaginary study of the reporting of crime in the local press, there is both the media item (for example,

one newspaper article) and the topic being coded (one of two offences). In practice, a researcher is interested in both but needs to keep the distinction in mind.

To enhance the quality of a coding scheme, it is advisable to conduct a pilot study to identify difficulties in applying it, such as having no code to cover a particular case (not exhaustive). Pilot tests also help to reveal if one category of a dimension includes an extremely large percentage of items. When this occurs, it may be necessary to break that category down to allow for greater specificity.

As mentioned, the reliability of coding is a further concern. An important part of pre-testing the coding scheme is examining consistency between coders (*inter-coder reliability*) and, if time permits, intra-coder reliability. The process of gauging reliability is more or less identical to how it is done in structured observation, discussed in Chapter 6.

Qualitative content analysis

Qualitative content analysis comprises a search for underlying themes in the materials analyzed and was used in several of the studies referred to earlier, such as Beharrell's study of the reporting of AIDS in the press (1993), and the Giulianotti (1997) study of soccer hooligans. Kennedy (2006), in his study of the Canadian fathers' rights movement 'Fathers For Justice,' used content analysis in conjunction with participant observation and semi-structured interviews to examine how the movement developed a collective identity. The content analysis was conducted on newsletters, position papers submitted to government agencies, pamphlets, minutes from meetings, and other documents, and was used mainly to make sense of the data gathered through participant observation and interviews. Similarly, Bell (2007) used pamphlets, speeches, newsletters, and other texts to arrive at an overall assessment of western-Canadian separatism as a neo-liberal movement. The processes through which the themes are extracted in a content analysis are often left implicit, although they are usually illustrated with quotations from the text being analyzed.

Lynch and Bogen (1997) examined core sociological textbooks to show that they contained recurring themes that present an upbeat and scientific view of the discipline, one that is, in the researchers' view, biased and value-laden. Seale (2002: 109) examined newspaper reports about people with cancer. One of the phases of his analysis entailed an 'NVivo coding exercise, in which sections of text concerning themes of interest were identified and retrieved.' He was especially interested in gender differences in how sufferers are represented, and demonstrated that stories about men are much more likely to discuss how a person's character is important in dealing with the disease.

Altheide (1996) outlined an approach he called *ethnographic content analysis* (ECA), which is typical of qualitative content analysis. He described his approach as differing from quantitative content analysis in that the researcher is constantly revising the themes or categories distilled from the examination of documents. As he put it:

> ECA follows a recursive and reflexive movement between concept development-sampling-data, collection-data, coding-data, and analysis-interpretation. The aim is to be systematic and analytic but not rigid. Categories and variables initially guide the study, but others are allowed and expected to emerge during the study, including an orientation to *constant discovery* and *constant comparison* of relevant situations, settings, styles, images, meanings, and nuances (1996: 16; emphases in original).

While quantitative analysis typically entails applying predefined categories to the sources, ECA allows a greater refinement of those categories and the generation of new ones. For example, Parnaby's (2003) study of squeegee kids included a reflexive examination of the documents used, which was done while still forming and confirming theoretical concepts; it was a process of constant discovery and comparison. In addition, ECA emphasizes the context within which documents are generated. For instance, a study of newspaper reports of crime would require an appreciation of things like news organizations and the work of journalists (Altheide 2004).

Semiotics

Another form of qualitative content analysis is semiotics, the *science of signs*. In social research, semiotics involves an analysis of the signs and symbols encountered in everyday life. It can be employed in relation to documentary sources and to many other kinds of data. The main terms employed in semiotics are as follows:

- the *sign* is something that stands for something else, such as a yellow traffic light; it is made up of a *signifier* and the *signified*;
- the *signifier* is the thing (here the yellow light) that points to an underlying meaning;
- the *signified* is the meaning to which the signifier points (Caution: Stop if possible);
- a *denotative meaning* is the manifest or more obvious meaning of a signifier and as such indicates its function (here to regulate traffic);
- a *connotative meaning* is a meaning that can arise in addition to its denotative meaning (for example, speed up to beat the coming red light); and
- *polysemy* refers to the notion that signs can be interpreted in many different ways.

Semiotics seeks to uncover the hidden meanings that reside in texts, broadly defined. Consider, by way of illustration, the curriculum vitae (CV) in academic life. The typical academic CV contains such features as: personal details; education; previous and current posts; administrative responsibilities and experience; teaching experience; research experience; research grants acquired; and publications. One can treat the CV as a system of interlocking signifiers denotatively providing a summary of the individual's experience (its sign function). At the connotative level, it as an indication of an individual's value, particularly in connection with employability. Each CV is capable of being interpreted in different ways and is therefore polysemic, but there is a shared code among academics whereby certain attributes of CVs are seen as especially desirable and are therefore less contentious in terms of their meaning. Applicants for posts know this and devise their CVs to highlight the desired qualities and to downplay others, so that the CV becomes a presentation of self, as Miller and Morgan (1993) suggested.

Box 16.2 provides an illustration of a semiotic study (Gottdiener 1997), with Disneyland as a text. The chief strength of semiotics lies in its invitation to see beyond and beneath the apparent ordinariness of everyday life and its manifestations. The main difficulty with a semiotic analysis is that, although it may result in a compelling exposition of some aspect of everyday life, the interpretation may be somewhat

---

Box 16.2   A semiotic Disneyland

Gottdiener (1997: 108–15) proposed that California's Disneyland can be fruitfully analyzed through a semiotic analysis, which examines signs and symbols. He concluded that Disneyland's meaning is based on the contrast between the alienated daily lives of nearby Los Angeles residents and the experiences they get at the facility. He identified, through this principle, several sign systems contrasting the park with its surrounding environment: transportation, food, clothing, shelter, entertainment, social control, economics, politics, and family. The first of these sign systems—transportation—reveals a difference between the Disneyland visitor as pedestrian (walking with others in a group) and the Los Angeles resident as passenger (a car is necessary; danger on the congested freeways). A further component of his research entailed an analysis of the connotations of the different 'lands' that make up the park. He suggested that each land is associated with signifiers of capitalism, for example:

- Frontierland—predatory capital, conquering;
- Adventureland—colonialism/imperialism; and
- Tomorrowland—state capital for space exploration.

---

arbitrary. For example, Gottdiener's assessment of 'Adventureland' at Disneyland as colonialism/imperialism may not be shared by other analysts. However, the results of a semiotic analysis may be no more arbitrary than any other kind of interpretation of documentary materials or any other data. Indeed, it would be surprising not to be struck by a sense of arbitrariness in interpretation, in view of the principle of polysemy that lies at the heart of semiotics.

Hermeneutics

Hermeneutics is an approach that has been used in understanding and interpreting the Bible, but it has also been employed in the analysis of other texts. It was influential in the formation of interpretivism as an epistemology (see Chapter 1) and has much in common with Weber's notion of *Verstehen*. The central idea behind hermeneutics is that the analyst of a text must seek its meanings from the perspective of its author. This entails considering the social and historical context within which the text was produced. Qualitative content analysis and semiotics are hermeneutic when they are sensitive to context.

Phillips and Brown's (1993) hermeneutic study of the corporate image advertisements of a Canadian synthetic crude oil company was a 'formal analysis of the structural and conventional aspects of the text' (1993: 1563). For them this meant examining the texts in terms of their constituent parts and the writing conventions employed. They also employed a large database of magazine and newspaper articles relating to the company, giving them additional documentary materials. They showed how corporate image advertisements were attempts to mobilize support for company activities from government and the public, and to ward off the environmental legislation that threatened them.

Readers and audiences — active or passive?

Audience reception is a prominent area of inquiry in media and cultural studies. The key point is whether audiences/readers are active interpreters of what they see or hear. Do they passively derive the meanings that authors or designers infuse into their texts, as in the oil company advertisements just described, or do they resist those meanings and arrive at independent readings? Do they arrive at a middle point that incorporates both passive and active elements? Much of the research on this issue suggests that audiences frequently come up with readings different from those intended by authors (see Fenton *et al.* 1998 for a summary of some of this research).

Although the idea of the 'active audience' has not gone unchallenged (for example, McGuigan 1992), it is so well supported that many of the interpretations of texts offered by social scientists have been questioned. This suggests caution in reading Giulianotti's (1997) study of 'fanzines' or Hier's (2002) examination of city council minutes to understand the rave issue. Are their interpretations the same as what other social scientists would make? Do they match those of the original readers or audiences? The social researcher is always providing a personal 'spin' on the texts analyzed. The same is true of all social science data: the conclusions derived from questionnaire or ethnographic data are always going to be one particular interpretation. The point is that

close scrutiny and critical thinking are required when reading renditions of any text.

Two approaches to the study of language

In this section two approaches to the study of language are examined: conversation analysis (CA) and discourse analysis (DA). While CA and DA do not exhaust the range of possibilities for studying language, they do represent two of the most prominent approaches and each includes quantitative and qualitative aspects. Both have evolved a technical vocabulary and a set of techniques. This section outlines some of their basic elements and draws attention to their contrasting features.

Conversation analysis

The roots of CA lie in ethnomethodology, a sociological approach to communication that focuses on the 'practical, common-sense reasoning' people use in their everyday lives. It includes notions of cause and effect (if I do this, then that will happen) and the generalizations that allow people to perform everyday tasks. This reasoning and communication is presented as a way in which social order is created. Social order is not seen as a pre-existing force constraining individual action, but as something that is worked at and accomplished by people through interaction. Garfinkel, one of its founders, claims that the role of sociology is not to uncover 'objective' social facts as Durkheim suggested, but to see them as an accomplishment, as the eventually taken-for-granted patterns arising from the activities of ordinary people going about their daily lives (Garfinkel 1967: vii).

Two ideas are particularly central to ethnomethodology and find clear expression in CA: *indexicality* and *reflexivity*. The former suggests that the meanings of words or utterances, including pauses and sounds, depend on the context in which they are used. Reflexivity means that talk is not a 'mere' representation of the social world, standing for something else, but is itself a reality. In these ways, ethnomethodology fits squarely with two aspects of qualitative research—a preference for a contextual understanding of action (see Chapter 8) and an ontological position associated with constructionism (see Chapter 1).

In the years following its introduction, ethnomethodological research sought to conduct fine-grained analyses of the sequences of interaction revealed in conversations recorded in naturally occurring contexts. As such, CA is a multifaceted approach—part theory, part method of data acquisition, part method of analysis. The predilection for the analysis of talk gleaned from naturally occurring situations suggests that CA fits well with another preoccupation among qualitative researchers—a commitment to naturalism (see Chapters 2 and 8).

Conversation analysts have developed a variety of procedures to study talk. Psathas (1995: 1) described them as 'rigorous, systematic procedures' that can 'provide reproducible results.' Such a framework brings to mind the procedures used to generate valid, reliable, and replicable findings in quantitative research. It is not surprising, therefore, that CA is sometimes described as having a positivist orientation. Thus a cluster of features that are broadly in tune with qualitative research (contextual and naturalistic analysis without prior theoretical commitments) are married to traits that are found in quantitative research.

However, the emphasis on context in CA is somewhat at variance with the way in which contextual understanding is normally thought of in qualitative research. For CA practitioners, context refers to the specific here-and-now context of immediately preceding talk, whereas for most qualitative researchers it has a much wider focus, encompassing things like the broader culture of the group within which the social action occurs, including their values, beliefs, and typical modes of behaviour. This is precisely the kind of attribution that CA practitioners seek to avoid. To import elements that are not specifically grounded in the here and now of what has just been said during a conversation risks implanting an understanding that is not grounded in the participants' own terms. It is no wonder, therefore, that writers like Gubrium and Holstein (1997) treated CA as a separate tradition within qualitative research, whereas Silverman (1993) found it difficult to fit CA into broad descriptions of qualitative research.

Assumptions of conversation analysis

A route to CA often begins with the analyst noticing something significant about how a speaker says something, a recognition that generates an interest in the function that the turn of phrase serves. Clayman and Gill (2004) gave the example of how children often begin a conversation by saying 'You know what, Daddy [or whoever]?' when among adults. The question generally produces a 'What?' reply that allows the child to find a slot in a sequence of communications, or to inaugurate such a sequence. The use of this strategy, instead of a straight declarative statement, may reflect a child's lesser power.

Once such a focus has been identified, conversation analysts typically follow certain basic assumptions. Heritage (1984, 1987) proposed three:

- *Talk is structured*. Talk comprises patterns, and participants are implicitly aware of the rules that underpin these patterns. As a result, conversation analysts do not attempt to infer the motivations of speakers from what they say, or to ascribe their talk to purely personal characteristics. Such information is unnecessary, since the conversation analyst is oriented to the underlying structures of talk revealed in its pauses, emphases, questions preceding answers, etc.
- *Talk is forged contextually*. Talk must be analyzed in terms of its context and understood in terms of the talk that has preceded it.
- *Analysis is grounded in data*. Conversation analysts shun prior theoretical schemes and instead argue that the characteristics of talk and social order must be derived from the data.

In doing a project based on CA, be careful not to collect too much data. The real work of CA goes into the painstaking analysis that its underlying theoretical stance requires. It may be that just one or two portions of transcribed text will be sufficient to answer the research questions.

Transcription and attention to detail

The transcript in Box 16.3 uses some basic symbols employed by conversation analysts:

We:ll A colon indicates that the sound that occurs directly before the colon is prolonged. More than one colon means further prolongation (e.g., : : : :).

.hh h's preceded by a dot indicate an intake of breath. If no dot is present, it means breathing out.

(0.8) A figure in parentheses indicates a period of silence, usually measured in tenths of a second. Thus, (0.8) signals eight-tenths of a second of silence.

<u>you</u> and I An underline indicates an emphasis in the speaker's talk.

(.) Indicates a very slight pause.

The attention to detail in the sequence of talk in Box 16.3 is striking, but what is significant in it? Silverman (1994) drew two main inferences. First, *P* initially tries to deflect any suggestion that there may be a special reason why she needs an HIV test. As a result, the disclosure that she has been engaging in potentially risky behaviour is delayed. Second, *P*'s use of '*you*' depersonalizes her behaviour. Silverman argued that sequences like these show how 'people receiving HIV counselling skilfully manage their talk about delicate topics' (1994: 75). The hesitations are designed by patients to establish that issues like these are not the subject of normal conversation. The rather general replies to questions indicate that the speaker is not the kind of person who immediately launches into a discussion about difficult sexual matters with a stranger. As an aside, Silverman suggested that *P*'s hesitancy and depersonalization are minimal. Others stall more, lie, or totally refuse to answer (1994: 76).

Some basic tools of conversation analysis

There are recurring features in how talk is organized that can be discerned in sequences of conversation. The following ones are presented to provide a flavour of the ways in which CA proceeds.

Turn-taking
One of the most basic ideas in CA is that taking turns is one of the ways in which order is achieved in everyday conversation. This is a particularly important tool of conversation analysis, because it illustrates that talk depends on shared codes indicating the ends of utterances. If such codes did not exist, there would not be smooth transitions in conversation. Hutchby and Wooffitt (1998: 47) summarized this model as indicating that only one speaker tends to talk at a time, the other listening, and turns are taken with minimal gaps between them.

Of course, things do go wrong in conversations, as occurs when people speak at the same time. Silverman (1993: 132) noted several repair mechanisms for instances in which turn-taking conventions are not followed:

- when someone starts to speak before the other has finished, the interrupted speaker stops talking before completing his or her turn;
- when a turn transfer does not occur at an appropriate point (for example, when someone does not respond to a question), the speaker may speak again, perhaps reinforcing the need for the other person to speak (for example, by re-phrasing the question).

The crucial point to note about such repair mechanisms is that they allow the rules of turn-taking to be maintained in spite of the fact that they have been breached.

Adjacency pairs
One of the ways in which turn-taking is revealed is through the examination of *adjacency pairs*, the tendency for talk to have two linked phases, for instance: a question followed by an answer, as in Box 16.3; an invitation followed by a response (accept/decline); or a greeting followed by a returned greeting. The first phase implies that the other part of the adjacency pair will be forthcoming, for example, that an invitation will get a response. The second phase is of interest to the conversation analyst not just because it invites a response in its own right but because compliance indicates an appreciation of how one is supposed to respond to the initial phase. In this way 'intersubjective understandings' are continuously reinforced. This does not mean that the second phase *always* follows the first. The failure to respond properly, as when one answers a question with another question, has itself been the focus of attention for conversation analysts.

Preference organization
Some responses are clearly preferred to others. An example is when an invitation or a request is proffered: acceptance is the *preferred response* and refusal the *non-preferred response*. For example, Potter (1996: 59) contrasted a sequence in which an offer is met with a straightforward acceptance—'thank

Box 16.3   Conversation analysis showing a question and answer adjacency pair

Silverman (1994: 72) provided the following extract from a conversation between an HIV counsellor (C) and a patient (P):

1. C Can I just briefly ask why: you thought about having

2. an hiv test done:

3. P .hh We:ll I mean it's something that you have these

4. I mean that you have to think about these da: ys, and

5. I just uh: m felt (0.8) you- you have had sex with

6. several people and you just don't want to go on (.)

7. not knowing.

Box 16.4   Conversation analysis in action: a non-preferred response

1. B: Uh if you'd care to come over and visit a little while

2. this morning I'll give you a cup of coffee.

3. A: hehh

4. Well

5. that's awfully sweet of you,

6. I don't think I can make it this morning. hh uhm

7. I'm running an ad in the paper and-and uh I have to

8. stay near the phone (Potter 1996: 59).

you'—with the sequence in Box 16.4 in which an invitation is declined.

Potter argued that this kind of response by *A* is fairly typical of rejections, which have features that contrast with the preferred response of unequivocal acceptance. For example, *A* delays the start of the response and fills it with 'hehh.' Also, the rejection is 'softened' by *A* saying that he or she doesn't 'think' he or she can make it (leaving a chance that an acceptance is still possible) and is accompanied by an explanation for failing to provide the preferred response. The key point is that the participants recognize the preference structure of this kind of adjacency pairing and that this affects the response (hesitancy, acknowledgment of the invitation, and providing an explanation). An acceptance does not have to be justified, whereas a refusal generally does, to allow the relationship between the two parties to be unharmed by the non-preferred response.

Research can be done by students on things like repair mechanisms to see if different groups, like men and women, or students and professors exhibit varying patterns. Status hierarchies can sometimes determine who the interrupters are, who defers to the interrupters, etc. Your class could go to an eating area on campus to collect data, each student listening to different conversations. To catch body movements, video recordings can be used (Heath 1997), so long as ethical protocols have been followed.

A final note on conversation analysis

CA considers the use of cultural factors to understand conversations to be illegitimate. However, some researchers see that as unnecessarily restrictive. For the participants in an exchange, much of their talk is informed by their mutual knowledge of contexts, including cultural contexts. The prohibition against cultural arguments limits CA to research questions that pertain only to talk itself. On the other hand, CA reduces the risk of making unwarranted speculations about what is happening in social interaction, and has contributed to our understanding of how social order is created, one of the classic concerns of social theory.

Discourse analysis

Although it incorporates aspects of CA, discourse analysis goes beyond it and can be applied to forms of communication other than talk, making it more flexible. Moreover, in DA there is less emphasis on naturally occurring talk, so that the talk in research interviews can be a legitimate target for analysis. According to Potter, DA 'emphasizes the way versions of the world, of society, events and inner psychological worlds are produced in discourse' (1997: 146). For continental philosophers like Foucault

(1926–84), discourse refers to the way a particular set of linguistic categories relating to an object, and the ways of depicting it, frame the way people comprehend that object.

For example, a certain discourse concerning mental illness produces conceptions of what mentally ill persons are like, the nature of their illness, how they should be treated, and who is legitimately entitled to treat them. Discourse can become a framework for justifying the power of those who provide such treatment and for their treatment regimens. In this way, discourse is much more than language: it is part of the social world of mental illness. Foucault took a broad, historical view of discourse. Discourse analysts, however, provide much more detailed analyses of talk and texts than Foucault did.

Several different approaches fall under the DA heading (Potter 1997). The version discussed here is one that is associated with such writers as Potter (1997), Potter and Wetherell (1994), and Billig (1991). This version of DA exhibits two distinctive features at the level of epistemology and ontology (Potter 1997).

- It is generally *anti-realist*; in other words, it denies that there is an external reality awaiting a definitive portrayal by the researcher. It therefore disavows the notion that researchers can arrive at accurate and objective accounts of the social world.
- It is *constructionist*; that is, the emphasis is placed on the versions of reality propounded by members of the social setting being investigated. More specifically, the constructionist emphasis recognizes that discourse analysis entails a selection from many viable renditions. For example, is a person who speaks to herself dangerous or harmless? Is she more in need of treatment than a handout? In the process of answering such questions, a particular reality is built up.

Discourse is not simply a neutral device for imparting meaning—people seek to accomplish many things when they talk or write. DA is concerned with the strategies they employ in trying to create different kinds of effect. This is illustrated in three basic discourse-analytic questions:

- What is this discourse doing?

- How is this discourse constructed to make this happen?
- What resources are available to perform this activity? (Potter 2004: 609).

This action orientation is revealed in a study of the first few moments of telephone calls to a National Society for the Prevention of Cruelty to Children helpline. Through an analysis of these call openings, Potter and Hepburn (2004) showed that these first few moments perform certain actions:

- They are an opportunity for the caller to specify the details of his or her concerns.
- They seek to establish that the child protection officer who receives the call is someone who, as an expert, can verify the caller's concerns.
- The caller makes it clear that he or she is concerned, but is not so concerned or certain about the situation that the police should be contacted.
- The child protection officer shows an ability to treat the report as serious, without making a judgment as to the actual truth or seriousness of the report.

Through an analysis of these brief moments of conversation, the flow of discourse achieves a number of objectives for both parties and is therefore action. On the other hand, as Gill (1996) suggested, what is said is always a way of *not* saying something else. Either way, discourse can be seen as providing a solution to a problem (Widdicombe 1993).

DA shares with CA a preference for locating contextual understanding in terms of the situational specifics of talk. As Potter (1997: 158) put it, discourse analysts prefer 'to see things as things that are worked up, attended to, and made relevant in interaction rather than being external determinants.' However, DA practitioners are less wedded to this principle than are conversation analysts.

Discourse analysts resist the idea of codifying their procedures and instead argue that such a codification is probably impossible. They prefer to see their style of research as an 'analytic mentality' and as 'a craft skill, more like bike riding or chicken sexing than following the recipe for a mild chicken *rogan josh*' (Potter 1997: 147–8).

Gill (2000) suggested adopting a posture of 'skeptical reading.' This means searching for a purpose

Box 16.5   Four themes in discourse analysis

Gill (2000) drew attention to four prominent themes in DA:

1. *Discourse is a topic.* This means that discourse is a focus of inquiry itself and not just a means of gaining access to aspects of social reality that lie behind it. Such a view contrasts with a traditional research interview in which language is a way of revealing what interviewees think, or a mechanism to learn about their behaviour and the reasons for it.

2. *Language is constructive.* This means that discourse is a way of constituting a particular view of social reality. Moreover, in rendering that view, choices are made regarding the most appropriate way of presenting it, and these reflect the disposition of the person devising it.

3. *Discourse is a form of action.* As Gill put it, language is viewed 'as a practice in its own right' (2000: 175). Language is a way of accomplishing acts, such as attributing blame, presenting oneself in a particular way, or getting an argument across. Moreover, a person's discourse is affected by the situation he or she is in. For instance, the reasons given for wanting a job may vary according to whether one is addressing interviewers in a job interview, family members, or friends.

4. *Discourse is rhetorically organized.* This means that DA practitioners recognize that discourse is concerned with 'establishing one version of the world in the face of competing versions' (Gill 2000: 176). In other words, there is a recognition that people want to persuade others when they present a version of events.

lurking behind the way things are said or presented. Gill proposed that DA can be usefully thought of as comprising four main themes, outlined in Box 16.5.

The bulk of the exposition of DA that follows is based on a study of a television program about success in the treatment of cancer (see Box 16.6).

Producing facts

In this section, the emphasis is on the resources employed in conveying allegedly factual knowledge. Once such resource is *quantification rhetoric*, by which is meant the ways in which numerical and non-numerical statements are made to support or refute arguments. The interest in this issue lies in part in the importance of quantification in everyday life, and also in the tendency for many social scientists to make use of this strategy themselves (John 1992). In the analysis of their data, such as the portions of transcript cited in Box 16.6, Potter *et al.* (1991) and Potter and Wetherell (1994) employed several devices.

Using variation as a lever
The authors drew attention to the phrase '1 per cent of a quarter of a million,' because it incorporates two quantitative expressions: a relative expression (a percentage) and an absolute frequency (quarter of

a million). The change in portraying quantification is important, because it allows the program-makers to make their case about the low cure levels (just 1 per cent) compared with the large number of new cases of cancer. Also, they could have pointed to the absolute number of people who are cured (2500), but the impact would have been less. And the 1 per cent is not being contrasted with 243 000 but with a quarter of a million. Not only does this citation allow the figure to grow by 7000, but also 'a quarter of a million' sounds larger.

Reading the detail
Discourse analysts incorporate the CA practice of attending to the details of discourse. For example, Potter and Wetherell suggested that the description of the three 'curable cancers' as 'amongst the rarest cancers' was deployed to make the point that these are atypical cancers, and that it would be unwise to generalize from them to all cancers.

Looking for rhetorical detail
Attention to rhetorical detail entails being sensitive to how arguments are constructed. During the editing of the film, the program-makers' discourse suggested they were looking for ways to provide a convincing argument to show that cancer remains

Box 16.6   Discourse analysis in action: producing facts through quantification rhetoric

The study of the television program *Cancer: Your Money or Your Life* (Potter *et al.* 1991; Potter and Wetherell 1994) used a variety of different sources, including:

- a video recording of the program;
- the observations of one of the people making the program (who acted as a participant observer while it was being made);
- drafts of the script;
- recordings of editing sessions;
- entire interviews (of people such as cancer research specialists and heads of charities) conducted for the program; and
- research interviews with some of the latter people and with some of the people involved in making the program.

With regard to the coding process, the authors said:

We made a list of about a dozen keywords and phrases that related to the sequence—percentage, cure rates, death rates, 1 per cent, etc.—and then ran through each of the interview and interaction files, looking for them with a standard word-processor. . . . Whenever we got a 'hit' we would read the surrounding text to see if it had relevance to our target sequence. When it did we would copy it across to an already opened coding file . . . noting the transcript page numbers at the same time. If we were not sure if the sequence was relevant we copied it anyway, for, unlike the sorts of coding that take place in traditional content analysis, the coding is not the analysis itself but a preliminary to make the task of analysis manageable (Potter and Wetherell 1994: 52).

Below is a prominent sequence used in the research. It occurred roughly halfway through the program, following the interviews with cancer scientists who had cast doubt on whether their research, much of it funded by charities, resulted in successful treatment:

Commentary: The message from these scientists is clear—exactly like the public—they hope their basic research will lead to cures in the future—although at the moment they can't say how this will happen. In the meantime, their aim is to increase scientific knowledge on a broad front and they're certainly achieving this. But do their results justify them getting so much of the money that has been given to help fight cancer? When faced with this challenge the first thing the charities point to is the small number of cancers which are now effectively curable.

[on screen: *Dr. Nigel Kemp Cancer Research Campaign*]

Kemp: The outlook for individuals suffering from a number of types of cancer has been totally revolutionized. I mean for example—children suffering from acute leukemia—in the old days if they lived six months they were lucky—now more than half the children with it are cured. And the same applies to a number of other cancers—Hodgkin's Disease in young people and testicular tumours in young men (Potter and Wetherell 1994: 52–3).

At this point a table showing the annual incidence of 34 types of cancer begins to scroll on the screen. The total incidence is 243 000 and the individual incidences range from placenta (20) to lung (41 400). The three forms of cancer mentioned by Kemp and levels of incidence are highlighted in yellow: childhood leukemia (350), testis (1000), and Hodgkin's Disease (1400). The program continues while the table is scrolling.

Commentary: But those three curable types are amongst the rarest cancers—they represent around 1 per cent of a quarter of a million cases of cancers diagnosed each year. Most deaths are caused by a small number of very common cancers.

Kemp: We are well aware of the fact that [pause] once people develop lung cancer or stomach cancer or cancer of the bowel sometimes—the outlook is very bad and obviously one is frustrated by the s[low], relatively slow rate of progress on the one hand but equally I think there are a lot of real opportunities and positive signs that advances can be made—even in the more intractable cancers (Potter and Wetherell 1994: 53).

largely incurable in spite of the money spent on it. The program-makers very consciously devised the strategy outlined in the discussion of 'using variation as a lever' of playing down the numerical significance of those cancers amenable to treatment. Moreover, Potter *et al.* (1991) pointed out that one element of their argument is to employ a tactic they call a 'preformulation,' whereby a possible counter-argument is discounted in the course of presenting an argument, as when the commentary says: 'When faced with this challenge the first thing the charities point to are the small number of cancers which are now effectively curable.'

Overview

DA draws on insights from CA, particularly when analyzing strings of talk. The CA injunction to focus on the talk itself and the ways in which intersubjective meaning is accomplished in sequences of talk is also incorporated into DA. But DA practitioners come perilously close to invoking speculations not directly discernible in the sequences being analyzed—that is, speculations about motives. It is precisely this to which conversation analysts object, as when Schegloff (1997: 183) wrote about DA: 'Discourse is too often made subservient to contexts not of its participants'

making, but of its analysts' insistence.' For their part, discourse analysts object to the restriction that this injunction imposes, because it means that conversation analysts 'rarely raise their eyes from the next turn in the conversation, and, further, this is not an entire conversation or sizeable slice of social life but usually a tiny fragment' (Wetherell 1998: 402).

Both CA and DA practitioners dismiss the notion of a pre-existing material reality that can constrain individual behaviour. This anti-realist inclination has been a source of controversy, as a lack of attention to material reality has proved to be too much for some social researchers and theorists. Writing from a critical realist position, Reed (2000) argued that discourses should be examined in relation to social structures, such as the power relationships that create the discourses. Similarly, Hier (2002) described his analysis of raves as critical discourse analysis. These studies showed how discourses worked through existing structures, thereby transforming the concept of discourse from a self-referential one in which nothing of significance exists outside it, into a 'generative mechanism.' Thus while many DA practitioners are anti-realist, a realist position in relation to discourse is feasible. That position is perhaps closer to the classic concerns of the social sciences than an anti-realist stance.

Box 16.7 A content analysis of qualitative research on the workplace

Hodson reported the results of a content analysis of 'book-length ethnographic studies using sustained periods of direct observation' (1996: 724). The idea of ethnography was explored in detail in Chapter 9. As a method, ethnography entails a long period of participant observation in order to understand the culture of a social group. Hodson (1996) performed a content analysis on ethnographic studies of workplaces published in book form (articles were excluded because they rarely included sufficient detail). Thousands of case studies from around the world were assessed for possible inclusion in the sample, but in the end 86 ethnographies were selected and 106 cases analyzed (several published ethnographies were of more than one case). Each case was coded into one of five types of workplace organization: craft, direct supervision, assembly line, bureaucratic, and worker participation. That was the independent variable. Various dependent variables were also coded. Here is one of the variables and its codes:

Autonomy

1 = none (workers' tasks are completely determined by others, by machinery, or by organizational rules); 2 = little (workers occasionally have a chance to select among procedures or priorities); 3 = average (regular opportunities to select procedures or to set priorities within definite limits); 4 = high (significant latitude in determining procedures and setting priorities); 5 = very high (significant personal interpretation is needed by the worker to reach broadly specified goals) (Hodson 1996: 728).

Hodson's findings suggest that some pessimistic accounts of worker participation schemes (for example, that they do not genuinely permit participation and do not necessarily have a beneficial impact on the worker) are incomplete. A more detailed treatment of this research is in Hodson (1999).

Advantages of content analysis

Content analysis has several advantages:

- In its most quantitative form, it is a very transparent research method, making replication easy. It is this transparency that often causes content analysis to be referred to as an 'objective' method of analysis.
- It allows for a longitudinal analysis with relative ease. For example, a crime study can be expanded to examine changes in newspaper crime reporting over two different time periods.
- Content analysis is an *unobtrusive method*, a term previously defined (Webb *et al.* 1966) as a method that does not change the behaviours of participants in any way. It is therefore a *non-reactive method* (see Box 6.5). Newspaper articles and television scripts are generally not written with the expectation that a content analysis may one day be carried out on them. On the other hand, if the content analysis is being conducted on interview transcripts or ethnographies (for example, Box 16.7), the documents may have been at least partly influenced by the anticipation of such scrutiny and thus may contain some reactive error.
- It is a highly flexible method, applicable to several different kinds of unstructured information. While content analysis is primarily associated with the analysis of mass media outputs, it has a much broader applicability. Box 16.8 illustrates a rather unusual but still interesting application.
- Content analysis can permit the study of social groups that are difficult to access. For example, much of the knowledge of the social backgrounds of elite groups, such as senior clergy, company directors, and top military personnel, comes from content analyses of publications such as *Who's Who* and the business pages of newspapers.

Disadvantages of content analysis

Like all research techniques, content analysis suffers from certain limitations:

- A content analysis can only be as good as the documents with which the practitioner works. Recall that Scott (1990) recommended assessing documents in terms of criteria such as: authenticity (the document is what it purports to be); credibility (there are no grounds for thinking that the contents of the document have been distorted in some way); and representativeness (the specific documents examined are representative of all possible relevant documents). These issues were explored in Chapter 7.
- Even in quantitative content analysis, it is almost impossible to devise coding manuals that do not require some coder interpretation. To the extent that this occurs, it is questionable whether there is a perfect correspondence of interpretation between different coders.
- Particular problems are likely to arise when the aim is to impute *latent* meanings (as opposed to the more readily apparent *manifest* content). For example, in searching for traditional markers of masculinity and femininity (see Box 16.1), the potential for invalid conjecture is magnified. A related distinction is sometimes made between a more mechanical analysis (in particular, counting certain words) and an emphasis on themes in the text, which entails a higher level of abstraction and a correspondingly greater chance of invalidity.

Box 16.8 Just burp the cover and you get a perfect seal

Vincent (2003) combined qualitative and quantitative strategies in her study of Tupperware. She did a qualitative content analysis of the available literature on Tupperware, including literature produced by the company itself. What image of women did the company show? A housewife who did not work outside the home and would sell Tupperware for a bit of pin money? A woman too busy juggling career and family and thus in need of time-saving and economical Tupperware? Vincent then turned to census data to acquire macro-sociological information on women's economic roles over the previous fifty years. She concluded that '[h]alf a century after the invention of Tupperware, it continues to solve the problems of preserving freshness and maintaining order in the kitchen, at the same time as it helps women mediate tensions between their domestic and income-earning roles,' adding that '[a]s long as women must contend with responsibilities in both spheres, Tupperware's success seems secure.'

- It can be difficult to answer 'why?' questions through content analysis. For example, Jagger found that 'the body of their partner, its attractiveness, shape and size, is of less importance to advertisers when in the buying mode [advertising for a partner]' (1998: 807) than when selling oneself (see Box 16.1). But why? And finding that this is true of both men and women is, as Jagger suggested, even more surprising. Again, why does this occur? Answers are usually speculations at best. Similarly, Fenton *et al.* (1998) found that sociology was only the fourth most common discipline referred to when social science research is being reported in the mass media, but by far the most frequently *inferred* discipline. Again, while interesting, the reasons for it are only speculative (Fenton *et al.* 1998). Sometimes, users of content analysis have been able to shed some light on 'why?' questions raised in their investigations by collecting more data (for example, Fenton *et al.* 1998).

- Some content analysis studies are accused of being atheoretical and it is easy to see why. The emphasis on measurement in content analysis can easily and unwittingly result in a focus on what is measurable rather than what is theoretically significant or important. However, content analysis is not necessarily atheoretical. Jagger (1998) placed her findings on dating advertisements in the context of current ideas about consumerism and the body. Hodson's (1996) content analysis of workplace ethnographies (Box 16.7) was underpinned by theoretical ideas deriving from research on developments in workplace organization and their impact on workers.

— Key Points —

- Frequently, content analysis is located within the quantitative research tradition, but it can be qualitative as well.

- While traditionally associated with the analysis of mass media content, it is a flexible method applicable to a wide range of phenomena.

- It is important to produce clear research questions and to be explicit about what is to be analyzed.

- The preparation of a coding schedule and coding manual are crucial steps in content analysis.

- Content analysis can become particularly controversial when it is used to search for latent meanings and themes.

- Semiotics and hermeneutics are qualitative approaches to content analysis.

- There is disagreement over whether readers of documents are active or passive consumers of the messages they receive.

- Both CA and DA approaches use language itself as a focus of research.

- CA is a systematic approach to conversation that sees talk as structured in that it follows certain rules.

- Practitioners of CA avoid making inferences about talk that are not grounded in its immediate context.

- DA shares many features with CA but comes in several different versions and can be applied to a wider variety of phenomena.

- Discourse is conceived of as a means of conveying meaning and generally relates meaning in talk to contextual factors.

- As with all research methods, there are advantages and disadvantages to content analysis.

— Questions for Review —

- To what kinds of documents and media can content analysis be applied?
- What is the difference between manifest and latent content? What are the implications of that distinction for content analysis?

Research questions

- Why are precise research questions crucial in content analysis?
- What kinds of things can be counted in a content analysis?

Coding

- What is the difference between a coding schedule and a coding manual?
- What potential pitfalls need to be guarded against when devising coding schedules and manuals?

Qualitative content analysis

- What is a sign? How central is it to semiotics?
- What is the difference between denotative and connotative meaning?
- What lessons can be learned from the hermeneutic approach used by Phillips and Brown (1993)?

Conversation analysis

- What is meant by each of the following: turn-taking, adjacency pairs, preference organization, repair mechanism? How do they relate to the production of social order?
- Evaluate the argument that CA should examine a participant's motives.

Discourse analysis

- What is the significance of saying that DA is anti-realist and constructionist?
- What are the chief differences between CA and DA?

Advantages of content analysis

- 'One of the most significant virtues of content analysis is its flexibility, that is, that it can be applied to a wide variety of documents.' Discuss.

Disadvantages of content analysis

- To what extent does the need for coders to interpret meaning undermine latent content analysis?
- Must content analysis be atheoretical?

17 Writing Up Social Research

Chapter overview

One of the main tasks of any research project, regardless of its size, is reporting the findings. Writing is crucial, because an audience must be persuaded that the research is credible and important. This chapter explores:

- why writing, and especially good writing, is important to social research;

- how quantitative and qualitative research are typically written up;
- the influence and implications of postmodernism for writing; and
- key issues in the writing of ethnography, an area in which discussions about writing have been especially prominent.

Introduction

The main purpose of this chapter is to extract some principles of good writing that are relevant and useful to students. This is an important issue because many find writing up research to be more difficult than carrying it out, while others treat the writing-up stage as relatively unproblematic. But no matter how well research is conducted, readers have to be convinced about the credibility of the knowledge claims being made. Good writing is *persuasive* and *convincing*. Flat, lifeless, uncertain writing does not have the power to persuade and convince. In exploring these issues, rhetorical strategies in the writing of social research are outlined.

This chapter first considers whether quantitative and qualitative research need different approaches to writing. As will be seen, there are many similarities in how research is presented in these two research orientations. Two published articles are examined to uncover some helpful features, one based on quantitative research and the other on qualitative. When Bryman (1998) compared qualitative and quantitative research articles, he found the differences between them to be less pronounced than anticipated from his reading of the methodological literature. One difference he did notice,

however, is that quantitative researchers often give more detailed accounts of their research design and methods than qualitative researchers. This is surprising, because in *books*, qualitative researchers provide detailed accounts of these areas. Wolcott (1990: 27) also noticed this tendency: 'Our [qualitative researchers'] failure to render full and complete disclosure about our data-gathering procedures gives our methodologically-oriented colleagues fits. And rightly so, especially for those among them willing to accept our contributions if we would only provide more careful data about our data.' Being informed that a study is based on a year's participant observation or a number of semi-structured interviews is not enough to establish credibility. However, as mentioned, the differences between quantitative and qualitative articles may not be as great as one might anticipate.

Writing up quantitative research: an example

To illustrate some of the characteristics of writing up quantitative research for academic journals, take the article by Kelley and De Graaf (1997), referred to in several chapters (see especially Boxes 1.3 and 3.4). The article is based on a secondary analysis of survey data on religion in 15 nations and was accepted for publication in one of the most prestigious journals in sociology—the *American Sociological Review*. The vast majority of published articles in academic journals have undergone a blind review process, being read by two or three peers who confidentially comment on the article and give the editors a judgment about its merits and whether it is worthy of publication.

Many articles are rejected. With highly prestigious journals, that is the fate of more than 90 per cent of them. Moreover, it is unusual for an article to be accepted on its first submission. Usually, the referees suggest areas that need revising and the author is expected to respond to that feedback. Revised versions of articles may be sent back to the referees for further comment and this process may result in the author having to revise the draft yet again. It may even result in rejection. Therefore, an article like Kelley and De Graaf's is not just the culmination of a research process, it is also the outcome of a reviewer feedback process. The fact that it was accepted for publication when so many others are rejected testifies to its having met the standards of the journal. That does not mean that it is perfect, but passing the refereeing process is an indication that it does possess certain crucial qualities.

The article has the following components, aside from the abstract and bibliography:

1. introduction;
2. theory;
3. data;
4. measurement;
5. methods and models;
6. results; and
7. conclusion.

Introduction

The opening four sentences of the Introduction attempt to grab the reader's attention, give a clear indication of the article's focus, and provide an indication of the likely significance of the findings. This is what the authors wrote (Kelley and De Graaf 1997: 639):

> Religion remains a central element of modern life, shaping people's world-views, moral standards,

family lives, and in many nations, their politics. But in many Western nations, modernization and secularization may be eroding Christian beliefs, with profound consequences that have intrigued sociologists since Durkheim. Yet this much touted secularization may be overstated— certainly it varies widely among nations and is absent in the United States (Benson, Donahue, and Erickson 1989: 154–7; Felling, Peters, and Schreuder 1991; Firebaugh and Harley 1991; Stark and Iannaccone 1994). We explore the degree to which religious beliefs are passed on from generation to generation in different nations.

This is an impressive start, because in just over one hundred words, the authors set out what the article is about and what its significance is. Look at what each sentence achieves:

- The first sentence locates the research focus as addressing an important aspect of modern society, one which touches on many people's lives.
- The second sentence notes that there is variety among Western nations in the importance of religion and that the variations may have 'profound consequences.' But this sentence does more than that: it also suggests that this topic has long been of interest to sociologists. To support this point, Durkheim, one of sociology's most venerated figures, is mentioned.
- The third sentence suggests that there is a problem with the notion of secularization, a research focus for many sociologists of religion. Several fairly recent articles are cited to support the authors' contention that some commentators exaggerate secularization. In this sentence, the authors are moving towards a rationale for their article in terms of sociological concerns as opposed to social changes, which are the main concern of the two opening sentences.
- In the fourth sentence the authors set up their specific contribution to this area, the exploration of the passing on of religious beliefs between generations in different countries.

So, with just four sentences, the contribution the article is claiming to make has been outlined and situated within the established literature on the topic. This is quite a powerful start, because the reader now knows what the article is about and the case the authors are making for its contribution to the literature on the subject.

Theory

In this section, existing ideas and research on the topic of religious socialization are presented. The authors point to the impact of parents and other people on children's religious beliefs, but then assert that 'a person's religious environment is also shaped by factors other than their own and their parents' religious beliefs, and hence is a potential cause of those beliefs . . .' (Kelley and De Graaf 1997: 641). The authors go on to argue that 'prominent among these "unchosen" aspects of one's religious environment is birthplace' (1997: 641). Kelley and De Graaf's ruminations on this issue lead them to propose the hypothesis that contextual factors have an impact on religious beliefs. They suggest that in predominantly secular societies, family background has a greater impact on a person's religious beliefs than in devout societies. In the former, they suggest, parents and other family members are more likely to isolate children from secularizing influences. In devout societies, by contrast, this insulation process is less necessary and the influence of national factors greater. These hypotheses are derived directly from the research questions, which are stated in the article's Abstract: 'How much does a nation's religious environment affect the religious beliefs of its citizens? Do religious nations differ from secular nations in how beliefs are passed on from generation to generation?' (1997: 639).

Data

In this section, the authors outline the data sets they used. The sampling procedures are outlined along with sample sizes and response rates.

Measurement

Here Kelley and De Graaf explain how their main concepts are measured. The concepts are: *religious belief* (the questionnaire items used are in Box 3.4); *parents' church attendance; secular and religious nations* (that is, the scoring procedure for indicating the degree to which a nation is religious or secular

on a five-point scale); *other contextual characteristics of nations* (for example, whether or not it is a former Communist nation); and *individual characteristics* (for example, age and gender).

Methods and models

This is a very technical section, which outlines both the different ways in which the relationships between the variables can be conceptualized and the implications of using different mutivariate data analysis methods.

Results

Here the authors provide a general description of their findings and then consider whether their hypotheses are supported—it turns out they are. The significance of other contextual characteristics of nations and individual differences are discussed separately.

Conclusions

In this final section, Kelley and De Graaf return to the issues that have been driving their investigation, namely those presented in the Introduction and Theory sections. They began this section with a strong statement of their findings: 'The religious environment of a nation has a major impact on the beliefs of its citizens: people living in religious nations acquire, in proportion to the orthodoxy of their fellow citizens, more orthodox beliefs than those living in secular nations' (Kelley and De Graaf 1997: 654). They then reflect on the implications of the confirmation of their hypotheses for understanding the process of religious socialization and religious beliefs. They also address the ramifications of their findings for the theories about religious beliefs in modern society outlined in the Theory section:

> Our results also speak to the long-running debate about US exceptionalism (Warner 1993): They support the view that the United States is unusually religious. . . . Our results do not support Stark and Iannaccone's (1994) 'supply-side' analysis of differences between nations which argues that nations with religious monopolies have substantial unmet religious

needs, while churches in religiously competitive nations like the US do a better job of meeting diverse religious needs (Kelley and De Graaf 1997: 655).

The final paragraph spells out inferences about the impact of social change on a nation's level of religious belief. The authors suggest that factors such as modernization and the growth of education depress levels of religious belief, resulting in a precipitous rather than gradual fall in levels of religiosity. In their final three sentences, they discuss societies undergoing such change:

> The offspring of devout families mostly remain devout, but the offspring of more secular families now strongly tend to be secular. A self-reinforcing spiral of secularization then sets in, shifting the nation's average religiosity ever further away from orthodoxy. So after generations of stability, religious belief declines abruptly in the course of a few generations to the modest levels seen in many Western nations (Kelley and De Graaf 1997: 656).

It may be argued that these reflections are somewhat risky, because the data from which the authors derived their findings are cross-sectional rather than longitudinal. They were clearly extrapolating from their scoring of the 15 nations in terms of levels of modernization to the impact of social change on national levels of religiosity. However, these final sentences make for a strong conclusion, which may inspire further research.

Lessons

What lessons can be learned from Kelley and De Graaf's article?

- There is an attempt to grab the reader's attention with strong opening statements, which also act as signposts indicating what the article is about.
- The authors clearly spell out the rationale for their research. This entails pointing to the continued significance of religion in many societies and to the literature on religious beliefs and secularization.
- The research questions, and the hypotheses that are derived from them, are clearly formulated.

(However, as noted in Chapter 3, by no means is all quantitative research driven by hypotheses.)
- The nature of the data, the measurement of concepts, the sampling, the research methods employed, and the approaches to the analysis of the data are clearly and explicitly summarized.
- The presentation of the findings is oriented very specifically to the research questions and their related hypotheses.
- The conclusion returns to the research hypotheses and spells out the implications of the findings for them and for the theories cited. This is an important point. There should be a link between the findings of a study and the hypotheses and theories introduced earlier. The link allows the authors to discuss whether the hypotheses or theories are supported, and what the implications are for further research.

There is also a clear sequential process connecting the formulation of the research hypotheses, the description of the data, the presentation of the findings, and the presentation of the conclusions. Each stage follows from its predecessor. The structure used by Kelley and De Graaf is one commonly used in quantitative research in social science journals, although sometimes there is a separate Discussion section that appears between the Results and the Conclusion.

Writing up qualitative research: an example

Now consider at an example of a journal article based on qualitative research. The article is one that has been referred to in several previous chapters (see Chapter 2 and Box 10.3): a study of vegetarianism by Beardsworth and Keil (1992). The study is based on semi-structured interviews and was published in the *Sociological Review*, a leading British journal.

The structure runs as follows:

1. introduction;
2. the analysis of the social dimensions of food and eating;
3. studies of vegetarianism;
4. the design of the study;
5. the findings of the study;
6. explaining contemporary vegetarianism; and
7. conclusions.

What is immediately striking about the structure is that it is fairly similar to that of Kelley and De Graaf's (1997) article. Nor should this be surprising. After all, a structure that runs

Introduction ➔ Literature review ➔ Research design/methods ➔ Results ➔ Discussion ➔ Conclusions

is not associated with one research strategy rather than the other. One difference, however, is that the presentation of the results and their discussion are frequently more interwoven in qualitative research articles, as will be seen in our examination of Beardsworth and Keil's piece.

Introduction

The first four sentences give an immediate sense of what the article is about:

The purpose of this paper is to offer a contribution to the analysis of the cultural and sociological factors that influence patterns of food selection and food avoidance. The specific focus is contemporary vegetarianism, a complex of inter-related beliefs, attitudes and nutritional practices which has to date received comparatively little attention from social scientists. Vegetarians in Western cultures, in most instances, are not life-long practitioners but converts. They are individuals who have subjected more traditional foodways to critical scrutiny, and subsequently made a deliberate decision to change their eating habits, sometimes in a radical fashion (Beardsworth and Keil 1992: 253).

Like Kelley and De Graaf's, this is a strong introduction. Again look at what each sentence achieves:

- The first sentence makes it clear that the research is concerned with the study of food.
- The second sentence describes the specific research focus, the study of vegetarianism, and makes a claim for attention by suggesting that this topic has been underresearched by sociologists. Interestingly, this is almost the opposite of the claim made by Kelley and De Graaf in their second sentence, in that they point to a line of sociological interest in religion going back to

Durkheim. Each is a legitimate textual strategy for gaining the attention of readers.
- Attention is piqued even more by the idea of vegetarians as converts.
- The fourth sentence elaborates on the idea that for most people vegetarianism is an issue of choice rather than a tradition into which one is born.

After only about one hundred words, the reader has a clear idea of the focus of the research and has been alerted to the fact that there is not a great deal of pre-existing social research on the issue.

The analysis of the social dimensions of food and eating

This and the next section review existing theory and research; the contributions of various social scientists to social aspects of food and eating are discussed. The literature reviewed acts as a backcloth to the issue of vegetarianism. Beardsworth and Keil propose that 'there exists a range of theoretical and empirical resources which can be brought to bear upon the issue of contemporary vegetarianism' (1992: 255).

Studies of vegetarianism

This section examines the social scientific literature on vegetarianism. The review includes: opinion poll and survey data, which point to the likely percentage of vegetarians in the British population; debates about animal rights; a sociological analysis of vegetarian ideas; and a reference to a dated survey research study (Dwyer *et al.* 1974) of vegetarians in the US.

The design of the study

The first sentence of this section forges a link with the preceding one: 'The themes outlined above appear to warrant further investigation, preferably in a manner which allows for a much more richly detailed examination of motivations and experiences than is apparent in the study by Dwyer *et al.*' (Beardsworth and Keil 1992: 260). This opening gambit allowed the authors to suggest that the literature in this area is scant and that there are many unanswered questions. Also, they distance themselves from the one sociological study of vegetarians, which in turn leads them to set up the grounds for preferring qualitative research. The authors then explain:

- who was studied and why;
- how respondents were recruited and the difficulties encountered with recruitment;
- the semi-structured interviewing approach and its rationale;
- the number of people interviewed and the interview context; and
- the approach to analyzing the interview transcripts, largely through identifying themes.

The findings of the study

The chief findings are outlined under separate headings: respondents' characteristics, types of vegetarianism, the process of conversion, motivations, nutritional beliefs, social relations, and dilemmas. The presentation of the results is carried out so that the discussion of their meaning and significance leads to the next section, which provides a discussion of them. For example, in the final sentence reporting findings relating to nutritional beliefs, the authors write (Beardsworth and Keil 1992: 276):

> Just as meat tended to imply strongly negative connotations for respondents, concepts like 'fruit' and 'vegetable' tended to elicit positive reactions, although less frequently and in a more muted form than might have been anticipated on the basis of the analysis of the ideological underpinnings of 'wholefoods' consumption put forward by Atkinson (1980, 1983), or on the basis of the analysis of vegetarian food symbolism advanced by Twigg (1983: 28).

In this way, the presentation of the results points to some themes taken up in the remaining sections and demonstrates the significance of certain findings for some of the previously discussed literature.

Explaining contemporary vegetarianism

This section discusses the findings in light of the study's research questions on food selection and avoidance. The results are also related to many of the ideas encountered in the two literature sections. The authors develop an idea emerging from their

research which they call 'food ambivalence.' This concept encapsulates the anxieties and paradoxes concerning food that can be discerned in the interview transcripts (for example, food can be construed both as necessary for strength and energy and simultaneously as a source of illness). Vegetarianism is in many respects a response to the dilemmas associated with food ambivalence.

Conclusions

In this section, the authors return to many of the ideas and themes that drove their research. They spell out the significance of the idea of food ambivalence, which is probably the article's main contribution to research in this area. The final paragraph outlines the importance of food ambivalence for vegetarians, but the authors are careful not to imply that it is the sole reason for the adoption of vegetarianism. In the final sentence they write: 'However, for a significant segment of the population [vegetarianism] appears to represent a viable device for re-establishing some degree of peace of mind when contemplating some of the darker implications of the carefully arranged message on the dinner plate' (Beardsworth and Keil 1992: 290). The sentence neatly encapsulates one of the article's main themes—vegetarianism as a response to food ambivalence—and alludes through the reference to 'the carefully arranged message' to semiotic analyses of meat and food.

Lessons

As with Kelley and De Graaf's article, it is useful to review some of the lessons learned here.

- Like the example of quantitative research writing, there are strong opening sentences which attract attention and give a good indication of the nature and content of the article.
- The rationale for the research is clearly identified, a key point being the paucity of sociological investigations of vegetarianism.
- Research questions are specified but they are somewhat more open-ended than in Kelley and De Graaf's article, which is in keeping with the general orientation of qualitative research. The research questions revolve around the issue of vegetarianism as a dietary choice and the motivations for that choice.

- The research design and methods are outlined. The section in which these issues are discussed is more transparent than is usually the case with qualitative research articles.

- The presentation and discussion of the findings are geared to the broad research questions that motivated the researchers' interest in vegetarianism. The 'explaining contemporary vegetarianism' section provides an opportunity for the idea of food ambivalence and its dimensions to be articulated. The inductive nature of qualitative research means that the concepts and theories generated from an investigation must be clearly identified and discussed, as in this case.

- The conclusion elucidates in a more specific way the significance of the results for the research questions. It also explores the implications of food ambivalence for vegetarians so that one of the article's major theoretical contributions is clearly identified and emphasized.

Postmodernism and its implications for writing

Postmodernism is an extremely difficult idea to pin down. It questions the very notion of dispassionate social scientists seeking to uncover a pre-existing external reality, and views their accounts as only one among many different ways of seeing the world. As a result, 'knowledge' of the social world is relative; as Rosenau (1992: 8) put it, postmodernists 'offer "readings" not "observations," "interpretations" not "findings" . . .'

For postmodernists, reporting findings in a journal article provides merely one version of the topics investigated, so they are interested in investigating the bases and forms of those sorts of knowledge claims. While the writing of all types of social science is potentially in the postmodernist's firing line, it has been the texts produced by ethnographers that have been a particular target. The ethnographic text 'presumes a world out there (the real) that can be captured by a "knowing" author through the careful transcription and analysis of field materials (interviews, notes, etc.).' Postmodernists claim that such accounts are problematic because there 'can never be a final, accurate representation of what was meant or said, only different textual representations of different experiences' (Denzin 1994: 296).

However, it is wrong to depict the growing attention given to ethnographic writing as exclusively a product of postmodernism. Atkinson and Coffey (1995) argued that other intellectual trends in the social sciences also stimulated this interest. One is concerned with distinctions between rhetoric and logic and between the observer and the observed; another with doubts about the possibility of a neutral language through which the natural and social worlds can be revealed. Atkinson and Coffey also pointed to the antipathy within feminism towards the image of the neutral 'observer-author' who assumes a privileged stance in relation to members of the social setting being studied. This stance is regarded as one of domination by the observer-author over the observed that is inconsistent with the goals of feminism (revisit Chapter 8 for an elaboration of this general point). This concern has led to an interest in how 'privilege' is conveyed in ethnographic texts and how voices, particularly of marginal groups, are suppressed.

The concerns in these and other traditions have led to innovations in writing ethnography (Richardson 1994). An example is the use of a 'dialogic' form of writing that seeks to raise the profile of the multiplicity of voices that can be heard in the course of fieldwork. As Lincoln and Denzin (1994: 584) put it: 'Slowly it dawns on us that there may . . . be . . . not one "voice," but polyvocality; not one story, but many tales, dramas, pieces of fiction, fables, memories, histories, autobiographies, poems, and other texts to inform our sense of lifeways, to extend our understandings of the Other . . .'

Manning (1995) cited, as an example of the postmodern preference for allowing a variety of voices to come through within an ethnographic text, Stoller's (1989) research in Africa. Manning (1995: 260) described the text as a dialogue, not a monologue by the ethnographer, one 'shaped by interactions between informants or "the other" and the observer.' This postmodern preference for seeking out multiple voices and for turning the ethnographer into a 'bit player' reflects the mistrust among postmodernists of 'meta-narratives,' that is, positions or grand accounts that implicitly question the possibility of alternative versions of reality. On the other hand, 'mini-narratives, micro-narratives, local narratives are just stories that make no truth claims and are therefore more acceptable to postmodernists' (Rosenau 1992: xiii).

Postmodernism has also encouraged a growing reflexivity about the conduct of social research, and the growing interest in the writing of ethnography is very much a manifestation of this trend (see Box 17.1). This reflexivity can be discerned in how ethnographers turn inwards to examine the truth claims inscribed in their own classic texts, the focus of the next section.

In the end, what postmodernism gives, despite its recent decline, is an acute sense of uncertainty. It raises the issue of how one can ever know or capture a social reality that belongs to another. In so doing it points to an unresolvable tension that is further revealed in the issues raised in the next section. To quote Lincoln and Denzin (1994: 582) again: 'On the one hand there is the concern for validity, or certainty in the text as a form of . . . authenticity. On the other hand there is the sure and certain knowledge that all texts are socially, historically, politically, and culturally located. Researchers, like the texts they write, can never be transcendent.'

Writing up ethnography

The term 'ethnography,' as noted in Chapter 9, refers to both a method of social research and the finished product of that research. In recent years, the production of ethnographic texts has become a focus of interest in its own right, particularly the rhetorical conventions employed in their production.

Ethnographic texts are designed to convince readers of the *reality* of the events and situations described, and the plausibility of the analyst's explanations. The ethnographic text does not simply present a set of findings: it endeavours to provide an 'authoritative' account, with strong claims to truth, of the group or culture in question. Stylistic and rhetorical devices are used to persuade the reader to enter into a shared framework of facts, interpretations, observations, and reflections. Just like the writing found in reports of quantitative social research, the ethnographer typically uses a writing strategy imbued with *realism*. This means that the researcher tries to present an authoritative, dispassionate account of an external, objective reality. In this respect, there is very little difference between the writing styles of quantitative and qualitative researchers. Van Maanen (1988) called ethnography texts that conform to these characteristics *realist tales*. They represent the most common form of ethnographic writing, though he distinguished other types (see Box 17.2). However, the *form* that this realism takes can differ. Van Maanen distinguished four characteristics of realist tales: experiential authority, typical forms, the native's point of view, and interpretive omnipotence.

Box 17.1   What is reflexivity?

Reflexivity has several meanings in social science. To ethnomethodologists it refers to the way in which speech and action do more than merely act as indicators of deeper phenomena (see Chapter 16). Its other meaning carries the connotation that social researchers should reflect on the implications that their methods, values, biases, and decisions have for the knowledge of the social world that they generate. Reflexivity entails a sensitivity to the researcher's cultural, political, and social context. As such, 'knowledge' from a reflexive position is always a reflection of a researcher's location in time and social space. This notion is contained in Pink's (2001) formulation of a reflexive approach to the use of visual images (see Chapter 9).

There has been a growing reflexivity in social research, documented in books that collect details on the inner workings of the actual research process as distinct from the often sanitized portrayal in research articles (for example, Bryman 1988). The confessional tales referred to in Box 17.2 are manifestations of this same development. However, the rise of reflexivity largely predates the growing awareness of postmodern thinking. What distinguishes the reflexivity that has followed in the wake of postmodernism is a greater acknowledgment of the role of the researcher in the construction of knowledge. A researcher is not just someone who extracts knowledge from observations and conversations with others and then transmits knowledge to an audience. The researcher is viewed as implicated in the construction of knowledge both through the observer stance assumed in relation to the observed, and through the ways in which an account is transmitted in the form of a written text.

Experiential authority

As in much quantitative research writing, in ethnography the author disappears from view. Readers are told what the members of a group, the only people directly visible in the text, say and do. An invisible author provides the narrative, giving the impression that the findings presented are what any reasonable, similarly placed researcher would have found. Readers have to accept that this is what the ethnographer saw and heard. This strategy essentially plays down any suggestion of bias arising from the personal subjectivity of the author/ethnographer; for example, that the fieldworker may have become too involved with the people being studied. To this end, when writing up their ethnographic work, authors play up their academic credentials and qualifications, their previous experience, and so on. All this enhances the degree to which their accounts can be relied upon, making the authors/ethnographers appear as reliable witnesses.

A further element of experiential authority is that, when describing their methods, ethnographers often make a great deal of the intensity of their research—they spent so many months in the field, had conversations and interviews with countless individuals, worked hard to establish rapport, and so on. Drawing the reader's attention to such hardships of the fieldwork—the danger, the poor food, the disruptive effect on normal life, the feelings of isolation and loneliness, and so on—creates a sympathy for the author, or less charitably, deflects potential criticism of the findings.

Also worth mentioning are the extensive quotations from conversations and interviews that invariably form part of the ethnographic report. These are important ingredients in the author's use of *evidence* to support the points made. They are also a mechanism for establishing the credibility of the report in that they demonstrate the author's ability to encourage people to talk. The copious descriptive details—of places, patterns of behaviour, contexts, etc.—show that the author was an ideally placed witness for all the findings uncovered.

Typical forms

The author often generalizes about a number of recurring features of the group being studied in order to illustrate a typical behaviour or thought pattern. Examples based on particular incidents or people may be used, but basically the emphasis is upon recurrent forms of behaviour. For example, in her conclusion to her ethnographic research on female drug users, cited several times in Chapter 9, Taylor wrote: 'Yet the control exercised over women through the threat to remove their children highlights a major factor differentiating female and male drug users. Unlike male drug users, female drug

---

Box 17.2   Three forms of ethnographic writing

Van Maanen (1988) distinguished three major types of ethnographic writing:

- *Realist tales*—apparently definitive, confident, and dispassionate third-person accounts of a culture and the behaviour of its members. This is the most prevalent form of ethnographic writing.

- *Confessional tales*—personalized accounts in which the ethnographer is fully implicated in the data-gathering and writing-up processes. These are warts-and-all accounts of the trials and tribulations of doing ethnography. They have become more prominent since the 1970s and reflect a growing emphasis on reflexivity in qualitative research. Several of the sources referred to in Chapter 10 are confessional tales (for example, Armstrong 1993; Giulianotti 1995). However,

confessional tales are more concerned with detailing how research is carried out than with presenting findings. Very often the confessional tale is told in one context (such as an invited chapter in a book of similar tales) but the main findings are written up in realist tale form.

- *Impressionist tales*—accounts that feature 'words, metaphors, phrasings, and . . . the expansive recall of fieldwork experience' (1988: 102). There is an emphasis on stories of dramatic events that provide 'a representational means of cracking open the culture and the fieldworker's way of knowing it' (1988: 102). However, as Van Maanen noted, impressionist tales 'are typically enclosed within realist, or perhaps more frequently, confessional tales' (1988: 106).

users, like many other women, have two careers: one in the public sphere and one in the private, domestic sphere' (1993: 154). This statement portrays a pattern among women drug users, making any individual woman important only insofar as she can illustrate the general tendency.

The natives' points of view

A commitment to seeing through the eyes of the people being studied is important for qualitative researchers because it is part of their strategy for getting at the meaning of social reality held by those observed. However, it also represents an important element in creating a sense of authority on the part of the ethnographer. After all, claiming to have taken the natives' points of view implies that the author can speak authoritatively about the group in question. Ethnographies frequently include numerous references to the steps taken by the ethnographer to get close to the people studied, and their success in that regard. In her research on female drug users, Taylor (1993: 16) wrote:

> Events I witnessed or took part in ranged from the very routine (sitting around drinking coffee and eating junk food) to accompanying various women on visits to . . . the HIV clinic; I accompanied them when they were in court, and even went flat-hunting with one woman. I went shopping with some, helping them choose clothes for their children and presents for their friends. I visited them in their homes, rehabilitation centres, and maternity wards, sat with them through withdrawals, watched them using drugs, and accompanied them when they went 'scoring' (buying drugs).

Interpretative omnipotence

When writing an ethnography, the author rarely presents alternative interpretations of an event or pattern of behaviour. Instead, the phenomenon in question may be portrayed as having a single meaning or significance, which the fieldworker alone has cracked. Indeed, the evidence provided is carefully marshalled to support the singular interpretation placed on the event or pattern of behaviour. It seems obvious or inevitable that anyone would draw the same inferences the author drew when faced with such evidence.

These four characteristics of realist tales imply that the research process itself is only one stage in the creation of a sense of having figured out the nature of a culture. Creating that impression also depends on how the researchers, in their written ethnography, *represent* what they did in the field. Recall that for postmodernists, any realist tale is merely one 'spin'—that is, one interpretation that has been formulated in relation to the culture in question.

Bibliography

No one likes to make bibliographic entries. That is why most bibliographies contain an error or two. The problem with errors is that they indicate a lack of attention on the author's part. Here is a bibliography taken from an earlier version of this text with errors deliberately added. Look over all of the entries to see the form, and then see how many errors you can find. Errors in bibliographic entries will not stop true scholars from finding your source, they just slow them down a bit. The answers are at the end of the next chapter.

Abraham, J. (1994), 'Bias in Science and Medical Knowledge: The Opren controversy,' *Sociology*, 28: 717–36.
Armstrong, D, Gosling, A., Weinman, J., and Marteau, T. (1997), 'The Place of Inter-Rater Reliability in Qualitative Research: an Empirical Study,' *Sociology*, 31: 597-606
Atkinson, R. (1998), *The Life Story Interview* (Thousand Oaks, CA: Sage).
Barnard, M., and Frischer, M. (1995), 'Combining Quantitative and Qualitative Approaches: Researching HIV-Related Risk Behaviours among Drug Injectors,' *Addiction Research*, 351–62.
Barter, C., and E. Renold (1999) 'The Use of Vignettes in Qualitative Research,' *Social Research Update*, 25.
Blaikie, A. (2001), 'Photographs in the Cultural Account: Contested Narratives and Collective Memory in the Scottish Islands,' *Sociological Review*, 49- 345–67.

Practical Tip

Referring to websites

It is a common practice in academic work when referring to a website to include the date when it was last consulted. This convention has arisen because a subsequent researcher, perhaps wanting to follow up some findings, may find that the website is no longer there or that it has changed.

Buchanan, D. R. (1992), 'An Uneasy Alliance: Combining Qualitative And Quantitative Research Methods,' *Health Education Quarterly*, *19*: 117–35.

Charmaz, K., (2000), 'Grounded Theory: Objectivist and Constructivist Methods,' in Denzin, N.K. and Lincoln, Y.S. (eds.), *Handbook of Qualitative Research*, 2nd ed. (Thousand Oaks, CA: Sage).

B. Czarniawska. (1998), *A Narrative Approach to Organization Studies* (Thousand Oaks, XA: Sage).

Giulianotti, R. (1995), 'Participant Observation and Research into Football Hooliganism: Reflections on the Problems of Entrée and Everyday Risks,' *Sociology of Sport Journal*, 12: 1–20.

Reinharz, S, 1992, *Feminist Methods in Social Research* (New York).

Okely, J. (1994), 'Thinking through Fieldwork, in A. Bryman and R G. Burgess (eds.), *Analyzing Qualitative Data* (London: Routledge).

Sheehan, K. (2001), 'E-Mail survey response rates: A review,' *Journal of Computer-Mediated Communication*, 6. www.ascusc.org/jcmc/vol6/issue2/sheehan.html.

DO NOT ALPHABETIZE the authors' names in items with multiple authors. The existing order reflects their choice, or at least the choice of the most powerful one in the group. (The first author listed is generally considered to be the lead author; the remaining ones are presented in descending order of importance.) What ethical issues arise in determining authorship order? Some online bibliographies include only the first author, as does part of the *Social Science Citation Index*.

Key Points

- Good writing is probably just as important as good research practice. Indeed, it is probably better thought of as a part of good research practice.

- A clear statement of the research questions and an effective structure for the report are important in writing up research.

- The writings of social scientists do more than simply report findings; they are designed to convince and to persuade.

- The emphasis on writing to convince and persuade is not meant to imply that there is no external social reality. It merely suggests that the reader's understanding of that reality is profoundly influenced by the way the writer represents it.

- While postmodernism has exerted an influence on this last point, writers working within other traditions have also contributed to it.

- The basic structure of quantitative and qualitative research articles are broadly similar, as are the rhetorical devices used to produce them.

Questions for Review

- Why is it important to consider the ways in which social research is written up?

Writing up quantitative research: an example

- Read an article based on quantitative research in a Canadian sociology journal. To what extent does it exhibit the same characteristics as Kelley and De Graaf's (1997) article?

- Why are strategies to convince and persuade important in writing up quantitative social research?

Writing up qualitative research: an example

- Read an article based on qualitative research in a Canadian sociology journal. How far does it exhibit the same characteristics as Beardsworth and Keil's (1992) article?

- How is the structure of Beardsworth and Keil's article different from that found in Kelley and De Graaf's piece?

Postmodernism and its implications for writing

- Why has postmodernism produced a growth of interest in the writing of social research?

- What is reflexivity?

Writing up ethnography

- Is it true that typical ethnographic writing is imbued with realism?

- What forms of ethnographic writing other than realist tales can be found?

- What are the main characteristics of realist tales?

18 Conducting a Research Project

Chapter overview

The goal here is to provide advice to students in conducting small-scale research projects. The guidance offered goes beyond the discussions presented in previous chapters. A wide variety of issues is explored, including:

- time management when doing research;
- generating research questions;
- dealing with existing literature on the subject; and
- writing to produce compelling findings.

Introduction

This chapter provides some advice for those readers carrying out their own small-scale research projects. The previous 17 chapters have provided helpful information about the choices available and how to implement them. Here we will examine how one can use that knowledge to conduct a small project of one's own, such as an honour's thesis or a course assignment. Students in graduate programs will also find some of the observations helpful. Finally, the advice is tailored for students engaged in empirical research, that is, studies in which they collect new data or conduct an analysis of existing data.

Know what is expected by your institution

Quite often a course instructor will have specific guidelines and requirements for class projects. Look them over carefully and follow them. People doing undergraduate theses or those in graduate programs should be aware that their institution or department may have specific requirements concerning a wide variety of features, such as: the form of binding to be used, how a study is to be presented, whether an abstract is required, the size of page margins, the format for referencing, the structure of the presentation, plagiarism, and deadlines.

Identifying research questions

Most students want to conduct research in areas of personal interest. This is not a bad thing; as noted in Chapter 1, many professional social researchers start from this point as well (see also Lofland and Lofland 1995: 11–14). However, in qualitative research as well as quantitative, this beginning must include the formulation of the research questions. Even though Chapter 8 said that qualitative research is more open-ended than quantitative, and Chapter 9 referred to some studies not driven by specific research questions, open-ended research is risky. It can lead to collecting data that will never be used, and to major problems in data organization and analysis. In some cases it can lead to disaster, namely the project taking far too long or never being completed. So, unless your supervisor or instructor advises to the contrary, formulate some research questions. In other words, what is it about your area of interest that you want to know?

Research questions are important because they provide a focus that will:

- guide the literature search;
- limit the scope of the project (see Figure 18.1);
- guide decisions about what data to collect;

- guide the analysis of data;
- guide the writing up of the findings; and
- reduce the chances of going off in unnecessary directions and tangents.

Research questions should exhibit the following characteristics:

- They should be clear.
- They should be researchable, thus not formulated in terms so abstract that they cannot be investigated. Nor should they be so grand in scope that it would be impossible to answer them in the time available.
- They should have some connection with established theory and research. This means that there should be an existing literature both to help illuminate how the research questions should be approached and how they relate to the larger discipline. Even with a topic scarcely addressed by social scientists, it is unlikely that there will be no relevant literature whatever; normally there is material available on related or parallel topics.
- Research questions should be linked to each other so an argument can be developed in the paper.

Constructing a coherent argument for unrelated research questions is almost impossible, even for experienced researchers.

- They should hold out the prospect of making an original contribution—however small—to the knowledge on the topic.

If stuck about how to formulate research questions (or indeed other phases of the research), look at journal articles or research monographs to see how others have expressed them. Look at past student papers for ideas as well. Talk things over with your advisor or course instructor. Gary Marx (1997) suggested a wide range of sources for research questions (see Box 18.1).

Using a supervisor

While most institutions allocate students writing theses or dissertations to supervisors or advisors, the kind and amount of assistance that can be expected varies greatly. Equally, students vary in how frequently and for what reasons they will see them. The advice here is simple: use a supervisor or advisor to

Research area
(Example: Concerns about risks to personal safety)

Select aspect of research area
(Causes of the variations in concerns about risks to personal safety)

Possible research questions
(What personal safety risks are of greatest concern to people? Do age, gender, social class, or education affect the perception of risk? Do parents worry more than non-parents about risks to personal safety? What is the main source of people's knowledge about issues relating to such risk—newspapers, television, family? Do concerns about these risks have an impact on how people conduct their daily lives, and if so in what ways? Do worries about personal safety result in fatalism?)

Select research questions
(What personal safety risks are of greatest concern to people? Do age, gender, social class, or education affect the perception of risk? Do parents worry more than non-parents about risks to personal safety? Why?)

Figure 18.1 Steps in selecting research questions

the fullest extent allowable and give due consideration to their suggestions. Such people are usually well versed in the research process and can provide help and feedback at all stages of the research, subject to your institution's strictures in this regard. If there is criticism of your research questions, interview schedule, early drafts, or whatever, try to respond positively. It is not a personal attack. Such comments are usually accompanied by the reasons for them and some suggestions for revision. Be thankful for the opportunity to address the deficiencies *before* your work is formally examined. Supervisors have to go through the same process themselves when they submit an article to a peer-refereed journal or when they apply for a research grant.

Also relevant here is that students stuck at the start, or who fall behind in their work, sometimes respond by avoiding their supervisors. They then get caught up in a vicious circle that results in their work being neglected and then rushed at the end, or in some cases never completed. Try to avoid this situation by confronting any difficulties and getting advice on how to deal with them as soon as possible.

Undergraduate students doing course projects should follow a similar procedure. Consult the course instructor about your project if you run into difficulties, and the sooner the better. It is also worthwhile to discuss your research with the instructor even if there are no apparent problems, since he or she may pick up on issues you have missed.

Managing time and resources: start thinking early about the research area

Most students are asked to start thinking about a potential topic well before they are required to actually research it. That is worth doing because all research is constrained by time. Two points are relevant here:

- Work out a timetable, preferably with your supervisor or instructor, detailing the different stages of the research (including the review of literature and writing up). The timetable should specify the different stages and the specific dates for starting and finishing them (see Figure 18.2 for an example of a quantitative research outline). Some stages are likely to be ongoing—for example, searching the literature for references (see below)—but that should not delay the development of a timetable.

- Find out what, if any, resources are available for carrying out your research. For example, can the institution help with such things as photocopying,

---

Box 18.1   Marx's (not Karl) sources of research questions

Marx (1997) suggested the following possible sources of research questions:

- Intellectual puzzles and contradictions.

- The existing literature.

- Replication.

- A feeling that a certain theoretical perspective or notable piece of work is misguided. Your work presents the reasons for those shortcomings.

- A social problem, one needing a social scientific (for example, sociological) explanation.

- 'Gaps between official versions of reality and the facts on the ground' (1997: 113). Examine the explanations for social phenomena—such as poverty, substance abuse, or international relations—offered by governments, the media, or social researchers. Are those explanations consistent with what you know or have experienced?

If not, produce some research questions pertaining to the phenomenon in question, including questions about the validity of the conventional wisdom on the topic.

- The counterintuitive. For example, when common sense seems to fly in the face of social scientific truths, as it did when those who thought the world would end began to proselytize rather than slink away in embarrassment when life carried on as usual (Festinger *et al.* 1956).

- Related 'empirical examples that trigger amazement' (1997: 114), for example, cases that contradict widely accepted theories, atypical events, etc.

- New methods and theories. How can they be applied in new settings?

- 'New social and technical developments and social trends' (1997: 114).

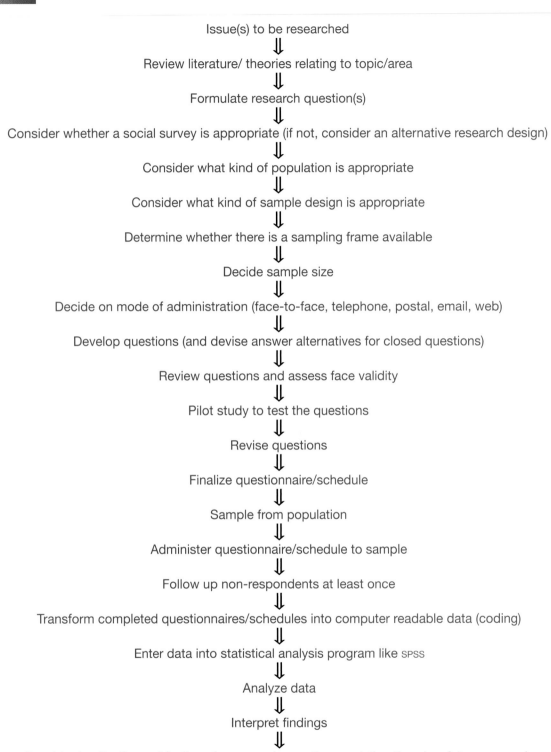

Issue(s) to be researched
⇓
Review literature/ theories relating to topic/area
⇓
Formulate research question(s)
⇓
Consider whether a social survey is appropriate (if not, consider an alternative research design)
⇓
Consider what kind of population is appropriate
⇓
Consider what kind of sample design is appropriate
⇓
Determine whether there is a sampling frame available
⇓
Decide sample size
⇓
Decide on mode of administration (face-to-face, telephone, postal, email, web)
⇓
Develop questions (and devise answer alternatives for closed questions)
⇓
Review questions and assess face validity
⇓
Pilot study to test the questions
⇓
Revise questions
⇓
Finalize questionnaire/schedule
⇓
Sample from population
⇓
Administer questionnaire/schedule to sample
⇓
Follow up non-respondents at least once
⇓
Transform completed questionnaires/schedules into computer readable data (coding)
⇓
Enter data into statistical analysis program like SPSS
⇓
Analyze data
⇓
Interpret findings
⇓
Consider implications of findings for research questions, existing theories, future research, and the discipline as a whole.

Figure 18.2 Steps in conducting a social survey

postage, stationery, and so on? Can it lend hardware to record and transcribe interviews? Has it got the necessary software, such as SPSS or NVivo? This kind of information helps to establish whether the research design and methods are financially feasible and practical. The imaginary 'gym study' in Chapter 12 is an example of an investigation feasible within the kind of time frame usually allocated to undergraduate projects. However, it would require resources for such things as: photocopying covering letters and questionnaires; postage for sending the questionnaires out and for follow-up letters; return postage for the questionnaires; quantitative data analysis, for example, software like SPSS.

Searching the existing literature

Online bibliographical databases accessible at most university libraries are an invaluable source of references. The best one for students is probably the *Sociological Abstracts*. It allows searches by keyword (topic), author, title, journal, and other descriptors. The focus is easily narrowed by specifying language, year, and type of presentation. For example, 'English, post-1998, journal articles only' can be searched and listed from latest to earliest. The 'journal articles only' restriction removes papers presented at meetings and dissertations, which are too hard for most students to access in any event. The searches use Boolean combinations of 'and,' 'or,' and 'not.' For example, a student can search keywords for articles on 'sexism and universities' to find articles that deal with both topics in the same piece. Choosing 'sexism or universities' gets those articles just referred to plus articles on either one alone. That is probably not a good choice—it's too broad. 'Universities and sexism or prejudice' is better because it expands the first option above to cover university prejudice in addition to university sexism. Finally, 'not' restricts the search. 'Sexism not universities' finds articles about sexism in places other than universities. Students should experiment with the use of keywords and Boolean options, and if unsuccessful, a librarian can help.

The output of these procedures gives details of journal articles in which the keyword (or journal, or year, etc.) appears. It may provide an abstract (if the journal concerned includes them) and full details of the article including references. Other indices are more specialized, for example, the *Canadian Periodical Index* and the *Population Index*, as are collections of abstracts, for example, *Sage Race Relations Abstracts* and *Women's Studies Abstracts*. (The *Readers' Guide to Periodical Literature* covers more popular pieces, those that would appear in magazines, etc., so it is generally not a good tool for finding academic research.) Mark the records you want and email them to yourself for a permanent record.

The bibliographies in the articles you find can provide additional sources to examine. A particularly interesting tool is the *Social Sciences Citation Index*, which looks forward from the original article to later ones that cite it, revealing what others think of it. Perhaps those who cited the article are critical, or maybe they accept it or expand on it. In this way a history of the research in the area of interest can be built up. To some professors, this index provides a measure of how often they have been cited. To those granting tenure and raises, it can be a crude indicator of merit: 'more citations, better researcher,' is the logic that is sometimes followed.

The library catalogue is an obvious route to find books, even those held at other universities. Again, ask a librarian if you are in difficulty. Too often, however, the books are checked out, dated, or contain too much information for student papers,

---

Practical Tip

Reasons for writing a literature review

The following are reasons for writing a literature review:

1. To find out what is already known in a research area, and what remains to be researched.
2. To learn from other researchers' mistakes.
3. To learn about different theoretical and methodological approaches to the research area.
4. To get help in developing an analytic framework.
5. To find additional variables to include in the research.
6. To search for further research questions.
7. To view examples of how findings can be interpreted.
8. To compare and contrast your findings with those of other researchers.
9. It is expected.

so the above sources may be preferable. The rule of thumb is to stop searching when the same items keep on appearing; this is similar to the idea of theoretical saturation in qualitative research.

The existing literature should be explored to identify the following issues:

- What is already known about this area?
- What concepts and theories are relevant?
- What research methods and strategies have been employed in studying this area?
- Are there any significant controversies?
- Are there any inconsistencies in the findings relating to this area?
- Are there any unanswered research questions?

Why review the existing literature? The most obvious reason is to find out what is already known about the area of interest in order to avoid 'reinventing the wheel.' You will also be able to revise and refine your research questions in the process of reviewing the literature. Beyond this, the existing literature on a topic will help you develop an argument about the significance of your research and where it will lead. The simile of a *story* is sometimes used in this context (see below).

A competent review of the literature is also a means of affirming your credibility as someone knowledgeable in your chosen area. When reading the existing literature, try to do the following:

- Take good notes, and record the full citation for all the materials used. It is infuriating to find that you forgot some detail, such as the volume number of an article in your Bibliography.
- The written review of the literature should be critical as well as descriptive. How does a particular piece relate to other things you have read? Is it contradictory? Are there any apparent strengths or deficiencies—for example, regarding the methods used or the conclusions drawn? What theoretical ideas have influenced the item?

In some areas of research, there are a huge number of references. Try to identify the major ones and work outwards from there. Move on to the next stage of the research at the point you identified in your timetable (see earlier) so that you can dig yourself out of the library. This is not to say that your search for the literature will cease, but that you need to force yourself to move on. Seek out your supervisor's or instructor's advice on whether you need to search the literature more.

Preparing for research

Once you have a methodology picked out, consider whether doing the research could lead to any ethical violations. Keep in mind the various ethical issues flagged throughout this book. (See Ethical issue 18.1.)

Do not begin your data collection until you have clearly identified your research questions. Develop data collection instruments with the research questions at the forefront of your thinking. If at all possible, conduct a small pilot study to see how well your research instruments work. You will also need to think about access to research sites. If the research requires entry to a closed setting like an organization, you need to get permission at the earliest opportunity. This usually takes so long that many advisors do not recommend using closed settings for student research. You also need to consider how you will go about gaining access to people. This issue leads you into sampling considerations, such as the following:

- Whom do you need to study in order to answer the research questions?
- Is an adequate sampling frame available?
- What kind of sampling strategy is feasible (for example, probability sampling, quota sampling, theoretical sampling, convenience sampling)?

Doing research and analyzing results

This is what the bulk of this book has been about. Here are some practical reminders:

- Keep good records. A research diary can be helpful, but there are several other things to bear in mind. For example, in a mailed questionnaire survey, keep track of who replied so you know who needs a reminder. If participant observation is a component of the research, it is imperative to keep good field notes and not to rely on memory.
- Become thoroughly familiar with any hardware to be used in collecting your data, such as tape recorders for interviewing, and make sure they are in good working order (for example, with batteries not close to being dead).

Ethical issue 18.1

Ethical approval for student work

By this point you have learned about many of the ethical issues involved in doing social research. Generally, for the type of work being described in this chapter, securing ethical approval is not necessary. Schools usually designate your supervisor or instructor as the person who should stop any unethical practices. Still, it is your work and you should pay attention to the rules. Supervisors and instructors have limited time to oversee your work, and situations may arise in the field that require quick decisions. In the end, the ethical responsibility is yours.

The following are examples of tricky ethical issues taken from actual research. To refresh your memory, see if you can identify the ethical dilemma and describe how it can be avoided or resolved.

- You are supposed to interview Ms Jones. Her mother answers the door and asks to be interviewed. She is lonely so you interview her and throw away the data; later you interview Ms Jones.

- Introductory psychology students are invited to participate in two experiments during the year. They are told that participation is optional, but those not taking part have to write a five-page paper.

- To reduce lying, rather than asking, 'Have you ever masturbated?' the question is rephrased as 'At what age did you begin masturbating?'

- To see if answers in an interview are truthful, some questions are repeated. In a variation, respondents are asked about reading books or seeing movies that do not exist.

- Respondents are told that a questionnaire is anonymous. Actually, the questionnaire can be identified by little pinholes in the last page, done to keep track of non-respondents needing a reminder. This will save a lot of time and money.

- A respondent asks after a three-hour interview that her case not be used, and that all the information she has provided be destroyed.

- Do not wait until all your data have been collected to begin coding. This recommendation applies to both quantitative and qualitative research. If using a questionnaire, begin coding data and entering them into SPSS, or an alternative package, after accumulating a reasonable number of completed questionnaires. In the case of qualitative data, such as interview transcripts, the same point applies; remember that in a grounded theory approach, data collection and data analysis should be intertwined.

- Recall that the transcription of recorded interviews takes a long time. Allow at least six hours for transcription for every one hour of recorded talk, at least in the early stages of the research.

- Become familiar with any needed software packages as early as possible.

- Do not put your personal safety at risk when doing research (see Box 18.2).

Writing up research

Once the data gathering and analysis have been completed, the findings must be conveyed to an audience. The first bit of advice is ...

Start early

There are good reasons for beginning the writing early on. It forces you to think about such issues as how best to present and justify the research questions, and how to structure the discussion of the literature cited. A further reason is an entirely practical one: many people find it difficult to get started and employ (probably unwittingly) procrastination strategies to put off the inevitable. This tendency can result in rushed, last-minute writing. Writing under this kind of pressure is not ideal, to say the least. How you present your findings and conclusions is a crucial aspect of the research process. Not providing a convincing account of your research due to time pressures does not do it justice.

Be persuasive

This point is crucial. Writing up research should not involve mechanically reporting findings and drawing conclusions. Above all, the writing must be *persuasive*, convincing readers of the credibility of the conclusions. Simply saying, 'it is interesting that ...' is not enough. Readers must be convinced that the findings and conclusions are plausible and significant.

Box 18.2   Safety in research

In 2002, a 19-year-old British female sociology student, thought to have gone to interview a homeless person, was reported missing. Because of safety concerns, her advisor had recommended that she take a friend with her and conduct the interview in a public place. However, it turned out that she had not gone to do the interview at all, and to everyone's relief showed up abroad (see Barkham and Jenkins, 'Fears for Fresher Who Vanished on Mission to Talk to the Homeless,' *The Times* [London], 13 December 2002).

Nonetheless, there is an important lesson in this incident: social research can place you in potentially dangerous situations. Avoid situations where personal harm is a real possibility. Just as you should ensure that no harm comes to research participants (as prescribed in the discussion of ethical principles throughout the book), individuals conducting research should not place themselves in unsafe situations. The advice given by the student's advisor—to take someone with you and conduct the interview in a public place—is sensible. If you have a cell phone, keep it nearby and switched on. Establish a routine whereby you keep in regular contact with friends or

family members. Even in seemingly safe situations, a researcher can be faced with a sudden outburst of abuse or threatening behaviour. This can arise when people react unpredictably to an interview question or to being observed. If there are signs that such behaviour is imminent (for example, through body language), withdraw from the situation. Further guidelines on these issues can be found in Craig (2004).

Lee (2004) drew an important distinction between two kinds of danger in fieldwork: ambient and situational. The former refers to situations in which danger is endemic to the context. Fieldwork in conflict situations of the kind encountered by the researcher who took on the role of a bouncer (Winlow *et al.* 2001) is an example. Situational danger occurs when a researcher attracts aggression, hostility, or violence from particular participants in an otherwise safe setting (Lee 2004). It is harder to foresee than ambient danger.

Sometimes one has to be extremely thorough in checking for possible hazards. For instance, it was only after she began her research in a hospital laboratory that Lankshear (2000) realized that she could be exposed to dangerous pathogens.

Practical Tip

Non-sexist writing

One of the biggest problems (but by no means the only one) when trying to write in a non-sexist way is avoiding those 'her/his' and 'his/her' formulations. The easiest way of dealing with this is to write in the plural where possible. For example:

'I wanted to give each respondent the opportunity to complete the questionnaire at a time and location that was convenient for him or her.'

This sentence, although grammatically correct, can be rephrased as:

'I wanted to give respondents the opportunity to complete their questionnaires at times and locations that were convenient for them.'

Get feedback

Try to get as much feedback on your writing as possible, and respond positively to the points made. Your supervisor or instructor is likely to be the main source of input; provide him or her with drafts of your work to the fullest extent that regulations allow, leaving plenty of time for a response. There are others like you who want your supervisor or instructor to comment on their work, and, if rushed, the comments may be less helpful. Also, you can ask others in your program or class to read your drafts and comment on them, and they may ask you to do the same. Their comments may be very useful, but, by and large, your supervisor's or instructor's comments are the main ones you should seek.

Avoid sexist, racist, and other prejudicial language

Remember that writing should be free of sexist, racist, and other prejudicial language. The Social Science and Humanities Research Council of

Canada publication *On the Treatment of the Sexes in Social Research* (1985) by M. Eichler and J. Lapointe is helpful.

Structure your writing

The following is typical of the structure of a 10 000- to 15 000-word research project entailing data collection.

Title page
Examine your institution's or class's rules about what should be included here.

Acknowledgments
You may want to acknowledge the help of various people, such as gatekeepers who gave you access to an organization, people who have read your drafts and provided you with feedback, or your supervisor or instructor for his or her advice.

Table of contents (if applicable)
Your institution or class may have recommendations or prescriptions about the form this should take.

An abstract
This is a brief (less than one page) summary of your work. Not all institutions or instructors ask for this component, so see if it is required. Journal articles usually have abstracts; draw on them for how to approach this task.

Introduction
- You should explain what you are writing about and why it is important.
- Describe in general terms the theoretical perspective you used and why.
- You should also outline your research questions. Remember that in qualitative studies, research questions are often more open-ended than is the case with quantitative work.
- The opening sentence or sentences are often the most difficult of all. Becker (1986) strongly advised against 'vacuous' opening sentences. He gave the example: 'This study deals with the problem of careers,' adding that this kind of sentence 'is evasive, pointing to something without saying anything, or anything much, about it. *What* about careers?' (Becker 1986: 51). He suggested that such evasions arise from concerns

about giving away the plot. He countered that it is much better to give readers a quick and clear indication of what is going to be presented. Kelley and De Graaf's (1997) and Beardsworth and Keil's (1992) opening sentences do rather well in this regard (see Chapter 17).

Literature review
This provides an overview of the main ideas and research done in the area of interest. However, you should do more than simply summarize the relevant literature.

- You should, whenever appropriate, be critical in your approach.
- You should use your review of the literature to show why your research questions are important. For example, if the basis for your research questions is the point that although a lot of research has been done on X (a general topic or area, such as food consumption), little research has been done on X_1 (an aspect of X, like vegetarianism), the literature review is where you justify this assertion. Alternatively, it may be that there are two competing positions with regard to X_1 and you are going to investigate which one provides a better understanding. In the literature review, you should outline the differences between the competing positions. The literature review, then, locates your own research within a tradition of related research.
- Bear in mind that you will return to much of the reviewed literature when you present your findings and write up the conclusions.
- Do not try to get everything you read into a literature review. Trying to force it all in (because of the great effort involved in uncovering and reading the material) is not going to help. The literature review is there to assist in developing an argument, and bringing in material of passing relevance may undermine your ability to get your argument across.
- Recall that reading the relevant literature should continue more or less throughout your research. This means that a literature review written before the data collection is provisional. Indeed, you may want to revise the initial review, *but do not make the new review conform to unexpected findings you have uncovered*. Leave that to another study.

- Further thoughts on producing a literature review are presented in Box 18.3. They were derived from a review of qualitative studies of organizations, but also apply to quantitative research.

Research methods

The term 'research methods' is meant here as a kind of catch-all for several things that need to be outlined: research design; sampling approach; how access was achieved (if applicable); specific procedures used (such as, if using a mailed questionnaire, whether it included a follow up of non-respondents); and, where relevant, the nature of the questionnaire, interview schedule, participant observation, observation schedule, or coding frame. Although detailed descriptions of these usually appear in an appendix, you should comment on such things as your style of questioning or observation and why you asked the things you did. Other issues to be discussed here include problems of non-response, note taking, and data-analysis procedures. When discussing each of these matters, describe and defend the choices made, such as why a mailed questionnaire rather than a structured interview was used, or why a particular population was chosen for sampling.

Results

In this section you present the gist of your findings. If you will have a separate Discussion section, the results are generally presented with little commentary on how the findings relate to the claims made in the literature. If there is no Discussion to follow, you

---

Box 18.3   Presenting the qualitative research literature

Further useful advice on literature reviews can be gleaned from examining how articles reporting qualitative research on organizations are composed. In their examination of such articles, Golden-Biddle and Locke (1993, 1997) argued that good articles in this area develop a story; that is, a clear and compelling framework around which the writing is structured. This idea is very much in tune with Wolcott's (1990: 18) recommendation to 'determine the basic story you are going to tell.' Golden-Biddle and Locke's research suggested that the presentation of the author's position in relation to the literature is an important component of storytelling, and distinguished two ways of conveying the literature.

- **Constructing inter-textual coherence**—the author shows how existing contributions to the literature relate to each other and to the research that will be reported. The techniques are:

  - *synthesized coherence*—theory and research previously regarded as unconnected are pieced together;
  - *progressive coherence*—portrays the building-up of an area of knowledge around which there is considerable consensus;
  - *non-coherence*—recognition that there has been considerable disagreement in the contributions to a certain research program.

Each of these strategies is designed to leave room for a contribution to be made by the writer's own research.

- **Problematizing the situation**—the literature is then criticized by identifying a problem, such as:

  - *incomplete*—the existing literature is not fully complete; there is a gap;
  - *inadequate*—the existing literature has overlooked useful ways of looking at the phenomenon; alternative perspectives or frameworks are then introduced.

Golden-Biddle and Locke argue that accounts of the literature are used by writers to achieve a number of things.

- They demonstrate their knowledge and competence by referring to prominent writings in the field.

- They develop their version of the literature in a way that highlights the contribution they will make in the article.

- The gap or problem identified in the literature corresponds to the research questions.

- The idea of writing up research as storytelling serves as a useful reminder that reviewing the literature, which is part of the story, should link seamlessly with the rest of the article and not be considered a separate element.

need to provide some reflections on the significance of your findings for your research questions and for the literature. Bear these points in mind:

- Whichever approach is taken, remember not to include *all* your results. You should present and discuss only those findings that relate to your research questions. This may mean a rather painful process of leaving out many findings, but it is necessary so that the thread of your argument is not lost.
- Your writing should point to particularly salient aspects of the tables, graphs, or other forms of analysis you present. Do not just summarize what a table shows; direct the reader to the parts of it that are especially striking from the point of view of your research questions. Try to ask yourself what story you want the table to convey, and then relay it to your readers.
- Do not simply present a graph or table without any comment whatsoever, leaving the reader to wonder why you think it is important.

- A particular problem in qualitative research is the need to leave out large parts of the data. As one experienced qualitative researcher put it: 'The major problem we face in qualitative inquiry is not to get data, but to get rid of it!' (Wolcott 1990: 18). You simply have to recognize that much of the data accumulated have to be jettisoned, or any sense of an argument in your work is likely to be lost. There is also the risk that the account of your findings will appear too descriptive and lack an analytical edge. This is why it is important to use the research questions as a focus and to orient the presentation of the findings to them.

Discussion

In the Discussion (if you have one), reflect on the implications of the findings for the research questions. If you have specified hypotheses, as Kelley and De Graaf (1997) did, the discussion should revolve around whether the hypotheses were confirmed or not. If not, you might speculate about why they were not supported. Was the sample too small? Did you

---

Answers   Bibliography errors in Chapter 17 are found at *X*

Abraham, J. (1994), 'Bias in Science and Medical Knowledge: The Opren *X*controversy,' *Sociology*, 28: 717–36.

Armstrong, D, Gosling, A., Weinman, J., and Marteau, T. (1997), 'The Place of Inter-Rater Reliability in Qualitative Research: *X*an Empirical Study,' *Sociology*, 31: 597-606*X*

Atkinson, R. (1998), *The Life Story Interview* (Thousand Oaks, CA: Sage).

Barnard, M., and Frischer, M. (1995), 'Combining Quantitative and Qualitative Approaches: Researching HIV-Related Risk Behaviours among Drug Injectors',*X* Addiction Research, *X*351–62.

Barter, C., and *X*E. Renold (1999)*X* 'The Use of Vignettes in Qualitative Research,' *Social Research Update*, 25*X*.

Blaikie, A. (2001), 'Photographs in the Cultural Account: Contested *X* Narratives and Collective Memory in the Scottish Islands,' *Sociological Review*, 49*X*- 345-67.

Buchanan, D. R. (1992), 'An Uneasy Alliance: Combining Qualitative *X*And Quantitative Research Methods,' *Health Education Quarterly, X(font)* 19: 117–35.

Charmaz, K., (2000), 'Grounded Theory: Objectivist and Constructivist Methods,' in Denzin, *X*N.K. and Lincoln, *X*Y.S. (eds.), *Handbook of Qualitative Research*, 2nd ed. (Thousand Oaks, CA: Sage).

*X*B. Czarniawska. (1998), *A Narrative Approach to Organization Studies* (Thousand Oaks, *XX*A: Sage).

SPACING*X*

Giulianotti, R. (1995), 'Participant Observation and Research into Football Hooliganism: Reflections on the Problems of Entrée and Everyday Risks,' *Sociology of Sport Journal*, 12: 1–20.

Reinharz, S. *X*1992, *Feminist Methods in Social Research* (New York*X*).

*X*ALPHABETIZATION

Okely, J. (1994), 'Thinking through Fieldwork*X*, in A. Bryman and R*X* G. Burgess (eds.), *Analyzing Qualitative Data* (London: Routledge).

Sheehan, K. (2001), 'E-Mail *X*survey *X*response *X*rates: A *X*review,' *Journal of Computer-Mediated Communication,* 6*X*. www.ascusc.org/jcmc/vol6/issue2/sheehan.html

Checklist of issues to consider for writing up research

☑ Is there a good correspondence between the title of the project and its contents?

☑ Have you clearly specified your research questions?

☑ Have you clearly linked the literature cited to your research questions?

☑ Is your discussion of the literature critical and not just a summary of what you have read?

☑ Have you clearly outlined your research design and research methods, explaining:

- why you chose a particular research design or method?

- why you implemented your research in a particular way (for example, how the interview questions relate to the research questions, or why you observed people in particular situations)?

- how you selected your research participants?

- whether there were any issues to do with cooperation (for example, response rates)?

- if your research required access to an organization, how and on what basis the agreement was achieved?

- any difficulties encountered in implementing your research?

- the steps taken to ensure that the research was ethical?

- how the data were analyzed?

☑ Have you presented your data so it relates to your research questions?

☑ Are the interpretations of your data fully supported with tables, figures, or segments from transcripts?

☑ Are those tables and/or figures properly labelled with a title and number?

☑ Does the discussion of the findings relate to the research questions?

☑ Does that discussion show how the findings shed light on the literature presented?

☑ If presenting tables and/or figures, are they commented upon in the text?

☑ Do the conclusions clearly establish what your research contributes to the literature?

☑ Have you explained the limitations of your study?

☑ Do your conclusions consist solely of a summary of findings? If so, rewrite them, explaining their significance.

☑ Do the conclusions provide clear answers to your research questions?

☑ Have you broken up the text in each chapter or section with appropriate subheadings?

☑ Do you provide signposts so that readers are clear about what to expect next, and why it is there?

☑ Does the writing avoid sexist, racist, and other prejudicial language?

☑ Have you checked to ensure that there is not excessive use of jargon?

☑ Have you included all necessary appendices (for example, interview schedule, letters requesting access, communications with research participants)?

☑ Does the list of references include all items referred to in your text?

☑ Does the format of the references follow precisely the style your institution or instructor requires?

☑ Have you ensured that your institution's or instructor's requirements for submitting projects are fully met on such issues as number of words (so that it is neither too long nor too short) and whether an abstract and table of contents are required?

☑ Have you ensured that you do not quote excessively when presenting the literature?

☑ Have you fully acknowledged the work of others so that you cannot be accused of plagiarism?

☑ Have you acknowledged, preferably in a preface, the help of others where appropriate (for example, your supervisor, people who may have helped with interviews, people who read drafts)?

☑ Finally, go back and check for consistency of style. Is the tense consistent, the margins, pagination, and capitalization? Many forms are acceptable, but all must be consistently applied.

forget a key variable? In this section you can also bring out the main theoretical contributions of the research and explore their implications.

Conclusion

The main points are as follows:

- A Conclusion is not the same as a summary. However, it is frequently useful to briefly recapitulate your main arguments at the beginning of the Conclusion. Once that is done, hammer home to readers the significance of your research.
- You may also draw attention to any limitations of your work, now apparent with the benefit of hindsight.
- Suggest avenues for further research.

Two things to avoid are engaging in speculations that take you too far from your data or that cannot be substantiated by the data, and discussing issues or ideas not previously introduced.

Appendices

In appendices you may want to include such things as the questionnaire, coding frame, observation schedule, letters sent to those sampled, and letters sent to and received from gatekeepers.

References

Include here all references cited in the text. Follow the format suggested by your department or instructor. The format is usually a variation of the one used in this book.

Finally

Remember to fulfill any obligations you have made, such as supplying a copy of your report to those who have been promised one. Maintain the confidentiality of the information given and the anonymity of informants and other research participants by securing and later destroying all the primary data.

Appendix

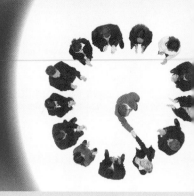

The Ideal Stages of Research

The word 'ideal' is used here to convey the idea that what is presented is an abstraction, a simplification of a more complex reality. These stages are not ideal in the sense that they are necessarily the best way to do things. Like building a house or painting a portrait, there is no single best way to do research. Sometimes the order of the tasks presented in Figure 1 can be rearranged. Also, it is not uncommon to go from one step to the next, and then backtrack and change what was done in a previous step. Nonetheless, some general points and observations can be made that outline how research may progress from its initial stages to its completion.

In the beginning: motivation

Where does research begin?

Sometimes research begins with a sense of wonder, a feeling of amazement with the social world that is accompanied with a strong desire to understand it. That amazement may be tinged with a sense of tragedy, for example, when a society is in crisis and scholars are trying to find solutions to the issues—a motivation that has been around since the beginnings of social science in the eighteenth century. The challenges posed by urbanization, industrialization, ethnic conflict, gender relations, and many other forms of social strain have long provided the impetus for research.

Sometimes the enthrallment occurs in the absence of calamity, as when one wonders how it happens that humans acquire speech or how people maintain democratic freedoms. At other times, inquiry is the result of rank curiosity—as one wag put it, if you walk by a house that has its curtains drawn and

wonder what goes on inside, you'd probably make a good social scientist.

Of course not all research begins with lofty motivations. Quite often the reasons for conducting a study are rather mundane. Research can enhance the career of the researcher, especially if it is conducted with substantial funding. Sometimes researchers compete with one another to see who can produce the most publications. Similarly, graduate students (and some undergraduates) may do research in order to fulfill degree requirements. In most instances, one would think, research is done out of some combination of exalted and mundane motivations.

The research question(s)

Once a decision has been made to do research, one must then decide *what* to delve into. The first thing to do is to come up with a research question, or a set of research questions, that will give the study a specific focus or goal. As mentioned in various places in this textbook, quite often research questions in quantitative studies are much more precise and explicit than those found in qualitative research. But even with the latter, there has to be at least a general idea of what one is trying to accomplish. With both types of inquiry, it is fairly common for research questions to be revised as the research proceeds, especially in the early stages of the project. Asking appropriate research questions should allow you to contribute to the existing knowledge of the topic, if only in a modest way.

Literature review

Chances are you will not be the first person to investigate your topic or to use the methodology you have in mind. Reading up on what others have done will

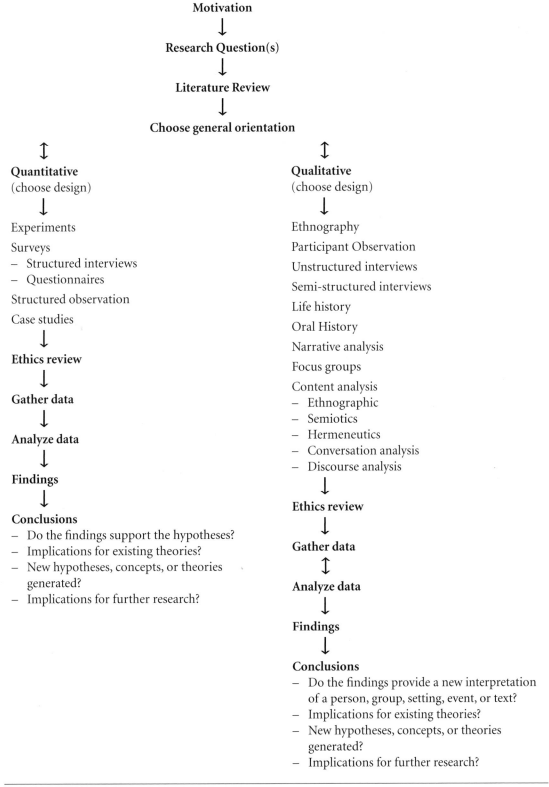

Figure 1 The Ideal Stages of Research

help you understand your topic more fully and will prevent 're-inventing the wheel.' A good knowledge of the literature may also reveal contradictions or gaps in the existing understanding of your topic, which can form the basis of your project. Sometimes doing a review of the literature can lead to substantial revisions in the research questions, for example, when one encounters a finding related to one's topic that lacks a compelling explanation and which can then be the focus of the inquiry. Reviewing the literature may also provide ideas about how various methodologies can be applied to your topic.

Choosing a general research orientation: quantitative and/or qualitative

Once one has come up with a research question or questions, and has reviewed existing works on the topic or related topics, a decision on a general research orientation can be made. However, it is not uncommon for researchers to begin with the idea that they are going to take a particular orientation, even before the research question is formulated or the literature review is done. For example, researchers specializing in qualitative studies may start with the assumption that their research will be qualitative rather than quantitative in nature. Likewise, a person who has done a number of survey projects may have surveys in mind when designing a study, and may not even review the qualitative literature that relates to the topic of interest.

Of course both quantitative and qualitative research can be combined in a single study, and that is why two-way arrows appear above and below 'Choose general orientation' in Figure 1, although in reality most studies are predominantly of one sort or the other.

Picking a research design from the ones available within a general research orientation

After the choice has been made to pursue the research from a quantitative or qualitative orientation (or both), a number of research designs are available for consideration. The choice of the research design depends on a number of things, but your first concern should be to find a design that is appropriate for your research questions. For example, if you've chosen a quantitative orientation

and want to produce findings on political attitudes that can be applied to some larger population, a survey design would be appropriate. Similarly, if qualitative research is to be pursued and the goal is to understand how professional jazz dancers cope with the pressures of auditions, then unstructured or semi-structured interviews would be a reasonable choice of design. Another consideration is whether a cross-sectional or longitudinal design would be most appropriate to answer the research questions.

Other factors that affect the choice of design include things like the availability of funding, time, and other resources. Perhaps one cannot afford to select a large probability sample, so a full-blown survey analysis may be out of reach. Ethnography may be your design of choice, but time and travel constraints could rule that out. In most cases, some sort of compromise has to be made between the best possible research design and what is feasible under the circumstances.

Ethics review

As highlighted at various points in this text, ethics are an important consideration when designing and conducting a study, and must also be kept in mind when writing up the results. Once the design of a study has been picked, researchers usually have to provide an ethics committee with a research proposal that outlines how ethical considerations will be handled at each stage of the project. However, this step can usually be skipped if the research does not involve human or animal subjects, for instance, if one is offering a new synthesis or interpretation of a body of theoretical work without gathering empirical data.

Gather data

If the ethics committee has approved the study, data gathering can begin. As discussed at length in this book, a wide variety of data-gathering techniques are available for both quantitative and qualitative studies. Sometimes a pilot study is conducted to determine whether the method of gathering data needs any refinement. For example, a pilot study can be used to find out whether the questions in a survey are understood by respondents, or whether potential participants in a qualitative study react strongly to the presence of the observer.

Analyze data

In quantitative studies, data analysis usually begins after all the data have been gathered. In qualitative research, there can be an iterative process in which some data are gathered and analyzed, with this preliminary analysis leading to a change in what sort of information is to be sought or how more data are to be gathered. That is why there is a two-headed arrow between 'Gather data' and 'Analyze data' in the qualitative section of Figure 1. At this stage software may be used, for example, SPSS for quantitative analysis or NVivo for qualitative.

Findings

The findings are the results of the data analysis. For instance, a quantitative researcher may find that support for a particular government policy is strongly associated with age and ethnicity. Someone conducting a qualitative study may find that heroin addicts in Vancouver's downtown east side resent the people from whom they purchase their drugs.

Conclusions

Finally, what does it all mean? At this point an effort is usually made to relate the findings of the study to existing theories or knowledge on the topic. This is where you enter the debate about the subject matter with other scholars.

Quantitative social scientists will discuss whether their findings support their hypotheses (if they had specific hypotheses to begin with, and not all do). Support for a hypothesis could provide substantiation for a particular theory, for example, when the findings indicate that economic development leads to greater similarity in gender roles, thus supporting a version of modernization theory. If the hypotheses are not supported or if the findings are not consistent with a particular theory, a case can be made that the theory has to be revised or abandoned. Sometimes the findings will generate new hypotheses, concepts, or theories. In virtually all cases, the researcher is able to come up with suggestions as to the ways in which further research may be beneficial—perhaps different variables should be examined or maybe the key variables should be measured differently.

Qualitative researchers will discuss whether their findings offer a new interpretation of the subject matter. For example, the findings derived from interviewing 15-year-old single mothers may help to understand how some young people view sexuality and their relationships with their peers, and those findings may be very different from what is currently believed about the topic. As with quantitative work, qualitative analysis may produce new hypotheses, concepts, or theories. Similarly, qualitative researchers can usually outline the ways in which further research would be desirable, for instance, by expanding the preceding study to include 15-year-old boys.

Glossary

Terms appearing elsewhere in the Glossary are in *italic*.

Action research Approach in which the researcher and client collaborate to diagnose a problem and develop a solution based on the diagnosis.

Adjacency pair Two kinds of talk activity that are linked together, such as an invitation and a response.

Analytic induction Approach to the analysis of qualitative data in which the collection of data continues and the hypothesis is modified until no cases inconsistent with it are found.

Arithmetic mean Also known simply as the **mean**, this is the 'average' in everyday usage—namely, the total of a distribution of scores divided by the number of scores.

Biographical method See **life history method**.

Bivariate analysis The examination of the relationship between two variables, as in *contingency tables*; *correlation*.

CAQDAS An abbreviation of **c**omputer-**a**ssisted (or -aided) **q**ualitative **d**ata **a**nalysis **s**oftware.

Case study A *research design* that entails a detailed and intensive analysis of a single case or a small number of cases for comparative purposes.

Causality Causal connections between variables, as opposed to the mere *correlation* between them.

Cell The area in a table, such as a *contingency table*, where the rows and columns intersect and data are inserted.

Census The enumeration of an entire *population*; unlike a *sample*, which comprises a count of some units in a population, a census relates to all of them.

Chi-square test Chi-square (χ^2) is a test of *statistical significance*, employed to establish confidence that a finding displayed in a *contingency table* can be generalized from a *probability sample* to the *population* from which it is drawn.

Closed question A question employed in an *interview schedule* or *questionnaire* that presents the respondent with a fixed set of possible answers to choose from; also called **fixed-choice question**.

Cluster sample A sampling procedure in which the researcher first samples sets of cases (that is, clusters) and then samples units from within these clusters, usually using a *probability sampling* method.

Code, coding In *quantitative research*, codes act as tags to assign the data on each *variable* to a category of the variable in question. Numbers are usually assigned to each category to allow easier computer processing. In *qualitative research*, coding breaks data down into component parts, which are then given names.

Coding frame A listing of the codes used in the analysis of data. For answers to a structured interview schedule or questionnaire, the coding frame delineates the categories used for each *open question*. With *closed questions*, the coding frame is essentially incorporated into the pre-given answers, hence the frequent use of the term 'pre-coded question' to describe such questions.

Coding manual This is the statement of instructions to coders that outlines all the possible categories for each dimension being coded.

Concept A name given to a category that organizes observations and ideas by virtue of their possessing common features.

Concurrent validity One of the main approaches to establishing *measurement validity*. It entails relating a measure to an existing criterion or different indicator of the concept to see if one predicts the other.

Connotation A term used in *semiotics* to refer to the meanings of a *sign* associated with the social context within which it operates: a sign's connotations are supplementary to and less immediately apparent than its *denotation*.

Constant An attribute on which cases do not differ; compare with *variable*.

Constructionism, constructionist An *ontological* position (often referred to as **constructivism**) that asserts that social phenomena and their meanings are continually being created by social actors. It is antithetical to *objectivism*.

Content analysis An approach to the analysis of documents and texts that seeks to quantify content in terms of predetermined categories in a systematic and replicable manner. The term is sometimes used in connection with qualitative research as well—see *qualitative content analysis*.

Contingency table A table, comprising rows and columns, that shows the *relationship* between two *variables*. Usually, at least one of the variables is a *nominal variable* or *ordinal* *variable*. Each *cell* in the table shows the number (usually percentage) of cases for that specific combination of the two variables.

Control group See **experiment**.

Convenience sample A sample that is selected because of its availability to the researcher; a form of *non-probability sample*.

Conversation analysis The fine-grained analysis of (recorded and then transcribed) talk as it occurs in naturally occurring situations, to uncover the underlying structures in interaction that make social order possible. Conversation analysis is grounded in *ethnomethodology*.

Correlation An approach to the analysis of relationships between *interval/ratio variables* and/or *ordinal variables* that seeks to assess the strength and direction of the relationship between the variables concerned. *Pearson's r* and *Spearman's rho* are both correlational measures. The corresponding term **measure of association** is often used with *nominal variables*.

Covert research A term frequently used in connection with *ethnographic* research in which the researcher does not reveal his or her true identity and/or intentions. Such research may violate the ethical principle of *informed consent*.

Cramér's V A statistical measure for assessing the strength of the relationship between two *nominal variables*.

Critical realism A *realist* epistemology that asserts that the study of the social world should be concerned with the identification of social structures in order to change them and thereby counteract inequalities and injustices. Unlike a *positivist* epistemology that is *empiricist*, critical realism maintains that the structures may not be directly perceivable.

Cross-sectional design A *research design* that entails the collection of data at a single point in time.

Deductive An approach to inquiry that begins with the statement of a theory from which hypotheses may be derived and tested; compare with *inductive*.

Denotation A term used in *semiotics* to refer to the principal and most manifest meaning of a *sign*; compare with *connotation*.

Dependent variable A *variable* that is caused or is assumed to be caused by an *independent variable*.

Diary A written memoir. Three types of diary can be distinguished: diaries written at the behest of a researcher; spontaneously produced personal diaries that can be analyzed as *personal documents*; and diaries written by researchers to log their activities and reflections.

Dichotomous variable A variable with just two categories.

Dimension An aspect of a *concept*.

Discourse analysis An approach to the analysis of talk and other forms of communication that emphasizes the way language can create versions of reality.

Ecological fallacy The error of assuming that inferences about individuals can be made from aggregate data.

Ecological validity Achieved if social scientific findings are applicable to people's everyday, natural social settings.

Empiricism An approach to the study of reality that suggests that only knowledge gained by observation through the senses is acceptable.

Epistemology, epistemological A branch of philosophy concerned with what constitutes knowledge and how knowledge is to be acquired; see *positivism*, *realism*, and *interpretivism*.

Eta A test of the strength of the *relationship* between two *variables*. The *independent variable* is usually a *nominal variable* while the *dependent variable* must be an *interval variable* or *ratio variable*.

Ethnography, ethnographer Like *participant observation*, a research method in which the researcher is immersed in a social setting for an extended period of time, observing behaviour, asking questions, and analyzing what is said in conversations both between others and with the fieldworker. The term has a more inclusive sense than participant observation, which emphasizes the observational component. The term is also frequently used to refer to the written output of ethnographic research.

Ethnomethodology A sociological perspective concerned with the way in which social order is accomplished through talk and interaction. It provides the intellectual foundations of *conversation analysis*.

Evaluation research Research that is concerned with the evaluation of real-life interventions, such as policy changes.

Experiment A *research design* that rules out alternative explanations of findings deriving from it (that is, possesses *internal validity*) by having at least (*a*) an experimental group, which is exposed to a treatment, and a control group, which is not, and (*b*) *random assignment* to the two groups.

Experimental group See **experiment**.

External validity Achieved if the results of a study can be generalized beyond the specific research context in which they were generated.

Face validity Achieved if, on inspection, an *indicator* appears to measure the *concept* in question.

Facilitator See **moderator**.

Factor analysis A statistical technique used for large numbers of *indicators* to establish whether there is a tendency for groups of them to be interrelated. It is often used with *multiple-indicator measures* to see if they cluster into one or more groups (factors).

Field experiment A study in which the researcher directly intervenes in and/or manipulates a natural setting to observe what happens as a consequence.

Field notes A detailed chronicle by an *ethnographer* of events, conversations, and behaviour, and the researcher's initial reflections on them.

Focus group A form of group interview in which: there are several participants (in addition to the *moderator/facilitator*); there is an emphasis in the questioning on a particular topic or related topics; and interaction within the group and the joint construction of meaning is observed.

Frequency table A table that displays the number and/or percentage of units (for example, people) in different categories of a variable.

Gatekeeper A non-researcher who controls researcher access to a research setting.

Generalization, generalizability A concern with the *external validity* of research findings.

Grounded theory An approach to the analysis of qualitative data that aims to generate theory out of research data by achieving a close fit between the two.

Hermeneutics A term taken from theology concerned with the theory and method of the interpretation of texts and emphasizing the need to understand them from the perspective of the authors.

Hypothesis An informed speculation, which is set up to be tested, about the possible relationship between two or more variables.

Independent variable A *variable* that has a causal impact on a *dependent variable*, or is assumed to do so.

Index See **scale**.

Indicator Something employed to measure to a *concept* when no direct measure is available.

Inductive An approach to inquiry that begins with data collection; the data gathered are used to develop theories, hypotheses, and concepts; compare with *deductive*.

Informed consent A key principle in social research ethics implying that prospective participants should be given as much information as needed to make an informed decision about whether to participate in a study.

Inter-coder reliability The degree to which two or more individuals agree about the *coding* of an item; likely to be an issue when *coding* answers to *open questions* in research based on *questionnaires* or *structured interviews*.

Internal reliability or **internal consistency** Degree to which the items that make up a *scale* or *index* are consistent or correlated.

Internal validity Is achieved if there is sufficient evidence that a *causal* relationship exists between two or more variables.

Interpretivism An *epistemological* position that requires the social scientist to grasp the subjective meanings people attach to their actions and behaviours.

Interval variable A *variable* where the distances between the categories are identical across its range of categories.

Intervening variable A *variable* that is affected by another one and that in turn has a causal impact on yet a third variable. Taking an intervening variable into account often facilitates the understanding of the relationship between two variables. It is Y in the following: X → Y → Z.

Interview guide The brief list of memory prompts of areas to be covered in *unstructured* and *semi-structured interviewing*.

Interview schedule A collection of questions designed to be asked by an interviewer; one is always used in a *structured interview*.

Intra-coder reliability The degree to which an individual coder is consistent over time in the *coding* of an item; likely to be an issue when *coding* answers to *open questions* in research based on *questionnaires* or *structured interviews*.

Kendall's tau A test of the strength of the *relationship* between two *ordinal variables*.

Key informant Someone who offers the researcher, usually in an *ethnography*, particularly perceptive information about the social setting, important events, and individuals.

Life history interview Similar to the *oral history interview*, but the aim of this type of *unstructured interview* is to glean information on the entire biography of a respondent.

Life history method Also often referred to as the *biographical method*, this method emphasizes the inner experience of individuals and its connections with larger societal events throughout the life course. The method usually entails *life history interviews* and the use of *personal documents* as data.

Likert scale A widely used format in which respondents are typically asked their degree of agreement with a series of attitude statements that together form a *multiple-indicator* measure. The scale is deemed to measure the intensity of respondents' feelings about an issue.

Longitudinal research A *research design* in which data are collected on a *sample* (of people, documents, etc.) on at least two occasions.

Mail questionnaire Traditionally this term was synonymous with the *postal questionnaire*, but with the arrival of email-based questionnaires, many have abandoned it for *postal questionnaire*.

Mean See **arithmetic mean**.

Measure of central tendency A measure, like the *arithmetic mean*, *median*, or *mode*, that summarizes a set of scores.

Measure of dispersion A measure, like the *range* or *standard deviation* that summarizes the amount of variation in a set of scores.

Measurement validity The degree to which a measure of a concept actually measures what it is supposed to measure; see also *face validity* and *concurrent validity*.

Median The mid-point in a set of scores that is arranged in order.

Meta-analysis A method for determining the relationship between variables by drawing together the findings from several research studies. It is typically achieved through quantitative measurement and the use of statistical procedures.

Missing data Data relating to a case that are not available, for example, when a respondent in *social survey* research does not answer a question. These are referred to as 'missing values' in SPSS.

Mode The score that occurs most frequently in a set of scores.

Moderated relationship A *relationship* between two *variables* is said to be moderated when the effect of the independent variable varies at different levels of a second independent variable (also known as a statistical interaction).

Moderator The person who guides the questioning of a *focus group*, also called a *facilitator*.

Multiple-indicator measure A measure that employs more than one *indicator* to measure a *concept*.

Multi-strategy research A term used to describe research that combines *quantitative* and *qualitative research*.

Multivariate analysis The examination of relationships among three or more *variables*.

Narrative analysis An approach concerned with the search for and analysis of stories that people use to understand their lives and the world around them.

Naturalism A style of research in which the natural or everyday social world is left as undisturbed as possible.

Negative relationship A *relationship* between two *variables*, whereby as one increases, the other decreases.

Nominal variable Also known as a *categorical variable*, it is comprised of categories that cannot be ranked.

Non-probability sample A sample not selected using a random sampling method. Essentially, this implies that some units in the population are more likely than others to be selected.

Non-response A source of *non-sampling error* that occurs when someone in a sample refuses to cooperate, cannot be contacted, or for some other reason cannot supply the required data.

Non-sampling error Differences between the *population* and a *sample* that arise either from deficiencies in the sampling approach, such as an inadequate *sampling frame* or *non-response*, or from such problems as poor question wording, poor interviewing, or flawed data processing.

Null hypothesis A *hypothesis* of no relationship between two variables, the one you hope to disprove.

Objectivism An *ontological* position that asserts that social phenomena have an existence independent of social actors; compare with *constructionism*.

Observation schedule A device used in *structured observation* that specifies the categories of behaviour that are to be observed and gives instructions on how behaviour should be allocated to those categories.

Official statistics Data compiled by or on behalf of state agencies in the course of conducting their business.

Ontology, ontological A branch of philosophy concerned with the nature of reality; for example, whether social entities can and should be considered objective entities with a reality external to specific social actors, or as social constructions built up from the perceptions and actions of these actors. See *objectivism* and *constructionism*.

Open question In an *interview schedule* or *questionnaire*, a format that does not present the respondent with a set of possible answers to choose from; compare with *closed question*.

Operational definition Spells out the operations that are to be performed to measure a *concept*.

Oral history interview A largely *unstructured interview* in which respondents are asked to recall and to reflect on events they have experienced.

Ordinal variable A variable whose categories can be rank-ordered, but the distances between the categories are not equal or known across the range.

Outlier An extreme value in a distribution of scores. If a *variable* has one—either very high or very low—the *arithmetic mean* or the *range* will be distorted by it.

Paradigm A cluster of often unstated beliefs and assumptions that influence views on what should be studied, how research should be done, and how results should be interpreted.

Participant observation Research in which the researcher is immersed in a social setting for an extended period of time, observing behaviour, asking questions, and analyzing what is said in conversations both between others and with the fieldworker. It usually includes interviewing *key informants* and studying documents. In this book, participant observation is employed to refer to the observational aspect of *ethnography*.

Pearson's r A measure of the strength and direction of the *relationship* between two *interval/ratio variables*.

Personal documents Things such as *diaries*, letters, and autobiographies not written for an official purpose that provide first-person accounts of the writer's life and events within it.

Phenomenology A philosophy concerned with how individuals make sense of the world around them and how social research must take that into account.

Population All cases or people covered by a theory or explanation—the universe of units from which a *sample* is selected.

Positive relationship A *relationship* between two *variables*, whereby as one increases the other increases as well, or both simultaneously decrease.

Positivism An *epistemological* position that advocates the application of the methods of the natural sciences to the study of social reality.

Postal questionnaire A form of *questionnaire* that is sent out and returned by non-electronic mail.

Postmodernism A position that questions the notion of dispassionate social scientists seeking to uncover a pre-existing external reality; it views their accounts as only one among many different ways of seeing the world. Postmodernists display a preference for qualitative methods.

Pre-coded question Another name for a *closed question*, but often preferred, because it shows the lack of necessity of a *coding frame;* the range of answers is predetermined and a numerical *code* pre-assigned for each possible answer.

Probability sample One selected using *random sampling* and in which each unit in the population has a known probability of being selected.

QSR NVivo A CAQDAS package that derives from but goes beyond NUD*IST (Non-numerical Unstructured Data Indexing Searching and Theorizing).

Qualitative content analysis An approach to constructing the meaning of documents and text that allows categories to emerge out of data analysis, and recognizes the significance of the context in which an item being analyzed appears.

Qualitative research Inquiry using mainly words, images, and other non-numerical symbols as data, and which involves little or no quantification. As a *research strategy* it tends to be *inductivist, constructivist,* and *interpretivist,* but qualitative researchers do not always subscribe to all three features; compare with *quantitative research.*

Quantitative research Inquiry using quantitative data-gathering techniques and statistical analysis. As a *research strategy* it tends to be *deductivist* and *objectivist* and to incorporate a natural science model of the research process (in particular, one influenced by *positivism*), but quantitative researchers do not always subscribe to all three features; compare with *qualitative research.*

Quasi-experiment A *research design* that is close to being an *experiment* but that does not meet the requirements fully and therefore does not exhibit complete *internal validity.*

Questionnaire A collection of written questions or response items that the respondent answers without the aid of an interviewer.

Quota sample A type of *non-probability sample,* it provides samples that match the proportions of people in different categories in the *population.*

Random assignment The random allocation of research participants to the experimental or control groups in *experiments.*

Random sampling The form in which the inclusion of any unit of a *population* occurs entirely by chance.

Range The difference between the maximum and the minimum score in a set of scores associated with an *interval* or *ratio variable.*

Ratio variable An *interval variable* with a true zero point.

Reactivity, reactive effect A term used to describe the effect on research participants of knowing that they are being studied, which may result in atypical or inauthentic behaviour.

Realism An epistemological position that posits a reality that is independent of the senses but is to some degree accessible to the researcher's tools and theoretical speculations. See also *critical realism.*

Reflexivity A term used to refer to an awareness of social researchers of the implications, for the knowledge of the social world they generate, of their methods, values, biases, decisions, and mere presence in the situations they investigate.

Relationship An association between two variables whereby the variation in one variable coincides with variation in another variable.

Reliability The degree to which a measure of a concept is stable or consistent.

Replication, replicability The degree to which a study can be repeated using the same methods.

Representative sample A sample that is similar to the *population* in all important respects.

Research design This term is employed in this book to refer to a framework for the collection and analysis of data. A choice of research design reflects decisions about the priority being given to a range of dimensions of the research process (such as *causality* and *generalization*).

Respondent validation Sometimes called **member validation,** a process whereby researchers provide the people on whom they conducted research with an account of their findings and request their feedback on it.

Response set The tendency among some respondents to *multiple-indicator measures* to reply in the same way to each constituent item, not according to how they actually feel about them but out of some other motive. Three of the most prominent types of response set involve the 'acquiescence,' 'social desirability,' and 'laziness or boredom' effects.

Sample The segment of the *population* selected for research, a subset of the *population.* The selection may be based on *probability* or *non-probability sampling.*

Sampling error Differences in data between a *random sample* and the *population* from which it is selected.

Sampling frame A listing of units in a *population* from which a *sample* is to be selected.

Scale A term usually used interchangeably with **index** to refer to a *multiple-indicator measure* in which the score a person gives for each component *indicator* is summed to provide a composite score for that person.

Secondary analysis The analysis of quantitative or qualitative data by researchers not involved in their original collection, often for purposes that may not have been envisaged by those responsible for the original data collection.

Semiotics An approach to the analysis of documents and other symbolic materials that emphasizes the importance of *signs* by seeking out their deeper meaning and revealing how signs are designed to have an effect on those who use them.

Semi-structured interview A term that covers a variety of types of interview, it typically refers to interviews in which the interviewer has a series of questions in the general form of an *interview guide* and is able to vary the sequence of questions. The questions are usually more general than those found in a *structured interview* schedule and the interviewer usually has some latitude to ask further questions in response to what are seen as significant replies.

Sensitizing concept A *concept* treated as a guide to an investigation in that it points in a general way to what is relevant or important. This contrasts with the idea of an *operational definition*, in which the meaning of a concept is fixed in advance of the investigation.

Sign A term employed in *semiotics*. A sign is made up of a signifier (manifestation of a sign) and the signified (that deeper meaning to which the signifier refers).

Simple random sample A *sample* in which each unit selected from the *population*, and each combination of units, has an equal probability of being included.

Snowball sample A *non-probability sample* in which the researcher makes initial contact with a small group of people who are relevant to the research topic and then uses them to establish contacts with others.

Social desirability bias A distortion of data caused by respondents' attempts to construct accounts that conform to a socially acceptable model of behaviour.

Spearman's rho [ρ] A measure of the strength and direction of the *relationship* between two *ordinal variables*.

SPSS **S**tatistical **P**ackage for the **S**ocial **S**ciences, a widely used computer program that allows quantitative data to be managed and analyzed.

Spurious relationship A *relationship* in which two *variables* are *correlated* but not *causally* related. It is produced by the impact of a common third variable on each of the two variables. When the third variable is controlled, the relationship disappears.

Standard deviation A measure of how dispersed a set of scores is around its ***mean***.

Standard error of the mean An estimate of the amount that a *sample mean* is likely to differ from the *population mean*.

Statistical significance (test of) Allows analysts to estimate their confidence that the results of a study of a randomly selected *sample* are generalizable to the *population* from which the sample was drawn. Such a test has nothing to do with substantive significance or importance. The *chi-square test* is an example of this kind of test. Using a test of statistical significance to generalize from a sample to a population is known as **statistical inference**.

Stratified random sample A *sample* in which units are *randomly sampled* from a *population* that has been previously divided into sub-groups (strata).

Structured interview One in which all respondents are asked exactly the same questions in the same order with the aid of a formal *interview schedule*.

Structured observation Often called ***systematic observation***, it is a technique in which the researchers employ explicitly formulated rules for what they should look for, including when and where, and how they should record what they have observed.

Survey research A *research design* in which data are collected from respondents, predominantly by *questionnaire* or by *structured interview*; usually, the data are then examined to detect *relationships* among *variables*.

Symbolic interactionism A theoretical perspective in sociology that views social interaction as being based on the meanings actors attach to their actions and the contexts in which they occur.

Systematic sample A *probability sampling* method in which units are selected from a *sampling frame* according to fixed intervals, such as every fifth unit.

Text A written work or, in more recent years, any symbol or image (such as a building or even Disneyland).

Theoretical sampling A term used mainly in relation to *grounded theory* to refer to sampling carried out in such a way that emerging theoretical considerations guide the collection of data and/or the selection of cases (usually research participants). It is supposed to continue until a point of *theoretical saturation* is reached.

Theoretical saturation In *grounded theory*, the point when emerging *concepts* have been fully explored and no new insights are being generated. See also *theoretical sampling*.

Thick description A term devised by Geertz (1973) to refer to detailed accounts of a social setting that can form the basis for creating general statements about a culture and its significance in peoples' social lives.

Transcription, transcript The verbatim written record of a taped *interview* or *focus group* session.

Triangulation The use of more than one method or source of data in the study of a social phenomenon so that findings may be cross-checked.

Trustworthiness A set of criteria advocated by some writers for assessing the quality of *qualitative research*.

Turn-taking The notion from *conversation analysis* that order in everyday conversation is achieved through taking turns in conversations.

Univariate analysis The analysis of a single *variable* at a time.

Unobtrusive methods Those that do not make research participants aware of their being studied and therefore are not subject to *reactivity*.

Unstructured interview One in which the interviewer is free to explore any topic, although an *interview guide* is often used. The questioning is usually informal and the content, phrasing and sequencing of questions may vary from interview to interview.

Validity A concern with the integrity of the conclusions generated from a piece of research. There are different types of validity. See, in particular, *measurement validity, internal validity, external validity*, and *ecological validity*. When used on its own, *validity* is usually taken to refer to *measurement validity*.

Variable An attribute or characteristic that may vary over time or from case to case. See also *dependent variable* and *independent variable*; compare with *constant*.

Vignette technique A method involving the presentation of hypothetical scenarios to individuals, who are then asked how they would respond if confronted with the circumstances depicted in the scenario.

References

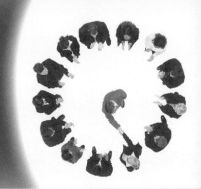

Abraham, J. (1994), 'Bias in Science and Medical Knowledge: The Opren Controversy,' *Sociology*, 28: 717–36.

Achille, M., and Ogloff J. (1997), 'When Is a Request for Assisted Suicide Legitimate?' *Canadian Jour. of Behavioural Sci.* 29: 19–27.

Adams, M. (2003), *Fire and Ice* (Toronto: Penguin).

Adriaenssens, C., and Cadman, L. (1999), 'An Adaptation of Moderated E-mail Focus Groups to Assess the Potential of a New Online (Internet) Financial Services Offer in the UK,' *Jour. of the Market Research Society*, 41: 417–24.

Agresti, A., and Finlay, B. (2009), *Statistical Methods for the Social Sciences* (Upper Saddle River, NJ: Prentice-Hall).

Altheide, D.L. (1996), *Qualitative Media Analysis* (Thousand Oaks, CA: Sage).

——— (2004), 'Ethnographic Content Analysis,' in M. Lewis-Beck, A. Bryman, and T. Liao (eds.), *The Sage Encycl. of Soc. Sci. Research Methods* (Thousand Oaks, CA: Sage).

Anderson, K., Sebaldt, R., Lohfeld, L., Burgess, K., Donald, F., and Kaczorowski, J. (2006), 'Views of Family Physicians in Southwestern Ontario on Preventive Care Services and Performance Incentives,' *Family Practice,* 23: 469–71.

Andrews, K., Smith, L., Henzi, D., and Demps, E. (2007), 'Faculty and Student Perceptions of Academic Integrity at U.S. and Canadian Dental Schools,' *Jour. of Dental Education*, 71: 1027–39.

Armstrong, D., Gosling, A., Weinman, J., and Marteau, T. (1997), 'The Place of Inter-Rater Reliability in Qualitative Research: An Empirical Study,' *Sociology*, 31: 597–606.

Armstrong, G. (1993), 'Like that Desmond Morris?' in D. Hobbs and T. May (eds.), *Interpreting the Field: Accounts of Ethnography* (Oxford: Clarendon Press).

——— (1998), *Football Hooligans: Knowing the Score* (Oxford: Berg).

Atkinson, M. (2002), 'Pretty in Ink: Conformity, Resistance and Negotiation in Women's Tattooing,' *Sex Roles*, 47: 219–35.

——— (2004), 'Tattooing and Civilizing Processes,' *Canadian Rev. of Sociology and Anthropology*, 41: 125–46.

Atkinson, P. (1981), *The Clinical Experience* (Farnborough: Gower).

——— (1990), *The Ethnographic Imagination: Textual Constructions of Society* (London: Routledge).

——— (2004), 'Life Story Interview,' in M. Lewis-Beck, A. Bryman, and T. Liao (eds.), *The Sage Encycl. of Soc. Sci.* *Research Methods* (Thousand Oaks, CA: Sage).

——— and Coffey, A. (1995), 'Realism and Its Discontents: On the Crisis of Cultural Representation in Ethnographic Texts,' in B. Adam and S. Allan (eds.), *Theorizing Culture: An Interdisciplinary Critique after Postmodernism* (London: UCL Press).

Baer, D., Curtis, J., and Grabb, E. (2001), 'Has Voluntary Association Membership Declined? Cross-national Analyses for Fifteen Countries,' *Canadian Rev. of Sociology*, 38: 249–74.

Bahr, H., Caplow, T., and Chadwick, B. (1983), 'Middletown III: Problems of Replication, Longitudinal Measurement, and Triangulation,' *Annual Rev. of Sociology*, 9: 243–64.

Bales, Robert (1951), *Interaction Process Analysis* (Cambridge, MA: Addison-Wesley).

Bampton, R., and Cowton, C.J. (2002), 'The E-Interview,' *Forum Qual. Social Research*, 3 (2): www.Qual.-research.net/fqs/.

Barnard, M., and Frischer, M. (1995), 'Combining Quantitative and Qualitative Approaches: Researching HIV-Related Risk Behaviours among Drug Injectors,' *Addiction Research*, 2: 351–62.

Barter, C., and Renold, E. (1999), 'The Use of Vignettes in Qualitative Research,' *Social Research Update*, 25.

Beagan, B. (2001), 'Micro Inequities and Everyday Inequalities: "Race," Gender, Sexuality and Class in Medical School,' *Canadian Jour. of Sociology*, 26: 583–610.

Beardsworth, A., and Keil, T. (1992), 'The Vegetarian Option: Varieties, Conversions, Motives and Careers,' *Sociological Rev.*, 40: 253–93.

——— (1997), *Sociology on the Menu: An Invitation to the Study of Food and Society* (London: Routledge).

——— Bryman, A., Ford, J., and Keil, T. (n.d.), '"The Dark Figure" in Statistics of Unemployment and Vacancies: Some Sociological Implications,' discussion paper, Department of Social Sciences, Loughborough Univ.

——— Keil, T., Goode, J., Haslam, C., and Lancashire, E. (2002), 'Women, Men and Food: The Significance of Gender for Nutritional Attitudes and Choices,' *Brit. Food Jour.*, 104: 470–91.

Becker, H. (1958), 'Problems of Inference and Proof in Participant Observation,' *Amer. Sociological Rev.*, 23: 652–60.

——— (1963), *Outsiders: Studies in the Sociology of Deviance* (NY: Free Press).

—— (1967), 'Whose Side Are We On?' *Social Problems*, 14: 239–47.

—— (1970), 'Practitioners of Vice and Crime,' in R. Habenstein (ed.), *Pathways to Data* (Chicago: Aldine).

—— (1986), *Writing for Social Scientists: How to Start and Finish Your Thesis, Book, or Article* (Chicago: Univ. of Chicago Press).

—— and Geer, B. (1957), 'Participant Observation and Interviewing: A Comparison,' *Human Organization*, 16: 28–32.

Beharrell, P. (1993), 'AIDS and the British Press,' in J. Eldridge (ed.), *Getting the Message: News, Truth and Power* (London: Routledge).

Belk, R., Sherry, J., and Wallendorf, M. (1988), 'A Naturalistic Inquiry into Buyer and Seller Behaviour at a Swap Meet,' *Jour. of Consumer Research*, 14: 449–70.

Bell, E. (2007), 'Separatism and Quasi-Separatism in Alberta,' *Prairie Forum*, 32: 335–55.

—— Jansen, H., and Young, L. (2007), 'Sustaining a Dynasty in Alberta: The 2004 Provincial Election,' *Canadian Poli. Sci. Rev.*, 1: 27–49.

Berthoud, R. (2000a), 'Introduction: The Dynamics of Social Change,' in R. Berthoud and J. Gershuny (eds.), *Seven Years in the Lives of British Families: Evidence on the Dynamics of Social Change from the British Household Panel Survey* (Bristol: Policy Press).

—— (2000b), 'A Measure of Changing Health,' in R. Berthoud and J. Gershuny (eds.), *Seven Years in the Lives of British Families: Evidence on the Dynamics of Social Change from the British Household Panel Survey* (Bristol: Policy Press).

Bhaskar, R. (1989), *Reclaiming Reality: A Critical Introduction to Contemporary Philosophy* (London: Verso).

Billig, M. (1991), *Ideology and Opinions: Studies in Rhetorical Psychology* (Cambridge: Cambridge Univ. Press).

Blaikie, A. (2001), 'Photographs in the Cultural Account: Contested Narratives and Collective Memory in the Scottish Islands,' *Sociological Rev.*, 49: 345–67.

Blaxter, M. (1990), *Health and Lifestyles* (London: Routledge).

Bloor, M. (1997), 'Addressing Social Problems through Qualitative Research,' in D. Silverman (ed.), *Qualitative Research: Theory, Method and Practice* (London: Sage).

—— , Frankland, S., Thomas, M., and Robson, K. (2001), *Focus Groups in Social Research* (London: Sage).

Blumer, H. (1954), 'What Is Wrong with Social Theory?' *Amer. Sociological Rev.*, 19: 3–10.

—— (1956), 'Sociological Analysis and the "Variable,"' *Amer. Sociological Rev.*, 21: 683–90.

—— (1962), 'Society as Symbolic Interaction,' in A. Rose (ed.), *Human Behavior and Social Processes* (London: Routledge & Kegan Paul).

Bottomore, T.B., and Rubel, M. (1963), *Karl Marx: Selected Writings in Sociology and Social Philosophy* (Harmondsworth, UK: Penguin).

Brannigan, A. (2004), *The Rise and Fall of Social Psychology: The Use and Misuse of the Experimental Method* (Hawthorne, NY: Aldine de Gruyter).

Brannigan, A., Gemmell, W., Pevalin, D., and Wade, T. (2002), 'Self-control and Social Control in Childhood Misconduct and Aggression: The Role of Family Structure and Hyperactivity,' *Canadian Jour. of Criminology*, 44: 119–42.

Braverman, H. (1974), *Labour and Monopoly Capital: The Degradation of Work in the Twentieth Century* (London: Monthly Rev. Press).

Brayfield, A., and Rothe, H. (1951), 'An Index of Job Satisfaction,' *Jour. of Applied Psych.*, 35: 307–11.

Bridgman, P. (1927), *The Logic of Modern Physics* (NY: Macmillan).

Brown, A. (1998), 'Narrative, Politics and Legitimacy in an IT Implementation,' *Jour. of Management Studies*, 35: 35–58.

Brown, S., and Lightfoot, G. (2002), 'Presence, Absence, and Accountability: E-mail and the Mediation of Organizational Memory,' in S. Woolgar (ed.), *Virtual Society? Technology, Cyperbole, Reality* (Oxford: Oxford Univ. Press).

Bryman, A. (1988a), *Quantity and Quality in Social Research* (London: Routledge).

—— (1992), 'Quantitative and Qualitative Research: Further Reflections on Their Integration,' in J. Brannen (ed.), *Mixing Methods: Qualitative and Quantitative Research* (Aldershot: Avebury).

—— (1994), 'The Mead/Freeman Controversy: Some Implications for Qualitative Researchers,' in R. Burgess (ed.), *Studies in Qual. Methodology, Volume 4* (Greenwich, CT: JAI Press).

—— (1995), *Disney and His Worlds* (London: Routledge).

—— (1998), 'Quantitative and Qualitative Research Strategies in Knowing the Social World,' in T. May and M. Williams (eds.), *Knowing the Social World* (Buckingham: Open Univ. Press).

—— (1999), 'Global Disney,' in P. Taylor and D. Slater (eds.), *The American Century* (Oxford: Blackwell).

—— and Burgess, R. (1994a), 'Developments in Qualitative Data Analysis: An Introduction,' in A. Bryman and R. Burgess (eds.), *Analyzing Qualitative Data* (London: Routledge).

—— (1994b), 'Reflections on Qualitative Data Analysis,' in A. Bryman and R. Burgess (eds.), *Analyzing Qualitative Data* (London: Routledge).

—— (1999), 'Introduction: Qualitative Research Methodology: A Review,' in A. Bryman and R. Burgess (eds.), *Qualitative Research* (London: Sage).

—— and Cramer, D. (2001), *Quantitative Data Analysis with SPSS Release 10 for Windows: A Guide for Social Scientists* (London: Routledge).

—— (2004), 'Constructing Variables,' in M. Hardy and A. Bryman (eds.), *Handbook of Data Analysis* (London: Sage).

—— Haslam, C., and Webb, A. (1994), 'Performance Appraisal in UK Universities: A Case of Procedural Compliance?' *Assessment and Evaluation in Higher Educ.*, 19: 175–88.

—— Stephens, M., and Campo, C. (1996), 'The Importance of Context: Qualitative Research and the Study of Leadership,' *Leadership Quarterly*, 7: 353–70.

Buckle, A., and Farrington, D. (1994), 'Measuring Shoplifting by Systematic Observation,' *Psych., Crime and Law*, 1: 133–41.

Bulmer, M. (1980), 'Why Don't Sociologists Make More Use of Official Statistics?' *Sociology*, 14: 505–23.

—— (1984), 'Facts, Concepts, Theories and Problems,' in M. Bulmer (ed.), *Social Research Methods* (London: Macmillan).

Burman, M., Batchelor, S., and Brown, J. (2001), 'Researching Girls and Violence: Facing the Dilemmas of Fieldwork,' *Brit. Jour. of Criminology*, 41: 443–59.

Burrell, I., and Leppard, D. (1994), 'Fall in Crime a Myth as Police Chiefs Massage the Figures,' *Sunday Times*, 16 Oct., 1, 5.

Bury, M. (2001), 'Illness Narratives: Fact or Fiction?' *Sociology of Health and Illness*, 23: 263–85.

Buston, K. (1997), 'NUD*IST in Action: Its Use and Its Usefulness in a Study of Chronic Illness in Young People,' *Sociological Research Online*, 2: www.socresonline.org. uk/socresonline/2/3/6.html.

Butcher, B. (1994), 'Sampling Methods: An Overview and Review,' *Survey Methods Centre Newsletter*, 15: 4–8.

Camerer, C. (1997), 'Taxi Drivers and Beauty Contests,' *Engineering and Sci.*, 60: 11–19.

Catterall, M., and Maclaran, P. (1997), 'Focus Group Data and Qualitative Analysis Programs: Coding the Moving Picture as well as Snapshots,' *Sociological Research Online*, 2: www.socresonline.org.uk/socresonline/2/1/6.html.

Charles, N., and Kerr, N. (1988), *Women, Food and Families* (Manchester: Manchester Univ. Press).

Charlton, T., Gunter, B., and Coles, D. (1998), 'Broadcast Television as a Cause of Aggression? Recent Findings from a Naturalistic Study,' *Emotional and Behavioural Difficulties*, 3: 5–13.

—— Coles, D., Panting, C., and Hannan, A. (1999), 'Behaviour of Nursery Class Children before and after the Availability of Broadcast Television: A Naturalistic Study of Two Cohorts in a Remote Community,' *Jour. of Social Behaviour and Personality*, 14: 315–24.

Charmaz, K. (1983), 'The Grounded Theory Method: An Explication and Interpretation,' in R. Emerson (ed.), *Contemporary Field Research: A Collection of Readings* (Boston: Little, Brown).

—— (1997), 'Identity Dilemmas of Chronically Ill Men,' in A. Strauss and J. Corbin (eds.), *Grounded Theory in Practice* (Thousand Oaks, CA: Sage).

—— (2000), 'Grounded Theory: Objectivist and Constructivist Methods,' in N. Denzin and Y. Lincoln (eds.), *Handbook of Qualitative Research*, 2nd ed. (Thousand Oaks, CA: Sage).

—— (2002), 'Qualitative Interviewing and Grounded Theory Analysis,' in J. Gubrium and J. Holstein (eds.), *Handbook of Interview Research: Context and Method* (Thousand Oaks, CA: Sage).

—— (2004), 'Grounded Theory,' in M. Lewis-Beck, A. Bryman, and T. Liao (eds.), *The Sage Encycl. of Soc. Sci. Research Methods* (Thousand Oaks, CA: Sage).

Chin, M., Fisak, B., and Sims, V. (2002), 'Development of the Attitudes Toward Vegetarianism Scale,' *Anthrozoös*, 15: 333–42.

Christakis, T., Christakis, P., Chipman, M., and Christakis, J. (2008), 'Medical Students' Attitudes on Diversity When Applying to Toronto's Ophthalmology Residency Program,' *Canadian Jour. of Ophthalmology*, 43: 218–21.

Cicourel, A. (1964), *Method and Measurement in Sociology* (NY: Free Press).

—— (1982), 'Interviews, Surveys, and the Problem of Ecological Validity,' *Amer. Sociologist*, 17: 11–20.

Clairborn, W. (1969), 'Expectancy Effects in the Classroom: A Failure to Replicate,' *Jour. of Educational Psych.*, 60: 377–83.

Clancey, W. (2001), 'Field Science Ethnography: Methods for Systematic Observation of an Arctic Expedition,' *Field Methods*, 13: 223–43.

Clapper, D., and Massey, A. (1996), 'Electronic Focus Groups: A Framework for Exploration,' *Information and Management*, 30: 43–50.

Clayman, S., and Gill, V.T. (2004), 'Conversation Analysis,' in M. Hardy and A. Bryman (eds.), *Handbook of Data Analysis* (London: Sage).

Cobanoglu, C., Ward, B., and Moreo, P.J. (2001), 'A Comparison of Mail, Fax and Web-based Survey Methods,' *Intnatl. Jour. of Market Research*, 43: 441–52.

Coffey, A. (1999), *The Ethnographic Self: Fieldwork and the Representation of Reality* (London: Sage).

—— and Atkinson, P. (1996), *Making Sense of Qualitative Data: Complementary Research Strategies* (Thousand Oaks, CA: Sage).

—— Holbrook, B., and Atkinson, P. (1996), 'Qualitative Data Analysis: Technologies and Representations,' *Sociological Research Online*, 2: www.socresonline.org. uk/socresonline/1/1/4.html.

Coleman, C., and Moynihan, J. (1996), *Understanding Crime Data: Haunted by the Dark Figure* (Buckingham: Open Univ. Press).

Coleman, H., Grant, C., and Collins, J. (2001), 'Inhalant Use by Canadian Aboriginal Youth,' *Jour. of Child and Adolescent Substance Abuse*, 10: 1–20.

Collins, M. (1997), 'Interviewer Variability: A Review of the Problem,' *Jour. of the Market Research Society*, 39: 67–84.

Collins, R. (1994), *Four Sociological Traditions*, rev. ed. (NY: Oxford Univ. Press).

Conger, J., and Kanungo, R. (1998), *Charismatic Leadership in Organizations* (Thousand Oaks, CA: Sage).

Cook, T., and Campbell, D. (1979), *Quasi-Experimentation: Design and Analysis for Field Settings* (Boston, MA: Houghton Mifflin).

Corti, L. (1993), 'Using Diaries in Social Research,' *Social Research Update*, 2.

Coté, J., and Allahar, A. (1994), *Generation on Hold: Coming of Age in the Late Twentieth Century* (Toronto: Stoddart).

Couper, M. (2000), 'Web Surveys: A Review of Issues and Approaches,' *Public Opinion Quarterly*, 64: 464–94.

—— and Hansen, S. (2002), 'Computer-assisted Interviewing,' in J. Gubrium and J. Holstein (eds.), *Handbook of Interview Research: Context and Method* (Thousand Oaks, CA: Sage).

Coxon, A. (1994), 'Diaries and Sexual Behaviour: The Use of Sexual Diaries as Method and Substance in Researching Gay Men's Response to HIV/AIDS,' in M. Boulton (ed.), *Challenge and Innovation: Methodological Advances in Social Research on HIV/AIDS* (London: Taylor & Francis).

Craig, G. (2004), 'Managing Safety in Policy Research,' in S. Becker and A. Bryman (eds.), *Understanding Research for Social Policy and Practice: Themes, Methods, and Approaches* (Bristol: Policy Press).

Cramer, D. (1998), *Fundamental Statistics for Social Research* (London: Routledge).

Crook, C., and Light, P. (2002), 'Virtual Society and the Cultural Practice of Study,' in S. Woolgar (ed.), *Virtual Society? Technology, Cyperbole, Reality* (Oxford: Oxford Univ. Press).

Curasi, C. (2001) 'A Critical Exploration of Face-to-face Interviewing vs. Computer-mediated Interviewing,' *Intnatl. Jour. of Market Research*, 43: 361–75.

Czaja, R., and Blair, J. (1996), *Designing Surveys: A Guide to Decisions and Procedures* (Thousand Oaks, CA: Sage).

Dale, A., Arber, S., and Proctor, M. (1988), *Doing Secondary Analysis* (London: Unwin Hyman).

Davies, P. (2000), 'Doing Interviews with Female Offenders,' in V. Jupp, P. Davies, and P. Francis (eds.), *Doing Criminological Research* (London: Sage).

Deacon, D., Bryman, A., and Fenton, N. (1998), 'Collision or Collusion? A Discussion of the Unplanned Triangulation of Quantitative and Qualitative Research Methods,' *Intnatl. Jour. of Social Research Methodology*, 1: 47–63.

———, Pickering, M., Golding, P., and Murdock, G. (1999), *Researching Communications: A Practical Guide to Methods in Media and Cultural Analysis* (London: Arnold).

Demers, A. (1996), 'Effect of Support Groups on Family Caregivers to the Frail Elderly,' *Canadian Jour. on Aging*, 15: 129–44.

Deng, J. (2006), 'A Comparison of Environmental Values and Attitudes Between Chinese in Canada and Anglo-Canadians,' *Environment and Behavior*, 38: 22–47.

Denzin, N. (1970), *The Research Act in Sociology* (Chicago: Aldine).

——— (1994), 'Evaluating Qualitative Research in the Poststructural Moment: The Lessons James Joyce Teaches Us,' *Intnatl. Jour. of Qual. Studies in Educ.*, 7: 295–308.

Desroches, F. (1990), 'Tearoom Trade: A Research Update,' *Qual. Sociology* 13: 39–61.

Dickinson, H. (1993), 'Accounting for Augustus Lamb: Theoretical and Methodological Issues in Biography and Historical Sociology,' *Sociology*, 27: 121–32.

Dinovitzer, R., Hagan, J., and Parker, P. (2003), 'Choice and Circumstance: Social Capital and Planful Competence in the Attainments of Immigrant Youth,' *Canadian Jour. of Sociology*, 28: 463–88.

Ditton, J. (1977), *Part-time Crime: An Ethnography of Fiddling and Pilferage* (London: Macmillan).

Dommeyer, C., and Moriarty, E. (2000), 'Comparison of Two Forms of an E-Mail Survey: Embedded vs. Attached,' *Intnatl. Jour. of Market Research*, 42: 39–50.

Dunning, E., Murphy, P., and Williams, J. (1988), *The Roots of Football Hooliganism: An Historical and Sociological Study* (London: Routledge).

Durkheim, E. (1938), *The Rules of Sociological Method*, trans. S. Solavay and J. Mueller (NY: Free Press).

——— (1952), *Suicide: A Study in Sociology*, trans. J. Spaulding and G. Simpson (London: Routledge & Kegan Paul).

Dwyer, J., Mayer, L., Dowd, K., Kandel, R., and Mayer, J. (1974), 'The New Vegetarians: The Natural High?' *Jour. of the Amer. Dietetic Assoc.*, 65: 529–36.

Dyer, W., and Wilkins, A. (1991), 'Better Stories, Not Better Constructs, to Generate Better Theory: A Rejoinder to Eisenhardt,' *Academy of Management Rev.*, 16: 613–19.

Eichler, M., and Lapointe, J. (1985), *On the Treatment of the Sexes in Research* (Ottawa: Social Sciences and Humanities Research Council of Canada).

Elliott, H. (1997), 'The Use of Diaries in Sociological Research on Health Experience,' *Sociological Research Online*, 2, http://www.socresonline.org.uk/socresonline/2/2/7.html.

Fenton, N., Bryman, A., and Deacon, D. (1998), *Mediating Social Science* (London: Sage).

Festinger, L., Riecken, H., and Schachter, S. (1956), *When Prophecy Fails* (NY: Harper & Row).

Finch, J. (1985), '"It's Great to Have Someone to Talk to": The Ethics and Politics of Interviewing Women,' in C. Bell and H. Roberts (eds.), *Social Researching: Politics, Problems, Practice* (London: Routledge & Kegan Paul).

——— (1987), 'The Vignette Technique in Survey Research,' *Sociology*, 21: 105–14.

——— and Hayes, L. (1994), 'Inheritance, Death and the Concept of the Home,' *Sociology*, 28: 417–33.

——— and Mason, J. (1990), 'Decision Taking in the Fieldwork Process: Theoretical Sampling and Collaborative Working,' in R. Burgess (ed.), *Studies in Qual. Methodology*, 2: 25–50.

Fine, G. (1996), 'Justifying Work: Occupational Rhetorics as Resources in Kitchen Restaurants,' *Administrative Sci. Quarterly*, 41: 90–115.

Foddy, W. (1993), *Constructing Questions for Interviews and Questionnaires: Theory and Practice in Social Research* (Cambridge: Cambridge Univ. Press).

Forster, N. (1994), 'The Analysis of Company Documentation,' in C. Cassell and G. Symon (eds.), *Qualitative Methods in Organizational Research* (London: Sage).

Foster, J. (1995), 'Informal Social Control and Community Crime Prevention,' *Brit. Jour. of Criminology*, 35: 563–83.

Fowler, F. (1993), *Survey Research Methods*, 2nd ed. (Newbury Park, CA: Sage).

——— and Mangione, T. (1990), *Standardized Survey Interviewing: Minimizing Interviewer-Related Error* (Beverly Hills, CA: Sage).

Frazer, R., and Wiersma, U. (2001), 'Prejudice vs. Discrimination in the Employment Interview: We May Hire Equally, but Our Memories Harbour Prejudice,' *Human Relations*, 54: 173–91.

Frean, A. (1998), 'Children Read More after Arrival of TV,' *The Times*, 29 April: 7.

Frey, J. (2004), 'Telephone Surveys,' in M. Lewis-Beck, A. Bryman, and T. Liao (eds.), *The Sage Encycl. of Soc. Sci. Research Methods* (Thousand Oaks, CA: Sage).

Frohlich, K., Potvin, L., Chabot, P., and Corin, E. (2002), 'A Theoretical and Empirical Analysis of Context: Neighbourhoods, Smoking, and Youth,' *Social Sci. and Medicine*, 54: 1401–17.

Gabor, T., Hung, K., Mihorean, S., and St-Onge, C. (2002),

'Canadian Homicide Rates: A Comparison of Two Data Sets,' *Canadian Jour. of Criminology*, 44: 351–63.

Gabriel, Y. (1998), 'The Use of Stories,' in G. Symon and C. Cassell (eds.), *Qualitative Methods and Analysis in Organizational Research* (London: Sage).

Gans, H. J. (1962), *The Urban Villagers* (NY: Free Press).

——— (1968), 'The Participant-Observer as Human Being: Observations on the Personal Aspects of Field Work,' in H. Becker (ed.), *Institutions and the Person: Papers Presented to Everett C. Hughes* (Chicago: Aldine).

Garfinkel, H. (1967), *Studies in Ethnomethodology* (Englewood Cliffs, NJ: Prentice-Hall).

Gazso-Windlej, A., and McMullin, J. (2003), 'Doing Domestic Labour: Strategising in a Gendered Domain,' *Canadian Jour. of Sociology*, 28: 341–66.

Geertz, C. (1973), 'Thick Description: Toward an Interpretive Theory of Culture,' in C. Geertz, *The Interpretation of Cultures* (NY: Basic Books).

Gephart, R. (1988), *Ethnostatistics: Qualitative Foundations for Quantitative Research* (Newbury Park, CA: Sage).

Gerson, K., and Horowitz, R. (2002), 'Observation and Interviewing: Options and Choices,' in T. May (ed.), *Qualitative Research in Action* (London: Sage).

Giddens, A. (1984), *The Constitution of Society* (Cambridge, UK: Polity).

Gidengil, E., Everitt, J., Blais, A., Fournier, P., and Nevitte, N. (2006), 'Gender and Vote Choice in the 2006 Canadian Election,' paper prepared for the Annual Meeting of the American Political Science Association, Philadelphia.

Gilbert, G., and Mulkay, M. (1984), *Opening Pandora's Box: A Sociological Analysis of Scientists' Discourse* (Cambridge: Cambridge Univ. Press).

Gill, R. (1996), 'Discourse Analysis: Practical Implementation,' in J. Richardson (ed.), *Handbook of Qualitative Research Methods for Psychology and the Social Sciences* (Leicester: BPS Books).

——— (2000), 'Discourse Analysis,' in M. Bauer and G. Gaskell (eds.), *Qualitative Researching with Text, Image and Sound* (London: Sage).

Ginn, J., and Arber, S. (1995), 'Exploring Mid-life Women's Employment,' *Sociology*, 29: 73–94.

Giulianotti, R. (1995), 'Participant Observation and Research into Football Hooliganism: Reflections on the Problems of Entrée and Everyday Risks,' *Sociology of Sport Jour.*, 12: 1–20.

——— (1997), 'Enlightening the North: Aberdeen Fanzines and Local Football Identity,' in G. Armstrong and R. Giulianotti (eds.), *Entering the Field: New Perspectives on World Football* (Oxford: Berg).

Gladney, A., Ayars, C., Taylor, W., Liehr, P., and Meininger, J. (2003), 'Consistency of Findings Produced by Two Multidisciplinary Research Teams,' *Sociology*, 37: 297–313.

Glaser, B. (1992), *Basics of Grounded Theory Analysis* (Mill Valley, CA: Sociology Press).

——— and Strauss, A. (1967), *The Discovery of Grounded Theory: Strategies for Qualitative Research* (Chicago: Aldine).

Glock, C. (1988), 'Reflections on Doing Survey Research,' in H. O'Gorman (ed.), *Surveying Social Life* (Middletown, CT: Wesleyan Univ. Press).

Glucksmann, M. (1994), 'The Work of Knowledge and the Knowledge of Women's Work,' in M. Maynard and J. Purvis (eds.), *Researching Women's Lives from a Feminist Perspective* (London: Taylor & Francis).

Goffman, E. (1956), *The Presentation of Self in Everyday Life* (NY: Doubleday).

——— (1963), *Stigma: Notes on the Management of Spoiled Identity* (Harmondsworth, UK: Penguin).

Gold, R. (1958), 'Roles in Sociological Fieldwork,' *Social Forces*, 36: 217–23.

Golden-Biddle, K., and Locke, K. (1993), 'Appealing Work: An Investigation of how Ethnographic Texts Convince,' *Organization Sci.*, 4: 595–616.

——— (1997), *Composing Qualitative Research* (Thousand Oaks, CA: Sage).

Goode, E. (1996), 'The Ethics of Deception in Social Research: A Case Study,' *Qual. Sociology*, 19: 11–33.

Gottdiener, M. (1997), *The Theming of America: Dreams, Visions and Commercial Spaces* (Boulder, CO: Westview Press).

Gouldner, A. (1968), 'The Sociologist as Partisan,' *Amer. Sociologist*, 3: 103–16.

Goyder, J., Guppy, N., and Thompson, M. (2003), 'The Allocation of Male and Female Occupational Prestige in an Ontario Urban Area: A Quarter-century Replication,' *Canadian Rev. of Sociology and Anthropology*, 40: 417–39.

Grabb, E., and Curtis, J. (2004), *Regions Apart: The Four Societies of Canada and the U.S.* (Don Mills, ON: Oxford University Press).

Graham, C.A., Sanders, S.A., Milhausen, R.R., and McBride, K.R. (2004), 'Turning On and Turning Off: A Focus Group Study of the Factors That Affect Women's Sexual Arousal,' *Archives of Sexual Behavior*, 33: 527–38.

Greene, J. (1994), 'Qualitative Program Evaluation: Practice and Promise,' in N. Denzin and Y. Lincoln (eds.), *Handbook of Qual. Research* (Thousand Oaks, CA: Sage).

——— (2000), 'Understanding Social Programs through Evaluation,' in N. Denzin and Y. Lincoln (eds.), *Handbook of Qual. Research*, 2nd ed. (Thousand Oaks, CA: Sage).

Griffin, J. (1961), *Black Like Me* (Boston: Houghton Mifflin).

Guba, E., and Lincoln, Y. (1994), 'Competing Paradigms in Qualitative Research,' in N. Denzin and Y. Lincoln (eds.), *Handbook of Qual. Research* (Thousand Oaks, CA: Sage).

Gubrium, J., and Holstein, J. (1997), *The New Language of Qualitative Method* (NY: Oxford Univ. Press).

Guppy, L., and Siltanen, J. (1977), 'A Comparison of the Allocation of Male and Female Occupational Prestige,' *Canadian Rev. of Sociology and Anthropology*, 14: 320–30.

Halford, S., Savage, M., and Witz, A. (1997), *Gender, Careers and Organisations: Current Developments in Banking, Nursing and Local Government* (London: Sage).

Hallgrimsdottir, H., Phillips, R., and Benoit, C. (2006), 'Fallen Women and Rescued Girls: Social Stigma and Media Narratives of the Sex Industry in Victoria, B.C., from 1980 to 2005,' *Canadian Rev. of Sociology and Anthropology*, 43: 265–80.

Hammersley, M. (1992a), 'By What Criteria Should Ethnographic Research Be Judged?' in M. Hammersley, *What's Wrong with Ethnography* (London: Routledge).

——— (1992*b*), 'Deconstructing the Qualitative-Quantitative Divide,' in M. Hammersley, *What's Wrong with Ethnography* (London: Routledge).

——— (1996), 'The Relationship between Qualitative and Quantitative Research: Paradigm Loyalty versus Methodological Eclecticism,' in J. Richardson (ed.), *Handbook of Research Methods for Psychology and the Social Sciences* (Leicester: BPS Books).

——— (1997), 'Qualitative Data Archiving: Some Reflections on Its Prospects and Problems,' *Sociology*, 31: 131–42.

——— and Atkinson, P. (1995), *Ethnography: Principles in Practice*, 2nd ed. (London: Routledge).

——— Scarth, J., and Webb, S. (1985), 'Developing and Testing Theory: The Case of Research on Pupil Learning,' in R. Burgess (ed.), *Issues in Educational Research: Qualitative Methods* (London: Farwin).

Healey, J. (2002), *Statistics: A Tool for Social Research,* 6th ed. (Belmont, CA: Wadsworth).

——— (2009), *Statistics: A Tool for Social Research*, 8th ed. (Belmont, CA: Wadsworth).

Heath, C. (1997), 'The Analysis of Activities in Face to Face Interaction Using Video,' in D. Silverman (ed.), *Qualitative Research: Theory, Method and Practice* (London: Sage).

Heritage, J. (1984), *Garfinkel and Ethnomethodology* (Cambridge, UK: Polity).

——— (1987), 'Ethnomethodology,' in A. Giddens and J. Turner (eds.), *Social Theory Today* (Cambridge, UK: Polity).

Hesse-Biber, S. (1995), 'Unleashing Frankenstein's Monster? The Use of Computers in Qualitative Research,' *Studies in Qual. Methodology*, 5: 25–41.

Hessler, R., Downing, J., Beltz, C., Pelliccio, A., Powell, M., and Vale, W. (2003), 'Qualitative Research on Adolescent Risk Using E-mail: A Methodological Assessment,' *Qual. Sociology*, 26: 111–24.

Hier, S. (2000), 'The Contemporary Structure of Canadian Racial Supremacism; Networks, Strategies, and New Technologies,' *Canadian Jour. of Sociology*, 25: 471–94.

——— (2002), 'Raves, Risks and the Ecstacy Panic: A Case Study in the Subversive Nature of Moral Regulation,' *Canadian Jour. of Sociology*, 27: 33–57.

Hiller, H., and DiLuzio, L. (2004), 'The Interviewee and the Research Interview: Analyzing a Neglected Dimension in Research,' *Canadian Rev. of Sociology and Anthropology*, 41: 1–26.

Hine, V. (2000), *Virtual Ethnography* (London: Sage).

Hirsch, J. (1981), *Family Photographs* (NY: Oxford Univ. Press).

Ho, K., Baber, Z., and Khondker, H. (2002) 'Sites of Resistance: Alternative Websites and State-society Relations,' *Brit. Jour. of Sociology*, 53: 127–48.

Hobbs, D. (1988), *Doing the Business: Entrepreneurship, the Working Class and Detectives in the East End of London* (Oxford: Oxford Univ. Press).

——— (1993), 'Peers, Careers, and Academic Fears: Writing as Field-work,' in D. Hobbs and T. May (eds.), *Interpreting the Field: Accounts of Ethnography* (Oxford: Clarendon Press).

——— , Hadfield, P., Lister, S., and Winlow, S. (2003), *Bouncers: Violence and Governance in the Night-time Economy* (Oxford: Oxford Univ. Press).

Hochschild, A. (1983), *The Managed Heart* (Berkeley and Los Angeles: Univ. of California Press).

Hodson, R. (1996), 'Dignity in the Workplace under Participative Management,' *Amer. Sociological Rev.*, 61: 719–38.

——— (1999), *Analyzing Documentary Accounts* (Thousand Oaks, CA: Sage).

Holbrook, A., Green, M., and Krosnick, J. (2003), 'Telephone Versus Face-to-face Interviewing of National Probability Samples with Long Questionnaires: Comparisons of Respondent Satisficing and Social Desirability Response Bias,' *Public Opinion Quarterly*, 67: 79–125.

Holbrook, B., and Jackson, B. (1996), 'Shopping Around: Focus Group Research in North London,' *Area*, 28: 136–42.

Homan, R. (1991), *The Ethics of Social Research* (London: Longman).

——— and Bulmer, M. (1982), 'On the Merits of Covert Methods: A Dialogue,' in M. Bulmer (ed.), *Social Research Ethics* (London: Macmillan).

Houghton, E. (1998), 'Sex Is Good for You,' *Guardian*, 92 (Jan.): 14–15.

Howell, J., and Frost, P. (1989), 'A Laboratory Study of Charismatic Leadership,' *Organizational Behavior and Human Decision Processes*, 43: 243–69.

Huey, L. (2003), 'Explaining Odlin Road: Insecurity and Exclusivity,' *Canadian Jour. of Sociology*, 28: 367–86.

Hughes, E. (1943), *French Canada in Transition* (Chicago: Univ. of Chicago Press).

Hughes, G. (2000), 'Understanding the Politics of Criminological Research,' in V. Jupp, P. Davies, and P. Francis (eds.), *Doing Criminological Research* (London: Sage).

Hughes, J. (1990), *The Philosophy of Social Research*, 2nd ed. (Harlow: Longman).

Hughes, K., MacKintosh, A. M., Hastings, G., Wheeler, C., Watson, J., and Inglis, J. (1997), 'Young People, Alcohol, and Designer Drinks: A Quantitative and Qualitative Study,' *Brit. Medical Jour.*, 314: 414–18.

Hughes, R. (1998), 'Considering the Vignette Technique and its Application to a Study of Drug Injecting and HIV Risk and Safer Behaviour,' *Sociology of Health and Illness*, 20: 381–400.

Humphreys, L. (1970), *Tearoom Trade: Impersonal Sex in Public Places* (Chicago: Aldine).

Hutchby, I., and Wooffitt, R. (1998), *Conversation Analysis* (Cambridge, UK: Polity).

Jagger, E. (1998), 'Marketing the Self, Buying an Other: Dating in a Post Modern, Consumer Society,' *Sociology*, 32: 795–814.

——— (2001), 'Marketing Molly and Melville: Dating in a Postmodern, Consumer Society,' *Sociology*, 35: 39–57.

Jamieson, J. (2000), 'Negotiating Danger in Fieldwork on Crime: A Researcher's Tale,' in G. Lee-Treweek and S. Linkogle (eds.), *Danger in the Field: Risk and Ethics in Social Research* (London: Routledge).

Jayaratne, T., and Stewart, A. (1991), 'Quantitative and Qualitative Methods in the Social Sciences: Current Feminist

Issues and Practical Strategies,' in M. Fonow and J. Cook (eds.), *Beyond Methodology: Feminist Scholarship as Lived Research* (Bloomington, IN: Indiana Univ. Press).

John, I.D. (1992), 'Statistics as Rhetoric in Psychology,' *Australian Psychologist*, 27: 144–9.

Johnson, J., Bottorff, J., Moffat, B., Ratner, P., Shoveller, J., and Lovato, C. (2003), 'Tobacco Dependence: Adolescents' Perspectives on the Need to Smoke,' *Social Sci. and Medicine*, 56: 1481–92.

Jones, K. (2000), 'Constructing rBST in Canada: Biotechnology, Instability, and the Management of Nature,' *Canadian Jour. of Sociology*, 25: 311–41.

Kanayama, T. (2003), 'Ethnographic Research on the Experience of Japanese Elderly People Online,' *New Media and Society*, 5: 267–88.

Karabanow, J. (2002), 'Open for Business: Exploring the Life Stages of Two Canadian Street Youth Shelters,' *Jour. of Sociology and Social Welfare*, 29: 99–116.

Katz, J. (2002), 'From How to Why: On Luminous Description and Causal Inference in Ethnography (Part 2),' *Ethnography*, 3: 63–90.

Katz, J., Kuffel, S., and Coblentz, A. (2002), 'Are There Gender Differences in Sustaining Dating Violence?' *Jour. of Family Violence*, 17: 247–71.

Kelley, J., and De Graaf, N. (1997), 'National Context, Parental Socialization, and Religious Belief: Results from 15 Nations,' *Amer. Sociological Rev.*, 62: 639–59.

Kelly, L., Burton, S., and Regan, L. (1994), 'Researching Women's Lives or Studying Women's Oppression? Reflections on What Constitutes Feminist Research,' in M. Maynard and J. Purvis (eds.), *Researching Women's Lives from a Feminist Perspective* (London: Taylor & Francis).

Kendall, L. (1999), 'Recontextualizing "Cyberspace": Methodological Considerations for On-line Research,' in S. Jones (ed.), *Doing Internet Research: Critical Issues and Methods for Examining the Net* (Thousand Oaks, CA: Sage).

Kennedy, R. (2006), 'Researching the Intersection Between Collective Identity and Conceptions of Post-separation and Divorced Fatherhood: A Case Study; Fathers For Justice, Fathers For Just Us, or Fathers Are Us,' *Qualitative Sociology Rev.*, 2: 75–97.

Kent, R., and Lee, M. (1999), 'Using the Internet for Market Research: A Study of Private Trading on the Internet,' *Jour. of the Market Research Society*, 41: 377–85.

Kerr, D. (2004), 'Family Transformations and the Well-being of Children: Recent Evidence from Canadian Longitudinal Data,' *Jour. of Comparative Family Studies*, 35: 73–90.

Kerr, D., and Michalski, J. (2007), 'Family Structure and Children's Hyperactivity Problems: A Longitudinal Analysis,' *Canadian Jour. of Sociology*, 32: 85–112.

Kimmel, A. (1988), *Ethics and Values in Applied Social Research* (Newbury Park, CA: Sage).

Kitzinger, J. (1993), 'Understanding AIDS: Researching Audience Perceptions of Acquired Immune Deficiency Syndrome,' in J. Eldridge (ed.), *Getting the Message: News, Truth and Power* (London: Routledge).

—— (1994), 'The Methodology of Focus Groups: The Importance of Interaction between Research Participants,' *Sociology of Health and Illness*, 16, 1994: 103–21.

Krosnick, J., Holbrook, A. *et al.* (2002), 'The Impact of "No Opinion" Response Options on Data Quality: Non-Attitude Reduction or an Invitation to Satisfice?' *Public Opinion Quarterly*, 66: 371–403.

Krueger, R. (1998), *Moderating Focus Groups* (Thousand Oaks, CA: Sage).

Kuhn, T. (1970), *The Structure of Scientific Revolutions*, 2nd ed. (Chicago: Univ. of Chicago Press).

Kusow, A. (2003), 'Beyond Indigenous Authenticity: Reflections on the Insider/ Outsider Debate in Immigration Research,' *Symbolic Interaction*, 26: 591–9.

Kvale, S. (1996), *InterViews: An Introduction to Qualitative Research Interviewing* (Thousand Oaks, CA: Sage).

Lankshear, G. (2000), 'Bacteria and Babies: A Personal Reflection on Researcher's Risk in a Hospital,' in G. Lee-Treweek and S. Linkogle (eds.), *Danger in the Field: Risk and Ethics in Social Research* (London: Routledge).

Lantz, P., and Booth, K. (1998), 'The Social Construction of the Breast Cancer Epidemic,' *Social Sci. and Medicine*, 46: 907–18.

LaPiere, R.T. (1934), 'Attitudes vs. Actions,' *Social Forces*, 13: 230–7.

Laplante, B. (2006), 'The Rise of Cohabitation in Quebec: Power of Religion and Power over Religion,' *Canadian Jour. of Sociology*, 31: 1–24.

Lauder, M. (2003), 'Covert Participant Observation of a Deviant Community: Justifying the Use of Deception,' *Jour. of Contemporary Religion* 18: 185–96.

Laurenceau, J-P., and Bolger, N. (2005), 'Using Diary Methods to Study Marital and Family Processes,' *Jour. of Family Psychology*, 19: 86–97.

Layder, D. (1993), *New Strategies in Social Research* (Cambridge, UK: Polity).

—— , Ashton, D., and Sung. J. (1991), 'The Empirical Correlates of Action and Structure: The Transition from School to Work,' *Sociology*, 25: 447–64.

Leake, J. (1998), 'Police Figures Hide Poor Clear-up Rate,' *The Times*, 21 June: 1.

LeCompte, M., and Goetz, J. (1982), 'Problems of Reliability and Validity in Ethnographic Research,' *Rev. of Educational Research*, 52: 31–60.

Lee, R.M. (2000), *Unobtrusive Methods in Social Research* (Buckingham: Open Univ. Press).

—— (2004), 'Danger in Research,' in M. Lewis-Beck, A. Bryman, and T. Liao (eds.), *The Sage Encycl. of Soc. Sci. Research Methods* (Thousand Oaks, CA: Sage).

Lee-Treweek, G. (2000), 'The Insight of Emotional Danger: Research Experiences in a Home for the Elderly,' in G. Lee-Treweek and S. Linkogle (eds.), *Danger in the Field: Risk and Ethics in Social Research* (London: Routledge).

Leidner, R. (1993), *Fast Food, Fast Talk: Service Work and the Routinization of Everyday Life* (Berkeley and Los Angeles: Univ. of California Press).

Levitas, R., and Guy, W. (1996), in R. Levitas and W. Guy (eds.), *Interpreting Official Statistics* (London: Routledge).

Lewis, O. (1961), *The Children of Sánchez* (NY: Vintage).

Li, P. (2003), 'Initial Earnings and Catch-up Capacity of Immigrants,' *Can. Public Policy*, 29: 319–37.

Liebling, A. (2001), 'Whose Side Are We On? Theory, Practice and Allegiances in Prisons Research,' *Brit. Jour. of Criminology*, 41: 472-84.

Lincoln, Y., and Denzin, N. (1994), 'The Fifth Moment,' in N. Denzin and Y. Lincoln (eds.), *Handbook of Qual. Research* (Thousand Oaks, CA: Sage).

—— and Guba, E. (1985), *Naturalistic Inquiry* (Beverly Hills, CA: Sage).

Lipset, S. (1990), *Continental Divide: The Values and Institutions of the United States and Canada* (NY: Routledge).

Little, M. (2001), 'A Litmus Test for Democracy: The Impact of Ontario Welfare Changes for Single Mothers,' *Studies in Political Economy*, 66: 9–36.

Locke, K. (1996), 'Rewriting *The Discovery of Grounded Theory* after 25 Years?' *Jour. of Management Inquiry*, 5: 239–45.

Lofland, J., and Lofland, L. (1995), *Analyzing Social Settings: A Guide to Qualitative Observation and Analysis*, 3rd ed. (Belmont, CA: Wadsworth).

Lonkila, M. (1995), 'Grounded Theory as an Emergent Paradigm for Computer-Assisted Qualitative Data Analysis,' in U. Kelle (ed.), *Computer-aided Qualitative Data Analysis* (London: Sage).

Lupton, D. (1996), *Food, the Body and the Self* (London: Sage).

Lynch, M., and Bogen, D. (1997), 'Sociology's Asociological "Core": An Examination of Textbook Sociology in the Light of The Sociology of Scientific Knowledge,' *Amer. Sociological Rev.*, 62: 481–93.

Lynd, R., and Lynd, H. (1929), *Middletown: A Study in Contemporary American Culture* (NY: Harcourt Brace).

—— (1937), *Middletown in Transition: A Study in Cultural Conflicts* (NY: Harcourt Brace).

McCall, M.J. (1984), 'Structured Field Observation,' *Annual Rev. of Sociology*, 10: 263–82.

McGuigan, J. (1992), *Cultural Populism* (London: Routledge).

McKee, L., and Bell, C. (1985), 'Marital and Family Relations in Times of Male Unemployment,' in B. Roberts, R. Finnegan, and D. Gallie (eds.), *New Approaches to Economic Life* (Manchester: Manchester Univ. Press).

McKeganey, N., and Barnard, M. (1996), *Sex Work on the Streets* (Buckingham: Open Univ. Press).

MacKinnon, N., and Luke, A. (2002), 'Changes in Identity Attitudes as Reflections of Social and Cultural Change,' *Canadian Jour. of Sociology*, 27: 299–338.

Macnaghten, P., and Jacobs, M. (1997), 'Public Identification with Sustainable Development: Investigating Cultural Barriers to Participation,' *Global Environmental Change*, 7: 5–24.

Madge, C., and O'Connor, H. (2002), 'On-line with E-Mums: Exploring the Internet as a Medium of Research,' *Area*, 34: 92–102.

Madriz, M. (2000), 'Focus Groups in Feminist Research,' in N. Denzin and Y. Lincoln (eds.), *Handbook of Qual. Research*, 2nd ed. (Thousand Oaks, CA: Sage).

Malbon, B. (1999), *Clubbing: Dancing, Ecstasy and Vitality* (London: Routledge).

Malinowski, B. (1967), *A Diary in the Strict Sense of the Term* (London: Routledge & Kegan Paul).

Malkin, A.R., Wornian, K., and Chrisler, J.C. (1999), 'Women and Weight: Gendered Messages on Magazine Covers,' *Sex Roles*, 40: 647–55.

Mangione, T.W. (1995), *Mail Surveys: Improving the Quality* (Thousand Oaks, CA: Sage).

Mann, C., and Stewart, F. (2000), *Internet Communication and Qualitative Research: A Handbook for Researching Online* (London: Sage).

Manning, P. (1995), 'The Challenge of Postmodernism,' in J. Van Maanen (ed.), *Representation in Ethnography* (Thousand Oaks, CA: Sage).

Marcic, D. (2002), *Respect: Women and Popular Music* (NY: Texere).

Markham, A. (1998), *Life Online: Researching the Real Experience in Virtual Space* (London and Walnut Creek, CA: AltaMira Press).

Marsh, C., and Scarbrough, E. (1990), 'Testing Nine Hypotheses about Quota Sampling,' *Jour. of the Market Research Society*, 32: 485–506.

Marshall, G., Newby, H., and Vogler, C. (1988), *Social Class in Modern Britain* (London: Unwin Hyman).

Marx, G.T. (1997), 'Of Methods and Manners for Aspiring Sociologists: 37 Moral Imperatives,' *Amer. Sociologist*, 102–25.

Marx, K. (1998 [1845]), *The German Ideology including Theses on Feuerbach and Introduction to the Critique of Political Economy* (Amherst: Prometheus Books).

Mason, J. (1994), 'Linking Qualitative and Quantitative Data Analysis,' in A. Bryman and R. Burgess (eds.), *Analyzing Qualitative Data* (London: Routledge).

—— (1996), *Qualitative Researching* (London: Sage).

—— (2002), 'Qualitative Interviewing: Asking, Listening, Interpreting,' in T. May (ed.), *Qualitative Research in Action* (London: Sage).

Mauthner, N., Parry, O., and Backett-Milburn, K. (1998), 'The Data Are Out There, or Are They? Implications for Archiving and Revisiting Qualitative Data,' *Sociology*, 32: 733–45.

Mayhew, P. (2000), 'Researching the State of Crime' in R. King and E. Wincup (eds.), *Doing Research on Crime and Justice* (Oxford: Oxford Univ. Press).

Maynard, M. (1994), 'Methods, Practice and Epistemology: The Debate about Feminism and Research,' in M. Maynard and J. Purvis (eds.), *Researching Women's Lives from a Feminist Perspective* (London: Taylor & Francis).

—— (1998), 'Feminists' Knowledge and the Knowledge of Feminisms: Epistemology, Theory, Methodology and Method,' in T. May and M. Williams (eds.), *Knowing the Social World* (Buckingham: Open Univ. Press).

Mead, M. (1928), *Coming of Age in Samoa* (NY: Morrow).

Menard, S. (1991), *Longitudinal Research* (Newbury Park, CA: Sage).

Merton, R. (1938), 'Social Structure and Anomie,' *Amer. Sociological Rev.*, 3: 672–82.

—— (1967), *On Theoretical Sociology* (NY: Free Press).

Michaud, S. (2001), 'The National Longitudinal Study of Children and Youth—Overview and Changes after Three Cycles,' *Canadian Studies in Population*, 28: 391–405.

Midgley, C. (1998), 'TV Violence has Little Impact on Children, Study Finds,' *The Times*, 12 Jan.: 5.

Mies, M. (1993), 'Towards a Methodology for Feminist

Research,' in M. Hammersley (ed.), *Social Research: Philosophy, Politics and Practice* (London: Sage).

Miles, M.B. (1979), 'Qualitative Data as an Attractive Nuisance,' *Administrative Sci. Quarterly*, 24: 590–601.

Milgram, S. (1963), 'A Behavioural Study of Obedience,' *Jour. of Abnormal and Social Psych.*, 67: 371–8.

Milkman, R. (1997), *Farewell to the Factory: Auto Workers in the Late Twentieth Century* (Los Angeles: Univ. of California Press).

Millen, D. (1997), 'Some Methodological and Epistemological Issues Raised by Doing Feminist Research on Non-Feminist Women,' *Sociological Research Online*, 2: www.socresonline.org.uk/socresonline/2/3/3.html.

Miller, D., and Reilly, J. (1995), 'Making an Issue of Food Safety: The Media, Pressure Groups, and the Public Sphere,' in D. Maurer and J. Sobal (eds.), *Food and Nutrition as Social Problems* (NY: Aldine de Gruyter).

Miller, D. Disney (1956), *The Story of Walt Disney* (NY: Dell).

Miller, N., and Morgan, D. (1993), 'Called to Account: The CV as an Autobiographical Practice,' *Sociology*, 27: 133–43.

Miller, R.L. (2000), *Researching Life Stories and Family Histories* (London: Sage).

Miraftab, F. (2000), 'Sheltering Refugees: The Housing Experience of Refugees in Metropolitan Vancouver, Canada,' *Canadian Jour. of Urban Research*, 9: 42–63.

Morgan, D. (1998a), *Planning Focus Groups* (Thousand Oaks, CA: Sage).

——— (1998b), 'Practical Strategies for Combining Qualitative and Quantitative Methods: Applications for Health Research,' *Qual. Health Research*, 8: 362–76.

——— (2002), 'Focus Group Interviewing,' in J. Gubrium and J. Holstein (eds.), *Handbook of Interview Research: Context and Method* (Thousand Oaks, CA: Sage).

——— and Spanish, M. (1985), 'Social Interaction and the Cognitive Organization of Health-relevant Behaviour,' *Sociology of Health and Illness*, 7: 401–22.

Morgan, R. (2000), 'The Politics of Criminological Research,' in R. King and E. Wincup (eds.), *Doing Research on Crime and Justice* (Oxford: Oxford Univ. Press).

Myles, J., and Hou, F. (2004), 'Changing Colours: Spatial Assimilation and New Racial Minority Immigrants,' *Canadian Jour. of Sociology*, 29: 28–58.

Nemni, M., and Nemni, M. (2006), *Young Trudeau: Son of Quebec, Father of Canada, 1919–1944,* trans. W. Johnson (Toronto: Douglas Gibson Books).

Nettleton, S., Pleace, N., Burrows, R., Muncer, S., and Loader, B. (2002), 'The Reality of Virtual Social Support,' in S. Woolgar (ed.), *Virtual Society? Technology, Cyperbole, Reality* (Oxford: Oxford Univ. Press).

Neuman, W.L. (2003), *Social Research Methods* (Toronto: Pearson Canada).

Nixon, K., Tutty, L., Downe, P., Gorkoff, K., and Ursel, J. (2002), 'The Everyday Occurrence: Violence in the Lives of Girls Exploited through Prostitution?' *Violence against Women*, 8: 1016–43.

Norris, C. (1993), 'Some Ethical Considerations on Fieldwork with the Police,' in D. Hobbs and T. May (eds.), *Interpreting the Field: Accounts of Ethnography* (Oxford: Clarendon Press).

Oakley, A. (1981), 'Interviewing Women: A Contradiction in Terms,' in H. Roberts (ed.), *Doing Feminist Research* (London: Routledge & Kegan Paul).

——— (1998), 'Gender, Methodology and People's Ways of Knowing: Some Problems with Feminism and the Paradigm Debate in Social Science,' *Sociology*, 32: 707–31.

O'Connell Davidson, J., and Layder, D. (1994), *Methods, Sex, and Madness* (London: Routledge).

O'Connor, H., and Madge, C. (2001), 'Cyber-Mothers: Online Synchronous Interviewing Using Conferencing Software,' *Sociological Research Online*, 5: www.socresonline.org.uk/5/4/o'connor.html.

——— (2003), '"Focus Groups in Cyberspace": Using the Internet for Qualitative Research,' *Qual. Market Research*, 6: 133–43.

Okely, J. (1994), 'Thinking through Fieldwork,' in A. Bryman and R. Burgess (eds.), *Analyzing Qualitative Data* (London: Routledge).

O'Reilly, K. (2000), *The British on the Costa del Sol: Transnational Identities and Local Communities* (London: Routledge).

Orona, C.J. (1997), 'Temporality and Identity Loss due to Alzheimer's Disease,' in A. Strauss and J. Corbin (eds.), *Grounded Theory in Practice* (Thousand Oaks, CA: Sage).

Pahl, J. (1990), 'Household Spending, Personal Spending and the Control of Money in Marriage,' *Sociology*, 24: 119–38.

Parker, M. (2000), *Organizational Culture and Identity* (London: Sage).

Parnaby, P. (2003), 'Disaster through Dirty Windshields: Law, Order and Toronto's Squeegee Kids,' *Canadian Jour. of Sociology*, 28: 281–307.

Pawson, R., and Tilley, N. (1997), *Realistic Evaluation* (London: Sage).

Peñaloza, L. (1999), 'Just Doing It: A Visual Ethnographic Study of Spectacular Consumption at Niketown,' *Consumption, Market, and Culture*, 2: 337–400.

Perrucci, R., Belshaw, R., DeMerritt, A., Frazier, B., Jones, J., Kimbrough, J., Loney, K., Pappas, J., Parker, J., Trottier, B., and Williams, B. (2000), 'The Two Faces of Racialized Space at a Predominantly White University,' *Intnatl. Jour. of Contemporary Sociology*, 37: 230–44.

Pettigrew, A. (1997), 'What Is a Processual Analysis?' *Scandinavian Jour. of Management*, 13: 337–48.

——— and Whipp, R. (1991), *Managing Change for Competitive Success* (Oxford: Blackwell).

Phelan, P. (1987), 'Comparability of Qualitative and Quantitative Methods: Studying Child Sexual Abuse in America,' *Educ. and Urban Society*, 20: 35–41.

Phillips, N., and Brown, J. (1993), 'Analyzing Communications in and around Organizations: A Critical Hermeneutic Approach,' *Academy of Management Jour.*, 36: 1547–76.

Phoenix, A. (1994), 'Practising Feminist Research: The Intersection of Gender and "Race" in the Research Process,' in M. Maynard and J. Purvis (eds.), *Researching Women's Lives from a Feminist Perspective* (London: Taylor & Francis).

Pidgeon, N., and Henwood, K. (2004), 'Grounded Theory,'

in M. Hardy and A. Bryman (eds.), *Handbook of Data Analysis* (London: Sage).

Pink, S. (2001), *Visual Ethnography* (London: Sage).

Platt, J. (1986), 'Functionalism and the Survey: The Relation of Theory and Method,' *Sociological Rev.*, 34: 501–36.

—— (1996), *A History of Sociological Research Methods in America 1920–1960* (Cambridge: Cambridge Univ. Press).

Podsakoff, P., and Dalton, D. (1987), 'Research Methodology in Organizational Studies,' *Jour. of Management*, 13: 419–44.

Poland, B.D. (1995), 'Transcription Quality as an Aspect of Rigor in Qualitative Research,' *Qual. Inquiry*, 1: 290–310.

Porter, S. (1993), 'Critical Realist Ethnography: The Case of Racism and Professionalism in a Medical Setting,' *Sociology*, 27: 591–609.

—— (2002), 'Critical Realist Ethnography,' in T. May (ed.), *Qual. Research in Action* (London: Sage).

Potter, G. (2003), '*Sui generis* Micro Social Structures: The Heuristic Example of Poker,' *Canadian Jour. of Sociology*, 28: 171–202.

Potter, J. (1996), *Representing Reality: Discourse, Rhetoric and Social Construction* (London: Sage).

—— (1997), 'Discourse Analysis as a Way of Analysing Naturally Occurring Talk,' in D. Silverman (ed.), *Qual. Research: Theory, Method and Practice* (London: Sage).

—— (2004), 'Discourse Analysis,' in M. Hardy and A. Bryman (eds.), *Handbook of Data Analysis* (London: Sage).

—— and Hepburn, A. (2004), 'The Analysis of NSPCC Call Openings,' in S. Becker and A. Bryman (eds.), *Understanding Research for Social Policy and Practice: Themes, Methods, and Approaches* (Bristol: Policy Press).

—— and Wetherell, M. (1994), 'Analyzing Discourse,' in A. Bryman and R. Burgess (eds.), *Analyzing Qualitative Data* (London: Routledge).

—— and Chitty, A. (1991), 'Quantification Rhetoric —Cancer on Television,' *Discourse and Society*, 2: 333–65.

Pratt, A., and Valverde, M. (2002), 'From Deserving Victims to "Masters of Confusion": Redefining Refugees in the 1900s,' *Canadian Jour. of Sociology*, 27: 135–62.

Psathas, G. (1995), *Conversation Analysis: The Study of Talk-in-Interaction* (Thousand Oaks, CA: Sage).

Punch, M. (1994), 'Politics and Ethics in Qualitative Research,' in N. Denzin and Y. Lincoln (eds.), *Handbook of Qual. Research* (Thousand Oaks, CA: Sage).

Radley, A., and Chamberlain, K. (2001), 'Health Psychology and the Study of the Case: From Method to Analytic Concern,' *Social Sci. and Medicine*, 53: 321–32.

—— and Taylor, D. (2003*a*), 'Images of Recovery: a Photo-Elicitation Study on the Hospital Ward,' *Qual. Health Research*, 13: 77–99.

—— (2003*b*), 'Remembering One's Stay in Hospital: A Study in Photography, Recovery and Forgetting,' *Health: An Interdisciplinary Jour. for the Social Study of Health, Illness and Medicine*, 7: 129–59.

Rafaeli, A., Dutton, J., Harquail, C.V., and Mackie-Lewis, S. (1997), 'Navigating by Attire: The Use of Dress by Female Administrative Employees,' *Academy of Management Jour.*, 40: 9–45.

Reed, M. (2000), 'The Limits of Discourse Analysis in Organizational Analysis,' *Organization*, 7: 524–30.

Reiner, R. (2000*a*), 'Crime and Control in Britain,' *Sociology*, 34: 71–94.

—— (2000*b*), 'Police Research,' in R. King and E. Wincup (eds.), *Doing Research on Crime and Justice* (Oxford: Oxford Univ. Press).

Reinharz, S. (1992), *Feminist Methods in Social Research* (NY: Oxford Univ. Press).

Richardson, L. (1990), 'Narrative and Sociology,' *Jour. of Contemporary Ethnography*, 19: 116–35.

—— (1994), 'Writing: A Method of Inquiry,' in N. Denzin and Y. Lincoln (eds.), *Handbook of Qual. Research* (Thousand Oaks, CA: Sage).

Riches, G., and Dawson, P. (1998), 'Lost Children, Living Memories: The Role of Photographs in Processes of Grief and Adjustment Among Bereaved Parents,' *Death Studies*, 22: 121–40.

Riessman, C.K. (1993), *Narrative Analysis* (Newbury Park, CA: Sage).

—— (2004*a*), 'Narrative Interviewing,' in M. Lewis-Beck, A. Bryman, and T. Liao (eds.), *The Sage Encycl. of Soc. Sci. Research Methods* (Thousand Oaks, CA: Sage).

—— (2004*b*), 'Narrative Analysis,' in M. Lewis-Beck, A. Bryman, and T. Liao (eds.), *The Sage Encycl. of Soc. Sci. Research Methods* (Thousand Oaks, CA: Sage).

Rinehart, J. (1996), *The Tyranny of Work*, 3rd ed. (Toronto: Harcourt Brace).

—— , Huxley, C., and Robertson, D. (1998), *Not Just Another Auto Plant* (Ithaca, NY: Cornell Univ. Press).

Ristock, J. (2001), 'Decentring Heterosexuality: Responses of Feminist Counsellors to Abuse in Lesbian Relationships,' *Women and Therapy*, 23: 59–72.

Roberts, B. (2002), *Biographical Research* (Buckingham: Open Univ. Press).

Robinson, J., Shaver, P., and Wrightsman, L. (1999), *Measures of Political Attitudes* (Toronto: Academic Press).

Roethlisberger, F., and Dickson, W. (1939), *Management and the Worker* (Cambridge, MA: Harvard University Press).

Rojek, C. (1995), *Decentring Leisure: Rethinking Leisure Theory* (London: Sage).

Rose, G. (2001), *Visual Methodologies* (London: Sage).

Rosenau, P.M. (1992), *Post-Modernism and the Social Sciences: Insights, Inroads, and Intrusions* (Princeton: Princeton Univ. Press).

Rosenhan, D.L. (1973), 'On Being Sane in Insane Places,' *Science*, 179: 350–8.

Rosenthal, R., and Jacobson, L. (1968), *Pygmalion in the Classroom: Teacher Expectation and Pupils' Intellectual Development* (NY: Holt, Rinehart & Winston).

Rosnow, R.L., and Rosenthal, R. (1997), *People Studying People: Artefacts and Ethics in Behavioral Research* (NY: W.H. Freeman).

Rubin, H.J., and Rubin, I.S. (1995), *Qualitative Interviewing: The Art of Hearing Data* (Thousand Oaks, CA: Sage).

Rushton, J. (2000), *Race, Evolution and Behaviour: A Life History Perspective* (Port Huron, MI: Charles Darwin Research Institute).

Russell, R., and Tyler, M. (2002), 'Thank Heaven for Little

Girls: "Girl Heaven" and the Commercial Context of Feminine Childhood,' *Sociology*, 36: 619–37.

Sampson, H., and Thomas, M. (2003), 'Lone Researchers at Sea: Gender, Risk and Responsibility,' *Qual. Research*, 3: 165–89.

Sanjek, R. (1990), 'A Vocabulary for Fieldnotes,' in R. Sanjek (ed.), *Fieldnotes: The Making of Anthropology* (Ithaca, NY: Cornell Univ. Press).

Sarsby, J. (1984), 'The Fieldwork Experience,' in R. Ellen (ed.), *Ethnographic Research: A Guide to General Conduct* (London: Academic Press).

Schaeffer, D., and Dillman, D. (1998), 'Development of a Standard E-mail Methodology,' *Public Opinion Quarterly*, 62: 378–97.

Schegloff, E. (1997), 'Whose Text? Whose Context?' *Discourse and Society*, 8: 165–87.

Schlesinger, P., Dobash, R.E., Dobash, R.P., and Weaver, C. (1992), *Women Viewing Violence* (London: British Film Institute).

Schröder, K.C. (1999), 'The Best of Both Worlds? Media Audience Research between Rival Paradigms,' in P. Alasuutari (ed.), *Rethinking the Media Audience* (London: Sage).

Schuman, H., and Presser, S. (1981), *Questions and Answers in Attitude Surveys: Experiments on Question Form, Wording, and Context* (San Diego, CA: Academic Press).

Schutz, A. (1962), *Collected Papers I: The Problem of Social Reality* (The Hague: Martinus Nijhof).

Scott, J. (1990), *A Matter of Record* (Cambridge, UK: Polity).

Seale, C. (1999), *The Quality of Qualitative Research* (London: Sage).

—— (2002), 'Cancer Heroics: A Study of News Reports with Particular Reference to Gender,' *Sociology*, 36: 107–26.

Shalla, V. (2002), 'Jettisoned by Design? The Truncated Employment Relationship of Customer Sales and Service Agents under Airline Restructuring,' *Canadian Jour. of Sociology*, 27: 1–32.

Sharf, B.F. (1999), 'Beyond Netiquette: The Ethics of Doing Naturalistic Discourse Research on the Internet,' in S. Jones (ed.), *Doing Internet Research: Critical Issues and Methods for Examining the Net* (Thousand Oaks, CA: Sage).

Sharpe, K. (2000), 'Sad, Bad, and (Sometimes) Dangerous to Know: Street Corner Research with Prostitutes, Punters, and the Police,' in R. King and E. Wincup (eds.), *Doing Research on Crime and Justice* (Oxford: Oxford Univ. Press).

Sheehan, K. (2001), 'E-mail Survey Response Rates: A Review,' *Jour. of Computer-Mediated Communication*, 6: www.ascusc. org/jcmc/vol6/issue2/sheehan.html.

—— and Hoy, M. (1999), 'Using E-mail to Survey Internet Users in the United States: Methodology and Assessment,' *Jour. of Computer-Mediated Communication*, 4: www.ascusc.org/jcmc/vol4/issue3/sheehan.html.

Shuy, R.W. (2002), 'In-person versus Telephone Interviewing,' in J.F. Gubrium and J.A. Holstein (eds.), *Handbook of Interview Research: Context and Method* (Thousand Oaks, CA: Sage).

Silverman, D. (1984), 'Going Private: Ceremonial Forms in a Private Oncology Clinic,' *Sociology*, 18: 191–204.

—— (1985), *Qualitative Methodology and Sociology: Describing the Social World* (Aldershot: Gower).

—— (1993), *Interpreting Qualitative Data: Methods for Analysing Qualitative Data* (London: Sage).

—— (1994), 'Analysing Naturally Occurring Data on AIDS Counselling: Some Methodological and Practical Issues,' in M. Boulton (ed.), *Challenge and Innovation: Methodological Advances in Social Research on HIV/AIDS* (London: Taylor & Francis).

Silverman, R., Sacco, V., and Teevan, J. (2000), *Crime in Canadian Society* (Toronto: Harcourt Canada).

Skeggs, B. (1994), 'Situating the Production of Feminist Ethnography,' in M. Maynard and J. Purvis (eds.), *Researching Women's Lives from a Feminist Perspective* (London: Taylor & Francis).

—— (1997), *Formations of Class and Gender* (London: Sage).

—— (2001), 'Feminist Ethnography,' in P. Atkinson, A. Coffey, S. Delamont, J. Lofland, and L. Lofland (eds.), *Handbook of Ethnography* (London: Sage).

Smith, D.J., and McVie, S. (2003), 'Theory and Method in the Edinburgh Study of Youth Transitions and Crime,' *Brit. Jour. of Criminology*, 43: 169–95.

Smith, N., Lister, R., and Middleton, S. (2004), 'Longitudinal Qualitative Research,' in S. Becker and A. Bryman (eds.), *Understanding Research for Social Policy and Practice: Themes, Methods, and Approaches* (Bristol: Policy Press).

Smith, R. (2008), 'Pain in the Act: The Meanings of Pain Among Professional Wrestlers,' *Qualitative Sociology*, 31: 129–48.

Smith, T.W. (1995), 'Trends in Non-response Rates,' *Intnatl. Jour. of Public Opinion Research*, 7: 157–71.

Stacey, J. (1988), 'Can There Be a Feminist Ethnography?' *Women's Studies Intnatl. Forum*, 1: 21–7.

Stake, R.E. (1995), *The Art of Case Study Research* (Thousand Oaks, CA: Sage).

Stanley, L., and Temple, B. (1995), 'Doing the Business? Evaluating Software Packages to Aid the Analysis of Qualitative Data Sets,' *Studies in Qual. Methodology*, 5: 169–97.

Stoller, P. (1989), *The Taste of Ethnographic Things* (Philadelphia: Univ. of Pennsylvania Press).

Strauss, A. (1987), *Qualitative Analysis for Social Scientists* (NY: Cambridge Univ. Press).

—— and Corbin, J. (1990), *Basics of Qualitative Research: Grounded Theory Procedures and Techniques* (Newbury Park, CA: Sage).

—— (1998), *Basics of Qualitative Research: Techniques and Procedures for Developing Grounded Theory* (Thousand Oaks, CA: Sage).

—— Schatzman, L., Ehrich, D., Bucher, R., and Sabshin, M. (1973), 'The Hospital and Its Negotiated Order,' in G. Salaman and K. Thompson (eds.), *People and Organizations* (London: Longman).

Sudman, S., and Bradburn, N. (1982), *Asking Questions: A Practical Guide to Questionnaire Design* (San Francisco: Jossey-Bass).

Sugiman, P. (2004), 'Memories of the Internment: Narrating Japanese-Canadian Women's Life Stories,' *Canadian Jour. of Sociology*, 29: 359–88.

Sullivan, O. (1996), 'Time Co-ordination, the Domestic Division of Labour and Affective Relations: Time Use and the Enjoyment of Activities within Couples,' *Sociology*, 30: 79–100.

Sutton, R.I. (1992), 'Feelings about a Disneyland Visit: Photography and the Reconstruction of Bygone Emotions,' *Jour. of Management Inquiry*, 1: 278–87.

—— and Rafaeli, A. (1988), 'Untangling the Relationship between Displayed Emotions and Organizational Sales: The Case of Convenience Stores,' *Academy of Management Jour.*, 31: 461–87.

—— (1992), 'How We Untangled the Relationship between Displayed Emotion and Organizational Sales: A Tale of Bickering and Optimism,' in P. Frost and R. Stablein (eds.), *Doing Exemplary Research* (Newbury Park, CA: Sage).

Sweet, C. (2001), 'Designing and Conducting Virtual Focus Groups,' *Qual. Market Research*, 4: 130–5.

Tastsoglou, E., and Miedema, B. (2003), 'Immigrant Women and Community Development in the Canadian Maritimes: Outsiders Within?' *Canadian Jour. of Sociology*, 28: 203–34.

Taylor, A. (1993), *Women Drug Users: An Ethnography of an Injecting Community* (Oxford: Clarendon Press).

Taylor, S. (1999), 'Covert Participant Observation: Unguarded Moments in Organizational Research,' *Notework: The Newsletter of the Standing Conference on Organizational Symbolism*, May: 8–18.

Teevan, J., and Dryburg, H. (2000), 'First Person Accounts and Sociological Explanations of Delinquency,' *Canadian Rev. of Sociology and Anthropology*, 37: 77–93.

Teitler, J., Reichman, N., and Sprachman, S. (2003), 'Costs and Benefits of Improving Response Rates for a Hard-to-reach Population,' *Public Opinion Quarterly*, 67: 126–38.

Thompson, T., and Zerbinos, E. (1995), 'Gender Roles in Animated Cartoons: Has the Picture Changed in 20 Years?' *Sex Roles*, 32: 651–73.

Tilley, N. (2000), 'Doing Realistic Evaluation of Criminal Justice,' in V. Jupp, P. Davies, and P. Francis (eds.), *Doing Criminological Research* (London: Sage).

Totten, M. (2001) 'Legal, Ethical, and Clinical Implications of Doing Fieldwork with Youth Gang Members Who Engage in Serious Violence,' *Jour. of Gang Research*, 8: 35–49.

Tourangeau, R., and Smith, T.W. (1996), 'Asking Sensitive Questions: The Impact of Data Collection Mode, Question Format, and Question Context,' *Public Opinion Quarterly*, 60: 275–304.

Trow, M. (1957), 'Comment on "Participant Observation and Interviewing: A Comparison,"' *Human Organization*, 16: 33–5.

Tse, A. (1998), 'Comparing the Response Rate, Response Speed and Response Quality of Two Methods of Sending Questionnaires: E-mail vs. Mail,' *Jour. of the Market Research Society*, 40: 353–61.

—— (1999), 'Conducting Electronic Focus Group Discussions among Chinese Respondents,' *Jour. of the Market Research Society*, 41: 407–15.

Turnbull, P. (1973), *The Mountain People* (London: Cape).

Van Den Hoonaard, W.C. (2001), 'Is Research-ethics Review a Moral Panic?' *Canadian Rev. of Sociology and Anthropology*, 38: 19–36.

Van Maanen, J. (1988), *Tales of the Field: On Writing Ethnography* (Chicago: Univ. of Chicago Press).

—— (1991*a*), 'Playing Back the Tape: Early Days in the Field,' in W. Shaffir and R. Stebbins (eds.), *Experiencing Fieldwork: An Inside View of Qualitative Research* (Newbury Park, CA: Sage).

—— (1991*b*), 'The Smile Factory: Work at Disneyland,' in P. Frost, L. Moore *et al.* (eds.), *Reframing Organizational Culture* (Newbury Park, CA: Sage).

Vidich, A., and Bensman, J. (1968), *Small Town in Mass Society* (Princeton, NJ: Princeton Univ. Press).

Vincent, S. (2003), 'Preserving Domesticity,' *Canadian Rev. of Sociology and Anthropology*, 40: 171–96.

Wachholz, S., and Miedema, B. (2000), 'Risk, Fear, Harm: Immigrant Women's Perceptions of the "Policing Solution" to Woman Abuse,' *Crime, Law, and Social Change*, 34: 301–17.

Wacjman, J., and Martin, B. (2002), 'Narratives of Identity in Modern Management,' *Sociology*, 36: 985–1002.

Walby, S., and Myhill, A. (2001), 'New Survey Methodologies in Researching Violence against Women,' *Brit. Jour. of Criminology*, 41: 502–22.

Walklate, S. (2000), 'Researching Victims,' in R. King and E. Wincup (eds.), *Doing Research on Crime and Justice* (Oxford: Oxford Univ. Press).

Walsh, M., Hickey, C., and Duffy, J. (1999), 'Influence of Item Content and Stereotype Situation on Gender Differences in Mathematical Problem,' *Sex Roles*, 41: 219–40.

Walters, D. (2004), 'A Comparison of the Labour Market Outcomes of Postsecondary Graduates of Various Levels and Fields over a Four-cohort Period,' *Canadian Jour. of Sociology*, 29: 1–27.

Warde, A. (1997), *Consumption, Food and Taste* (London: Sage).

Weaver, A., and Atkinson, P. (1995), *Microcomputing and Qualitative Data Analysis* (Aldershot: Avebury).

Webb, E.J., Campbell, D.T., Schwartz, R.D., and Sechrest, L. (1966), *Unobtrusive Measures: Non-reactive Measures in the Social Sciences* (Chicago: Rand McNally).

Weber, M. (1947), *The Theory of Social and Economic Organization*, trans. A.M. Henderson and T. Parsons (NY: Free Press).

Weick, K.E. (1990), 'The Vulnerable System: An Analysis of the Tenerife Air Disaster,' *Jour. of Management*, 16: 571–93.

Weinholtz, D., Kacer, B., and Rocklin, T. (1995), 'Salvaging Quantitative Research with Qualitative Data,' *Qual. Health Research*, 5: 388–97.

Westergaard, J., Noble, I., and Walker, A. (1989), *After Redundancy: The Experience of Economic Insecurity* (Cambridge, UK: Polity).

Wetherell, M. (1998), 'Positioning and Interpretative Repertoires: Conversation Analysis and Post-structuralism in Dialogue,' *Discourse and Society*, 9: 387–412.

White, J. (1990), *Hospital Strike* (Toronto: Thompson Educ. Publishing).

Whitehead, P., and Carpenter, D. (1999), 'Explaining Unsafe Sexual Behaviour: Cultural Definitions and Health in the Military,' *Culture, Health, and Sexuality*, 1: 303–15.

Whyte, W.F. (1955), *Street Corner Society*, 2nd ed. (Chicago: Univ. of Chicago Press).

Widdicombe, S. (1993), 'Autobiography and Change: Rhetoric and Authenticity of "Gothic" Style,' in E. Burman and I. Parker (eds.), *Discourse Analytic Research: Readings and Repertoires of Text* (London: Routledge).

Wilkinson, P., and Whitworth, D. (1998), 'Fat Is Fanciable, Says the Body of Evidence,' *The Times*, 7 Jan.: 3.

Wilkinson, S. (1998), 'Focus Groups in Feminist Research: Power, Interaction, and the Co-production of Meaning,' *Women's Studies Intnatl. Forum*, 21: 111–25.

——— (1999a), 'Focus Group Methodology: A Review,' *Intnatl. Jour. of Social Research Methodology*, 1: 181–203.

——— (1999b), 'Focus Groups: A Feminist Method,' *Psych. of Women Quarterly*, 23: 221–44.

Williams, M. (2000), 'Interpretivism and Generalization,' *Sociology*, 34: 209–24.

Wilson, B. (2002), 'The Canadian Rave Scene and Five Theses on Youth Resistance,' *Canadian Jour. of Sociology*, 27: 373–412.

Winkler, C. (1995), 'The Ethnography of the Ethnographer,' in C. Nordstrom and A. Robben (eds.), *Fieldwork under Fire: Contemporary Studies of Violence and Survival* (Berkeley: Univ. of California Press).

Winlow, S., Hobbs, D., Lister, S., and Hadfield, P. (2001), 'Get Ready to Duck: Bouncers and the Realities of Ethnographic Research on Violent Groups,' *Brit. Jour. of Criminology*, 41: 536–48.

Wolcott, H. (1990), *Writing up Qualitative Research* (Newbury Park, CA: Sage).

Wolf, D. (1991), 'High Risk Methodology: Reflections on Leaving an Outlaw Society,' in W. Shaffir and R. Stebbins (eds.), *Experiencing Fieldwork: An Inside View of Qualitative Research* (Newbury Park, CA: Sage).

Yin, R. (1984), *Case Study Research: Design and Methods* (Beverly Hills, CA: Sage).

Yun, G.W., and Trumbo, C.W. (2000) 'Comparative Response to a Survey Executed by Post, E-mail, and Web Form,' *Jour. of Computer-mediated Communication*, 6: www.ascusc.org/ jcmc/vol6/issue1/yun.html.

Index

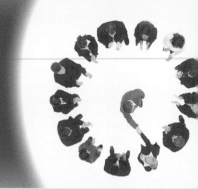

Abraham, J., 113–14
absolute sample size, 193–4
abstract, 333
access to research setting: closed settings, 143–4, 145–6; ongoing, 147–8; open settings, 143–4; 146–7; politics and, 15–17; soccer hooligans, 146
Achille, M.: and Ogloff, J., 94
acquiescence, 76–7
adjacency pairs, 304
Adriaenssens, C.: and Cadman, L., 174
aide mémoire, 160
Alberta Survey, 65, 77
Altheide, D.L., 300
ambiguous terms: in questions, 85–6
analytic memos, 152, 253, 255–6, 257
Anderson, K.: and Sebaldt, R., Lohfeld, L., Burgess, K., Donald, F., and Kaczorowski, J., 71
Andrews, K.: and Smith, L., Henzi, D., and Demps, E., 73
anecdotalism, 283
anonymity, 68, 75, 105. *See also* confidentiality
answers: balanced, 89; 'don't know'/'no opinion' option, 89; forced-choice, 83; identifying response sets, 92; pausing for, 163; recording, 69, 166–7; symmetrical, 88–9; vertical/horizontal format, 91–2
archive material: as unobtrusive measure, 124
'argot', 179
argumentative interactions, 172–3
Armstrong, D.: and Gosling, A., Weinman, J., and Marteau, T., 134
Armstrong, G., 134, 135, 147, 148, 151–2, 182, 203
articles. *See* journal article
Atkinson, M., 135, 144, 161, 271
Atkinson, P., 161; and Coffey, A., 319
attitudes: questions about, 84; racial prejudice, 58; *v.* behaviour, 58; to vegetarians, 55
attrition, 37, 76
audience reception, 302
auditing, 133
authenticity: criterion, 109, 110; official documents, 114; personal documents, 110
autobiography, 110
axial coding, 253

Baer, D.: and Curtis, J., and Grabb, E., 36
Bales, Robert, 100
Bampton, R.: and Cowton, C.J., 67

bar chart, 225, 226
Beagan, B., 16, 31, 96, 196, 198
Beardsworth, A.: and Keil, T., 35, 160, 167, 316–19
Becker, H., 14, 179, 198–9; and Greer, B., 182
Beharrell, P., 203, 300
behaviour: observation strategies, 102; sampling, 201; structured observation, 99; survey research, 100; *v.* attitudes, 58; *v.* meaning, 140, 279–80
behaviour sampling, 201
Bell, E., 100, 135, 144, 160, 288, 289, 300; and Jansen, H., and Young, L., 38, 113, 149
Berthoud, R., 52, 53
biases, 14, 90
bibliography, 322–3, 335
Billig, M., 306
biography, 110
bivariate analysis, 232–40; Cramér's *V*, 238–9; eta, 239; Kendall's tau-b, 237, 238; means, 239; Pearson's *r*, 234, 237; scatter diagrams, 234–7; Spearman's rho, 238; variation, 239–40
Blaikie, A., 113
Blaxter, M., 34
Bloor, M., 132–3; and Frankland, S., Thomas, M., and Robson, K., 173
Blumer , H., 9, 48, 59, 130–1
breast cancer: and social construction, 10
Brown, A., 272
Brown, S.: and Lightfoot, G., 116
Bryman, A., 93, 199, 313; and Cramer, D., 51, 222; and Haslam, C., and Webb, A., 137; and Stephens, M., and Campo, C., 147, 257
Buckle, A.: and Farrington, D., 102
Bulmer, M., 124
Burman, M.: and Batchelor, S., and Brown, J., 135
Bury, M., 272

Cambridge-Summerville Youth Study, 29
Camerer, C., 124
Canadian National Election surveys, 117
Canadian Periodical Index, 329
Canadian Sociology and Anthropology Association, 15
case studies: multiple-case study approach, 39–40; research design, 38–40, 41; types of case, 39; validity, 38–9
categorical variables. *See* nominal variables
categories, 254
Catterall, M.: and Maclaran, P., 259

causality: cross-sectional design and, 34, 56; erroneous assumption of, 233; experimental method and, 24; inferences of, 35–6, 56; internal validity, 22–3; quantitative research and, 55–7

census, 187

central tendency: measures of, 230, 231

Charles, N.: and Kerr, N., 81

Charmaz, K., 164, 203, 253, 256, 258, 278

Chin, M.: and Fisak, B., and Sims, V., 55

chi-square test, 242–3

Christakis, T.: and Christakis, P., Chipman, M., and Christakis, J., 50, 51, 53

Cicourel, A., 59, 60

Clairborn, W., 28

Clancey, W., 154

Clayman, S.: and Gill, V.T., 303

closed-ended question, 63, 64, 71, 82–4, 87

closed settings, 143–4, 145–6

cluster sampling, 192–3

coding, 47, 63, 331; closed questions, 82–4; computer-assisted, 258–71; in content analysis, 297–300; errors, 63–4, 76, 299–300; fragmentation of, 269–70; for grounded theory, 253–4; open questions, 81; principles of, 82; steps in, 257–8; types of, 253–4

coding frame, 64

coding manual, 298–9

coding stripes, 263

Coffey, A.: and Atkinson, P., 259, 272; Holbrook, B., and Atkinson, P., 270

Cohen's kappa, 102

cohort study, 36–7

Coleman, C.: and Moynihan, J., 121

comparison: cross-cultural studies, 40; experiments and, 33; multiple-case study approach, 39–40

complementary interactions, 172

complete observer, 150

complete participant: ethnographer as, 148–9

computer-assisted interviewing, 65, 66–7. See also online surveys

computer-assisted personal interviewing (CAPI), 66–7

computer-assisted qualitative data analysis software (CAQDAS), 251, 258–9, 270. See also NVivo

computer-assisted telephone interviewing (CATI), 66

concepts, 48–52, 130; dimensions of, 51–2; generating, 254; measurement of, 49–51; multiple-item measures, 49–51; nominal definition, 49; operational definition, 49; sensitizing, 131–2

concurrent validity, 53–4

confessional tales, 320, 321

confidentiality, 29, 68, 75, 103

confirmability: criterion, 23; and trustworthiness, 133–4

connotative meaning, 301

constant comparison: of indicators and concepts, 253, 255

constructionism, 10–11, 14, 49, 128, 278–9

construct validity, 22, 54, 55. See also measurement validity

content analysis: advantages of, 310; audience reception, 302; coding, 297–300; described, 295–6; disadvantages of, 310–11; ethnographic, 300; hermeneutics, 300–1; omissions in coverage, 295; qualitative, 300–2; of qualitative research, 310; sampling, 203–5; semiotics, 300–1; subject and themes, 297; value positions, 297; word counting, 296–7. See also conversation analysis (CA); discourse analysis (DA)

contextual understanding, 135–6, 140, 302, 303, 306

contingency tables, 232–3, 244

control group, 25, 26

convenience sample, 197–8

convergent validity, 54

conversation analysis (CA), 129, 302–5; adjacency pairs, 304; anti-realism, 309; assumptions of, 303; contextual understanding, 302, 303; preference organization, 304–5; transcription of, 303–4, 305; turn-taking, 304

Cook, T.: and Campbell, D., 26, 27

correlation coefficient: and statistical significance, 241–2

Corti, L., 74, 76

Coté, J.: and Allahar, A., 115

covert ethnography, 143–5

covert observation: ethics of, 105

Coxon, A., 74

Craig, G., 332

Cramér's V, 238–9

credibility: criterion, 23, 109, 110–11; government documents, 114; mass media outputs, 115; official documents, 114; personal documents, 110–11; and trustworthiness, 132–3

crime statistics, 54–5, 122, 123, 124

critical case: hypotheses testing, 39

Cronbach's alpha coefficient, 53, 60

Crook, C.: and Light, P., 76, 115

cross-cultural studies, 40, 119–20

cross-sectional design, 33–6, 41; non-manipulable variables, 34–5; replicability, 34; structure of, 36; validity, 34, 56, 57

Curasi, C., 67

Dale, A.: and Arber, S., and Proctor, M., 117

data: analysis, 47–8; in cross-sectional design, 34; and generation of theory, 6, 130; interpretation of, 129; missing, 72, 212–14; photographs as, 112, 154; quantitative v. qualitative, 140; secondary analysis, 117–21; statistics, 121–5; and theory testing, 5–6, 130. See also qualitative data analysis; quantitative data analysis

data collection: naturalism, 23, 128, 168, 180

Davies, P., 164

Deacon, D.: and Bryman, A., and Fenton, N., 288

deception, use of, 25, 28, 30

deductive approaches, 5–6

definitive concepts, 130–1

Deng, J., 53

denotative meaning, 301

Denzin, N., 287

dependability: criterion, 23; and trustworthiness, 133

dependent variable, 23, 25, 56

de-skilling, 58

Desroches, F., 105, 142

deterministic statements, 3

diagrams, 225–6, 234

diaries: as documents, 110–11, 161; of Mackenzie King, 112; researcher-driven, 74–5

dichotomous variables, 225

Dickinson, H., 110

Dinovitzer, R., 31; Hagan, J., and Parker, P., 37, 197, 225
discourse, 129
discourse analysis (DA), 305–9; anti-realism, 306, 309; approaches to, 305–7; constructionism, 306, 307; contextual understanding, 306; producing facts, 307, 308; reading the detail, 307–8
Disney, Walt, 110
dispersion: measures of, 230
Ditton, J., 143
documents: citing online sources, 116, 322; evaluating, 109–10, 116; government, 113–14; mass media outputs, 115; official, 114; personal, 110–13; selective survival of, 111, 113; virtual outputs, 115–17; visual objects, 111–13
Dommeyer, C.: and Moriarty, E., 72–3
'don't know'/'no opinion' option, 89
double-barrelled questions, 86, 87, 88
Dunning, E.: and Murphy, P., and Williams, J., 296
Durkheim, E., 3, 13, 122, 305
Dyer, W.: and Wilkins, A., 39

ecological fallacy, 121
Elliott, H., 74
email surveys, 72–3
embarrassing questions, 90, 100
embedded methods argument: against multi-strategy research, 286
emotional labour, 131
emotions: and sales, 56
empiricism, 7, 277
epistemology, 7–9, 279, 286
error variance, 243
eta, 239
ethics: of covert observation, 105; ethics committees and qualitative research proposals, 138; experiments and, 24, 25, 28–30; and harm to participants, 29–30; informed consent, 28; and monetary incentives, 31; moral universalism, 144; pervasive transgression view, 144, 179; random response technique, 106; and research, 15; research funding, 68; in research on prostitution, 179, 181; revising hypotheses, 293; sampling, 207; situation ethics, 144; stances on, 144; and use of deception, 25, 28, 30
ethnographic content analysis, 300
ethnography, 128, 129; access to research setting, 143–8; advantages of, 179–80; critical realism, 277, 278; end point of research, 154–5; ethical research, 28; feminist, 155–6; field notes, 129, 143, 145, 151–2; key informants, 148; micro research, 142; nature of research, 142–3; overt v. covert, 143–5; and participant observation, 142; qualitative interview v., 179–82; roles of ethnographer, 148–51; unstructured approach of, 136–7; visual, 152–4; writing, 320–2
ethnomethodology, 302–3
ethnostatistics, 281
evaluation research, 33
existing questions, 96–7
experiential authority: ethnographic writing and, 322
experimental design, 24–33, 41; classic, 24–30; ethical concerns, 24, 25, 28–30; field experiments, 24, 30–1; and internal validity, 24; laboratory experiments, 24, 30–1;

logic of comparison, 33; significance of, 32–3; and social research, 24
experimental group, 25
explained variance, 243
external reliability, 132
external validity, 23, 24; case study design, 38; cross-sectional design, 34; laboratory experiments, 30–1; qualitative research, 132; quantitative research and, 57, 59; threats to, 27–8. See also validity
extreme case, 39

face-to-face interview, 65–6, 67, 68, 70
face validity, 53
facilitator, 168
factual questions, 84
feminism: critique of survey research, 77–8; and ethnography, 155–6; and focus group research, 178–9; and interviewing, 175–9; and quantitative methods, 15, 292; and semi-structured interview, 164; value-laden research, 14–15
Fenton, N.: and Bryman, A., and Deacon, D., 289, 291, 311
Festinger, L.: and Riecken, H., and Schachter, S., 29, 39, 277
field experiments, 24, 30–1, 104–6
field notes, 129, 143, 145, 151–2
filter questions, 66
Finch, J., 95, 291; and Hayes, L., 187
Fine, G., 150
fixed-choice question, 63. See also closed-ended question
focus group, 64–5, 129, 168–75; as feminist method, 178–9; group interaction, 172–3; group size, 169–71; limitations of, 173–4; moderator involvement, 171; and naturalism, 168, 178, 281; online, 174–5; recording and transcription, 171–2; selecting participants, 169–71
Foddy, W., 81
formal theory, 254
Forster, N., 114
Foster, J., 9, 129–30, 135
Foucault, M., 305–6
Fowler, F., 70, 196
free-text diary, 74, 75–6
frequency tables, 222, 224, 226
full field notes, 152

Gabriel, Y., 283
Gans, H.J., 128, 144, 150
Garfinkel, H., 302
Gazso-Windlej, A.: and McMullin, J., 47, 53
Geertz, Clifford, 133
generalizability of research findings, 140. See also external validity
General Social Survey, 65, 75, 118, 119
Gephart, R., 281
Gerson, K.: and Horowitz, R., 143, 147, 150, 167
Giddens, A., 4
Gidengil, E.: and Everitt, J., Blais, A., Fournier, P., and Nevitte, N., 117
Gilbert, G.: and Mulkay, M., 281
Gill, R., 306–7
Ginn, J.: and Arber, S., 119
Giulianotti, R., 115, 146, 147, 149, 151, 203, 300, 302

Gladney, A.: and Ayars, C., Taylor, W., Liehr, P., and Meininger, J., 134
Glaser, B., 278; and Strauss, A., 155, 253
Glock, C., 280
Glucksmann, M., 144
Goffman, E., 4
'going native'. *See* participant-as-observer role
Golden-Biddle, K.: and Locke, K., 334
Goode, E., 28, 144
Gottdiener, M., 301
Gouldner, A., 14
government documents, 113–14
Goyder, J.: and Guppy, N., and Thompson, M., 36, 58, 66
Grabb, E.: and Curtis, J., 119
grand theories, 3–4
Griffin, J., 35
grounded theory, 6, 130, 252–7, 277; coding for, 253–4; criticisms of, 256–7; defined, 252; outcomes of, 254–5; tools for, 252–3
Gubrium, J.: and Holstein, J., 303
guinea pig effect, 103

Halford, S.: and Savage, M., and Witz, A., 292
Hallgrimsdottir, H.: and Phillips, R., and Benoit, C., 10, 14, 49, 115, 135
Hammersley, M., 287; Scarth, J., and Webb, S., 138, 148
harm: ethical questions, 29–30
'Hawthorne effect', 103
Heritage, J., 303
hermeneutics, 300–1
Hessler, R., 28; and Downing, J., Beltz, C., Pelliccio, A., Powell, M., and Vale, W., 74, 150
heterogeneity: and sampling, 197
Hier, S., 12, 115, 297, 302, 309
Hiller, H.: and DiLuzio, L., 134
Hine, V., 175
Hirsch, J., 111
histograms, 225–6, 228
history: effect of, 26; and interaction with treatment, 27
Ho, K.: and Baber, Z., and Khondker, H., 116
Hobbs, D., 133, 149
Hochschild, A., 4, 131
Hodson, R., 282, 309, 311
Holbrook, A.: and Green, M., and Krosnick, J., 66
Holbrook, B.: and Jackson, B., 171
Homan, R., 28, 105
Horowitz, R., 147
Howell, J.: and Frost, P., 30–1, 33
Hughes, E., 38
Hughes, G., 16
Hughes, K.: and MacKintosh, A.M., Hastings, G., Wheeler, C., Watson, J., and Inglis, J., 287
Hughes, R., 165–6
Humphreys, L., 105, 149
Hutchby, I.: and Wooffitt, R., 304
hypotheses: generating, 254; null, 240, 241; revising, 293; testing, 5, 39, 277. *See also* theory testing

idiographic explanations, 22
impressionist tales, 321

incidents: recording, 102
independent variable, 23, 25, 56. *See also* variables
in-depth interview. *See* qualitative interview
indexicality, 302
indicators: in measurement of concepts, 49–51
inductive approaches, 5–6, 12, 39, 128, 140
inferential statistics, 240–3
informal social control, 9
informed consent, 28
instrumentation, 26, 47
interaction, 244
interaction effects, 27
inter-coder variability, 64
inter-interviewer variability, 63
internal consistency. *See* internal reliability
internal reliability, 52–3, 132
internal validity, 22–3; cross-sectional design, 34; experimental method, 24; threats to, 26–7
Internet documents, 115–17
inter-observer consistency, 53, 132
interpretative omnipotence: ethnographic writing and, 322
interpretivism, 7–9, 128, 278
intersubjectivity, 7
interval variables, 221–2
intervening variable, 243–4
interview: computer-assisted, 65, 66–7; conducting, 67–71; contexts, 64–7; errors, 63–4; face-to-face, 65–6, 67, 68, 70; in feminist research, 175–9; filter questions, 66; flexible approach, 167–8; guide, 160, 166; introductory rationale, 67–8; introductory statement, 68; leaving, 70; life history, 161; multiple interviewees, 64–5; notes from, 129, 162; online, 174, 176–7; oral history, 161; preparation, 162; qualitative, 128, 158–9, 158–82; question order, 69; rapport, 68; recording answers, 69, 166–7; schedule, 67, 89–90, 97; semi-structured, 159–60, 164; silence during, 163; structured, 33, 62–5, 69; telephone, 65–6, 72; transcript, 165; transcription, 162, 167; unstructured, 159–60; wording of questions, 69
interviewer: effects, 64; training, 70–1; traits of effectiveness, 163; use of multiple interviewers, 64–5; variability, 63, 69
intra-coder variability, 64
intra-interviewer variability, 63
iterative strategy, 6

Jagger, E., 204, 296, 297, 311
Jamieson, J., 289
Jones, K., 113
jotted field notes, 152
journal article: blind review process, 313; qualitative research, 316–19; quantitative research, 313–16

Kanayama, T., 151
Karabanow, J., 136, 138
Kelley, J.: and De Graaf, N., 5, 51, 52, 53, 119, 313–16, 335
Kendall, L., 174
Kendall's tau-b, 237, 238
Kennedy, R., 300
Kerr, D., 36; and Michalski, J., 36
key informants, 148
Kimmel, A., 29

King, William Lyon, 111, 112
King diaries, 112
Kitzinger, J., 169, 170, 173
knowledge: questions about, 84
Krueger, R., 173
Kuhn, T., 286
Kvale, S., 162

laboratory experiments, 24, 30–1
Lamb, Augustus, 110–11
language-based research, 129
Lankshear, G., 332
Lantz, P.: and Booth, K., 10, 278, 279
LaPiere, R.T., 58, 102
Lauder, M., 145
laziness/boredom: as respondent problem, 77
leading questions, 87
LeCompte, M.: and Goetz, J., 132
Lee, R.M., 332
Lee-Treweek, G., 149
Leidner, R., 131, 145
letters: as documents, 110–11, 161
Lewis, O., 38, 136, 161
Li, P., 117
Liebling, A., 14
life history interview, 161
Likert scales, 50, 55, 84, 92
Lincoln, Y.: and Denzin, N., 319; and Guba, E., 23, 132, 133, 134
literature review, 329, 330, 333–4
literature search, 329–30
Little, M., 178
loaded questions, 87. See also leading questions
Lofland, J.: and Lofland, L., 135, 152, 160, 167
longitudinal designs, 36–8, 41
Longitudinal Immigration Data Base (IMBD), 117
losing information, 225
Lupton, D., 159
Lynch, M.: and Bogen, D., 300
Lynd, R.: and Lynd, H., 37

McCall, M.J., 104
McGuigan, J., 302
McKee, L.: and Bell, C., 136
McKeganey, N.: and Barnard, M., 4, 181
MacKinnon, N.: and Luke, A., 198, 289
macro research, 140. See also micro research
Madriz, M., 173
magazines, 115
Malbon, B., 159
Mangione, T.W., 205
Mann, C.: and Stewart, F., 66, 174
Manning, P., 319
Markham, A., 174
Marshall, G.: and Newby, H., and Vogler, C., 52
Marx, G.T., 325, 327
Marx, Karl, 87, 280
Marxist research, 8
Mason, J., 131, 165, 291
maturation: effect of, 27
Mayhew, P., 89

Mead, George Herbert, 8
Mead, Margaret, 39
mean, 213, 230, 239, 243
meaning: behaviour v., 140, 279–80; connotative, 301; denotative, 301; of evidence, 109, 114; personal documents, 111; photographs, 112–13, 154; problem of, 77, 100
measurement: of concepts, 47, 49–51; reasons for, 55
measurement validity, 22, 53–5, 60; concurrent validity, 53–4; construct validity, 22, 54, 55; convergent validity, 54; face validity, 53
median, 230, 231
member validation. See respondent validation
memory problems, 89, 100
memos. See analytic memos
Menard, S., 37
mental field notes, 152
Merton, R., 4
meta-ethnography, 282
micro research: ethnography, 142; v. macro research, 140
middle range theories, 3–4
Mies, M., 14
Miles, M.B., 251
Milgram, S., 28, 29
Milkman, R., 289–90, 293
Millen, D., 176, 177
Miller, D.: and Reilly, J., 295, 301
Miller, Diane Disney, 110
Miller, R.L., 161, 272, 278
missing data, 72, 205–6
mode, 230, 231
moderator, 168
monetary incentives: use of, 31
moral universalism, 144
Morgan, D., 169, 171, 173, 289; and Spanish, M., 172
Morgan, R., 16
mortality, 26. See also attrition
multiple-case study approach, 39
multiple-item measures, 49–51
multi-strategy research: approaches, 287–92; arguments against, 285–6; complementarity, 287, 289–92; defined, 285; facilitation, 287, 288–9; increasing use of, 292–3; limitations, 293; technical argument, 287; triangulation, 287–8
multivariate analysis, 243–8
Myles, J.: and Hou, F., 119

narrative analysis, 271–3
National Graduates Surveys, 117
National Longitudinal Studies of Children and Youth (NLSCY), 36, 37, 117
National Population Health Survey, 117
natives' points of view, 322. See also participant-as-observer role
'natural experiments', 31–2. See also quasi-experiments
naturalism, 23, 128, 168, 180, 280–1, 303
Nemni, M.: and Nemni, M., 38
neo-positivism, 278
Nettleton, S.: and Pleace, N., Burrows, R., Muncer, S., and Loader, B., 116

newspapers, 115
Nietzsche, F., 10
Nixon, K.: and Tutty, L., Downe, P., Gorkoff, K., and Ursel, J., 138
nodes, 261–2
nominal definition, 49
nominal variables, 119–20
nomothetic approach, 21
non-manipulable variables, 34–5
non-participant observation, 100
non-probability sample, 187, 197–200
non-response, 187, 196–7, 205–6
non-sexist writing, 332
non-spurious relationship, 243
Norris, C., 149
NUD*IST (Non-numerical Unstructured Data Indexing Searching and Theorizing), 258–9
null hypothesis, 240, 241
NVivo, 259–71; coding, 261–3; coding problems, 269–70, 271; memos, 268–9; nodes, 261–2; saving and retrieving in, 269; searching text, 263–8

Oakley, A., 14
objectivism, 10
objectivity, 7. See also intersubjectivity
observation research: ethics of covert observation, 105; non-participant observation, 100; participant observation, 100, 128; simple observation, 124; strategies for observing behaviour, 102. See also structured observation
observation schedule, 100–2, 104
observation strategies, 102
observer-as-participant role, 149
O'Connell Davidson, J.: and Layder, D., 179
O'Connor, H.: and Madge, C., 175
official statistics, 121–5
online focus groups, 174–5, 176–7
online interview, 174, 176–7
online sources. See Internet documents
online surveys, 72–4, 75, 206–7. See also computer-assisted interviewing
ontology, 9–11, 279
open coding, 253
open-ended question, 63, 80–1
open-ended research, 325
operational definition, 49
operationalization, 47
oral history interview, 161
ordinal variables, 221
O'Reilly, K., 137, 147
Orona, C.J., 254
outliers, 230

Pahl, J., 65
panel conditioning effect, 37
panel design, 119
panel study, 36–7
paradigm argument: against multi-strategy research, 286
Parnaby, P., 18, 115, 297
participant-as-observer role, 149, 150
participant observation, 100, 128, 142. See also ethnography

Pawson, R.: and Tilley, N., 33
Pearson's r, 234, 237
Peñaloza, L., 153
Perrucci, R.: and Belshaw, R., DeMerritt, A., Frazier, B., Jones, J., Kimbrough, J., Loney, K., Pappas, J., Parker, J., Trottier, B., and Williams, B., 100
personal, factual questions, 84
personal documents, 110–13
pervasive transgression view, 144, 179
Pettigrew, A., 136
Phelan, P., 288
phenomena of interest, 3
Phillips, N.: and Brown, J., 302
Phoenix, A., 281
photographs: as documents, 111–13, 154, 161
physical traces: as unobtrusive measure, 124
Pidgeon, N.: and Henwood, K., 253–4
pie chart, 225, 226–8
pilot studies, 95–6
Pink, S., 153, 320
Platt, J., 279
Poland, B.D., 167
politics: in social research, 15–17
polysemy, 301
population, 187
Population Index, 329
Porter, S., 277, 278
positivism, 7, 12, 277
post-coding, 81, 82
postmodernism, 319–20
Potter, J., 11, 304, 305, 306; and Chitty, A., 306, 309; and Hepburn, A., 306; and Wetherell, M., 306, 307, 308
Pratt, A.: and Valverde, M., 14, 38, 39
pre-coded question, 63. See also closed-ended question
pre-coding, 82
preference organization, 304–5
pre-testing, 28
probabilistic statements, 3
probability sample, 187, 189–93
probability sampling, 57, 61
probing, 69–70
probing questions, 163
prompting, 70, 166
Psathas, G., 303
publication, 16, 48
public policy shifts: as quasi-experiments, 32, 33
Punch, M., 144

QRS NVivo. See NVivo
qualitative data analysis, 251–73; analytic induction, 252; basic operations in, 257–9; computer software for, 251, 258–9, 270; general strategies, 252–7; narrative analysis, 271–3. See also coding
qualitative evaluation, 33
qualitative interview: advantages of, 180–2; flexible approach, 167–8; interview guide, 160, 166; life history interview, 161; nature of, 158–9; online, 174; oral history interview, 161; questions, 161–2, 163–6; transcription, 162, 165; types of, 159–60; v. structured interview, 159–68; without immersion v. ethnography, 179–82

qualitative research, 11–12, 21–2; contrasted with quantitative research, 139–40; criteria for evaluating, 23–4; critiques of, 137–9; cross-sectional design, 35–6; description and contextual understanding, 135–6, 140; difficulty of replication, 137–8; empathy, 134–5; emphasis on process, 136; ethics committees and, 138; evaluation criteria, 132–4; facilitation of quantitative research, 288–9; features of, 128–9; general orientation of, 11–13; inductive approach, 128, 140; and lack of transparency, 139; longitudinal design, 37; main goals of researchers, 134–7; main steps in, 129–30; natural model and, 277–8; notes, 129, 151–2; problems of generalization, 138–9; qualitative approach to quantitative research, 281–2; quantification in, 282–3; researcher involvement, 140; subjectivity, 137; theory and concepts in, 130–2; theory testing, 130; unstructured nature of, 136–7, 140
qualitative sampling, 202–5
quantitative data analysis: bivariate analysis, 232–40; multivariate analysis, 243–8; survey project, 210–14; univariate analysis, 222–31. *See also* Statistical Package for the Social Sciences (SPSS)
quantitative interview. *See* structured interview
quantitative research, 11–12, 133; and causality, 55–7; contrasted with qualitative research, 139–40; criteria for evaluating, 22–3; critiques of, 15, 58–9; facilitation of qualitative research, 289; feminism and, 15, 292; and generalizability of findings, 57; general orientation of, 11–13; and interpretivism, 278; main goals of researchers, 55–8; main steps in, 46–8; measurement validity, 22, 53–5, 60; non-manipulable variables in, 34–5; objectivist ontology, 59; quantitative approach to qualitative research, 282; reality and practice of, 60; and replication, 57–8; research design, 21; researcher involvement, 140; research question in, 18
quasi-experiments, 31–2, 33
quasi-quantification, 282–3
questionnaires, 34, 71–6; advantages of, 71; attached, 72–3; bad example, 96; clear instructions, 92, 94; designing, 91–4; disadvantages of, 71–2; email surveys, 72–3; embedded, 72–3; mailed, 71–2, 205–6; response rates, 205–6; types of questions in, 84–5; web surveys, 73–4. *See also* survey research
questions: about attitudes, 84; about beliefs, 84; about knowledge, 84; ambiguous terms in, 85–6; asking, 69–70, 80–97; balanced answers to, 89; closed, 63, 64, 71, 82–4, 87; common mistakes, 93; in content analysis, 295; direct, 163; double-barrelled, 86. 87, 88; embarrassing, 90, 100; ending, 164; existing, 96–7; factual, 84; filter, 66; follow-up, 163; indirect, 163; initial open-ended, 164; intermediate, 164; interpreting, 163–4; introducing, 163; leading, 87; long, 86; negatives in, 88; open, 63, 80–1, 83; order of, 69, 89–91; that overstretch memory, 89; personal, factual, 84; pre-testing, 95–6; probing, 163; in qualitative interviews, 161–2, 163–6; and requisite knowledge, 88; research, 17–18, 129, 130, 325–6; rules for designing, 85–9; specifying, 163; in structured interviews, 84–5; structuring, 163; symmetrical with answers, 88–9; technical terms in, 88; very general, 86–7; vignette, 94–5, 103–4, 166; wording of, 69

quota sampling, 199–200
Radley, A.: and Taylor, D., 154
random digit dialling, 65
random response technique, 106
random selection, 25, 26, 27, 57, 188
range, 230
ratio variables, 221–2
raves, 12, 154
reactive effects: of experimental arrangements, 28; in interviews, 64; in social science research, 103–4
readers, active/passive, 302
Readers' Guide to Periodical Literature, 329
realist tales, 320–2
Reed, M., 309
reflexivity, 14, 153, 302, 320
Reinharz, S., 155, 176
relational statements, 3
relevatory case, 39
reliability: criterion, 22, 34, 38; internal, 52–3; inter-observer consistency, 53, 102; qualitative research and, 131–2, 134; quantitative research and, 52–3, 55; stability over time, 52–3; statistics, 123; structured observation, 102–4
replicability, 22, 28, 30, 34, 57
replication of research, 30, 57–8
representativeness: criterion, 109, 111, 113; mass media outputs, 115; official documents, 114; photographs, 113
representative sample, 23, 57, 187
research: artificial v. natural contrast, 280–1; behaviour v. meaning, 279; criteria for evaluating, 22–4; epistemological assumptions, 7–9, 279; funding of, 16, 68; micro v. macro studies, 140; mutual analysis of quantitative and qualitative research, 281–2; naturalism, 23, 128, 168, 180, 280–1, 303; numbers v. words, 280; ontological considerations, 9–11, 279; politics and, 15–17; practical considerations, 17; problems with quantitative/qualitative contrast, 278–81; question, 17–18, 129, 130, 325–6; role of photographs, 112, 154; site, 47, 129; theory and, 3–6, 46–7; theory testing v. theory construction, 253, 280; values and, 13–15
'research bargain', 16, 146
research design, 47; case study, 38–40; cross-sectional, 33–6; experimental, 24–33; longitudinal, 36–8; qualitative v. quantitative articles, 313; quasi-experiments, 31–2, 33; and research orientation, 40–1; types of designs, 21–43
researcher-driven diaries, 74–5
research project: conducting, 325–36; ethical approval, 330, 331; personal safety concerns, 332; practical reminders, 330–1; preparing for research, 330; structure of, 333–6; time management, 327, 329. *See also* writing
research question, 17–18, 129
respondent problems, 71, 72, 76–7, 103–4
respondents, 47; probing, 69–70; prompting, 70; rapport, 68
respondent validation: member validation, 132–3
response rates, 196–7, 205–6
response sets, 76–7, 92
Riches, G.: and Dawson, P., 112
Riessman, C.K., 269–70, 271, 272
Rinehart, J., 38
Ristock, J., 178
Roberts, B., 271

role selection, 103
Roosevelt, Franklin D., 112
Rosenau, P.M., 319
Rosenhan, D.L., 104–5, 203
Rosenthal, R.: and Jacobson, L., 24–5, 27, 29, 30
Russell, R.: and Tyler, M., 39

Sage Race Relations Abstracts, 329
sample: absolute size of, 193–4, 196; biased, 186–9; convenience, 197–8; defined, 187; generalizing from, 194–5, 201–2; multi-step cluster, 192–3; non-probability, 187; probability, 187, 189–93; relative size of, 193–4, 196; simple random, 189–90; size, 193–4, 196–7; snowball, 198–9; stratified random, 191; systematic, 191
sample attrition, 37. *See also* attrition
sampling: analysis and, 197; content analysis, 203–5; dates, 204–5; distributions, 195; ethics, 207; media, 203–4; probability, 57, 61; problems, 201–2; qualitative, 202–5; quota, 199–200; structured observation and, 200–1; terms and concepts, 187; theoretical, 202–3; time, 102, 201; virtual, 206–7
sampling error, 187, 189, 194, 196, 202
sampling frame, 187, 188
Sanjek, R., 152
scatter diagrams, 234–7
schedule: coding, 297, 298; interview, 67, 89–90, 97; observation, 100–2, 104
Schegloff, E., 309
Schlesinger, P.: and Dobash, R.E., Dobash, R.P., and Weaver, C., 169, 170, 172
Schuman, H.: and Presser, S., 81, 83, 87
scientific method, 7
Scott, J., 109, 111, 112, 113, 114, 310
secondary analysis, 117–21; advantages of, 117–20; limitations of, 120–1
selection: effect of, 27; and interaction with treatment, 27; random, 25, 26, 27, 57, 188
selective coding, 253
semiotics, 300–1
semi-structured interview, 159–60, 164. *See also* qualitative interview
sensitizing concepts, 130–1
sex-trade workers: constructionism and, 10, 14, 49; ethics in research, 179, 181
Shalla, V., 38
Sharpe, K., 147
Sheehan, K.: and Hoy, M., 72
show cards, 70
sign, 301
signified, 301
signifier, 301
Silverman, D., 130, 181, 280, 303, 304, 305
simple observation: as unobtrusive measure, 124
simple random sample, 189–90
situation ethics, 144
Skeggs, B., 133, 135, 155, 156
Smith, D.J.: and McVie, S., 71
Smith, N.: and Lister, R., and Middleton, S., 38
Smith, T.W., 196
snowball sample, 198–9

soccer hooliganism, 115, 146, 147–8
social desirability, 71, 77, 100
Social Sciences Citation Index, 329
Sociological Abstracts, 329
sources of data. *See* documents
Spearman's rho, 238
split-half method, 53
stability of measures, 52, 53, 60
Stacey, J., 155, 156
standard deviation, 230
Stanley, L.: and Temple, B., 271
Statistical Package for the Social Sciences (SPSS), 215–19; bar chart, 226; basic operations in, 215; bivariate analysis, 233–9; computing new variable, 222–3; contingency tables, 233–4, 244; Cramér's *V*, 238–9; defining variables, 217–19; entering data, 216–17; frequency table, 226; histogram, 228; measures of central tendency, 230, 231; measures of dispersion, 230; pie chart, 226–8; printing output, 228–9; recording variables, 222–3; retrieving data, 219; saving data, 219; scatter diagrams, 234–7; univariate analysis, 226–31
statistical significance, 240–3
statistics. *See* crime statistics; official statistics
stratified random sample, 191
Strauss, A., 11; and Corbin, J., 202, 252, 253, 254
structured diary, 74–5
structured interview: characteristics of, 62–4; cross-sectional design, 33; multiple interviewers, 64–5; potential problems, 69; questions in, 63; standardization in, 62–3; types of questions in, 84–5; *v.* qualitative research interviews, 158–9; *v.* questionnaires, 71–2. *See also* questions
structured observation, 99–107; behavioural studies, 99; checklist for, 105; criticisms of, 106–7; field experiments as, 104–6; reliability, 102–4; and sampling, 200–1; validity, 104. *See also* observation research
subgroup analysis, 119
substantive theory, 254, 255
Sudman, S.: and Bradburn, N, 87
Sugiman, P., 111, 161
suicide statistics, 123
Sullivan, O., 74, 76
survey research, 62–78; questionnaires; questions; and behavioural studies, 100; feminist critique of, 77–8; online surveys, 72–4, 75, 206–7; researcher-driven diaries, 74–5; respondent problems, 72, 76–7. *See also* interview
Sutton, R.I., 112; and Rafaeli, A., 56, 233
Sweet, C., 175
symbolic interactionism, 8–9, 59
systematic sample, 191

Tastsoglou, E.: and Miedema, B., 14, 160, 198, 199, 259, 290
Taylor, A., 135, 147, 148, 151, 154, 202, 321, 322
teacher expectations, 24–30
Teevan, J.: and Dryburgh, H., 4, 47
Teitler, J.: and Reichman, N., and Sprachman, S., 196
telephone interviews, 65–6, 72
testing: effect of, 26
test-retest method, 52

'text', 115
thematic analysis, 282
theoretical sampling, 202–3
theoretical saturation, 203, 252
theories: components of, 3; construction of, 6; grand, 3–4; grounded, 6, 130; middle range, 3–4. *See also* hypotheses
theory testing, 3–5, 6, 130, 253, 277, 280
thick description, 133
Tilley, N., 33
time management, 327, 329, 331
time sampling, 102, 201
time-use diary, 74, 76
Totten, M., 150
Tourangeau, R.: and Smith, T.W., 71
transcription, 331; of conversation analysis, 303–5, 305; focus group, 171–2; of interview, 162, 167; qualitative interview, 162, 165
transferability: criterion, 23; and trustworthiness, 133
treatment group, 25
triangulation, 125, 287–8
Trow, M., 182
trustworthiness: confirmability and, 133–4; credibility and, 132–3; criterion, 23–4; dependability and, 133; transferability and, 133
Turnbull, R., 14
turn-taking, 304
Type I error, 241
Type II error, 240–3

unemployment statistics, 123
univariate analysis, 222–31; frequency tables, 222, 224, 226; histograms, 225–6, 228; measures of central tendency, 230, 231; measures of dispersion, 230; pie chart, 225, 226; with SPSS, 227–31
unobtrusive measure, 124–5
unstructured interview, 159–60. *See also* qualitative interview
unstructured observation, 100

validity: case study research, 38–9; classic experimental design and, 26–30; criterion, 22–3; external, 23, 24, 27–8, 30–1, 34, 57, 132; internal, 22–3, 26–7, 34; in qualitative research, 131–2; statistics, 123; structured observation, 104; threats to, 26–8
values: influence of, 13–15
Van den Hoonaard , W.C., 138
Van Maanen, J., 144, 147, 320, 321
variables, 3, 22; analysis of variance, 243; concepts as, 48; dependent variable, 23, 25, 56; dichotomous, 225; independent variable, 23, 25, 56; interaction, 244; intervening variable, 243–4; interval, 221–2; manipulation, 24, 25–7, 34, 35; new, 222–3; nominal, 119–220; non-manipulable, 34–5; non-spurious relationship, 243; ordinal, 221; ratio, 221–2; relationships between, 233; statistical significance, 240–3; types of, 219–22; univariate analysis, 222–6
variance: analysis of, 243
variation, 239–40
Verstehen, 8, 301
victimization surveys, 54–5
video-recording: as observation strategy, 102
Vidich, A.: and Bensman, J., 29
vignette questions, 94–5, 103–4, 166
Vincent, S., 310
virtual sampling. *See* online surveys
visual ethnography, 152–4
visual objects: as documents, 111–13, 152–4; realist framework, 153; reflexive framework, 153

Wachholz, S.: and Miedema, B., 178
Wacjman, J.: and Martin, B., 290, 291
Walklate., S., 97, 288
Walsh, M.: and Hickey, C., and Duffy, J., 30
Walters, D., 37, 119, 121
WANE study, 47
Warde, A., 204
Webb, E.J.: and Campbell, D.T., Schwartz, R.D., and Sechrest, L., 103, 124–5, 287
Weber, M., 8
web surveys, 73–4. *See also* online surveys
White, J., 38
Whitehead, P.: and Carpenter, D., 252
Whyte, W.F., 103, 128, 146–7, 148
Wilkinson, S., 172, 178–9
Williams, M., 138
Wilson, B, 6, 12, 167, 277
Wolcott., H., 313
Wolf, D., 147
Women's Studies Abstracts, 329
writing, 313–23; abstract of research, 333; bias-free language, 332–3; Discussion section, 334–5; ethnographic, 320–2; feedback, 332; finding/conclusions, 129, 315, 318, 334–5, 337; introduction, 314, 317, 333; literature review, 333–4; persuasion, 313, 332; research methods, 334; research project, 331–6; structure of articles, 314–18; time management, 331

Yin, R., 39